A NEW BOUNDARY STONE

OF

NEBUCHADREZZAR I.

The Ancient Near East: Classic Studies

K.C. Hanson
Series Editor

Albert T. Clay
Light on the Old Testament from Babel

Albert T. Clay
The Origin of Biblical Tradition

Leonard W. King
Legends of Babylon and Egypt in Relation to Hebrew Tradition

Friedrich Delitzsch
Babel and Bible

George Smith
Assyrian Discoveries

George Smith & A. H. Sayce
The Chaldean Account of Genesis

T. Eric Peet
A Comparative Study of the Literatures of Egypt, Palestine, and Mesopotamia

Raymond Philip Dougherty
Nabonidus and Belshazzar

James B. Pritchard
Archaeology and the Old Testament

A. T. Olmstead
History of Palestine and Syria

W. J. Hinke
A New Boundary Stone of Nebuchadrezzar I

A NEW BOUNDARY STONE

OF

NEBUCHADREZZAR I.

from Nippur
with a Concordance of Proper Names and
a Glossary of the Kudurru
Inscriptions thus
far Published

William J. Hinke

New Foreword and Bibliography by
K. C. Hanson

WIPF & STOCK · Eugene, Oregon

A NEW BOUNDARY STONE OF NEBUCHADREZZAR I. FROM NIPPUR WITH A CONCORDANCE OF PROPER NAMES AND A GLOSSARY OF THE KUDURRU INSCRIPTIONS THUS FAR PUBLISHED

The Ancient Near East: Classic Studies

ISBN 13: 978-1-60899-099-3

Cataloging-in-Publication data

Hinke, William John, 1871–1947.

A new boundary stone of Nebuchadrezzar I. from Nippur with a concordance of proper names and a glossary of the kudurru inscriptions thus far published / William J. Hinke. New foreword and bibliography by K. C. Hanson.

The Ancient Near East: Classic Studies

ISBN: 978-1-60899-0993

xxxv + 323 p.; 1 folded leaf of plates; ill.; 25 cm.

Reprint, with new material, of the edition published by University of Pennsylvania, 1907.

1.Boundary stones—Iraq—Babylonia. 2. Akkadian language—Texts. 3. Akkadian language—Glossaries, vocabularies, etc. I. Hanson, K. C. (Kenneth C.). II. Title. III. Series.

PJ3861 .H55 2009

Manufactured in the U.S.A.

SERIES FOREWORD.

The archaeological discoveries of ancient cities and texts in Mesopotamia, Egypt, and Syria-Palestine began in earnest in the nineteenth century and only accelerated in the twentieth and twenty-first centuries. A few of the most significant early explorations and excavations make the point:

- In 1838, Edward Robinson explored and inaugurated the geographical study of Palestine, especially exploring Jerusalem, including Hezekiah's Tunnel.[1]
- Funded by King Friedrich Wilhelm IV of Prussia, Richard Lepsius discovered several monuments from the Old Kingdom of Egypt during his three-year expedition (1843–1845).[2]
- The earliest treasures of Assyria were excavated by Austen Henry Layard at Calah (Nimrud) and Paul Émile Botta at Nineveh (the Kuyunjik mound in Mosul) in the 1840s.[3]
- Sir W. K. Loftus carried out the earliest explorations of Ur (Tell Muqqayyar) in 1849. But it was Sir C. Leonard Wooley who did the systematic excavations (1922–34).[4]
- Charles Warren surveyed the topography of Jerusalem and the temple mount in 1867 and 1870.
- The ancient Egyptian sites of Tanis and Gizeh were explored by Sir Flinders Petrie in the 1880s.[5]
- The University of Pennsylvania began excavations of

[1] Edward Robinson and Eli Smith, *Biblical Researches in Palestine and in the Adjacent Regions: A Journal of Travels in the Year 1838*, 3 vols. (Boston: Crocker & Brewster, 1841).

[2] C. R. Lepsius, *Denkmäler aus Aegypten und Aethiopien*, 12 vols. (Berlin: Nicolaische Buchhandlung, 1849–56).

[3] Austen Henry Layard, *Nineveh and Its Remains*, 2 vols. (New York: Putnam, 1849); Layard, *Discoveries in the Ruins of Nineveh and Babylon* (New York: Harper, 1853); Paul Émile Botta, *Monument de Ninive* (Paris: Imprimerie Nationale, 1849–50).

[4] C. L. Wooley, *Ur Excavations*, 10 vols. (London: Oxford University Press, 1927–74).

[5] W. M. Flinders Petrie, *Tanis*, 2 vols. (Egypt Exploration Fund, 1880–1888); Petrie, *The Pyramids and Temples of Gizeh* (London: Field & Tuer, 1883).

Nippur (southeast of Baghdad) in 1889.[6]

- Under the auspices of the Deutsche Orient-Gesellschaft (German Orient Association), Robert Koldewey excavated Babylon (part of modern Baghdad) from 1899 to 1918.[7]

The remains of ancient societies often require decades to unearth, but much longer to interpret and understand. The methods of archaeology have progressed dramatically in recent years. Archaeologists have continuously refined their tools, methods, and techniques. Today archaeology is characterized by pottery identification, classification, and cataloging; disciplined excavation of "squares"; use of sophisticated electronics, such as GPS, infrared, and computer-aided design; and the integration of multiple methodologies, such as epigraphy, art history, physical anthropology, paleobotany, and climatology.

The interpretation of ancient Near Eastern history and cultures has also progressed. An increasing number of documents has been unearthed. The vast document collections from Tel el-Amarna, Nippur, Mari, Nuzi, Ebla, Ugarit, and the Dead Sea caves are just some of the more spectacular examples. These provide an enormous amount of detail about royal administrations, business transactions, land tenure systems, taxes, political propaganda, mythologies, marriage practices, and much more. And things that sometimes seem unique about one culture at first look often fit into larger patterns of relationship when the surrounding cultures are better understood.

The Ancient Near East: Classic Studies (ANECS) reprints classic works that have brought the results of archaeology, textual, and historical investigations to audiences of scholars, students, and the general public. While the discussions continue and the

[6] Clarence S. Fisher, *Excavations at Nippur* (Philadelphia: Babylonian Expedition of the University of Pennsylvania, 1905).

[7] Robert Koldewey, *The Excavations at Babylon*, trans. Agnes S. Johns (London: Macmillan, 1914).

results of earlier investigations are continuously re-examined, these classic works remain of interest and importance.

K. C. HANSON

Series Editor

SELECT BIBLIOGRAPHY.

Bienkowski, Piotr, and Alan Millard, editors. *Dictionary of the Ancient Near East*. Philadelphia: University of Pennsylvania Press, 2000.

Brinkman, J. A. "Kudurru. A. Philologisch." *In Reallexikon der Assyriologie* , edited by D. O. Edzard, 6:268–74. Berlin: de Gruyter, 1980–83.

———. *A Political History of Post-Kassite Babylonia, 1158–722 B.C.* Analecta Orientalia 43. Rome: Pontificium Institutum Biblicum, 1968.

———, and Stephanie M. Dalley. "A Royal Kudurru from the Reign of Aššur-nādin-šumi." *Zeitschrift für Assyriologie* 78 (1988) 76–98.

Frankfort, Henri. T*he Art and Architecture of the Ancient Orient*. 5th ed. New Haven: Yale University Press, 1996.

Hallo, William W., and William Kelly Simpson. *The Ancient Near East: A History*. 2nd ed. Fort Worth: Harcourt Brace College, 1998.

Hallo, William W., and K. Lawson Younger Jr., editors. *The Context of Scripture. Vol. 1: Canonical Compositions from the Biblical World.* Leiden: Brill, 1997.

———. *The Context of Scripture. Vol. 2: Monumental Inscriptions from the Biblical World*. Leiden: Brill, 1999.

———. *The Context of Scripture. Vol. 3: Archival Documents from the Biblical World*. Leiden: Brill, 2002.

Hinke, William J. *Selected Babylonian Kudurru Inscriptions. Semitic Studies Series 14*. Leiden: Brill, 1911.

King, L. W. *Babylonian Boundary Stones and Memorial Tablets in the British Museum (BBSt)*. London: British Museum, 1912.

Kuhrt, Amélie. *The Ancient Near East, 3000–332 B.C. 2 vols. Routledge History of the Ancient World*. London: Routledge, 1995.

Lambert, W. G. "Babylonians and Chaldaeans." In *Peoples of Old Testament Times*, edited by D. J. Wiseman, 179–96. Oxford: Clarendon, 1973.

Leick, Gwendolyn. *Who's Who in the Ancient Near East.* London: Routledge, 1999.

Nissen, Hans J. *The Early History of the Ancient Near East, 9000–2000 B.C.* Translated by Elizabeth Lutzeier. Chicago: University of Chicago Press, 1990.

Rogers, Robert William. *Cuneiform Parallels to the Old Testament.* 2nd ed. 1926. Reprinted with new foreword and bibliography by K. C. Hanson, Ancient Texts and Translations. Eugene, OR: Wipf & Stock, 2005.

Roux, Georges. *Ancient Iraq*. 3rd ed. New York: Penguin, 1993.

Saggs, H. W. F. Babylonians. Peoples of the Past. London: British Museum Press, 1995.

———. *Civilization before Greece and Rome.* New Haven: Yale University Press, 1989.

———. *The Greatness That Was Babylon: A Survey of the of the Ancient Civilization of the Tigris-Euphrates Valley.* Rev. ed. Great Civilizations Series. London: Sidgwick & Jackson, 1988.

Sasson, Jack M., editor. *Civilizations of the Ancient Near East.* 4 vols. New York: Scribners, 1995.

Slanski, Kathryn E. *The Babylonian Entitlement Narus (Kudurrus): A Study of Their Form and Function.* ASOR Books 9. Boston: American Schools of Oriental Research, 2003.

———. "Classification, Historiography and Monumental Authority: The Babylonian Entitlement Narûs (Kudurrus)." *Journal of Cuneiform Studies 52* (2000) 95–114.

Snell, Daniel C. *Life in the Ancient Near East, 3100–332 B.C.E.* New Haven: Yale University Press, 1997.

Steinmetzer, Franz Xaver. *Über den Grundbesitz in Babylonien zur Kassitenzeit nach den sog. Grenzsteinen Dargestellt.* Der Alte Orient 19/1-2. Leipzig: Hinrichs, 1918.

Tuman, V. S. "Astronomical Dating of the Nebuchadnezzar *kudurru* found in Nippur in February, 1896." In *Nippur at the Centennial: Papers Read at the 35e Rencontre Assyriologique Internationale,* 281–85. Philadelphia: University Museum, 1988.

Van de Mieroop, Marc. *The Ancient Mesopotamian City*. Oxford: Clarendon, 1997.

———. *Cuneiform Texts and the Writing of History*. Approaching the Ancient World. London: Routledge, 1999.

———. *A History of the Ancient Near East, ca. 3000–323 BC*. Blackwell History of the Ancient World. Malden, MA: Blackwell, 2004.

Williamson, H. G. M., editor. *Understanding the History of Ancient Israel*. Proceedings of the British Academy 143. Oxford: Oxford University Press, 2007.

PREFACE.

THAT part of this book which relates directly to the boundary stone of Nebuchadrezzar I. from Nippur was originally presented to the Faculty of Philosophy of the University of Pennsylvania, in partial fulfillment of the requirements for the degree of Ph.D. The author has since continued his studies of the Babylonian boundary stones, and now offers Chapter One as a general introduction into this interesting field of Babylonian studies. The questions which the Babylonian boundary stones open up are so numerous and varied that their contents are not only of interest to the specialist, but their legal enactments offer material to the student of ancient law, their religious features are of interest to the student of ancient religion, while their symbols claim the attention of the student of ancient astronomy. When we realize that these symbols are the oldest astronomical charts which are in existence, they are seen to possess an unusual importance. The attempt seemed, therefore, warranted to secure, if possible, a complete collection of all the symbols and to present them in the form of an astronomical atlas. This original plan, however, had to be given up, because the Museums of Berlin and London declined to permit the publication of the material in their possession, inasmuch as it had been "reserved for publication by the Museum." As a result the author was compelled to restrict himself to a collection of all the material that had been published thus far. In the case of the boundary stones discovered by the French at Susa, and now preserved in the Louvre at Paris, photographs of several originals were secured through the kind assistance of Dr. Léon Heuzey, Director of the Louvre, for whose valuable help the author wishes to express publicly his gratitude. Through these photographs it was possible to give not only an improved drawing of the important stone, Susa No. 1 (fig. 24), and to offer accurate drawings of Susa Nos. 16 and 20 (see figs. 10 and 30), but also to substitute several halftone pictures in place of the drawings given in the *Délégation en Perse* (see figs. 2, 17, 18). The publication of the symbols on the boundary stone of Merodach-baladan II., now at Berlin, was made possible through the kindness of Prof. Clay, who placed at my disposal a set of photographs which he had secured from Berlin. The symbols on III R. 41 and 43 (see III R. 45, Nos. 1 and 2) were redrawn from casts of these stones in the Museum of the University of Pennsylvania, by which a more accurate representation of these important monuments was secured. The excellent drawings, prepared under the direction of the author, were made by Mr. P. F. Goist, an artist of Philadelphia, who spared no pains in making them as accurate as possible.

The new boundary stone of Nebuchadrezzar I., whose "important inscription" was announced in 1901 by Prof. Hommel, will doubtless fulfill all expectations, as there are few *Kudurru* inscriptions which surpass it in interest. Inasmuch as the boundary stone of Marduk-aḫê-erba had never received an adequate treatment and its inscription had not been translated in full, it was thought fitting to add it as an Appendix, with some brief notes on its linguistic features.

The Concordance will be found to contain the proper names which occur in all the *Kudurru* inscriptions published thus far. In order to make it as complete as possible two lists of symbols were added. Although the symbols are given at length in Hommel's *Aufsätze*, yet inasmuch as his list does not include the latest finds since made at Susa, and as it seemed desirable to have one place in which all this information could be found conveniently grouped together, the author concluded to repeat the list, with such additions as were necessary, and to add another alphabetical list, which brings out more prominently the number and variety of the symbols represented.

The Glossary, while not aiming at absolute completeness, was prepared to include all the words used in the inscriptions and most of the passages in which the words occur, with the exception of some of the most common words, for which it seemed unnecessary to quote any passages.

In conclusion, the pleasant duty remains to express my gratitude to my teachers and friends who have aided me in my study. Prof. Hilprecht not only permitted me most kindly to publish the important inscription of Nebuchadrezzar I., but he has also given me during the whole course of my study his generous assistance and encouragement. He has still further increased my obligation by reading the proof-sheets as they passed through the press, to which he added many valuable suggestions, the most important of which are duly acknowledged in their respective places. With Prof. Clay I spent many delightful hours, discussing with him the problems connected with these inscriptions. I owe much to his stimulating suggestions. Prof. Jastrow has given me the benefit of his thorough knowledge of the literature involved and has supplied me with a number of references for the list of the gods. Through the kind mediation of my friend, Dr. Ranke, of the Egyptological Department of the Royal Museums at Berlin, Dr. Ungnad kindly undertook the task of collating a number of passages for me on the stones in the Berlin Museum. His readings have been credited in the Concordance as well as in the Glossary. Finally, I wish to thank the Publication Committee of the University for generously undertaking the publication of my book, and especially the liberal founder of this Fund, Mr. Eckley Brinton Coxe, Jr. To all these friends I owe much, and I can only hope that the result of my studies may be worthy of their interest.

WILLIAM J. HINKE.

PHILADELPHIA, November 13, 1907.

CONTENTS.

LIST OF ILLUSTRATIONS.

BIBLIOGRAPHY OF THE BABYLONIAN KUDURRU INSCRIPTIONS.

I. TEXT EDITIONS.

H. C. RAWLINSON, "Cuneiform Inscriptions of Western Asia," Vol. I, 1861, pls. 66, 70; Vol. III, 1870, pls. 41–43; Vol. IV, 1875, pl. 41; 2d ed., pl. 38; Vol. V, 1884, pls. 55, 56.

H. V. HILPRECHT, *Freibrief Nebukadnezar's I.*, Leipzig, 1883.

TH. G. PINCHES, "On an Edict of Nebuchadnezzar I." (in "Proceedings of the Soc. for Bibl. Arch.," Vol. VI, 1884, pp. 151–170).

S. A. SMITH, "Assyrian Letters from the Royal Library at Nineveh," Leipzig, 1888, Pt. IV, pls. VIII–IX.

F. E. PEISER, *Keilschriftliche Acten-Stücke aus babylonischen Städten,* Berlin, 1889, pls. I–II, photos 1–5.

C. W. BELSER, *Babylonische Kudurru Inschriften* (in *Beiträge zur Assyriologie,* Vol. II, 1891, pp. 165–203).

H. V. HILPRECHT, "Old Babylonian Inscriptions," Vol. I, Pt. 1, 1893, Nos. 80, 83; Pt. 2, 1896, Nos. 149, 150.

L. W. KING, "Cuneiform Texts of the British Museum," Vol. IX, 1900, pls. IV–V; Vol. X, 1900, pls. III; IV–VII.

V. SCHEIL, *Délégation en Perse,* Memoirs, Vol. II, 1900, pls. 16–19; 20; 21–24; pp. 93, 97, 113, 116. Vol. IV, 1902, pl. 16. Vol. VI, 1905, pls. 9, 10; 11*a*.

F. DELITZSCH, *Vorderasiatische Schriftdenkmäler der Königlichen Museen zu Berlin,* Heft I, Leipzig, 1907, Nos. 35, 36, 37, 57, 58, 70, autographed by Dr. Ungnad.

II. TRANSLITERATIONS, TRANSLATIONS AND DISCUSSIONS.

J. OPPERT, *Premiers déchiffrements de la langue cunéiforme* (in *Annales de Philosophie Chrétienne,* Vol. 53, 4th S., 1856, XIV, contains a translation of the Caillou de Michaux). *Les Mesures de longueur chez les Chaldéens* (in *Bulletin Archéologique de l'Athénœum français,* 1856, pp. 53ff.).

F. TALBOT, "The Inscription of Michaux" (in "Journal of the Royal Asiatic Society," Vol. XVIII, 1861, pp. 53–75).

G. SMITH, "Assyrian Discoveries," 1875, pp. 237–241.

J. OPPERT and J. MENANT, *Documents juridiques de l'Assyrie et de la Chaldée*, 1877 pp. 117–138.

J. OPPERT, "Records of the Past," Vol. IX, 1877, pp. 31–36, 91–107.

H. V. HILPRECHT, *Freibrief Nebukadnezar's I.*, Leipzig, 1883.

TH. G. PINCHES, "On an Edict of Nebuchadnezzar I." (in the "Proceedings of the Soc. of Bibl. Arch., Vol. VI, 1884, pp. 144–170).

F. HOMMEL, *Geschichte Babyloniens und Assyriens*, 1885, pp. 443–468.

W. ST. BOSCAWEN, "A Babylonian Land Grant" (in the "Babylonian and Oriental Record," Vol. I, 1888, pp. 66–68).

B. MEISSNER, *Ein Freibrief Nebukadnezar's II.* (in *Zeitschrift für Assyriologie*, Vol. IV, 1889, pp. 259–267; cf. also p. 403f.).

F. E. PEISER, *Keilschriftliche Acten-Stücke*, 1889, pp. 2–17.

A. BOISSIER, *Recherches sur quelques contracts babyloniens*, Paris, 1890, pp. 21–36.

C. W. BELSER, *Babylonische Kudurru Inschriften* (in *Beiträge zur Assyriologie*, Vol. II, 1891, pp. 111–156).

F. DELITZSCH, *Der Berliner Merodach-baladan Stein* (in *Beiträge zur Assyriologie*, Vol. II, 1891, pp. 258–273).

P. JENSEN, *Gulkischar, König von Babylon*, etc. (in *Zeitschrift für Assyriologie*, Vol. VIII, 1893, pp. 220–224).

J. OPPERT, *La Fondation consacrée à la déesse Nina* (in *Zeitschrift für Assyriologie*, Vol. VIII, 1893, pp. 360–374).

H. V. HILPRECHT, *Assyriaca*, 1894, pp. 1–58.

V. SCHEIL, *Notes d'epigraphie et d'archéologie Assyriennes* (in *Recueil de Travaux*, Vol. XVI, 1894, p. 32f.).

H. WINCKLER, *Altorientalische Forschungen*, I *Serie*, 1897, pp. 497–503.

V. SCHEIL, *Délégation en Perse*, Memoirs, Vol. II, 1900, pp. 86–116.

R. F. HARPER, *Assyrian and Babylonian Literature*, New York, 1901, pp. 8–11, 64–68.

C. H. W. JOHNS, "Babylonian and Assyrian Laws, Contracts and Letters," New York, 1904, pp. 191–205.

V. SCHEIL, *Délégation en Perse*, Memoirs, Vol. IV, 1902, pp. 163–164; Vol. VI, 1905, pp. 31–47.

E. CUQ, *La propriété foncière en Chaldée d'après les pierres-limites* (extrait de la *Nouvelle Revue historique de Droit français et étranger*, de November-December, 1906, pp. 701–738).

OTTO WEBER, *Die Literatur der Babylonier und Assyrer*, Leipzig, 1907, pp. 245–247.

III. DESCRIPTION AND DISCUSSION OF THE SYMBOLS.

TH. G. PINCHES, "The Guide to the Nimroud Central Saloon," 1886, pp.40–60.

M. J. DE MORGAN, *Délégation en Perse*, Memoirs, Vol. I, 1900, pp. 165–182.

F. Hommel, *Ursprung des Tierkreises* (in *Aufsätze und Abhandlungen*, 1900, pp. 236–268). *Astronomie der alten Chaldäer, l.c.*, 1901, pp. 434–474.

F. Ball, *Sphæra*, Leipzig, 1903, pp. 198–208.

R. Redlich, *Vom Drachen zu Babel* (in *Globus*, Vol. LXXXIV, 1903, pp. 364–371, 384–389).

O. Gilbert, *Babylons Gestirndienst* (in *Globus*, Vol. LXXXVI, 1904, pp. 225–231).

M. J. De Morgan, *Délégation en Perse*, Memoirs, Vol. VII, 1905, pp. 137–153.

K. Frank, *Bilder und Symbole der babylonisch-assyrischen Götter* (in *Leipziger Semitistische Studien*, Vol. II, 2, Leipzig, 1906).

H. Zimmern, *Die Göttersymbole des Nazimaruttash-Kudurru* (in *Leipziger Semitische Studien*, Vol. II, 2, 1906, pp. 33–44).

F. Delitzsch, *Vorderasiatische Schriftdenkmäler der Königlichen Museen zu Berlin*, Heft I, Beiheft, Leipzig, 1907, pls. I–V.

IV. CHRONOLOGICAL LIST OF THE BABYLONIAN KUDURRU INSCRIPTIONS WITH BIBLIOGRAPHICAL NOTES.

I. Kudurru of Nazi-Maruttash.

Provenance: Susa, found 1898.

Present location: Louvre, Paris.

Text: Scheil, *Délégation en Perse*, Vol. II, pls. 16–19.

Translation: Scheil, *l.c.*, pp. 86–92.

Symbols: Published by De Morgan, *Délégation en Perse*, Vol. I., pls. 14–15, *Koudourrou*, No. 2; see also figs. 27, 28 of this book; described by De Morgan, *l.c.*, pp. 170–172; Hommel, *Aufsätze*, pp. 438–440, No. 20; our List of Symbols, p. 231; discussed also by Zimmern, in *Leipziger Semitistische Studien*, Vol. II, 2, pp. 33–44.

Quoted as Susa, No. 2.

II. Kudurru of Bitiliâshu.

Provenance: Susa, found 1898.

Present location: Louvre, Paris.

Text: Scheil, *Délégation en Perse*, Vol. II, p. 93f.

Translation: *ibidem*, 36 lines, fragmentary.

Symbols: Published by De Morgan, *Délégation en Perse*, Vol. I, p. 179, fig. 386, *Koudourrou*, No. 9; see also fig. 21 of this book; described by Hommel, *Aufsätze*, p. 445; our List of Symbols, p. 231.

Quoted as D. E. P., II, 93, 94.

III. Stone tablet of Agabtaḫa.

Provenance: Susa.

Present location: Louvre, Paris.

Text: Scheil, *Délégation en Perse*, Vol. II, pl. 20.

Translation: Scheil, *l.c.*, p. 95.
Symbols: None.
Quoted as D. E. P., II, pl. 20.

IV. Kudurru of Rammân-shum-uṣur.
Provenance: Susa.
Present location: Louvre, Paris.
Text: Scheil, *Délégation en Perse*, Vol. II, p. 97.
Translation: Scheil, *ibidem*, 19 lines, fragmentary.
Symbols: None preserved.
Quoted as D. E. P., II, 97.

V. First Kudurru of Meli-Shipak.
Provenance: (?).
Present location: British Museum, No. 103 (90,827).
Text: Belser, in B. A., Vol. II, pp. 187–203.
Translation: Peiser, K. B., Vol. III, 1, pp. 154–163.
Symbols: Unpublished, described by Pinches, "Guide to the Nimroud Central Saloon," 1886, p. 54f.; Hommel, *Aufsätze*, pp. 244–246, No. 1; our LIST OF SYMBOLS, p. 231f.
Quoted as London, 103.

VI. Second Kudurru of Meli-Shipak.
Provenance: (?).
Present location: British Museum, No. 101 (90,829).
Text: Belser, in B. A., Vol. II, pp. 165–169.
Translation: Peiser, in K. B., Vol. IV, pp. 56–61.
Symbols: Unpublished, described by Pinches, "Guide," pp. 50–52; Hommel, *Aufsätze*, pp. 246–248, No. 2; our LIST OF SYMBOLS, p. 232.
Quoted as London, 101.

VII. Third Kudurru of Meli-Shipak.
Provenance: Susa, found 1899.
Present location: Louvre, Paris.
Text: Scheil, *Délégation en Perse,* Vol. II, pls. 21–24.
Translation: Scheil, *l.c.*, pp. 99–111.
Symbols: Published by De Morgan, *Délégation en Perse*, Vol. I, pl. 16; *Koudourrou*, No. 3; described by Hommel, *Aufsätze*, p. 440f., No. 21; our LIST OF SYMBOLS, p. 232f.
Quoted as Susa, No. 3.

VIII. Fourth Kudurru of Meli-Shipak.
Provenance: Susa.
Present location: Louvre, Paris.
Text: Transliterated by Scheil, *Délégation en Perse*, Vol. II., p. 112.

Translation: Scheil, *ibidem,* 10 lines, fragmentary.

Symbols: Broken off.

Quoted as D. E. P., II, 112.

IX. First Kudurru of Marduk-apal-iddina I.

Provenance: Opposite Bagdad, found by George Smith and presented to the British Museum by the "Daily Telegraph" in 1873.

Present location: British Museum, No. 99.

Text: IV R.[1] 41; IV R.[2] 38.

Translations: George Smith, "Assyrian Discoveries," 1875, pp. 237ff.; Oppert and Menant, *Documents juridiques,* 1877, pp. 129–138; Rodwell, "Records of the Past," Vol. IX, pp. 31ff.; Peiser, K. B., Vol. IV, pp. 60–63.

Symbols: Published IV R.[1] 43; see also fig. 6 of this book; described by Pinches, "Guide," p. 46; Hommel, *Aufsätze,* p. 248f., No. 3; our LIST OF SYMBOLS, p. 233.

Quoted as IV R.[2] 38.

X. Second Kudurru of Marduk-apal-iddina I.

Provenance: Susa.

Present location: Louvre, Paris.

Text: Scheil, *Délégation en Perse,* Vol. VI, pls. 9, 10.

Translation: Scheil, *l.c.,* pp. 32–39.

Symbols: Published by Scheil, *l.c.,* pls. 9, 10; see also fig. 10 of this book; described in our LIST OF SYMBOLS, p. 233.

Quoted as Susa, No. 16.

XI. Third Kudurru of Marduk-apal-iddina I.

Provenance: Susa.

Present location: Louvre, Paris.

Text: Scheil, *Délégation en Perse,* Vol. VI, pl. 11.

Translation: Scheil, *l.c.,* pp. 39–41; fragmentary.

Symbols: Published by De Morgan, *Délégation en Perse,* Vol. VII, p. 140; see also fig. 40 of this book; described in our LIST OF SYMBOLS, p. 234.

Quoted as Susa, No. 14.

XII. Fourth Kudurru of Marduk-apal-iddina I.

Provenance: Susa.

Present location: Louvre, Paris.

Text: Unpublished, transliterated by Scheil, *Délégation en Perse,* Vol. VI, pp. 42–43.

Translation: Scheil, *ibidem,* 71 lines; fragmentary.

Symbols: None preserved, cf. De Morgan, *Délégation en Perse,* Vol. VII, p. 145; *Koudourrou,* No. XVII.

Quoted as D. E. P., VI, 42, 43.

XIII. Cassite Dynasty, first fragment.

Provenance: Susa.

Present location: Louvre, Paris.

Text: Scheil, *Délégation en Perse,* Vol. II, p. 113f.

Translation: Scheil, *ibidem,* 23 lines; fragmentary.

Symbols: Published by De Morgan, *Délégation en Perse,* Vol. I, pp. 174–175, figs. 380–381; *Koudourrou,* No. 4; see also fig. 23, p. 76, of this book; described by Hommel, *Aufsätze,* p. 443f., No. 22; our LIST OF SYMBOLS, p. 234.

Quoted as D. E. P., II, 113.

XIV. Cassite Dynasty, second fragment.

Provenance: Susa.

Present location: Louvre, Paris.

Text: Unpublished, transliterated by Scheil, *Délégation en Perse,* Vol. II, p. 115.

Translation: Scheil, *ibidem,* 7 lines.

Quoted as D. E. P., II, 115.

XV. Cassite Dynasty, third fragment.

Provenance: Susa.

Present location: Louvre, Paris.

Text: Scheil, *Délégation en Perse,* Vol. II, p. 116.

Translation: Scheil, *ibidem,* 6 lines.

Quoted as D. E. P., II, 116.

XVI. Cassite Dynasty, fourth fragment.

Provenance: Susa.

Present location: Louvre, Paris.

Text: Transliterated by Scheil, *Délégation en Perse,* Vol. VI, pp. 44–45.

Translation: Scheil, *ibidem,* 58 lines.

Symbols: Published by De Morgan, *Délégation en Perse,* Vol. VII, p. 145, fig. 456; *Koudourrou,* No. 18; see also fig. 4, p. 14, of this book; described in our LIST OF SYMBOLS, p. 235f.

Quoted as D. E. P., VI, 44, 45.

XVII. Cassite Dynasty, fifth fragment.

Provenance: Susa.

Present location: Louvre, Paris.

Text: Transliterated and translated by Scheil, *Délégation en Perse,* Vol. VI, p. 46.

Quoted as D. E. P., VI, 46.

XVIII. Cassite Dynasty, sixth fragment.

Provenance: Susa.

Present location: Louvre, Paris.

Text: Transliterated and translated by Scheil, *Délégation en Perse,* Vol. VI, p. 47.

Symbols: Published by De Morgan, *Délégation en Perse,* Vol. VII, p. 146, fig. 457; *Koudourrou,* No. 19; see also fig. 39, p. 104, of this book; described in our List of Symbols, p. 236.

Quoted as D. E. P., VI, 42.

XIX. First Charter of Nebuchadrezzar I.

Provenance: Abu Habba, found by Rassam in 1882.

Present location: British Museum, No. 100 (90,858).

Text: Hilprecht, *Freibrief Nebukadnezar's I.;* V R. 55, 56.

Translations: Hilprecht, *Freibrief N's,* Leipzig, 1883; Pinches, P. S. B. A., Vol. VI, pp. 144–170; Peiser, K. B., Vol. III, 1, pp. 164–171; C. D. Gray, in R. F. Harper's "Assyrian and Babylonian Literature," New York, 1901, pp. 8–11.

Symbols: Published V R. 57; "Guide to the Babylonian and Assyrian Antiquities," London, 1900, pl. VI, etc.; see also fig. 49, p. 131, of this book; described by Hommel, *Aufsätze,* p. 249f., No. 4; our List of Symbols, p. 236.

Quoted as V R. 55, 56.

XX. Second Charter of Nebuchadrezzar I.

Provenance: (?)

Present location: British Museum, No. 92, 987 (82–7–4, 34).

Text: Published by S. A. Smith, "Assyrian Letters," 1888, Pt. IV, pls. VIII–IX; C. T., IX, pls. IV, V.

Translations: B. Meissner, Z. A., IV, 259–269 (cf. Winckler, Z. A., IV, 403); Peiser, K. B., Vol. III, 1, pp. 172–173.

Quoted as C. T., IX, pls. IV–V.

XXI. Kudurru of Nebuchadrezzar I.

Provenance: Nippur, found by the Babylonian Expedition of University of Pennsylvania, 1896.

Present location: In possession of Mrs. Hilprecht.

Text: Transliterated, pp. 142–155 of this book.

Translation: *ibidem.*

Symbols: Published fig. 47, p. 120, of this book; described pp. 121f.; 236f.

Quoted as Neb. Nippur.

XXII. Stone Tablet of Ellil-nâdin-aplu.

Provenance: Presumably neighborhood of Babylon.

Present location: Museum of Archæology, University of Pennsylvania.

Text: Hilprecht, O. B. I., Vol. I, Pt. 1, pls. 30, 31; No. 83.

Translations: Oppert, Z. A., Vol. VIII, pp. 360–374; Hilprecht, *Assyriaca,* pp. 1–58; Peiser, K. B., Vol. IV, pp. 64–66 (cf. also Jensen, Z. A., VIII, 221).

Quoted as O. B. I., No. 83.

XXIII. Second Isin (PA.SHE) Dynasty.

Provenance: (?)

Present location: British Museum, No. 105 (90,841).

Text: III R. 41.

Translations: Oppert, *Documents juridiques*, pp. 117–125; "Records of the Past," Vol. IX, pp. 103ff.; Belser, B. A., Vol. II, pp. 124–129; Peiser, K. B., Vol. IV, pp. 74–79.

Symbols: III R. 45, No. 1; see also fig. 14 of this book; described by Hommel, *Aufsätze*, pp. 250ff., No. 5; our LIST OF SYMBOLS, p. 237.

Quoted as III R. 41.

XXIV. Second Isin (PA.SHE) Dynasty.

Provenance: Bagdad, found by C. Michaux, brought to Paris in 1800.

Present location: Cabinet des Medailles, Paris, No. 702 (Caillou de Michaux).

Text: I R. 70.

Translations: Millin, *Monuments antiques inédits ou nouvellement expliqués*, 1802, Vol. I, pp. 58–68; Lichtenstein, *Braunschweigisches Magazin*, 1802; *Tentamen Palæographiæ Assyrio-Persicæ*, Helmstaedt, 1803, pp. 117–137; Münster, *Religion der Babylonier*, Kopenhagen, 1827, pp. 102–134, tab. III; Oppert, *Bulletin Archéologique de l'Athénæum français*, 1856; *Annales de Philosophie Chrétienne,* Vol. LIII, 1856, 4th, XIV; *Documents juridiques,* 1877, pp. 85–97; "Records of the Past," 1878, Vol. IX, pp. 92ff.; Talbot, J. R. A. S., Vol. XVIII, 1861, pp. 53–75; Babelon, *Histoire ancienne de l'Orient,* Vol. V, pp. 79–81; Boissier, *Recherches sur quelques Contracts Babyloniens*, Paris, 1890, pp. 21–36; Peiser, K. B., Vol. IV, pp. 78–83.

Symbols: First published by Millin, *l.c.*, pls. VIII–IX; repeated by Lichtenstein, Münster and elsewhere; see also fig. 13 of this book; described by Hommel, *Aufsätze*, p. 252f., No. 6, and our LIST OF SYMBOLS, p. 237.

Quoted as I R. 70.

XXV. Stone Tablet of Marduk-nâdin-aḫê, first year.

Provenance: Za'aleh, near Babylon.

Present location: British Museum, No. 96 (90,938).

Text: I R. 66.

Translations: Oppert, *Documents juridiques,* pp. 81ff.; "Records of the Past," Vol. IX, pp. 91; Peiser, K. B., Vol. IV, pp. 66–68.

Symbols: None.

Quoted as I R. 66.

XXVI. Kudurru of Marduk-nâdin-aḫê, tenth year.

Provenance: (?)

Present location: British Museum, No. 106 (90,840).

Text: III R. 43.

Translations: Oppert, *Documents juridiques*, pp. 98–116; "Records of the Past," Vol. IX, pp. 96ff.; Belser, B. A., Vol. II, pp. 116–125; Peiser, K. B., Vol. IV, pp. 68–75.

Symbols: Published III R. 45, No. 2; see also fig. 12 of this book; described by Hommel, *Aufsätze*, p. 253; and our List of Symbols, p. 237f.

Quoted as III R. 43.

XXVII. Kudurru of Marduk-aḫê-erba.

Provenance: Unknown.

Present location: Unknown, perhaps Constantinople.

Text: Hilprecht, O. B. I., Vol. I, Pt. 2, pls. 65–67, No. 149.

Translations: Scheil, *Recueil de Travaux*, Vol. XVI, p. 32f. (partial), and pp. 190–195 of this book.

Symbols: Unpublished, described by Hilprecht, O. B. I., Vol. I, Pt. 2, pp. 65–66; Hommel, *Aufsätze*, p. 434f., No. 16; and our List of Symbols, p. 238.

Quoted as O. B. I., 149.

XXVIII. Kudurru of Second Isin (PA.SHE) Dynasty.

Provenance: Nippur.

Present location: Imperial Ottoman Museum, Constantinople.

Text: Hilprecht, O. B. I., Vol. I, Pt. 1, pl. 27, No. 80.

Translation: None, fragment of four lines.

Symbols: O. B. I., Vol. I, Pt. 1, pl. XII, Nos. 32, 33; see also fig. 44 of this book; described in our List of Symbols, p. 238.

Quoted as O. B. I., 80.

XXIX. Kudurru of Second Isin (PA.SHE) Dynasty.

Provenance: Perhaps Nippur.

Present location: Berlin Museum, V. A., 213.

Text: Hilprecht, O. B. I., Vol. I, Pt. 2, pl. 68, No. 150; *Vorderasiatische Schriftdenkmäler, Heft* I, No. 58.

Translation: None.

Symbols: O. B. I., Vol. I, Pt. 2, pl. XXV, No. 69; described in our List of Symbols, p. 238.

Quoted as V. A., 213.

XXX. Kudurru of the Second Isin (PA.SHE) Dynasty.

Provenance: (?)

Present location: Berlin Museum, V. A., 211.

Text: *Vorderasiatische Schriftdenkmäler, Heft* I, No. 57.

Translation: None, transliterated by Ungnad, *l.c.*, p. IXa.

Symbols: *l.c., Beiheft*, pl. V, described by Hommel, *Aufsätze*, p. 258f., No. 14; our LIST OF SYMBOLS, p. 238.

Quoted as V. A., 211.

XXXI. Kudurru of Nabû-mukîn-aplu.

Provenance: (?)

Present location: British Museum, No. 102 (90,835).

Text: Belser, B. A., Vol. II, pp. 171–185.

Translation: Peiser, K. B., Vol. IV, pp. 82–93.

Symbols: Unpublished, described by Pinches, "Guide," p. 53f.; Hommel, *Aufsätze*, p. 253f., No. 8; and our LIST OF SYMBOLS, p. 238f.

Quoted as London, 102.

XXXII. Stone Tablet of Nabû-apal-iddina.

Provenance: (?)

Present location: British Museum, No. 12,051 (90,922).

Text: C. T., X, pl. 3.

Translation: Boscawen, "Babylonian and Oriental Record," Vol. I, pp. 66–68; Peiser, K. B., Vol. IV, pp. 92–95.

Symbols: Published by Boscawen, *l.c.*, facing p. 65; see also fig. 9 of this book; described by Hommel, *Aufsätze*, p. 255f., No. 10; and our LIST OF SYMBOLS, p. 239.

Quoted as C. T., X, pl. 3.

XXXIII. Stone Tablet of Marduk-shum-iddina.

Provenance: (?)

Present location: Berlin Museum, V. A., 208.

Text: Peiser, *Keilschriftliche Acten-Stücke*, pls. 1–2; *Vorderasiatische Schriftdenkmäler, Heft* I, No. 35.

Translation: Peiser, *l.c.*, pp. 2–6; K. B., Vol. IV, pp. 94–97.

Symbols: Published in *Vorderasiatische Schriftdenkmäler, Heft* I, *Beiheft* pl. II; described by Hommel, *Aufsätze*, p. 256f., No. 11; and our LIST OF SYMBOLS, p. 239f.

Quoted as V. A., 208.

XXXIV. Kudurru of Sargon.

Provenance: (?)

Present location: Berlin Museum, V. A., 209.

Text: Peiser, *Keilschriftliche Acten-Stücke*, photos 1–5; *Vorderasiatische Schriftdenkmäler, Heft* I, No. 70.

Translation: Revillout, *Mélanges assyr. babyl.*, I, No. 1; Peiser, *l.c.*, pp. 6–17; Peiser, K. B., Vol. IV, pp. 158–164.

Symbols: Published by Peiser, *l.c.*, photos 1–5; *Vorderasiatische Schriftdenkmäler, Heft* I, *Beiheft*, p. V; see also fig. 15 of this book; described by Hommel, *Aufsätze*, p. 257f., No. 12; and our LIST OF SYMBOLS, p. 240.

Quoted as V. A., 209.

XXXV. Kudurru of Marduk-apal-iddina II.

Present location: Berlin Museum, V. A., 2663.

Text: *Vorderasiatische Schriftdenkmäler, Heft* I, No. 37; transliterated by Delitzsch, B. A., Vol. II, pp. 258–273; Peiser, K. B., Vol. III, pp. 184–193 (cf. Peiser and Winckler, Z. A., Vol. VII, 182–190).

Translations: Delitzsch, *l.c.*; Peiser, *l.c.*; R. F. Harper, "Assyrian and Babylonian Literature," New York, 1901, pp. 64–68.

Symbols: Published in part by Bezold, *Nineve und Babylon*, p. 63; in full, *Vorderasiatische Schriftdenkmäler, Heft* I, *Beiheft*, pls. III, IV; also fig. 8 of this book; described by Hommel, *Aufsätze*, p. 258, No. 13; our LIST OF SYMBOLS, p. 240.

Quoted as V. A., 2663.

XXXVI. Kudurru of Shamash-shum-ukîn.

Present location: British Museum, No. 87,220.

Text: C. T., X, pls. IV–VII.

Translation: Winckler, *Altorientalische Forschungen*, Vol. I, pp. 497–503.

Symbols: Unpublished.

Quoted as C. T., X, pls. IV–VII.

FRAGMENTARY BOUNDARY STONES, WHOSE INSCRIPTIONS ARE BROKEN OFF OR UNPUBLISHED.

I. Fragments of the Cassite Dynasty.

Provenance: Susa.

Present location: Louvre, Paris.

Symbols: Published by De Morgan, D. E. P., Vol. I, figs. 379, 382–388; Vol. VII, fig. 453, pls. 27, 28.

1. Susa, No. 1, De Morgan, D. E. P., I, p. 168, fig. 379, *Koudourrou*, No I; see also fig. 24 of this book; described by Hommel, *Aufsätze*, p. 437f., No. 19; our LIST OF SYMBOLS, p. 231.
2. Susa, No. 5, De Morgan, D. E. P., I, p. 176, fig. 382; see figs. 17, 18, pp. 40, 41 of this book, and the description in the LIST OF SYMBOLS, p. 234.
3. Susa, No. 6, De Morgan, D. E. P., I, p. 177, fig. 383; see fig. 38, p. 103 of this book, and the description in the LIST OF SYMBOLS, p. 234.
4. Susa, No. 7, De Morgan, D. E. P., I, p. 178, fig. 384; see fig. 21, p. 73 of this book, and the description in the LIST OF SYMBOLS, p. 234.

5. Susa, No. 8, De Morgan, D. E. P., I, p. 178, fig. 385; see fig. 21, p. 73 of this book, and the description in the List of Symbols, p. 235.
6. Susa, No. 10, De Morgan, D. E. P., I, p. 179, fig. 387; see fig. 41, p. 112 of this book, and the description in the List of Symbols, p. 235.
7. Susa, No. 11, De Morgan, D. E. P., I, p. 179, fig. 388; see fig. 44, p. 112 of this book, and the description in the List of Symbols, p. 235.
8. Susa, No. 12, no symbols preserved.
9. Susa, No. 13, De Morgan, D. E. P., VII, p. 139, fig. 451; see also fig. 29 of this book, and the description in our List of Symbols, p. 235.
10. Susa, No. 15, De Morgan, D. E. P., VII, p. 142, fig. 453; see fig. 2, p. 6 of this book, and the description in the List of Symbols, p. 235.
11. Susa, No. 20, De Morgan, D. E. P., VII, pls. 27, 28; see fig. 16, p. 38, and fig. 30, p. 95 of this book, and the description in the List of Symbols, p. 236.

II. Second Isin (PA.SHE) Dynasty.

Provenance: ʿAmrân (Babylon).

Present location: Berlin Museum.

Text: Fragmentary, unpublished.

Symbols: Published in *Mitteilungen der Deutschen Orient Gesellschaft*, No. 7, p. 25; see also fig. 19, p. 45 of this book; described by Hommel, *Aufsätze*, p. 436, No. 18; our List of Symbols, p. 238.

III. Elamite Boundary Stone.

Discovered at Susa, where it remained.

Symbols: Published by Walpole, "Travels in Various Countries of the East," London, 1820, pl. facing p. 426; described by Hommel, *Aufsätze*, p. 259f., No. 15; reproduced there p. 474.

UNPUBLISHED BOUNDARY STONES.

I. British Museum, No. 94 (90,833), c. 1400 B. C.

See *Guide to the Babylonian and Assyrian Antiquities*, London, 1900, p. 85.

II. British Museum, No. (?).

Dated in the reign of Kurigalzu, *šar Bâbili mâr Ka-daš-man-ḫar-bi šarri lâ šanân*; cf. Winckler, Z. A., Vol. II, p. 309; *Altorientalische Forschungen*, Vol. I, p. 117 (perhaps identical with No. I).

III. British Museum, No. 104 (90,834).

Of the reign of Marduk-balâṭsu-iqbi, c. 830 B.C., given as a boundary stone in *Guide*, 1900, p. 88, but cf. E. Cuq, *La propriété foncière en Chaldée*, p. 703.

IV. Paris, Louvre. Boundary Stone of Meli-Shipak. Containing three deeds. See *Académie des Inscriptions et Belles Lettres, Comptes Rendus*, June, 1906, p. 279.

ABBREVIATIONS.

A. D. D..............Johns, *Assyrian Deeds and Documents.*
A. J. S. L............*American Journal of Semitic Languages.*
A. P......................Meissner, *Altbabylonisches Privatrecht.*
A. S. K. T...........Haupt, *Akkadische und Sumerische Keilschrifttexte.*
B. A......................*Beiträge zur Assyriologie.*
B. E......................The *Babylonian Expedition of the University of Pennsylvania,* Series A, Cuneiform Texts.
Br. M....................*British Museum.*
B. O. R...............*Babylonian and Oriental Record.*
Br..........................Brünnow, *A Classified List.*
C. T......................*Cuneiform Texts from Babylonian Tablets in the British Museum.*
Del. H. W...........Delitzsch, *Handwörterbuch.*
D. E. P.................*Mémoires de la Délégation en Perse.*
G. G. A.................*Göttinger Gelehrten Anzeiger.*
I. S. A.................Thureau-Dangin, *Les Inscriptions de Sumer et d'Akkad,* Paris, 1905.
J. A. O. S............*Journal of the American Oriental Society.*
K. B.......................*Keilinschriftliche Bibliothek.*
J. R. A. S............*Journal of the Royal Asiatic Society.*
K. A. T.................Schrader, *Die Keilschriften und das alte Testament.*
M. D. O. G..........*Mitteilungen der Deutschen Orient Gesellschaft.*
M. V. A. G..........*Mitteilungen der Vorderasiatischen Gesellschaft.*
O. B. I.................Hilprecht, *Old Babylonian Inscriptions.*
O. L. Z.................*Orientalistische Literatur-Zeitung.*
P. N.......................Ranke, *Early Babylonian Personal Names, from the published Tablets of the so-called Ḫammurabi Dynasty.*
P. S. B. A...........*Proceedings of the Society of Biblical Archæology.*
R...........................Rawlinson, *Cuneiform Inscriptions of Western Asia.*
R. A.......................*Revue d'Assyriologie.*
R. P.......................*Records of the Past.*
R. T.......................*Recueil de Travaux.*
S. B. B. A...........*Sitzungsberichte der Berliner Akademie der Wissenschaften.*

S. B. O. T...........Haupt, *Sacred Books of the Old Testament.*
V. A.....................*Vorderasiatische Abteilung der Kgl. Museen in Berlin.*
V. S.....................*Vorderasiatische Schriftdenkmäler der Königl. Museen zu Berlin.*
Z. A.....................*Zeitschrift für Assyriologie.*
Z. D. M. G..........*Zeitschrift der Deutschen Morgenländischen Gesellschaft.*
Z. K.....................*Zeitschrift für Keilschriftforschung.*

Delitzsch, *Kossäer* = *Die Sprache der Kossäer,* Leipzig, 1884.

Hommel, *Aufsätze* = *Aufsätze und Abhandlungen,* Pts. 1–3, München, 1892–1901.

Hommel, *Geographie* = *Grundriss der Geographie und Geschichte des alten Orients,* München, 1904.

Hrozný, *Mythen* = *Sumerisch-Babylonische Mythen von dem Gotte Ninrag (Ninib)* (in *Mitteilungen der Vorderasiatischen Gesellschaft,* Vol. VIII, No. 5, 1903).

Langdon, *Building Inscriptions* = *Building Inscriptions of the Neo-Babylonian Empire,* Paris, 1905.

Reisner, *Hymnen* = *Sumerisch-Babylonische Hymnen nach Thontafeln griechischer Zeit,* Berlin, 1896.

Zimmern, *Beiträge* = *Beiträge zur Kenntniss der Babylonischen Religion,* Leipzig, 1899–1900

I.

BABYLONIAN BOUNDARY STONES.

Babylonian boundary stones and their inscriptions have long been the subject of study and investigation. Among the earliest Babylonian monuments which arrived in Europe was the now famous *Caillou de Michaux,* found by the French botanist, C. Michaux, at the Tigris, a day's journey below Bagdad, in the ruins of a palace, and brought by him to Paris in the year 1800. Published by A. J. Millin in 1802,[1] its inscription was at once studied and translated by the German professor, A. A. H. Lichtenstein, of Helmstädt. His attempt was, however, a failure, for he made out the inscription to be Aramaic, read it from right to left, and declared it to be a dirge addressed by a certain Archimagus to wailing women at an annual mourning festival.[2] After this unpromising beginning no progress was made in the interpretation of Babylonian boundary stone inscriptions until after the epoch-making decipherment of the great Behistun inscription by Sir Henry C. Rawlinson in 1851. Among the scholars who at that time devoted all their energies to the decipherment of the new language was Jules Oppert,

[1] *Monuments antiques inédits ou nouvellement expliqués,* Paris, 1802, Vol. I, pp. 58–68; pls. VIII, IX.

[2] *Tentamen Palæographiæ Assyrio-Persicæ,* Helmstædt, 1803, pp. 111–134; pls. III–VII. The inscription is rendered in a Latin poem. Its contents are described as follows:

Næniam quasi quamdam ab Archimago parentantibus feminis inter Sabæos, sive Persas eius ævi, quæ nuper maritos, fratres vel alios cognatos amiserant, et comitantibus præficis, die festo, quando sollemnia sacra luctus publici ob defunctos quotannis celebrantur, prælegendam, vel recitandam.

who in 1856 gave the first approximately correct rendering of the Michaux stone. During the next two decades the text of the first four *kudurru* inscriptions[1] was published by Sir H. C. Rawlinson in his monumental work, *Cuneiform Inscriptions of Western Asia*, Vols. I–IV, 1861–1870. An important step in advance was made in 1877 by the joint work of Oppert and Menant, *Documents juridiques de l'Assyrie et de la Chaldée*, in which the four inscriptions referred to were transliterated and translated.

A brief history of the publication and interpretation of boundary stones till 1891 was given by C. W. Belser in B.A., II, 112–114. Since that time the following scholars have made contributions to this subject: Prof. F. E. Peiser furnished transliterations and translations of fifteen *kudurru* inscriptions for the *Keilinschriftliche Bibliothek*, Vols. III–IV. Prof. H. V. Hilprecht published two boundary stones (O. B., I, 83, 149) and two fragments (O. B., I, 80, 150), together with an exhaustive discussion of the inscription of Ellil-nâdin-aplu (*Assyriaca*, pp. 1–58). Prof. H. Winckler gave a transliteration and translation of the stone of Shamash-shum-ukîn (*Altorientalische Forschungen*, I, 497–503). Dr. L. W. King published three boundary stones (C. T., IX, pls. IV–V; X, pls. III; IV–VII). Finally Prof. V. Scheil published three large Cassite stones

[1] The most common name applied to Babylonian boundary stones is *abnunarû*, literally "a stone (*NA*) that is engraved (*RU*)"; so Jensen, *Kosmologie*, pp. 349, note, 440, and K. B., III, 1, p. 37 note *. The name *kudurru* is employed less frequently with a direct reference to the stone on which the inscription is written (cf. London, 103, V, 39; VI, 21; London, 101, I, 1; Susa 3, III, 53; I R. 70, II, 8; Neb. Nippur, heading l. 2). Other names are *abnu*, "stone" (London, 101, III, 2; London, 103, III, 30; London, 102, V, 6), *asumittu*, "a sculptured and an inscribed stele" (London, 103, VI, 26), *tuppu*, "an inscribed tablet" (I R. 66, II, 5; C. T., X, pl. III, 23; V. A. 2663, IV, 56; V. A. 208, 48; V. A. 202, II, 11; V, 13), and *li'û*, "a tablet" or "document" (Neb. Nippur V, 8; Susa 9, II, 9, 12; *isuLI*, Susa 16, III, 11, 15; see Chap. I, p. 10). Finally, the term *kan-gi* (= kâniku) is used in the sense of "a sealed document" in London, 102, VI, 14.

and twelve fragments[1] (*Delegation en Perse,* Vols. II, IV, VI). For a full list of all the known boundary stones, together with their literature, see our *Bibliography.*

At the present time (June, 1906) we have twenty whole boundary stones with inscriptions more or less complete, together with sixteen fragments of other boundary stones. They cover the period from about 1350–650 B.C., or from the reign of Nazi-Maruttash to that of Shamash-shum-ukîn.

But while boundary stones, properly so called, do not make their appearance until the Cassite dynasty, we find other similar monuments at a much earlier period. The oldest monument of this kind is a *national* boundary stone, erected by Entemena,[2] one of the early rulers of Shirpula, about 3500 B.C., to mark the boundary between Shirpula and the neighboring city Gish-ḫú. Its important inscription closes, in perfect agreement with the later boundary stones, with a series of curses:

"Whenever the people of Gish-ḫú shall cross the boundary canal of Ningirsu or the boundary canal of Ninâ, in order to bring this land under their power—whether they be the men of Gish-ḫú or the men of the mountain—may Enlil destroy them, may the great net of Ningirsu overthrow them, may his sublime hand and sublime foot be lifted up high (over them), may the warriors of

[1] These fragments are: One of the reign of Bitiliâshu (D. E. P., II, 93f.), one of Rammân-šum-uṣur (D. E. P., II, 97f.), one of Meli-Shipak (D. E. P., II, 112), two of Marduk-apal-iddina I (D. E. P., VI, 39–41; 42, 43), and six undated Cassite fragments (D. E. P., II, 113f.; 115; 116; VI, 44f.; 46; 47). A boundary stone fragment is perhaps also the broken stone of Meli-Shipak (D. E. P., IV, pls. 16, 17). The phraseology of the curses points in that direction. Its shape resembles the stone of Marduk-apal-iddina I. = IV R.[2] 38. Finally, the stone of Agabtaḫa (D. E. P., II, 95) must also be included, for it is a private deed, recording a grant of land. Cf. below, p. 11.

[2] Published by Thureau-Dangin in R. A., IV, No. 11, pl. 2, and translated there pp. 42–50; cf. also his *Inscriptions de Sumer et d'Akkad,* Paris, 1905, pp. 62–69.

the city be filled with rage, and, in the midst of the city, may fury be in their hearts.''

Another series of monuments closely related to the later boundary stones are the doorsockets of the ancient kings of Agade and other early rulers. The doorsockets and thresholds of temples were evidently regarded as their boundary. A doorsocket of Ur-

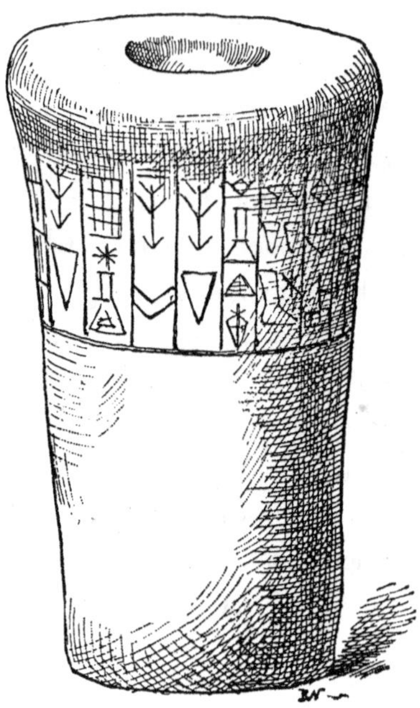

FIG. 1.—Doorsocket of Ur-Ninâ, shaped as a boundary stone.

Ninâ has actually the shape of a boundary stone,[1] while all their inscriptions close with the identical formula of the later boundary stone inscriptions. Thus, *e.g.*, the second doorsocket inscription of Shargâni-shar-âli, published by Prof. Hilprecht,[2] reads:

[1] Published by Heuzey in R. A., IV, 97; see also Thureau-Dangin, I. S. A., p. 18f.

[2] Hilprecht, O. B. I., Vol. I, No. 2; cf. also No. 1.

^{d}Šar-ga-ni-šar-âli mâr Itti(-ti)-^{d}En-lil,[1] *da-num šar Akkadi ù bá-ú-la-ti ^{d}En-lil bâni E-kur bît ^{d}En-lil in Nippur^{ki} ša duppa sù-a (u)-sa-za-ku-ni*[2] *^{d}En-lil ù ^{d}Šamaš išid-su li-zu-ḫa ù zêr-su li-il-gu-da—i.e.,* "Shar-gâni-shar-âli, the son of Itti-Ellil, the powerful king of Akkad and of the dominion of Ellil, (is) the builder of Ekur, the temple of Ellil in Nippur. Whoever shall alter this inscribed stone, may Ellil and Shamash tear out his foundation and carry off his seed."

Other inscriptions of Naram-Sin, the kings of Guti and Lulubi and of Gudea close with similar curses.[3] It seems in fact that most *public* monuments were placed by these imprecations under the protection of the gods, to guard them against destruction by ill-disposed persons. A conspicuous example is furnished by the famous stele of Ḫammurabi, containing his code of laws, in which twelve of the great gods are invoked (Col. XLII, 45–XLIV, 90) to punish anyone who abolishes his judgments, overrules his words, alters his statues, effaces his name and writes his own name in its place (Col. XLII, 27–35).

[1] Or perhaps better *Da-ti-^{d}En-lil*, as suggested by Thureau-Dangin (cf. I. S. A. 233, note 10), on the basis of R. T. C. No. 176, *Da-ti-^{d}En-lil*, as compared with C. T. 21335, 121, *Da-a-ti-^{d}En-lil*. For Ellil see article of Prof. Clay, "Ellil, the God of Nippur," in A. J. S. L., July, 1907.

[2] Thureau-Dangin calls attention to the fact (cf. I. S. A., 233) that *nazâku* alternates with *nakâru*, especially in the Code of Ḫammurabi: Col. XLI, 74, *u-zu-ra-ti-ia a u-ša-zi-iq*; Col. XLII, 10, *u-zu-ra-ti-ia la u-na-ki-ir.*

[3] For the inscriptions of Naram-Sin, containing curses, see (*a*) Hilprecht, O. B. I., 120, Col. III, 5–IV, 4; (*b*) Scheil, D. E. P., II, 55, note 1, Col. IV, 1ff.; (*c*) Scheil, D. E. P., VI, 3–4, Col. II, 20–30. For the inscription of King Lasirab of Guti see Hilprecht, O. B. I., Vol. I, 13f.; Thureau-Dangin, I. S. A., 244f. For the stele of Anu-banîni, King of Lulubi, see Thureau-Dangin, I. S. A., 246. The statue of Gudea, numbered C, contains also a curse, Col. IV, 5–17 (Thureau-Dangin, I. S. A., 119). Similar curses are found on a number of Elamite monuments, *e.g.*, the stelæ of Karibu of Shushinak: (*a*) Scheil, D. E. P., II, 64, Col. III, 1–6; (*b*) Scheil, D. E. P., IV, 6–7, Col. V, 1ff.; (*c*) Scheil, D. E. P., VI, 3–4, Col. II, 20–30, and the inscriptions given by Thureau-Dangin, *l.c.*, pp. 252–258. An example of a Sumerian curse during the Cassite period occurs on an inscription of Kadashman-Turgu (Hilprecht, O. B. I., Vol. I, 63, 14–20).

Turning now to the boundary stones, properly so called, the first question that engages our attention is the probable origin and introduction of boundary stones into Babylonia to mark the limits of private property. All that is known for certain is that they first make their appearance during the third or Cassite dynasty. But when we consider the fact that, although there are many transfers

FIG. 2.—Symbols on a fragmentary boundary stone of the Cassite period. (Susa, No. 15.)

of land in the earlier periods, no traces of boundary stones for private land have come to light, and when we consider furthermore that there was no marble, basalt or limestone in the alluvial soil of Babylonia to provide the material for boundary stones, but that they had to be imported, we are almost forced to the conclusion that the erection of boundary stones on private lands was a foreign custom, which originated in a mountainous country where there were plenty of stones to supply the demand. As the Cassite rulers were foreigners, who came most likely from the mountainous regions east of Babylonia,[1] it is natural to conclude that they caused the introduction of this custom.[2] This conclusion is somewhat supported by the interesting fact, which ought to be emphasized, that all the twelve boundary stones of the Cassite period which have come down to us, in whole or in part,[3] contain either the record of a royal grant or the confirmation of such a grant when no earlier deed had been

[1] Cf. Hommel, *Geographie*, p. 36.

[2] While this book was passing through the press I had an opportunity of consulting Edouard Cuq, *La propriété foncière en Chaldée d'apres les pierres-limites* (extrait de la *Nouvelle Revue historique de Droit français et étranger*, de November-December, 1906, pp. 701–738). Unfortunately I am unable to agree with the author in many of his positions. His statement (§ 10, p. 735) that the introduction of boundary stones was a sign of a degeneration of law, and was caused by the inability of the Cassite kings properly to protect land, does not seem to be borne out by the facts. A number of the later Cassite rulers have the determinative *ilu* before their names, which implies that they enjoyed divine honors (Hilprecht, B. E., XX, pt. 1, p. 51f.). If they were regarded as divine surely their power was sufficient to protect property. Again, several of these kings, *e.g.*, Nazi-Maruttash (Susa 2, I, 2), Rammân-shum-uṣur (D. E. P., II, 97, 8), Meli-Shipak (London, 101, I, 13) and Marduk-apal-iddina (D. E. P., VI, 42, Col. I, 24), used the title *šar kiššati*, which implied a claim of supremacy over Babylonia, Assyria and Mesopotamia (cf. Winckler, *Forschungen*, I, 222–232). If they could rule practically all of Western Asia, they could surely protect the property of their subjects at home. There may have been a degeneration of law at the close of the Cassite period, but the introduction of boundary stones had nothing to do with it. Finally, no inferences of that kind can be drawn from the stone of Meli-Shipak (London, 103), which contains the record of several lawsuits, for it does not appear that the case was reopened by the *same* party after the king had rendered an adverse decision, but *different* parties made claims under different reigns.

[3] As the *Bibliography* shows, eighteen boundary stones of the Cassite period have been published thus far. Six of them are, however, so fragmentary that the name of the king has not been preserved, nor is enough of their inscriptions left to enable us to classify them as to the nature of the grants they contained.

executed or when the land had been in dispute. Gradually, however, during the second Isin (PA.SHE) dynasty, these stones were also used to record transfers of private property, while still later their use was even further extended.[1] It is also interesting to note that all the boundary stones published thus far come from Babylonia; none have as yet been found in Assyria. Even the stone of Sargon is dated in the Babylonian city of Dêr (Col. II, 25). There are a number of similar grants of land by the Assyrian kings Adad-nirari, Tiglath-pileser III, Ashur-bân-aplu and Ashur-êtil-ilâni, but they are written on clay tablets.[2]

Documents for Public and Private Use.

From the evidence at hand it seems that at least in all royal grants of land two documents were used[3]—one a large conical block, to be placed as a public monument upon the field for the information of the people in general, the other a private document, to be

[1] A stone, dated in the reign of Nabû-shum-ishkun (M. D. O. G., No. 4, March, 1900, pp. 14–17), has the shape of a boundary stone. It has also the various symbols on top (see p. 97) and its inscription contains the usual curses. It is, however, no boundary stone, but a document recording the investiture of a Nebo priest of Borsippa, Nabû-mutakkil, with certain rights and privileges pertaining to his office. The analogy of the stone of Nazi-Maruttash (see p. 22) and of the Nippur stone (see p. 123) leads to the inference that the priest himself wrote the inscription and caused the selection of this undoubtedly sacred monument bearing the symbols of the gods, because the transaction was one of great importance, at least for himself and his family.

[2] For the Assyrian land grants see Johns, *Assyrian Deeds and Documents*, (*a*) Adad-nirâri, A. D. D., Nos. 651–656; (*b*) Tiglathpileser III, A. D. D., Nos. 658–659; (*c*) Aššur-bân-aplu, D. D. D., Nos. 646–48; (*d*) Aššur-etil-ilâni, A. D. D., Nos. 649–650. See also Meissner, *Assyrische Freibriefe*, B. A., II, 566–570, and Peiser, K. B. IV, 142–147.

[3] This fact had already been recognized before, *e.g.*, by Prof. Hilprecht, O. B. I., Vol. I, pt. 1, p. 38, note 8. The inscriptions on the private documents were, however, not exact copies of the public boundary stones. As to the differences see below, p. 13.

held by the owner of the field as a proof of his ownership. Of the former class there was in each case but one copy.[1] This is evident from the repeated references in the inscriptions to the boundary stone of the field (*ku-dur-ri eqlu šu-a-tu*); the plural of *kudurru* is never used in this connection. The same inference can be drawn from the name of the stone of Nazi-Maruttash: *dNabû-nâṣir-kudur-eqlâti*, and also from the curses of Ninib. That the boundary stones were actually placed on the fields appears from the curses, which show that they were public monuments which could be removed from their place; hence we find provisions that the stone shall not be removed from its place (London, 101, III, 2), that it shall not be placed in a secret place where it cannot be seen (Susa, 3, Col. V, 43, 44), that it shall not be hidden in the earth (III R. 41, II, 12). It can also be inferred from the fact that the lowest part of the stones was not covered with writing (cf. D. E. P., II, pls. 21–23; VI, pls. 9, 10; 11*a*; IV R. 43; I R. 70, etc). But the

[1] This is in contrast to Egyptian custom, where a number of boundary stones seem to have been used for one tract of land. In a number of cases at least we have clear proof that such was the case. A cemetery at Abydos was marked by two stelæ (Breasted, *Ancient Records of Egypt*, Vol. I, §§ 766–772). At Tell-el-Amarna were fourteen landmarks to indicate the extent of the city (Breasted, *l.c.*, II, §§ 949–972). The extent of the jackal nome was marked by fifteen boundary stones (Breasted, *l.c.*, I, § 632). Egyptian boundary stones resemble those of Babylonia in several respects: (*a*) They are elaborate stone monuments, set up on the boundaries of fields (Breasted, *l.c.*, IV, § 332). (*b*) Frequently the stone had a name (Breasted, *l.c.*, IV, 479). A list of such names is given by Maspero, *Dawn of Civilization*, 3d ed., p. 329. (*c*) The inscriptions of the boundary stones carefully define the demarkations of the fields on all four sides (Breasted, *l.c.*, IV, §§ 479–483). (*d*) The historical circumstances leading to the grant are sometimes given (Breasted, *l.c.*, I, § 768; II, § 1043). (*e*) In some cases there are also curses uttered in the name of the gods or prohibitions not to erase the inscription (Breasted, *l.c.*, II, §§ 925, 968; IV, § 483). (*f*) Not only the land but also immunity from taxation was granted by the king in some instances (Breasted, *l.c.*, IV, §§ 147–150). All these features appear also on the Babylonian boundary stones, see below, pp. 37–39.

clearest proof consists in the repeated reference to the actual removal of the stone from the field in the course of a litigation (cf. Susa, 16, III, 5-10; London, 103, II, 20–III, 2; O. B. I., 83, I, 10–14).

The existence of the second class of documents, dealing with land grants, depends upon the following evidence: The stone of Bitiliâshu refers to a field granted in the reign of Kurigalzu (D. E. P., II, 94, Col. II, 8–12). A duplicate copy of the original grant was produced during a litigation in the reign of Bitiliâshu. Again we learn that of the grant of Nazi-Maruttash a record was written on a tablet of terra cotta and set up before the god (*narâ ša haṣbi išṭurma maḫar ilišu ušziz*, D. E. P., II, 91; Med., I, 3–5). The latter refers evidently to a private document and does not exclude the existence of a public boundary stone. Both the public and the private documents are referred to on the new stone of Marduk-apal-iddina I, which reads: 𒉌 *Ú u tup-pi eqli ka-nik di-ni ik-nu-uk-ma a-na* ^m^*Mu-un-na-bit-tum id-din. I-na ka-nak* 𒉌 *Ú u tup-pi eqli* ^abnu^*kunukki di-ni šú-a-tum . . . . iz-za-az-zu* (D. E. P., VI, 34, Col. III, 11–15). The group 𒉌 *Ú* cannot be read with Scheil I *ammatu* and rendered ''l'aune,'' from which he concludes that there is here a reference to the sealing of the yardstick alongside of the sealing of the tablet. This is clearly excluded, for on the new stone of Nebuchadrezzar I. the phrase: *Ina ka-nak* 𒉌 *Ú šú-a-tu*, etc. (Col. V, 8), occurs alone, which, following Scheil's rendering, would lead us to the impossible conclusion that no sealing of a tablet took place. The true reading of the signs in question can be inferred from the stone of Merodach-baladan II, where Bâbili (Gen.) is written Bâbi + li (𒉌) while ili, resp. ilê, "gods," appears as 𒉌𒉌 (V. A., 2663, I, 26; II, 2); hence (𒉌) has the value *li* and the signs under discussion ought to be read li-ú.[1] While the term *li'û* refers to the public boundary

[1] I owe this explanation to Prof. Hilprecht. In support of it he calls attention to the fact that the use of *NI* and *NI.NI* is exactly parallel. The single *NI* is often read *li*, while *NI.NI* is used for *ili* (Br. 5356) and *ilê*, *e.g.*, in the name *Shamash-bêl-NI.NI*, see Ranke, *Personal Names*, p. 213, note 3.

stone (cf. D. E. P., II, 94, 8, 12), the term *tuppu* refers to the private tablet,[1] both of which were sealed in the presence of witnesses.[2]

But, what is more important, the existence of private documents recording grants of land cannot only be inferred from the inscriptions; we are also in the possession of actual copies that have come down to us. Being stored in the temple (cf. D. E. P., II, 91; Med., I, 5) or held by the owner, they were not exposed to destruction by strangers, and hence the most characteristic feature of the public boundary stones, the long-drawn-out curses, are naturally wanting on the private monuments. Taking this absence of the curses as our guide, we can classify the following stones as documents kept privately: (1) The tablet of Agabtaḫa (D. E. P., II, pl. 20), recording a grant of ten *gur*[3] of cultivated land by King *Bi-ti-li-ia-a-šu* to Agabtaḫa, a fugitive of Ḫaligalbat. (2) The charter of Nebuchadrezzar I (C. T., IX, pls. 4, 5), granting land and immunity from levies to two priests of Eria. (3) The stone of Ellil-nâdin-aplu (O. B., I, 83), confirming the grant of a tract of land to a temple of the goddess Ninâ at Dêr. (4) The stone of Za'aleh (I R. 66), granting exemption from levies to one called the Ishnunakean. (5) The grant of King Nabû-apal-iddina to the temple officer Nabû-apal-iddina.[4] (6) The grant of land, made in the eleventh year of King Marduk-shum-iddina, by Bêl-iddina to his son Kidîni (V. A. 208). (7) To this

[1] There are of course cases in which *tuppu* refers to the public monument (see above, p. 2, note 1). The statement in the text has only reference to its use on the stone of Marduk-apal-iddina I. (Susa 16).

[2] Another reference to a private document occurs in a stone of Meli-Shipak (London, 103), where it is distinctly stated that the sealed document had been deposited in the house of the owner of the field (*kunuk šîmi eqli ša ana bîti ša mBêlâni šaknu*, Col. III, 9–10).

[3] The reading of *gur* is made certain by the interesting discovery of Prof. Clay that it is represented in the Aramaic endorsements of the Murashû tablets by כר; cf. his forthcoming article on the "Aramaic Endorsements of the Murashû Tablets" in the William R. Harper Memorial Volumes.

[4] See C. T., X, pl. 3.

FIG. 3.—Stone tablet of Ellil-nâdin-aplu, confirming a grant of land to a temple of the goddess Ninâ at Dêr. (O. B. I., No. 83)

same class of private records belongs also the stone of Nazi-Maruttash (Susa, 2 = D. E. P., II, pls. 16–19). Its inscription states distinctly that it was a copy of a terra cotta tablet which had been set up in the temple, and in perfect harmony with this is the fact that it has no curses against the removal of the stone. Nevertheless when a new copy was made it was written upon a block like those of the public boundary stones. Originally then, as we may infer from this case, private deeds were written upon terra cotta or perhaps clay tablets.[1] In course of time stone tablets were substituted, and in exceptional cases even stone blocks, such as were commonly used for public boundary stones. The characteristic features of these private deeds during the Cassite and PA.SHE dynasties were as follows: (1) With the exception of the stone block of Nazi-Maruttash, they are stone tablets and not conical blocks. (2) Their inscriptions contain no curses against the removal of the boundary stone. At most there are curses against any change in the status of the field (D. E. P., II, pl. 17; III, 11–15), or admonitions not to change the boundary nor to curtail the field (O. B. I., 83, II, 21–24). (3) No witnesses are mentioned. (4) There is no demarcation of the field. (5) All but the Nazi-Maruttash stone have no symbols. The two later private deeds, made under Nabû-apal-iddina and Marduk-shum-iddina, differ in several respects from the earlier tablets. They have both witnesses and demarcations

[1] It is of course *possible* that the introduction of boundary stones was earlier than the Cassite period, and that even in the earlier period stone tablets were used. The above inferences are drawn from the material now at our disposal. Later discoveries may compel us to modify our statements. Such a modification would even now be necessary if the statements on the stone of Ellil-nâdin-aplu (Col. I, 11, 12) implied that the governor of Bît-Sin-mâgir took away the original boundary stone granted under Gulkishar. This, however, is not at all necessary; because, when the custom was once introduced during the Cassite period, it would be quite natural to have copies of the private documents made, in order to erect them on the fields.

noted in their inscriptions, and in addition the one of Nabû-apal-iddina has also symbols. The close connection of all these stone tablets with the public boundary stones is proved by their similarity of language and the fact that both record grants of land, originally royal grants alone.

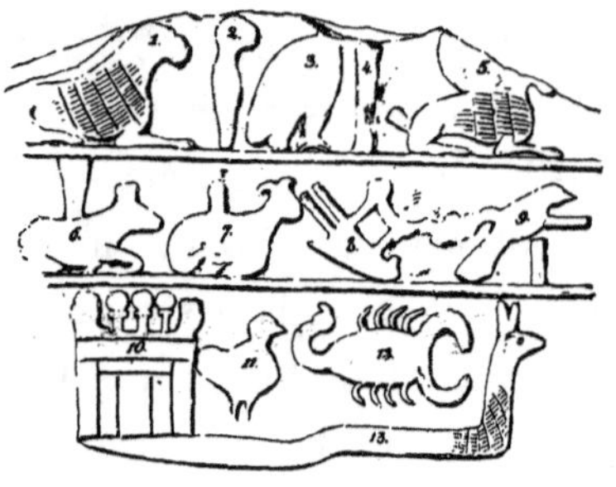

Fig. 4.—Symbols on a Cassite boundary stone. (Susa, No. 18.)

Babylonian boundary stones and boundaries were sacred to the god NIN.IB, hence he is called *bêl kudurri* (D. E. P., II, 113) or *bêl miṣri u kudurri* (Neb. Nippur, IV, 19). Sometimes his wife Gula is associated with him (O. B. I., 149; III, 1) and mentioned with him in the curse to tear out the boundary stone of the enemy (V R. 56, 39–40). In at least one case, however, the boundary stone is placed under the protection of Nabû, the god of agriculture,[1] for this is clearly implied in the name of the stone of Nazi-Maruttash: *ᵈNabû-nâṣir-kudur-eqlâti* (Col. IV, 34).

An interesting reference to boundary stones in the religious literature occurs in the *Shurpu* series, in a prayer which is remarkable for its ethical contents. In this prayer the priest intercedes for the worshiper, and implores the deity to forgive him by asking the following questions: *Kudurru lâ ketti uktadir, kudurru ketti ul uktadir, usa miṣra u kudurru uštêli—i.e.*, "Has he drawn a false

[1] For Nabû as the god of agriculture see Jastrow, *Religion*, Vol. I, p. 118, and the article on Nebo by A. Jeremias in Roscher's *Lexicon*, III, 60.

boundary? Has he omitted to draw a true boundary? Has he removed the confines, the limits or the boundary stone?''[1]

Fig. 5.—Symbols on a fragmentary boundary (?) stone of Meli-Shipak, carried to Susa by Sutruk-naḫunte. (D. E. P., IV, pl. 16.)

[1] Shurpu II, 45–46. It is remarkable that no punishment for the removal of the boundary is referred to in the *kudurru* inscriptions aside from the curses. Only once, in an inscription of Sennacherib, do we find a threat of hanging in case a man tears down his old house and rebuilds the new extending into the royal highway (*ša bîtsu labiru inaqqaruma eššu ibannû ša uššê bîtišu ana girri šarri irruba ṣîr bîtišu ana gašîši illalûšu*, I R. 7 F 24–27; cf. Peiser, *Acten-Stücke*, p. IX, note 2).

Legal Transactions in the Kudurru Inscriptions.

According to the various legal transactions recorded on the boundary stones, they naturally group themselves into two general divisions—first, those which represent royal grants; second, those which represent transfers of private land from one individual or family to another.

(I) In the first group there are again several sub-divisions:

(a) Royal grants to faithful and distinguished officials, of which we have the following specimens:

King Rammân-shum-uṣur granted a tract of land to an official whose name is partly broken off (D. E. P., II, 97).

From the reign of Meli-Shipak we have three grants of this kind:

The longest and most interesting inscription (Susa, 3 = D. E. P., II, pls. 21–24) records in seven columns (52 + 54 + 60 + 60 + 57 + 53 + 51 = 387 lines) a grant of 84 *gur* 160 *qa* of cultivated land of the city of Tamakku, the communal land (*ugâru*) of the city of Akkad (A-ga-de), situated at the royal canal, belonging to Bît-Pir-*ᵈ*Amurru.[1] It was deeded by the king to his son and

[1] The translation of *bîtu* as "tribe" by Scheil and the far-reaching conclusions of Edouard Cuq, based on this translation, that the royal grants during the Cassite period were essentially transfers of tribal land to private property, are not justified. The land granted was always taken from the *ugâru* or communal land of some city or district (for this use of *ugâru* see Meissner, A. P., 123). That the term *bîtu* refers to a district consisting of smaller villages and towns appears from its usage. The stone of Marduk-nâdin-aḫê (III R. 43) refers to twenty *gur* of seed land, the communal land of Alnirêa, at the banks of the canal Zirzirri, in (*ina*) Bît *ᵐ*A-da. In other cases the term *piḫâtu* (French: *gouvernement*; in German: *Regierungsbezirk*) is prefixed to *bîtu*, as *piḫât Bît-ᵐᵈSin-ma-gir* (Susa 2, I, 28), which is parallel to *piḫât mât ᵃˡᵘḪu-da-di* (Col. II, 4). Again, *piḫât Dupliaš* (Col. II, 9) is placed alongside of *piḫât Bît-ᵐᵈSin-ašaridu* (Col. II, 14). There can hardly be any question that these are all districts. Moreover, the curses contain provisions that the land is not to be returned to the *piḫâtu* (III R. 41, II, 2; Neb. Nippur, III, 28; C. T. X., pl. VII, 34, etc.), but there is no reference to any tribe. The communal land of the cities was evidently public land of which the king could make disposition.

FIG. 6.—Symbols on a boundary stone of Marduk-apal-iddina I., found by George Smith opposite Bagdad in 1873. (IV R.[1] 43.)

successor Marduk-apal-iddina I. The grant embraced four tracts, for which a compensation was given (Col. I, 26).

A second grant of 50 *gur* of cultivated land, the communal land (*ugâru*) of the city Shaluluni, at the banks of the royal canal, in the district of Bît-^{n}Pir(?)-^{d}Amurru(MAR.TU), was made to Ḫasardu, a *sukallu*, son of Sumê (London, 101).

A third grant was made by Meli-Shipak to [Me]li-Ḫala, son of Zumê[a]. Unfortunately but a fragment of the inscription remains (D. E. P., II, 112), which does not enable us to give the exact size or location of the field.

Of the reign of Marduk-apal-iddina I. two grants to officials have come to light:

One, now in the British Museum (London, 99 = IV R.^{2} 38), records a grant of 10 *gur* of cultivated land, the communal land of the city Dûrzizi, at the banks of the Tigris, in the district of the city Gur-^{d}Ninni, to Marduk-zâkir-shumu, a governor (*bêl paḫâti*).

By another stone, Marduk-apal-iddina I. confirmed a grant of land, which had originally been made by King Rammân-shum-uṣur to Rammân-bêl-kala, a royal officer (*šaq-šarri*). The reason for this confirmation was that no sealed document had been given by the former king (Susa, 17 = D. E. P., VI, 42, 43).

During the period of the second Isin (PA.SHE) dynasty we also find several royal grants to distinguished officials.

Nebuchadrezzar I. granted 22 *gur* and 170 *qa* of cultivated land, at the Tigris, of the communal land of the town of Mâr-Aḫattûa, in the district of Bît-Sin-sheme, to Nusku-ibni, the son of Upaḫḫir-Nusku, a priest of Ellil at Nippur, perhaps for aid rendered in the reorganization of the temple services at Nippur.

Marduk-nâdin-aḫê ordered the grant of 20 *gur* of cultivated land at the Zirzirri canal, of the communal land of Alnirêa, in the district of Bît-Ada, to Rammân-zêr-iqîsha, a *shaq-shuppar*, for valuable services in a war with Assyria. The transfer of the land

Fig. 7.—Boundary stone of Marduk-nâdin-aḫê. (III R. 43.)

was made by Marduk-il-napḫari (DUL), the chief of Bît-Ada (London, 106 = III R. 43).

Under Marduk-aḫê-erba 12 *gur* of the royal domain, in the district Bît-Pir-^{d}Amurru, was granted by the king to Kudurra, a Ḫabirean (O. B. I., Vol. I, No. 149, pls. 65–67).

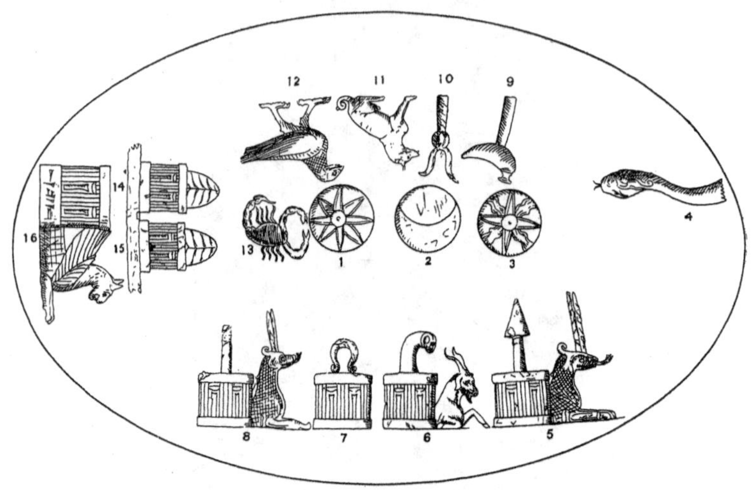

Fig. 8.—Symbols on the boundary stone of Marduk-apal-iddina II. (Berlin, V. A. 2663.)

Finally, Marduk-apal-iddina II., the Biblical Merodach-baladan,[1] granted four tracts of land of the royal domain, in all 109 *gur* 126 *qa*, to Bêl-aḫê-erba, a dignitary (^{h}*ša-ku*) of Babylon. The transaction took place at Babylon, in the seventh year of Merodach-baladan (714 B.C.), in the presence of Iqîsha-Marduk, son of the king, and nine high dignitaries of the realm (V. A., 2663 = B.A., II, 258–271).

(b) Two other stones record grants of land to fugitives.

Agabtaḫa, a fugitive of Ḫaligalbat, fled to King Bitiliâshu, and after having made for the king some object of leather (*pa-gu-mi*)

[1] Cf. Isa. 39 : 1ff.; II K. 20 : 12–19.

the king granted him 10 *gur* of cultivated land in the city of Padan (D. E. P., II, pl. 20).

Shamûa and Shamai, two priests of the god Eria, fled from Elam to Nebuchadrezzar I., who not only received them, but accompanied by them went to Elam, devastated the country and transferred the statues of Marduk[1] and Eria to Babylon. From there the statue of Eria was taken to Ḫuṣṣi, in the district Bît-Sin-asharidu, not far from Opis. There the priests were settled and a tract of land was granted to them, to be held by them as temple property. It was moreover freed from all imposts and territorial obligations (London, 92, 987 = C. T., IX, pls. 4, 5).

(c) The last forms a natural transition to two others which are royal grants to temples.

The earliest known boundary stone of Nazi-Maruttash, c. 1350 B.C., records a grant of several tracts of land opposite Babylon, in all 700 *gur*, to the god Marduk. But only 494 *gur*, divided into eight sections, which were located in six different districts (Bît-Sin-mâgir, Dûr-Papsukal, Ḫudâdu,[2] Dupliash, Bît-Sin-asharidu and Upê), were given directly to the god; the remaining 206 *gur* were given to Kashakti-Shugab, the son of Aḫu-bânî. The reason for the last act is not stated. But the two "medallions," which form the distinguishing feature of this monument, state that "Kashakti-Shugab, the son of Aḫu-bânî, wrote a memorial tablet of terra cotta[3] (*narû ša ḫaṣbi*) and set it up before his god. In the reign of Marduk-apal-iddina, the son of Meli-Shipak, a wall fell upon that tablet and

[1] The god written *iluEN* is always Marduk, never Enlil of Nippur; see Schrader, K. A. T.², 174; also article of Prof. Clay on "The God Ellil of Nippur" in A. J. S. L., July, 1907.

[2] Not to be read *Bagdadu*, a Persian word, but *Ḫu-dâdu*, the opposite of *Ḫu-aibu*; see Hommel, *Geographie*, pp. 252², 345.

[3] The meaning of *ḫaṣbu* is definitely established by a terra cotta dog, found by Scheil at Sippar (*Fouilles à Sippar*, p. 90, fig. 13), which bears the inscription: *Ana dME.ME* (*Gula*) *bêlti kalbu ḫaṣbi êpušma aqîš; l.c.*, p. 92.

broke it. Shuḫuli-Shugab, the son of Nibi-Shipak, wrote upon a new monument of stone a copy of the original and set it up.'' This interesting statement shows (1) that Kashakti-Shugab, the new owner of the land, himself wrote the tablet recording the grant; (2) that he placed it before his god, *i.e.*, he put it into the temple archives; (3) that the original tablet was of terra cotta. All this makes it very probable that Kashakti-Shugab was one of the priests of Marduk. His ability to write, his anxiety to preserve a record of the transaction, and his setting it up in the temple, all point in that direction. This also explains why he is mentioned on this document which purports to record a grant to Marduk: he was one of his priests. The reference to the original terra cotta tablet is distinctly interesting. Does it imply that there was no public boundary stone? This can hardly be inferred from the statement of Shuḫuli-Shugab, because the copy which he executed on stone was the transcript of the original *private* record of the transaction, and therefore leaves the question of a *public* record out of consideration.

Another grant in favor of a temple of the goddess Ninâ, located in the city of Dêr, which had originally been made by Gulkishar,[1] a king of the sea country (*šar mât tâmdi*), was partly set aside by E-karra-iqîsha, the then governor of the district Bît-Sin-mâgir, in which the land was located. Thereupon the priest of Ninâ, Nabû-shum-iddina, appealed to the king Ellil-nâdin-aplu (c. 1130 B.C.), who ordered at once the governor to restore the land to the temple (O. B. I., Vol. I, pls. 30, 31).

(d) There are several other grants which involve restorations.

King Nabû-apal-iddina (c. 865 B.C.) granted the restoration of three *gur* of cultivated land and five gardens to a priest, Nabû-apal-iddina, the son of Atnai, after they had been bought by his

[1] The reading *GUL.KI.SHAR* is most likely to be retained. The sign *gir* has also the value *gul* (kul), see Code of Ḫammurabi, XLIII : 19, in *tu-kul-ti* and *Concordance*.

FIG. 9.—Stone tablet of King Nabû-apal-iddina, restoring land to one of his officials. (Br. M. 90,922.)

uncle. Nabû-apal-iddina, the priest, appealed to the king for their restoration, basing his request on the plea that the king should not allow a part of his paternal estate to be alienated from the family. It was granted at Babylon, in the presence of five witnesses, in the twentieth year of Nabû-apal-iddina, the king of Babylon (London, 90, 922 = C. T., X, pl. 3).

The latest boundary stone, of the reign of Shamash-shum-ukîn, dated in his ninth year (658 B.C.), records the restoration of a certain estate which had been taken away from a Chaldean nobleman, Mushêzib-Marduk, during the political disturbances under Esarhaddon, but which had been restored to him by Esarhaddon. Before, however, this king could give him a proper deed, both he and Mushêzib-Marduk died. Hence the nobleman's son Rammân-ibni appealed to king Shamash-shum-ukîn, who restored to him Bît-Ha'raḫu with all its fields, and gave him a proper deed confirming the restoration by Esarhaddon (London, 87, 220 = C. T., X, pls. 4–7).

(e) Several of the boundary stones contain royal grants, involving lawsuits.

To this class may belong the stone of Bitiliâshu, by which he confirmed 120 *gur* of cultivated land at the town Rishshagidi to Uzub-Shipak. This grant had originally been made to him by Kurigalzu, for services in a war with Assyria. It was confirmed by Bitiliâshu, either because one of the neighbors of the grantee had contested the grant by a lawsuit or, what is just as likely, Kurigalzu had failed to give him a sealed document, or perhaps both reasons were involved, as in the following case (Susa, 9 = D. E. P., II, 93).

A stone of Marduk-apal-iddina I. (Susa, 16 = D. E. P., VI, pls. 9, 10) begins by stating that a certain tract of land, situated within the limits of the town Shaknanâ, at the banks of the canal Mê-dandan, in the district of Ḫudâdu, had been given by King Meli-

Shipak to his servant Munnabittu, the son of Ṭâbu-melû. Officials of the king having surveyed the field it had passed into the possession of Munnabittu. Unfortunately the king failed to draw up a document recording his grant. Meanwhile Munnabittu remained in peaceful possession of the field till the first year of Marduk-apal-iddina I., when one of his neighbors, Aḫunêa, the son of Daian-

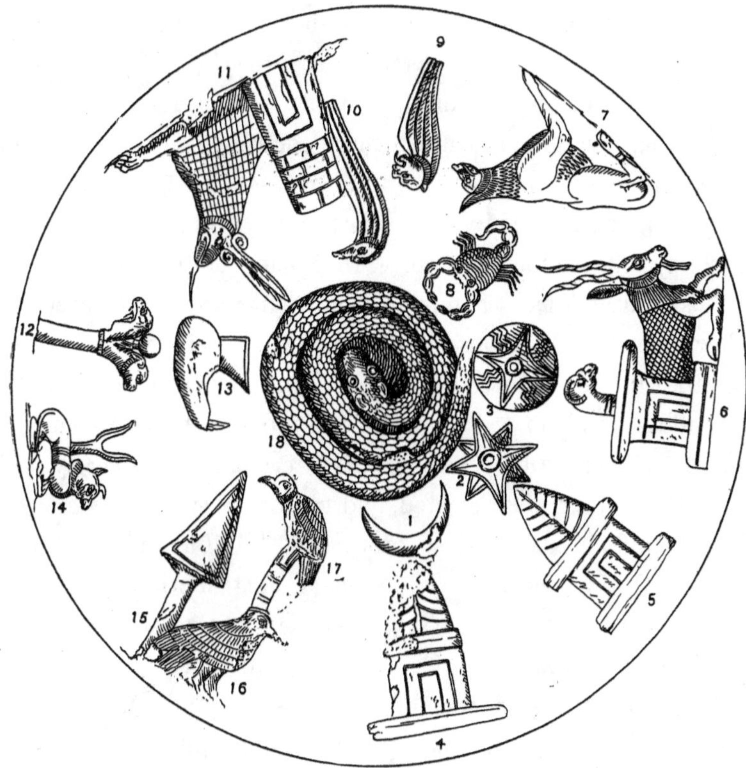

Fig. 10.—Symbols on a boundary stone of Marduk-apal-iddina I., discovered at Susa. (Susa, No. 16.)

Marduk, claimed a part of the field, namely three *gur* and twenty *qa*. Munnabittu appealed to the king, who summoned Kidin-NINIB, the former governor of Ḫudâdu, under whom the field had been granted, and Ṣir-shum-iddina, his successor in office, and the old city officials (*paršê labirûti*),[1] whom the king questioned about the field. They were unanimous in saying that the field belonged to Munnabittu. The king thereupon sent the governor, Ṣîr-shum-iddina, and the scribe, Bêl-bashmê, who measured the field and found it to be thirty *gur* as Munnabittu claimed. The king then confirmed the land to Munnabittu. This inscription gives us an interesting insight into the workings of a Babylonian court; we notice the summoning of witnesses and the taking of testimony. The part played by the elders (the *šîbû* of the Code of Ḫammurabi) reminds us of the modern jury.

Another lawsuit of a much more complicated nature dragged through the reigns of the kings Rammân-shum-iddina, Rammân-shum-uṣur and Meli-Shipak. Unfortunately the stone in question (London, 103) is much broken, so that many of the details of the various transactions escape us. From what remains we gather the following facts. The house of Tâkil-ana-ilishu being without direct heirs, the question of succession arose. During the reign of Rammân-shum-iddina a claim was made for the property by two men (Col. I, 26, 27). But as they had not been recognized as sons by their father their claim was rejected, and the property was awarded to Ur-Bêlit-muballiṭat-mîtûti, a brother of Tâkil-ana-ilishu (Col. I, 37–39). During the reign of the next king another attempt to secure a share of the property was made by another person, who claimed to be a grandson of Tâkil-ana-ilishu (Col. I, 40–43). But his effort, as it seems, was likewise unsuccessful. Meanwhile a part of the land, ten *gur*, had passed through purchase (Col. III, 9, 10) into the hands of Bêlâni, but upon an appeal of Ur-Bêlit-

[1] The reading *paršû* is to be preferred to *maššû* (Br. 1930), because it connects the word with the well-known stem *parâšu*, which occurs frequently in the Code of Ḫammurabi (*e.g.*, Col. VI : 9; XLI : 90; VIII : 65) and in the Letters of Ḫammurabi (King, *Letters of Ḫam.*, Vol. III, p. 287), as a synonym of *parâsu*. The ideogram *BAR.SU(D)* points in the same direction.

muballiṭat-mîtûti to the king, Bêlâni was compelled to surrender the land again, upon the payment of a certain amou t of grain equivalent in value to the purchase price (Col. III, 25–36). After the death of Ur-Bêlit-muballiṭat-mîtûti, Aḫu-dârû, another brother of Tâkil-ana-ilishu (Col. IV, 23), took the field by force, whereupon Marduk-kudur-uṣur, a son of Ur-Bêlit-muballiṭat-mîtûti, appealed to the king, Meli-Shipak, who, after some delay and after the death of Aḫu-dârû, decided the case in favor of Marduk-kudur-uṣur. All of which, with many other details, too much effaced to be deciphered, was duly engraved upon the stone.

Another lawsuit seems to have been involved in a stone of Marduk-apal-iddina I. (Susa, 14 = D. E. P., VI, 39–41), in which the king is referred to as listening to an appeal (Col. I, 15), and a certain sum of money is mentioned as having been paid as a fee (*atru*). The land in question was a part of the district Bît-Pir-Amurru, adjoining with its eastern side the canal Ṛadanu. The name of the grantee is broken off.

(f) Besides the royal grants of land already considered, there is still another class by which not only the land in question was conveyed, but also special favors were secured, such as exemption from taxation or immunity from forced labor, or, as in some cases, this freedom from territorial obligations alone was granted.

Of the first kind we have the grant of King Meli-Shipak to his son Marduk-apal-iddina, granting to him not only four tracts of land, but also freedom from all territorial obligations. No levies were to be raised to build, maintain and dyke the royal canal, or guard the cities of Bît-Sikkamidu and Dâmiq-Rammân against inundation (Col. II, 18–27). The people were not to be compelled to work at the sluices of the royal canal, to close or open them or dig up the bed of the canal (Col. II, 28–33). No governor of Bît-Pir-Amurru had the right to draft farmers, sojourners, citizens or councilmen (Col. II, 34–42). Neither king nor governor nor any other

Fig. 11.—Boundary stone of King Meli-Shipak, granting land to his son Marduk-apal-iddina I. (Susa, No. 3.)

official had the right to forage wood or grass, straw, wheat or any other grain (Col. II, 43–50). Nor could they for this purpose demand wagons with harness, asses to draw them or men to drive them (Col. II, 51–53). During the low water level of the connecting canal, which joined the canal Râṭi-Anzan with the royal canal, no water could be taken from its canal or reservoir, nor could its system of irrigation be diverted to other fields (Col. II, 54–III, 2). The grass of its fields could not be cut by king or governor, nor were they allowed the right of pasturage (Col. III, 13–21). Neither roads nor bridges could be constructed for king or governor (Col. III, 22–27). Neither king nor governor could order any new work or the reparation of the old (Col. III, 28–41).

Similar immunities were granted by King Marduk-nâdin-aḫê to Rammân-zêr-iqîsha (III R. 45, No. 2). No river or land officers were to take away the freedom of the town Alnirêa from forced labor. No (royal) officials, who were appointed over Bît-Ada, had the right of entry in Alnirêa; the government of Bît-Ada was not to be introduced there; the canal was not to be stopped up; asses and oxen were not to be taken into the city by the tax collector.

Nebuchadrezzar I. granted to the priest Nusku-ibni certain immunities. None was allowed to make use of the pasture lands (III, 21); no canal officer was to seize a canal digger under the pretext of a levy (III, 25); no land officer was to cut any grass (III, 26). The same king exempted the land granted to the priests Shamûa and Shamai from several obligations, ordering that "officers of the canals and officers of the land shall not go into the city; its servants, oxen and asses they shall not bind (*i.e.*, impress them to forced labor); its sheep they shall not seize; its chariots they shall not hitch up; from all forced labor whatsoever he has freed them" (C. T., X, pl. V, 33–39).

The stone of Za'aleh records a similar grant of freedom (*zakûtu*) from forced labor. Unfortunately much of the section in which it was recorded (Col. I, 6–II, 1) has been effaced (Col. I, 11–20).

The most notable charter of freedom is that granted by Nebuchadrezzar I. to his distinguished officer, Ritti-Marduk, the chief of Bît-Karziabku. Here we find the following immunities. The

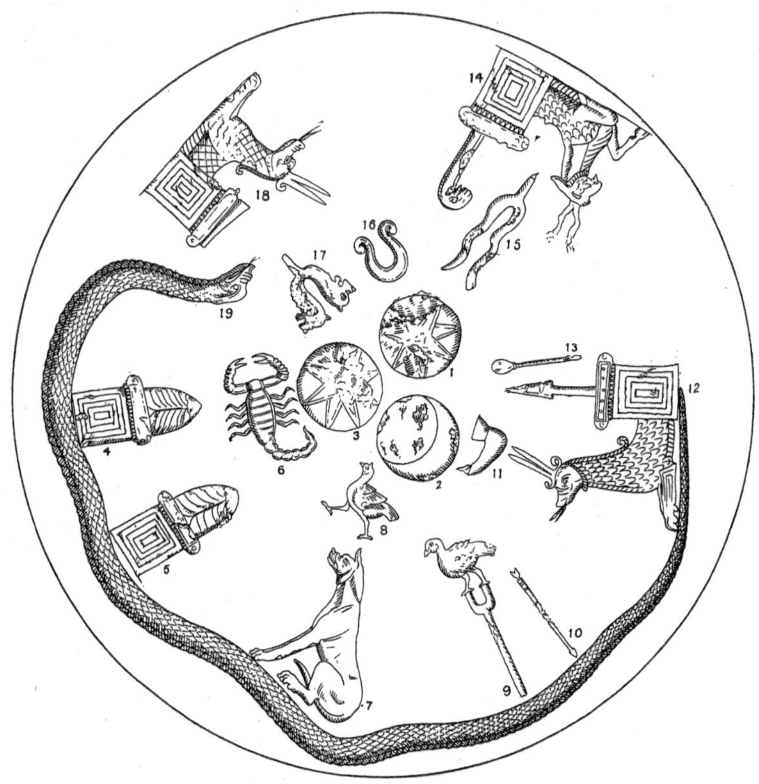

Fig. 12.—Symbols on the boundary stone of Marduk-nâdin-aḫê, in the British Museum. (III R. 45, *b* = London 106 and No. 90,840.)

officers of the king and of the governor of Namar have no right of entry (Col. I, 51, 52). Neither stallions nor mares are to be taken into the cities of Bît-Karziabku by the master of the horse (Col. I, 53–54). Taxes on oxen or sheep are not to be levied for the king or governor (Col. I, 55). Dues on gardens are not to be given to the tax-gatherer (Col. I, 56–57). The master of the royal horse cannot enter the cities to take out mares for riding horses (Col. I, 58, 59). The hedges(?) of the parks and date palm groves are not to be cut down, and the walls of the cities Bît-Shamash and Bît-Shanbasha are not to be torn down (Col. I, 60–II, 1). Bridges are not to be built and roads are not to be constructed (Col. II, 2). Nor shall the soldiers of the king who live in the district have the right to impress any one into service (Col. II, 3–5). From all the territorial obligations of Namar Nebuchadrezzar freed the cities of Ritti-Marduk (Col. II, 6–8), but the soldiers stationed in its cities he assigned to the extraordinary support of the governor and palace commander (Col. II, 9, 10).

An analysis of these provisions shows that the ordinary territorial obligations in Babylonia were threefold[1]—to the king, to the governor and to the community. (1) The king could levy men to keep up the royal canal, to work its sluices, to dig its bed or to preserve its embankments. By forced labor he could build bridges and roads and carry on any government work that was needed. He could draft men for service in the army. His master of horse could demand horses for the royal stable. The king had the right of forage, for which he could demand wagons, asses and men. He had also the right of pasturage. His privilege to cut the herbage (Neb. Nippur, III, 26; Susa, 3, Col. III, 13, 14) was no doubt parallel to the Hebrew "king's mowings" (Amos 7 : 1), which appear to have been a tribute levied by the kings of Israel on the spring herbage, to be used as provender for their horses (cf. I K. 18 : 5). (2) The governor had the right to levy a tax on wood, grass, straw, wheat or any other grain. He had also the right of pasturage. He could demand wagons and their harness, asses and men for forced labor. He levied taxes on oxen and sheep and dues on gardens. (3) The community could make use of private

[1] Cf. Edouard Cuq. *La propriété foncière en Chaldée*, p. 730.

canals during the period of low water level. It could use private reservoirs and cut branches from any system of irrigation to water neighboring fields.

(II) Having exhausted the list of the royal grants we turn to the remaining stones dealing with the transfer of private property.

(a) There are two boundary stones which record the grant of land to daughters as their dowry.

The famous Caillou de Michaux (I R. 70) records the grant of twenty *gur* of cultivated land, of the communal land of the town Kar-Nabû, at the banks of the canal Mêdandan, in the district Bît-^{m}Ḫabban, by Ṣîr-uṣur, son of Ḫabban, to his daughter Dûr-sharru-kênaiti, the bride of Ṭâb-ashâb-Marduk, as her dowry (*mulugu*). In connection with this transaction the bridegroom had to swear, "by the great gods and the god Ṣîru," not to raise any claim against that field.

A similar grant of land was made in the reign of Nabû-mukîn-aplu (London, 102) by Arad-Sibitti, son of Atrattash, to his daughter SAG-mudammiq-sharbi, wife of Shamash-nâdin-shum. This grant of three *gur* of cultivated land was made by Arad-Sibitti in the fourth year of king Nabû-mukîn-aplu, in the presence of seven sons. But not all the children having been present at the transaction it was confirmed by the others in the following year. Besides this dowry grant the monument also contained the record of several earlier transactions, extending from the second year of NINIB-kudur-uṣur to the fifth year of Nabû-mukîn-aplu, parts of which are so badly defaced that it is impossible to make out the details. It is at all events certain, that Burusha, father of Shamash-nâdin-shumu, and Arad-Sibitti were engaged in litigation, which seems to have been ended by the marriage of the two children and the settlement of the tract of land upon the daughter of Arad-Sibitti as her dowry.

(b) There finally remain several cases in which land was acquired through purchase.

FIG. 13.—Symbols on the Caillou de Michaux, now in Paris. (I R. 70.)

A boundary stone from the reign of one of the kings of the second Isin (PA.SHE) dynasty, most likely Nebuchadrezzar I. (III R. 41), records the purchase of five *gur* of land, belonging to the district of Bît-Ḫanbi, by Marduk-nâṣir, an officer of the king (*ʰšaq šarri*), from Amel-Ellil, son of Ḫanbi, for one wagon, several horses,

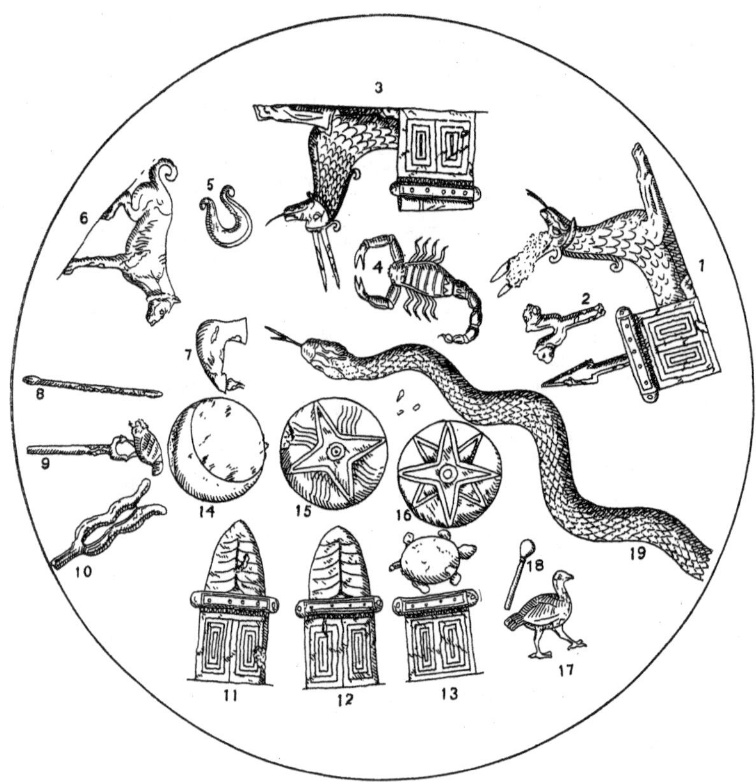

FIG. 14.—Symbols on III R. 41. (III R. 45*a* = London 105 and No. 90,841.)

asses, oxen, harness, grain and clothing, in all worth 816 pieces of silver.

Another stone, dated in the reign of Marduk-shum-iddina (c. 850 B. C.), records the purchase of a field by Kidîni, son of Bêliddina, from Iddinâ, for one and five-sixths mines of silver.

But this purchase occupies only the latter part of the inscription. The former is taken up with a bequest of Bêl-iddina, a priest of Dilbat, to his younger son Kidîni, giving him his share in the paternal property. It consisted of three parts. First, an income derived from his position as priest ([amelu]TU) of the temple of the goddess Lagamal (l. 33). Second, a piece of land, consisting of

Fig. 15.—Symbols on the boundary stone of Sargon, dated 711 B. C. (V. A. 209.)

four *gur* of uncultivated land and an orchard. Third, a lot with a house on it in the city of Dilbat. The first transaction is dated in the twenty-eighth year of Nabû-apal-iddina, the second in the eleventh year of Marduk-shum-iddina (V. A., 208).

A still larger number of transactions is recorded on the stone of

Sargon (V. A., 209).[1] Nabû-ile'i, the son of Nûr-Sin, owned a piece of land in the city of Dêr. But as he desired to enlarge its size, he offered to his neighbor, Ina-eshê-êṭir, another property at the new canal in exchange for the one next to his own lot. At the same time he asked him to give him a sealed document for his own lot. This may have been due to the fact that Ina-eshê-êṭir was its former owner, who sold it to Iddina-Nabû, and the latter in turn to Nabû-ile'i. To this exchange and request Ina-eshê-êṭir consented, with the condition that Nabû-ile'i give him six sheqels as a fee for concluding the transaction, which was done. A second property, adjoining his own, Nabû-ile'i bought from Sharâni for fifty-six sheqels of silver. A third property, adjoining that of Sharâni, Nabû-ile'i bought from Uṣalli, for one and one-third mines and four sheqels of silver. A fourth property, adjoining the one bought from Sharâni, Nabû-ile'i acquired from Iddina and Shamâ, sons of Erbâ, for one and one-third mines and five sheqels. Then Nabû-ile'i won a lawsuit against Bêl-usâtu; but instead of taking the sum of money awarded to him he accepted several lots (*bîtâti*) which Bêl-usâtu had in Dêr. Another claim for one mine and thirteen sheqels was settled in a similar way. Nabû-ile'i gave his creditors fifty sheqels in exchange for a house and an orchard in the confines of the city of Dêr. All these six transactions are duly recorded on this stone, which is dated in the eleventh year of Sargon or 711 B.C. The combination of so many transactions upon one document is a well-known Babylonian custom, which may have been dictated by a desire on the part of Nabû-ile'i to have a permanent record of all the transactions involving his property.[2]

[1] Thus according to a kind communication of Dr. Ungnad; not 202 as given formerly.

[2] For a similar instance see Ranke, B. E., VI, pt. 1, pl. 71.

Contents of the Kudurru Inscriptions.

The different parts of a kudurru inscription are usually as follows:

(1) In a number of cases the stone has a name. It is called *ᵈNabû-nâṣir-kudur-eqlâti* (Del., II, pl. 17; III, 34, 35), or *ᵈRammân-limuttu(?)-pattinu-da(?)-riš* (London, 101, Col. I, 3), or *ᵈNIN.IB-u-ᵈNusku-mukîn-kudurri* (Neb. Nippur), or *Mukîn-kudurri-dârâti* (III, R. 41).

(2) Then follows the description of the field or fields in question; the total area is given and the different sides are carefully bounded by referring to the adjoining properties. In a few cases the exact length of each side is added.

(3) Next we find a statement of the circumstances which led to the grant. The grantor and the grantee are mentioned. In this section we often find important historical information, as well as elaborate eulogies on the king from whom the grant proceeded.

(4) The next section contains the most characteristic feature of these inscriptions, namely, elaborate curses against all kinds of officials and persons who might interfere with the land, its area, its privileges and its owners. This section has usually several well-marked subdivisions:

(*a*) An enumeration of the individuals admonished not to raise claims or warned not to interfere with the land—kings, princes, governors, prefects, judges, overseers, counselors, magistrates, relatives and neighbors. Thirty different officials are found in this section on the various stones.

(*b*) Next follow the acts of violence which are forbidden. No claim or lawsuit is to be made against the land. It cannot be confiscated, turned over to the state, nor given to a temple. The extent of the field is not to be changed. Its ditches and boundaries are not to be removed. Its canals are not to be closed up, nor its water supply to be diverted to other fields. The boundary stone, more-

FIG. 16.—Uninscribed boundary stone of the Cassite period, showing symbols and a sacrificial procession. (Susa, No. 20.)

over, is not to be touched, not to be thrown into fire, water or a dark place. It is not to be broken nor to be hidden in the dust. The inscription finally is not to be erased, nor anything else put in its place. No irresponsible person is to be engaged to carry out any evil intentions against the land or the boundary stone.

(*c*) Then the great gods are invoked, either by enumerating them first and then ascribing one curse to them all, or by giving a separate curse to each deity. The latter is the more common method. In the curses themselves all kinds of diseases or calamities are threatened to the would-be offenders. Although there is some regularity in ascribing the various curses to the different deities, yet there is considerable variation.

(5) The last section usually contains a list of the witnesses present during the transaction, and sometimes even the date is added.

These various sections follow by no means in a set order, but it was left to the individual scribe to arrange them as he saw fit. In some instances one or more sections are omitted. In other cases new sections are added, as, *e.g.*, the hymn to Ellil on the new boundary stone of Nebuchadrezzar from Nippur (Col. I, 1–22), the glorification of Marduk on the stone of Merodach-baladan II. (V. A., 2663, I, 1–24), together with the elaborate eulogy on Merodach-baladan (I, 25–III, 35). On the various charters (D. E. P., II, pls. 21–24; V R. 55, 56; Neb. Nippur; C. T., IX, pls. 4, 5; I R. 66; III R. 45, No. 2) the section treating of the territorial immunities and exemptions is also peculiar to these stones.

Several of the above sections are important enough to deserve further discussion.

As to the orientation of the fields, there is considerable difference on the various stones. Most of them begin the enumeration of the sides of the fields with the upper length (*šiddu elû*); only three start with the upper width (*pûtu elû*), namely, D. E. P., II, 112; IV R.[2] 38, and O. B. I., 150. Taking the upper length as the determining factor, we find that eight stones locate that side towards north (*iltânu*), namely, London, 103; 101; Susa, III; Susa, XVI; III R. 41; III R. 43–45; O. B. I., 149; 150. Five stones locate it towards west (*amurrû*), namely, Neb. Nippur; IV R.[2] 38; London, 102; Br. M. 87,220; V. A., 208. Three locate it towards

FIG. 17.—A priest standing before the symbol of Marduk, on a fragmentary boundary stone. (Susa, No. 5, *a*.)

east (*šadû*), namely, D. E. P., II, 112; I R. 70; Br. M. 90,922. On two stones (V. A., 209, and V. A., 2663) several fields are mentioned, which are differently oriented. Three fields on V. A., 209, have the upper length towards south (Col. II, 31; III, 2, 19); one field has it towards east (Col. IV, 9), and one towards west (Col.

V, 26). On V. A., 2663, three fields are oriented towards south (Col. III, 44; IV, 23; IV, 35) and one towards west (Col. IV, 7).

Fig. 18.—The god Rammân and other symbols, on a fragmentary boundary stone found at Susa. (Susa, No. 5, *b*.)

Officials of the Kudurru Inscriptions.

To show the number and variety of the various officials mentioned in the curses it will be best to reproduce the passages in full, leaving out the connecting particles and the names of the places in connection with which many of the titles occur. We shall quote the various lists in their chronological order.

1. Nazi-Maruttash (Susa II)
   ša-kin mâti, bêlê paḫâti (EN.NAM.MESH) ḫa-za-an-na-tim ù ki-pu-ú-tim ša qaq-qa-ra-tim añ-na-tim (D. E. P., II, 89; III, 5–10).
2. Rammân-shum-uṣur[1] (Susa, IV)
   aklu (PA) ša-pi-ru, laputtû[2] *(NU.TUR) dai[anu] di-ku-ú, na-gi-ru, man-za-az pân šarri,........ša rubû (NUN)* (D. E. P., II, 97, 11–14).
3. Meli-Shipak[3] (London, 101)
   ᵸšaqû(SAG) ᵸlaputtû, ᵸšak(k)anakku (NER.ARAD) (Col. II, 13–14).
4. Meli-Shipak (Susa, III)
   etellu (BE), rabû ma-lik šarri, ᵸšaq šarri, ša-kin ša i-na piḫâti........iš-šak-ka-nu, ḫa-za-an piḫâti (NAM), šakin[4] *(GAR) ṭe-mi, mu-še-ri-šu, gù-gal-lu* (D. E. P., II, 108; VI, 1–11).
5. Marduk-apal-iddina I. (IV R.² 38)
   aklu, laputtû, ḫa-za-an-nu ša eqlu šú-a-tum (Col. III, 1–3).
6. Marduk-apal-iddina I. (Susa, XVI)
   ᵸaklu, ᵸlaputtû, ša-pi-ru, šakin(-in) ṭe-mi, bêl paḫâti, ḫa-za-an-nu, PA.TE.SI, mu-ir-ru, USH.SA.DU, šakkanakku, (NER.TA!) ša i-na piḫât........iš-šak-ka-nu (D. E. P., VI, 35; III, 27–IV, 8).

[1] Or *Rammân-nâdin-aḫu.*

[2] The reading *labuttû* is also possible.

[3] For the reading *Meli-Shipak* instead of *Meli-Shiḫu* cf. Clay, B. E., XV, 3, note 4.

[4] That the reading *ša ṭe-mi* must be given up has long been apparent from the writing *ᵸšakin(GAR-in) ṭe-mi* on the stone of *Marduk-aḫê-erba*, O. B. I., 149, II, 3; cf. also Susa 16, III 30.

7. Marduk-apal-iddina I. (Susa, XIV)
   šakkanakku, ḫa-za-an-nu, mu-ir-ru, ša-kin (*Bît-*[m]*Pir-*[d]*Amurru*), *USH.SA.DU* (D. E. P. VI, 40; II, 1–5).
8. Nebuchadrezzar I. (Nippur)
   rê'û, šakkanakku, ak-lu, ša-pi-ru, ri-du-ú, ḫa-za-an-nu (Col. III, 19, 20).
9. Ellil-nâdin-aplu (O. B. I., 83)
   aklu, laputtu, šakkanakku (Col. II, 12).
10. Second Isin Dynasty (III R. 41)
    ak-lu, laputtû, ḫa-za-an-nu, mu-še-ri-šu, gù-gal-lu, ki-pu (Col. I, 31–33).
11. Second Isin Dynasty (I R. 70)
    laputtû (*NU.TUR.DA*), *i-tu-ú* (Col. II, 5–6).
12. Marduk-nâdin-aḫê (III, R. 43)
    bêl bîti, bêl paḫâti, ḫa-za-an-ni, šakin ṭe-mi, gu-ta-ku, lu-pu-ut-tu-ú, ak-lu, ki-pu-tu ar-ku-tu (Col. III, 8–14).

    Appendix to III R. 43 (III R. 45, No. 2)
    daianu (*DI.KUD*) *bêl paḫâti, bêl bîti, bêl paḫâti, ki-pu-tu, ḫa-za-an-nu ar-ku-tu, ki-pu-tu, sakin ṭe-mi, ḫa-za-an-nu* (l. 3–5).
13. Marduk-aḫê-erba (O. B. I., 149)
    ša-kin, bêl paḫâti, ḫa-za-an-nu, [h]*šakin(-in) ṭe-mi, PA.TE.SI* (Col. II, 2–4).
14. Marduk-apal-iddina II. (V. A., 2663)
    šarru, mâr šarri, [h]*ki-i-pu,* [h]*šak-nu* [h]*ša-tam, ḫa-za-an-nu* (Col. V, 19, 20).
15. Shamash-shum-ukîn (C. T., X, pls. 4–7)
    šarru, mâr šarri, [h][*ša*]*-kan,* [h]*ša-pi-*[*ru*], [h]*ḫa-za-an-nu* (Col. II, 32–33).

Here we have in fifteen inscriptions thirty officials and dignitaries from the king downwards. Arranged in alphabetical order they are as follows:

(1) *aklu*, (2) *etellu*, (3) *itû*, (4) *USH.SA.DU*,[1] (5) *bêl bîti*, (6) *bêl paḫâti*, (7) *gugallu*, (8) *gutaku*, (9) *daianu*, (10) *dikû*, (11) *ḫazannu*, (12) *la(u)puttû*, (13) *manzaz pân šarri*, (14) *mâr šarri*, (15) *mu'irru*, (16) *mušêrišu*, (17) *nâgiru*, (18) *PA.TE.SI* (*iššakku*), (19) *qîpu*, (20) *rabû*, *malik šarri*, (21) *rê'û*, (22) *ridû*, (23) *šaknu*, (24) *šakin ṭêmi*, (25) *šakkanakku*, (26) *šâpiru*, (27) *šaqû*, (28) *šaq šarri*, (29) *šarru*, (30) *šatam*.

The largest number of officials, ten, occurs on the stone of Marduk-apal-iddina I (D. E. P., VI, pls. 9, 10); the smallest number, namely two, is found on the *Caillou de Michaux* (I R. 70). No principle of arrangement can be detected except that *aklu* heads the list five times; *laputtû* occurs four times in second place, following *aklu*, and *ḫazannu* five times in third place. Several titles occur in pairs—*aklu* and *šâpiru* (Nos. 2, 8), *aklu* and *laputtû* (Nos. 5, 10), *ḫazannu* and *šakin ṭêmi* (Nos. 12, 13), *šarru* and *mâr šarri* (Nos. 14, 15).

Only a few of these officials appear in these *kudurru* inscriptions outside of the curses, and then only in the act of measuring the fields. In one case (London, 101, I, 18–21) a *ḫazannu*, a *tupšarru* and a *šaq šarri* measure the field, in another (Susa, 3, I, 28–38) a *šaq šarri* and a *ḫazannu*, in a third a *šaknu* and a *tupšarru* (Susa, 16, II, 5–10). In a fourth case it is an *amel paḫâti*, a *šakin ṭêmi* and two other men whose official position is not given (D. E. P., VI, 44; I, 9–15). Later a *sukallu*, who is also the *bêl bîti*, appears in the same act (III R. 43, I, 9–13), while in the last instance on record (O. B. I., 149, I, 15–20) two *tupšarru*, a *šakin ṭêmi* and a *ḫazannu* measure the field. In one case the measurement of the field is performed by a certain officer of Nippur, ideographically written *GÛ.EN.NA* (London, 103, III, 26).

[1] It seems doubtful whether *UŠ.SA.DU* has the meaning "neighbor" in this connection, especially as it appears in the midst of the officials on Susa 16. At any rate its occurrence among the officials should be noted.

It is evident that the enumeration of the officials in the curses was not arbitrary, but depended upon the actual number and character of the officials who held office in the district where the land granted was located. Whether they were royal officials

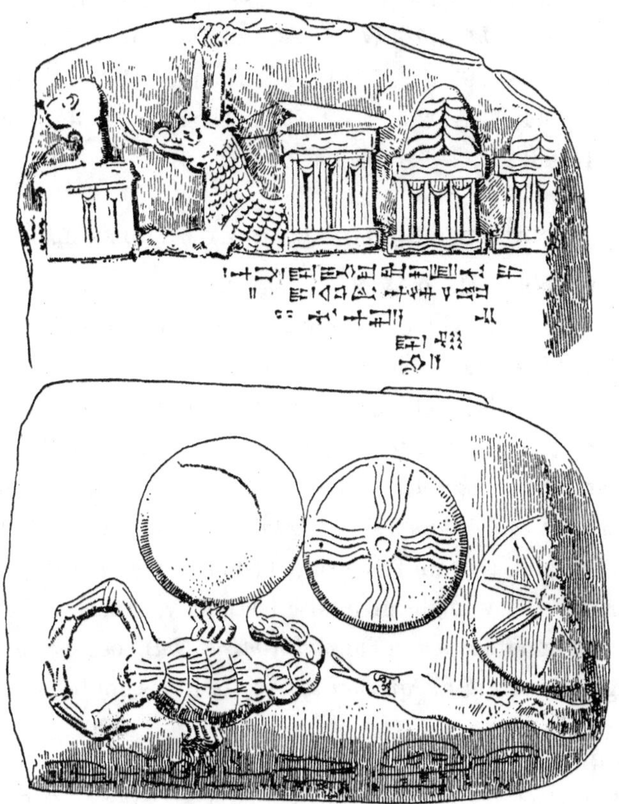

FIG. 19.—Boundary stone found by the German expedition at 'Amrân, in December, 1900, now at Berlin.

or chosen by the community in which they lived does not clearly appear, but from the fact that the king dealt directly with them it is more likely that they held office by the appointment of the king. As they are enjoined in the curses from engaging in certain acts, it must of necessity follow that under ordinary circumstances they enjoyed certain rights over the public lands and most likely derived income from them.

In private transfers of property, in which the king does not appear, these officials are omitted, but their place is taken by brothers, sons, family, members of household and relatives, male and female servants (*aḫê, mârê kimti, nišûti, salâti, ardên ù kinâti*; London, 103, V, 28, 29; I R. 70; II, 2–4; London, 102, IV, 36–37; V. A., 208, 43, 44; V. A., 209, I, 32, 33). The stone of Marduk-nâdin-aḫê (III R. 43; III, 2–3, 8–15) has both lists.

Injunctions against Acts of Violence.

The possible acts of violence against which the officials are warned, and from whose committal they are solemnly enjoined, may be classified under eight heads.

1. The officials might enter lawsuits against the land. They might direct their mind to the seizure of the field (*ana tabâl eqlâti annâti uzunšu išakkanu*).[1] They might sue or cause a suit to be made (*ina eli eqlu šu'atum idabbubu ušadbabu*).[2] They might raise a claim or cause a claim to be raised (*iraggumu ušargamu, ipaqqiru ušapqaru*).[3] They might give false testimony, saying the field has not been granted (*eqlu annû ul nadin-mi iqabbû*),[4] or it is not a gift of the king (*eqlu ul niditti šarri-mi iqabû*),[5] or it has not been measured

[1] III R. 41, I, 35, 36; cf. I R. 70, II, 7; V. A. 2663, V, 32.

[2] Susa 14, II, 7–9; Susa 16, IV, 13, 14; London, 101, II, 16, 17; cf. Susa 2, III, 11–13; London, 103, V, 33, 34; C. T., IX, pl. V, 32; O. B. I., 149, II, 6, 7; V. A. 209, I, 35–II, 1, IV R.[2] 38, III, 3–5.

[3] London, 103, V, 34, 35; Susa 14, II, 10, 11; III R. 41, I, 36, cf. D. E. P., II, pl. 20, 9–10.

[4] London, 103, V, 37, 38; London, 101, III, 1; V. A. 209, II, 2–4, cf. V. A. 208, 46, 47.

[5] Susa 14, II, 12, 13; Susa 16, IV, 20, 21; O. B. I., 149, II, 7, 8; C. T., X, pl. VII, 35.

(*iqabû eqlu ul mašiḫ*),[1] and a sealed document has not been given (*kunukku ul kanik iqabû*).[2]

2. The officials might not only raise claims against the field, but they might actually take it and thus change its ownership. They might turn it over to the state again (*eqlâti šinâti ana piḫâtišina utarrû*),[3] give it to a temple, to the king, to a representative of the king, to a representative of the governor, to a representative of his council or to any other person (*ana ili lu ana šarri lu ana iššakki šarri lu ana iššakki ḫšakin lu ana iššakki bît ṭêmišu lu ana mamma šanumma išarraqu*).[4] They might give it to a stranger (*ana aḫânu išarraqu*),[5] exchange it for another field (*eqlu kîmu ittanaššû*)[6] or appropriate it to their own use (*ana ramânišu išakkanu*),[7] and thus change the royal grant (*nidinti šu'atu ušannû*)[8] or overthrow it entirely (*šarqi eqlu šu'atu inamdû*)[9] by taking it away or causing it to be taken (*itabbalu ušatbalu*).[10]

3. The officials might change the extent of the field. They might curtail it or cut it up (*niširta qiṣṣata ina libbi išakkanu*).[11] They might change its ditches and boundary lines (*ika miṣra ittiqu*)[12] or alter its confines, limits and boundary (*usa miṣra ù kudurrašu ušannû*).[13]

[1] III R. 43, III, 16; perhaps also Neb. Nippur III, 33.

[2] III R. 43, III, 17.

[3] Neb. Nippur III, 28; III R. 41, II, 2; cf. Susa 3, V, 33; C. T., X, pl. VII, 34.

[4] III R. 41, II, 3–5; cf. I R. 70, II, 10; III R. 43, III, 18.

[5] C. T., X, pl. VII, 33.

[6] Susa 3, V, 33.

[7] I R. 70, II, 12; III R. 43, III, 19; cf. C. T., X, pl. VII, 34.

[8] C. T., X, pl. VII, 33.

[9] Neb. Nippur, III, 20, 21.

[10] Susa 16, IV, 15; III R. 41, I, 37; cf. London, 103; V, 37, 38; Susa 3, V, 28.

[11] I R. 70, II, 15, 16; cf. Susa 2, III, 14, 15; Susa 3, V, 29, 30; Susa 16, IV, 16, 17; III R. 41, II, 6; C. T., X, pl. VII, 34; III R. 43, III, 21, 22.

[12] Susa 16, IV, 18.

[13] III R. 43, III, 20; cf. O. B. I., 150, II, 1, 2.

4. The officials might damage the canals or divert them. They might stop up the canals with mud (*šakikki dalti u ašar milti nâri-šu isikkiru*)[1] or divert its waters (*šikizzu ubbalu*).[2]

5. The officials might change or damage the boundary stone. They might take it (*narâ annâ ušaššû*)[3] and change its location (*unakaru ina šubtišu*),[4] throw it into the water (*ana mê inamdû*)[5] or into the river (*ana nâri inamdû*),[6] or put it in a well (*ana bûri inassuku*),[7] hide it in the dust (*ina epiri itammiru*),[8] or bury it in the earth (*ina irṣiti iqabbiru*),[9] put it in a dark place (*ana bît eklîti ušerribu*),[10] or in a place where it cannot be seen (*ašar la amâri išakkanu*),[11] in a secret place (*puzra uštaḫiz*),[12] wall it up (*ina igari ipteḫi*),[13] or enclose it in an enclosure (*ina lipitti itte'i*).[14] They might

[1] Susa 16, V, 5–7. [2] Susa 16, V, 8.

[3] III R. 43, I, 32; III R. 41, II, 10; cf. Susa 16, IV, 29, 30.

[4] V. A. 2663, V, 28; cf. *ina ašrišu unakkaru*, London, 101, III, 2–3.

[5] I R. 70, III, 1; III R. 43, I, 33; O. B. I., 149, II, 11; V. A. 2663, V, 28; C. T., X, pl. VII, [36]; Neb. Nippur V, 1.

[6] III R. 41, II, 10; O. B. I., 150, II, 2; London, 102, V, 1; cf. *ana mê ušadû*, London, 103, V, 45; *ana mê ana išâti ušaddû*, IV R.[2] 38, III, 18–19; *ana mê ana išâti ina(m)dû (ittadi)*, London, 101, III, 3; Susa 3, V, 51; Susa 16, IV, 31–32; D. E. P., VI, 45, V, 14.

[7] III R. 41, II, 11; London, 102, V, 2; cf. *ana nâri inasuku*, V R. 56, 36.

[8] I R. 70, III, 2; III R. 43, I, 33; O. B. I., 150, II, 3; Neb. Nippur IV, 29, 30; cf. *ina irṣiti itammiru*, III R. 41, II, 12; *ina eqli lâ amâri itammiru*, V R. 56, 36; *eqlu lâ amâri itemiru*, O. B. I., 149, II, 13; *ina qaqqari itammiru*, Susa 16, IV, 33, 34; Susa 3, V, 52; *ina epiri ušatmaru*, London, 103, V, 46, 47.

[9] IV R.[2] 38, III, 20.

[10] IV R.[2] 38, III, 7, 8; cf. *ana bît a-sa-ki a-šar(!) lâ amâri ušêribu*, D. E. P. VI, 45 Col. V, 17–19.

[11] Susa 16, IV, 35–V, 1; I R. 70, III, 7, 8; V, 2663, V, 31; cf. *ašar lâ amâri šanamma ušakanu*, O. B. I., 150, II, 5; *ašar lâ amâri ušakkanu*, London, 101, III, 7; *ašar lâ amâri itammiru*, III R. 41, II, 12; *ina ašrim šanimma ki limutti iltakan*, Susa 3, V, 41, 42.

[12] Susa 3, V, 43, 44; cf. *ašar lâ a[ma]-ri puzri [ušaḫazu]*; C. T., X, pl. VII, 37; *puzru ušaḫazu*, V. A. 2663, V, 30, 31.

[13] Susa 3, V, 54; *ina igari ipi[ḫû]*, D. E. P., II, 113, 17.

[14] Susa 3, V, 53; cf. *ina lipitti ipiḫû*, Neb. Nippur V, 2.

think of breaking the stone (*ana ḫapê* ^{abnu}*narû šuatu išakkanu uznâšu*),[1] crush it and thus destroy it (*uptessisma ittaqar itabat uḫtallik*),[2] break it up with another stone (*ina abni inaqqaru*[3] or *ina abni ubbatu*)[4] burn it with fire (*ina išâti iqallû*),[5] or plan any other malicious act against it (*ina mimma šumišu mala bašû ibannû nikiltu mamman*).[6]

6. The officials might erase the inscription. They might erase the names of the gods and the king and put others in their places (*šum ili ù šarri ša šaṭru uptaššiṭuma šanam iltaṭru*).[7]

7. The officials might employ irresponsible persons to carry out their wishes.[8] This they might do out of fear of the terrible curses written on the stones (*aššu arrâti šinâti* (*limutti*) *ša ina* ^{abnu}*narî šaṭru iptalaḫ*),[9] or because the persons they sent did not fear the gods

[1] V. A. 2663, V, 22.

[2] Susa 3, V, 55, 56.

[3] V R. 56, 35; cf. *ušaqqaru unakkaru uḫalliqqu*, London, 103, V, 42, 43; *ušaqqaru inaqqaru*, IV R.^{2} 38, III, 16, 17.

[4] III R. 41, II, 11; I R. 70, III, 3; III R. 43, I, 34; London, 102, V, 2; cf. *ina abni uabbitsu*, London, 101, III, 4; *ina abni ubbaṣu*, Susa 16, V, 2; *ina abni upasasu*, V. A. 2663, V, 30; *upasasu*, O. B. I., 150, II, 3; *šipir nikilti ubbatu*, C. T., X, pl. VII, 36.

[5] III R. 41, II, 11; III R. 43, I, 34; O. B. I., 149, II, 12; London, 102, V, 3; C. T., X, pl. VII, 37; cf. *išâta ušaqqa*[*lû*], London, 103, V, 44; *ana išâti inadû*, London, 101, III, 3; D. E. P., VI, 45, Col. V, 12; *ana mê u išâti ittadi*, Susa 3, V, 51; *ana mê ana išâti ušaddû*, IV R.^{2} 38, 18, 19; *ana mê u išâti inamdû*, Susa 16, IV, 31–32; *išâti išaqlû*, V R. 56, 36; *ina išâti išarrapu*, I R. 70, III, 4; *išâti ušakalu*, O. B. I., 150, II, 4.

[6] V. A. 2663, V, 23, 24.

[7] V R. 56, 33; cf. *šumi šaṭra iptašiṭ*, Susa 3, V, 57; Susa 16, V, 3, 4; *upaššaṭuma šanamma išaṭṭaru*, I R. 70, III, 5, 6; *šumu šaṭru ipaššiṭu*, V. A. 2663, V, 32.

[8] From this point of view IV R.^{2} 38, III, 15 *mâr bêl eqli šu'atum*, must be understood. It is doubtless a minor whom the writer has in mind.

[9] Susa 3, V, 47, 48; I R. 70, II, 19, 20; cf. *aššu arr*[*at*] *ipallaḫuma*, London, 102, V, 3; *aššu arrâti šinâti*, Susa 16, IV, 22, 23; *aššu arrâti*, III R. 41, II, 8; *aššu* (*MU* = Br. 1226) *arrâti annâti ipallaḫuma*, London, 101, III, 5.

(*lâ pâliḫ ilâni rabûti*).[1] They might send strangers and enemies (*aḫâm, nakara*),[2] rascals (*gišḫabba*),[3] persons affected with bodily ailments, deaf and blind (*sakka, la šêmâ ša amâti, samâ, lâ nâṭil ša pâni-šu*), or persons with mental defects, fools, weak-minded and idiots (*sakla, nu'a, ulâla*)[4] who do not understand what they are doing (*lâ mûdâ*).

8. Officials might curtail or revoke the freedom of the land from certain territorial obligations. They might subject it again to the regular taxation (*ana ilki uštêrib*[5] or *utteruma ilka iltaknu*),[6] permit land officers to cut grass and canal officers to seize canal diggers (*ina ilki dikûti ṣabât amel ḫirê nâra baqân šammi kallê nâri u tabali ušaššû*),[7] and send some one to forage the pasture lands (*ana ikîli rî'ti uma'aru šanamma*).[8]

[1] V. A. 2663, V, 27; cf. V R. 56, 32, *šarru u ilânišu lâ iptalḫuma utteruma ilka iltaknu*.

[2] Susa 3, V, 49, cf. V. A. 2663, V, 25.

[3] III R. 41, II, 9.

[4] The order of the first three persons mentioned in this section is usually *sakla sakka* (*sukkuka*) *samâ*, cf. London, 101, III, 6; Susa 16, IV, 26, 27; Susa 14, II, 14, 15; V R. 56, 34; I R. 70, II, 21, 22; III R. 43, I, 31; but the order may also be *sakka sakla samâ*, Susa 3, V, 50, or *sakla sakka lâ šêmâ*, V. A. 2663, V, 25, 26, and perhaps IV R.[2] 38, III, 11, 12; or *sakka sakla lâ šêmâ*, D. E. P., VI, 45 Col. V, 20, 21, or *sakla sakka lâ mûdâ*, London, 103, V, 41, 42. When the series begins with *sakla sakka* (*sakka sakla*) *samâ* it is *always* followed by a fourth term, which may be *lâ mûdâ*, Susa 3, V, 50; Susa 16, IV, 26, 27; or *lâ šêmâ*, V R. 56, 34; I R. 70, II, 21, 22 (which may also be prefixed to this series, O. B. I., 149, II, 9, 10); or *ulâla*, Susa 14, II, 14, 15; or *ulâla* and *lâ šêmâ*, III R. 43, I, 43. The formula *sakla sakka lâ šêmâ* is varied in III R. 41, II, 8, 9 by the insertion of *nu'a* and *gišḫabba* after *sakka*, while V. A. 2663, V, 25–27 adds to this series *lâ nâṭil ša pâniša lâ mûdâ nu'a*. Finally, London, 102, V, 4, has only *sakla lâ šêmâ*, with perhaps a third term effaced.

[5] Susa 3, IV, 57, 58; V, 31.

[6] V R. 56, 32.

[7] Neb. Nippur, III, 25–27.

[8] Neb. Nippur, III, 21, 22. Other infringements of privileges and immunities granted by the king are mentioned in the various charters, see above, pp. 27–31.

Names and Titles of the Gods.

As to the names of the gods which are employed in the various curses, we can refer to the discussion of the subject by Prof. Jastrow in his *Religion Babyloniens und Assyriens*, Vol. I, pp. 182–187, and to our Index. Attention must be called to the longest list of gods that has been found thus far on any boundary stone. It occurs on a stone of Marduk-apal-iddina I. (Susa, XVI), recently published by Prof. V. Scheil (D. E. P., VI, pls. 9, 10). It begins with the four gods, Anu, Ellil, Ea and NIN.ḪAR.SAG, a title of the Bêlit of Nippur. Then follow a series of pairs, Sin and his wife NIN.GAL, the gods of Ur; Shamash and his wife Ai, the gods of Sippar, together with three lesser gods, forming the court of Shamash, Bunene, Kittu (NIN.GI.NA) and Mêsharu (NIN.SI), and two gods the reading of whose name is not yet certain, AT.GI.MAḪ[1] and SHE.-RU.SHISH. These are followed by Marduk and his wife Zarpanîtum, the gods of Babylon; Nabû and his wife Tashmêtum, the gods of Borsippa; NIN.IB and his wife NIN.KAR.RA.AG, a title of Gula, worshipped chiefly at Nippur; Zamama and his wife Bau, the gods of Kish. The next group consists of five goddesses, Damu and GESHTIN.NAM (GESHTIN is explained as *bêlit ṣêri*,[2] see Br. 5008), Ishtar, Nanâ and Anunîtum. Then follow Rammân and his wife Shala, together with Mi-šar-ru (the latter is also associated

[1] Perhaps to be read *malku ṣîru*, since *AT.GI* = *ma-lik*, cf. Br. 4170, and belonging with *ŠE.RU.ŠIŠ* to the attendants of Shamash. Their position between Bunene and Kittu points in that direction.

[2] *Bêlit ṣêri* occurs in the Gilgamesh epic as the scribe of the under world, kneeling before Ereshkigal (col. V, 47, cf. K. B., VI, 190). In IV R. 27, No. 5, 29, 30, *dNIN.GEŠTIN.NA DUB.SAR MAḪ* corresponds to *dbe-lit ṣi-ri tup-šar*, cf. also II R. 59, Rev. 10–11, *b*, *c*, where *dGEŠTIN* is given as the equivalent of *dbe-lit ṣêri*, as well as *dGEŠTIN.AN.NA*. *dNIN.GEŠTIN.NA* is placed alongside of Nanâ on K 2613, Obv. II, 13, cf. B. A., V, 701. *dGAŠ.TIN.NAM* appears alongside of *NIN.KA.SI*, a wine goddess, =Siris, in Reisner, *Hymnen*, IV, 64, 65. In I R. 43, 32, *dGAŠ.TIN.NAM* is mentioned among the deities of Erech (*ilâni âšibût Uruk*).

with Rammân and Shala[1] in D. E. P., VI, 46, III, 2); Nergal and his wife Laṣ, the gods of Kutha; Ishum and Shubula, the latter being known as the goddess of Shumdula.[2] Their juxtaposition here proves them husband and wife. Next come LUGAL.GIR.RA and SHIT.LAM.TA.E, two forms of Nergal, here perhaps regarded as male and female; LUGAL.GISH.A.TU.GAB.LISH (to be read Bêl-ṣarbi),[3] also a form of Nergal, the god of Baṣ, and his wife Ma-'-me-tum, usually named as the wife of Nergal.[4] Next LIL and NIN.BAD,[5] together with Tishḫu,[6] and probably his wife KA.DI, the goddess of Dûr-ilu, and finally the three pairs Nusku and his wife Sadarnunna, IB (or Urash) and his wife NIN.E.GAL (also called Mama, according to the Code of Ḫammurabi, II, 29), the gods of Dilbat, and Shuqamuna and his wife Shumalia.

The number of all the gods invoked in the curses on the various boundary stones published thus far is fifty-eight. This large number is mainly due to the new stone of Marduk-apal-iddina I. (Susa, XVI), which alone enumerates forty-seven deities. Omitting this stone the number on all the other stones is but thirty-six, and even of these hardly a dozen occur frequently. The deities invoked on the *Caillou de Michaux* give a fair representation of the most favored gods, because all of them occur more than six times. They are Anu, Ellil, Ea and NIN.MAḪ (a title of the Bêlit

[1] The same association occurs also in Craig, *Religious Texts*, pls. 57, 22; 58, 24.

[2] Cf. II R. 60, 18, *a*, *b*. Ishum and Shubula are mentioned together as the gods of the Tigris and Euphrates, see Craig, *Religious Texts*, pl. 57, 11.

[3] Cf. Langdon, *Building Inscriptions*, Nebuch. 1, II, 29, 30, and 9, II, 48.

[4] Cf. Böllenrücher, *Gebete an Nergal*, No. III, 8, p. 20; but *LUGAL.GIŠ.A.-TU.GAB.LIŠ* is placed alongside of *dMa-mi-tum* also in *Shurpu Series*, VIII, 14.

[5] *dNIN.BAD.NA* is called the wife of *LUGAL.AB.BA*, cf. III R. 68, 73, *a*, and *LUGAL.A.AB.BA* is a title of Nergal, cf. II R. 59, 37, 38, *e*; hence *dLIL* must also be a title of Nergal, which agrees very well with the context, in which various forms of Nergal are enumerated.

[6] For the pronunciation *Tishḫu* see Ranke, *Personal Names*, pp. 169 and 207; Thureau-Dangin, I. S. A., 249, note 9.

of Nippur), Marduk, Shamash, Sin and Ishtar, NIN.IB, Gula, Rammân and Nabû. Besides these nearly all the stones of the Cassite period mention the Cassite gods Shuqamuna and Shumalia. As lesser gods, which occur at least three times, are invoked Nergal and Nusku, NIN.E.GAL and Zamama, Bau and Zarpanîtum.

Numerous titles are applied to the gods on the boundary stones.

Anu, the father of the gods (*abi ilâni*),[1] the king, the father of the gods (*šarru abi ilâni*),[2] Anu the prince, the great lord (*Anu rabû bêlu rabû*),[3] the king of heaven (*šar šamê*).[4]

Anunît, the one inhabiting heaven (*âšibat* [*šamê*]).[5]

Bêlit, the mistress of the gods who creates all (*bêlat ilâni bânat napḫari*).[6]

Bunene, the son of Shamash, the exalted king, the hero, the counselor of his father (*apil Šamaš šarru tizkaru qardu malik abišu*).[7]

Ea, the creator of men (*pâtik nišê*),[8] the creator of all (*bân kala*),[9] the king of the ocean, the lord of wisdom (*šar apsî bêl tašîmti*),[10] and perhaps "the king of springs" (*šar naqbê*).[11]

Ellil, the great lord, the command of whose mouth cannot be altered and whose grace is steadfast (*bêlu rabû ša qibît pîšu la innennû u annašu kînu*),[12] the lord of lands (*bêl mâtâti*),[13] the king of all (*šar gimri*),[14] the sublime lord who determines the fate of the gods (*bêl šaqû mušîm šîmat ilâni*).[15]

[1] London, 101, III, 9.
[2] Neb. Nippur, IV, 3.
[3] III R. 43, IV, 30.
[4] Susa 2, IV, 2.
[5] London, 101, III, 15.
[6] D. E. P., II, 113, 1. *Bêlat* is written *NIN-at;* cf. V. A. 2663, II, 52f.
[7] D. E. P., II, 115, 5, 6. The ideogram from Shamash is *ALAM*, see Br. 7298 and cf. Br. 7296.
[8] London, 101, III, 11.
[9] O. B. I., 83, II, 17.
[10] Neb. Nippur, IV, 9.
[11] D. E. P., VI, 43, IV, 4. Cf. *Ea, bêl naq-bi kup-pi ù ta-mir-ti*, Sennach., Bavian, 28.
[12] Susa 3, VII, 44–48.
[13] Susa 2, IV, 4.
[14] London, 101, III, 10.
[15] Neb. Nippur, IV, 5, 6.

Gula, the glorious mistress, the mistress of all mistresses (*bêltu šurbûtum etillit kala bêlêti*),[1] the great mistress (*bêltu rabîtu*),[2] the great mistress, the wife of NIN.IB (*bêltu rabîtu ḫîrat NIN.IB*),[3] the great physician (*azugallatu rabîtum*),[4] the physician, the great mistress (*azugallatu bêltu rabîtu*),[5] the bride of Esharra (*kallat Ešarra*).[6]

Girru, the terrible Girru (BIL.GI), the child of Nusku (*Girru izzu mêru ša Nusku*).[7]

Išḫara, the mistress of victory over lands (*bêlit lêti dadma*).[8]

Ištar, the mistress of heaven and earth (*bêlit šamê u irṣiti*),[9] the mistress, the princess among the gods (*bêltu rubâ ilâni*),[10] the mistress of lands (*bêlit mâtâti*),[11] the mistress of lands whose fury is like a storm flood (*bêlit mâtâti ša rûbša abûbu*).[12]

Marduk, the leader of the gods (*abkal ilâni*),[13] the leader of heaven and earth (*abkal šamê u irṣiti*),[14] the great lord (*bêlu rabû*),[15] the great lord whose command no god can annul (*bêlu rabû ša ṣît pîšu ilu mamma la ušpellum*),[16] the king of the gods (*šar ilâni*),[17] the king of heaven and earth (*šar šamê u irṣiti,*)[18] the mighty one, the lord (owner) of this field (*alîlu bêl eqli šu'atum*),[19] the lord of constructions (*bêl liptêti*),[20] and *bêl*

[1] Susa 3, VII, 14–17.

[2] London, 102, II, 20; D. E. P., VI, 47, 11; Neb. Nippur, IV, 20.

[3] III R. 43, IV, 15; I R. 70, IV, 5.

[4] Susa 14, IV, 5, 6.

[5] III R. 41, II, 29.

[6] D. E. P., II, 113, 13; V R. 56, 39.

[7] Susa 2, IV, 18, 19. The rendering of Scheil, *šibru* (=*šibirru*) *ša Nusku*, *i.e.*, "the weapon of Nusku," is also possible.

[8] III R. 43, IV, 28; called thus as the goddess of war.

[9] I R. 70, III, 22; III R. 43, IV, 12.

[10] III R. 41, II, 21.

[11] Susa 2, IV, 16; London, 103, VI, 18.

[12] Neb. Nippur, IV, 22.

[13] London, 101, III, 13.

[14] Susa 14, III, 14.

[15] I R. 70, III, 13; III R. 43, III, 31.

[16] Susa 3, VI, 29–32.

[17] London, 102, I, 40.

[18] III R. 41, II, 25.

[19] Susa 2, III, 30–32.

[20] O. B. I., 149, II, 21.

qat(?)-ta-ti.[1] Marduk and Zarpanîtum together are addressed as the lords who determine fate (*bêlê mušimmu šîmti*).[2]

Nabû, the overseer of the universe (*pa-qid kiṣ[šat]*),[3] the overseer of the totality of heaven and earth (*pa[qid kiššat šamê u irṣiti]*),[4] the lofty messenger (*sukallu ṣîru*),[5] the firstborn son of Esagila (*[aplu] reštû ša Esagila*),[6] the king of Ezida, the scribe of Esagila, the shepherd of the totality of heaven and earth (*šar Ezida tupšar Esagila rê'i kiššat šamê u irṣitim*).[7]

Nanâ, together with Rammân and Nergal, called "the gods of Namar" (*ilâni ša mâtuNamar*).[8]

Nergal, the lord of weapons and bows (*bêl bêlê u qašâti*),[9] the lord of war and battle (*bêl qabli u taḫâzi*).[10]

Ninâ, the mistress of the goddesses (*bêlit eštarâtu*).[11]

NIN.E.GAL, together with Nusku, Shuqamuna and Shumalia, called "the gods of the king" (*ilâni šarri*)[12] and "the gods of the kingdom and of his land" (*[ilâni] šarrûti u mâtišu*).[13]

NIN.IB, the lord of the boundary, limit(?) and boundary stone (*bêl apli šûmi u kudurri*),[14] the lord of the boundary stone (*bêl kudurri*),[15] the lord of boundary stones (*bêl kuddurrêti*),[16] the lord of the boundary and of the boundary stone (*bêl miṣri u kuddurri*)[17] (so alone and also with Gula), the king of heaven and earth (*šar šamê u irṣiti*),[18] the son of Ešarra, the sublime son of Ellil (*apil Ešarra, mâr Enlil ṣîru*).[19]

[1] D. E. P., II, 113, 4; written *bêl ŠÚ-ta-ti*.
[2] V. A. 2663, V, 40–42.
[3] London, 101, III, 14.
[4] London, 102, I, 44.
[5] I R. 70, IV, 16; III R. 41, II, 34, III R. 43, IV, 1.
[6] London, 102, I, 45.
[7] D. E. P., VI, 46, 4–6.
[8] V R. 56, 48.
[9] III R. 43, IV, 21.
[10] London, 102, II, 3.
[11] O. B. I., 83, II, 15.
[12] Susa 14, IV, 11.
[13] D. E. P., VI, 47, 5, 6.
[14] Susa 3, VII, 5–8.
[15] D. E. P., II, 113, 3; London, 103, VI, 11.
[16] III R. 43, IV, 19; London, 102, II, 14.
[17] Neb. Nippur, IV, 19; III R. 41, II, 27; O. B. I., 149, III, 1.
[18] V R. 56, 39.
[19] I R. 70, IV, 1, 2.

Nusku, the powerful lord, the mighty scorcher (*bêl gašrum, ârirum karûbu*).[1] Nusku, NIN.E.GAL, Shuqamuna and Shumalia are called "the gods of the king"[2] (Marduk-apal-iddina I.) and "the gods of the kingdom and of his land" (*ilâni šarrûti u mâtišu*).[3]

Papsukal, the messenger of the great gods, who walks in the service of the gods, his brothers (*sukalli ilâni rabûti, âlik kiširri ilâni aḫêšu*).[4]

Rammân, the leader of heaven and earth (*gugal šamê u irṣiti*),[5] the leader of heaven and earth, the lord of fountains and rain (*gugal šamê u irṣiti bêl naqbî u zunni*),[6] the leader of the gods (*gugal ilâni*),[7] the son of Anu, the hero (*mâr Anum qardu*),[8] the lord of right(?) (*bêl ki-ta-a-ti*).[9] Rammân, Nergal and Nanâ are called "the gods of Namar" (*ilâni ša* $^{m\hat{a}tu}$*Namar*).[10]

Sin, the terrible lord, who among the great gods is brilliant (*bêlum izzu ša ina ilâni rabûti šupû*).[11] The inhabitant of the bright heavens (*ašâb šamê ellûti*),[12] the light of the bright heavens (*nannar šamê ellûti*),[13] the light, the inhabitant of the bright heavens (*nannaru âšib šamê ellûti*),[14] the light delivering decrees (*nannari pâris purussê*),[15] the eye of heaven and earth (*în šamê u irṣitim*),[16] the lord of the crown of splendor (*bêl agê namerûti*),[17] the father of the great gods (*abi ilâni rabûti*).[18]

1 Neb. Nippur, IV, 25.
2 Susa 14, IV, 11.
3 D. E. P., VI, 47, 5, 6.
4 III R. 43, IV, 25, 26.
5 V R. 56, 41; III R. 43, IV, 3; III R. 41, II, 32; I R. 70, IV, 9; Susa 14, III, 9.
6 V R. 56, 41.
7 D. E. P., II, 113, 7.
8 I R. 70, IV, 10.
9 D. E. P., VI, 47, 7.
10 V R. 56, 48.
11 Susa 3, VI, 41–43.
12 III R. 43, IV, 7. The text has *a-šab*, but we expect *a-šib*, and it was probably intended; cf. I R. 70, III, 18.
13 III R. 41, II, 16.
14 I R. 70, III, 18.
15 Susa 14, III, 7.
16 O. B. I., 149, III, 6; London, 102, I, 46.
17 Neb. Nippur, IV, 13.
18 D. E. P., II, 113, 6.

Ṣîru, the child of KA.DI (*mêru ša KA.DI*),[1] the brilliant god, the *mâr bîtu* of Dêr (*ilu šûpû mâr bîtu ša* $^{\hat{a}lu}$*Dêr*).[2]

Shamash, the judge of heaven and earth (*daian šamê u irṣiti*),[3] the judge, the prince of heaven and earth (*daianu rabu šamê u irṣitim*),[4] the judge, the strong one over men, the great one in heaven and earth (*daianu kaškaš nišê rabu šamê u irṣiti*),[5] the great judge of the great gods (*daianu rabû ša ilâni rabûti*),[6] the creator of heaven and earth (*pâtik šamê u iršitim*).[7] Shamash and Rammân together are called "the powerful gods, the lofty judges" (*ilâni gašrûtu daianê ṣîrûti*)[8] and "the gods, the lords of right" (*ilâni bêlê dîni*).[9]

Shumalia, the mistress of the bright mountains, dwelling on the mountain tops and walking by the springs (*bêlit šadê ellûti âšibat rêšêti kâbisat kuppâti*).[10]

Shuqamuna and *Shumalia*, the gods of the king (Meli-Shipak) (*ilâni ša šarri*),[11] called the gods of war (*ilâni qabli tamu*).[12]

Zamama, the king of battle (*šar taḫâzi*),[13] the powerful one among the gods (*kaškaš ilâni*).[14]

Zarpanîtum, the mistress of Esagila (*bêlit Esagila*),[15] the great mistress ([*bêltu*] *rabîtum*).[16] Marduk and Zarpanîtum, the lords who appoint fate (*bêlê mušimmu šîmti*).[17]

[1] Susa 2, IV, 23; or perhaps *šibru ša KA.DI*, "the weapon of KA.DI."

[2] V R. 56, 49. [3] London, 101, III, 12; III R. 41, II, 19; London, 102, II, 1.

[4] I R. 70, III, 15. [5] III R. 43, IV, 10. [6] Susa 14, III, 3.

[7] D. E. P., II, 113, 5. [8] Neb. Nippur, IV, 15, 16.

[9] London, 103, VI, 9. [10] V R. 56, 46, 47.

[11] London, 103, VI, 15, 16, cf. also Susa 14, IV, 10, 11, and the title "the gods of the kingdom and of his land" ([*ilâni*] *šarrûti u mâtišu*), which they share with Nusku and NIN.E.GAL, cf. D. E. P., VI, 47, 5, 6.

[12] Susa 2, IV, 22, or perhaps "the gods of war, the twins," as suggested by Zimmern, see Frank, *Bilder und Symbole*, p. 40.

[13] III R. 43, IV, 23. [14] London, 102, II, 6. [15] London, 102, I, 43.

[16] O. B. I., 149, II, 22. [17] V. A., 2663, V, 40–42.

Anu, Ellil and Ea,[1] and in some cases also NIN.ḪAR.SAG[2] or NIN.MAḪ,[3] are called the great gods (*ilâni rabûti*).

Of all these titles only a few of a more general nature are exchanged between the gods; *bêlu rabû* is common to Anu, Ellil and Marduk; *abi ilâni* is attributed to Anu and Sin, and *šar šamê u irṣiti* to Marduk and NIN.IB. In the other cases the titles seem to have become firmly attached to the several gods. At least no transfer can be observed.

The Curses of the Kudurru Inscriptions.

The calamities and disasters which the gods are asked to send down upon would-be offenders are even more numerous and varied than their titles. We quote them under the names of the gods with whom they are connected.

Anu is asked:

a. May he overthrow him in anger and destroy his soul (*aggiš litallikšuma napšatuš liballi*, Neb. Nippur, IV, 3, 4).

b. May he cause him to take a road that is obstructed (*harranna parikta lišeṣbisu*, III R. 43, IV, 30, 31).

Anunît:

May she destroy his foundation (*išidsu lîbit*, London, 101, III, 15).

Bunene:

May his command tear him out (*qibîsu lisuḫšuma*, D.E.P., II, 115, 6).

Ea:

a. May he give him an evil fate (*šîmtašu lilamman*, London 101, III, 11).

[1] V. A. 2663, V, 36, 37; C. T., X, pl. VII, 38; London, 103, V, 48–VI, 1; III R. 43, III, 26, 27; London, 102, I, 37; V. A. 209, II, 8, 9.

[2] Susa 3, VI, 16–20.

[3] I R. 70, III, 9, 10; III R. 41, II, 13, 14.

b. May he take away from him gladness of heart, happiness of mind, abundance and fullness, so that lamentation may seize him (*nûgu kabitti numur libbi naḫâša ḫabâṣa lîkimšuma nissatu lilqišu,* Neb. Nippur, IV, 10–12).

Ellil:

a. May they (the curses) not miss him, but overtake him (*lâ išettâšu likšudâšu,* Susa 3, VII, 50, 51).

b. May he appoint for him an evil fate, so that calamity, misfortune and the words of men may oppress him (*šîmat marušti lišîmšuma lubnâ nelmenâ amât nišê ligisâšu,* Neb. Nippur, IV, 6–8).

c. May he lay his punishment upon him (*še-ri-[it-su li]-mi-is-su,* London, 101, III, 10).

Gula:

a. Destructive sickness may she put into his body, so that he may pass dark and bright red blood as water (*simma laz(za) in zumrišu liškumma (lišabšima) dama u šarka kî mê lirmuk (lirtammuk),* I R. 70, IV, 6–8; III R. 43, IV, 16–18; III R. 41, II, 30, 31).

b. *idem* till body, then adding: So that as long as he lives he may pass dark and bright red blood as water (*adi ûm balṭu šarqa u dama kî mê lirmuk,* Susa 3, VII, 19–25).

c. *idem* as *a,* then adding: And may she not cause his corpse to have burial (*ša[lamtašu] qibîra ai[ušaršišu],* London, 102, II, 20–25; cf. Susa 16, VI, 21, *ša-lam-ta-šu i-na irṣiti ai ik-ki-bir*).

d. A painful, destructive disease, a depression that does not go away, may she let loose into his body (*simma akṣa lazza miqta la tabâ ina zumrišu lišêṣi,* Susa 14, IV, 6–9).

Išhara:

May she not hear him in mighty battle (*ina taḫâzi danni lâ išemišu,* III R. 43, IV, 29).

Ištar:

a. Before the gods and the king of Babylon may she bring him into evil (*ana maḫri ilâni u šar Bâbili ana limutti lirtedišu*, III R. 43, IV, 13–14).

b. Daily before god and the king may she lead him into evil (*ûmišamma ana maḫar ili u šarri ana limutti lirteddišu*, I R. 70, III, 23–24).

c. In conflict and in battle to the weapon of the enemy may she surrender him (*a-šar qa-tuš u taḫâzi ana* ^{isu}*kakki nakiri limnuš*, London, 103, VI, 18–20).

d. May she send him despair and.... her message of anger, day and night he may multiply his words, like a dog pass the night in the street(s) of his city (*tâlîtum lispuršuma.... našpartaša ša uzzi urra u mûša lima'ida atmêšu kîma kalbi libta'ita ina rêbit âlišu*, III R. 41, II, 21–24).

e. May she cause him to see difficulties, so that he may not escape from misfortune (*namraṣa likallimšuma ai ûṣi ina ušaki*, Neb. Nippur, IV, 23, 24).

Marduk:

a. May he pursue him with evil (*ina limutti lirdišu*, London, 101, III, 13).

b. May he pour out his life like water (*napištašu kîma mê litbuk*, Susa 2, III, 33–35).

c. May he inflict famine as his severe punishment upon him. Seeing angry faces and holding out his hand, without being fed, may he wander through the streets of his city (*bubûta šêrtašu rabîta limissuma ina naṭâl kammali tiriṣ qâti ù lâ epêri sûq âlišu lissaḫḫar*, Susa 3, VI, 33–40).

d. May he cause him to bear dropsy as a bond that is unbreakable (*agalâtillâ riksu (rikissu) lâ paṭêra lišiššišu*, III R. 43, III, 31–32; I R. 70, III, 13, 14; London, 102, I, 41).

e. May he stop up his canals(?) (*nârâte*(?)-*šu liskirma*, O. B. I., 149; II, 21).

f. May he fill his body with dropsy, whose hold cannot be broken (*agalâtillâ ša rikissu lâ ippaṭaru liṣân karassu*, III R. 41, II, 25, 26).[1]

g. *Marduk* and *Zarpanîtum*:

May they cause him to bear dropsy as his severe punishment, and with the bloating of his flesh may his body perish (*šêritsu kabittu agalâtillâ lišiššûšuma ina šîḫat šêri liqta zumuršu*, V. A., 2663, V, 42–44).

Nabû:

a. May he change his confines, limits and boundary stone (*usa miṣra u kudurrašu lišenni*, III R. 43, IV, 1–2).

b. May he appoint for him days of want and drought as his fate (*ûm sugê u arrati ana šîmâtišu lišîmšu*, III R. 41, II, 34–35).

c. May he bring want and famine upon him, so that he may not attain whatever his throat desires (*sugâ u nibrîta liškunaššumma mimma uttû ana ḫurri pîšu lâ ikaššad*, I R. 70, IV, 17–20).

d. May he lead(?) his children into famine ([*mârê*]*šu ana ḫušaḫḫi* [*lirteddi*?], London, 102, I, 45).

Nergal:

a. May he break his weapons (*kakkêšu lišêbir*, III R. 43, IV, 22).

b. May he slay him in his battle (*ina taḫâzišu lišgissu*, London, 102, II, 5).

NIN.GIRSU and *Bau*:

May they not appoint for him cheerful hilarity(?) as his lot (*alâla ṭâba ana šîmtišu lâ imannû*, London, 103, VI, 6–8).

[1] Cf. D. E. P., II, 113, 18-19, May the head be sick, may dropsy like a band of fire enclose him (*qaqqadu* [*mar*(?)]-*zi-ma agalâtillâ mêsir maqlûti likmi*-[*šu*]).

NIN.KAR.RA.AG (or *Gula*):

Of his seed may she snatch away (*ina zêrišu lilqut*, London, 101, III, 17).

NIN.IB:

a. The son, the water pourer, may he take away from him, and may he not cause him to have seed and offspring (*aplam naq mê lîkimšuma še'uzêru u pira ai ušaršišu*, Susa 3, VII, 9–13).

b. May he tear out his boundary stone (*kudurrašu lissuḫ*, Neb. Nippur, IV, 19; D. E. P., II, 113, 3).

c. May he deprive him of his son, his water pourer (*apilšu naqa mêšu lišêli*, III R. 43, IV, 20).

d. May he tear out his boundary stone, tread down his boundary line and change his plot (*kudurrašu lissuḫ miṣiršu likabis pilikšu lîni*, III R. 41, II, 27–28).

e. May he tear out his confines, limits and boundary stone (*ussu miṣiršu u kudurrašu lissuḫ*, I R. 70, IV, 3, 4).

f. May he tear out his boundary stone, destroy his name, his seed, his offspring, his descendants from the mouth of men, and may he not let him have a son and a pourer of water (*kudurrašu lissuḫ šumišu zêrišu pir'šu u nannabšu i(na) pî nišê liḫalliq aplu ù naq mê ai ušaršišu*, London, 102, II, 15–19).

g. May he destroy his boundary stone (*kudurrašu linaqir*, London, 103, VI, 12).

h. *NIN.IB* and *Gula*:

May they destroy his boundary stone and annihilate his seed (*lîbutû kudurrašu liḫalliqû zêrišu*, V R. 56, 40).

i. *NIN.IB* and *Gula*:

May they cause destructive sickness to be in his body and, as long as he lives, may he pass dark and bright red blood as water (*simmu laz[za ina] zumrišu lišabšûma ûm balṭu dama u šarka kîma mê lirmuk*, O. B. I., 149, III, 3–5).

Nusku:

a. May he be his evil demon and burn up his root (*lu rabiṣu limuttišu šuma liqamme šuršišu*, Neb. Nippur, IV, 26, 27).

b. *Nusku* and *NIN.E.GAL*:
May they cause the kingdom and his land to make him sick (*šarrûtu u mâtišu lišamriṣûšu*, D. E. P., VI, 47, 5, 6).

c. *Nusku*, *NIN.E.GAL*, *Shuqamuna* and *Shumalia*:
May they fill his head with sickness (*qaqqadsu lišamriṣûšu*, Susa 14, IV, 9–12).

Papsukal:

May he bar his gate (*bâbšu liparriki*, III R. 43, IV, 27).

Rammân:

a. May he destroy his fields with weeds, keep back the grain, so that no blade of grass may come forth (*eqlâtišu idra[nu] lišasḫîma lizammi ^{d}Ašnan ai ušêṣi urqîti*, Susa 14, III, 9–13).

b. May he fill his canals with mud, bring upon him hunger and want, and surround him day and night with distress, frailty and misery, so that frailty fasten its grip upon the inhabitants of his city (*nârâtišu limillâ sakîkê bubûta u ḫušaḫḫa liškunšumma lubnu makû u limînu urra u mûšu lû râkis ittišu ana âšib âlišu makî qâtsu limgug*, V R. 56, 41–45).

c. May he fill his canals with mud and his acres may he fill with thorns, may his feet tread down vegetation and pasturage (*nârâti sakîkê limili u tamirâtišu limilâ puqutta šir bîrâ likabbisa šêpâšu*, III R. 43, IV, 3–6).

d. May he flood his fields and instead of green herbs may weeds, instead of grain may thorns grow luxuriantly (*ugâršu lirḫiṣma kîmû urqêti idranu kîmû Nisâba puquttu liḫnubi*, III R. 41, II, 32, 33).

e. May he flood his field, and destroy his grain so that thorns may grow in abundance, and may his foot tread down vegetation and pasturage (*ugâršu lirḫiṣma Nisâba liḫalliqa puquttu lišmuḫ šerâ bîrîta likabbisa šêpâšu*, I R. 70, IV, 11–14).

f. May he cause barrenness instead of grain and weeds instead of water to be there (*[kî]mû ŠE.BAR la širiš kîmû mê idrâna lišabšî*, London, 102, II, 11–14).

Sin:

a. May he cause him to bear dropsy, whose hold cannot be broken, may he clothe his body with leprosy as with a garment and as long as he lives bar him from his home, so that like a beast of the field he lie down and may not tread upon the streets of his city (*agalâtillâ ša rikissu la ippaṭṭaru lišeššišu išrubâ kîma ṣubati pagaršu lilabišma adi ûm balṭu bîtsu lizamima kîma umâm ṣêri lirpud rebît âlišu ai ikbus*, Susa 3, VI, 44–VII, 4).

b. May he clothe his body with leprosy as with a garment (*išrubâ kîma lubâri lilibiša zumuršu*, III R. 43, IV, 8, 9).

c. May he cause leprosy to be in his body, so that he may not lie down within the wall of his city (*išrubâ ina zumrišu lilabšuma ina kamât âlišu ai irbiṣ*, O. B. I., 149, Col. III, 6–8).

d. May he clothe his whole body with never yielding leprosy, so that he may not be clean till the day of his death, but, like a wild ass, stretch himself out at the wall of his city (*išrubâ la tebâ gimir lânišu lilabbišma adi ûmi šîmâtišu ai ibib u kîma purîmi ina kamât âlišu lirtappud*, III R. 41, II, 16–18).

e. With leprosy as with a garment may he clothe him, so that, as a wild ass, he may stretch himself out at the wall of the city (*išrubâ kî lubâri lilabbisuma kî purîmi ina kamât âlišu lirtappud*, I R. 70, III, 19–21; London, 102, I, 46, 47).

f. May he darken his face so that he may not have merriment (*bûnišu liṭṭešuma lilli ai îši*, Neb. Nippur, IV, 13, 14).

Shamash:

a. May he destroy his name (*liḫalliq šumišu*, London, 101, III, 12).

b. Blindness of eyes, deafness of ears and lameness of limbs may he present to him for a present (*zût pâni sakâk uzni u ubbur mešrêti* [*ana ši*]*riqti lišruqšu*, Susa 14, III, 4–6).

c. May he decree the denial of his right and oppose him with violence (*lûdî*(*n*) *kul dînišu ina par*(*ik*)*ti lizzis*(*s*)*u*, III, R. 43, IV, 10, 11; I R. 70, III, 15–17).

d. May he not decide his right and his judgment, *i.e.*, give him a favorable decree (*dînšu u purussûšu ai iprus*, London, 102, II, 2–3).

e. May he smite his face so that his clear day may turn for him to darkness (*pânišu limḫaṣma ûmišu namru ana da'ummati lîturšu*, III R. 41, II, 19, 20).

Shamash and *Marduk*:

When he calls upon Shamash and Marduk may they not hear him (*êma* ^{d}*Šamaš ù* ^{d}*Marduk išassû ai* (*iš*!)-*mu-šu*, IV R.[2] 38, III, 42–44).

Shamash and *Rammân*:

May they not let his cause succeed (*dînšu lâ ušteššerû*, London, 103, VI, 9, 10).

May they spoil his plans, and with a judgment of justice and righteousness may they not judge him (*lu mulammenû igirrêšu šunuma dîn kitti u mêšari ai idînûšu*, Neb. Nippur, IV, 15–18).

Shuqamuna and *Shumalia*:

May they place him before the king and the nobles (as a culprit) (*ina pân šarri u rubûti lišaškinûšu*, London, 103, VI, 15, 16).

Urash and *NIN.E.GAL*:

May they pursue him with evil (*ina limutti lirtedûšu*, London, 103, VI, 13, 14).

Zamama:

May he not take his hand in battle (*ina taḫâzi qâtsu lâ iṣabat*, III R. 43, IV, 24).

Zamama and [*Bau*]:

May they look upon him in anger, so that they may not let him have a name (child) ([*izz*]*iš likkilmûšuma u šumu ai ušaršûšu*, D. E. P., VI, 47, 1–3).

Zarpanîtum:

May she spoil his plans (*igirrâ*[*šu*] *l*[*ila*]*mman*, O. B. I., 149, II, 23).

There are still a series of curses left, uttered in the name of a number of gods:

1. *Anu*, *Ellil* and *Ea* are asked:
   a. May they in the anger of their heart look upon him (*ina aggi libbišunu likkilmûšu*, London, 103, V, 48–VI, 2).
   b. May they tear out and destroy his foundation, tear out his offspring, carry off his descendants (*ešissu lissuḫḫû liḫalliqû piriḫšu lissuḫḫû lišêlû nannabšu*, III R. 43, III, 26–30).
   c. May they in anger look upon him and destroy his soul and the children of his seed (*izziš likkilmûšuma napi*[*štašu*] *mârê zêrišu liḫalliqû*, O. B. I., 149; II, 18–20).
   d. May they curse him with an evil curse that cannot be broken ([*arrat*] *la napšuri marušta liru*[*rûšu*], London, 102, I, 38, 39).

e. [The gods] as many as there are, may they curse him ([*ilâni*] *mala ibšimu lirurûšu*, C. T., X, pl. 7, 40).

f. A curse from which there is no escape, blindness of eyes, deafness of ears, lameness of limbs, may they present to him, so that he may drag along evil (*arrat la napšuru turti îna sakâk uznâ ubbur mešrêti lišruqûšumma lišdud marušti*, V. A., 2663, V, 36–40).

2. *Anu, Ellil, Ea* and *NIN.ḪAR.SAG* (or *NIN.MAḪ*):

a. May they look upon him with their angry face and with an evil curse from which there is no escape, may they curse him (*ina bûnišunu izzûti likkilmûšuma arrat la napšuri limutta lirurûš*, Susa 3, VI, 23–28, or *izziš likkilmûšuma arrat la napšuri marušta lirurûšu*, III R. 41, II, 13–15).

b. May they look upon him in anger, tear out his foundation and destroy his offspring (*izziš likkilmûšuma išidsu lissuḫû liḫalliqû pir'išu*, I R. 70, III, 9–12).

3. *Anu, Ellil, Ea, NIN.IB* and *Gula*:

May they look upon him in anger, and with a curse, from which there is no escape, curse him, tear out his boundary stone, snatch away his seed in misery, and in poor bodily health may he end the few days which he has to live (*izziš likkilmûšu arrat la pašâri lirurûšu kudurrašu lissuḫû zêrišu lilqutû(m) ina limutti u lâ-ṭûb šêri adi ûmi iṣûti ša balṭa liqtima*, IV R.[2] 38, III, 26–41).

4. *Sin, Shamash, Rammân* and *Marduk*:

May they tear out his foundation (*išidsu lissuḫû*(!), London, 103, VI, 4).

5. Of the (great) gods which are mentioned on this stone:

a. May they curse him with an evil curse, destroy his name, and may his seed not have a resting place for reposing(?) (*arrat limutti lirurûšu šumšu liḫalliqû zêršu ana šulî ai iršû nida aḫi*, Susa 2, III, 23–29).

b. May they destroy his name and cause him to come to naught (*šumišu liḫalliqû ana mimma lâ bašê lišâlikûšu*, London, 103, VI, 23–25).

c. May they curse him with a curse that is without escape, and may they not prolong his life a single day, may they not let him, his name, his seed live, may they appoint days of drought, years of famine for him as his fate, before god, king, lord and prince may his whining be long and may he end in misery (*arrat la napšuri lirurûšuma ûma ištên lâ balâṭsu liqbû šâšu šumišu ù zêrišu ai*(?) *ušabšû*(?) *ûmê arurti šanâte ḫušaḫḫi ana šîmâtišu lišîmû eli ili šarri* [*bêli*?] *u rubî lîrik rininšuma ina limutti likla*, London, 101, IV, 6–14).

d. May they appoint for him a fate of not seeing (blindness), stopping up of ears (deafness) and dumbness of mouth forever (*šîmat lâ naṭâli sakâk uzni ù ṣibît pî ana ṣât ûmi lišîmûšu*, Susa 3, VII, 35–40).

e. May they tear out his name, his seed, his posterity (*šumšu zêršu pir'išu lissuḫû*, D. E. P., IV, pl. 16, II, 9, 10).

f. May they look upon him in anger, . . . curse him with an evil curse that is without escape, with a deadly leprosy, a serious condition, may they envelop his body, from the gate of his city may he be driven captive, at the wall of his city may they make him crouch, as long as he lives may he cling to(?) the country, may he not come near to his people, may they afflict him with dropsy, so that his body may not be buried in the earth, [his spirit] may not press the hand of another spirit, decreeing life may they not grant his life, but destroy his name, tear out his foundation, snatch away his seed and may they not spare his children (*izziš lik*[*kil*]*mûšuma. . . . literrûšu arrat la napšurim marus-ta lirurûšu išrubâ mûti ân kabitta zumuršu lillab*[*biš*]*ma abulli âlišu kameš liṭṭarid ina kamât âlišu lišarbiṣûšuma adi ûm baldu lis(?)niq mâta ana nišêšu ai iṭḫi agallatillâ lišamriṣûšuma šalamtašu ina irṣiti ai ikkibir [ekimmušu] ana ekimmi rittišu ai isniq [mu]šîm balâṭi lâ balazzu [liqb]û šumšu liḫalliqû [išidsu] lizziḫû [zêršu] lilqutû a[i] îzibû daddašu,* Susa 16, VI, 11–27).

g. With a curse may they be cruel and may he not have offspring (*ina arrat limrirû piri ai iršu,* Susa 14, IV, 17).

h. May they curse him in anger, may god and the king look upon him in anger (*aggiš lirurûšu ilu u šarru izziš likkilmûšu,* V R. 56, 37, 38). In the anger of their heart may they plan evil against him, so that another may own the house he built. With a dagger in his neck and a poniard in his eyes, may he cast down his face before his captor and may the latter, unmindful of his pleading, quickly cut off his life. In the collapse of his house may his hands get into the mire, as long as he lives may he drag along misery, and as long as heaven and earth exist may his seed perish (*ina uzzat libbi ana limutti liḫtassûšuma bîtu ippušu libêl šanumma ultu paṭru ina kišâdišu u kuppû ina înišu ana ṣabitânišu appašu lilbimma unnînišu ai imḫuršu ḫanṭiš likkisa napšat[su] ina hipê bîtišu qâtâšu ṭîṭa lîrubâ adi ûm balṭu marušta lišdud u adi šamê ù irṣiti bašû zêršu liḫliq,* V. R. 56, 51–60).

i. May they lead him into evil and misfortune, and may they destroy his name, his seed, his offspring, his posterity from the mouth of the people far and near (*ana limutti u lâ ṭâbti lirteddûšu šumšu zêršu pirišu nannabšu ina pî nišê dišâti liḫalliqû,* III R. 41, II, 37–39).

j. May they curse him with an evil curse that is without escape, and may they destroy his seed forever (*arrat la napšuri limutta lirurûšuma adi ûm ṣâti lippuṣû zêršu,* I R. 70, IV, 23–25).

k. May they curse him with a curse that is without escape (*arrat lâ napšuri* (*limutta*) *lirurûšu,* III R. 43, III, 25; IV, 34–35; O. B. I., 149, II, 16, 17). For a single day may they not grant him life (*kî ištên ûmi lâ balâṭsu liqbû,* O. B. I., 149, III, 10, 11).

l. May they destroy his name, his seed, his offspring from the mouth of the people, may they cut off his future (*šumšu zêršu piri'šu ina pî nišê liḫalliqû lunakkisû arkâtsu,* V. A., 2663, V, 46, 47).

Here then we have nearly one hundred curses, uttered in the name of nearly thirty gods. It will be of interest to review briefly the most characteristic of these curses. Ea is asked to send melancholy, Gula a destructive sickness, Ishtar loss of weapons in battle, Marduk dropsy, Nabû want and famine, Nergal death in battle, NIN.IB removal of boundary and death of children, Nusku burning of root and headache, Rammân destruction of fields through floods, Sin leprosy, Shamash blindness, deafness and lameness or unfavorable decision in law, Zamama bad luck in battle. The other curses are couched in vague and general terms.

It is remarkable that the presence of witnesses was not always recorded upon the boundary stones. In view of Ḫammurabi's law (§§ 7 and 123) that a contract without witnesses was invalid, it is hardly possible to infer from these instances that no witnesses were present. We can only note the fact that on some of the finest boundary stones their names are omitted. The stone of Meli-Shipak (D. E. P., II, pls. 21–24), the sale of land to Marduk-nâṣir (III R. 41), the *Caillou de Michaux* (I R. 70), and the stone of Marduk-aḫê-erba (O. B. I., 149) omit this feature. When witnesses were present and their signatures were added, their number varied from at least three (IV R.[2] 38) to sixteen (III R. 43).

Several stones have a pictorial representation of the king who made the grant. III R. 41 shows the picture of one of the first kings of the second Isin (PA-SHE) dynasty. London, 102, represents Nabû-mukîn-aplu. C. T., X, pl. III, shows Nabû-apal-iddina, and V. A., 2663, Merodach-baladan II. Finally, the stone of 'Amrân (M. D. O. G., No. 7, p. 26) shows the picture of a king, who resembles the one on III R. 41 so much that they are most likely pictures of the same king, perhaps of Nebuchadrezzar I.

THE SYMBOLS OF THE BOUNDARY STONES.

The last remarkable feature of the boundary stones are the symbols which are sculptured either on top or on one of the sides of the stones. They are found on all the public boundary stones and on three of the private documents (the stone of Nazi-Maruttash, D. E. P., II, pls. 18, 19; that of Nabû-apal-iddina, B. O. R., I, 65; and the one of Marduk-šum-iddina, V. A., 208). They also occur on the stone of Nabû-šum-iškun, which records the appointment of Nabû-mutakkil as priest of Nebo at Borsippa.

Various theories have been proposed as to the meaning and purpose of these symbols. According to one theory (*Guide to Babylonian and Assyrian Antiquities*, 1900, p. 85f.) they are "representations of certain powers of evil from which the owners of the lands wished to preserve their property, or powers of good whose favor they wished to secure." According to another theory they are the representatives of the gods invoked in the inscription. This is the view of Prof. Scheil (*Recueil de Travaux*, 1901, Vol. XXIII, pp. 95–97), of Dr. Ward ("The Asherah," A. J. S. L., XIX, 33, 44), of George Thiele (*Antike Himmelsbilder*, Berlin, 1898), and partly of Prof. Jastrow (*Religion Babyloniens und Assyriens*, Vol. I, p. 191f.). According to a third view they represent the signs of the zodiac. This was first suggested by Oppert (*Documents juridiques*, 1877, p. 85f.). It was adopted by Pinches (*Guide to*

Fig. 20.—Boundary stone of Marduk-apal-iddina II. (V. A. 2663.)

the Nimroud Central Saloon, 1886, pp. 40–60), and more fully developed by Epping and Strassmaier, who identified three emblems as belonging to the zodiac (*Astronomisches aus Babylon,* 1889, pp. 149, 150). It was most fully elaborated by Prof. Hommel (*Aufsätze und Abhandlungen,* 1900, pp. 236–272, 350–372, 434–474). It has since been accepted by Prof. H. Winckler (*Preussische Jahrbücher,* Vol. 104 (1901), p. 226) and by F. K. Ginzel (*Beiträge zur Alten Geschichte,* Vol. I, p. 7f.). A fourth view recognizes in them only in part signs of the zodiac and in part other stars. This is held by Franz Boll (*Sphaera,* Leipzig, 1903, pp. 198–208).

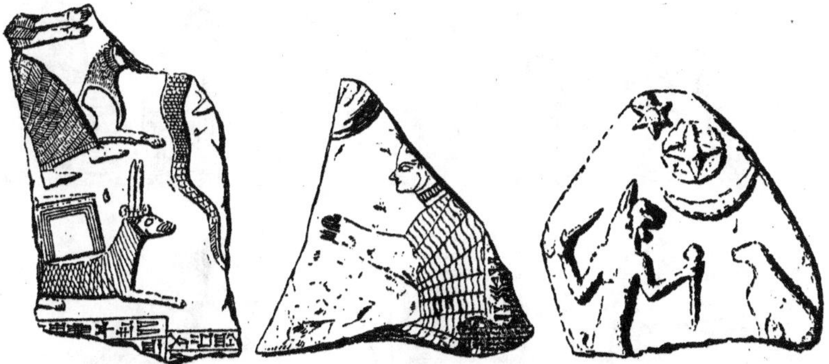

FIG. 21.—Fragments of boundary stones found at Susa, Nos. 7–9.

In view of this uncertainty it is not surprising that many scholars agreed with Oppert, who declared: "It would be rash to pretend to explain these symbols." Recently, however, the problem has passed into a new stage through the discovery by the French expedition at Susa of a number of new boundary stones, on which the symbols are repeatedly referred to. Before that time there was but one reference to the symbols on IV R.[2] 38, III, 29–31: *ilâni ma-la i-na narî šú-a-tum eš-ri-tu-šú-nu ud-da-a—i.e.,* "the gods whose shrines are shown on this stone." Now we read on the stone of Nazi-Maruttash (D. E. P., II, pl. 17, III, 19–22): *šum-šú-nu za-ak-ru* ^{iṣu}*kakku-šú-nu kul-lu-mu ù šú-ba-*

tu(m)-šú-nu ud-da-a—i.e., "whose names are mentioned, whose weapons are shown, whose seats are indicated."

Meli-Shipak, VII, 26–34 (D. E. P., II, pl. 23) reads: *ilâni rabûti ma-la i̤-na* *abnunarî an-ni-i šú-um-šú-nu za-ak-ru šú-ba-tu-šu-nu ud-da-a* *iṣukakkê-šú-nu ku-ul-lu-mu ù ú-ṣu-ra-tu-šu-nu uṣ-ṣu-ra—i.e.,* "the great gods as many as are mentioned on this stone by their names, whose seats are indicated, whose weapons are shown, whose reliefs are sculptured."

D. E. P., II, 89, note 3, reads: *ilâni mala [ina eli n]arî annî*

Fig. 22.—Babylonian temples as they appear on the boundary stones.

šum-šu-nu [šuṭṭ]uru KI.DUR.MEŠ-šunu uddâ u *iṣuDIB.MEŠ-šunu [u]-zu-[zu]*, and the fragment D. E. P., II, 113, 20, 21 reads: *ilâni mala i[na narî annî šum-šunu] za-ak-ru u-ṣu-ra-[tu-šu-nu uṣ-ṣu-ra]*.

These passages make it plain that the symbols represent three different things: (1) The seats or shrines of the gods, called *šubâti* or *ešrêti*; (2) the weapons of the gods, called *iṣukakkê* and *iṣuDIB.MEŠ*,[1] and (3) the bas-reliefs of the gods, called *uṣurâti*. The shrines are no doubt to be recognized in what scholars (Pinches

[1] This ideogram is perhaps only a scribal error for *iṣuKU* = *kakku*.

and Hommel) have been in the habit of calling altars. That these shrines actually represent ziggurats appears not only from the names *ešrêti*, "sanctuaries," which is applied to them, but also from the fact that a ziggurat is clearly drawn on IV R.[1] 43, third row,[1] last figure. The dragon, crouching before the stage tower, with a wedge standing upright on its back, corresponds to the wedge lying flat on the usual form of shrines (London 100; 106; 105; I R 70, etc.).[2] The stage tower on IV R.[1] 43, has four stories, and when we examine the other shrines more closely we find that they also contain four oblong squares within each other. It is the ground plan of a stage tower (cf. Bezold, *Nineve und Babylon*, p. 102).

These shrines, however, are not the stations of the planets or of the moon (Hommel, *Aufsätze*, pp. 244, 272, 435[1]), but more generally the seats of stellar deities (Boll, *Sphaera*, p. 203). This is particularly clear in the figure of the seated goddess on the stone of Nebuchadrezzar I. (V R. 57, fifth row),[3] which is not King Nebuchadrezzar, but the goddess Gula, as is definitely stated on a new stone from Susa (D. E. P., VII, p. 140, fig. 452).[4] Here the shrine evidently indicates the dwelling place of the deity; however, not an earthly temple (for all Babylonian deities are stellar in their nature), but a heavenly sanctuary. As the prototypes of all earthly conditions are to be found in heaven, according to the belief of the Babylonians, so earthly temples had their heavenly models.[5]

The shrines are not represented in connection with all the symbols. The largest number of shrines (ten) occurs on the stone of Meli-Shipak (D. E. P., II, pl. 24).[6] There we have two shrines with

[1] See fig. 6, p. 17; and fig. 22, second row.

[2] See fig. 49[8], p. 131; fig. 14[3], p. 34; fig. 12[18], p. 30; fig. 13[9], p. 33. The upper figures refer to the numbers of the symbols on the various pictures.

[3] See fig. 49[14], p. 131. [4] See fig. 40[1], p. 105.

[5] Cf. Winckler, *Himmels- und Weltenbild der Babylonier*, p. 12; Winckler, *Die Weltanschauung des alten Orients*, p. 11; A. Jeremias, *Das alte Testament im Lichte des alten Orients*, ed. 1, p. 12. [6] See fig. 11, p. 28.

tiaras, one with a ram's head, one with a pin and a horseshoe-like figure, one with a spear, one with a brick[1] and a wedge, one with a goddess, one with a lightning fork, one with a chisel, and one with a sea-shell. Besides these, there are shrines with a tortoise (London

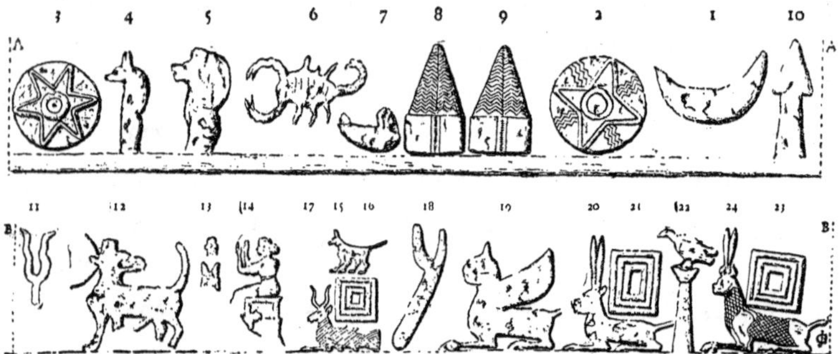

Fig. 23.—Symbols on a boundary stone discovered at Susa. (Susa, No. 4.)

106),[2] with a winged dragon beside it (V.A. 2663),[3] with a pyramid-shaped object (Susa 15),[4] with a square object (Susa 15),[5] with a round object with two horns (Susa 15),[6] with another round object (Susa 13),[7] one on the back of a monster carrying a vase on its

[1] Instead of one brick there may also be several rows of bricks, cf. Susa 16^{11} (fig. 10, p. 25), which shows twelve bricks in four rows. Compare also Susa 20^{6}, where three rows of bricks are given. It is the symbol of Nabû, which follows the spear, the symbol of Marduk. The same arrangement seems to be followed on Susa No. 15 (fig. 2, p. 6). The spearhead of Marduk in the third row is there followed by a pyramid-shaped figure, which is no doubt a variant representation of the bricks of Nabû.

[2] See fig. 14^{13}, p. 34.

[3] See fig. 8^{16}, p. 20.

[4] See fig. 2^{9}, p. 6.

[5] See fig. 2^{10}, p. 6.

[6] This object is probably a variant form of the horseshoelike figure, which follows usually the symbols of Anu, Ellil and Ea (cf. Susa 3^{7}, Susa 20^{4}, I R. 70^{7}, V. R. 57^{9}). It is the symbol of Ninḫarsag. See below, p. 95.

[7] This round object is perhaps identical with the tortoise, see London, 106 (fig. 14, p. 34).

head (Susa I), and one with a stylus-like object[1] (V. A. 2663). The shrines occur therefore thus far in connection with eighteen symbols. It seems to have been left to the choice of the artist to reproduce the shrine or to omit it. Accordingly we find the spear of Marduk on a shrine (V R. 57),[2] or on a dragon (IV R.[1] 43),[3] or alone (Susa 16);[4] the ram's head of Ea is on a shrine (London 105),[5] or on a goatfish (IV R.[1] 43);[6] the lightning fork of Rammân is on a shrine (Susa III),[7] or on a crouching ox (IV R.[1] 43),[8] or it stands alone (I R. 70).[9] Indeed a close examination of the symbols reveals the fact that they can be represented in three ways, corresponding to the three classes of objects mentioned on the stone of Meli-Shipak (shrines, weapons and reliefs of the gods, VII, 23–34). Either the weapon is shown alone, or, secondly, the weapon and the shrine or the weapon and the animal figure are placed together, or, thirdly, weapon, shrine and animal figure are combined into one group. In other words, either one, two or three figures constitute the symbol.

A few examples will show the nature of this variation. (1) The spear of Marduk is found alone on Susa I, II, Susa IV.[10]

[1] The stylus is a substitute for the wedge, the symbol of Nabû. This appears from the following considerations: (1) The symbol of Nabû would otherwise be wanting on this stone (V. A. 2663), while it occurs on nearly every other stone. (2) Nabû is frequently represented as holding the stylus, cf., *e.g.*, *tâmeḫ qân tuppi âḫizu šukâmi* (I R. 35, No. 2, 4) *ṣâbit qân tuppi elli nâši tupšîmât ilâni* (K. B., IV, 102, 3). (3) On the stone of Sargon (fig. 15, p. 35) the stylus standing erect follows the spearhead of Marduk. It here takes the place of the wedge, the usual symbol of Nabû. On Assyrian monuments the symbol of Nabû is a single (rock relief of Bavian) or double (Esarhaddon stele of Sendschirli) column. On the boundary stone of Nabû-apal-iddina (fig. 9, p. 23) the two columns are joined so that they form an H-like figure.

[2] See fig. 49^{7}, p. 131.

[3] See fig. 6^{13}, p. 17.

[4] See fig. 10^{15}, p. 25.

[5] See fig. 12^{14}, p. 30.

[6] See fig. 6^{17}, p. 17.

[7] See fig. 11^{16}, p. 28.

[8] See fig. 6^{12}, p. 17.

[9] See fig. 13^{10}, p. 33.

[10] See fig. 24^{1}, p. 86; fig. 28^{11}, p. 91; fig. 23^{10}, p. 76.

It appears on a shrine, London, 90922;[1] on a dragon, London, 99.[2] Dragon, shrine and spear on top are found on London, 100, 105, 106, I R. 70[3] and on most of the other stones. (2) The wedge appears standing alone on the new stone of Nebuchadrezzar I. (Neb. Nippur),[4] on the dragon (London, 99),[5] on the shrine without the dragon (V. A. 208),[6] on the shrine with the dragon alongside (London, 100, 105, 106, I R. 70).[7] (3) The ram's head is on a shrine (London, 90922),[8] on a goatfish (London, 99).[9] Ram's head, shrine and goatfish are seen together on London, 105, V. A. 2663, Susa I, etc.[10] (4) The arrow, pointing downwards, occurs alone I R. 70.[11] It is held by a scorpion man with a bow (London, 100),[12] or by a centaur with a bow (London, 101).[13] (5) The fork of Rammân occurs alone (London, 106, 101, I R. 70),[14] or on the crouching ox (London, 99, 100, Susa II),[15] or on a shrine (V. A. 208),[16] or on a shrine with crouching ox alongside (Susa III).[17] These variations might be multiplied, but enough have been given to show that a considerable number of symbols appear in three possible forms.

From the shrines we pass to a discussion of the weapons. A number of these weapons can readily be recognized on the boundary stones, others are more difficult to identify, because the Babylonians did not limit the term "weapons" to what we commonly include in that term. Of the more obvious weapons on the boundary stones may be mentioned the spearhead (fig. 24^1), the lightning

[1] See fig. 9^1, p. 23.
[2] See fig. 6^{13}, p. 17.
[3] See fig. 49^7, p. 131; fig. 12^{12}, p. 30; fig. 14^1, p. 34; fig. 13^8, p. 33.
[4] See fig. 47^2, p. 120.
[5] See fig. 6^{14}, p. 17.
[6] See Hommel, *Aufsätze*, p. 256.
[7] See fig. 49^8, p. 131; fig. 12^{18}, p. 30; fig. 14^3, p. 34; fig. 13^9, p. 33.
[8] See fig. 9^2, p. 23.
[9] See fig. 6^{17}, p. 17.
[10] See fig. 12^{14}, p. 29; fig. 8^6, p. 20; fig. 24^6, p. 86.
[11] See fig. 13^{10}, p. 13.
[12] See fig. 49^{15}, p. 131.
[13] See fig. 32, p. 98.
[14] See fig. 14^{10}, p. 34; fig. 13^{11}, p. 33.
[15] See fig. 6^{12}, p. 17; fig. 49^{16}, p. 131; fig. 28^{16}, p. 91.
[16] See Hommel, *Aufsätze*, p. 250.
[17] See fig. 11^{16}, p. 28.

fork (fig. 28^{16}), the mace with the double head (fig. 24^{11}), the mace with the square top (fig. 24^{10}), the mace with the vulture head (fig. 24^{14}), the mace with the lion head (fig. 24^{12}), the lion standing erect, holding two daggers (fig. 21), the mace with the globular end (fig. 12^{13}, fig. 14^{18}) and the arrow (fig. 12^{10}, fig. 14^{8}, fig. 13^{11}). The three scepters or shafts with round balls on top, pictured on the new boundary stone from Nippur (fig. 47, Nos. 3, 6, 9), belong perhaps to the same category.

When we turn to the historical and religious texts[1] we find that the Babylonians included among the weapons of the gods a number of mythological forms and natural phenomena.

Anu has a weapon called *e-ri*, which was held by the sorcerer in incantations (*e-ri* ^{iṣu}*kakku ṣîri ša* ^{d}*A-num ina qâtâ-ia našâku*, C. T., XVI, pl. 3, 87; cf. also pl. 6, 211; pl. 21, 202). A bow of Anu is spoken of in the Creation Story (*îmurû-ma* ^{iṣu}*qaštu kî nukkalat* [*epšetsa*], K. 3449, a Rev. 2, cf. K. B., VI, 1, 32).

Anunît, as the goddess of battle, carries a bow and a quiver (^{d}*Anunîtum bêlit taḫâzi našâta* ^{iṣu}*qašti u išpati*, V R. 64, III, 22, cf. K. B., III, 2, 104).

Ea has a net (*gišparru ša* ^{d}*Ea*, C. T., XVII, 34, 26).

Ishtar is supplied with a "powerful bow, a mighty spear, which cuts down the disobedient" (^{iṣu}*qaštu dannatu* ^{iṣu}*tartaḫu gišru mušamqit lâ mâgiri*, Esarhaddon stele of Sendschirli, Rev. 29, 30, see *Ausgrabungen in Sendschirli*, p. 38). Aššurbânaplu describes an appearance of Ishtar in a dream, "on the right and left she had quivers hanging, she held a bow in her hand and drew a sharp sword" (*imna u šumêla tullâta išpâti tamḫat* ^{iṣu}*qaštu ina idiša šalpat namṣaru zaqtu*, Cyl. B., Col. V, 53–55, cf. K. B., II, 250). The same king killed four lions with "the

[1] Cf. for this section especially Frank, *Bilder und Symbole*, pp. 7–32.

terrible bow of Ishtar, the mistress of battle" (*tilpânu izzitu ša ᵈIštar bêlit taḫâzi*, I R. 7, No. 9, *a*, 2).

Lugal Maradda is mentioned by Nebuchadrezzar II., who refers to his "terrible weapons which spare not the foe, truly advance and are sharp" (*kakkêka ezzûtim ša lâ igammilû nakiri lû tibû lû zaqtû*, Langdon, *Building Inscriptions*, Nebuch. 2, Col. III, 42–43; cf. 3, Col. II, 27f.).

Marduk's weapons are described in the Creation Story. Before he went into the fight with Tiâmat "the gods gave him a weapon without equal, which overwhelms enemies" (*iddinûšu kakku lâ maḫra dâ'ipu zaiari*, IV, 30). To prepare himself for the conflict Marduk "formed a bow and appointed it for his weapon; he laid the arrow on it; he took up the *miṭṭu*-weapon and caused his right hand to seize it, he hung a bow and a quiver at his side; he placed lightning before him and filled his body with burning fire; he prepared a net to enclose Tiâmat" (*ibšimma* ^{iṣu}*qašta kakkašu uaddî mulmullum uštarkiba iššîma* ^{iṣu}*miṭṭa imnašu ušâḫiz* ^{iṣu}*qaštu u* ^{mashku}*išpatum iduššu îlul iškun birqu ina pânišu nablu muštahmiṭu zumuršu umtallâ êpušma sapara šulmû kirbiš Tiâmat*, IV, 35–41). The same weapons of Marduk occur in several other passages (cf. Frank, *Bilder und Symbole*, p. 23).[1]

Nabû has a weapon of which it is said: "Thy weapon is a dragon from whose mouth runs no poison," *kak-ka-ka ú-šum-gal-lu ša iš-tu pî-šu im-tu la i-na-at-tu-ku*, IV R.[2] 20, No. 3, 15,

Nanâ had a bare sword and a pointed *ulmû* as the adornment of her divinity ([*na*]*mṣaru pitû* [*u*]*lmû zaqtu simat ilûtiša*, Craig, *Rel. Texts*, I, 55, Col. I, 2).

Nergal is called "the lord of weapons and bows" (*bêl bêlê u qašâti*, III R. 43, IV, 21, cf. above, p. 55). Tiglathpileser declares

[1] See also Hehn, *Hymnen an Marduk*, B.A., V, 309, 19; 327, Obv. 16; 329, Obv. 10, 15; 330, 20; 339, Obv. 1; 349, 23.

that he received from Ninib and Nergal "their terrible weapons and their sublime bows" (*[iṣu]kakkêšunu ezzûti ù [iṣu]qašâtsunu ṣîrtu,* I R. 14, 58, 59, cf. K. B., I, 38). Again he is represented as holding "the merciless *abûbu* weapon" (*tâmeḫ, abûbi lâ pâdê,* Böllenrücher, *Gebete an Nergal,* No. 8, 8, p. 50). Of Nudimmud (Ea) it is said, "he presented to thee a weapon without equal" (*[iṣu]kakku lâ mâḫiru iqîšku [d]Nudimmud,* Böllenrücher, No. 8, 12. He is "the hero whose whip[cracks" (?)] and people cry out, "The noise of his weapon" (*qarradu ša qinazzu* . . . . *iqabbû rigim kakkišu,* Böllenrücher, No. 5, 46). He is the one "who lifts up the weapon, who urges on to battle" (*naš [iṣu]kakki dikû anantum,* Böllenrücher, No. 4, 13, p. 21).

NIN.IB's weapons are the most numerous and best known at present. Upon what is perhaps the third tablet of the *Ana-gim gim-ma* series (Hrozný, *Mythen von dem Gotte Ninrag,* p. 13f.) twenty-two weapons (perhaps originally twenty-four) are enumerated. Some are given in Assyrian, others only in Sumerian. Not all of the latter can be explained. The weapons given in Assyrian are: "The heavy weapon of Anu" (*[iṣu]kakku kabtu ša [d]Anum,* Obv. 30); "the wide net of the hostile land" (*alluḫappu mâti nukurtim,* Obv. 34); "the sword, the dagger of my divinity" (*namṣaru paṭru anûtîa,* Rev. 1); "the net of the battle" (*šuškal taḫâzi,* Rev. 4); "the long bow" (*ariktu,* Rev. 6); "the girdle clasping men and the bow of the storm (battle)" (*šibba ša ana ameli iṭeḫḫu qaštu abûbi,* Rev. 8); "the bow and the shield" (*tilpânu u kakâbu,* Rev. 10).[1] The weapons whose names are only

[1] These weapons have a series of ornamental names: "The destroyer of lords," *muabbit šadî,* Obv. 30; "The overthrower of lords," *mušakniš šadî,* Obv. 32; "The victor in battle," *litti taḫâzi,* Obv. 34; "The one cutting off necks," *muṣṣir kišadâti,* Rev. 2; "The lord from whose power there is no escape," *ša šadû ina qâtišu la ipparšiddu,* Rev. 4; "The helper of heroes," *rêṣat edli,* Rev. 6; "The overwhelmer of the houses of the hostile land," *ḫatû bît mât nukurtim,* Rev. 10.

given in Sumerian are: ^{d}*Šar-ur* in his right and ^{d}*Šar-gaz* in his left hand (Obv. 19–22); ^{d}*Ud-ka-ninnû*, "the storm with fifty edges" (Obv. 23); ^{d}*Ud-ba-nu-illa*, "the merciless storm" (Obv. 25, cf. also II R. 26, 38*c–d*, and II R. 57, 61*a* = *ûmu lâ pâdû*); *mir-silig-ga* (Obv. 27); the *nu-na* weapon (Obv. 31); *Ku-šag-ninnû*, "the weapon with fifty heads" (Rev. 11); *Giš-ga-šag-imin-na*, "the weapon with seven heads" (Rev. 13); *Ku-šag-ia*, "the weapon with five heads" (Rev. 16); ^{d}*Kur-ra-šu-ur-ur*, "which makes the lords tremble" (Rev. 19); ^{d}*Erim-a-bi-nu-tuk*, "whose enemy has no strength" (Rev. 21); *ŠI+UM-tila*, "support of life" (Rev. 28) and once more *Ku-šag-ninnû* (Rev. 29, cf. Rev. 12).

NIN.IB is also called "the spear, the great hero, the son of Ellil, with his arrow he cuts off life" (^{d}*NIN.IB tartaḫu qarradu rabû apil* ^{d}*En-lil ina uṣṣišu zaqti uparri' napištim*, V R. 9, 84–85). In Shurpu IV, 75, he has the title "the lord of the weapon" (*bêl* ^{iṣu}*kakki*).

Nisaba, like Ea, has a net (*saparu ša* ^{d}*Nisaba*, C. T., XVII, 34, 30).

Rammân's weapon is the lightning, hence one form of Rammân (^{d}*UMUN-IM*) is called ^{d}*Rammân ša birqi*, III R. 67, 47*c–d*, and the curse of Rammân is "that he may strike his (the evil-doer's) land with awful lightning" (^{d}*Rammân ina birqi limutti mâtsu libriq*, Tigl., VIII, 83, 84). Rammân is also pictorially represented with the lightning fork on the boundary stones (most clearly on Susa, No. 5, *b*, see fig. 18, p. 41). Another weapon of Rammân, as has been suggested by Zimmern (cf. K. A. T.^{3}, 448^{6}), may be the axe, which is once referred to on a fragmentary boundary stone (O. B. I., No. 80, 1).

Shamash has a snare by which he overthrows all lands (*sâḫip šuškallaka puḫur mâtâti*, IV R. 17, Rev. 13). The net (*šêtu*) of Shamash occurs in the *Etana* myth (I, a, 11, cf. K. B., VI, 1,

104) and a synonym, *gišparru,* is also mentioned (*gišparru mamît* *ᵈŠamaš, Etana* Myth, 1, a, 12).

Sibitti, they are described by Esarhaddon as holding bow and arrow (*ᵈSibitti ilâni qardûti tâmeḫu tilpânu u uṣṣi,* K. 2801, 12, Esarhaddon's *Bauinschriften,* cf. B. A., III, 228). Cf. also Hehn, *Siebenzahl und Sabbat bei den Babyloniern,* pp. 19ff.

Sin, his symbol is the crescent, *usqaru=asqaru,* also called the basket (*bugîna*) and the ship (*maqurru,* Susa 2, IV, 10, 11). Although it is probable that the crescent was regarded as Sin's weapon, it is not definitely called by that name in the inscriptions published thus far.

Ùr-ra, "the powerful weapon of the terrible Ùr-ra," is mentioned by Nabopolassar (*ⁱṣᵘkakku dannu ša ᵈÙr-ra rašubbu,* O. B. I., No. 84, Col. I, 24, 25).

A fragmentary list of divine weapons together with their names is given III R. 69, 3, 75–83. As it has not been used in this connection before, as far as I know, it is reproduced entire:

[*ⁱṣᵘkakku ᵈEn-lil mar-šar-ú*
ⁱṣᵘkakku ᵈMarduk qa-qu-ul-tu
ⁱṣᵘkakku ᵈNabû(UR) iṭ-ṭi-it-[*tum*]
ⁱṣᵘkakku ᵈNIN.IB ḫi-ḫi-nu
ⁱṣᵘkakku ᵈZa-mà-mà ṣi-il-lu
ⁱṣᵘkakku] *ᵈNergal(UGUR) pal-s*[*u?-u?*]
. . . . *pu-qut-*[*tum?*]
. . . . *ma-aš-*[*šú*(?)*-u*(?)]

As to the names only a few suggestions can be ventured at the present time because none of them, with perhaps a single exception, appear elsewhere. It seems that several of the names indicate different species of thorns. *Iṭ-ṭi-it-ti* occurs in the Gilgamesh Epic (XI, 284) as the "bramble," by means of which Gilgamesh is enabled to return home.[1] *Puquttu* is also a thorn, which occurs on the boundary stones in the curses of Rammân (cf. p. 64f.). With *ḫiḫinu* we may perhaps compare *ḫa-ḫi-in* which is mentioned as a synonym of *puquttu* (II R. 41, 58*a*, *b*). *Maššû* (if the restoration is correct) is perhaps the *maš-šú-u* mentioned II R. 47, 14, *b*, as a synonym of *kak-ku*. For *qa-qu-ul-tu*, the weapon of Marduk, we can offer no explanation, unless it has something to do with *qaq-qul-ti la pa-te-e*, "a closed vessel," mentioned in an incantation text, cf. C. T., XVII, 35, 79. It is tempting to restore the weapon of Nergal to *pal-s*[*u-u*], because of the occurrence of this name in an omen text, to which we shall presently refer.

The Babylonians did not only picture the divine weapons on the boundary stones, but they fancied that they could also detect them in the markings found on sheep livers. Hence they appear frequently in omen texts. In one of these (C. T., XX, 42) which has recently been discussed by Prof. Jastrow (A. J. S. L., XXXIII, (January, 1907), pp. 111–115) we find a similar series of divine weapons. The destructive weapon (*iṣukakku iššitu*) of Ellil is called *kak-su-ú*, the weapon of Shamash *ud-di-su-ú* and the weapon of Ea *gab-laḫ-ḫu*.[2] In the case of three other weapons, the names

[1] Cf. also the god *Id-di-tum* (or *Iṭ-ṭi-tum*) in the Cassite texts published by Prof. Clay, B. E., XV, p. 54. For the deification of the divine weapons see the weapons of NIN.IB, cf. p. 82.

[2] The view of Prof. Jastrow that the names of these weapons are written ideographically does not seem to me to be fully established. The other names found in Col. VI of the tablet under discussion (K 2235) are all written phonetically. Moreover the name of the weapon of Ea, written *gab-laḫ-ḫu*, is not necessarily connected with the ideogram *GAB.LAḪ*, for which the reading *saḫ-maš-tum* seems probable, or, if they are the same, it might be argued that *gablaḫḫu* is only a synonym of *saḫmaštum*, but not identical with it. Finally the fact that four of the names end in *su-ú* does not necessarily prove them to be ideograms, especially since the ideogram *SU-Ú* is unknown and no possible meaning can be attached to it. For these reasons I prefer to regard the names as written phonetically.

of the respective deities to whom they belonged have been effaced. They are: *pal-su-ú, di-di-su-ú* and *[iṣu]kakku* III-*tuš*, perhaps to be read with Prof. Jastrow *šalaltuš*.

Besides the weapons mentioned on this tablet there are numerous other references to divine weapons in omen texts. As Prof. Jastrow has shown, there is a weapon of Ishtar called *di-e-pu*, "the overthrower" (V R. 63, II, 30), a weapon of Shamash called *ma-ak-ša-ru*, perhaps "the helper," from *kašâru* to support. A second weapon of Shamash is called *at-mu-u ki-e-nu*, "the faithful word" (Rm.[2] 106), and a double weapon is named *ûmu šaqû*, "the mighty storm" (Stele of Nabonidus, XI, 11f.). As one of the weapons of NIN.IB is called *Ud-ba-nu-illa* = *ûmu lâ pâdû* (cf. above p. 82), "the merciless storm," and as the double-headed club is the symbol of NIN.IB, it is probable that the *ûmu šaqû* here mentioned is also a weapon of NIN.IB. We also find a "sevenfold *zibu*," the weapon of Shamash (C. T., XX, 48, 33–36), a "fifteen-fold *zibu*," the weapon of Ishtar (C. T., XX, 48, 39), a "threefold *zibu*," the weapon of Sin (C. T., XX, 48, 42). Three other names appear on the tablet referred to above (C. T., XX, 42, 33), namely, *šú-šú-ru*, *šul-mu* and *[iṣu]kakku KU.ŠI*. To these may be added a name occurring in the omens of Sargon and Narâm-Sin, namely *su-ḫu-ru-ni* (IV R.[2] 34, Rev. 4). Altogether the omen texts have thus far furnished us with seventeen names of divine weapons.

Finally divine weapons appear also in the heavens. The Babylonians spoke of certain constellations as the weapons of the gods. Thus both the *mulmullu* star and the *gamlu* star were called "the weapon of the hand of Marduk" (*[iṣu]kakku ša qât [d]Marduk*, V R. 46, Obv. 3, 26, *a*), and the star *GIŠ.GAN.URU* was called the weapon of the God A-e(mal), (V R. 46, 25, *a*). One of the weapons of NIN.IB was the *tartaḫu* (V R. 9, 84), but there was also a *tartaḫu* star, which was identified with Ninib (II R. 57, 52, *a, b*).[1] Ishtar held a bow in her hand (see above, p. 79), but there was also a bow star (=Sirius), identified with Ishtar, cf. V R. 46, 23, *a, b*, and Jensen, *Kosmologie*, pp. 53, 149. *Šar-ur* and *šar-gaz* are two weapons of NIN.IB (see above, p. 82), but they are also two

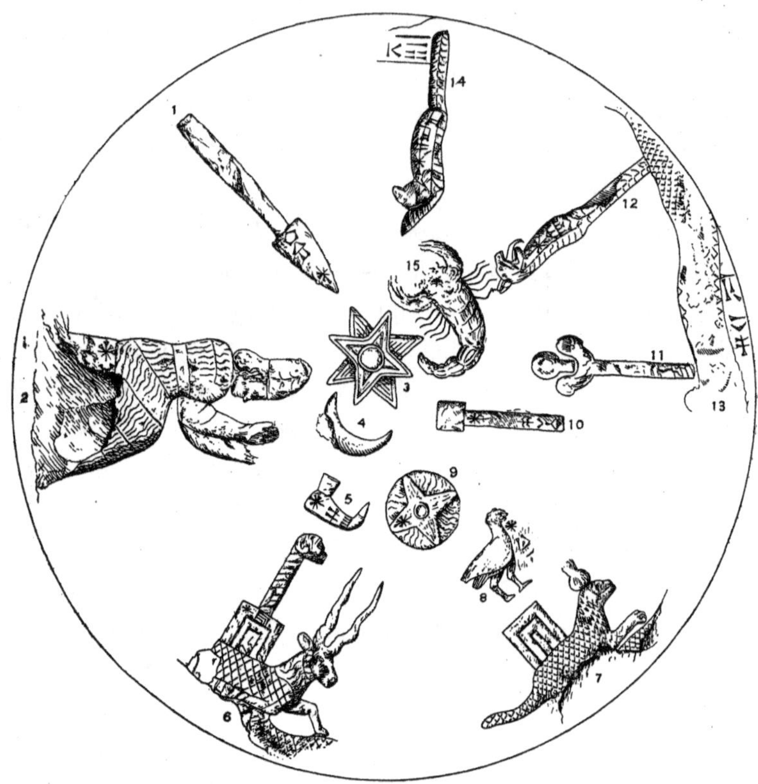

FIG. 24.—Symbols on a boundary stone found at Susa, with the names of the gods written on the symbols. (Susa, No. 1.)

stars, cf. V R. 46, 32, *a*, and Jensen, *Kosmologie*, p. 145f.

A review of these divine weapons has shown that the Babylonians did not only represent them pictorially upon their boundary stones, but they also believed that they could detect their

[1] For the *tartaḫu* star (=Saturn) see Jensen, *Kosmologie*, p. 150.

shape in the markings of sheep livers and in the forms of certain constellations.

There can no longer be any question that not only the weapons but all the varying figures on the stones are symbolic representations of certain gods. This is not only stated in the inscriptions, as quoted above, but one of the new stones from Susa (D. E. P., I, fig. 379) has actually the names of the gods written on the symbols. We now know that the spear represents Marduk, the mace with a vulture head Za-mà-mà, the mace with a lion head Nergal,[1] the mace with the square top Shuqamuna, the walking bird most likely Bau, the shrine with the goat-fish and ram's head Ea, the lamp Nusku, the seated goddess Gula, the crescent Sin, the sun disk Shamash, the eight-pointed star Ishtar and the serpent Ṣîru. The inscriptions on the scorpion, on the mace with twin-headed dragons, on the crocodile-like monster with a shrine on its back and a vase on its head, have become illegible (cf. fig. 24).

There are other symbols which can be identified with certain gods. On the stone of Nebuchadrezzar I. (V R. 57)[2] we find three shrines with tiaras in the first row. These correspond to the two shrines followed by the symbol of Ea (a shrine and a goatfish), on Susa III, Susa XV, I R. 70, Susa XX.[3] This makes it probable that the first two symbols stand for Anu and Ellil. The proof for

[1] The sign is , as determined by an examination of a photograph of the original, which I secured through the kind assistance of Dr. Heuzey, the Director of the Louvre. I submitted the photograph also to Prof. Hilprecht, who independently reached the same conclusion. The sign is a variant of *GIR* (cf. Br. 9190), as can be seen by a comparison with the older forms, cf. Amiaud et Méchineau, *Tableau comparé*, No. 203. This conclusion is important because it shows that the twin lion heads, as on the rock relief of Bavian, can only be NIN.IB. It also proves that the lion standing erect with daggers in his fore claws, as shown on Susa No. 9 (fig. 21, p. 73), is a symbol of Nergal.

[2] See fig. 49, p. 131.

[3] See fig. 11^{4-6}, p. 28; fig. 2^{4-6}; fig. 13^{4-6}, p. 33; fig. 30^{1-3}, p. 95.

this identification is found on the rock relief of Sennacherib at Bavian. In this case the symbols agree with the gods mentioned

Fig. 25.—Rock relief of Sennacherib at Bavian.

on the stone. As the list is important for our later discussion we reproduce it:

1.	Shrines with horned caps	Aššur,
2.		Anu,
3.		Ellil.
4.	Shrine with ram's head	Ea.
5.	Crescent	Sin.
6.	Winged disk	Shamash.
7.	Forked lightning	Rammân.
8.	Column with spear head	Marduk.
9.	Square column	Nabû.
10.	Column with two lion heads	[NIN.IB].
11.	Venus star	Ištar.
12.	Seven stars	Sibitti.[1]

[1] The god Sibitti is written in this as well as in other inscriptions ^{d}VII-Bi, which should not be read ^{d}*Sibi*(*-bi*). The Semitic reading is determined by IV R.^{2} 21 (B) Rev. 21–22 (= Zimmern, *Ritualtafeln*, No. 54, p. 168), where to ^{d}VII-Bi in the Sumerian line corresponds *ilâni Si-bit* in the Semitic line. Cf. also Winckler, *Altorientalische Forschungen*, II, 10, ^{d}*Si-bit-ti*; Zimmern, K. A. T.^{3}, p. 620, and Hehn, *Siebenzahl*, p. 24, note. For the inscription on the Bavian relief see III R. 14.

In this inscription, as Hommel has already shown (*Aufsätze*, p. 442), Anu and Ellil are clearly represented by the shrines with tiaras. To the identifications made on Susa I are here added: Rammân with the lightning fork, Nabû with the square column,

FIG. 26.—Stele of Esarhaddon found at Sendschirli, giving the symbolic representations of the gods current in Assyria.[1]

Ishtar with the four-cornered star, which on Babylonian monuments appears usually as eight-cornered. The identification of NIN.IB with the twin lion heads has now become certain, because Susa I has shown that the single lion head stands for Nergal, hence there is no other god but NIN.IB left for the twin lion heads.

[1] The gods represented are as follows: (1) The seven stars, the Sibitti; (2) Aššur (Anu) standing on two animals; (3) Bêlit seated on a lion; (4) Ellil standing on a dragon, similar to that of Anu; (5) Rammân holding the lightning fork and standing on an ox; (6) The crescent of Sin; (7) The winged disk of Shamash; (8) The sixteen-pointed star of Ištar; (9) The spearhead of Marduk; (10) The double staff of Nabû; (11) The ram's head of Ea; (12) The twin-headed mace of NIN.IB.

Fig. 27.—Boundary stone of King Nazi-Maruttash found at Susa, No. 2, face C.

FIG. 28.—Boundary stone of King Nazi-Maruttash found at Susa, No. 2, face D.

These are all the identifications that can be made with any degree of certainty. Recently, however, Prof. Zimmern has attempted to increase the number considerably by a study of the stone of Nazi-Maruttash. I should be glad to follow the ingenious explanation of this distinguished scholar, but it seems to me there are fatal objections to his identifications: (1) His whole theory is based on the supposition that the seventeen terrible figures (*šuripât*) of the gods are actually represented on the stone. But there is no justification for this supposition in the text. The strongest argument that can be found for the view of Prof. Zimmern is the fact that there are actually seventeen figures on the stone. But this is in itself not sufficient to warrant their identification, especially when we find that *on no other boundary stone do the figures and the gods quoted in the text agree.* This point is important enough to warrant the full presentation of the evidence on hand.

Stone		Symbols			Gods			
London, 103	has	17	symbols	and	15	gods	in the	text.[1]
London, 101	"	19	"	"	13	"	"	"
London, 99	"	18	"	"	7	"	"	"
London, 100	"	20	"	"	12	"	"	"
London, 106	"	19	"	"	12	"	"	"
I R. 70	"	19	"	"	12	"	"	"
London, 105	"	19	"	"	16	"	"	"
London, 102	"	19	"	"	14	"	"	"
London, 90922	"	8	"	"	0	"	"	"
Berl. V. A. 208	"	9	"	"	0	"	"	"
Berl. V. A. 209	"	6	"	"	4	"	"	"
Berl. V. A. 2663	"	16	"	"	5	"	"	"
O. B. I. 149	"	14	"	"	8	"	"	"

[1] The number of gods might possibly be increased to seventeen by counting twice Shamash and Rammân, whose names are repeated. There are only fifteen *different* gods enumerated in the curses.

Neb. Nippur	has	20 symbols	and	10 gods	in	the	text.
Susa III	"	24 "	"	9 "	"	"	
Susa XVI	"	18 "	"	47 "	"	"	

This list shows that the supposition that the gods and the symbols are identical is not favored by the other boundary stones. (2) But when we analyze Prof. Zimmern's identifications we meet still more objections. The first two symbols are two identical shrines with tiaras; hence we should expect, if symbols and text correspond, that the text should have the same or at least similar statements about these two symbols. But this is not the case. While the first is described as *šub-tum u šú-ku-zu šá Anum(-num) šarri šamê*, the second is said to be *gir-gi-lu al-la-ku ša* ^{d}*En-lil bêl mâtâti*. Hence Prof. Zimmern is forced to the assumption that the second symbol "*in der bildlichen Darstellung nur implicite vorhanden ist.*" This is equivalent to a confession that his theory does not agree with the evidence. (3) It may well be doubted that the third symbol, which is entirely erased, consisted of the shrine and the goatfish. There is room for the shrine with the ram's head, but for the goatfish is hardly any room, as a glance at the upper row will show. (4) He identifies the two lion heads with Shuqamûna, while Susa I shows that the mace with the square end represents Shuqamuna. To call the latter simply "*eine weitere Zuthat*" seems again due to the exigencies of a theory. (5) Shar-ur and Shar-gaz represent the personified weapons of NIN.IB, of which Shar-ur is held in his right hand and Shar-gaz in his left (Frank, *Bilder und Symbole*, p. 28); but how can the vulture head alone be said to fit that description? It demands rather that the two lion heads represent the weapons of NIN.IB. (6) The *ma-sab ru-ba-ti*, or "censer of the princess," is also absent, and Prof. Zimmern must again have recourse to the supposition that it is implied. (7) The identification of the *mar-ka-su rabû(-ú) ša bît si-kil-*

Fig. 29.—Symbols on a boundary stone found at Susa, from the Cassite period. (Susa, No. 13.)

la with the shrine carrying the horseshoe-like, or Ω-like, figure is also doubtful, and would hardly have been made if the theory had not demanded it. It will be observed that this last symbol occurs frequently in fourth place after the symbols of Anu, Ellil and Ea (*e.g.*, V R. 57, Susa XX, Susa XV, Susa III, I R. 70,

Fig. 30.—Symbols on an uninscribed boundary stone found at Susa, No. 20.

III R. 41).[1] And as in several of these cases (I R. 70, III R. 41, Susa III) NIN.ḪAR.SAG or NIN.MAḪ follows Anu, Ellil and Ea, it is likely that this symbol is a representation of *Ninḫarsag*. Although the identifications of Prof. Zimmern as a whole can hardly

[1] See fig. 49[9], p. 131; fig. 30[4], p. 95; fig. 2[7], p. 6; fig. 11[7], p. 28; fig. 13[7], p. 33; fig. 14[13], p. 34.

be accepted, there are several which are correct. His identification of Išḫara with the scorpion is very happy. Both have the same ideogram, GIR.TAB (Br. 315-316). The lion-headed dragon undoubtedly represents Nergal or Shit-lam-ta-ë (Frank, *Bilder und Symbole*, p. 30).

Recently Dr. Leon Heuzey has made it very probable (*Revue d'Assyriologie*, VI, 95–104) that the shrine with the brick and the wedge, which is frequently (Susa III, XX, V R. 57, IV R.[1] 43, III R. 41, I R. 70, etc.)[1] placed alongside of the lance of Marduk, is the symbol of Nabû, the god of writing and architecture.

To sum up, we have thus far been able to make twenty identifications of symbols with their respective deities;[2] that is, nearly half of the symbols have been identified. But these symbols are more than gods, for all the gods of Babylonia are astral. They represent certain stars with which the gods were identified. This should have been plain long ago, for sun, moon and the eight-pointed Venus star, which occur on all these monuments, clearly point to the heavens as the place where we should look for all the other symbols.

The most prominent of the symbols is the serpent, which is either coiled up on top of the monument or extends along the

[1] See fig. 11[14], p. 28; fig. 30[6], p. 95; fig. 49[8], p. 131; fig. 6[14], p. 17; fig. 14[3], p. 34.

[2] These identifications are: (1) The spearhead stands for Marduk; (2) the mace with vulture head for Zamama; (3) the mace with lion head for Nergal; (4) the mace with the square top for Shuqamuna; (5) the lamp for Nusku; (6) the shrine with goatfish and ram's head for Ea; (7) the seated goddess with dog (or dog alone) for Gula; (8) the crescent for Sin; (9) the sundisk for Shamash; (10) the eight-pointed star (five-pointed on Neb. Nippur, No. 13, six-pointed on Susa, No. 4, seven-pointed on the stone of Nabû-shum-ishkun) for Ishtar; (11) the serpent for Ṣîr; (12) the walking bird for Bau; (13–14) the two shrines with tiaras for Anu and Ellil; (15) the shrine with the wedge, brick(s) or stylus for Nabû; (16) the mace with the twin lion heads for NIN.IB; (17) the scorpion for Ishḫara; (18) the forked lightning and the ox for Rammân; (19) the shrine with the yoke or horseshoelike figure for Ninḫarsag; (20) the seven stars for the Sibitti.

lower edge of the symbols or winds through the centre and hangs downwards with its tail. The meaning of this serpent has been determined by three separate facts: (1) In a list of rivers (II R. 51, 45–47) the river of the serpent (*nâr Ṣir*) is explained as "the river of the great band of heaven" (*nâr* DUR.AN.GAL) and as "the river of the great ocean" (*nâr* ZU.AB.GAL). (2) Another text (Rm. 282) represents Ellil as drawing the picture of the great serpent, called Labbu, upon the firmament (see Hroznў, *Mythen

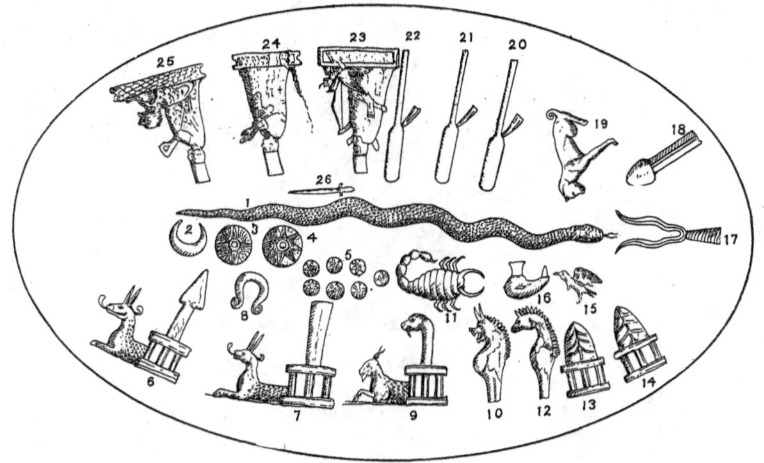

Fig. 31.—Symbols on the stone of King Nabû-shum-ishkun, now at Berlin.

von dem Gotte Ninrag, p. 108, obv. 7–10). (3) Franz Delitzsch has added the observation that Jewish tradition identified the serpent defeated by God (Job 23:16) with the milky way (so Rabbi Levi Ben Gersom; see Delitzsch, "Commentary on Job," 2d ed., p. 339[1]). Prof. Hommel was the first to infer from the first and the third of these facts that the serpent was identical with Tiâmat and her eleven helpers, and recognized them in the milky way and the signs of the zodiac (Hommel, *Aufsätze*, pp. 360, 370). On the basis of this identification Prof. Hommel has argued that all the other symbols are signs of the zodiac. This theory has recently been subjected to an able criticism by Boll in his valuable work, *Sphaera*, Leipzig, 1903. He raises two strong objections to Hommel's theory:

(1) The symbols do not occur in a fixed order, such as we naturally expect to be followed if they represented the signs of the zodiac. In all other known zodiacs the order is fixed, while the arrangement of the symbols on the boundary stones varies constantly. (2) There are more symbols than twelve represented

FIG. 32.—The archer from a Babylonian boundary stone. (London, 101.)

on fifteen stones, while at least five have less than twelve symbols. In view of this evidence we must come to the conclusion that the zodiac as such is not represented on the boundary stones.

A different answer, however, must be given to the inquiry whether separate signs of the zodiac are to be found on the stones. This is certainly the case. The most striking symbol on the boundary stone of Nebuchadrezzar I. (V R. 57)[1] is the scorpion man or archer. It also occurs on the stone of Meli-Shipak (London, 103).[2] The human part ends with the belt, below which is the body

[1] See fig. 49[15], p. 131. [2] See Hommel, *Aufsätze*, p. 245.

and the tail of a scorpion, with the feet of a lion. To this symbol corresponds a centaur drawing a bow on two other stones. In one case (London, 101)[1] he has a double head, one human, the other that of a dragon. He is also provided with wings and a double tail, the lower of a horse, the upper of a scorpion, and under his fore feet is a scorpion. In the second case (D. E. P., I, p. 175, fig. 381)[2] the wings are left off and there is but one tail. All these remark-

FIG. 33.—The archer from the Egyptian zodiac of Dendera.

able features appear on Egyptian and the Greek zodiacs. On the square zodiac of Dendera, *e.g.*, which dates from the time of the Emperor Nero, we see the same double-headed centaur drawing a bow, winged and having two tails, the lower of a horse and the upper of a scorpion. Here, too, the scorpion follows as the next sign of the zodiac. Moreover, there is the same transition from a centaur to a human form. The *sagittarius,* which Boll gives from a Latin MS. (p. 131), is a two-legged satyr with a horse-tail. These

[1] See fig. 32, p. 98.

[2] See fig. 23[12], p. 76.

Fig. 34.—Rectangular zodiac of Dendera from the time of Emperor Nero.

remarkable agreements cannot be accidental. They rather prove conclusively that the Egyptian zodiac was influenced by the Babylonian, and that by this symbol on the Babylonian boundary stones a sign of the zodiac, the *sagittarius* or archer, is meant. If one symbol of the zodiac is unquestionably represented on the

Fig. 35.—Round zodiac of Dendera from the time of Emperor Augustus.

boundary stones, it is reasonable to suppose that there are more.

In this connection the round zodiac of Dendera deserves special attention. Here we find along the inside circle, besides the planets, the thirty-six decani and some other stars, the signs of the zodiac in the usual order: *aries, taurus, gemini, cancer, leo, virgo, libra, scorpio, sagittarius, capricornus, aquarius* and *pisces.* The planets are arranged as follows: Mercury between lion and virgin, Saturn between virgin and balance, Mars above the capricorn,

Fig. 36.—The goatfish (Capricorn) from a boundary stone of Meli-Shipak (Susa, No. 3).

Fig. 37.—The goatfish (Capricorn) from the round zodiac of Dendera.

Venus between waterman and fishes, Jupiter between twins and cancer. Several of these signs are found in similar forms on the Babylonian monuments. The goatfish, combining the head and body of a goat with the tail of a fish, is found repeatedly on the boundary stones as the symbol of Ea (I R. 70, London, 99, Susa I, Susa XV, Susa XX, etc.).[1] The close similarity in form absolutely demands a common origin. Another symbol which shows close similarity is the lion walking on a serpent. It may correspond to the winged lion walking on a serpent on Br.M. 99.[2] Again, the waterman pouring water out of two vases reminds us very much

Fig. 38.

The god Ea on Susa, No. 6.

The waterman from the round zodiac of Dendera.

of the similar figure on Susa VI, most likely Ea, standing on a goat. In front of his breast he holds a vase, out of which two streams are running. A similar figure of Ea with vases, out of which water is bubbling in two streams, is published by Heuzey in *Revue d'Assyriologie,* Vol. VI, p. 95. This identification, however, can hardly be said to be certain, because we found that the

[1] See fig. 13^6, p. 33; fig. 6^{17}, p. 17; fig. 24^6, p. 86; fig. 2^6, p. 6; fig. 30^3, p. 95.

[2] See fig. 6^{18}, p. 17.

goatfish, the symbol of Ea, corresponds to the Greek capricorn, while here we would have the God Ea identified with the waterman. It will be noticed, however, that the goatfish and waterman are two adjoining signs, and it might well be that the figure of Ea himself stood for the waterman, while his symbol, the goatfish, expressed the neighboring sign of the capricorn.[1]

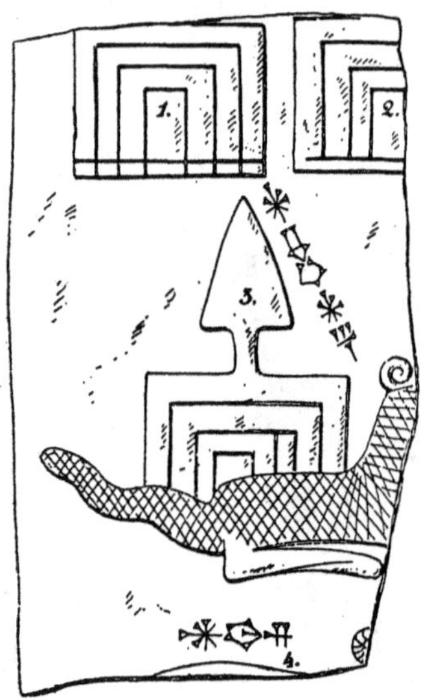

Fig. 39.—The symbol of the god Marduk. (Susa, No. 19.)

Other identifications that have been proposed are still less certain. Attention has been called to the fact that in a number of cases the spear of Marduk opens the series of symbols (V. A. 2663, Susa I[1], Susa 106[1]), and that on the Sargon stone the inscription AM, the "ox," is placed alongside of it (Hommel, *Aufsätze*, p. 257). Now when we recall the fact that at 1100 B.C., when the boundary

[1] The symbol of Gula seems to be a parallel case which probably stands for the virgin, while her dog represents the next zodiacal sign, the lion. The same combination of two symbols into one group may be seen in the centaur holding the bow, which represents the sagittarius, under whose fore feet is the scorpion, the next sign in the zodiac (see fig. 32, p. 98).

stones were engraved, the vernal equinox fell into the sign of the bull (*taurus*), it may be argued with some degree of probability that the spear represents the first zodiacal sign or *taurus*. It is often preceded or followed by the shrine with the wedge, and, as a glance at the northern hemisphere of heaven shows, the triangle is a part of the sign of the *ram*. Therefore the wedge represents perhaps the *aries*. Again, the spear of Marduk is at least twice associated with the twin lion heads (London, 105, Susa II), but the twins (*gemini*) adjoin the *taurus;* hence the twin lions may stand for the *gemini*. All these identifications are rendered uncertain by the fact that the spearhead stands for Marduk, the wedge most

Fig. 40.—The goddess Gula, the scorpion of Ishḫara, and the walking bird of Bau on Susa, No. 14.

likely for Nabû and the twin lion heads for NIN.IB. These are the gods of the three planets Jupiter, Mercury and Mars. Hence it would be more natural to identify them with these planets.

To sum up, the only certain identifications of the boundary stone symbols with signs of the zodiac are, the archer with the *sagittarius*, the scorpion with the *scorpio* and the goatfish with the *capricorn*. The rest cannot be regarded as fully established—the god pouring out water with the waterman, the walking or sitting lion (dog) with *leo*, the spearhead with *taurus*, the wedge with the *aries*, the twin dragon heads with the *gemini*. The goddess Gula may stand for the virgin. But that the mace with the globular end is a substitute for the *cancer*, the Ω like figure on the shrine for the *libra*, and the walking bird for the *fishes* does not appear to have been proved by the arguments of Hommel.[1]

But even if all the twelve signs of the zodiac were fully established it would by no means exhaust the list of the symbols, as there are more than forty different symbols. What are the rest?

We naturally expect to find besides the signs of the zodiac the five planets that were known to the ancients. Now, it is highly probable that they are represented. We have seen that the spear-head is attributed to Marduk, who was in later times identified with Jupiter; the wedge is most likely the symbol of Nabû, identified with Mercury; the twin lion heads are the symbol of NIN.IB, identified with Mars; the lion-headed dragon is the symbol of Nergal, identified with Saturn, while the eight-pointed star is certainly the symbol of Išhtar, identified with Venus, the morning and evening star.

As neither the signs of the zodiac nor the planets exhaust the list of symbols found on the boundary stones, we must look for other constellations which might possibly be represented. At this stage of our investigation an astrological text of a Greek writer named Teucros the Babylonian, which was published recently by Boll,[2] seems to show us the right way. In this text we find each sign of the zodiac associated with an animal name, which is called ἡ δωδεκάωρος. These animals, therefore, are symbols of a series of twelve hours. The hours must have been double hours, because it takes twenty-four hours for one revolution of all the twelve parts of the ecliptic, and each animal represents one-twelfth

[1] I do not mean to question the many and valuable contributions of Prof. Hommel on this subject. But in the points enumerated he does not seem to have established his contention. See also article of C. Bezold in *Archiv für Religionsgeschichte,* X (1907), p. 115f., and Frank, *Bilder und Symbole der Babylonisch-Assyrischen Götter,* p. 3.

[2] Cf. Ball, *Sphæra,* pp. 17–21, 41–52.

part or thirty degrees. Moreover, these twelve double hours could not originally have referred to the ecliptic, because each twelfth part of the ecliptic rises in unequal intervals of 1 hour 20 minutes, to 2 hours 24 minutes in the latitude of Babylon. To secure equal

Fig. 41.—Marble plate from Egypt showing the zodiac and the "Dodekaoros."

divisions the twelve parts must have been applied to the heavenly equator.[1]

Now it is well known that the system of double hours called *kaš(s)-bu* (KAŠ.GID) was used in Babylonia, as the tablet III R.

[1] Ball, *l.c.*, p. 315.

51, Nos. 1 and 2, and other passages plainly show. The Babylonians must, therefore, first have measured the dodekatemoria of the equator, and from this division determined that of the ecliptic; so also in Egypt the division of the thirty-six decani referred originally to the equator.[1]

This juxtaposition of the zodiacal circle with the *dodekaoros* circle has recently been found pictorially represented on a marble plate discovered in Egypt.[2] The centre is occupied by the two heads of Apollo and Phœbe, around which is a double circle. The outer circle represents the signs of the zodiac, the inner circle agrees completely with *dodekaoros* animals mentioned by Teucros. They are as follows:

1.	ram, with belt	αἴλουρος,	cat, sitting.
2.	bull	κύων,	dog (or jackal).
3.	twins (man and woman)	ὄφις,	serpent.
4.	crab	κάνθαρος,	crab (cancer).
5.	lion	ὄνος,	ass.
6.	virgin	λέων,	lion, walking.
7.	balance (borne by man)........	τράγος,	goat (or gazelle)
8.	scorpion	ταῦρος,	ox.
9.	archer (centaur)..............	ἱέραξ,	falcon.
10.	goatfish	κυνοκέφαλος,	ape.
11.	waterman	ἶβις,	ibis.
12.	fishes	κροκόδειλος,	crocodile.

It is strange to notice that while the idea of a twelve-hour circle goes back to Babylonia, several of these animals at least (cat, ibis, crocodile) are no doubt due to Egyptian influence. The best theory to account for this phenomenon is, as Boll has pointed out, to suppose that the *dodekaoros* was carried from Babylonia to Egypt, where several of the animals were renamed. That there

[1] Ball, *l.c.*, p. 316.

[2] Ball, *l.c.*, pl. VI; see fig. 41.

was such a renaming process seems to be supported by the East Asiatic cycle. This cycle of twelve animals represented: (1) A cycle of twelve successive years. (2) A cycle of twelve months. (3) The twelve hours of the calendar day. In all these relations the Chinese substituted the twelve *tschi* or characters in their places which (4) designated the twelve signs of the zodiac and

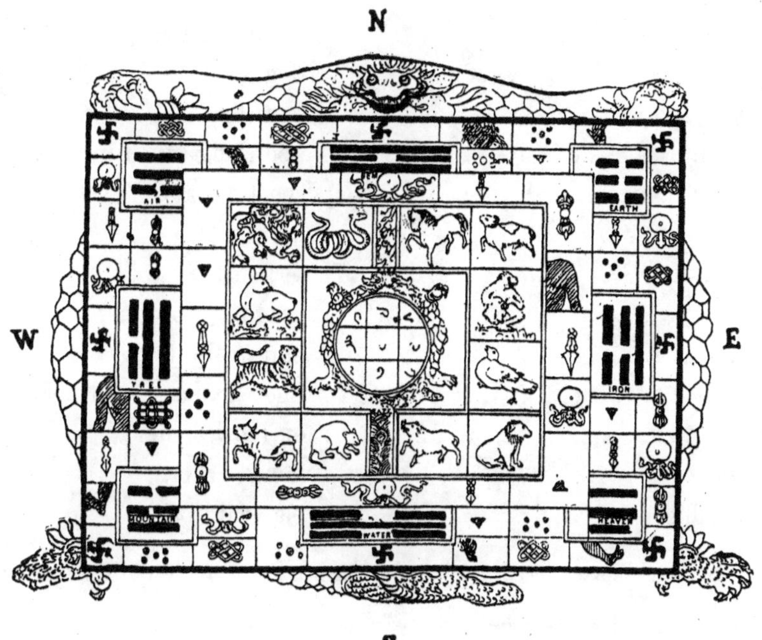

Fig. 42.—East Asiatic circle as represented in Tibet.

(5) twelve successive days.[1] The same uniform designation of hours, days, months and years, corresponding to the twelve parts of the zodiac, is not only a part of ancient astrology, but we know that the Babylonians divided the calendar day into twelve double hours, they had twelve months, over which presided the same gods

[1] Ball, *l.c.*, p. 333.

as those attributed to the signs of the zodiac (Diodor., II, 30),[1] while Censorinus testifies to the "Chaldaic" origin of a cycle of twelve years. From all this it is highly probable that the East Asiatic cycle, with all the ideas connected with it, goes back to Babylonia. A comparison of the two series of animals, those of the *dodekaoros* and of the East Asiatic cycle, will further corroborate this view. They are as follows:

Dodekaoros.	*East Asiatic Cycle.*
cat	dog.
dog	hen (bird).
serpent	ape (long-tailed monkey).
scarab (cancer)	sheep (goat).
ass	horse
lion	serpent.
he-goat	dragon (crocodile).
bull	hare (rabbit).
falcon	tiger (leopard, panther).
ape	ox (cow, heifer).
ibis	mouse (rat).
crocodile	pig (wild boar).

In both cases we have twelve animals, of which nine are the

[1] He says: *τῶν θεῶν δὲ κυρίους εἶναί φασι δώδεκα τὸν ἀριθμόν, ὧν ἑκάστῳ μῆνα καὶ τῶν δώδεκα λεγομένων ζῳδίων ἓν προσνέμουσι*, *i.e.*, "the chief of these gods (the thirty-six decani), they say, are twelve in number, to each of whom they attribute a month and one sign of the twelve in the zodiac." With this statement of Diodorus ought to be compared the list of months and their gods in IV R.[2], 33 (= K 2049 + K 129). It reads: (1) *Nisannu ša dA-num u dEn-lil* (2) *Airu ša dE-a bêl te-ni-še-e-ti* (3) *Sîmânu ša dSin mâru rêštî ša dEn-lil* (4) *Dûzu ša qu-ra-du dNIN.IB* (5) *Abu ša dNin-giš-zi-da bêl* . . . (6) *Ulûlu ša dIš-tar be-lit* . . . (7) *Tašrîtu ša dŠamaš qu-ra-du* (8) *Araḫsamnu ša abkal ilâni dMarduk* (9) *Kisilîmu ša qarradu rabû dNergal* (10) *Ṭêbitu ša dPap-sukal sukal dA-num u dIštar* (11) *Šabâṭu ša dRammân gù-gal šamê(-e) u irṣitim(-tim)* (12) *Addaru ša dSibitti ilâni rabûti* (13) [*arḫumaḫ-ru ša Addaru*] *ša Aš-šur a-bi ilâni.*

Fig. 43. – Zodiac of a Sivaite pagoda at Trichinopoly, India, showing the zodiac and the Karanas

Vadouca
Bhérava
Hasta
Outtara Phalgouni
Pourva Phalgouni
Canya
Toula
Sinha

same or at least similar in both lists. Only three of the *dodekaoros* have no parallels, the cat, the scarab and the falcon, and three on the East India circle are unique, the hare, the mouse and the pig.

An intermediate link between these two circles, found on an Indian zodiac, is preserved on a wall in a pagoda at Trichinopoly,[1] India. It shows six circles, of which the fourth contains the signs of the zodiac and the third, corresponding to them, eleven animal figures called Karana. Here we find the following animals corresponding to the zodiacal signs:

Zodiac.	*Karana.*	
ram—bull	lion (*Bhava*)[2]	D[3] (lion, cat).
bull—twins	tiger (*Bhalava*)	A
twins—crab	boar (*Côlava*)	A
crab—lion	ass (*Têttila*)	D (a horse).
lion—virgin	elephant (*Carasey*)	
virgin—balance	bull (*Banij*)	DA
balance—scorpion	hen (*Bhadra*)	A
scorpion—bow	hawk (*Saccouni*)	D (ibis, falcon).
bow—sea monster	dog (*Tchatouchpad*)	DA
sea monster—urn	serpent (*Naga*)	DA
urn—fish	rat (*Kintoughna*)	A
fish—ram		

Of these animals the lion, ass, bull, hawk, dog, serpent are found on the *dodekaoros* in the same or similar forms, while the tiger, wild boar, horse, bull, hen, dog, serpent and rat occur on the East Asiatic circle. Only the elephant is represented on neither, while bull, dog and serpent occur on all three circles.

[1] Cf. E. Morien in *Mémoires présentés par divers savants à l'Académie des Inscriptions et Belles Lettres*, I Serie, Tom. III (1853), pl. No. 4, facing p. 276.

[2] I reproduce the spelling as found on Morien's plate.

[3] D stands for Dodekaoros, A for Asiatic circle.

When we now ask the question, What is the possible bearing of these figures upon those of the Babylonian monuments? we must remember that while the arrangement and also the names of these animals differ, they all agree in the fact that they represent constellations parallel to the signs of the zodiac. This parallel circle, which in its full form numbers twelve animals and represents a division of the heavenly equator, points unmistakably to Babylonia as the place of its origin. If this is true, we are fully warranted in seeking a representation of this *dodekaoros* circle on Babylonian monuments.

FIG. 44.—A group of fragments: (1) From Nippur, O. B. I., Vol. I, Pt. 1, pl. XII. (2) From Susa, No. 10. (3) From Susa, No. 11.

It is evident that, as has already been pointed out, some of these animals are due to native influences—the cat, ibis and crocodile to Egypt, the tiger and elephant to India—but after making due allowance for such native influences, there remain certain of these animals, common to the different circles, which must go back to a common origin. It is at least interesting to note that we find on the boundary stones a lion (the sitting lion on London 105, 106)[1] and an ox (the crouching ox of Rammân with lightning fork), also two birds, corresponding to the falcon and ibis of the *dodekaoros* and to the hen and hawk on the Indian circle (the walking bird of Bau and the bird perched on a pole). We find also a horse (V R. 57)[2] and a dragon with wings (IV R.[1] 43, Susa III).[3] There is also a sheep with a shrine bearing a chisel (Susa III) and a crocodile-like creature (Susa I, XV).[4] In view of these resemblances it is altogether probable that some of the symbols on the boundary stones represent constellations belonging to the *dodekaoros*.[5]

The attempt of Richard Redlich[6] to explain all these symbols as constellations of the equator circle must be regarded as a failure, because the archer, the scorpion and the goatfish point decidedly to the ecliptic; nor is their position close enough to the equator circle that they could represent equatorial constellations. But he seems to be right in claiming that the equatorial circle was more original than the ecliptic, and that constellations of the equatorial circle are represented on the boundary stones, not, however, to the exclusion of the signs of the zodiac.

[1] See fig. 12[7], p. 30; fig. 13[6], p. 34. [2] See fig. 49[12], p. 131.

[3] See fig. 6[18], p. 17; fig. 11[12], p. 28. [4] See fig. 24[7], p. 86; fig. 2[10], p. 6.

[5] Cf. also the chart given by Hommel at the end of his *Aufsätze und Abhandlungen* III, 1.

[6] Redlich, *Der Drache zu Babel* in the *Globus*, Vol. 84 (1903), Nos. 23, 24. The identifications of Redlich are as follows: (1) Spearhead of Marduk—Pleiades, (2) Twin lion heads—Orion, (3) Sitting dog—Prokyon, (4) Serpent—Hydra, (5) Bird on perch—Raven, (6) Lightning fork—Spica of virgin, (7) Scorpion—Balance, (8) Tortoise—Ophiuchus, (9) Walking bird—Eagle, (10) Mace with round knob—Dolphin, (11) Lamp—Pegasus and Andromeda, (12) Horseshoelike form—Aries. Compare with these the remarks of Hommel, *Geographie*, p. 239.

We may summarize the results of our investigation as follows:

(1) The symbols on the Babylonian boundary stones represent

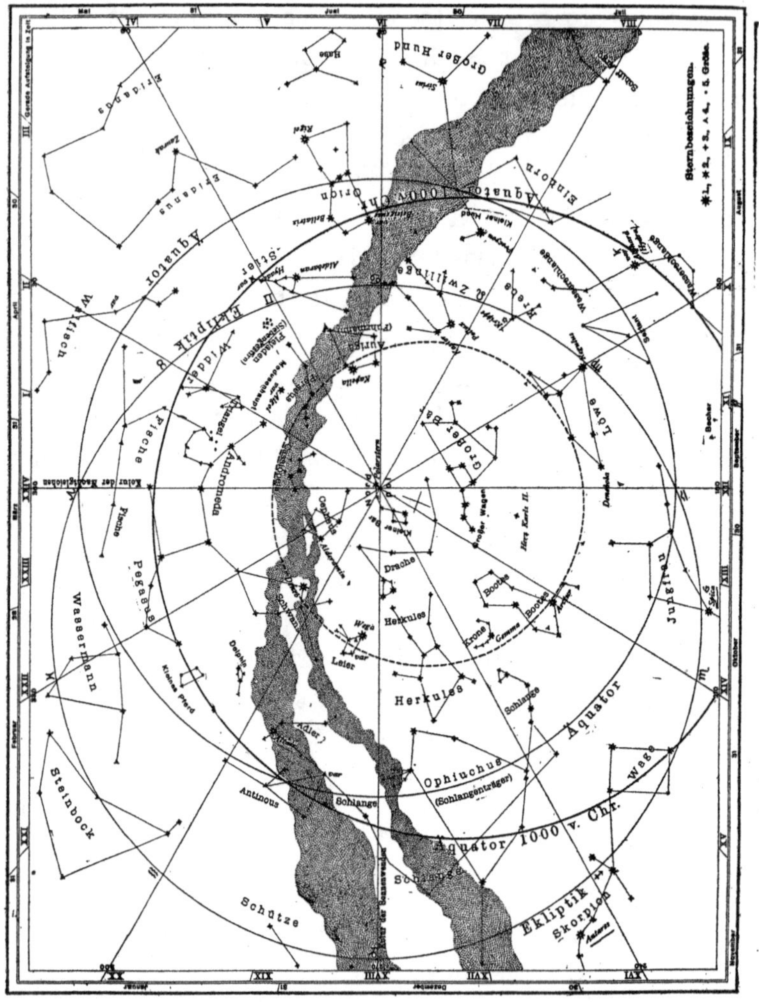

Fig. 45.—Northern hemisphere showing the ecliptic and the equatorial circles at 1000 B. C.

primarily certain deities, as is now definitely known from Susa I, XIV and XIX. The deities thus symbolically represented are independent of the deities enumerated in the texts. The two series never agree. The symbols represent the deities either by their shrines, their weapons, their sacred animals or in human form.

(2) Babylonian deities being also stellar in their nature, the symbols represent by implication certain constellations. Some signs of the zodiac are represented, but not the zodiac itself, for there is no order such as we expect if the zodiac as such were represented.[1]

(3) There being more than forty symbols, other constellations besides the zodiac are included. These are most likely the planets and the constellations of the *dodekaoros*. Here again there is no representation of the full series, but, as in the case of the zodiacal signs, only a selection is made.

The problems in connection with these symbols which still await future solution are: (1) The compete identification of all the symbols with the gods they represent. (2) The identification of the symbols with their respective constellations. (3) The determination of the principle which guided the Babylonian sculptors in their selection and arrangement of the symbols on the stones. When these problems are solved the mystery of the symbols shall have found its complete and satisfactory solution.

[1] According to Prof. Hilprecht, the rounded top of the boundary stones, as also frequently seen in Etruscan monuments (cf. Milani, *Studi e Materiali di archeologia e numismatica*), represents the firmament of heaven with various well-known stars and constellations.

II.

A NEW BOUNDARY STONE OF NEBUCHADREZZAR I. FROM NIPPUR c. 1140 B.C.

1. Inscription and Symbols.

This magnificent boundary stone was found at Nippur, "on the northwest side of the Ziggurat, within the temple area,"[1] in February, 1896, at the close of the third Babylonian expedition of the University of Pennsylvania. It was presented by the Imperial Ottoman Government to Prof. Hilprecht for his services in organizing the Assyriological Section of the Sultan's Archeological Museum in Constantinople.[2]

It is a conical block of black limestone, being 49 cm. in height and 73.2 cm. in circumference around the center. It tapers towards the top, being 68.4 cm. along the upper edge of the inscription. The latter consists of a heading of two lines, placed among the symbols on top, and five columns, containing 32 + 32 + 33 + 30 + 26 = 155 lines of text. The stone is slightly damaged, a piece having been broken off at the lower end, by which the latter part of six lines from column three and the beginning of four lines from column four have been lost. Fortunately their contents can be restored almost completely.[3]

This boundary stone has several peculiar features not found on

[1] According to a note entered by Dr. Haynes in his diary, to accompany the photographs taken of the stone at the time of its discovery. It was found on the last day while closing up one of the ditches.

[2] The text will be published in B. E., Series A, Vol. I, Part 3.

[3] See the translation and transliteration for the restoration of these passages.

Fig. 46.—Boundary stone of Nebuchadrezzar I. from Nippur.

other monuments of this kind. In the first place, it contains a drawing of the field in question, together with an accompanying description, which precedes the inscription proper. Similar plots of fields and plans of buildings are, however, found on numerous clay tablets.[1] A second peculiarity is a beautiful hymn to Ellil, at the beginning of the inscription. It was no doubt taken from the liturgical collections of hymns in use at Nippur. It is the finest Ellil hymn which has been found thus far,[2] fitly celebrating the majesty and power of the god of Nippur. In some of its expressions it approaches the Psalms of the Old Testament.[3] A similar hymn to Nanâ, opening a legal document, is found on a stone tablet, dated in the reign of Nabû-shum-ishkun, which records the investiture of a priest of Nebo at Borsippa with certain rights and privileges.[4] The nearest approach to a hymn on other boundary stones is the glorification of Marduk on the stone of Merodach-baladan II., now at Berlin.[5]

The inscription is also remarkable for certain peculiar signs, as *e.g.* the sign to be read perhaps *saḫ* in *saḫ-pu-ú*, (I, 13), the sign for *rabiṣu* (IV, 26), the sign for *išdu* (V, 7), and the sign *NISAG* in *nisakku* (V, 18). A large number of ideograms is used, and several new words occur. Of the latter the following may be mentioned: *alâku*, "to throw down" (IV, 4); *nelmenu*, "misfortune" (IV, 7); *lillu*, "laughter" or "smile" (IV, 14); *ušaku*, "calamity" (IV, 24). Other words are written in an unusual way—*baqânu* (because of following *š*) = *baqâmu* (III, 26); *nazuzzu* (under accent) = *nanzuzu* (I, 8); *šuzuzzu* (half accent) but *šuzu-*

[1] Compare the full literature quoted by Prof. Hilpreċht, B.E., Vol. XX, Pt. 1, p. 11, note 9.

[2] For other hymns to Ellil see Dr. Jastrow's *Religion Assyriens und Babyloniens*, I, 488–492.

[3] See Commentary for detailed comparisons.

[4] Cf. M.D.O.G., No. 4, March, 1900, pp. 14–17, Col. I, 1–20.

[5] V.A. 2663, cf. B.A., II, 258–273, Col. I, 1–24.

zatma (II, 19 and II, 30); *maḫḫar* = *maḫar* (II, 18); *nanzaz* = *manzaz* (II, 18); *nugu kabitti* = *nug kabitti* (IV, 10); *bannûa* = *bânûa* (IV, 26); *ikîlu* (probably = *ekêlu*) = *akâlu* (III, 21) as *libênu* = *labânu* (II, 10).[1]

The stonecutter has not always been accurate in engraving the inscription. There are several erasures, as *ina* written on an erasure of *ši* (III, 23); the sign preceding *i-tar-ra-ṣu* (III, 24); the second last sign following the *nu* in *i-din-nu-šu* (IV, 18); *šup-par* written on an erasure of *bît* (V, 9). Even some mistakes occur—*at-pi* instead of *ap-pi* (II, 10); *ta* instead of *ša* (II, 11); *ŠA.SAG* instead of *ŠA.DUG(KA*, II, 3); and probably also *me-su-šu* instead of *par-su-šu* (I, 18) and *A.ḪA.ME* instead of *ḪA.A.ME* (V, 7).

The inscription consists of the following divisions:

(1) The heading, containing the name of the stone, in two lines, written between the symbols.

(2) The plot of the field, accompanied by a description of eight lines.

(3) A hymn in honor of Ellil, the god of Nippur, Col. I, 1–22.

(4) The historical circumstances under which the land was given to Nusku-ibni, a high dignitary of Ekur, the temple of Ellil at Nippur, Col. I, 23–II, 16.

(5) The measuring of the land under the supervision of Bau-shum-iddina, the governor of Bît-Sin-sheme, in response to a royal command; a more detailed description of the field and its actual transfer to Nusku-ibni, Col. II, 17–III, 16.

(6) The curses: (*a*) Introduction to the curses, forbidding any official to appropriate the land or interfere with the privileges of the owner, Col. III, 17–IV, 2. (*b*) Invocation of the gods and the punishments they are asked to mete out to any offender, Col. IV,

[1] Several of these forms (*baqânu, nanzaz, libênu*) occur also elsewhere, but rarely. See Commentary.

3–27. (*c*) Curses directed against any one removing or destroying the boundary stone, Col. IV, 28–V, 7.

(7) The fourteen witnesses present at the transaction, Col. V, 8–25.

(8) The date of the inscription, Col. V, 26.

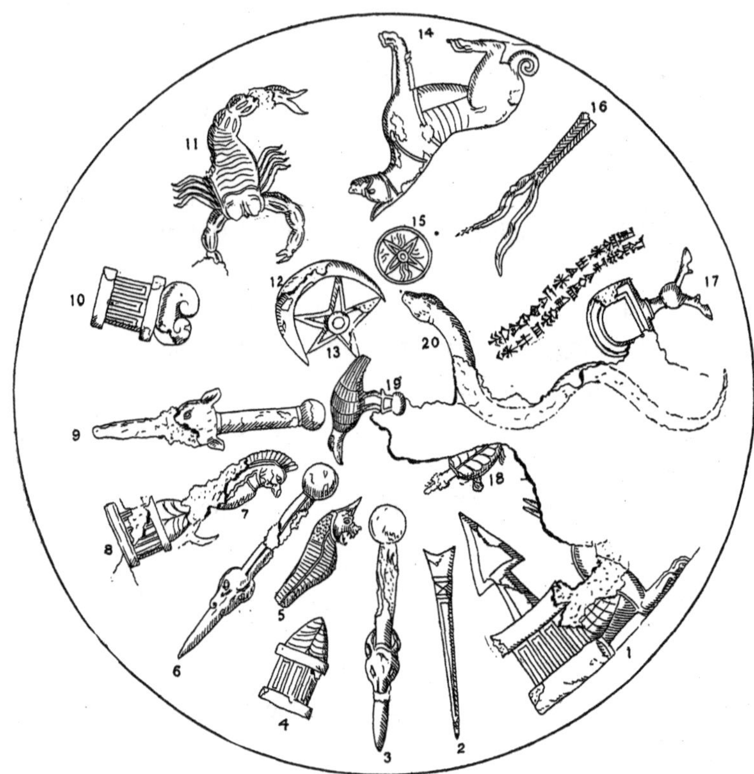

Fig. 47.—Symbols of the boundary stone of Nebuchadrezzar I. from Nippur.

As the symbols covering the top have not been described very accurately by Prof. Hommel,[1] who had only photographs to guide him, which evidently did not show all the objects, a full description is herewith given:

[1] *Aufsätze und Abhandlungen,* München, 1901, p. 435f.

(1) A shrine with the spearhead of Marduk, before which lies a crouching dragon, whose head is broken off. (2) A pointed shaft, wedge-shaped, standing upright, most likely the symbol of Nabû.[1] (3) A scepter, erect, with a knob at the upper end and the head of a horned animal in the center. (4) A shrine with a tiara on it, the symbol of Anu. (5) The neck and head of a lion above the shrine, the symbol of Nergal. (6) A scepter (like No. 3) standing erect, a knob on top and an animal head in the center. (7) A shrine with a tiara on it, the symbol of Ellil. (8) The head and neck of a vulture above the shrine, the symbol of Zamama. (9) A scepter, standing erect, with a knob and the head of an animal (partly defaced) in the center. (10) A shrine with a yoke-shaped figure, reversed (as on V R. 57, third symbol, second row, and Susa No. 20), most likely the symbol of Ninḫarsag.[2] (11) A scorpion, the symbol of Ishḫara. (12) The crescent, the symbol of Sin, partly surrounding (13) a five-pointed star, the symbol of Ishtar. (14) A sitting dog, the symbol of Gula.[3] (15) The sundisk, the

[1] See Chap. I., p. 96; R. A., VI, 95–104.

[2] Dr. Hayes Ward, of New York, has called my attention to the fact that this symbol, which represents most likely the goddess Ninḫarsag (cf. p. 95), shows a remarkable resemblance to the plaits of hair adorning the Egyptian goddess Hathor. Compare, *e.g.*, the picture given by Prof. W. Max Müller in his *Egyptological Researches*, Washington, 1906, p. 14 (cf. fig. 48). The similarity is striking, to say the least. If the figure on the Babylonian boundary stones really represents plaits of hair, it would furnish an adequate reason why this peculiar symbol stands for the goddess Ninḫarsag. There is but one difficulty in the explanation—if it was intended for plaits of hair, why was it reversed and even flattened out, cf. fig. 11^7; 30^4; 47^{10}; 49^9?

[3] The dog is not only associated with Gula on numerous boundary stones, but there is definite evidence in the inscriptions that the dog was sacred to her. Nebuchadrezzar II. set up two gold dogs, two silver dogs and two bronze dogs at the entrance of Gula's temple E-sa-bad in Babylon. Cf. *Neb. Wady Brissa*, B, VI, 20–24; and in the temple E-ul-la in Sippar he found her name written upon a terra cotta figure of a dog (*šu-um ša dNin-kar-ra-ag* [*a-ši-bat*] *E-UL.LU* [*ṣi-i-ri*] *kalbu ḫa-aṣ-ba ša-ṭi-ir-ma*); cf. K. B., III, pt. 2, p. 50. Finally Scheil

symbol of Shamash, above the dog. (16) The lightning fork of Rammân, ending in two serpents. (17) A curious figure, consisting of some kind of a vessel supported by two animal feet, perhaps a censer.[1] (18) A tortoise above the partly effaced dragon of Marduk. (19) The serpent, winding over the top of the stone. (20) A bird, perched on a pole alongside of the serpent.

FIG. 48.—Symbol of Ninḫarsag and symbol of Hathor.

The three scepters which appear here for the first time may simply be marks of division, as Hommel thinks.[2] However, attention must be called to the fact that the animal heads, placed in the

found at Sippar (see *Fouilles à Sippar*, p. 90, fig. 13) a terra cotta dog with the inscription: *Ana* ^{d}*ME.ME.* (= ^{d}*Gula*, cf. V R. 44, c–d, 10) *bêlti kalbu ḫaṣbi êpušma aqîš.*

[1] It is remarkable that the symbol of Ea, the goatfish with the shrine carrying a ram's head, is wanting. Its place may be taken by this new symbol, which may be intended for a brazier or censer, called *kinûnu* in Babylonian. If this is true, the remarks of Hommel may be compared (*Aufsätze*, p. 241) who places the star called *Kinûnu* near the Capricorn, the symbol of Ea.

[2] *L.c.*, p. 436. The horned animal head in the first scepter is perhaps that of an antelope, the second can hardly be recognized, the third is perhaps a lion head. With these three scepters the three fans or fly flaps on the stone of Nabû-shum-ishkun may perhaps be compared. See p. 97.

center of the scepters, differ. It is therefore more probable that they may turn out to be separate symbols.

The finding of this boundary stone within the confines of the temple at Nippur raises the interesting question, How can we explain its presence there? An examination of the inscription shows that the priest to whom the land was granted was Nusku-ibni, the son of Upaḫḫir-Nusku, who was officially connected with the Nusku worship at Nippur,[1] being the *pašiš apsî* or *UḪ.ME.-ZU.AB* of Nusku. Hence the name of this boundary stone contains the name of the god Nusku, while at the same time Nusku is invoked in the curses. This is remarkable, as it is thus far the only instance of a separate curse being uttered in the name of Nusku. But the key to the whole situation lies in the title which is ascribed to Nusku. It is *bannûa*, "my creator." Now, as the name of the priest was Nusku-ibni, he is evidently playing on his own name. This conclusion leads us to the further inference that he himself wrote the inscription. This is at once the explanation of all the peculiarities. It explains the repeated use of the god Nusku in the title and in the curses. It also furnishes the reason for the plot of the field. It was a measure of precaution, adopted by the priest to locate and describe his land as exactly as possible. It also explains why this inscription begins with a hymn of Ellil. Nusku-ibni, the priest (*nisak*) of Ellil (Col. II, 13; III, 11), had access to the hymnological collections of the temple, and by its insertion wanted to glorify his god and place the land and stone under his special protection. Finally we can also infer from it why the stone was found in the temple precincts. It had evidently been deposited

[1] The earliest reference to Nusku that has come to my notice occurs on a seal cylinder, dedicated to Nusku by a patesi of Nippur, for the life of Dungi, king of Ur. Collection de Clercq, No. 86; cf. Thureau-Dangin, *Inscriptions de Sumer et d'Akkad*, p. 278, Sceau, B.

by Nusku-ibni in the temple.[1] The land itself was located between the royal canal and the Tigris, probably at some distance from Nippur.[2]

A comparison between this inscription, written under Nebuchadrezzar I., and the inscription of Nebuchadrezzar II. reveals the fact that there is a remarkable similarity between them, and makes it very probable that the scribes of Nebuchadrezzar II. intentionally imitated the style and phraseology of his great predecessor and namesake.

The following table contains the most important parallels:[3]

Nebuchadrezzar I.	Nebuchadrezzar II.
ú-taq-qu-ú pal-ḫiš, I, 6.	*pa-al-ḫi-iš ú-ta-qu*, 1, I, 15; 13, I, 26. *pa-al-ḫi-iš lu ú-ta-aq-qu*, 9, I, 11. *pa-al-ḫi-iš ú-ta-ak-ku-šu*, 15, II, 61.
na-zu-uz-zu ša-aḫ-tiš, I, 8.	*ka-am-su iz-za-zu maḫ-ru-uš-šu*, 15, II, 62.
Ellil is called: *ka-bit mâtâti*, I, 12.	Marduk is called: *ka-ab-tu*, 15, II, 2.
me-gir-šu, I, 23. *me-gir dEn-lil*, II, 15.	*mi-gi-ir dMarduk*, 19a, I, 3.
muš-te-'-ú aš-ra-ti-šú, I, 24.	*mu-uš-te-'-ú aš-ra-a-ti*, 13, I, 8; 19b, V, 2.
a-na hrê'û-ut mâtuŠú-me-ri u Akkadîki, II, 1.	*a-na ri-e-ú-ti i-ti-nam*, 9, I, 10. *a-na ri-'i-ú-ti id-di-na*, 10, I, 10.
a-na ud-du-uš eš-rit ma-ḫa-az da-ad-me, II, 2.	*za-na-an ma-ḫa-zi ud-du-šu eš-ri-e-tim*, 1, I, 13; 3, I, 14; 12, I, 22; 13, I, 24; III, 28; 16, I, 5.
sa-dar satuk E-kur, II, 3.	*mu-ki-in sa-at-tu-uk-ku*, 13, I, 20.
iṣukakku na-ki-ri-šú ú-šib-bir-ma, II, 4.	*mu-šab-bir ka-ak-ku na-ki-ri-ia*, 13, II, 39; 15, IV, 49; 19b, VI, 30. *šu-ub-bi-ir kakkê-šu-nu*, 2, III, 38.

[1] A parallel case is furnished by the stone of Nazi-Maruttash, whose inscription states explicitly that it was set up in the temple, before the god (*maḫar ilišu ušziz*, D. E. P., II, pl. 18, 5). For the picture of such a temple treasure vault, see Hilprecht, *Excavations in Assyria and Babylonia*, facing p. 390.

[2] See Commentary, p. 158f.

[3] The passages from the inscriptions of Nebuchadrezzar II. are quoted from the *Building Inscriptions of the Neo-Babylonian Empire*, by Stephen Langdon, Paris, 1905.

ṣir-rit nakri-šú qa-tu-uš-šú it-muḫ, II, 5.	*ši-bi-ir-ri u-šat(-at)-mi-iḫ ga-tu-uš-šu*, 16, I, 10. *iṣuḫaṭṭu i-ša-ar-tum ú-ša-at-mi-iḫ ga-tu-ú-a*, 11, I, 12; 14, I, 17; 15, I, 45; cf. 19*a*, II, 1–2.
balâṭ ûmê da-ru-ú-ti iš-ruq-šum-ma, II, 6.	*ba-la-ṭam da-ir-a(am) . . . . a-na ši-ri-iq(-tim) šu-ur-qam*, 4, II, 19–23; 5, II, 21–22; 8, II, 16–22. *ba-la-aṭ ûm(-um) ri-e-ku-ú-tim . . . . a-na ši-ri-iq-tim šu-ur-qam*, 2, I, 33–36.
eli šarri a-lik maḫ-ri ú-ša-tir šùm-šu, II, 7.	*šu-um-šum u-ša-te-ir*, 9, II, 17. *ša e-li šarrâni ab-bi-e u-ša-ti-ru*, 13, II, 77. *e-li ša pa-nim u-ša-te-ir*, 9, I, 15. *šarrâni a-lik maḫ-ri-ia*, 15, VII, 13.
ina igisê (Ši.Di) ḫab-ṣu-ú-ti, II, 9.	*i-gi-sa-a šu-um-mu-ḫu*, 15, II, 37; 19*a*, III, 31. *ba-bi-il i-gi-se-e rabûti (ra-be-u-tim)*, 17, I, 10; 13, I, 27.
ina ut-ni-ni-šu, II, 16.	*ut-ni-en-šu-um*, 12, II, 15. *ana dMarduk ut-ni-en*, 15, I, 51. *mu-ut-ni-en-nu-u*, 7, I, 11; 10, I, 2; 14, I, 11.
ki-niš ippalis-su-ma, II, 16.	*ki-ni-iš na-ap-li-is-ma*, 12, III, 2.
šar me-ša-ri, II, 22.	*šar mi-ša-ri-im*, 9, I, 1.
mu-ki-in iš-di ma-a-ti, II, 24.	*mu-ki-in iš-di mâti*, 16, I, 4; Nabop, 3, I, 6.
ilu]ban-nu-ú-a, IV, 25.	*bêl ilâni i-lu ba-nu-ú-a*, 4, II, 14; 7, I, 15. *i-lu ba-ni-ia*, 15, I, 30. *a-bi ba-nu-ú-a*, 15, VII, 48; 14, II, 7.

Some of these phrases are also found in other inscriptions, but it is impossible to duplicate any considerable number of them from the inscriptions of any other king. The scribes of Nebuchadrezzar II. adopted, therefore, not only the archaic script, but imitated also the style of older kings, notably that of Nebuchadrezzar I.

2. Identity of PA.SHE with Isin.

This inscription of Nebuchadrezzar I. brings again the questions and problems still surrounding the fourth Babylonian dynasty to the front.

One of these problems refers to the proper pronunciation of the name of the dynasty written PA.SHE in the king's list.[1] It seems to be tacitly assumed by some scholars (Winckler, *Forschungen*, I, 130, 138)[2] that *Pa-še* is to be read phonetically and that it represents, therefore, the actual name of the dynasty. This, however, is far from certain. On the contrary, it is most probable that PA.SHE is an ideogram. Not only are most of the other dynastic names written ideographically in the king's list (*TIN.TIR*^{ki}; *URU.AZAG*, or *URU.ḪA* according to list A, and *E*), but other considerations point in the same direction.

As early as 1888 Sayce regarded PA.SHE identical with the cities of Isin and Patesi.[3] The same view was maintained by Pinches.[4] It was further developed by Jensen,[5] who observed that (1) according to K. 4995, 20f.[6] (*PA.ŠE GAL.LA.BA* = *ša i-ši-in-šu ib-šú-ú*) *PA* (= *aru*, the tassel) + *ŠE* (corn) is equivalent to *išinšu*. This seems to be confirmed by another passage[7]

[1] Winckler, *Untersuchungen*, p. 147; Rost, *Untersuchungen*, pl. III (who, however, writes by mistake PA.MU); Knudtzon, *Gebete an den Sonnengott*, p. 60, and Lehmann, *Zwei Hauptprobleme*, pls. 1, 2.

[2] Hommel formerly held this view, *Geschichte*, pp. 170, 488, but he has since expressed himself in favor of Isin being a synonym of Pashe; cf. *Geographie und Geschichte des alten Orients*, p. 297.

[3] R.P.[2], Vol. I, 17[3], quoting II R. 53, 13*a*. This passage, however, does not prove the identity of Isin and Patesi, just as Kutha and Nippur (l. 4) or Sippar and Dilbat (l. 8), though placed in the same juxtaposition, are not identical.

[4] J.R.A.S., 1894, p. 833.

[5] Z.A., XI, p. 90.

[6] Haupt, A.S.K.T., p. 124; see also Böllenrücher, *Gebete und Hymnen an Nergal*, p. 43.

[7] Haupt, *l.c.*, p. 22; cf. Z.A., VII, 199, l. 4.

in which *PA* + *X* is followed by the gloss *i-ši-in*. (2) That in the charter of Nebuchadrezzar I. (V R. 56, 17–18), who was a member of the PA.SHE dynasty, the name of the governor of Ishin precedes that of the governor of Babylon, which argues for the great political importance of Ishin at that time. (3) That according to Reissner, V.A.TH. 408 + 2178, Obv. 5, *PA.ŠE* is = *i-ši-in*. From these facts Jensen concluded that the city of PA.SHE*ki* was also to be pronounced Ishin. This conclusion, however, while very ingenious, was not absolutely necessary, for what was true of the word *iš(i)nu*, cstr. *išin*, meaning the blossom of the grain,[1] was not necessarily true of the city of Ishin. But as the Babylonians were very fond of playing with their ideograms, it is *à priori* probable that the sameness of sound in the two words caused a transferring of the ideogram, originally intended for *iš(i)nu*, blossom, to the name of the city of Ishin.

This probability can be increased by other evidence. In 1897 Craig published two tablets,[2] preserved in the British Museum, which shed more light on this question. From the first tablet (80–7–19, 126) we learn that the later pronunciation of *NI.SI.IN.ki* is *I-si-in*[3] (l. 9–10), that Gula was the "Lady of Isin" (l. 1), which is called "the city of her dominion" (*âl bêlûtiša*, l. 9–10).

These statements are supplemented by another inscription, published by Craig (Sm. 289, Obv. 17), in which we read: *Bît-dGu-la ša PA.ŠEki*. Combining these statements we are naturally brought to the conclusion that PA.SHE and Ishin are identical.

The name of this city is written either I-si-in (so in the tablet 80–7–19, 126, quoted above) or I-ši-in (V R. 56, 17; I R. 66, II, 7) or I-šin (*Babylonian Chronicle*, IV, 18; see Winckler, *Forschungen*, I, 303). In the Sumerian texts the same variation occurs between

[1] See also *shami-ši-in eqli*, *Hebraica*, XIII, 221.

[2] A.J.S.L., XIII, 200f. A more recent publication of the first of these tablets is given by Macmillan, B.A., V, p. 644f., and translation, p. 586.

[3] Cf. Bezold in Z.A., IV, 430.

NI.SI.IN (so usually) or *NI.ŠI.IN* (K. 3811 + 3833 and K. 10844, see Bezold, *Catalogue*, pp. 566, 1118). In this connection it is noteworthy that the word *išinu*, "the blossom of the grain," is also written *isinu* (Reissner *Hymnen*, 73, 5*a*, compared with *ibid.*, pp. 21, 27). Finally it may be mentioned that alongside of the personal name *PA.ŠE*^{ki}*-ai* also the form *I-sin-na-ai* is found.[1]

On the basis of the above evidence Isin may well be adopted as the *probable* pronunciation of PA.SHE.[2]

The dynasty was called Pa-she, according to some scholars,[3] from a certain quarter in the city of Babylon, which is inferred from Nebuchadrezzar I.'s statement that he was "the offspring of Babylon" (V R. 55, 2), and it is further assumed that the names of the other dynasties (*TIN.TIR.KI*, *URU.AZAG* and *E*) refer to Babylon. On the other hand, those scholars who identify PA.SHE and Isin naturally connect the origin of the fourth dynasty with that city as the ancestral home of its princes. They look for the city somewhere in Southern Babylonia.[4]

In favor of a city of PA.SHE or Isin as entirely different from Babylon the following considerations may be urged. The argument based upon the title of Nebuchadrezzar, "the offspring of Babylon," is not absolutely convincing, for this personal title may have nothing to do with the origin of his dynasty. Nebuchadrezzar may have been born in Babylon as the son of a younger royal prince, perhaps Ninib-nâdin-shum,[5] who held a priestly office, for it is noteworthy that Nebuchadrezzar bears the titles *iššakku*

[1] See Hilprecht and Clay, B.E., IX, p. 61; X, p. 60.

[2] See Hommel, *Geographie und Geschichte*, p. 297; Hilprecht in B.E., X, 60; Rogers, *History of Assyria and Babylonia*, Vol. I, p. 425.

[3] See Rost, *Untersuchungen*, p. 10, note 2; Winckler, "Ancient Nearer Asia,' in Helmholt's *History of the World*, Vol. III, p. 19.

[4] Jensen, *Göttinger Gelehrten Anzeiger*, 1900, p. 864, note 1; Delitzsch, *Wo lag das Paradies*, p. 225; Winckler, *Altorientalische Forschungen*, I, p. 203; Hommel, *Geographie und Geschichte*, p. 297, looks for it either east of the Tigris in the "Sea Land," or near Bagdad.

[5] Cf. p. 129, below.

(*PA.TE.SI*) *qardu šakkanak Bâbili*[1] and also *nisakku* (Neb. Nippur, II, 12), the same title as borne by the priest Nusku-ibni. Moreover, the new stone of Nebuchadrezzar I. distinctly implies (Col. II, 1–4) that the causes which placed him on the throne were largely of a religious nature.

Nor is the argument drawn from the names of the other dynasties more conclusive, because several dynasties, the fifth, sixth and seventh, had nothing to do with Babylon. Why should the fourth? Besides, the name of the second dynasty is very uncertain (*URU.-AZAG* or *URU.ḪA*) and not well suited to draw far-reaching conclusions from it. Cf. King, "Chronicles," pp. 70f., 107ff.

On the other hand, it must be remembered that the city of Isin appears prominently during the fourth (PA.SHE) dynasty. On the charter of Nebuchadrezzar I. (V R. 56, 17) Shamash-nâdin-shumu, the son of Atta-iluma, the governor of Ishin, is placed in a conspicuous position before the governor of Babylon. On the stone of Za'aleh (I R. 66, II, 6–7) E-karra-iqîsha, the then governor of Ishin, is the very first among the witnesses, and on the new stone of Nebuchadrezzar I. (Neb. Nippur, V, 21) we find among the witnesses a native of Ishin, named Amel-Ishin. To complete the references mentioning the city of Isin during this period, we may recall the fact that at the close of the Cassite period Ishin was entered by a victorious Elamite army under Kidin-ḫutrutash (*Babylonian Chronicle*, IV 18).

As to its location we know nothing definite, but the various lists of cities seem to locate it in Southern Babylonia. On K 3811 + 3833 (Bezold, *Catalogue*, p. 566) NI.ŠI.IN appears between Shirpurla and Girsu (= Telloh, cf. Hommel, *Geographie*, p. 189). On

[1] That *âluHI(DUG)*, "the good city," is a term applied to Babylon appears from the parallel expression *šakkanak Bâbili*, applied to Nebuchadrezzar I. on the new stone from Nippur (Col. II, 20). This corroborates the view of Winckler, K.B., III, pt. 1, p. 165, note 2 Cf. also IV R.[2] 21,* No. 1 (C), Col. III, 1.

K. 4541 (*Catalogue*, p. 640) it follows Shirpurla and Nippur. On K. 10844 (*Catalogue*, p. 1118) it precedes Larsa. In another text (Rass. 2, 417, see *Catalogue*, p. 1674) PA.ŠE is preceded by Eridu, Adab (*UD.NUN*^{ki}) and Ur, while in still another passage (80–7–19, 126) it is in close parallelism with Nippur.

3. The Succession of the Isin Kings.

Another problem of the Isin (PA.SHE) dynasty is the succession of its kings.

Our knowledge of the dynasty is based on the kings' list, the synchronistic history and the inscriptions of the various rulers belonging to this dynasty.

The kings' list is unfortunately very incomplete at this point. We only know that there were in all eleven kings belonging to it, who reigned 132 years and six months.[1] The names of the last three kings are partially preserved, only one of which can be restored with certainty. This is the name of the last king, *Nabû-shum-[li-bur]*, the same king to whom the inscription upon a duck-weight found by Layard in the North-West palace at Nimrûd belongs. Cf. King in *P. S. B. A.*, Vol. XXIX (1907), p. 221, and "Chronicles," Vol. II, p. 159. Of the eight kings whose names are missing entirely six are known to us from their own inscriptions, Nabû-kudurri-uṣur I., Ellil-nâdin-aplu, Marduk-nâdin-aḫê, Marduk-shâpik-zîrim, Rammân-apal-iddina and Marduk-aḫê-erba.

Nebuchadrezzar I. is now represented by three boundary stones (V R. 55–57; C. T., IX, pls. 4, 5, and the new stone from Nippur). Two hymns glorify his military achievements (K. 3426, published

[1] The sum total was long in doubt. It was read 72 by Pinches, Winckler and Delitzsch. Peiser first proved (Z.A., VI, 269) that the number 72 was impossible. Later Knudtzon and Lehmann read 132, while Rost still considers it as doubtful (*Untersuchungen*, p. 3). Taking, however, everything into consideration, the figure 132 (or perhaps 133) seems to be the most probable and has, therefore, been generally accepted.

last in *C.T.*, XIII, pl. 48, and III R. 38, 4; see Winckler, *Forschungen*, I, 534–538). Winckler also translates two other inscriptions (K.

Fig. 49.—Boundary stone of Nebuchadrezzar I. from Abu Habba. V R. 57.

3444 = IV R. 20 and D.T. 71), which seem to refer to Nebuchadrezzar's successes over Elam. Finally an inscription published by Strassmaier (Br. M., Sp. II, 407, in *Hebraica*, Vol. IX, p. 5) must be mentioned. It refers to a king, *Nabû-kudurri-uṣur šar Bâbili mâr NIN.IB-nâdin-šumu*. This seems to refer to Nebuchadrezzar I., because it can neither apply to Nebuchadrezzar II., the son of Nabopolassar, nor to the usurper Nebuchadrezzar III.

From the reign of Ellil-nâdin-aplu we have one *kudurru* inscription (*O.B.I.*, Vol. I, 83). To the reign of these two kings belong also III R. 41 and I R. 70, as we shall show below in discussing the succession of the various kings.

The reign of Marduk-nâdin-aḫê is represented by two boundary stones, the stone of Za'aleh from his first year (I R. 66) and III R. 43–45, from the tenth year of his reign. An inscription, dated in the fifth year of this king has been discovered at Nippur, as announced by Prof. Hilprecht (see his *Excavations in Assyria and Babylonia*, p. 519).

The king Marduk-shâpik-zîrim (or Marduk-shâpik-zêr-mâti, of which the first is an abbreviation; see Rost, *Untersuchungen*, p. 26, note 1)[1] is represented by a fragmentary inscription (*O.B.I.*, Vol. I, No. 148).

Of Rammân-apal-iddina we have a short inscription, preserved in the Louvre (Place, *Ninive et Assyrie*, III, 78, note 4; cf. Winckler, *Untersuchungen*, p. 28, note 2). An inscription dated in the tenth year of this king has been found at Nippur (see Hilprecht, *Excavations in Assyria and Babylonia*, p. 519).

A boundary stone of Marduk-aḫê-erba was published by Prof. Hilprecht (*O.B.I.*, Vol. I, No. 149).

Four of these kings are also mentioned in the *Synchronistic History* (II R. 65, 1 and III R. 4, 3; see also Winckler, *Untersuchungen*,

[1] For the use of "m" as a hypocoristical ending see note of Prof. Hilprecht in Ranke's *Early Babylonian Personal Names*, p. 186.

pp. 148–152), namely, Nebuchadrezzar, Marduk-nâdin-aḫê, Marduk-shâpik-zêr-mâti and Rammân-apal-iddina. Of the last two it is definitely stated that they followed each other immediately. That leaves us to determine the succession of the other four kings. From the inscription of Ellil-nâdin-aplu it is evident (Col. I, 7–15) that he was the immediate successor of Nebuchadrezzar, for the land in question had been for 696 years in peaceful possession of the temple of Ninâ up to the reign of Nebuchadrezzar, but in the fourth year of Ellil-nâdin-aplu its area was reduced by E-karra-iqîsha. It is also evident that the reign of Ellil-nâdin-aplu was of short duration and was followed immediately by that of Marduk-nâdin-aḫê, for Ardi-Nanâ, son of Mudammiq-Rammân, occurs both on the charter of Nebuchadrezzar (V R. 56, 13) and the stone of Za'aleh (I R. 66, II, 13) dated in the first year of Marduk-nâdin-aḫê. Ṭâb-ashâb-Marduk, son of Ina-Esagila-zêru, is mentioned on three stones, on V R. 56, 22, as governor of Ḫalmân, but on I R. 70, I, 15 and I R. 66, II, 11 as *sukallu*. Moreover, E-karra-iqîsha, son of Ea-iddina, is found as governor of Bît-Sin-mâgir in the reign of Ellil-nâdin-aplu (*O.B.I.*, 83, I, 10), but as governor of Ishin (I R. 66, II, 6, 7) in the reign of Marduk-nâdin-aḫê. Perhaps Ellil-nâdin-aplu had transferred him to another province as the result of his high-handed actions in Bît-Sin-mâgir. Again, Ṣîr-uṣur, brother of Ellil-nâdin-shumu, and son of Ḫabban, mentioned V R. 56, 23, is also found on the *Caillou de Michaux* (I R. 70, I, 13), while Nabû-zêr-lîshir, son of Itti-Marduk-balâṭu and grandson of Ardi-Ea, who served as surveyor of the field, mentioned on the new stone of Nebuchadrezzar I. (Col. III, 13, 14), is no doubt a brother of Shâpiku, son of Itti-Marduk-balâṭu and grandson of Ardi-Ea, the surveyor of the field mentioned in III R. 41, Col. I, 13. All these links would be impossible if Ellil-nâdin-aplu and Marduk-nâdin-aḫê had not succeeded Nebuchadrezzar immediately. They also prove that III R. 41 and I R. 70 were written either in the reign of Nebuchadrezzar I. or his immediate successor, as Hommel had already concluded in his *Geschichte*, p. 459. The position of Marduk-aḫê-erba is less easy to determine. Rost (*Untersuchungen*, p. 65) places him with a question mark at the head of the Isin (PA.SHE) dynasty. Lehmann (*Zwei Hauptprobleme, Tabelle IV*) inserts him between Marduk-nâdin-aḫê and Marduk-shâpik-zêr-mâti. Assyrian synchronism does not favor the latter arrangement, because Tiglath-pileser, the contemporary of Marduk-nâdin-aḫê, is followed immediately by his son Ashur-bêl-kala, the contemporary of Marduk-shâpik-zêr-mâti. This would argue that, as in Assyria, so in Babylonia there was an immediate succession of the two kings in question. It is therefore more natural to place Marduk-aḫê-erba either at the beginning of the dynasty or after Rammân-apal-iddina. The latter seems to me preferable, because none of the persons named on the stone occur on any of the other boundary stones of this period.[1] It was, therefore, most likely separated from them by a considerable number of years.

4. Place of Nebuchadrezzar I. in the Dynasty of Isin.

The last question that needs discussion is the position of Nebuchadrezzar I. in the dynasty. It appeared in our discussion that he heads the six kings whose names are broken off from the kings' list; but where is he to be placed in the dynasty? It is now generally agreed that he did not occupy the first place. A renewed examination of this passage in the kings' list seems to have placed that beyond doubt.[2] On the other hand, there is strong and even irresistible evidence to show that he was actively engaged in freeing his country from the chaos and disorder such as we know prevailed

[1] This is also the judgment of Hommel, who identifies him with the ninth king of the PA.SHE dynasty, see his article, "Eine neuer Babylonischer König," in *Sitzungsberichte der Königl. böhm. Ges. d. Wissensch.*, 1901, pp. 18, 24.

[2] See Prof. Hilprecht's statement in B.E., Vol. XX, Pt. 1, p. 44, note 1.

at the close of the Cassite period. This appears first of all in the remarkable titles that are attributed to him. He is called "the sun of his land who makes prosperous his people" (*dŠamaš mâtišu mušammiḫu nišêšu,* V R. 55, 4)[1]; "the protector of boundary stones, who fixes the boundaries" (*nâṣir kudurrêti mukinnu ablê,*[2] V R. 55, 5); "the king of right who judges a righteous judgment" (*šar kinâti ša dîn mêšari idinnu,* V R. 55, 6). The last two statements clearly imply previous lawlessness and disorder, which he brought to an end. The titles applied to him in the new inscription from Nippur point even more strongly to a change of dynasty. It is said that "Ellil broke the weapon of his (Ellil's) enemy and laid the scepter of his enemy into his (Nebuchadrezzar's) hand" (Col. II, 4, 5). These statements show that the Ellil cult at Nippur had been neglected by the previous rulers, that this neglect had roused the anger of Ellil, and that the downfall of the Cassite dynasty was attributed to it. In perfect agreement with this is the fact that after Bitiliâshu no monuments of Cassite kings have been found at Nippur. But the new inscription from Nippur is even more explicit in its statements as to the causes which led to the elevation of Nebuchadrezzar to the throne of Babylonia. We are told that it was done for a threefold purpose: "that he might shepherd Shumer and Akkad, renew the sanctuaries of the city of dwellings and regulate the tithes of Ekur and Nippur" (Col. II, 1–3). Here the religious character of the movement is plainly indicated. Another significant title applied to Nebuchadrezzar is "the one who lays the foundation of the land," *mukîn išdi mâti* (Col. II, 24). As Nebuchadrezzar was not the first of the dynasty, it can hardly mean "the founder of the dynasty," as Winckler interpreted it,[3] but perhaps

[1] Ḫammurabi uses a similar title, *dŠamaš Bâbili mušêzi nûrim ana mâtuŠumêrim u Akkadim,* Code V, 4–9.

[2] For the meaning of *ablê,* see Glossary and Lau, J.A.O.S., Vol. 27, pp. 301f.

[3] Cf. Winckler, *Forschungen,* I, 519.

"the one who established the autonomy of the land," for we find the title used by Agukakrime (K.B., III, 136; Winckler, *Forschungen,* I, 517f.), the seventh Cassite king. It is also used by

Fig. 50.—Figure of a king, probably Nebuchadrezzar I., on the Stone of 'Amrân, now at Berlin.

Nebuchadrezzar II. (Langdon, *Building Inscriptions,* 16, I, 4), neither of whom were founders of dynasties. Nor could this title, in the sense of founder of a dynasty, be properly applied to Sargon,

FIG. 51.—Figure of a king, probably Nebuchadrezzar I., on III R. 41 (London, 106).

as we find it done by Shamash-shum-ukîn (C.T., X, pl. IV, 7), nor to Merodach-baladan II. (B.A., II, 261, Col. II, 44). Nabopolassor is the only one using this title (Sippar inscription, A.H., 82, 7–14, Col. I, 5) who can properly be called the founder of a dynasty. In view of these facts the translation, "the one who establishes the autonomy of the land," seems to be more appropriate, because it fits every case. Of great importance for the relation of Nebuchadrezzar I. to his contemporaries is the interesting inscription K. 2660 (III R. 38, 2), translated and discussed by Winckler (*Forschungen*, I, 534–38). Here we find that Zamama-shum-iddina, the next to the last Cassite king, was driven away by an Elamite king, whose name we now know from the inscriptions found at Susa[1] to have been Sutruk-naḫunte, who, it seems, had entrusted his son Kudur-naḫunte with the conquest of Babylonia. In the course of the following lines, which are badly broken, Ellil-nâdin-aḫu, the last Cassite king, is twice referred to, and it is stated that he (most likely the Elamite conqueror) swept away all the people of Akkad like a storm flood and devastated all their large cities (*nišê* *mâtu**Akkadi kul-lat-si-na a-bu-biš is-pu-nu* . . . . [*ma-ḫa*]-*zi ṣi-ru-ti na-gab-šu-nu u-še-me* [*kar-miš*], Obv. 7–8). By this same Elamite invasion another king suffered, who called Ellil-nâdin-aḫu "the king my predecessor" (*šarru pa-na maḫ-ri-ia*, Obv. 5). His name is broken off, but his title, "the offspring of Babylon" (*nabnît Bâbili*), still remains. Winckler is undoubtedly correct in restoring the missing name to Nebuchadrezzar, whose wars against Elam form the theme of several other hymns. This inscription, by connecting Ellil-nâdin-aḫu and Nebuchadrezzar so closely, implies clearly that they are contemporaneous. It constitutes, therefore, a valuable corroboration of the view recently advanced by Prof. Hilprecht that the first kings of the Isin (PA.-

[1] Cf. Scheil, D. E. P., V, pp. XV–XVI.

SHE) dynasty were contemporaneous with the last Cassite kings.[1] This view reconciles also the otherwise contradictory statements of the kings' list and Nebuchadrezzar's own inscriptions. From the evidence now at hand we can conclude that Nebuchadrezzar was a usurper, for his father is not given any royal titles; that at first he battled in vain against the Elamite and Assyrian supremacy, but after repeated reverses and late in his reign he was able to throw off the foreign yoke, ascend the throne of Babylonia and even extend his conquests to the Lulubeans in the east and the land *Amurru* in the west. This enabled him to assume the proud title, "king of the world" (*šar kiššati*). The case of Nebuchadrezzar I., fighting against the Elamites and only succeeding in the latter part of his reign in defeating them, has a close parallel in the history of Ḫammurabi, who only in the thirtieth year of his reign defeated the Elamites and in the following year Rim-Sin, king of Larsa, by which he was able to unite all of Babylonia under his rule.

If it is true that Nebuchadrezzar followed the last Cassite king immediately, it should be possible to remove the chronological objections which have been raised against this view by Winckler and others. These chronological difficulties are caused almost exclusively by assigning to the Assyrian kings more years than the inscriptions demand. Thus, *e.g.*, Winckler assigned at first[2] approximately twenty years to Ninib-apal-Ekur and about thirty-five years to Ashur-dân. Recent discoveries, however, have compelled him[3] to lower the reign of the first king to twelve years, and that of the latter to not more than twenty. The probabilities are that at least the reign of Ninib-apal-Ekur must be reduced still more. The following table offers the probable synchronisms of this period:

[1] Hilprecht, B.E., Vol. XX, Pt. 1, pp. 44f.

[2] Cf. *Forschungen*, Vol. I, pp. 135–138, 266–268.

[3] Cf. *Forschungen*, Vol. III, p. 347.

Babylonia.	Assyria.
Bitiliâshu Reign of eight years. Defeated by Tukulti-Ninib. Captured and brought to Assyria. All of Shumer and Akkad conquered (*Inscr. of Tukulti-Ninib,* Obv. 30–36; *Synchron. History,* S. 2106; *Babyl. Chronicle,* IV, 1).	**Tukulti-Ninib** Victorious war against Babylonia.
Ellil-nâdin-shum Reign of one year and six months. Elamite invasion by Kidin-ḫutrutash. Nippur and Dûrilu devastated. Ellil-nâdin-shum's rule overthrown (*Babyl. Chron.,* IV, 14–16).	
Kadashman-Ḫarbe Reign of one year and six months. Babylon taken by Tukulti-Ninib. Marduk statue taken to Assyria. Governors over Babylonia appointed (*Babyl. Chron.* IV, 3–8).	
Rammân-shum-iddina Reign of six years. Second Elamite invasion. Ishin captured. Battle at [Marad]da (*Babyl. Chron.* IV, 17–21). Nobles revolt and place on throne (*Babyl. Chron.,* IV, 8, 9).	**Tukulti-Ninib** rules Babylonia through governors seven years (*Babyl. Chron.,* IV, 3–7).
Rammân-shum-uṣur Reign of thirty years.	Nobles of Assyria revolt, dethrone and kill king and place on the throne **Aŝhur-nâṣir-aplu,** his son (*Babyl. Chron.,* IV, 9–11). **(Ninib)-tukulti-Ashur** flees to Babylonia and returns statue of Marduk and scepter of Shagaṙakti-Shuriash. Ashur-shum-lîshir entrusted with the government (IV R.[2] 34, No. 2). The nobles of Assyria place on throne

Meli-Shipak

Reign of fifteen years.

Writes letter (IV R.[2] 34, No. 2) to neighboring prince.

Isin dynasty begins.

The first two local kings reign 18 + 6 years at Isin.

Marduk-apal-iddina I.

Reign of thirteen years.

Zamama-shum-iddina

Reign of one year.

He is driven off by the Elamites (III R. 38, 21).

Ellil-nâdin-aḫu

Reign of three years.

Defeated by Elamites.

Akkad devastated (III R. 38, 2, 5–7).

ISIN DYNASTY.

Nebuchadrezzar I.

Reign of at least sixteen years.

Defeated by Elamites (III R. 38, 2, R. 4–15).

Drives out the Cassites (V R. 55, 10).

Defeated by Assyrian King Ashur-rishishi (*Syn. Hist.*, K. 4401*a* + R. 854).

Victorious over Elamites.

Marduk statue brought back (IV R. 20, 1, 10–14).

Conquers the Lulubeans and the West Land (V R. 55, 9–10).

Ellil-kudur-uṣur

(*J.R.A.S.*, 1904, 415.)

He is killed in war (*Synchron. History*, K. 4401*b*).

Ninib-apal-ekur

"Whose might like an *urinnu* spread over the land and who led the soldiers of Ashur aright" (*Tigl.*, VII, 57–59).

Conquered Ashur with help of Babylonian(?) king (*Synchr. Hist.*, K. 4401*b*).

Ashur-dân

"Who reached gray hairs and old age" (*Tigl.* VII, 54).

Invasion of Babylonia by Ashur-dân. The cities Zâban, Irria, Arsallu captured. Much booty carried to Assyria (*Syn. Hist.*, K. 4401*b*).

Mutakkil-Nusku

Ashur-rishishi

Compels Nebuchadrezzar to give up attack on Assyrian fortress Zanqi.

Defeats Nebuchadrezzar.

Captures forty of his chariots (*Syn. Hist.*, K. 4401*a* + R. 854).

TRANSLITERATION.

Šùm ^{abnu}narî[1] *an-ni-i ^{d}NIN.IB-*
u-^{d}Nusku-mu-kin-ku-dur[2]*-ri šùm-šu.*[3]

XXII (gur) 170 (qa) ^{sheu}zêru $\frac{1}{18}$ *GAN* 30 *qa I ammatu*[4] *rabîtu*[5]

<table>
<tr><td rowspan="3">nâru I-diq-lat</td><td colspan="4">IV UŠ šiddu elû amurrû UŠ.SA.DU</td></tr>
<tr><td>I UŠ pûtu šaplû šûtu kišâd[6] ^{nâru}Idiq-lat</i></td><td><i>Bît-^{md}Ṣir-ap-pi-li</td><td>nâr šarri</td><td>II UŠ X GAR pûtu elû iltânu UŠ.SA.DU bêl mâtâti[7]</td></tr>
<tr><td colspan="4">III UŠ LV GAR (šiddu šaplû)[8] šadû UŠ.SA.DU Bît-^{m}Su-ḫur-Gal-du</td></tr>
</table>

Col. I

^{d}En-lil[9] *bêl šá-qu-ú e-til šamê(-e) u irṣiti*
rubû[10] *bêl gim-ri*
šàr ilâni rabûti šá ina šamê(-e) u irṣiti
la i-ba-aš-šú-ú ilu ša-nin-šú
šá a-na na-dan ur-ti-šú ^{d}I-gí-gí
ap-pa i-lab-bi-nu ú-taq-qu-ú pal-ḫiš[11]
ù a-na ši-tul-ti-šú ^{d}A-nun-na-ku
aš-riš šú-ḫar-ru-ru na-zu-uz-zu šá-aḫ-tíš
be-el bêlum[12] *ša i-piš pî*[13]*-šú la ú-šam-sa-ku*
ilu ai-um-ma
ra-šub-bi ^{d}A-nun-na-ku be-el ṣal[14]*-mat qaqqadi*[15]

1 *NA.RÚ.A.*
2 *ku, dur.*
3 *MU.NE.*
4 *Ú.*
5 *GAL.*
6 *TIK.*
7 *EN.KUR.MEŠ.*
8 Omitted by scribe, see III, 2.
9 See Commentary.

TRANSLATION.

The name of this stone: "NIN.IB and Nusku establish the boundary," (such) is its name.

XXII (gur) 170 (qa) of seedfield, $\frac{1}{18}$ GAN (reckoned) at 30 qa of seed, (equivalent to) a large cubit

<table>
<tr><td rowspan="3">River Ti-gris.</td><td colspan="4">IV USH, upper length, west, adjoining</td></tr>
<tr><td>I USH, lower width south (adjoining) the bank of the Tigris</td><td>Bît-Ṣir-appili</td><td>Royal Canal</td><td>II USH, X GAR upper width, north, adjoining (the property of) the lord of countries.</td></tr>
<tr><td colspan="4">III USH, LV GAR (lower length) east, adjoining Bît-Suḫur-Gal-du.</td></tr>
</table>

Col. I

Ellil,—the lofty lord, the ruler of heaven and earth,
the prince, the lord of all,
the king of the great gods, whose equal as a god
does not exist in heaven and on earth,
upon the giving of whose command the Igigi
prostrate themselves, reverently pay homage,
and upon whose decision the Anunnaki
wait in submissive awe, stand in humble fear,
the lord of lords, the word of whose mouth
no god can set aside,
the potentate of the Anunnaki, the lord of the blackheaded,

[10] *NUN.* [11] *ut, tu tam.* [12] *EN.* [13] *KA.*
[14] *ni, ṣal.* [15] *SAG.DU.*

ka-bit mâtâti[16] *mut-tar-ru-ú ba-'-ú-la-ti*
ilu šá melammi[17]*-šú saḫ(?)*[18]*-pu-ú nam-ri-ir-ri ṣa-'-nu*

šá-ru-ru-šú ka-la si-ḫi-ip ša-ma-me
nap-ḫar qin-ni-e u kal da-ad-me lit-bu-uš-ma
ša-qum[19]*-mat-su mâtâti*[16] *ka-at-ma*
be-lut-su la iš-ša-na-nu la um-daš-ša-lu ilu-su

par(?)[20]*-su-šú šit-ru-ḫu billudû*[21]*-šú ṣîru*
šak-ku-šú riš-tu-ú al-ka-ka-tù-šu nak-la
mu-ma-'-ir šamê(-e) u irṣiti mu-kil mâtâti[16]
na-bu-ú rê'û[22] *ki-nu mu-ad-du-ú ša-kan irṣiti*

a-na šat-ti ina nûr[23] *pânû*[24]*-šu damqûti*[25] *ina bu-ni-šu nam-rù-ti*

^{d}*Nabû-kudurri*[26]*-uṣur*[27] *rubû*[28] *me-gir-šú*

muš-te-'-ú aš-ra-ti-šu ki-niš ip-pa-lis-ma

Col. II

a-na ^{h}*rê'û*[22]*-ut* ^{mâtu}*Šú-me-ri u Akkadi*[29]^{ki}
a-na ud-du-uš eš-rit ma-ḫa-az da-[a]d-me
ù sa-dar satuk[30] *E-kur u Nippur*[31]^{ki}
^{iṣu}*kakku*[32] *na-ki-ri-šú ú-šib-bir-ma*
ṣir-rit ^{h}*nakri*[33]*-šú qa-tu-uš-šú it-muḫ*
balâṭ[34] *ûmê da-ru-ú-ti iš-ruq-šum-ma*
eli šarri a-lik maḫ-ri ú-ša-tir šùm-šu.
Ina sa-dar satuk[35] *E-kur ina niqê*[36] *šum-du-li*

[16] *KUR.MEŠ.* [17] *M[E].LAM.* [18] Sign

[19] *lum.* [20] Text has *ME*, probably mistake of scribe.

[21] *PA+AN(GARZA).* [22] *SIB.* [23] *LAḪ.*

[24] *ŠI.MEŠ.* [25] *ŠI.BIR.MEŠ* [26] *ŠA.DU*

the sovereign of lands, the ruler of kingdoms,
The god, whose splendor is overwhelming(?) and filled with brilliancy,
with whose glory the whole extent of heaven,
all habitations and all dwellings are clothed,
with whose majesty the lands are covered,
whose rule cannot be rivalled, whose divinity cannot be equaled,
whose decision is weighty, whose command is lofty,
whose law is supreme, whose ways are wonderful,
who rules heaven and earth, who sustains the lands,
who calls the faithful shepherd, who appoints the governor of the earth,
forever,—with the light of his gracious countenance, with his shining face
he looked faithfully upon Nebuchadrezzar, the prince, his favorite,
who is devoted to his sanctuaries, and

Col. II

that he might shepherd Shumer and Akkad,
that he might renew the sanctuaries of the city of dwellings
and regulate the tithes of Ekur and Nippur
he broke the weapon of his enemy and
the sceptre of his enemy he placed in his hand,
a life of eternal days he granted to him and
above any preceding king he magnified his name.
Because of the regulation of the tithes of Ekur, because of the magnificent sacrifices,

[27] *ŠEŠ.* [28] *NUN.* [29] *URI.*
[30] Original reads *ŠÀ.SAG*, mistake for *ŠÀ.DUG.* [31] *EN.LIL.KI.*
[32] ^{iṣu}*KU.* [33] *KUR* (*PAP*). [34] *TI.LA.*
[35] *ŠÀ.DUG.* [36] *SIGIŠ.*

ina igisê[37] *ḫab-ṣu-ú-ti ina na-kín*[38]*-ti maḫ-ri* ^{d}*En-lil*
ina li-bi-en ap[39]*-pi ša a-na bêli u mâr bêli*

šá[40] *ana* ^{d}*En-lil u* ^{d}*NIN.IB pal-ḫi-iš ú-taq-qu-ú*
ina zu-ru-ub ZI.ŠAG.GAL-li ina amât[41] *šarri nisakki*[42]

^{md}*Nusku-ib-ni mâr* ^{m}*Upaḫḫir*[43]*-*^{d}*Nusku nisak*[42] ^{d}*En-lil*
[UḪ.ME][44]*.ZU.AB* ^{d}*Nusku laputtû*[45] *DUR.AN.KI*
[a]-na šarri rê'î[28] *ki-ni rubû* [51] *me-gir* ^{d}*En-lil*

ina ut-ni-ni-šú ki-niš ippalis[46]*-su-ma*
^{md}*Ba-ú-šùm-iddina*[47]*(-na) mâr* ^{m}*Ḫu-un-na i-bir bêli-šu*
na-an-za-az maḫ-ḫar šarri ki-zu-ú ša ultu[48] *ul-la*
at-mu-šú na-as-qu-ma šú-zu-uz-zu ina maḫ-ri
šakkanak[49] *Bâbili*[50]^{ki} *ša-kìn Bît-*^{md}*Sin-še-me*
rubû[51] *me-gir-šú ú-ma-ir-ma*
ina qa-bi-e šar me-ša-ri
^{d}*Nabû-kudurri*[52]*-uṣur*[53] *šàr kiššati*[54]
mu-kin iš-di ma-a-ti
XXII (gur) 170 (qa) ^{šeu}*zêru eqlu qi-ru-ba-a*
šá a-na bu-tuq-ti šaknu[55]*(-nu)*
ugâr[56] *âli ša Mâr-*^{m}*Aḫ*[53]*-at-tu-ú-a*
ina kišâd[57] ^{nâru}*Idiqlat*[58] *ina piḫât*[59] *Bît-*^{md}*Sin-še-me*
ša ultu[48] *ûmi(-mi) pa-na i-ku la šap-ku*
abšênu[60] *la šú-zu-za-at-ma a-na me-riš-ti*
la šú-lu-ku-ú-ma a-na me-te-iq mê šaknu[55]*(-nu)*

I[V]UŠ šiddu elû amurrû[61] *UŠ.SA.DU*

[37] *ŠI.DI.* [38] *ḫar, mur.* [39] Text has *at*, by mistake.
[40] Text has *ta*, by mistake. [41] *KA.*
[42] *NU.AB.* [43] *KIL.* [44] Cf. III, 11.
[45] *NU.TUR.* [46] *ŠI.BAR.* [47] *SE.*
[48] *TA.* [49] *NER.ARAD.* [50] *KA.DINGIR.RA.KI.*

because of the rich gifts and the treasures (laid) before Ellil,
because of the prostrations, with which to the lord and the son of the lord,
with which to Ellil and NIN.IB he showed his respectful reverence,
because of the utterance of supplications, because of the prayer of the king, the priest,
Nusku-ibni, the son of Upaḫḫir-Nusku, the priest of Ellil,
the UḪ.ME.ZU.AB of Nusku, the chief of *Duranki*,
to the king, the faithful shepherd, the prince, the favorite of Ellil,
because of his (the king's) supplication, he looked faithfully, and
Bau-shum-iddina, the son of Ḫunna, the friend of his lord.
who stood before the king, the servant whose word
was always weighty and respected before the
potentate of Babylon, the governor of Bît-Sin-sheme,
the prince, his favorite, he sent and
upon the command of the king of righteousness,
Nebuchadrezzar, the king of the world,
who has laid the foundation of the land,
XXII (gur) 170 (qa) of seedfield, arable land,
which had been exposed to flooding,
a field of the town of Mâr-Aḫattûa,
on the bank of the Tigris, in the district of Bît-Sin-sheme,
where since ancient days no ditch had been dug,
no vegetation had grown up and which had not been brought
under cultivation, but had been exposed to the inroads of the water,—namely
IV USH, upper length, west, adjoining

51 *NUN.* 52 *ŠA.DU(NIN.GUB).* 53 *ŠES.*
54 *ḪI(SAR).* 55 *ŠA-nu.* 56 *A.KAR.*
TIK. 58 *MAŠ.TIK.ḲAR.* 59 *NAM.*
60 *AB.SIM.* 61 *IM.MAR.TU.*

Col. III

Bît-^{md}Ṣir-ap-pi-li u piḫât[62] *Bît-^{md}Sin-še-me*
III UŠ LV GAR šiddu šaplû šadû
UŠ.SA.DU Bît-^{m}Su-ḫur-Gal-du
II UŠ X GAR pûtu elû iltânu UŠ.SA.DU
Bît-^{m}Uš-bu-la ša a-na bêl mâtâti nadnu[63]*(-nu)*
I UŠ pûtu šaplû šûtu kišâd[57] *^{nâru}Idiqlat*[58]
napḫar[64] *XXII (gur) $168\frac{2}{3}$ (qa) 5 (gin) ^{sheu}zêru $\frac{1}{18}$ GAN 30 qa*
I ammatu[65] *rabîtu*
ugâr[56] *âli ša Mâr-^{m}Aḫ*[53]*-at-tu-ú-a piḫat*[62] *Bît-^{md}Sin-še-me*

^{md}Ba-ú-šùm-iddina(-na) ša-kìn Bît-^{m}Sin-še-me
im-šú-uḫ-ma ^{md}Nusku-ib-ni mâr ^{m}Upaḫḫir[66]*-^{d}Nusku*
^{h}nisak[67] *^{d}En-lil UḪ.ME.ZU.AB ^{d}Nusku*
ḫa-za-an ^{âlu}Nippur^{ki} arad[68]*-su ana ûmê(-me) ṣa-a-ti*
i-ri-im. pa-lik eqlu šú-a-tu ^{md}Nabû-zêr-lîšir[69]
mâr ^{m}Itti-^{d}Marduk-balâṭu[70] *ŠÀ.BAL.BAL ^{m}Ardi-^{d}Ea*
u ^{md}Nabû-un-na mâr ^{m}A-ḫi ^{h}ša-kin ṭe-me
ša Bît-^{md}Sin-še-me.
Ma-ti-ma ana ûmê(-me) da-ru-ú-ti
a-na aḫ-rat nišê[71] *a-pa-ti*
lu-ú rê'û[72] *lu-ú šakkanakku*[73] *lu ak-lu lu ša-pi-ru*
lu ri-du-ú lu ḫa-za-an-nu ša-ar-qi eqlu šú-a-tu
i-nam-du-ma a-na i-ki-li ri-'-ti
ú-ma-'-a-ru ša-nam-ma
ina[74] *lim-ni-ti ú-šá-ḫa-zu*
ubâni[75]*-šú a-na limutti*[76]*(-ti) i-tar-ra-ṣu*
ina il-ki di-ku-ti ṣa-bat amêlu ḫi-ri-e nâra
ba-qa-an šam-mi kal-li-e nâri u ta-ba-li

[62] *NAM.* [63] *SE-nu.* [64] *ŠÚ.NIGIN.* [65] *Ú GAL*
[66] *KIL.* [67] *NU.AB.* [68] *ARAD.*
[69] *SI.DI.* [70] *TI.LA.* [71] *UN.MEŠ.*

Col. III

Bît-Ṣir-appili and the district of Bît-Sin-sheme III USH, LV GAR, lower length, east, adjoining Bît-Suḫur-Gal-du, II USH, X GAR, upper width, north, adjoining Bît-Ushbula, which had been given to the Lord of countries, I USH, lower width, south, on the bank of the Tigris, in all XXII (gur) $168\frac{2}{3}$ (qa) 5 (gin) of seedfield, $\frac{1}{18}$ GAN (reckoned) at 30 qa of seed, (equivalent to) a large cubit, a field of the town of Mâr-Aḫattûa, in the district of Bît-Sin-sheme, Bau-shum-iddina, the governor of Bît-Sin-sheme, measured and to Nusku-ibni, son of Upaḫḫir-Nusku, the priest of Ellil, the UḪ.ME.ZU.AB of Nusku, the magistrate of Nippur, his servant, forever granted. The surveyors of this field were Nabû-zêr-lîshir, son of Itti-Marduk-balâṭu, a descendant of Ardi-Ea and Nabunna, son of Aḫi, the commander of Bît-Sin-sheme. For all future days! Whenever one (who dwells) in human habitations, be it a ruler or a potentate, a governor or a regent, a levymaster or a magistrate, overthrows the grant of this field and in order to secure the use of the pasture land sends some one and with evil intent causes (its) seizure, stretches out his finger to do evil, under the obligation of a levy permits a canal or land-officer to seize a canal digger or to cut down plants,

72 *SIB.* 73 *NER.ARAD.*

74 Written on erasure of *ši.*

75 *ŠU.SI.* 76 *ḪUL.*

uš-aš-šú-ú ú[-šad-ba-bu(?)][77]*-ma eqlu šú-a-t[u]*
ik-ki-mu ú[-ša-aš-ra-qu(?)[77] *a-na] piḫâti i-t[u-ur-ru]*
ul ri-ḫu. . . . .
u ^{md}*Ba-[ú-šùm-iddina(-na) ša-kìn Bît-*^{md}*Sin-še-me]*[78]
a-na ^{md}*[Nusku-ib-ni mâr* ^{m}*Upaḫḫir-*^{d}*Nusku.*[79] . . . .]
ḫa-za[-an ^{âlu}*Nippur*$^{80 ki}$ *ul i-ri-im-šu i-qab-bu-ú(?)]*[77]
eqlu [šú-a-tu ul ma-ši-iḫ(?)][81]

Col. IV

ul ša-ri-iq ul na-di-in
ul ma-ḫi-ir-mi i-qab-bu-ú
^{d}*A-nu šarru abi*[82] *ilâni ag-giš li-tal-lik-šu-ma*

nap-šá-tuš[83] *li-bal-li.*
^{d}*En-lil*[84] *bêl ša-qu-ú mu-šim*
ši-mat ilâni ši-mat ma-ru-uš-ti
li-šim-šú-ma lu-ub-na ni-el-me-na
a-mat nišê[85] *li-gi-sa-šú.*
^{d}*E-a šàr apsî*[86] *bêl ta-šim-ti*
nu-gu ka-bit[87]*-ti nu-mur libbi na-ḫa-ša*
ḫa-ba-ṣa li-kim-šú-ma
ni-is-sa-tu li-ilqî[88]*-šú.*
^{d}*Sin*[89] *bêl agê*[90] *na-me-ru-ti*
bu-ni-šú liṭ-ṭe-šú-ma lil-li ai îši.[91]
^{d}*Šamaš u* ^{d}*Rammân ilâni ga-aš-ru-tu*
daianê[92] *ṣîrûti*[93] *lu mu-lam-me-nu*
i-gir-ri-šu šú-nu-ma di-in kit-ti
u me-ša-ri ai i-di-nu-šu.
^{d}*NIN.IB bêl me-iṣ-ri u kudurri*[94] *kudurra-šu lissuḫ*[95]*(-uḫ).*

[77] See Commentary. [78] Cf. Col. III, 9. [79] Cf. Col. III, 10.
[80] Cf. Col. III, 12. [81] Cf. Col. III, 10, and Commentary.
[82] *AD.* [83] *ku, tuš.* [84] *EN.LIL.*
[85] *UN.MEŠ.* [86] *ZU.AB.* [87] *be, bad.*

who [makes a claim] and takes
that field [who gives it away or] returns it to the crown
and says it has not.................................
or [Bau-shum-iddina, the governor of Bît-Sin-sheme]
has not [given it to Nusku-ibni, son of Upaḫḫir-Nusku,]
the ma[gistrate of Nippur.......],
says that [field has not been measured]

Col. IV

has not been presented, has not been given,
has not been received—
May Anu, the king, the father of the gods, in anger overthrow him
and annihilate his life,
Ellil, the lofty lord, who appoints
the fate of the gods, appoint for him
an evil fate, so that calamity, misfortune
and the commands of men may oppress him.
Ea, the king of the ocean, the lord of wisdom,
take away from him gladness of heart, happiness of mind,
abundance and fullness, so that
lamentation may seize him.
Sin, the lord of the crown of splendor
darken his face, so that he may not have merriment(?).
Shamash and Rammân, the powerful gods,
the lofty judges, give him
evil plans, and with a judgment of justice
and righteousness may they not judge him.
NIN.IB, the lord of confines and boundaries, tear out his boundary-stone.

[88] *ŠU.TI.* [89] *dXXX.* [90] *MIR.*
[91] *TUK.* [92] *DI.KUD.* [93] *MAḪ.MEŠ.*
[94] *ŠA.DU.* [95] *ZI*

^{d}*Gu-la bêltu*[96] *rabîtu si-im-ma la-az-za*
ina zumri[97]*-šu liškun*[98]*-ma dâma*[99] *u šarqa*[100] *kîma*[101] *mê*[102] *li-ir-muk.*
^{d}*Iš-tar bêlit*[96] *mâtâti ša ru-ub-ša a-bu-bu*
nam-ra-ṣa li-kal-lim-šu-ma ai ú-ṣi
ina ú-ša-ki.
^{d}*Nusku*[103] *bêl ga-aš-rum a-ri-rum ka-ru-bu*
[*ilu*] *ban-nu-ú-a lu rabiṣu*[104] *limutti*[105]*-šu šú-ma*
li-qa-am-me šur-ši-šú
[*ša* ^{abnu}[106]] *narâ*[107] *an-na-a*
........*ŠIM.MEŠ ina e-pi-ri*
i-tam-me-ru

Col. V

ina išâti[108] *i-qal-lu-ú a-na mê*[102] *inamdû*[109](*-ú*)
ina ^{iṣu}*lipitti*[110] *i-pi-ḫu-ú sa-ak-la*
sa-ak-ka lâ šêmâ[111] *ú-ša-aš-šú-ma*
a-šar la a-ma-ri i-ša-ka-nu
ilâni rabûti ma-la ina ^{abnu}*narî*[112]
an-ni-i šùm-šu-nu zakrû[113] *ar-rat limutti*[114]
li-ru-ru-šu išid[115]*-su lissuḫû*[116](*-ḫu*) *u zêri-šu liḫalliqû.*[117]
I-na ka-nak li-ú[118] *šú-a-tu*
^{md}*Šamaš-nâṣir*[119] ^{h}*šaq-šup-par*[120] ^{md}*Sin-še-me*
^{m}*Ku-bu-bu amel bâb*[121] *êkalli*[122] *Bît-*^{md}*Sin-še-me*
^{m}*Ši-ta-ri-ba* ^{h}*šaq*[123] *Bît-*^{md}*Sin-še-me*
^{m}*Ta-qi-šú mâr* ^{m}*Ki-in-pî*[124]*-*^{d}*Šamaš*
^{h}*ša-kin bu-ši Bît-*^{md}*Sin-še-me*
^{m}*A-tu-'-ú mâr* ^{m}*Ki-diš*(*daš*) ^{h}*bârû*[125] *Bît-*^{md}*Sin-še-me*

96 *GAŠAN.* 97 *SU.* 98 *ŠA*, cf. Susa 3, Col. VII, 21
99 *BE.* 100 *BE.UD.* 101 *KIM.*
102 *A.MEŠ.* 103 *dPA.KU.* 104 *MAŠKIM.*
105 *ḪUL.* 106 See Commentary. 107 *NA.RÚ.A.*
108 *NE.* 109 *RU.* 110 *LIBIT.*
111 *ŠI.NU.TUK.* 112 *TAḲ NA.RÚ.A.* 113 *MU.*

Gula, the great mistress, put lingering sickness
into his body, so that dark and bright red blood he may pour out as water.
Ishtar, the mistress of lands, whose fury is like a flood,
reveal difficulties to him, so that he may not escape from misfortune.
Nusku, the powerful lord, the mighty scorcher,
[the god], my creator, be his evil demon and may he burn his root.
Whoever [removes?] this stone
hides it in the dust,

Col. V

burns it with fire, throws it into water,
shuts it up in an enclosure, causes a fool,
a deaf man, a witless man to take it,
places it in an invisible place,
may the great gods as many as are mentioned
by their names on this stone, curse him
with an evil curse, tear out his foundation and destroy his seed.
At the sealing of this document
Shamash-nâṣir, the *shaq-shuppar* of Sin-sheme,
Kububu, the gatekeeper of the palace of Bît-Sin-sheme,
Shi-tariba, the dignitary of Bît-Sin-sheme,
Taqîshu, son of Kîn-pî-Shamash,
the administrator of the property of Bît-Sin-sheme,
Atu'u, son of Kidish, the seer of Bît-Sin-sheme,

[114] *ḪUL.* [115] Br. 4811. [116] *ZI.*
[117] The original reads *A.ḪA.ME* instead of *ḪA.A.ME.*
[118] See Commentary. [119] *ŠEŠ.*
[120] Written on erasure of *bît.* [121] *KÀ.*
[122] *E.GAL.* [123] *SAG.* [124] *KA.* [125] *hḪAL.*

^{m}*Ri-mut-*^{d}*Gu-la bêl paḫâti*[126] *Bît-*^{md}*Sin-še-me*
^{md}*Nabû*[127]*-un-na mâr* ^{m}*A-ḫi* ^{h}*ša-kin*
ṭe-me ^{âlu}*Dûr-Rîm*[128]*-*^{d}*Sin Bît-*^{md}*Sin-še-me*
^{m}*Kaš-šú-ú tup-šar nisak*[129] *Bît-*^{md}*Sin-še-me*
^{md}*Sin-zêr-ib-ni ḫa-za-an* ^{âlu}*Dûr-Rîm*[128]*-*^{d}*Sin*
Bît-^{md}*Sin-še-me* ^{m}*Pir*[130]*-šá* ^{h}*nâgir*[131] *Bît-*^{md}*Sin-še-me*
^{m}*Amel-*^{âlu}*I-ši-in mâr* ^{m}*Ḫu-un-na*
^{m}*Kaš-šu-ú mâr* ^{m}*Ḫu-un-na*
^{md}*Gu-la-zêr-iqîša*[132]*(-ša) mâr* ^{m}*Ḫu-un-na*
u ^{md}*Nabû*[127]*-zêr-lîšir*[133] *mâr* ^{m}*Ardi-*^{d}*E-a*
iz-za-zu.
šattu XVI ^{kan} ^{d}*Nabû-kudurri-uṣur*[134] *šarru.*

[126] *EN.NAM.*
[127] *dAG.*
[128] *AM.*
[129] *NISAG.GA.*
[130] *ut, tu, tam.*
[131] *LIGIR,* see Br. 6966.
[132] *BA-ša.*
[133] *SI.DI.*
[134] *dAG.ŠA-DU.ŠEŠ.*

Rimût-Gula, the governor of Bît-Sin-sheme,
Nabunna, son of Aḫi, the commander
of Dûr-Rîm-Sin in Bît-Sin-sheme,
Kashshû, the scribe, the priest of Bît-Sin-sheme,
Sin-zêr-ibni, the magistrate of Dûr-Rîm-Sin
in Bît-Sin-sheme, Pirsha, the prefect of Bît-Sin-sheme,
Amel-Ishin, son of Ḫunna,
Kashshû, son of Ḫunna,
Gula-zêr-iqîsha, son of Ḫunna,
Also Nabû-zêr-lîshir, son of Ardi-Ea,
were present.
The 16th year of King Nebuchadrezzar.

COMMENTARY.

THE heading of the inscription written among the symbols is a nominal sentence, whose predicate, for emphasis sake, has been placed at the head of the sentence. Cf. the other nominal sentences in this inscription, Col. IV, 15–17, 26, and Delitzsch, Gr., § 140. For similar constructions in Hebrew see Gesenius-Kautzsch, *Hebr. Gram.*,[26] p. 446*d*.

The gods NIN.IB and Nusku are combined in this heading as guardians of the boundary, because they were, alongside of Ellil, the chief gods worshipped at Nippur. The earliest references to both of them are found in the reign of Dungi, the first king of the second dynasty of Ur (cf. Thureau-Dangin, *Inscriptions de Sumer et d'Akkad*, pp. 278, B; 330, 1) . Their worship became prominent at Nippur during the Cassite dynasty. Not only do we find numerous votive objects, dedicated to Nusku (O. B. I., Vol. I, Nos. 51, 54, 58, 59, 64, 71, 75, 138) and NIN.IB (O. B. I., Vol. I, Nos. 31, 32, 61, 62, 76), but they also occur together in the oath formula of contract tablets dated in the Cassite period. For example, Clay (B. E., XIV, 40, 22–24) reads: *niš(MU) ᵈEn-lil ᵈNIN.IB ᵈNusku ù Ku-ri-gal-zu šarru (LUGAL.E) mitḫâriš (UR.BI) itmû (IN.PAD.DE.EŠ)*, *i.e.*, "by the name of Ellil, NIN.IB, Nusku and King Kurigalzu together they swore" (cf. also B. E., XIV, 1, 18–20; 7, 28–30).

As to the pronunciation of *NIN.IB* see the Aramaic transliteration אנושת (Clay, B. E., X, pp. XVIII, 8), for which Prof. Clay offers the ingenious explanation: *ên-waštu* = *ên-maštu* = *ên-martu*, *i.e.*, "Lord of the West Land" (cf. J. A. O. S., July, 1907).

MU.NE = *MU.NI* = *šùm-šu*, see Br. 4,600, 5,330.

The drawing of the field is not a correct geometrical figure, corresponding to the measurements as given in the text, but the stonecutter adapted it to the space at his disposal. The correct drawing would have been as follows:

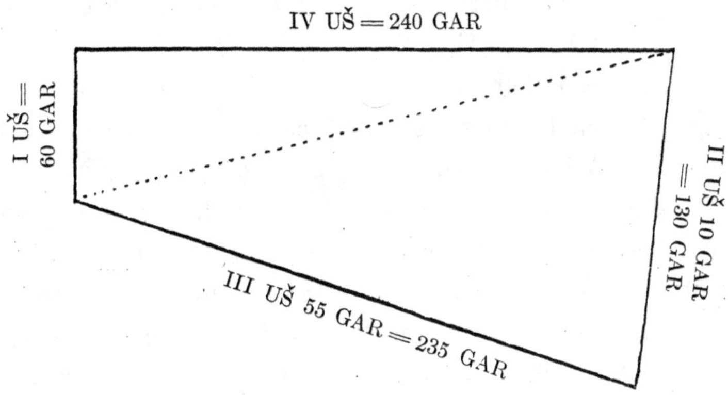

This would give a square area of $60 \times 120 = 7{,}200$ GAR² + $235 \times 65 = 15{,}275$ GAR², in all 22,475 GAR².

Now assuming the correctness of the usual statements (Reissner, in S. B. B. A., 1896, p. 477f., and Z. A., XI, p. 422; Thureau-Dangin, R. A., IV, pp. 18ff.; IV, p. 80, and Z. A., XI, p. 428; Johns, A. D. D., II, p. 231) that 1 gur = 300 QA, 1 QA = 3 GAR, 1 gur = 900 GAR², 1 GAN = 1,800 GAR², we obtain the following result:

$$
\begin{array}{l}
900 : 22475 \text{ GAR}^2 = 24 \text{ GUR} \\
\quad\;\; 1800 \\
\hline
\quad\;\;\; 4475 \\
\quad\;\;\; 3600 \\
\hline
3 : 875 = 291\tfrac{2}{3}\text{QA}
\end{array}
$$

This sum, 24 GUR, 291⅔ QA, shows that a mistake has been made, either by the scribe or possibly by the surveyor, in giving the length of one or several of the sides. If it were possible to take

1 GUR at 1,000 GAR² we would come much nearer to the 22 (gur) 168⅔ (qa) 5 (gin), the result of the measurement of the surveyors (Col. III, 7), for we would obtain on that basis 22 (gur) 158⅓ (qa), which differs only by 10⅓ qa, 5 gin from the sum given by the surveyors. For a similar error see the *Caillou de Michaux* (I R. 70); cf. Johns, A. D. D., Vol. II, p. 232.

From the fact that the ancient formula *DIL.GAN.AŠ* is used, it may be concluded that the old system of measurement, making 1 gur = 300 QA, is employed. The phrase *DIL.GAN.AŠ* has caused considerable discussion. Delitzsch (B. A., II, 273) and others read: *ina KAR.AŠ I ammatu rabîtu*, and explain the whole phrase as meaning "according to the square yard." But the investigations of Thureau-Dangin have shown that the first two signs are used in the GAN.SAR scale to denote $\frac{1}{18}$ GAN (according to Oppert, 1 GAN), while AŠ denotes 30 qa of seed, used to seed $\frac{1}{18}$ GAN. Hence Thureau-Dangin explains the whole expression as meaning "$\frac{1}{18}$ GAN is reckoned at 30 qa of seed and equal to one *ammatu rabîtu*." The latter is 32,400 Ú² = 100 GAR (DU)² = $\frac{1}{18}$ GAN (cf. R. A., IV, 19). According to this interpretation two systems of measurements have been combined in this expression—one which determined the size of the field by the amount of seed it took to sow it, the other by the number of yards it contained.

The reading of *Ú-GAL(-tum)* is now certain from the stone of Agabtaḫa (D. E. P., II, 95, ll. 4, 5), which reads: 10 *zêrê i-na am-ma-ti ra-bi-i-ti.*

The field, presented by Nebuchadrezzar to Nusku-ibni, was not situated in the neighborhood of Nippur, as might be expected, but it lay most likely in Northern Babylonia. This seems to follow from the fact that the field was bounded on its northwestern side (*iltânu*) by the royal canal and on the southwest (*šûtu*) by the Tigris. All the references to the "Royal Canal" point to Northern Babylonia. The Semitic name *nâr šarri* appears first in the

Cassite period. The boundary stone of Nazi-Maruttash informs us that the city of Pilarî, in the government of Ḫudâdi (Col. II, 2–4), and the city of Karî in the government of Upî (Col. II, 17–19), were located at the royal canal. The latter is the classical Opis at the mouth of the Adhem river (cf. Winckler, *Altor. Forsch.*, II, 509ff., and Hommel, *Geographie und Geschichte*, 346ff.). According to the new boundary stone of Meli-Shipak from Susa (Susa, No. 3) the city Tamakku, belonging to the environs of Akkad in the government of Bît-Pir'-[d]Amurru (Col. I, 3–6) and the town Shalḫi, belonging to the land of the goddess Ishtar of Akkad (Col. II, 47–54), bordered on the royal canal. The same inscription records the immunity of the people of Akkad from conscription to repair the sluices of the royal canal (Col. II, 25–29). It also refers to a connecting canal (*mê ša mušêbiri*), which joined the canal Râṭi-Anzan with the canal of the royal province (*nâr piḫâti ša šarri*, Col. III, 1–3). Another inscription of Meli-Shipak (London, 101) locates the town Shaluluni, in the government of Bît-Pir'-[d]Amurru, at the royal canal (Col. I, 5, 6). The royal canal is also most likely meant by the *kišâd na-ga-ar šarri*, referred to on a fragmentary boundary stone, D. E. P., II, 112, 5. On the charter of Nebuchadrezzar I., granted to the priests Shamûa and Shamai (C. T., IX, pls. 4, 5), the district *Bît-[m]Ma-zi* (or perhaps better *Bît-[m]Ba-zi*), "of the royal canal," is mentioned (pl. IV, 24).

The new boundary stone of Nebuchadrezzar I. from Nippur locates the town of Mâr-Aḫ-attûa, in the government of Bît-Sin-sheme, at the royal canal, and places Bît-Ṣir-appili and Bît-Suḫur-Gal-du in its immediate vicinity. It also shows that the land was bordered on its southeastern side (*šûtu*) by the Tigris, and on its northwestern side by Bît-Ushbula, which was temple property. The land of Nusku-ibni adjoined this temple land, while, according to the plot of the field, the royal canal passed through its northwestern end. On the boundary stone of Marduk-aḫê-erba (O. B. I., 149,

Col. I, 6, 11) the canal *nâr* $^{(\hat{a}lu)}$*Ša-šar-ri*^{ki} is mentioned, which Streck (*Deutsche Lit. Zeit.*, 1905, p. 618) includes among the references to the royal canal. But it is safer to take *Šašarri* as one word which does not refer to the royal canal (cf. p. 196). Under Merodach-baladan II. (668-648 B.C.) we find the field (*ugâru*) of Dun-ni-edinni and Nurzu (perhaps also a city) situated on the royal canal.

Unfortunately the references to the royal canal in the contract tablets do not help us materially to fix its location. Strassmaier, Nbn., 483, refers to tithe (*ešrû*), the property of Shamash, of the tenth year of King Nabû-na'id. In the text occurs this passage: *a-di* $^{\hat{a}lu}$*Za-za-an-nu* 50 *gur ultu muḫ-ḫi nâr šarri a-di muḫ-ḫi* $^{n\hat{a}ru}$*Idiqlat* (Nbn., 483, 6, 7). This statement, which does not go beyond the new boundary stone from Nippur, except that it seems to locate the town Zazannu in the neighborhood of the royal canal, is the most definite that occurs; all the others are indefinite. Cyrus 26 : 17, a text dated at Sippar, refers to the *nâr šarri* in a broken passage. Cyrus 181 : 11, *suluppu GIŠ.BAR ša muḫ-ḫi nâr šarri*. Camb. 44 : 5 locates a field at royal canal, but the boundaries of the other three sides are unfortunately broken off. Cf. also Darius 198 : 4 and Dar. 411 : 7–9. The latter refers to a royal canal in Elam. It reads: *a-di-i u-il-tim maḫrîtim(-tim) ša* 1½ *ma-na kaspi ša a-na dul-lu ša nâr šarri ša* $^{m\hat{a}tu}$*Êlamti nadna(SE-na)*. Finally one of the Murashû texts refers to the royal canal, but again in such general terms that no definite inference is possible. B.E., IX, 73, 1–3, reads: *II gur* 24 *qa* $^{she'u}$*šamaššammu zitti šarri ša ina uz-ba-ri ša šarri ša ina muḫ-ḫi nâr šarri ša ina pâni* ^{m}*Rimut-*^{d}*NIN.IB aplu ša Mu-ra-šú-ú*. The same is true of a passage in the Harper Letters, No. 275, Rev. 4. For a recent discussion of the "royal canal" see Hommel, *Geographie*, pp. 284–6.

UŠ.SA.DU. The pronunciation of this word is still unknown. Oppert (*Doc. jur.*, p. 99) proposed *emêdu*; Belser (B. A., II, p. 135) *ṭîḫ*. The former, however, is a verb, while *UŠ.SA.DU* is here used as a preposition. The latter is admittedly only a hypothetical reading. The form *UŠ.SA* is used in the date list of the first dynasty, published by King (*Letters of Ḫammurabi*, Vol. III, pp. 212–253), in the sense of "after" or "next" (King, p. 310), *DU* = *nazâzu* (Br. 4,893), hence the ideogram means literally "standing after" or "standing next." See Daiches, *Altbabylonische Rechtsurkunden*, p. 21, and the discussion of Arno Poebel as to the use of *MU.US.SA* in the contract tablets of the first dynasty (Z. A., XX, pp. 234–238).

Col. I, 1. The recent investigations of Prof. Clay ("Ellil, the God of Nippur," in A. J. S. L., XXIII (July, 1907), pp. 269–279) have shown that in the Aramaic endorsements of the Murashû tablets the name, which was formerly read *Bêl-nâdin-shumu*, is transliterated אלל שו אדן, *i.e.*, *Ellil-šum(w)-iddin* (cf. B. E., IX, 66*a*), which proves that the god ^{d}En-lil is not to be pronounced Bêl, but Ellil. This is corroborated by the equation, *Il-lil* = ^{d}*En-lil* in V R. 37 : 21 and the transliteration Ἴλλινος of Damascius.

Many of the titles applied in this hymn to Ellil are in other hymns transferred to other gods. *Etil šamê u irṣiti* is applied to Shamash by Agu-kakrime, Col. VIII, 7–9.

I, 2. The title *bêl gimri* is also applied to Ea. Cf. IV R.[2] 56, II, 9, *bân kullati bêl gimri*, "creator of everything, lord of all."

I, 3. With the title *šar ilâni rabûti* may be compared the titles of Marduk, *šar ilâni* (B. A., V, 381, No. 2, Col. II, 1), *bêl ilâni rabûti* (B. A., V, 375, No. 24, 10), *etil ilâni* (B. A., V, 325, No. 3, 1), *qarrad ilâni* (B. A., V, 330, No. 5, 18).

I, 4. To *lâ ibaššu ilu šâninšu* corresponds Marduk's title *ša šânina la išû* (B. A., V, 334, No. 7, 18) and *ša šin-na-as-su la ibaššû* (B. A., V, 329, No. 5, 12).

I, 6. *appa ilabbinû*. The same phrase is applied to the Igigi before Nabû, Rm. III, 15 (*[ina ilu]-ti-šu ka-bit-ti Igigi ap-pi i-lab-bi-*

na-šu, cf. Winckler, *Altorientalische Forschungen*, I, 254, l. 12). Of Nergal it is said, [d]*A-nun-na-ki ap-pa i-lab-bi-nu-ka*, Böllenrücher, *Gebete an Nergal*, No. 7, II, 36, p. 44. Similarly of Sin, cf. IV R.[2] 9, 59, 60*a*. Cf. also Schrank, *Priester und Büsser in Babylonischen Sühnriten*, pp. 58f.

The verb *ú-taq-qu-ú* stands here in parallelism with *appa ilabbinû*, from which it may be argued that it has the same or a similar meaning. This raises at once the question, whether the usual derivation from אקה or וקה (see Delitzsch, H. W., 123*a*) is correct. In favor of Delitzsch's rendering it may be urged that the syllabaries connect it with *še-mu-ú*, "obedient" (in S[d] 24 *ú-te-ku-ú* follows *še-mu-ú*), and with *pu-uq-qu* (פוק) and *nu-up-pu-qu*, "to pay attention, to await" (the ideograms [*ḪAR*].*DA* and [*ḪAR.DA*]. *AG.A* are shared in common by them, see K. 4,188, III, 55–59). But the historical inscriptions clearly connect it with "bowing," *e.g.*, Nebuch. E. H., II, 61, reads: *ilâni šu-ut šamê u irṣiti pa-al-ḫi-iš ú-tak-ku-šu ka-am-su iz-za-zu maḫ-ru-uš-šu*. Here it stands in parallelism to the phrase, "bowed they stood before him." To do justice to all the passages I propose to connect *utaqqû* with a verb *taqû*, which corresponds to the Arabic تَقَى, "to fear god," which in turn is the eighth form of وَقَى, "to fear or reverence God." Accordingly *utaqqû* is the Piel (II, 1) of תקה, and means "to show reverence or obedience." If this explanation is correct, the phrase *utaqqû palḫiš* is not absolutely synonymous with *appa ilabbinû*, but rather gives the reason for the prostration; it was to show their reverence.

I, 7. The form *A-nun-na-ku* is exceptional. It is not singular but plural, hence *Anunnakû* (cf. IV R. 45, 30f., *ilâni rabûti* [ilâni]*I-gi-gu ša ša-me-e* [ilâni]*A-nun-na-ku ša irṣiti*). The meaning of the Sumerian *A.NUN.NA* is given (K. 4,829, Rev. 5f. = Hrozný, *Mythen*, pp. 18, 19) as *riḫût rubê*, *i.e.*, "offspring of the great," namely "abyss." Compare with this *DAM.GAL.NUN.NA*, "the great mistress of the abyss." For recent discussions of the Igigi and Annunaki see Hrozný, *Mythen*, pp. 84–89; Zimmern, K. A. T.[3], 451–56; Morgenstern, *The Doctrine of Sin in the Babylonian Religion*, M. V. A. G., X (1905), pp. 161–167.

I, 8. *šuḫarrurû* and *nazuzzû* are both permansives, 3d pl., *nazúzzû* = *nazuzû* = *nazzuzû* = *nanzuzû*, IV, 1 of נזז. The metrical accent has caused the form *nazúzzû* instead of *nánzuzû*. The parallelism and metrical form of ll. 6 and 8 are evident. They are as follows:

áppa ilábbinû, utáqqû pálḫiš
ášriš šuḫárrurû, nazúzzû šáḫtiš.

I, 9. *be-el bêlû(m)*, the singular *bêlu(m)* agreeing with the plural *bêlû(m)* in form, is used as a substitute for it. The same expression is applied to Marduk, IV R. 20, No. 1, 25, *be-el be-lum* (cf. Hehn, *Hymnen*, B. A., V, 340, 25). This title is also applied to Aššur, see Craig, *Religious Texts*, pl. 34, 15.

As to the meaning of *ušamsaku*, I would like to propose starting with the meaning of the corresponding Arabic word مَسَكَ "to lay hands on," "to seize." From this can easily be derived the meanings to remove, to set aside and to keep back.

These meanings suit all the known instances of its occurrence. It is applied: (1) To the removal of the statues and memorial tablets. Cf. Adad-nirari, I, Rev. 16, 17, *lu na-ri-ia ú-šam-sa-ku a-na ša-aḫ-lu-uq-ti i-ma-nu-ú*, *i.e.*, "who will remove my inscribed stone and give it over to destruction." Cf. also Aššur-naṣir-apal, *Monolith*, Col. V, 57, 58; Sargon, Cylinder, 76, and Sargon, Bull Inscription, 104. (2) It is applied to the removal of sin, *šu-ṣi-i mur-ṣi šum-si-ki ḫi-te-ti*, Br. M., 81, 2–4, 188, Rev. 21 (Z. A., V, 68), *i.e.*, "let my sickness come forth, remove my sin." (3) It is applied to shouting, Br. M., 81, 2–4, 188, Rev. 11, *rig-ma šum-sa-ku si-mat u ḫa-da-a ša balâṭi zu-um-ma-ku*, "I am removed (*i.e.*, kept) from shouting, from the beauties and pleasures of life I am debarred." (4) It is applied to the contents of the inscriptions. K. 2,727, Rev. 35 (B. A., II, 366f.), *rubû arku(-ú) ša pi-i dan-ni-te šu-a-tu la ú-šam-sak*, "a later prince who will not remove (*i.e.*, set aside) the contents of this document." Cf. K. 382, 13, 14 (Str., A. V., 5,065). (5) It is applied to the commands of the gods, Neb. Nippur, I, 9f., *i-pis pî-šú la ú-šam-sa-ku ilu aiumma*, "his command no god can set aside." V R. 66*b*, 11, *ina qibîti-ka kit-ti ša la uš-tam-sa-ku*, "by thy righteous command, which cannot be set aside." Cf. also K. 2,852 + 9,662, Col. I, 25, *la uš-tam-sa-ku a-mat ru-bu-ti-ša*. A substitute for this phrase is *ṣi-it pi-i-šu la uš-te-pi-il ilu ai-um-ma*, Creation Epos, VII, 132, and Susa, 3, VI, 29–32, *ša ṣi-it pi-šu ilu ma-am-ma la uš-pi-el-lum*, "what issues from his mouth (*i.e.*, his command) no god can annul." (6) It is applied to the removal, *i.e.*, the keeping back of tribute, Tigl. II, 92, *Šu-ba-ri-i šap-ṣu-te . . . ša bilat-su-nu ù ma-da-at-ta-šu-nu u-šam-si-ku-ni*, "the powerful Shubarites, who had kept back their taxes and their tribute." (7) It is applied to the thoughts in one's heart, IV R.[2], 60, III, Obv. 15, *ša ina lib-bi-šu mu-us-su-kat*, "what is kept back in one's heart."

I, 11. *rašubbi* [d]*Anunnakû*, literally "one who fills the Anunnakû with terror," from which develops the more general meaning, the powerful one, the potentate. In this line beings, including gods and men, in the next line lands and kingdoms indicate the extent of the god's rule. *ka-bit* is the construct of *kabtu*, "powerful," not yet registered in the dictionaries.

I, 13. The value of the sign is unknown. It is the simple form of which Br. 2,706 is the double. As the noun *melammu* is frequently joined with the verb *saḫâpu*, *e.g.*, *a-na ša-a-ri ir-bit-ti me-lam-me saḫ-pu*, "to all four directions they spread terror" (for other passages see Muss-Arnolt, *Dict.*, p. 550), it is probable that the verb used here was *saḫâpu*, or at least a synonym.

I, 14. *ka-la si-ḫi-ip ša-ma-me.* The rendering of the word *si-ḫi-ip* has caused translators considerable difficulty. It occurs: Aššurb. (Smith) 285, 7; 274, 28, *si-ḫi-ip mâti ka-la-mu a-na si-ḫir-ti-šu um-da-al-lu ana pâṭ gim-ri-ša.* To this passage corresponds V R. 9, 44, 45, *nap-ḫar mâti-ia um-dal-lu-ú ana pâṭ gim-ri-ša.* In the first passage Delitzsch (H. W., p. 494*a*) is inclined to see in *si-ḫi-ip* a scribal error of George Smith. But the word occurs again in a Shamash hymn (A. J. S. L., XVII, 134), Col. I, 20, *nam-ri-ru-ka im-lu-ú si-ḫi-ip mâtâti,* and again Col. III, 41, *kal si-ḫi-ip da-ad-me.* The former passage is translated by Gray: "Thy brilliancy fills and overwhelms countries," taking *si-ḫi-ip* evidently as equivalent to *sâḫip* (cf. I, 40). But there can be little question that *siḫip* in these passages is the construct of *siḫpu* and means "extent." The fundamental meaning of *saḫâpu* would, therefore, be to stretch out; applied to an area it is that which is stretched out, the extent; in a hostile sense it becomes "to overthrow." This is corroborated by our passage, where *kala siḫip šamâme* is in parallelism to *napḫar qinnê u kal dadmê.* The phrase must therefore be translated literally: "the totality of the extent of heaven." In agreement with this we find the expressions *kiššat da-ad-me* (K. 8,235 + 8,234, Col. I, 6; cf. Z. A., IV, 22, 8) and *gi-mir da-ad-me* (K. 8,717 + D. T. 363, Col. I, 8; cf. Z. A., IV, 230) substituted in similar passages. The accuracy of G. Smith is once more vindicated, and his passage becomes particularly valuable because it shows that *siḫip* actually exchanges with *napḫar.*

Namrirri ṣa'nu is the governing sentence, whose thought is further elaborated by the two lines that follow (cf. Hilprecht, *Assyriaca,* pp. 14, 16).

I, 15. *qinnê* is here used with reference to human habitations, a usage which is also found in the O. T. (cf. Jer. 46 : 16; Hab. 2 : 9; Ob. 4; Job 29 : 18).

The etymology of *dadmê* is not given by lexicographers, as far as

I know.[1] I would suggest that it belongs to the same root as *admânu*, dwelling (cf. Tigl., VII, 74, 90; VIII, 17, etc.), namely *adâmu*, to build. It is, therefore, a *t* formation, whose *t* under the influence of the following *d* has been softened to *d*. The same formation is probably to be found in *da(d)daru*, "the stench," whose root, according to Jaeger (B. A., II, 299), is *adâru*.

Parallel passages, comparing the glory of a god to a garment, are [*ša puluḫ*]-*tu lit-bu-šu ma-lu-ú ḫar-ba-šu*, King, *Magic*, No. III, 11; cf. II, 13, and *ḫa-lip ša-qum-ma-ti ša lit-bu-šu nam-ri-ri*, King, *Magic*, No. 46 : 15, pl. 61. There are also Hebrew parallels to this thought, compare especially Hab. 3 : 3, כסה שמים הודו ותהלתו מלאה הארץ; also Ps. 104 : 1–2, "With honor and glory thou art clothed, using light as a garment," and Ps. 93 : 1; 148 : 13.

I, 16. As Prof. Hilprecht was the first to recognize (*Assyriaca*, p. 57), the word *šalummatu* does not exist in Assyrian. The reasons for this are as follows: (1) If we read *šalummatu* it is impossible to connect the word with the verb *šalâmu*, "to be whole." Nor can any other satisfactory etymology be suggested. (2) We never find the word written *ša-lu-um-ma-tu*, but there are frequent cases in which we find the writing *ša-qu-um-ma-tu*. (3) The sign *lum* has also the value *gum*, *qum*, cf. Strassm., Neb., 135 : 24, *a-pi-il ru-gúm-ma-a*, and Oppert, Z. K., I, 61; Tallquist, *Contracte Nabû-na'ids*, p. 127, *sub rugummû*; Hilprecht, *Assyriaca*, p. 57, note.[2] (4) The meaning of *šaqummatu* appears from the explanation of its ideogram *SU.ZI* as *puluḫtu*, "terror." From this develops the secondary meaning, "that which inspires terror," hence "majesty, glory." We must, therefore, translate the passage of Aššur-bân-apal (V R. III, 3) *ša-qu-um-ma-tu at-bu-uk*, "terror I poured out."

[1] This was written before the appearance of Prof. Hilprecht's latest book, which offers the same etymology, cf. B. E., Vol. XX, Pt. 1, p. 44, note 1.

[2] Cf. also *sin-niš-tum šag-gum*(*LUM*)-*ma*, Reisner, *Hymnen*, 115 : 24; *be-el-šu iš-gum*(*LUM*)-*ma*, Reisner, *Hymnen*, 62, 17.

For the discussion of Jensen, who makes the original meaning of שקמם, "to be quiet," see K. B., VI, 1, 354f. Compare also Macmillan, B. A.,V, 564, who arrives at the meaning, "to be in distress."

katmâ, permans. 3 pl. fem., agreeing with *mâtâti.* A thought parallel is: *puluḫti melammeka bît* ^d^*Enlil kîma ṣubâti iktum,* which is said of NIN.IB, cf. Hrozný, *Mythen,* p. 10, Obv. 30.

um-daš-ša-lu, II, 2 pres. of *mašâlu.* For other examples of this form see King, *Seven Tablets of Creation,* III, 86; II, 24, and Muss-Arnolt, *Dict.,* 605*a.* This same idea is also found in the O. T., *e.g.,* Ex. 15 : 11, "Who is like thee of Yahweh among the gods?" Cf. further Ps. 71 : 19; 89 : 6; 113 : 5; II Chron. 6 : 14. *ilu-su* = *ilu-us-su* = *ilûti-šu,* cf. Delitzsch, Gr., § 51.

I, 18. *me-su-šu.* There are three possibilities as to the reading of this word. (1) The signs may be read syllabically *me-su-šu* or *šip-su-šu,* for which, however, no satisfactory explanation can be offered. (2) *ME.SU* may be an ideogram. *ME* is *parṣu* (Br. 10,374) and *ME.ZU* is *mûdê têrti* (Br. 10,385), "expert in omina," a title applied to the *bârû.* In the same way *ME.SU* might be an ideogram for *parṣu* or one of its synonyms, possibly *purussû.* If the latter word was intended *su* might also be regarded as a phonetical complement (cf. *KUD-su* = *ipparasu(-su)*). (3) The text contains a scribal error, *me-su-šu* for *par-su-šu.* The word *par-si-e* occurs on the boundary stone of Ellil-nâdin-aplu, II, 9 (*Assyriaca,* p. 5). In that case the ideogram *ME* for *parṣu* probably contributed to the confusion, as well as the similar form of the signs [cuneiform sign] and [cuneiform sign]. The last alternative seems to me to be the most probable, especially as the most common word for law *parṣu* (of which *parsu* is a synonym) would otherwise be wanting. Moreover, the inscription contains other inaccuracies (cf Col. II, 3, 11; V, 10).

šit-ru-ḫu. For other passages in which this word occurs see Zimmern, G. G. A., 1898, 826; B. A., V, 311, l. 20; Muss-Arnolt, *Dict.,* p. 1137*a.*

billudûšu (*GARZA.MEŠ*). The plural sign is only attached to the singular in this case because plural happens to agree in form with the singular. For this playful use of the plural sign see Hilprecht, *Assyriaca*, p. 55[1].

I, 19. For similar glorifications of the "word" of the gods see a hymn to Sin, IV R. 9, Col. I, 48–62; a hymn to Nergal, K. 69 (cf. Böllenrücher, *Gebete und Hymnen*, pp. 30–42), and the "word" of Ellil and Marduk in the Reissner collection, see Macmillan, B. A., V, 539f. A similar description of the law of Yahweh is found Ps. 19 : 7–9.

naklâ is perm., 3. pl. fem., agreeing with *alkakâtu.*

I, 20. With *muma'ir šamê u irṣiti,* cf. Gen. 14 : 24, אל עליון קנה שמים וארץ, and Ezra 5 : 11.

mukîl mâtâti. The verb *kâlu* is here used in the sense of uphold, sustain, as, *e.g.*, in IV R. 5, 37–39c, *na-piš-ti mâti ú-kal-lu,* "he (Sin) sustains the life of the land." Of Ishtar it is said: *mukillat napišti,* K. 3,477, Obv. 19, cf. B. A., V, 592; cf. also the statement of Ḫammurabi, Code XL, 49, 50, *ina utlia nišê* *mâtu**Šumêrim u Akkadim ukîl.* The various meanings of כול are discussed by Meissner, A. P., p. 138.

I, 23. With *ana šatti* the various appositions to Ellil, extending I, 1–23, come to an end. With the next words the apodasis begins, whose first predicate is *ippalisma.*

ina BIR.ŠI.MEŠ. In view of the parallelism which characterizes this hymn, we should expect, corresponding to *bûnisu namrûti,* a noun followed by an adjective, so that *BIR.ŠI* would be the ideogram of a word synonymous with *bûnu.* This synonym might be *zîmu,* for it occurs in parallelism with *bûnu* in V R. 61, Col. IV, 43–46, *ina bu-ni-šu nam-ru-ti zi-me-šu ru-uš-šu-ti damqâti inâ(ŠI + II)-šu ḫa-diš ip-pa-lis-su-ma.* In accordance with the analogy of this sentence we should read: *ina zîmêšu damqûti ina bûnišû namrûti.* Over against these considerations we have the expression in the O. T., Prov. 16 : 15, באור פני מלך חיים; cf. also Ps. 4 : 7; 44 : 4; 89 : 15; 90 : 8. Now *BIR* (as *LAḪ*) is an ideogram of *nûru*, "the light." Hence it is equally possible to read: *Ina nûr panûšû damqûti.* This reading I regard as preferable in view of the Hebrew expression quoted above, and the absence of any evidence that *BIR.ŠI* is an ideogram for *zîmu*.

II, 2. *eš-rit* is pl. cstr. = *ešrêt.* The phrase *ana udduš ešrêti* is common in the inscription of Nebuchadrezzar II. (cf. p. 124).

II, 3. *ŠA.SAG* is certainly a scribal error for *ŠÀ.DUG* (cf. II, 8). It is a new form of the usual ideogram for *satukku SA.DUG*, cf. Delitzsch, H. W., 513. The ideogram is artificial, having the appearance of a Sumerian word, but *satukku* is no doubt Semitic, corresponding to Arabic صَدَقَة, "poor tax," Talmudical צדקת and South Arabic *ṣadaqat.* See Hommel, *Aufsätze*, p. 274, and Leander, *Ueber die Sumerischen Lehnwörter im Assyrischen*, p. 31. A synonymous expression: *su-ud-du-ru gug-ga-ni-e qut-ri-ni niknakkê* occurs in Craig, *Religious Texts*, I, pl. 30, 6.

II, 5. *qâtuššu itmuḫ* = *ina qâti-šu itmuḫ*, cf. Delitzsch, Gr., § 80*e*.

II, 7. *ú-ša-tir šum-šu.* This phrase ends the first long sentence, containing the hymn to Ellil and the appointment of Nebuchadrezzar as king.

II, 9. *ina igisê*, the singular, is here again used as a substitute for the plural, cf. I, 9.

The adjective *ḫabṣûti* is in parallelism with *šum-du-li.* The exact meaning of *ḫabâṣu* has been in dispute. Jensen (K. B., VI, 1, 20, 323) translates "to swell," Zimmern "to strengthen," Delitzsch "to fill, burst." Nebuchadrezzar II. connects *igisê* with the adjective *rabûti* (*Délégation en Perse*, II, 123), *ba-bi-il i-gi-si-e ra-be-ù-tim*, Col. I, 10, or with *summuḫu*, cf. E. H., II, 37, *i-gi-sa-a šu-um-mu-ḫu*, while in this inscription *ḫabâṣu* stands in parallelism with *naḫâšu*, "to be abundant." This establishes also for *ḫabâṣu* the meaning "to fill to overflowing," a meaning which fits very well the context of the Creation Epos, III, 136, *ši-ik-ru ina ša-te-e ḫa-ba-ṣu ṣu-um-[ru]*.

The word *na-kin-ti* appears now in four different forms: *bît na-kam-te* (Layard, 34, 21), *na-kan-ti* (Aššurb., Sm., 132, 22), *kîma na-kim-tum* (V R. 47, 21*b*), and *na-kin-ti* in our passage.

II, 10. The inf. *libênu* instead of *labânu* occurs also in the new Ishtar hymn, Rev. 91, *mug-ri li-bi-en ap-pi-ia, i.e.,* "received favorably my prostration," cf. King, *Seven Tablets of Creation,* I, 234.

The expression *bêl u mâr bêli* is also applied to Marduk and Nebo in an inscription of Sargon, *a-na* *ilu**Bêl* *ilu**mâri* (it ought to be *mâri* *ilu*) *Bêl ú-ki-in* (cf. Winckler, *Inschriften Sargons,* pl. X, No. 20, l. 7).

II, 12. The verb *zarâbu* means to be pressed or oppressed, hence it shares with *šaḫarratu,* "anguish," the same ideogram (*SIG*), while *zurub ša libbi* has the same ideogram as *marâru,* "to be sad." In the stem II, 1, it means "to press out," so in Sennach. VI, 20, not "to keep back," or it may be applied to the expression of sounds. Regarding *zurub* as the cstr. of *zurbu,* "anguish," we should translate: "In the anguish of fervent prayer." But it is perhaps better to explain it as the inf. cstr. II, 1 = *zur(r)ub,* and translate "in the utterance of prayer." For the omission of the doubling see *li-gi-sa-šu,* IV, 8.

For *ZI.ŠAG.GAL-li* compare O. B. I., 83, I, 17, and Hilprecht, *Assyriaca,* p. 13[6]. This Sumerian word (also written *ZI.ŠAG.GAL.-LA,* cf. Gudea, B, III, 1) is no doubt correctly explained by Jensen (K. B., III, 1, 29††, 208) as *ZI* = *napištu, ŠAG* = *libbu, GAL* = *bašû,* hence "breath being in the heart." It is a synonym of *ikribu,* see Jensen, Z. A., VIII, 221, and also Leander, *Sumerische Lehnwörter,* p. 18, No. 135.

II, 14. *UḪ.ME.ZU.AB* is rendered by Jensen as *pašîš apsî, Weltmeer-Gesalbter,* while Meissner (A. P., 154) and Haupt (in

Cheyne, Isaiah, S. B. O. T., p. 82) transcribe *pâšišu*, "the anointer." But in view of K. 4,328 (= C. T., XIX, 41) and K. 10,194 (= C. T., XVIII, 47), happily joined by Meissner (M. V. A. G., Vol. X (1905), p. 254), it is perhaps better to regard *UḪ.ME.ZU.AB* as the pronunciation which was actually used in Assyrian, for the word which is in the left-hand column is there accompanied (l. 6) in the right-hand (or Semitic) column by the remark *šú-u*, *i.e.*, "the same."[1] For this use of *šú* see, *e.g.*, Hommel, *Geographie*, p. 281. Or we should at least expect, following the analogy of *UḪ.ME.ŠIK.BAR.RA* = *šú-'-ú-ru* and *UH.ME.-TUR.RA* = *lu-ma-ak-ku* (*l.c.*, ll. 7, 8), that there is one Semitic word to correspond to the Sumerian *UḪ.ME.ZU.AB*; but as none has as yet appeared the first alternative seems to me preferable, hence I retain *UH.ME.ZU.AB*. For a recent discussion of the meaning of this title as "one who anoints himself with the water of the *apsû*, perhaps a large basin standing in the temple," see Morgenstern, M. V. A. G., Vol. X (1905), p. 117[7].

NU.TUR. This shorter ideogram occurs on a number of stones —London, 101, II, 14; D. E. P., II, 97, 11; IV R.[2] 38, III, 1; O. B. I., 83, II, 12, and Code of Ḫam., XI, 49, 52, 63. The longer form *NU.-TUR.DA* is found III R. 41, I, 32; I R. 70, II, 5. The phonetic spelling *lu-b(p)u-ut-tu* occurs III R. 43, III, 13. For the explanation of Jensen as "deputy governor," see K. B., III, 1, 31**o, and *Kosmologie*, 78[1]. But why should we not rather follow the Assyrian lexicographers, who translate *TUR.DA* (read *ba-an-da*, V R. 38, 19, *a*, *b*) by *ek-du*, cf. IV R. 27, 19, 20*a*: *AMAR.BAN.DA* = *ri-mi ek-du*, hence *NU.BAN.DA* = *zikaru ekdu*, *Machthaber*, here the "chief" of the temple. See also Leander, *Lehnwörter*, p. 26.

II, 14. *DUR.AN.KI*, "the link of heaven and earth," was one

[1] This "ditto" note can hardly refer to the preceding word in the Semitic column, for that is *zer-ma-ši-tum* = *NU.BAR*, which in turn is preceded by *NU.GIG* = *qa-diš-tum*.

of the names of the stage tower of the temple *E.KUR* at Nippur. See Hilprecht, *Explorations in Assyria and Babylonia*, p. 462. The same name also occurs in K. 3,454, Col. II, 8, 10, 50, 73; III, 73 (cf. B. A., II, 409); Br. M. 80, 7–19, 126, ll. 11, 12 (cf. B. A. V., 586); IV R. 24, No. 1, 50, 51; King, *Babylonian Magic and Sorcery*, No 6, 18; Craig, *Religious Texts*, I, pl. 19, 9, *EŚ.EN.LIL*[ki] *DUR.AN.KI*; *Laws of Ḫammurabi*, I, 59, where we should not translate "*Dûrilu*," as Nippur precedes immediately. For other passages see Hommel, *Geographie*, 351².

II, 15. To *ana šarri rê'i kîni* the verb *ippalissuma* belongs. The whole section wants to say that, because the king was so pious (as shown by his restoration of all the gifts and tithes to the temple), Nusku-ibni, the high priest of Ellil, gathered courage and addressed his petition to the king through the governor, Bau-shum-iddina.

II, 16. *ut-ni-ni-šu* is inf. II, 2 of אנן; it ought to be written *utninnu*, cf. Delitzsch, H. W., 101*b*.

II, 17. Bau-šum-iddina, son of Ḫunna, the governor (*šaknu*) of *Bît-Sin-šeme*, was no doubt identical with Bau-šum-iddina, son of Ḫunna, the governor (*šaknu*) of Babylon, mentioned on the first boundary stone of Nebuchadrezzar, V R. 56, 18.

II, 18. In *na-an-za-az* we have an assimilation of *m* to *n*.[1] The same forms occur R. M. III, 105, *na-an-za-az maḫ-ri-šu*; see Winckler, *Forschungen*, I, 256, 11; also Nabû-shum-ishkun, Edge 7, *ilâni mala ina eli narî annî šuršudû na-an-za-zu*, *i.e.*, "the gods as many as on this stone have been caused to take a place." The usual form of this title occurs on a boundary stone of Rammân-shum-uṣur, *lu man-za-az pân šarri*, D. E. P., II, 97, 13. *maḫ-ḫar* is an unusual writing for *ma-ḫar*, perhaps due to the accent.

[1] Prof. Hilprecht, however, informs me that he prefers to explain *nanzaz* as a *fa''al* form *nazzaz*, dissolved into *nanzaz*, *i.e.*, "a man whose business it is to stand before one."

II, 19. *at-mu-šu na-as-qu-ma*, with which compare *a-wa-tu-ú-a na-aš-ga*, *Code of Ḫammurabi* (Harper), 40 : 81; 41 : 99.

II, 20. *šakkanak Bâbili*, "the viceroy of Ellil over Babylon," cf. *Annals of Aššur-nâṣir-apal*, who calls Adad-nirari *šakkanak ilâni rabûti*, Col. I, 29, and Winckler, *Keilschrifttexte Sargons*, Vol. I, p. XXXVI[6].

šakkanakku, literally *ša kanakku*, "the man of the door," like *šangû* = *šá naqû*, "the man of sacrifice," and *šabrû* = *ša barû*, "the man of sight," so Jensen, Z. A., VII, 174[1]. In V R. 55, 3, this title is placed alongside of *iššakku (PA.TE.SI) qardu*, while in our inscription the king is distinctly called *nisakku* (II, 12), which is the same title as that of the priest Nusku-ibni (II, 13). With this compare the priestly titles of the Assyrian kings, see M. D. O. G., No. 22, p. 74.

II, 23. For a discussion of *šar kiššati* see Hilprecht, O. B. I., Vol. I, Pt. 1, pp. 23ff., and Winckler, *Forschungen*, I, 90–97, 140–158, 222–232. See also Chapter II, p. 137.

II, 25. With *qirubû* compare the Aramaic כרובא, "an area that can be plowed in a day," from כרב, "to plow." In view of *qir-bi-tum*, pl. *qir-ba-a-ti* and *ga-ar-ba-a-tim*, the root must be קרב in Assyrian.[1] For a discussion of the word see Streck, Z. A., XVIII, 174[2].

II, 26. With *bu-tuq-ti* compare Talmudical בדקא, "flooding."

II, 27. *Ugâr âli* means here as in Old Babylonian law (Meissner, A. P., 123) "the land belonging to a city." It is therefore usually followed by the name of the city, I R. 70, I, 2; III R. 43, I, 2; Susa 2, I, 23, 30, 33; II, 2, 7, 12, etc.

II, 29. *iku* and *palgu* are the little ditches of irrigation drawn through a field, so in *Shurpu*, V/VI, 63, which treats of an onion, "around which a furrow and ditch is not drawn" (*ina iki u palgi*

[1] Compare also the Arabic كَرِيبٌ and جَرْبٌ

lâ innimmedu). For the earliest occurrence of *šapâku* compare the stele of Narâm-Sin from Diarbekr, O. B. I., 120, III, 3–4, *KI.GAL iš-pu-uk*.

II, 30. *mêrištu* from *erêšu*, "to plant," cf. Arabic غرس, "to plant." The fundamental meaning of this verb, as proposed by Jensen (*Theol. Lit. Zeitung*, 1895, Sp. 250), is "to irrigate," but this is not accepted by Zimmern (*Beiträge*, p. 58). The Arabic does not support the meaning "to irrigate," nor the Assyrian lexicographical lists, which give *na-du-ú* as a synonym of *e-re-šu* (cf. V R. 24, 12, *c, d*). Its connection with *a-ga-di-ib-bi* (Haupt, A. S. K. T., p. 73: 8, 9), whose exact meaning is still uncertain, can hardly be used to reach a definite conclusion.

III, 1. *Ṣîr-ap-pi-li*, perhaps "O Ṣîru, answer," Imp. II, 1 of אפל, cf. *a-pal-an-ni*, "answer me," Knudtzon, *Gebete an den Sonnengott*, 286.

III, 3. The last part of the name *Su-ḫur-Gal-du* is most probably a Cassite god. The same name occurs in the Cassite tablets from Nippur, *e.g.*, *Ḫa-aš-mar-Gal-du* (Clay, B. E., XV, 154 : 30); cf. also Clay, B. E., XIV, Introduction, p. 4[5].

III, 5. *bêl mâtâti*, *i.e.*, Ellil of Nippur, to whose temple the land in question belonged; see also plan of field, l. 7. Even this peculiar title of Ellil was transferred to Marduk by the priests at Babylon (K. 3,505, 8, see B. A., V, 325; K. 2,962, 14, see B. A., V, 334; IV R. 57, 1, see B. A., V, 349, etc.).

III, 12. A *ḫazannu* was originally the chief of a village or township, cf. Winckler, *Forschungen*, I, 246.

III, 14. A comparison of this line with III R. 41, I, 14–15, shows that *ŠÀ.BAL.BAL* has here the force of "grandson," for in III R. 41, we find Shâpiku, son of Itti-Marduk-balâṭu, son (*mâru*) of Ardi-Ea, Shâpiku and the Nabû-zêr-lîshir of our stone were no doubt brothers. This places III R. 41 either in the reign of Nebuchadrezzar I. or of his immediate successor. Other names point to the same conclusion, see p. 133.

A discussion of the different meanings of *ŠÀ.BAL.BAL* is given by Weissbach, *Babylonische Miscellen,* p. 3; cf. also Winckler, *Forschungen,* I, 518[1]; II, 20. The Semitic pronunciation is perhaps *liplîpu,* which like *ŠÀ.BAL.BAL* may be used of grandson (*Agum-kakrime,* I, 14), great-grandson (Adad-nirari, Obv. 27), or descendant in general; so hesitatingly Delitzsch, *Lesestücke*[4], 27, No. 224, and Winckler, *Forschungen,* II, 20, 23.

III, 15. *[h]ša-kin ṭe-me.* The name of this official is not *ša ṭe-me,* so Belser (B. A., II, 118, Col. II, 3; p. 120, Col. III, 11), and still retained by Scheil (D. E. P., II, 108, Susa 3, VI, 9), but as O. B. I., 149, I, 18; II, 3, and Susa 16, III, 30, has shown, it is *[h]ŠA-in* = *šakin(-in) ṭe-me.* Inasmuch as *šakânu ṭêmu* means always "to have, to hold a command" (Delitzsch, H. W., 297*b*), I prefer to translate *[h]šakin ṭême* "commander" instead of "councillor."

III, 17. Most of the boundary stones begin the section of the curses with *mâtima.* In two cases (III R. 43, III, 1; I R. 70, II, 1) *im-ma-ti-ma* is used. Two other stones introduce this section with *man-nu ar-ku-u,* V. A. 2663, V, 18; also the stone of Nabû-shum-ishkun, II, 16; IV, 3. One has *ma-na-ma arkû(-ú),* C. T., X, pl. VII, 32. A stone of Marduk-apal-iddina I. (IV R.[2], 38) leaves out the line with *mâtima* altogether and starts at once with the enumeration of the officials (*lu aklu lu laputtu,* etc., IV R.[2], 38, III, 1). Finally the smaller charter of Nebuchadrezzar (C. T., IX, pl. 5, 31) opens this section with *ša.*

The phrase *ana ûmê* is most frequently used, but *ina arkât ûmê* occurs six times (D. E. P., II, 112, 10; I R. 70, Col. II, 1; London, 102, I, 29; V. A. 202, I, 31). On III R. 43, III[1], we find *ina ar-ka-ti ûmi(-mi)* and on V. A. 208, Rev. 43, *ina (ar)-kat ûmâ(-ma).*

III, 18. To *ana aḫrât nišî apâti* corresponds *a-na ni-ši aḫ-ra-a-ti* on London 101, II, 13. *Nišê apâti* is peculiar to the new boundary stone from Nippur, but the same phrase is found, in a different connection, in the new hymn to Ishtar (King, *Seven Tablets of Creation,* Vol. I, 226, Obv. 27), where Ishtar is called *ri-e-a-at nišê a-pa-a-ti.* An etymology for *apâti* is offered by Zimmern, Z. A., VIII, 84, from the root ופה, "to unite," to which also *šutapû,* "the companion," belongs.

III, 19. It is to be noted that *rê'û* occurs here for the first time among the officials enumerated in the passage introduced by *lu* (cf. pp. 42, 43). Its absence on other boundary stones was commented on by Prof. Hilprecht, *Assyriaca,* p. 19[1]. A similar phrase occurs in the new stone of Meli-Shipak (Susa 3), Col. III, 59f., *ša ilâni rabûti inambûšuma ana rê'ût mâti inaššûšu,* "whom the great gods will call and to the rule (shepherding) of the land will raise."

lu aklu lu šâpiru lu ridû. The same succession of officers is found on K. 7599, Obv. 3 (cf. Winckler, *Forschungen,* I, 530). With *aklu* we can compare the Arabic وَكِيل, "*Agent, Verwalter*" (Wahrmund, H. W., 1217*b*); for *šâpiru* (= Hebrew ספר), see Johns, *Deeds and Documents,* II, 160f.; with *ridû,* cf. the Hebr. רדה בעם, I K. 5 : 30; 9 : 23, literally "one who drives the people, the levy-master," see Hastings, *Bible Dict.,* Vol. V, 590*b*; B. A., IV, 85, and Daiches, in Z. A., XVIII, pp. 202–222.

III, 20. *ša-ar-qi eqlu šú-a-tu i-nam-du-ma.* As there is a noun *šurqu,* "the gift," used in the phrase *šarâqu šurqu* (*Shurpu,* II, 86), so this passage establishes the word *šarqu,* "the gift, grant."

The context demands for *inamdûma* the meaning "to overthrow, to set aside"; cf. the use of *inamdû* in the curses, p. 48.

a-na i-ki-li ri-'-ti. Thus I would read the somewhat broken signs of this line. The *ki* might possibly be *di* and the *'i* perhaps *ḫi* or *iḫ,* but after studying the signs carefully I have come to the conclusion that the proposed reading is the most probable. I regard *ikîlu* (*ekêlu*) as equivalent to *akâlu,* as *libênu* (II, 10) = *labânu, ḫi-ri-e* (III, 25) = *ḫarû,* "to dig," and *limênu* (from which the noun *ni-el-me-na*, IV, 7) = *lamânu*; *ă* and *ā* become *ĕ* and *ē* when standing in proximity of *l*, (*m*), *n* and *r*, cf. *ramênu, nadênu, naṣêru*, etc. (Prof. Hilprecht's lectures). *akâlu* is used in the Code of *Ḫammurabi* (XIII, 1; XV, 57; cf. also XV, 48, 59) and in contract tablets of the first dynasty in the sense of "*Nutzniessung nehmen*," "to obtain the usufruct of something." Cf. C. T., VIII, 6*b*, *iš-ri-ku-ma i-ku-lu*, l. 6; C. T., VIII, 49*b*, *a-di ba-al-ṭi-at i-ka-al*, l. 14; cf. Meissner, *Assyriologische Studien*, in M. V. A. G., Vol. X (1905), pp. 260, 291.

III, 24. After the word *limutti(-ti)* appears the trace of a little wedge, but it is no doubt an erasure, due to a small hole which the scribe wished to avoid.

III, 25. *ina ilki dikûti* is synonymous with *ina ilki tupšiki* used on the second charter of Nebuchadrezzar I. (C. T., IX, 4, 38). *ilku* means here "obligation service," see Streck, Z. A., XVIII, 198[3], Daiches, Z. A., XVIII, 212–217. It is the Biblical הֲלָךְ, tax, Ezra 4 : 14 (cf. Zimmern, K. A. T.[3], 651). Prof. Clay discovered הלכא in the Aramaic endorsements of the Murashû tablets, corresponding to *ilki gamrutu*, see B. E., X, 78, where ה in the first line of the Aramaic endorsement is written on an erasure of שׁ.

As to the liabilities incumbent upon land in Babylonia see Chapter I, pp. 27–31, and Johns, *Assyrian Deeds and Documents*, II, 174–178.

III, 26. The verb *baqânu* occurs also on Susa 3, III, 13, 14, *šammê eqlišu la ba-qa-ni*. It is a variant of *baqâmu*, a synonym of *qaṣâṣu*, "to cut off"; cf. Delitzsch, H. W., 181*b*. The imper. occurs B. A., II, 393–4, Obv. 28, *bu-qu-un-šu-ma*. The change of *m* to *n* is caused by the following *š*, see Delitzsch, Gr. § 49, p. 114.

kal-li-e nâri u ta-ba-li. The same phrase is found on several other boundary stones. I R. 66, I, 6, 7, *kal-li-e nâri kal-li-e ta-ba-li*; III R. 45, No. 2, *ka-al-li-e nâri ka-al-li-e ta-ba-li*. On the second charter of Nebuchadrezzar I. (C. T., IX, pl. 5, 32f.) the expression is followed by officials: *kal-li nâri kal-li ta-ba-li* ^{h}*pa-nu-ú* ^{h}*šanû*(?) ^{h}*ṣu-hi-li*, while V R. 55, 51, 52, shows plainly that *kallû* is also an official, *kal-li-e šarri u ša-kin* ^{mâtu}*Na-mar* ^{h}*nâgiru*. The juxtaposition of *šakin* ^{mâtu}*Namar* with *kallê šarri* leaves no doubt that both are officials. On the new stone from Nippur "the seizing of a canal digger" goes evidently with the canal officers (*kallê nâri*); hence the cutting of plants must refer to the other group of officials. This leads to the natural conclusion that the noun *tabâlu* means land, and is in that case related to the Hebrew תבל, "the world." In this sense *tabâlu* is evidently a synonym of *nabâlu*, "the dry land."[1]

III, 27. The verb following *uš-aš-šu-ú* and introducing *ik-ki-mu* of the next line is probably *ú-šad-ba-bu*, for (1) this verb occurs usually on the boundary stones in this connection (Susa 2, III, 13; London 103, V, 36; London 101, II, 17; IV R.² 38, III, 5; III R. 43, III, 6; O. B. I., 149, II, 7; V. A. 209, II, 1). (2) It would be natural to have the taking away (*ekêmu*) preceded by a legal action.

III, 28. The phrase [*a-na*] *piḫâti i-t*[*u-ur-ru*] is probably preceded by *ušašraqu*, which is found in the parallel passages, III R. 41, II, 2, *a-na piḫâti-ši-na ú-tar-ru lu-ú ana ili . . . . i-šar-ra-qu*. C. T., X, pl. 7, 34, *a-na a-ḫa-*[*n*]*u i-šar-ra-*[*qu*] *lu-ú ana pi-ḫat i-man-nu-u*, cf. also V R. 61, VI, 40; I R. 70, II, 10.

III, 32. As Bau-shum-iddina is the subject of the dependent clause, and is followed by *a-na* ^{md}[*Nusku-ibni mâr Upaḫḫir-Nusku*] it is necessary that the predicate be active, and as the main act of Bau-shum-iddina (Col. III, 13) is not mentioned in the other lines, it is probable that it stood here, hence we read: [*ul i-ri-im-šu i-qab-bu-ú*]. For the repetition of *iqabbû* see III R. 43, III, 6, 7, and V. A. 208, 45, 47.

IV, 2. *ma-ḫi-ir-mi*. The enclitic *ma* has here become *mi* under the influence of the preceding syllable. For other examples of

[1] Cf. Meissner in Z. A., Vol. IV, p. 266.

this change see O. B. I., 149, II, 7, *šarri-mi*; London, 103, V, 38, *na-din-mi*, and London, 101, III, 1. We ought to read *i-qab-bu-ú* not *i-gab-bu-ú*, and *i-qal-lu-ú* (V, 1) not *i-gal-lu-ú*, because the *q* is not softened to *g* in this inscription, see *na-as-qu-ma*, II, 19; *qa-tu-uš-šu*, II, 5; *qa-bi-e*, II, 22; *ba-qa-an*, III, 26; *li-qa-am-ma*, IV, 27.

IV, 3. *li-tal-lik-šu-ma*, II, 2, pret. of *alâku*. The sign *tal* is Br. 7. For its syllabic use (*dal*) *tal* see Jensen, *Kosmologie*, 468[4]. The meaning of the verb cannot be "to go," for the following reasons: (1) The context demands a stronger verb than *alâku*, "to go." (2) *alâku*, "to go," is intransitive, hence always constructed with the preposition *ana*, but not with the direct accusative, such as we find here. (3) There is another verb *alâku*, whose meaning appears from V R. 24, 11–13, *c–d: a-la-ku* = *e-re-šu*; *e-re-šu* = *na-du-ú*; *na-du-ú* = *ma-qa-tu*(*m*). This passage shows that this verb *alâku* has the meaning "to throw down." The prt. I, 1, of this verb seems to occur in a text published by Craig, *Religious Texts*, I, 23, 31, *šamnu ṭâbu i-za-ar-ri-qu immerî niqê ip-pu-šu rikkê il-lu-ku*, *i.e.*, "good oil they shall sprinkle, sheep as sacrifices they shall offer, herbs they shall lay down." Martin compares the vulgar Arabic علق, "to throw into the fire" (cf. Martin, *Textes religieux Assyriens et Babyloniens*, p. 97).

Like this curse was perhaps London, 101, III, 9, *ᵈA-nu-um a-bi ilâni* [*ag-giš li-tal*(?)]-*lik-šu* or [*li-ḫal*]-*lik-šu*.

Against the suspicion that the text contains an error, *li-ḫal-lik-šu-ma* instead of *li-tal-lik-šu-ma* (the *tal* sign is quite plain), it may be urged that if *li-ḫal-lik-šu-ma* were intended there would be a tautology, for it is followed by *nap-ša-tuš li-bal-li*.

The phrase *nap-ša-tuš li-bal-li* occurs also in the *Creation Epos*, IV, 103: *nap-ša-taš* (var. *tuš*) *ú-bal-li*.

IV, 5. The title *mušîm šîmâti* is also applied to other gods, *e.g.*, to Anu, Monolith of Aššur-nâṣir-apal, I, 2; to Aššur, Craig,

Religious Texts, I, 32, 2; to Marduk, D. T., 109, 5 (cf. B. A., V, 375); to NIN.IB, Hrozný, *Mythen*, p. 28, Obv. 4.

IV, 7. *ni-el-me-na*, an *m* formation from the root למן. The *m* has become *n* under the influence of the labial (Barth's law, see Delitzsch, Gr. 174).

Both *lubnâ* and *nelmenâ* are fem. pl.

IV, 8. *li-gi-sa-šu*, prt. I, 1, third pl. fem. of *nagâšu*, "to throw down." The pret. of this verb is *ig(g)iš*, like *ik(k)is* of *nakâsu*. The *s* before *š* is due to dissimulation. For other examples see Nabopol. (Hilprecht), Col. III, 32, *ri-e-si-šu*; cf. I, 36, *ri-e-si-ša*; *ú-ša-ar-sa-an-ni*, II, 19. The meaning of *nagâšu* in this passage is, like the Hebrew נגש, "to oppress," so in Isa. 14 : 2; I Sam. 13 : 6. With this curse compare Susa 3, VII, 44–51; London, 101, Col. III, 10.

IV, 10. *nu-gu* is inf. II, 1, of נגא. It is treated as a noun, cf. Delitzsch, Gr., p. 339. To avoid the coming together of two "k" sounds (*nug kabitti*) we have here *nugu kabitti*. *Naḫâša ḫabâṣa* are also two inf., which, like *maḫâru*, govern a double accusative, cf. Delitzsch, Gr., p. 347f. The parallelism with *naḫâša* establishes for *ḫabâṣa* the meaning "to fill to overflowing," see Commentary on II, 9. Usually the curses of Anu, Ellil and Ea are combined, cf. Chapter I, p. 66f.

IV, 14. *liṭ-ṭe-šu-ma*, II, 1, pret. of אטה₅, "to darken," thus far not found in this stem. The result of the face being darkened is naturally that he does not smile, hence the meaning of "smile, laughter," suggests itself for *lil-lu*. The passages quoted for *lil-lu* by Muss-Arnolt, *Dictionary*, 481*a*, hardly belong to this word, cf. Martin, *Textes religieux*, pp. 172, 76; 184, 218.

IV, 15. Shamash and Rammân are combined only on the Nippur stone and on London, 103, VI, 9, 10. For the other parallel passages see Chapter I, p. 65.

I retain the reading Rammân for Babylonia, because there is no proof thus far that it was pronounced Adad, as in Assyria. Compare on this question Zimmern, K. A. T.[3], 444; Hommel, *Aufsätze*, 270; Ranke, *Personal Names*, 206[1].

IV, 16. With the nominal sentence *lu mulammenû igirrê-šu šunuma* compare the heading of this inscription, IV, 26; B. E., X, 94: 14, 15; 119 : 10, 11; and Amos 7 : 13, כי מקדש מלך הוא.

IV, 17. *kitti u mêšari*, also personified as the companions of Shamash, standing before him, cf. V R. 65, Col. II, 29; with which compare the Old Testament expressions: "Righteousness (צדק) and judgment (משפט) are the foundation of thy throne, mercy (חסד) and truth (אמת) go before thee," Ps. 89 : 15; Ps. 97 : 2.

IV, 20. *simma* can hardly be connected with the Aramaic סמא and the Arabic سُمّ, "the poison," as Belser suggested (B. A., II, 146–7), because (1) If poison is injected into the body it does not have the results mentioned in IV, 21. (2) The curses uttered in the name of several other gods refer to sickness. Marduk is called upon to send dropsy (III R. 43, III, 31; III R. 41, II, 25; I R. 70, III, 13; London, 102, I, 40f.; V. A. 2663, V, 43; cf. Chapter I, pp. 61, 62). Anu, Ellil and Ea shall send blindness, deafness and lameness (V. A. 2663, V, 36–40). *simma* does not mean "blindness," but it is a synonym of *marṣu*, Br. 9235, 9238; cf. also Jäger in B. A., IV, 287, and Jensen in K. B., VI, 1, 413f. Scholars have differed about the derivation and meaning of *la-az-za*. Jäger derives it from *lâ âs (sa)*, *asa* = *assa* = *asia*, "healing," from *asû*, "to heal," cf. B. A., II, 288. It is also derived from *aṣû*, cf. Muss-Arnolt, *Dict.*, while Belser (B. A., II, 146–7) and Delitzsch (H. W., 357*a*) prefer to read *la-az-za*, from the root לזז.

The word is written *la-zu* (Winckler, *Forschungen*, II, 10), or *la-az* (Susa 3, VII, 19; III R. 43, IV, 16), or *la-az-za* (III R. 41, II, 30; I R. 70, IV, 6; London 102, II, 20), and *la-az-zu* (Labartu, III, *a*, 54). On the boundary stones it is applied to sickness, but in the Labartu series to a plan, *a-nam-di šipta a-na la-az-za me-lik-ki* (Labartu, III, *a*, 54; *b*, 4, 14), and to heat, *umma(NE) la-az-za*

(Labartu, I, *a*, 21; cf. Z. A., XVI, 156). As to the meaning the Arabic لَظًّ , "evil," and the verb لَظَّ , "to follow one persistently, to press upon," supply a satisfactory etymology. As لَزَّ has similar meanings, it is impossible to decide the nature of the sibilant. I retain therefore the spelling preferred by Delitzsch. Judging from the symptoms of the disease, it may be consumptoin accompanied by hemorrhages.

IV, 22. As *šarqu* means "bright red blood," cf. the Sumerian *BE.UD* and the Arabic شُقْرَةٌ , "bright red, fox color," it refers perhaps to the blood of the arteries, in which case *dâmu* would mean the darker blood of the veins.

As to the derivation of *rûb* in *ša ru-ub-ša a-bu-bu*, there are two possibilities. It may be derived from ראב or רוב. The former would lead to the translation: "Whose rage is (like) a stormflood," and the latter "whose destruction is (like) a stormflood." In favor of the first rendering the following may be urged: (1) The anger of the gods is often compared to a stormflood. Cf. *e.g.*, King, *Babylonian Magic*, No. 11, pl. 23, 1, [d]*Marduk ša e-zis-su a-bu-bu*. (2) The verb *ra'âbu*, "to rage," is applied to Ishtar, *e.g.*, in the new hymn to Ishtar, Rev. 94 (King, *Seven Tablets of Creation*), *a-di mâti* [d]*Bêlti-ia ra-'-ba-ti-ma uz-za-za-at kab-ta-at-ki*. (3) The writing of the א is frequently omitted, cf. *e.g.*, *ú-za-in* and *ú-za-'-in* (Del., H. W., 249*a*), *bi-i-ši* and *bi-'i-šu* (Del., H. W., 165*a*), *ta-a-ú* and *ta-'a-ú* (Del., H. W., 697*a*), *da-a-tim* and *da-'a-ti* (Del., H. W., 208*a*). (4) We must take into consideration the possibility that, as in Hebrew, ע guttural verbs, and ע"ו, verbs having the same meaning, may have existed side by side. Cf. Hebrew ראב and דוב, כאר and כור, ראם and רום, תאר and תור and the nouns ראשׁ and רושׁ, "poison," באר and בור, "the pit."

In favor of a derivation from רוב may be urged that this verb is also applied to Ishtar. *mu-rib-bat šamê mu-nar-ri-ṭa-at irṣitim*, Sm. 954, Obv. 45, 46 (Del., H. W., 615*a*), and M. I. Hussey, *Some Sumerian-Babylonian Hymns of the Berlin Collections*, A. J. S. L., XXIII (1907), p. 170.

On the whole the first alternative appears to me to be preferable, especially as the anger of the gods is dwelt upon in these curses (cf. IV, 3). Moreover Ishtar's anger would be the natural cause of what is stated in the next line.

IV, 24. The word *ušaku* is evidently used here as a synonym of *namraṣu*. It is no doubt to be connected with the Hebrew חֹשֶׁךְ, as Prof. Hilprecht suggested to me. It is here used, like the Hebrew word in some cases, in a figurative sense, "trouble, misfortune," cf. Isa. 9 : 1; Job 15 : 22. To the same root belongs *ašakku*, "a demon of sickness and misfortune," cf. the Ašakku series of incantation texts in C. T., XVII, pls. 1–11, and their discussion by Prof. Jastrow, *Religion Babyloniens*, I, 348–351.

IV, 25. On the other boundary stones no curse is uttered in the name of Nusku; he is only referred to in Susa 2, IV, 19. As to the reason for the insertion of Nusku here, cf. Chapter II, p. 123, Com., p. 156. For Nusku hymns see IV R.[2] 26, No. 3; Craig, *Religious Texts*, I, pls. 35, 36. For translations and discussion see Jastrow, *l.c.*, I, 485–88.

The title *a-ri-ru* is also applied to the fire god *GIŠ.BAR*; cf. Craig, *Religious Texts*, I, 40, 13, *ᵈGIŠ.BAR a-ri-ru bu-kur ᵈA-num*; cf. also 41, 40. A similar title of Nusku is *ilu qar-du qa-mu-ú limnûti*, Craig, *Religious Texts*, I, 35, 4.

IV, 26. The sign *ban* in *ban-nu-ú-a* is No. 145 in Amiaud and Méchinau, *Tableau comparé; bannua* = *bânua*. The phrase *ilu bânua* or *abu bânua* is of frequent occurrence, especially in the inscriptions of Nebuchadrezzar II. (see Chapter II, p. 125).

IV, 27. In this line I assume that nothing is wanting, although the break has carried away a small part of this line.

IV, 28. The section which begins here is usually opened by

man-nu (see Nabû-shum-ishkun, Col. IV, 13; V. A. 2663, V, 18), or *man-na-ma* (C. T., X, pl. VII, 32), but as *man-nu* is always followed by *ša*, *man-nu* cannot have stood here. The section opened therefore with a simple *ša*, such as we find O. B. I., No. 1, 12; 2, 12; C. T., IX, 5, Rev. 31; V. A. 208, Rev. 45. It occurs also in contract tablets Nbk. 198 : 9; 283 : 19; 368 : 8, and on Assyrian inscriptions, Pudi-ilu, ll. 5, 6; Adad-nirari, Rev. 14; Tiglathpil., VIII, 63.

IV, 29. *ŠIM.MEŠ* stands probably for a verb. The parallel passages suggest *nakâru*, *abâtu* or *našû*, V. A. 2663, V, 28, *ú-na-ka-ru ina sub-ti-šu*; Nabû-shum-ishkun, IV, 18, *ina abni ubbatu*; I R. 70, II, 24, *abnu**narâ annâ ú-ša-aš-ša-ma*; so also III R. 41, II, 10; III R. 43, I, 32; *ina abni i-naq-qa-ru*, V. R 56, 35.

V, 2. With *ina* *iṣu**lipitti* (*LIBIT*) *i-pi-ḫu-ú* should be compared Susa 3, V, 52–54: *i-na qaq-qa-ri it-te-mi-ir*, *i-na lipitti* (*LIBIT*) *it-te-'i* (נ'א, I, 2) *i-na i-ga-ri ip-te-ḫi*, *i.e.*, "who hides it in the dust, surrounds it by an enclosure or shuts it up in a wall." *Ina LIBIT* cannot be read, as is done by Scheil, *ina libnâti*, as there is no plural sign. Our passage shows that it is something made of wood and no bricks. We must therefore take *lipittu* (Br. 11,193), which forms with *agurru*, "the enclosure," and *amâru*, "to enclose," a group, cf. II R. 36, 23–25, *h*. A similar expression is found D. E. P., II, 114, 16, 17, *lu a-na išâti i-na-du-*[*ú*] *lu i-na i-ga-ri i-p*[*i-ḫu-ú*].

V, 3. For the persons here mentioned see Chap. I, p. 50.

V, 7. The text reads *u zêri-šu a-ḫa-me*. In view of the fact that *aḫameš*, a synonym of *aḫame*, is always used of two persons, but never of things, while here "the foundation" and "the seed" would be joined by *aḫame*, I am inclined to see in the last three signs a scribal error. To this must be added the fact that most of the other inscriptions close with *ḫalâqu*; see V R. 56, 60, *zêra-šu li-iḫ-liq*; O. B. I., 149, II, 20, *zêra-šu li-*[*hal*]-*li-*[*qu*]; cf. also Susa 2, III, 25; London, 103, VI, 23; London, 101, III, 9, 12; but especially

V. A. 2663, V, 47, *zêri-šu piri-'šu ina pî nišê liḫalliqû* (*ḪA.A.ME*). The phrase occurs also on Assyrian monuments: Tukulti-Ninib, Rev. 29, 30; Adad-nirari, Rev. 55. All these passages make it probable that the scribe intended to write *ḪA.A.ME* = *liḫalliqû*.

With these curses compare the interesting passage in the history of the Arabic historian Maṣûdi, *Kitâb Marûj el Dhahabi*, Paris, 1861, p. 22f.: "He who dares to change the sense of this book, to remove one of the foundations upon which it rests, to obscure the clearness of the text or to cast doubt upon a passage by alteration or removal, by extract or résumé, and finally who shall allow it to be attributed to another author, may he be the object of divine wrath and of swift punishment," etc.

V, 8. For the reading of 𒁹 *Ú* as *li-ú*, see Chap. I, p. 10.

V, 9. The title *šaq-šup-par* occurs on I R. 66, No. 2, Col. II, 10; III R. 43, I, 30; II, 30; Edge IV, 4; London, 102, IV, 48; VI, 17. By transposing the elements of the name we get *[h]šu-par-šaq*, "the commander." This reading has long been maintained by Guyard, *Notes de lexicographic Assyrienne*, Paris, 1883, § 33, and Winckler, *Forschungen*, I, 476[2]. It has become more probable by the observation of the possible connection between these two titles (*šaq-šup-par* and *šup-par-šaq*) and the plausible emendation of Ezra 4 : 9 and 5 : 6, reading ספרסכיא instead of the unintelligible אפרסכיא, see Hoffmann, Z. A., II, 54f., and Marti, *Gram. des Bibl. Aram.*, p. 53. This makes it probable that the usual reading of the word as *šud-šaqû* (see Delitzsch, H. W., 685*a*) has to be given up. For a full discussion of the word see Muss-Arnolt in A. J. S. L., 1904, p. 192; and Johns, A. D. D., II, 163.

V, 10. With the name *Ku-bu-bu* we may compare *Ku-ub-bu-bu*, on the Cassite tablets from Nippur, Clay, B. E., XV, 44 : 8; 157, 3, and the *fu''ulu* formations on p. 29[3] of the same work; cf. also Ranke, *Personal Names*, p. 21[6].[1]

[1] See also Tallquist, in O. L. Z., Vol. IX (1906), p. 467.

The interchange of the title *amel bâb êkalli* with *amêlu ša bâb êkalli* (V R. 56, 16) shows that *amelu* should not be taken as a determinative, but as a part of the title.

V, 11. *Ši-ta-ri-ba*, "She has increased." Compare with this name *Ši-la-ma-zi* and *Ši-lu-da-ri*, Ranke, *Personal Names*, 194; also *fŠi-lu-da-ra-at* (Tallquist, N. B.), and for *ta-ri-bi* see *Ištar-ta-ri-bi*, Johns, A. D. D., No. 89; cf. III, 149. A different form is in *Mil-ḫi-ta-ri-bi* (B. E., IX), *Nabû-taribi(-SU)-uṣur;* in both cases it must be second person singular pret.; cf. Tallquist, *Namenbuch*, pp. 264, 317.

V, 12. *Taqîšu*, an abbreviated name, cf. *Ta-qiš-dGu-la*, Clay, B. E., X, 65. For such hypocoristica see Tallquist, *Namenbuch*, p. xxx.

V, 15. *Ri-mut-dGu-la*, usually regarded as an abbreviated name, but in view of the fact that *irîm* (pret. I of *râmu*) is always used on the boundary stones of the "granting" of land, and also the noun *ri-mut* occurs (O. B. I., 149, I, 2; V. A. 2663, V, 33; also V. A. 66, 25 = Peiser, *Acten-Stücke*, p. 20) in the sense of "grant, gift," I would suggest that *Ri-mut-Gula* means "the gift of Gula."

V, 16. *A-hi*, abbreviated perhaps from *A-ḫi-ba-ni* (Clay, B. E., XV, 26*a*), *Aḫu-iddina* (Clay, B. E., X) or a similar name.

V, 18. With *mKaššû* the name *mKaš-ša-a* (O. B. I., 149, I, 18) should be compared. There are but few names on the boundary stones of the second Isin (*PA.SHE*) dynasty which can clearly be recognized as Cassite, *e.g.*, *Na-zi-dMarduk mâr Shad-dak-me*, V R. 56, 12; *Ka-šak-ti-ia-an-zi*, III R. 43, II, 10; *Mi-li-Ḫar-be*, III R. 43, II, 14, 18; *Šar-bi-dEnlil*, O. B. I., 149, I, 19. *NISAG.GA* is here used instead of the usual *NISAG*, cf. Br. 6710.

V, 20. If the reading *Pir-šá* is correct we may compare *Pir(-ir)-dŠamaš*, D. E. P., II, 93, of which it is perhaps an abbreviation; cf. the remarks of Prof. Hilprecht in Ranke's *Personal Names*,

p. 19[3], calling attention to the Palmyrene name אמרשא, transcribed in Greek αμαρι σαμσου; see Lidzbarski, *Handbuch.*, p. 223.

[h]*Nâgiru,* for the ideogram see Amiaud, *Tableau,* No. 127, and remarks under No. 126; also Thureau-Dangin, *Ecriture,* No. 91. For a discussion of this official see Johns, A. D. D., II, 70.

V, 24. The earlier passages (III, 14) in which the name *Ardi-Ea* occurred showed that he was the grandfather of *Nabû-zêr-lîšir,* son of *Itti-Marduk-balâṭu.* Whether this *Ardi-Ea* is identical with persons of the same name mentioned on other stones (V R. 56, 19; III R. 43, II, 4; I R. 66, II, 15; O. B. I., 149, I, 15) cannot be determined.

III.

BOUNDARY STONE OF MARDUK-AḪÊ-ERBA.

O. B. I., Vol. I, Pt. 2, No. 149.

The discovery of this boundary stone was announced in the year 1894 by Prof. V. Scheil. It was then for sale in one of the bazaars of Constantinople. Scheil published a transliteration of the first column of the inscription in the *Recueil de Travaux*, Vol. XVI (1894), p. 32f. In 1896 the text itself was published by Prof. Hilprecht in his *Old Babylonian Inscriptions*, Vol. I, Part 2, No. 149. As a full transliteration and translation has not yet appeared, as far as I know, it will be appropriate to present one in this volume, as an appendix.

This boundary stone of Marduk-aḫê-erba belongs evidently to the second Isin (PA.SHE) dynasty. This appears not only from the fact that there is no room for Marduk-aḫê-erba at the end of the Cassite dynasty, to which its paleography might possibly permit us to place him, but on closer examination we find that the paleographical evidence points distinctly to the second Isin (PA.SHE) dynasty. Many of the signs, like *kat* (II, 1), *bi* (I, 18, 19; III, 18), *bir* (I, 22), *gu* (III, 1), *sa*, (I, 6), *šar* (I, 16), *zu* (III, 3), *ḫa* (I, 19), *SIS* (I, 14), *tuk* (II, 9), *šal* (I, 16), and others, occur in the same form on the boundary stones of Nebuchadrezzar I., while other signs, like *gir* (II, 23), *ḫar* (I, 11), *tim* (III, 6), etc., appear also on III R. 41 and III R. 43. An exhaustive comparison of all the signs of this inscription with those of the other *Kudurru* inscriptions of the fourth dynasty shows that, with but few exceptions, they can all be found in them. As to the exceptions, it is difficult to say whether they are due to the idiosyncrasy of the scribe or to his inexperience in engraving inscriptions. The signs for *il* (II, 5), *iš* (I, 15, 20; II, 19), *ṣar* are not found in exactly the same form in Amiaud, *Tableau comparé.* Two other signs are remarkable. One of them, *liq* (III, 11), looks much like *ba* (II, 7), but that it is meant for *liq* appears clearly from the context (see p. 199). The strangest sign is *zi* (II, 19), which has exactly the same form as *gab* (Neb. Nippur, IV, 2). It is either due to an error, or, what is more likely, the scribe represents by his upper horizontal wedge two perpendicular wedges, as in the case of *liq*, where the uppermost horizontal wedge takes the place of the two usual perpendicular wedges, forming the first part of the sign (cf. Amiaud, *l.c.*, No. 276).

The scribe shows also a peculiar tendency to make two similar signs so much alike that there is practically no difference between them. Thus *di* (I, 2, 4, 7; II, 7) is made like *ki* (I, 5, 6, 9, 10, 12, etc.); *ri* (I, 2, 10, 11, 21; II, 13, 16, etc.) like *uš* (I, 7, 8, 9); *ni* (II, 15, 22; III, 2) like *kak* (II, 8, 14) and also like *ir* (III, 5); *ib* (I, 12) like *lu* (II, 3, 4). Again, the same signs vary constantly in form; compare, *e.g.*, *bi* (I, 18, 19 and III, 8), *ri* (I, 5 and I, 6 and I, 10), *ki* (I, 5, 8 and III, 6), *du* (I, 7 and II, 11), *tu* (I, 1 and II, 6, 14), *i* (II, 14 and III, 2) and *ir* (III, 5 and III, 8).

For a general statement of the contents of this inscription see Chap. I, p. 20. For the position of Marduk-aḫê-erba in the dynasty see Chap. II, p. 133f., and for the symbols see p. 238.

In the transliteration the most common ideograms are not indicated in the notes.

TRANSLITERATION.

Col. I

XII $^{she'u}$ *zêru* $\frac{1}{18}$ *GAN I ammatu rabîtu(-tu)*
a-di II $^{she'u}$*zêru ri-mut*
^{md}*Sin-bêl*[1]*-ilâni*$^{pl.}$
mâr ^{m}*Ka-an-di ša-kin Bît-*^{m}*Pir'-*^{d}*Amurru*[2]
ugâr ^{âlu}*Šá-šar-ri* ^{ki} *ḫa-ar-ri*
^{âlu}*Šá-sa-na* ^{ki}*kišâd nâr* ^{âlu}*Ša-šar-ri*^{ki}
šiddu êlû iltânu UŠ.SA.DU
Bît-^{m}*Šum-ili-a-šip-ú-uš*
šiddu šaplû šûtu ba-ba-at
ḫar-ri ^{âlu}*Šá-sa-na* ^{ki} *Bît-*^{m}*Pir'-*^{d}*Amurru*[2]
pûtu êlû kišâd nâri Šá-šar-ri^{ki}
pûtu šaplû ti-ib ^{âlu}*Šá-sa-na*^{ki}
Bît-^{m}*Pir'-*^{d}*Amurru*
šá ^{md}*Marduk-aḫê*$^{pl.}$*-erba*[3] *šarru*[4]
^{md}*Nabû[-eriš*[5]*](-iš) mâr* ^{m}*Ardi-*^{d}*E-a*
tup-šar ù ^{d}*Bêl*[6]*-mu-šal-lim* ^{h}*bârû*[7]
tup-šar ša-kin Bît-^{m}*Pir'-*^{d}*Amurru*[2]
^{m}*Kaš-šá-a* ^{h}*šakin*[8]*(-in) [ṭ]e-mi*
ù ^{m}*Šar-bi-*^{d}*En-lil ḫa-za-an-na*
iš-pu-ru-ma rêš[9] *eqli iš-šú-ma*
^{m}*Ku-dur-ra mâr* ^{m}*Ḫi(?)-ri-šú-ru*
Ḫa-bir-ai arad-su i-ri-mu.

Col. II

Ma-te-[ma a]-na ar-kat ûmi(-mi)

[1] BE. [2] KUR.GAL. [3] SU.
[4] LUGAL.E. [5] PIN erased. [6] EN.

TRANSLATION.

Col. I

XII (gur) of seedfield $\frac{1}{18}$ GAN (reckoned) at 30 qa (of seed),
(equivalent to) one large cubit,
including II (gur) of seedfield, a gift of Sin-bêl-ilâni,
son of Kandi, governor of Bît-Pir'-^{d}Amurru,
a field of the city of Sha-sharri, (at) the canal of
Shasana, (at) the bank of the canal of the city of Sha-sharri,
upper length, north, adjoining
Bît-Shum-ili-âšhipush,
lower length, south, the sluices of
the canal of Shasana, in Bît-Pir'-^{d}Amurru,
upper width, the bank of the canal of Sha-sharri,
lower width, the approach of Shasana
in Bît-Pir'-^{d}Amurru,
property of Marduk-aḫê-erba, the king,
(who) sent Nabû-êrish, son of Ardi-Ea,
the scribe, and Bêl-mushallim, the seer,
the scribe of the governor of Bît-Pir'-^{d}Amurru
Kashshâ, the commander,
and Sharbi-^{d}Ellil, the prefect,
and took the boundary stone of the field
and gave it to Kudurra, son of Hirishuru,
the Ḫabirean, his servant.

Col. II

For all future days!

HAL. GAR. SAG

lu-ú ša-kin lu-ú bêl paḫâti[10]
lu-ú ḫa-za-an-nu lu-ú ^{h}*šakin*[8]*(-in) ṭe-mi*
lu-ú iššakku[11] *lu-ú ai-um-ma*
šá Bît-^{m}*Pir'-*^{d}*Amurru*[2] *šá il-lam-ma*
i-na muḫ-ḫi eqli šú-a-tu i-da-bu-bu
ú-šad-ba-bu eqlu ul ni-di-it-ti šarri-mi
i-qa-bu-ú ù ^{abnu}*narâ*[12] *an-na-a*
lâ šêmâ[13] *sa-ak-la sa-ak-ka*
sa-ma-a ú-qar-ra-bu-ma ú-šá-aš-šú-ma
a-na mê$^{pl.}$[14] *i-nam-du-ú*
i-na i-šá-ti i-qal-lu-ú
eqlu la a-ma-ri i-te-mi-ru
ilâni$^{pl.}$ *rabûtu*$^{pl.}$[15]*(-tu) ma-la i-na* ^{abnu}*narî*[12]
an-ni-i šùm-šú-nu za-ak-ru
ar-rat la na-ap-šú-ri li-mut-ta
li-ru-ru-šú.
^{d}*A-nu* ^{d}*En-lil* ^{d}*E-a*
iz-zi-iš lik-kil-mu-šú-ma na-p[i-iš-ta-šu]
aplê$^{pl.}$[16] *zêri-šú li-[ḫal]-li-[qu]*
^{d}*Marduk bêl*[6] *lip-te-ti [na(?)-ra(?)-a(?)-t]e-šú*
li-is-kir-ma ^{d}*Ṣar-pa-ni-[tum bêltu] rabîtum(-tum)*
i-gir-ra-[šu?] l[i-la]m-man.

Col. III
^{d}*NI[N.I]B ù* ^{d}*Gu-la bêl*[6] *mi-iṣ-ri*
ù ku-d[ur]-ri an-ni-i
si-im-ma la-[az-za i-n]a zu-um-ri-šú
li-šab-šú-ma ûm[ba]l-[ṭ]u da-ma ú šar-ka
ki-[ma] mê$^{pl.}$[14] *li-ir-muq*
^{d}*Sin*[17] *in*[18]*(-in) šamê(-e) ù irṣitim(-tim) iš-ru-ba-a*

[10] EN.NAM. [11] PA.TE.SI. [12] NA.RU.A.
[13] ŠI.NU.TUK. [14] A.MEŠ. [15] GAL.MEŠ.

Whenever a governor or the chief of the district,
a prefect or a commander,
a prince or any one
of Bît-Pir'-^{d}Amurru shall arise and
against that field shall raise a claim
or cause a claim to be raised, shall say the field
is not the gift of the king and shall order
a thoughtless man, a fool, a deaf man,
a blind man to approach that inscribed stone
and shall throw it into the water,
burn it with fire,
hide it in a field where it cannot be seen—
May the great gods, as many as on this stone
by their names are mentioned,
with an evil curse, that is without escape,
curse him.
May Anu, Ellil and Ea
in anger look upon him and destroy
his life, (and) the children, his seed.
May Marduk, the lord of constructions(?), stop up
his rivers, and Zarpanîtum, the great mistress,
spoil his plans.

Col. III

May NIN.IB and Gula, the lords of the boundary
and of this boundary stone,
cause a destructive sickness to be
in his body, so that, as long as he lives,
he may pass dark and bright red blood as water.
May Sin, the eye of heaven and earth, cause

[16] TUR.UŠ.MEŠ. [17] *dXXX.* [18] UD, cf. Br. 7781.

i-na zu-um-ri-šú li-šab-šú-ma
i-na ka-mat âli[19]*-šú ai ir-bi-iṣ*
ilâni$^{pl.}$ *ka-li-šú-nu ma-la šùm-šú-nu*
za-ak-ru ki-i ištên ûmi(-mi) la balât[20]*-su*
liq-bu-ú.

[19] ER.KI. [20] TI.

leprosy to be in his body, so that
in the enclosure of his city he may not lie.
May the gods, all of them, as many as are mentioned
by their names, not grant him life for a single day.

COMMENTARY.

I, 2. For the noun *ri-mut*, "the grant, gift," compare also V. A. 2663, V, 33, *ri-mut . . . . i-ri-mu*; V. A. 66, 25 (see Peiser, *Acten-Stücke*, p. 20), and Muss-Arnolt, *Dictionary*, 969*a*.

I, 4. The name *Kandi* may perhaps be compared with *Gan-daš(diš)*, the first king of the Cassite dynasty.

For the deity ^{d}KUR.GAL, equivalent to ^{d}Amurru, see Clay, B. E., X, p. 7f.

I, 5. The word *ḫarri*, "canal," should also be recognized in the proper names, *Ḫar-ri-Pi-qu-du* (B. E., IX, p. 76), *Ḫa-ar-ri-Ba-ṣi*, "the canal of the city Baṣ" (Susa 3, I, 24), and $^{\hat{a}lu}$*Ḫar-ri-Ka-ri-e* (D. E. P., VI, 42, I, 3).

I, 6. The fact that after *šarri* in every case (ll. 5, 6, 11) the determinative *ki* is written decides in favor of the reading *nâru* $^{\hat{a}lu}$*Šá-šar-ri*^{ki}.

I, 12. I prefer to read *ti-ib*, cstr. of *têbu*, "approach," rather than *ti-lu*, as read by Scheil, which might be connected with *til(l)u*, "mound of ruins."

I, 15. The sentence beginning with Nabû-êrish I take to be a relative sentence with the *ša* understood, hence the overhanging *u* vowel in the verbs *iš-pu-ru-ma* (I, 20) and *i-ri-mu* (I, 22). Another possibility would be to take Nabû-erish and Bêl-mushallin as the subject and the other two persons as the object. Against this, however, militates the fact that the grant is distinctly said to be "a gift of the king" (*ni-di-it-ti šarri-mi*, II, 7), and then there is no apparent reason why the two scribes should have sent two men, who, to judge by their titles, held a superior office. Moreover, scribes are repeatedly referred to as engaged in measuring fields (cf. p. 44).

I, 19. I see no reason for the reading *Ḫar-bi-Ellil* as given by Scheil. The sign *šar* has the value *ḫir* (Br. 4287), but there is as yet no proof for the value *ḫar*.

I, 20. The reading *rêš eqli* for *SAG eqli* is determined by the new stone of Marduk-apal-iddina I. (Susa 16), Col. III, 6, 7, *iš-pur-ma ri-eš eqli šú-a-tum iš-šú-ma*. This has been rendered by Scheil, "the area of that field they took," but the meaning "area" for *rêš* can hardly be established. The verb *našû* means "to take up, to lift up," and refers evidently to a portable object. Moreover, the phrase *ri-iš eqli-šu i-ka-aš-ša-ad* occurs repeatedly in Hunger's texts of *Becherwahrsagungen*, and as Prof. Jastrow has shown (A. J. S. L., XXIII (1907), p. 100), is there used as a synonym of *zittam akâlu*, "to acquire possession"; but the taking of the area of a field could hardly be equivalent to gaining possession. It was rather the acquisition of the "boundary stone" which gave a man the title to a property. The term *rêš*, literally "the head-(piece)," was certainly appropriate for the boundary stone.

I, 21. The name of Kudurra's father might also be read *Tu*(?)-*uš-šu-ru*. The scribe made no distinction between *uš* (I, 6, 7, 8, 9) and *ri* (I, 2, 6, 10, 11, 22, etc.). The first character, however, looks more like a *ḫi* (I, 2; II, 5, 16) than an *ud, tu* (II, 1; III, 4, 10), whose final wedges are more perpendicular.

I, 22. *Ḫa-bir-ai* is literally "a man of (the country) *Ḫa-bir*," probably Elam, for IV R.[2] 34, No. 2, 5, mentions a *Ḫa-bir-ai*, called *Ḫar-bi-Shi-pak*, cf. Jensen, Z. D. M. G., Vol. 50 (1896), p. 246f.

II, 3. Finding a hole at the end of l. 3 the scribe wrote *ṭe-mi* at the end of l. 2.

II, 7. For *šarri-mi* see p. 178f.

II, 12. In view of *i-qa-bu-ú* (II, 8) I prefer the reading *i-qal-lu-û* to *i-gal-lu-ú*. Cf. p. 179.

II, 19. The form of *zi* in *iz-zi-iš* (on which see above p. 189) may throw some light on London, 103, VI, 3, 4, *ᵈSin ᵈŠamaš ᵈRammân ᵈMarduk išid-su GAB-ḫu.* Peiser (K. B., III, 1, 162) takes *GAB* here as the ideogram of *paḫû* (Br. 4486) and renders *lipḫu(-ḫu)* "may they loosen(?) his foundation," but as *GAB* has the same form as *zi* in *iz-zi-iš* (which is undoubtedly *zi*), and as *ZI-ḫu* is the ideogram of *nasâḫu,* used in connection with *išid-su* (cf. Neb. Nippur, V, 7; IV, 19 and I R. 70, III, 12; III R. 43, III, 27) I propose reading *išid-su lissuḫû* in London, 103, VI, 4.

II, 20. For the restoration of *zêri-šu li-[ḫal]-li-[qu]* cf. *zêri-šu li-iḫ-liq,* V R. 56, 60; *li-ḫal-li-qu zêri-šu,* V R. 56, 40; cf. also Neb. Nippur, V, 7; I R. 70, III, 12; III R. 43, III, 28.

II, 21. *Marduk bêl lip-te-ti.* This title does not appear elsewhere. But the phrase *li-bit ga-ti-ia* occurs repeatedly in the inscriptions of Nebuchadrezzar II. (cf. Langdon, *Building Inscriptions,* Nebuch., 2, III, 31; 3, II, 18; 5, II, 17; 7, II, 24; 10, I, 16, etc.) and *lip-ta-at qâtâ-ia* (Sargon, *Bullinscr.,* 101), cf. especially *li-pi-it ga-tim ᵈMarduk,* "the work of the hand of Marduk," in an omen text published by Prof. Clay, B. E., XIV, 4. 1. The dams and dykes, guarding fields and preserving cultivation, are therefore placed under the protection of Marduk, as is implied in this title. For this side of Marduk's character compare his titles *šâriq mêrišti mukîn isrâti* (from *esêru,* to enclose), *bânû šeam u qê mušêṣi urqîti,* "giver of vegetation, establisher of enclosures, creator of grain and herbs, producer of (green) grass" (King, *Seven Tablets of Creation,* Vol. I, pp. 92, 93), and Hehn, *Hymnen und Gebete an Marduk* (B. A., V, pp. 282, 319), *muš-te-šir nârâte ina ki-rib ša-di-i mu-pat-tu-ú bu-ur kup-pi ina ki-rib ḫur-sa-ni,* "the director of rivers in the mountains, the opener of the depth of the spring(s) in the hills."

With the restoration *[na-ra-a-t]e-šú lis-kir-ma* compare the following passages from other boundary stones: III R. 45, No. 2, 8, *nâri-šu a-na la sa-ka-ri,* "not to close his canal"; Susa 16, V, 5-8, *lu-ú ša-ki-i-ik-ki dal*[*-ti*] *u a-šar mi-il-ti nâri-šu i-si-ik-ki-ru-ma ši-ki-iz-zu ub-ba-lu,* "whoever closes up with mud the sluice, the place by which his canal is filled, and diverts its irrigation"; Susa 3, II, 28–33, *la e-pi-ši du-ul-li bâb nâr šarri lu-ú ša si-ki-e-ri lu-ú ša pi-te*(!)*-e ḫi-ru-tu nâr šarri la ḫi-ri-e,* "they are not to do the work at the sluice of the royal canal, neither that of closing, nor that of opening it, nor to dig the bed of the royal canal." Cf. also *Code of Ḫam.* (Harper), XLIII : 7–9, *nârâte-šu i-na na-ak-bi-im li-is-ki-ir,* "May he (Ea) dam up his rivers at the sources."

II, 23. With *i-gir-ra-šu l*[*i-la*]*m-man* compare the curse of Ea, *šîmti-šu li-lam-man,* London, 101, III, 11; and of Shamash and Rammân, *mu-lam-me-nu i-gir-ri-šu šú-nu-ma,* Neb. Nippur, IV, 16, 17.

III, 4. *ûm* [*ba*]*l-ṭu.* The last part of *bal* is clearly visible. The form of *ṭu,* not given by Amiaud et Méchinau, *Tableau comparé,* No. 275, is found Susa 3, VI, 52; VII, 23–25, in the identical phrase, *a-di ûm*(*-um*) *bal-ṭu šar-ka u da-ma ki-ma me-e li-ir-mu-uk.*

III, 6. With the title of Sin *în*(*-in*) *šamê*(*-e*) *u irṣitim*(*-tim*) compare the personal name *ᵈSin-i-na-ma-tim,* Tallquist *Namenbuch,* p. 274; and *ᵈŠamaš-în*(*ŠI*)*-âli-šu, l.c.,* p. 281.

III, 8. In view of the fact that the other parallel passages (cf. p. 64f.) and Susa 16, VI, 17, *i-na ka-mat âli-šu li-šar-bi-ṣu-šú-ma,* contain the positive statement that the criminal shall lie outside of the wall of his city, *i-na ka-mat âli-šú ai ir-bi-is* must mean "in the enclosure of," *i. e.,* "within his city may he not lie."

III, 10. Compare with the phrase *ki-i ištên ûmi*(*-mi*) *la balâṭ* (*TI*)*-su liq-bu-ú,* London, 101, IV, 7, *ûma*(*-ma*) *iš-tin la balâṭ*(*TI*)*-su liq-bu-ú;* London 102, V, 7, *ûmê-šu la ba-laṭ-su iq-*[*bu-ú*], and Susa 16, VI, 23, 24, [*mu*]*-šim balâṭi la ba-la-az-zu* [*liq-b*]*u-ú.*

III, 11. That the first sign of *liq-bu-ú* is really *liq* cannot be doubtful from the parallel passages quoted above and the context.

IV.

CONCORDANCE.

Abbreviations.

b., brother; **cf.,** confer; **d.,** daughter; **f.,** father; **s.,** son.
Determinatives: **d.,** *deus, dea*; **f.,** *femina*; **h.,** *homo*.

Transliteration.

Ai = ^{d}GAL.
Bêl = ^{d}EN.
Bêlit = ^{d}GAŠAN.
Bunene = ^{d}ḪAR.
Ellil = ^{d}EN.LIL.
Ellil[1] = ^{d}L.
Ištar = ^{d}RI.
Mâr-bîti = ^{d}TUR.E.
Marduk = ^{d}AMAR.UD.
Nabû[1] = ^{d}AG.
Nabû[2] = ^{d}PA.
Nergal = ^{d}*UGUR*.
Nusku = ^{d}PA+KU.
Rammân = ^{d}IM.
Sibitti = ^{d}VII – BI.
Sin = ^{d}XXX.
Šamaš = ^{d}UD.

I. Names of Persons.

A*b-ba-ti* (hypocor., cf. *Ab-ba-tum, Ib-ba-tum,* Ranke, P. N.)
  f. of *Bu-ru-ša,* London, 102, I, 28.
Abullu(KÀ.GAL)-ta-ta-par(?)-a-a-ú mâr šarri, III R. 43, II, 26.
A-da (hypocor., cf. Ranke, P. N.)
  in *Bît-*^{m}*A-da* III R. 43, I, 3, 15, 17, 21; II, 23, 25; III, 4, 8, 9, 10, 11, 12, 14; edge IV, 1, 4, 6; III R. 45, No. 2, 4, 7.
A-dal-la-li (cf. *A-da-lál-lum,* Ranke, P. N.)*
  f. of *Is-kal(?)-da-a,* London, 103, I, 41.
A-ga-ab-ta-ḫa
  Ha-li-gal-ba-tu-ú, D. E. P., II, pl. 20, 1, 8.
Aḫê(ŠEŠ.MEŠ)-šul-lim (abbrev., cf. *Šamaš-aḫê-šul-lim*)
  1. b. of ^{d}*Mâr-bîti-šum-ib-ni,* London, 102, I, 23; IV, 32.
  2. V. A. 2663, IV, 16.
A-ḫi (abbreviated)
  f. of ^{d}*Nabû-un-na,* Neb. Nippur, III, 15; V, 16.
Aḫu(ŠEŠ)-at-tu-ú-a, "My brother(?)" Neb. Nippur, II, 27; III, 8.
Aḫu-bânî† *(KAK-i)* (hypocor., as indi-

* Compare with this name the opening stanza of a hymn addressed to Marduk (Craig, *Religious Texts*, pl. 29): *a-dal-lal zi-kir-ka* ^{d}*Marduk*.

† Not *Nusku-na'id* as Scheil translates, because *ŠEŠ.KAK* is not preceded by the determinative *ilu*. For the correct reading see Tallquist, N. B., p. 4.

cated by use of final long *î* and *û*).
f. of *Ka-šak-ti-Šu-gab*, Susa 2, II, 31; Medallion I, 2.

Aḫu-ba-nu-ú(ni-i)
f. of *dṢîr-šum-iddina*, Susa, 16, II, 25; III, 2.

Aḫu-da-ru-ú(ri-i), (cf. *Šamaš-lu-da-ri*).
s. of *dEllil-ki-di-ni*, London, 103, IV, 12, 20, 40; V, 7, 13.

Aḫu-er-ba (abbreviated)
s. of *Ḫab-ban*, *hka-lu*, C. T., X, pl. III, 26.

Aḫu-iddina
s. of *Mu-šal-lim-aplu*, V. A. 2663, IV, 12.

A-ḫu-ni-e-a (hypocor.)
s. of *Daian-dMarduk*, Susa 16, I, 13; II, 15, 31; IV, 10.

dAi(GAL)-bêl-šumâti(MU.MEŠ)
s. of *Ra-ḫaṣ*, V. A. 209, IV, 16.

dAi(GAL)-mu-tak-kil, "Ai gives strength."
s. of *dNabû-iddina*, V. A. 209, V, 19.

Amel-dEllil
s. of *Ḫa-an-bi*, III R. 41, I, 10, 28.

Amel-E-ul-maš
s. of *Šam-(Û)-eš-ḫa-la*, III R. 43, I, 19; II, 19.

Amel-âluI-ši-in
s. of *Ḫu-un-na*, Neb. Nippur, V, 21.

*Amel-iššakkê(PA.TE.SI.MEŠ)-ša-Uš-tim**
London, 101, I, 9.

Amel-dNabû[1]
London, 103, II, 18.

Am-me-en-na (cf. *Am-men-ni*, Tallquist, N.B.)
hšaqû, London, 102, VI, 16.

dAmurri†(KUR.GAL)-e-a (hypocor.)
hâsû, III R. 43, II, 28.

Anu-bêl-aḫê-šu (better than *Ilu-bêl-aḫê-šu*)
s. of *Mi-li-Ḫar-be*, III R. 43, II, 17.

dA-num-nâṣir(PAP)
s. of *Nûr-dSin*, V. A. 209, II, 14; V. 15.

Aplâ(TUR.UŠ-a) (hypocor.)
hMUK, V.A. 209, II, 33.

Apli(TUR.UŠ)-ia
f. of *Mušabši-ilu*, III R. 43, II, 16.

A-qar-dNabû [1 2], "Nabû is dear."
1. f. of *At-na-ai*, C. T., X, pl. III, 2.
2. f. of *dNabû-šaqû(NIM)-ina-mâti*, C. T., X, pl. III, 16.

Ardi‡-dE-a (written *dBE* in No. 18)
1. f. of *Iqîša(-ša)-dBa-ú*, London, 101, II, 8; Susa, 16, III, 22; D. E. P., VI, 43, II, 17.
2. f. of *Ib-ni-dMarduk*, London, 101, I, 16; Susa 3, I, 29.
3. f. of *Û-bal-liṭ-su-dMarduk*, IV R.[2] 38, II, 3.
4. f. of *dNabû-ša-kin-šumu*, IV R.[2] 38, II, 37.
5. f. of *dE-a-ku-dur-ri-ib-ni*, III R. 43, II, 4.
6. f. of *dNabû-[eriš](-iš)*, O. B. I., 149, I, 15.
7. f. of *Iz-kur-dNabû*, Susa 16, II, 3.
8. f. of *Šu-zib-dMarduk*, Susa 16, II, 8.
9. f. of *Bêl-bašmê*, Susa 16, III, 5.
10. f. of *Zêr-ib-ni*, Susa 14, I, 16.

* This name, meaning "the man of the rulers of Ushtim," is hardly the real name of the man, but more likely his professional name. To the same class of names may belong the following of this list: *mhšaq šup-par*, *mRê'û piḫâti*, *mKa-nik-bâbi* and perhaps *mBêl-bašmê*, unless the latter is abbreviated.

† For this rendering of the ideogram *dKUR.GAL* see Clay, B. E., X, p. 8, and the hypocoristicon *A-mur-ri-ia*, which exchanges with *dKUR.GAL-êriš* in Peiser, *Urkunden aus der Zeit der dritten babylonischen Dynastie*, Berlin, 1905, p. 41.

‡ The most common writing is *Ar-di-dBêl*, cf. Tallquist, N. B., p. 12, although the form *Ar-du-dNusku* also occurs. See Clay, B. E., XV, 27, note 5.

11. f. of *Bi-ra-a*, D. E. P., VI, 44, I, 13.
12. f. of *Uballiṭ-su-dGu-la*, V R. 56, 19.
13. f. of *Itti-dMarduk-balâṭu*, III R. 41, I, 13; Neb. Nippur, III, 14.
14. f. of *dNabû-râ'im-zêru*, I R. 66, II, 14.
15. f. of *dNabû-zêr-lîšir*, Neb. Nippur, V, 24.
16. f. of *Er-ba-dMarduk*, C. T., X, pl. III, 29.
17. f. of *Ardi-dNabû*, London, 102, VI, 21.
18. f. of *dNabû-za-kir-šumu*, V. A. 2663, V, 3.

Ardi-dGu-la
s. of *Kal-bi*, V R. 56, 21.

Ardi-dIštar(RI)
s. of *Ellil-zêr-ke-ni*, III R. 43, I, 25.

Ardi-dMarduk(ŠU)
f. of *Mu-šal-lim-dMarduk*, London, 102, IV, 7.

Ardi-dNabû
s. of *Ardi-dE-a*, London, 102, VI, 20.

Ardi-dNa-na-a
s. of *Mudammiq(-iq)-dRammân*, I R, 66, II, 13; V R. 56, 13; Stone of Amrân II [1].

Ardi-nu-bat-ti, "The child of the *nubattu* day" (cf. *Ardu-ûmu* 3 *kan*, etc., Clay, B. E., XV).
f. of *dŠamaš-nâdin-šumu*, Susa 3, I, 31.

Ardi-dSibitti
s. of *At-rat-taš*, London, 102, I [10], 19, 20, 23, 33; II, 38; III, 1, 10, 16: IV, 13, 31; VI, 2, 7, 9, 11.

Arkât (*EGIR.MEŠ*)-*ilâni-damqâti* (*BIR.ME*).
s. of *dNabû-ile'i(DA)*, V. A. 2663, V, 10.

Ar-ra-ku-tu
f. of *Ina-ešê-êṭir*, V. A. 209, I, 4.

A-šab-šu (abbreviated, cf. *Ṭâb-a-šab-šu*, Clay, B. E., XV, 44)
f. of *dNabû-aḫu-ni*, V. A. 208, 51.

A-ša-ri-du (abbreviated, cf. *Bêl-aša-ridu*, Talquist, N. B.)
in *Bît-mA-ša-ri-du*, V. A. 208, 45.

dAššur(ḪI)-aḫ-iddina
šarru, C. T., X, pl. V, 6.

dAššur-bân(KAK)-aplu(A)
šar kiššati, C. T., X, pl. IV, 11.

At-na-ai
f. of *dNabû-apal-iddina*, C. T., X, pl. III, 1, 10, 20, 22.

At-rat-taš
f. of *Ardi-dSibitti*, London, 102, I, 11, 15, 19, 31, 32; III, 6, 21; IV, 15, 31, 37; VI, 2, 7.

At-ta-ilu-ma
1. f. of *dŠamaš-nâdin-šumu*, V R. 56, 17.
2. f. of *dŠamaš-šum-lîšir*, London, 101, II, 9.

A-tu-'-ú
s. of *Ki-diš(daš)*, Neb. Nippur. V, 14.

B*a-bi-la-ai(-ú)*
s. of *dSin-lîšir*, *ḫšaqû*, I R. 66, II, 8; III R. 43, II, 1.

Ba-laṭ-su (abbreviated, cf. *dBêl-balâṭsu-iqbi*, Tallquist, N. B.)
s. of *It-tab-ši*, V. A. 209, II, 21.

Ba-ni-ia (hypocor.)
1. s. of *E-ṭi-ru*, V. A. 209, IV, 27; V, 17.
2. s. of *Kan-dar-šam-(Ú)-ši*, V. A. 208, 28.

dBâniti(KAK-ti)-êriš (*PIN-eš*)*
s. of *Ulûlai*, V. A., 209, II, 18.

Ba-ri-ki-ilu (cf. Hebr. ברכאל)
C. T., X, pl. VI, 21.

dBa-ú-aḫ-iddina(-na)
1. s. of *Ni-ga-zi*, I R. 66, II, 9.
2. *ṭupšarru*, London, 101, I, 19.

dBa-ú-šum-iddina(-na)
s. of *Ḫu-un-na*, V R. 56, 18; Neb. Nippur, II. 17, 30; III, 9, 30

* Thus according to a suggestion of Dr. Ungnad.

Ba-zi (cf. city Baṣ.).
1. f. of *E-ul-maš-šurqi-iddina*, III R. 43, I, 30.
2. f. of *Kaš-šu-ú-mukîn-aplu*, London, 102, VI, 17.
3. in *Bît-mBa-zi*, D. E. P., VI, 42, I, 14; and perhaps in C. T., IX, pl. V, 24, instead of *Bît-mMa-zi*.

Be-la-ni (abbreviated, cf. *dBêl-bêl-a-ni*, Strassmaier, Neb., 135, 15)
f. of *Ri-mu-ti* and *Tab-nu-ti*, London, 103, II, 16; III, 3, 10, 12, 32, 44.

dBêl-aḫê-erba(SU)
hša-ku Bâbili, V. A. 2663, III, 36; IV, 50; V, 34.

Bêl-am-ma
mâr hišpari, V. A. 2663, IV, 29.

Bêl-ana-mâti-šu (abbrev. from perhaps *Bêl-ana-mâti-šu-utîr*)
V. A. 2663, III, 44.

dBêl-a (hypocor., cf. *Mar-duk-a*, B. E., X, 55).
s. of *dŠamaš-eriš(PIN)*, V. A. 208, 50.

Bêl-bašmê(BUR.RA) (cf. Br. 98 and 334), "The lord of serpents."
s. of *Ardi-dE-a*, Susa 16, III, 4.

dBêl-êpuš(KAK-uš)
V. A. 208, 22.

dBêl-er-ba
s. of *Ku-ri-gal-zu*, V. A. 208, 27.

dBêl-iddina(-na)
1. s. of *Ši-gu-ú-a*, C. T., X, pl. VII, 50.
2. s. of *dNabû-zêr-iddina(-na)*, V. A. 208, 1, 14, 18, 49.

dBêl-ile'i(DA)-kalâmi(KAK.A.BI), "Bêl is all powerful."
s. of *E-sag-ila-ai*, C. T., X, pl. VII, 48.

dBêl(?)-ili-ia
hša pân êkalli, C. T., X, pl. VII, 43.

dBêl-mu-šal-lim
hbârû, O. B. I., 149, I, 16.

dBêl-šum-iškun(ŠA-un)
in *Bît-mdBêl-šum-iškun*, V. A. 209, III, 6, 21.

dBêl-ú-sa-tu, "Bêl is help."
s. of *I-bu-nu*, V. A. 209, II, 15; IV, 2, 6, 13.

dBêl-ú-sip-pi, "Bêl I implored."
mâr hbârû, V. A. 209, V, 18.

dBêl-ušabši(GAL-ši), "Bêl has called into existence."
hNI.SUR, V. A. 209, III, 3, 20.

Bi-e-a
s. of *Šú-la-a*, V. A. 209, IV, 9.

Bi-ra-a (cf. *Bi-ri-ia*, Clay, B. E., XV)
s. of *Ardi-dE-a*, D. E. P., 44, I, 43.

mBît-dar(?)-da-ri-ib-nu
f. of *dNabû-zêr-ib-nu*, V. A. 209, II, 23.

mBît-di-bi-na
London, 101, II, 4.

Bi-til[-ia-aš] (cf. *Bi-ti-li-ia-a-šú*, D. E. P. II, pl. 20, 3, 4)
šarru, D. E. P., 93, II, 5.

Bur-na-Bu-ri-aš (*Bur-ra-Bu-ri-ia-aš*)
f. of *Ku-ri-gal-zu*, Susa 2, I, 5; D. E. P., II, 93, I, 19.

Bu-ru-ša (cf. Bi. ברושע).
1. f. of *dŠamaš-nâdin-šumu*, London, 102, I, 17.
2. s. of *Ab-ba-ti*, London, 102, I, 28, 35, 37, II, 32; IV, 20, 22, 25, 30; VI, 3, 7, 10, 12, 15.

D*a-bi-bi* (abbrev., cf. *Da-bi-bi-ni-ir* and *dNabû-dâbibi-ni-ir*, Tallquist, N. B.)
f. of *La-ba-ši-dMarduk*, V. A. 2663, V, 8.

Daian(DI.KUD)-dMarduk
1. f. of *A-ḫu-ni-e-a*, Susa 16, I, 14; II, 15; IV, 11.
2. perhaps f. of *Ellil-šum-im-bi*, London, 103, I, 47.

Da-ku-ru (cf. *Mâr-Da-ku-ru*, Bezold, Catalogue V, 1994).
f. of *dNabû-mušallim(GI)*, C. T., X, pl. V, 10; VII, 45.

Dâmiq(ŠI.BIR-iq)-dRammân
in *âlu ša mDâmiq-dRammân*, Susa 3, II, 24.

âluDûr-šarru-kên-ai-i-ti
d. of *dṢîr-uṣur*, I R. 70, I, 14.

*d*E*-a-iddina*
f. of *E-kar-ra-iqîša(-ša)*, O. B. I., 83, I, 10; I R. 66, II, 7.

dE-a-ku-dur-ri-ib-ni
s. of *Ardi-dE-a*, III R. 43, II, 3.

dE-a-ma-lik
hnangaru, in *Bît-mdE-a-ma-lik*, Susa 3, I, 22.

E-an-na-ellu(AZAG.GAL)
rê'û sisî, London, 102, III, 13.

E-an-na-šum-iddina(na)
ša-kin mât tâmdi, O. B. I., 83, II, 7.

E-gi-bi (cf. Tallquist, N. B., p. 57)
f. of *Ku-dur-ru*, V. A. 2663, IV, 12.

Êkalla-ai
s. of *At-rat-taš*, London, 102, I, 14.

E-kar-ra-iqîša(BA-ša)
s. of *dE-a-iddina*, O. B. I, I, 83, I, 10; II, 3, 6; I R. 66, II, 6.

dEllil-iddina(SE-na)
1. s. of *dRammân-šum-iddina, šarru*, London, 103, I, 19.

dEllil-ki-di-ni
1. f. of *Aḫu-da-ru-ú*, London, 103, IV, 13, 44; V, 1.
2. in *Bît-mdEllil-ki-di-ni*, London, 103, IV, 29; V, 31.

dEllil-mušallim(GI)-aplu, "Bêl has preserved a son."
s. of *hšaq-šup-par*, III R. 43, II, 5.

dEllil-nâdin-aplu
šarru, O. B. I., 83, I, 9, 18.

dEllil-nâdin-šumu
1. s. of *Aḫu-da-ru-ú*, London, 103, V, 12.
2. s. of *Ša-zu-ú-ti*, III R. 43, II, 11.
3. s. of *Ḫab-ban*, V R. 56, 23.

dEllil-šum-ib-ni
s. of *Rabâ(GAL-a)-ša-dMarduk*, C. T. X., pl. III, 24.

dEllil-šum-im-bi
perhaps s. of *Dai[ân]-dMarduk*, London, 103, I, 46; III, 6, 25, 34, 37.

dEllil-tab-ni-bu-ul-liṭ, "O Ellil, preserve what thou hast created."
hbârû, V R. 56, 25.

dEllil-zêr-ke-ni, "O Ellil, establish the seed."
s. of *Ardi-dIštar*, III R. 43, I, 24.

Er-ba (abbreviated)
1. s. of *Na-na-šu*, V. A. 208, 10.
2. s. of *Im-bu-pâni-ia*, V. A. 209, III, 24.

Er-ba-dMarduk
1. *šar Bâbili*, V. A. 2663, II, 43; III, 52.
2. s. of *Ardi-dE-a*, C. T., X, pl. III, 29.

E-sag-ila-ai
f. of *Bêl-ile'i-kalâmi*, C. T., X, pl. VII, 48.

E-sag-ila-bu-nu-ú-a
hḫa-za-an Bît-mA-da, III R. 43, II, 3.

E-sag-ila-zêru (identical with *Ina-E-sag-ila-zêru*)
f. of *Ṭâb-ašâb-dMarduk*, V R. 56, 22; cf. also I R. 70, I, 15, 19; I R. 66, II, 12.

E-ṭi-ru(ri)
s. of *Ba-ni-ia*, *hšangu dA-e*, V. A. 209, IV, 4, 26; V, 17.

E-ul-maš-nâṣir
s. of *Tu-na-mis-saḫ*, London, 102, VI, 19.

E-ul-maš-šurqi(ŠA-ki)-iddina
s. of *Ba-zi*, III R. 43, I, 29.

G*UL.KI.ŠAR**
šar mât tâmdi, O. B. I., 83, I, 3, 6.

dGu-la-zêr-iqîša(BA-ša)
1. s. of *Ḫu-un-na*, Neb. Nippur, V 23.
2. *hbâ'iru*, C. T., X, pl. III, 13.

* That the name of this king is to be read *Gul-ki-šar* and not *Gir-ki-šar* as claimed by Winckler (*Altorientalische Forschungen*, I, 130, note 3, p. 267) and Lehmann (*Zwei Hauptprobleme*, p. 18) has been shown by Jensen (*Göttinger Gelehrten-Anzeiger*, 1900, p. 860). Another instance, besides those given by Jensen, of the sign *gir* having the value *gul* (*kul*) is found in the Code of Ḫammurabi, Col. XLIII : 19, *tu-kul-ti*.

Ḫa-'-ra-ḫu
in *âluBît-mḪa-'-ra-ḫu*, C. T., X, pl. V, 12, 16; pl. VI, 29.
Ḫab-ban (cf. *Ḫan-bi*)
1. f. of *Ellil-nâdin-šumu*, V R. 56, 23, 27.
2. f. of *dṢîr-uṣur*, I R. 70, I, 13.
3. f. of *Aḫu-er-ba*, C. T., X, pl. III, 26.
4. in *Bît-mḪab-ban* (*Ḫab-ba-an*), V R. 56, 50; I R. 70, I, 3, 10, 12; II, 5.

Ḫa-li-e
in *Bît-mḪa-li-e*, C. T., X, pl. VI, 18.
Ḫa-an-bi
1. f. of *Amel-dEllil*, III R. 41, I, 11, 28.
2. in *Bît-mḪa-an-bi*, III R. 41, I, 2, 3, 7, 34.

Ḫar-ra. . . . .
V. A. 209, III, 5.
Ḫa-sar-du
1. s. of *Su-me-e*, *ḫsukkal mu-ni-ri*, London, 101, I, 14, 22.
2. *ḫsukkal*, Susa 16, III, 18.
3. D. E. P., VI, 43, II, 11.

Ḫi-ma-gu
in *Bît-mHi-ma-gu*, Susa 16, I, 20.
Ḫi(?)*-ri-šú-ru*
f. of *Ku-dur-ra*, O. B. I., 149, I, 21.
Ḫu-un-na (abbreviated, cf. *Aḫu-ú-na-a*, Clay, B. E., X, 39; Hilprecht, B. E., X, p. 51 note)
1. f. of *dBa-ú-šum-iddina*, V R. 56, 18; Neb. Nippur, II, 17.
2. f. of *Amel-âluI-ši-in*, Neb. Nippur, V, 21.
3. f. of *Kaš-šu-ú*, prob. same as No. 2, Neb. Nippur, V, 22.
4. f. of *dGu-la-zêr-iqîša*, prob. same as Nos. 2 and 3, Neb. Nippur, V, 23.

Ib-ni-dMarduk
s. of *Ardi-dE-a*, London, 101, I, 16; Susa 3, I, 28.
I-bu-nu (cf. *I-bu-ni*, Tallquist, N. B.)
f. of *Bêl-ú-sa-tu*, V. A. 20 , II, 15; IV, 2.
Iddina(*-na*) (abbreviated)
s. of *Er-ba*, V. A. 209, III, 23.
Iddinâ(*-na-a*) (hypocor., cf. Clay, B. E., X, 17)
1. s. of *Šâpik-zêru*(!), V. A. 208, 34, 37, 54.
2. s. of *sangû dMarduk*, V. A. 208, 52.

Iddina(*-na*)*-dNabû*[2]
V. A. 209, I, 6, 13.
Ilâni-uṣrâ(*ŠEŠ.*)*-šu*,* "O gods help him."
London, 102, VI, 4.
Ili-ia (abbreviated, cf. *Bêl-ili-ia*)
f. of *dNabû-bêl-šumâti*, C. T., X, pl. VII, 48.
dIllat-ai†
br. of *dMâr-bîti-šum-ibni*, London, 102, I, 23.
Ili-ia-ili-(*DA*)*-'*, "My god is powerful."
ḫša-kin Dêrki, V. A. 209, I, 2.
Ilu-ma-udammiq(*ŠI.BIR-iq*)
s. of *Nûr-dMarduk*, London, 102, VI, 22.
Im-bi-ia-ti, "He called me."
in *Bît-mIm-bi-ia-ti*, III R. 41, I, 15.
Im-bu-pâni-ia
s. of *Er-ba*, V. A. 209, III, 24.
Ina-E-sag-ila-zêru
1. f. of *dMarduk-ìl-napḫari*(*DUL*), *ḫsukkallu*, III R. 43, I, 9; Edge IV, **4**, 5.
2. f. of *Ṭâb-a-šab-dMarduk*, I R. 70, I, 16, 19; I R. 66, II, 12; Stone of Amrân, II, 1; cf. also V R. 56, 22.

Ina-ešê-êṭir(*KAR-ir*), "From destruction he has delivered."

* Cf. *Ilu-iṣ-ṣur-šu*, Clay, B. E., XV, 180, 20; or it might be read, as suggested by Prof. Hilprecht, *Ilî-aḫi-šhu*. On AN.MEŠ = ili (sing.) cf. Editorial Preface of B. E., Vol. X, p. xii.

† Zimmern (*Beiträge*, p. 60) suggests the reading *iluḪarrân-šadû*.

s. of *Ar-ra-ku-tu*, V. A. 209, I, 4, 16, 22, 23, 34; II, 26.

*Ina-ki-bi-dEN.AB**
hḫazan Bâbili, V. A. 2663, V, 5.

In-nu-ú-a (hypocor.)
f. of *Šàr-a-ni*, V. A. 209, II, 36; III, 8.

Iqîšâ(*BA-ša-a*) (cf. Clay, B. E., X, 19, אקשׁי).
s. of *Šùm-ukîn*, V. A. 209, II, 19.

Iqîša(*BA-ša*)-*dBa-ú*
s. of *Ardi-dE-a*, London, 101, II, 8; Susa 16, III, 21; D. E. P., VI, 43, II, 16.

Iqîša(*BA-ša*)-*dMarduk*
apil šarri, V. A. 2663, IV, 57.

Ir-ri-ga (cf. *Ir-ri-gi*, Clay, B. E., XV, 34) in *Bît-mIr-ri-ga*, Susa 3, I, 13.

Is-ba-dRammân(*IM*)
in *Bît-mIs-ba-dRammân*, Susa 3, I, 18.

I-sin-na-ai
f. of *Ú-ṣal-li*, V. A. 209, III, 10.

Is-kal(?)-*da-a*
s. of *A-dal-la-li*, London, 103, I, 41.

dI-šum-ba-ni
s. of *Sin-ka-rab-iš-me*, V. A. 2663, V, 12.

It-tab-ši (abbrev., cf. *It-tab-ši-lîšir*, "May that which has been created prosper!")
1. 1. of *Ba-laṭ-su*, V. A. 209, II, 21; IV, 11.
2. s. of *dNabû-ša-d*[*u-nu*(?)], V. A. 202, 25.

Itti-dMarduk-balâṭu (*TI.LA*)
1. f. of *dNabû-zêr-lîšir*, Neb. Nippur, III, 14.
2. f. of *Šâpiku*, III R. 41, I, 13 (identical with No. 1).
3. *hšaq šarri*, London, 101, I, 20.

Iz-kur-dNabû
s. of *Ardi-dE-a*, Susa 16, II, 3.

K*al-bi* (abbrev., cf. *Kalbi-dSin*)
f. of *Ardi-dGu-la*, V R. 56, 21.

Kan-dar-šam(*Ú*)-*ši*
f. of *Ba-ni-ia*, V. A. 208, 29.

Ka-an-di
f. of *dSin-bêl-ilâni*, B. O. I. 149, I, 4.

Ka-nik-bâbi, "notary."
f. of *Mar-duk*, V. A. 2663, IV, 27.

Ka-ri-e-a (hypocor., cf. *dNabû-ina-kâri-lûmur*, Nk. 402, 18)
f. of *dNabû-ga-mil* V. A. 2663, IV, 8.

Kar-zi-ia-ab-ku
1. f. of (*dŠu-*)*qa-mu-na-apal-iddina*, London, 102, IV, 6.
2. f. of *Zêr-ukîn* (perhaps identical with No. 1), London 102, IV, 15, 28, 33.
3. f. of *dEllil-i-za....*, D. E. P., VI, 44, I, 6.
4. in *Bît-mKar-zi-ia-ab-ku*, V R. 55, 25, 35, 45; 56, 4, 30.
5. f. of *Rit-ti-dMarduk*, V R. 56, 8.

Ka-šak-ti-ia-an-zi
f. of *Ú-bal-liṭ-su*, III R. 43, II, 10.

Ka-šak-ti-Šu-gab (Cassite)
s. of *Aḫu-bânî*(-*i*), Susa 2, II, 30; Med. I, 2.

Kaš-ša-a
hšakin(-*in*) *ṭe-mi*, O. B. I., 149, I, 18.

Kaš-ša-ai
s. of *At-rat-taš*, London, 102, I, 12; III, 16; IV, 31.

Kaš-šu-ú
1. *ṭupšarru*, Neb. Nippur, V, 18.
2. s. of *Ḫu-un-na*, Neb. Nippur, V, 22.

dKaš-šu-ú-mukîn-aplu
s. of *Ba-zi*, London, 102, VI, 17.

dKaš-šu-ú-nâdin-aḫê
s. of *At-rat-taš*, London, 102, I, 13; IV, 46.

dKaš-šu-ú-šum-iddina(-*na*)
s. of *Na-zi-dMarduk*, London, 102, VI, 18.

* Perhaps intended for *Ina-ki-bi-dEN.ZU.AB=Ea;* or *AB* might be a title, for the name *mIna-ki-bi-dBêl* occurs; cf. Nd. 753, 16.

Ki-bu-šik-nu
V. A. 209, III, 18, 22.
Ki-di-ni (hypocor., cf. *Ki-din-dMar-duk*)
s. of *dBêl-iddina,* V A. 208, 2, 6, 21, 32.
Ki-din-Dupliaš(AB.NUN.NAki)
V. A. 211, II, 13.
Ki-din-dMarduk, "The client of Marduk."
1. *hMIR.GAL,* London, 101, II, 11.
2. *hpaḫâtu,* D. E. P., VI, 44, I, 9.
Ki-din-dNIN.IB
1. s. of *Nam-ri,* Susa 16, II, 5, 21.
2. London, 103, I, 30.
Ki-diš(daš)
f. of *A-tu-'-ú,* Neb. Nippur, V, 14.
[*Ki*(?)]-*na-a* (cf. *Ki-na-a,* Clay, B. E., X, 54), C. T. X, pl. VI, 25.
Ki-in-pî(KA)-dŠamaš (cf. *I-ku-un-bi-Sin,* Ranke, P. N., p. 98)
f. of *Ta-qi-šú,* Neb. Nippur, V, 12.
Ku-bu-bu (cf. *Ku-ub-bu-bu,* Clay, B. E., XV)*
amel bâb êkalli, Neb. Nippur, V, 10.
Kud-da-ai (cf. *Qu-da-a, Qud-da-a,* Hilprecht in B. E., IX)
London, 102, III, 15.
Ku-dur-ra
s. of *Hi*(?)-*ri-šú-ru,* O. B. I., 149, I, 21.
Ku-du-ra-na (hypocor., cf. Ranke, P. N., p. 13)
s. of *dBêl....,* London, 103, I, 21.
Ku-dur-ru
s. of *E-gi-bi,* V. A. 2663, IV, 11.
Ku-ri-Gal-zu
1. f. of *Na-zi-Marut-taš,* Susa 2, I, 3; II, 28.
2. s. of *Bur-ra-Bu-ri-ia-aš,* D. E. P., II, 93, I, 6, 18 (identical with No. 1).
3. ancestor of *dMarduk-apal-iddina* I, IV R.[2] 38, I, 25.
4. s. of *dBêl-erba,* V. A. 208, 27.

Kur-za-bu
s. of *Su-me-e-a,* D. E. P., VI, 44, I, 14.

L*a-ba-ši-dMarduk* (cf. *Lâ-tu-ba-ša-ni-ilu,* Ps. 25 : 2; Tallquist, N. B., p. 308)
s. of *Da-bi-bi,* V. A. 2663, V, 8.
La-ba-šu (abbreviated)
1. s. of *Ú-ṣal-li,* V. A. 209, II, 20.
2. s. of *Ra-ḫaṣ,* V. A. 209, IV, 16.
âluLa-rak-zêr-ibni(KAK!)
s. of *At-rat-taš,* London, 102, I, 12.
La-ri-i(?)
V. A. 208, 40.
Li-bur-za-nin-E-kur, "May the restorer of Ekur be strong."
hšaqû, London, 101, II, 6; Susa 16, III, 17.
fLi-ki-im-ma-ai
V. A. 209 IV, 12.
Lûṣa(UD.DU)-a-na nûr-dMarduk
London, 101, II, 7.
Lûṣa(UD.DA)-ilu....
London, 103, I, 26.

*d***M***âr-bîti(TUR.E)-aḫê-iddina(-na)*
mâr šarri, London, 102, IV, 44.
dMâr-bîti(TUR.E)-ša-li-ti
s. of *Me-li-Ḫa-la,* London, 102, IV, 45.
dMâr-bîti(TUR.E)-šum-ibni(KAK)
s. of *Ardi-dSibitti,* London, 102, I, 19, 25 [35], III, 18; IV, 18, 19, 28, 32.
Mar-duk
1. s. of *Ka-nik-bâbi,* V. A. 2663, IV, 26, 41.
2. s. of *dSin-tab-ni,* V. A. 209, II, 12.
dMarduk-apal-iddina(-na)
1. *šarru,* s. of *Me-li-Ši-pak,* Susa 2, Med. 2, I, 2; Susa 16, II, 14, 20, 29, 34; IV R.[2] 38, I, 20; II, 18; Susa 3, I, 39; II, 4; Susa 14, I, 15; D. E. P., VI, 42, I, 23.
2. *šar Bâbili,* V. A. 2663, I, 25, 43; III, 39; IV, 49; V, 17, 33.

* A hypocoristicon, cf. *Puḫḫuru,* Tallquist, *Namenbuch,* p. xviii; O. L. Z., IX (1906), p. 467.

dMarduk-e-a (hypocor.)
f. of *Sa-mi-du*, III R. 43, II, 22.
dMarduk-aḫê-erba(SU)
1. *šarru*, O. B. I., 149, I, 14.
dMarduk-ibni
hḫa-za-an Bît-mPir'-dAmurru, Susa 14, I, 9.
dMarduk-ìl-napḫari(DUL)
s. of *Ina-E-sagila-zêru*, III R. 43, I, 8; Edge IV, 3, 4.
dMarduk-ku-dur-ri-uṣur(ŠA.DU.ŠEŠ)
1. s. of *Ur-dBêlit-muballiṭat-mîtûti*, London, 103, IV, 15; V, 9, 18, 24.
2. *hšaq bîti*, Susa 16, III, 19.
3. *hsukkal dBêl*, V R. 56, 14.
4. *hšaqû*, D. E. P., VI, 43, II, 12.
dMarduk-mukîn-aplu
s. of *Ṭâbu(ḪI)-mi-li-e*, V R. 56, 20.
dMarduk-nâdin-aḫê
šarru, I R. 66, I, 3; II, 18; III R. 43, I, 4, 22, 28; edge IV, 4.
dMarduk-nâṣir(PAP)
1. *hšaq šarri*, III R. 41, I, 11, 29.
2. s. of *Ga-mi*[-*il*]. . . ., III R. 43, II, 29.
dMarduk-šâpik(DUB)-zêru
s. of *Tam-ma-šad*(?)-*dar*, C. T., X, pl. III, 28.
dMarduk-šàr[-*ilani*(?)]
f. of *Šu-ma-a*, C. T., X, pl. VI, 25.
dMarduk-šum-iddina
šar Bâbili, V. A. 208, 53.
dMarduk-za-kir-šumu
1. *bêl paḫâti*, IV R.^{2} 38, I, 27; III, 21.
2. *Ardi-dEa*, V. A. 2663, V, 2.
dMarduk-zêr-ib-ni
s. of *dSin-ša-du-nu*, C. T., X, pl. VII, 46.
Mâr-âluIš-nu-nak
I R. 66, II, 3.
Ma-zi (perhaps better *Ba-zi*)
in *Bît-mMa-zi*, C. T., IX, pl. V, 25 (cf. *Bît-mBa-zi*, D. E. P., VI, 42, I, 14).
Me-li-Ḫa-la
1. f. of *Mâr-bîti-ša-li-ti*, London, 102, IV, 45.
2. [*Me*]-*li-Ḫa-la*, s. of *Zu-me-e*[-*a*], D. E. P., II, 112, 8; VI, 44; I, 2(?).
Me-li-Ši-pak
šarru, successor of *Rammân-nâdin-aḫê*, London, 103, IV, 17, 36; V, 11, 20, 21; VI, 31.
f. of *Marduk-apal-iddina* I., Susa 2, Med. 2, I, 3.
šarru, Susa 3, I, 27; II, 3, D. E. P., 112, 7; Susa 16, I, 5; II, 4, 12; *šar Bâbili*, IV R.^{2} 38, I, 23; *šar kiššati*, London, 101, I, 13.
Mi-li-Ḫar-be
1. f. of *Šu-qa-mu-na-aḫ-iddina*(-*na*), III R. 43, II, 14.
2. f. of *Anu-bêl-aḫê-šu*, III R. 43, II, 18.
Mudammiq(ŠI.BIR-iq)-dRammân
f. of *Ardi-dNanâ*, V R. 56, 13; I R. 66, II, 13; Stone of Amrân, II, 2.
Muk-kut-is-saḫ (cf. perhaps *Tu-na-mi-is-sa-aḫ*, IV R.^{2} 38, I, 14)
1. s. of *Ṣa(za)-ap-ri*, V R. 56, 16.
2. in *Bît-mMuk-kut-is-saḫ*, Susa 2, I, 12, 18.
Mu-un-na-bit-tu(ti), "fugitive."
s. of *Ṭâbu(DUG.GA)-me-lu-ú*, Susa 16, I, 6; II, 11, 19, 32; III, 9, 13.
Mu-ra-nu
s. of *Še-kib-si-bar*. . . ., V. A. 208, 42.
Mušabši(TUK)-ilu
s. of *Apli-ia*, III R. 43, II, 15.
Mu-šal-li-mu (abbrev., cf. *dNabû mušallim*)
s. of *dSin-apal-iddina*, V. A. 208, 23.
Mu-šal-lim-aplu
f. of *Aḫu-iddina*, V. A. 2663, IV, 13.
Mu-šal-lim-dMarduk
s. of *Ardi-dMarduk*, London, 102, IV, 7.
Mu-še-zib-dMarduk
f. of *dRammân-ibni*, C. T., X, pl. IV, 22; V, 14; VI, 31.
Mu-šib-ša
apil hḫa-za-an-na, V. A. 208, 41.

dNabû[1,2]*-apal-iddina*
1. *šarru*, C. T., X, pl. III, 2, 9, 21, 31; V. A. 208, 30.
2. s. of *At-na-ai*, C. T., X, pl. III, 1, 22.

dNabû[1]*-aḫu-ni*(!)*
s. of *A-šab-šu*, V. A. 208, 51.

dNabû[2]*-balâṭ(TIN)-su-iq-bi*
V. A. 2663, V, 4.

dNabû[1]*-bêl-šumâti(MU.MEŠ)*
s. of *Ili-ia*, C. T., X, pl. VII, 47.

dNabû[2]*-bêl-u-ṣur*
hša-kin, C. T., X, pl. VII, 42.

dNabû[1,2]*-ga-mil*
1. s. of *Ka-ri-e-a*, V. A. 2663, IV, 7.
2. *mâr hnangaru*, V. A. 208, 9.

dNabû[1]*[êriš](-iš)* (cf. *Šamaš-êriš* of this list)
s. of *Ardi-dEa*, O. B. I, 149, I, 15.

dNabû[2]*-ḫa-mat-ú-a*, "Nabû is my help"(?).
hnâgir êkalli, V. A. 2663, V, 7.

dNabû[1]*-iddina(SE-na)*
f. of *dAi(GAL)-mu-tak-kil*, V. A. 209, V, 19.

dNabû[1,2]*-ile'i(DA)*
1. s. of *Arkât-ilâni-damqâti*, V. A. 2663, V, 10.
2. s. of *Nûr-dSin*, V. A. 209, I, 3, 17, 20, 26; II, 35; III, 9, 23; IV, 1, 6, 15, 18, 31, 34, 38.

dNabû[1]*-iqîša(BA-ša)*
f. of *Mu-še-zib-dMarduk*, C. T., X, pl. VI, 31.

dNabû[1]*-ku-dur-ri-uṣur(ŠA.DU.ŠEŠ)*
1. *šarru*, V R. 55, 1, 23, 42, 49; C. T., IX, pl. IV, 4, 7, 15; V, 27; O. B. I., 83, I, 7; Neb. Nippur, I, 23; II, 23, V, 26.
2. *hnâgir mâtuNa-mar*, V R. 56, 24.

dNabû[1]*-mukîn(GI.NA)-aplu*
šarru, London, 102, I, 10, 18; II, 37; III, 9, 12, 22; IV, 1, 12, 14.

dNabû[2]*-mušallim(GI)*
s. of *Da-ku-ru*, C. T., X, pl. V, 10, 11; VII, 45.

dNabû[1]*-nâdin-aḫê*
1. s. of *Nam-ri*, I R. 66, II, 15.
2. IV R.[2] 38, I, 32.

dNabû[1]*-na-ṣi-ir*
s. of *Na-zi-dMarduk*, IV R.[2] 38, II, 34.

dNabû[2]*-ni-ir-da-bi-bi*
hṭupšarru, V. A. 2663, V, 14.

dNabû[1]*-râ'im-zêru*
s. of *Ardi-dEa*, I R. 66, II, 14.

dNabû[1]*-rim-an-ni*
C. T., X, pl. VII, 43.

dNabû[1]*-ša-d[u-nu(?)]*†
f. of *It-tab-ši*, V. A. 208, 25.

dNabû[1]*-ša-kin(šakin-in)-šumu*
1. s. of *Ardi-dEa*, IV R.[2] 38, II, 36.
2. London, 103, IV, 28.

dNabû[2]*-šaqû(NIM)-ina-mâti*
s. of *A-qar-dNabû*, C. T., X, pl. III, 15.

dNabû[1]*-šum-iddina*
1. s. of *Šu-zib-dMarduk*, Susa 16, II, 7.
2. *šangû dApsû(ENGUR)*, O. B. I., 83, I, 15.

dNabû[1]*-tab-ni-bul(!)-liṭ*
London, 102, VI, 20.

dNabû[1]*-un-na* (abbrev., cf. *Nabû-ú-ú-na-aḫ-ḫu*, Tallquist, N. B.)
s. of *A-ḫi*, Neb. Nippur, III, 15; V, 16.

dNabû[1]*-ú-šib-ši* (= *Nabû-ú-šab-ši*, II R. 67, 15)
s. of *dNabû-zêr-iddina*, V. A. 208, 19.

Na-bu-ti (cf. *Na-bu-tu*, Tallquist, N. B., 149; *Na-bu-ut-tu*, K. B. IV, p. 124)
br. of *dMâr-bîti-šum-ibni*, London, 102, I, 22.

dNabû[1]*-zêr-ib-nu*
s. of *Bît-dar(?)-da-ri-ib-nu*, V. A. 209, II, 23.

* Dr. Ungnad regards the last *ni* as a scribal error for *ir* and accordingly reads the name *dNabû-nâṣir(-ir)*.

† Read *dNabû-šâkin-šu[mu]* by Ungnad; see *Vorderasiatische Schriftdenkmäler*, Vol. I, p. vii, *a*; but compare the name *dSin-ša-du-nu* of this list.

dNabû²-zêr-iddina(-na)
1. f. of *dBêl-iddina*, V. A. 208, 1, 14, 18, 20, 32, 49.
2. f. of *dNabû-ú-šib-ši* (identical with No. 1), V. A. 208, 20.

dNabû¹-zêr-lîšir(SI.DI)
1. s. of *Ardi-dEa*, Neb. Nippur, V 24.
2. s. of *Itti-dMarduk-balâṭu*, Neb. Nippur, III, 13.

*Nam-gar(ŠA)-dûr-dEllil**
London, 103, III, 23.

Nam-mu-ú-a
apil šangû dRammân, V. A. 2663, IV, 39.

Namri (cf. *Nam-ru*, Clay, B. E., XV, "shining")
1. f. of *Ki-din-dNIN.IB*, Susa 16, II, 5.
2. f. of *dNabû-nâdin-aḫê*, I R. 66, II, 15.

Na-na-šu
f. of *Er-ba*, V. A. 208, 10.

Na-ṣi-bi-ilu
in *Bît-mNa-ṣi-bi-ilu*, C. T., X, pl. VI, 20.

Na-zi-d . . . .
f. of *Nim-gi-ra-bi-dMar[duk]*, D. E. P., II, 93, I, 10.

Na-zi-dEllil¹
f. of *dNIN.IB-bêl-šu-nu*, V. A. 2663, V, 1.

Na-zi-dMarduk
1. s. of *Šad-dak-me*, V R. 56, 12.
2. s. of *Zêri-ia*, London, 102, IV, 4.
3. f. of *dNabû-na-ṣi-ir*, IV R.² 38, II, 35.
4. f. of *dKaš-šu-ú-šùm-iddina-(na)*, London, 102, VI, 18.
5. in *Bît-mNa-zi-dMarduk*, IV R.² 38, I, 10.

Nazi-Marut-taš
s. of *Ku-ri-Gal-zu*, Susa 2, I, 1; II, 26.

dNergal-apal-uṣur
V. A. 211, II, 5.

dNergal(UGUR)-ašaridu(SAG.KAL)
s. of *dSin-karâbi-išme*, C. T., X, pl. VII, 49.

dNergal-êpuš(KAK-uš)
V. A. 209, IV, 29.

dNergal-ri-ṣu-ú-a
lušа-kin PA.ŠEki, V. A. 211, II, 1.

dNergal-ú-šib-ši (*ušibši(IG-ši)*)
1. s. of *Tu(tam)-ma-šad(lad)-dar*, C T., X, pl. III, 27.
2. V. A. 211, II, 8.

Ni-bi-Ši-pak
f. of *Šu-ḫu-li-Šu-gab*, Susa 2, Med. 2, 8.

Ni-ga-zi
f. of *dBa-ú-aḫu-iddina*, I R. 66, II, 10.

Nim-gi(!)-ra-bi dMar[duk]
s. of *Na-zi*. . . ., D. E. P., II, 93, I, 9.

dNIN.IB-apal-iddina
1. s. of *dRammân-na-ṣi-ir*, IV R.² 38, II, 31.
2. s. of *At-rat-taš*, London, 102, I, 13.

dNIN.IB(BAR)-bêl-šu-nu
s. of *Na-zi-dEllil*, V. A. 2663, V, 1.

dNIN.IB-kudurri-uṣur (*ŠA.DU-PAP* or *ŠEŠ*)
1. *šarru*, London, 102, II, 36; III, 21; VI, 1, 6, 8, 24.
2. *mâr šarri*, London, 102, IV, 42.

dNIN.IB-nâdin(SE)-šumu
London, 102, IV, 47.

dNIN.IB-nâṣir(PAP-ir)
London, 103, I, 27.

dNIN.IB. . . .tu-ú
f. of *Ta-kil-a-na-ili-šu*, London, 103, II, 2.

Nu-ur-aḫê-šu (abbreviated)
in *âlu ša mNu-ur-aḫê-šu*, Susa 3, I, 17.

Nûr(LAḪ)-dBunene(ḪAR)
f. of *Šal-man-la-ti-ku*, London, 102, IV, 9.

Nûr-e-a (hypocor.)
in *Bît-mNûr-e-a*, C. T., X, pl. VI, 24, 29.

* This name occurs as the name of a canal in the Murashû texts, cf. B. E., Vol. X, p. 70.

Nûr-dE-a
f. of *Zêri-ia*, C. T., X, pl. III, 15.
Nûr-lîšir(SI.DI)
f. of *Šamûa* and *Šamai*, C. T., IX, pl. IV, 2; V, 29.
Nûr-dMarduk
f. of *Ilu-ma-udammiq(-iq)*, London, 102, VI, 22.
Nûr-dSin (XXX)
1. f. of *dNabû-ile'i*, V. A. 209, I, 3; III, 9, 23; IV, 1, 18.
2. f. of *Ša-ba-ia*, V. A. 209, II, 13, 14; V, 14.
3. f. of *dA-num-nâṣir*, V. A. 209, II, 14; V, 15 (perhaps all three identical).
dNusku(PA+KU)-ib-ni
s. of *Upaḫḫir-dNusku*, Neb. Nippur, II, 13; III, 10, 31.

P*ir'-dAmurru(KUR.GAL)*
1. in *Bît-mPir'-dAmurru*, O. B. I., 149, I, 4, 10, 13, 17; II, 5; Susa 14, I, 11; Susa 3, I, 25; II, 40, 47; III, 17, 25, 32.
2. in *Bît-Pir*(?)*-dAmurru(MAR.TU)*, London, 101, I, 6, 7, 12.
Pir(UD)-ša (cf. perhaps *fPir(UD)-ša-ti*, Clay, B. E., XV, 49, or abbreviated from *Pir-dŠamaš*, see p. 186f.)
hnâgiru, Neb. Nippur, V, 20.
Pi-ir-dŠamaš
s. of *Šu-ma-at*(?)*-dŠamaš*, D. E. P., II, 93, I, 14.

R*abâ(GAL-a)-ša-dMarduk**
f. of *dEllil-šum-ib-ni*, C. T., X, pl. III, 24.
Ra-ḫaṣ
f. of *La-ba-šu*, V. A. 209, IV, 17, 35, 36.
dRammân(IM)-bêl-ka-la
šaq šarri, D. E. P., VI, 42, I, 19.
dRammân-ib-ni
s. of *Mušêzib-dMarduk*, C. T., X, pl. V, 14; VI, 31.
dRammân-da-an
hsukkallu, C. T., X, pl. VII, 42.
dRammân-na-ṣi-ir
f. of *dNIN.IB-apal-iddina*, IV R.[2] 38, II, 32.
dRammân-šum-êriš
s. of *dSin-apal-iddina*, V. A. 208, 22.
dRammân-šum-iddina
šarru, London, 103, I, 2, 4, 18, 24, 37; VI, 29.
dRammân-šum-uṣur (or perhaps *nâdin-aḫu*)
šarru, London, 103, I, 40, 45; II, 17; III, 2, 39; IV, 5, 31; VI, 30; D. E. P., VI, 42, I, 18.
šar kiššati, D. E. P., II, 97, 8.
dRammân-zêr-iqîša(BA-ša)
III R. 43, I, 6, 12; Edge IV, 3.
mhRê'û-piḫâti
f. of *Ta-ki-ša-dBêlit*, III R. 43, II, 8.
Ri-ḫa-nu
hki-i-pi ša E-sag-ila, C. T., X, pl. VII, 44.
Ri-ḫu-ša-ilâni, "The seed of the gods."
mâr šarri, London, 102, IV, 43.
Ri-me-ni-dMarduk, "Merciful is Marduk."
f. of *dNabû-na-din-aḫê*, IV R.[2] 38, I, 34.
Ri-mu-ta(ti) (abbreviated)
s. of *Be-la-ni*, London, 103, III, 11, 27, 31.
Ri-mut-dGu-la
bêl paḫâti, Neb. Nippur, V, 15.
Rit-ti-dMarduk, "My hand (= help) is Marduk."
bêl bîti ša Bît-mKar-zi-ab-ku, V R. 55, 25; 35, 45; VI, 7.
Ri-zi-in-ni
hšaq, London, 101, II, 5.

S*a-a-mi-pa*(?)
f. of *fUr-dBêlit-muballiṭat-mîtûti*, London, 103, IV, 8.
Sag-ga. . . .
D. E. P., II, 93, 9.

* For this reading see Tallquist, *Namenbuch*, p. 173*a*.

^{fd}SAG-mudammiq(ŠIBIR-iq)-šar-be
  d. of *Ardi-^{d}Sibitti*, London, 101, I, 16, 27, 34.
Sa-mi-du (cf. Clay, B. E., XIV, p. 51; XV, p. 41)
  s. of *^{d}Marduk-e-a*, III R. 43, II, 21.
^{d}Sin(XXX)-aḫê-erba(SU)
  s. of *Ra-ḫaṣ*, V. A. 209, IV, 16.
^{d}Sin-apal-iddina
  f. of *Mu-šal-li-mu*, V. A. 208, 23.
^{d}Sin-ašaridu (SAG.KAL) (abbreviated, cf. *^{d}Sin-a-ša-rid* and *^{d}Šamaš-a-ša-ri-id-ili(NI.NI)*; see Tallquist, N. B.; cf. also Hilprecht in Ranke's P. N., p. 129, under *Nannar-SAG-KAL*.
  1. O. B. I., 150, I, 2, 3, 4.
  2. in *Bît-^{md}Sin-ašaridu*, Susa 2, II, 14; C. T., IX, pl. IV, 22.
^{d}Sin-bêl(BE)-ilâni
  s. of *Ka-an-di*, O. B. I., 149, I, 3.
^{d}Sin-ib-nu
  ^{h}nuḫatimmu(MU), V. A. 209, II, 16.
^{d}Sin-ka-rab-iš-me
  f. of *^{d}I-šum-ba-ni*, V. A. 2663, V, 12.
^{d}Sin-karâbi(GAZ.GAZ)-iš-me
  f. of *^{d}Nergal-ašaridu*, C. T., X, pl. VII, 49.
^{d}Sin-lîšir(SI.DI)
  f. of *Ba-bi-la-ai(-ú)*, I R. 66, II, 8; III R. 43, II, 2.
^{d}Sin-ma-gir
  in *Bît-^{md}Sin-ma-gir*, Susa 2, I, 28; O. B. I., 83, I, 11, 12; II, 4, 6, 13.
^{d}Sin-mu-šal-lim
  s. of *Bu-ru-ša*, London, 102, VI, 15.
^{d}Sin-ša-du-nu
  f. of *^{d}Marduk-zêr-ibni*, C. T., X, pl. VII, 46.
^{d}Sin-še-me
  in *Bît-^{md}Sin-še-me*, Neb. Nippur, II, 20, 28; III, 1, 8, 9, 16 [30]; V, 9, 10, 11, 13, 14, 15, 17, 18, 20.
^{d}Sin-zêr-ib-ni
  ^{h}ḫa-za-an-nu, Neb. Nippur, V, 19.
^{d}Sin-tab-ni (abbreviated, cf. *Sin-tab ni-uṣur*)
  f. of *Mar-duk*, V. A. 209, II, 12.
Su-ḫur-Gal-du (cf. p. 174)
  in *Bît-^{m}Su-ḫur-Gal-du*, Neb. Nippur, Heading 9; III, 3.
Su-me-e
  f. of *Ḫa-sar-du*, London, 101, I, 15.
Su-me-e-a
  f. of *Kur-za-bu*, D. E. P., VI, 44, I, 14.
*Ša-ba-ia**
  s. of *Nûr-^{d}Sin*, V. A. 209, II, 13; V, 14.
Šad-dak-me†
  f. of *Na-zi-^{d}Marduk*, V R. 56, 12.
Ša-ga-rak-tum (abbrev., cf. *Šagarakti-Šuriaš*)
  ^{h}ša-kin ṭe-me mât ^{alu}Ir-ri-ḫa, D. E. P., VI, 44, I, 11.
Šal-man-la-ti-ku. . . .
  s. of *Nûr-^{d}Bunene*, London, 102, IV, 8.
Ša-ma-ai
  s. of *Ša-mu-ú-a*, C. T., IX, pl. IV, 1, 17; pl. V, 29.
Ša-mar-di
  br. of *^{d}Mâr-bîti-šum-ibni*, London, 102, I, 22.
^{d}Šamaš(UT)-êriš(PIN)
  f. of *^{d}Bêl-iddina*, V. A. 208, 50.
^{d}Šamaš-iddina (abbreviated)
  ^{h}ḫa-za-an-nu Ḫa-ni, London, 101, I, 18.
^{d}Šamaš-nâdin-šumu
  1. s. of *Ardi-nu-bat-ti*, Susa 3, I, 30.
  2. s. of *At-ta-ilu-ma*, V R. 56, 17.
  3. s. of *Bu-ru-ša*, London, 102, I, 17, 27, 36; IV, 30.
^{d}Šamaš-nâṣir(ŠEŠ) (abbreviated, see Tallquist, N. B., 142, under *^{d}Nabû-nâṣir*)
  ^{h}šaq-šup-par, Neb. Nippur, V, 9.

* Cf. the names *Ša-bu-ú-a* and *^{d}Marduk-ša-bu-šu*, see Tallquist, *Namenbuch*.

† Formerly read *Kur-kà-me*, but the second sign is not *KÀ*, from which it differs by the last two wedges. In the Cassite texts the name *Šad(Kur)-dak-me* occurs; see B. E., Vol. XV, 37, 8; 85 : 3; 90 : 20. That makes it probable that the doubtful sign is an older form of *dak*.

ᵈŠamaš-šum-lîšir(SI.DI)
1. s. of *At-ta-ilu-ma*, London, 101, II, 9.
2. s. of *Ul-tu-ilu*, Susa, 3, I, 33.

ᵈŠamaš(GIŠ.ŠIR)-šum-ukîn(GI.NA)
šarru, C. T., X, pl. V, 7; VI, 29; VII, 51.

Šam(Ú)-eš-Ḫa-la
f. of *Amel-E-ul-maš*, III R. 43, II, 20.

Ša-mu-ú-a
s. of *Nûr-lîšir*, C. T., IX, pl. IV, 1, 17; pl. V, 28.

*Šâpik(DUB-ik)-zêru** (abbreviated)
f. of *Iddinâ*, V. A. 208, 34, 37, 54.

Ša-pi-ku (abbreviated)
s. of *Itti-ᵈMarduk-balâṭu*, III R. 41, I, 13

ᵐʰŠaq-šup-par (cf. p. 201*)
s. of *ᵈEllil-mušallim-aplu*, III R. 43, II, 6.

Šàr-a-ni (abbrev., cf. *ᵈBêl-šàr-a-ni*, Tallquist, N. B.)
s. of *In-nu-ú-a*, V. A. 209, II, 35; III, 8.

Šar-bi ᵈEllil †
ḫazannu, O. B. I., 149, I, 19.

Šarru-ukîn(DU)(ú-kin)
šarru, C. T., X, pl. IV, 12; V. A. 209, II, 28; V, 4.

Ša-zu-ú-ti
f. of *ᵈEllil-nâdin-šumu*, III R. 43, II, 13.

Še-kib-si-bar....
f. of *Mu-ra-nu*, V. A. 208, 42.

Še-li-bi
in *âlu ša Mâr-ᵐŠe-li-bi*, Susa 3, I, 44.

ŠEŠ-a-pa....
in *Bît-ᵐŠEŠ-a-pa....*, London, 103, III, 48.

Ši-gu-ú-a (cf. *Še-gu-su*, Nk. 305, 14, and *šegû*, lamentation)
f. of *ᵈBêl-iddina(-na)*, C. T., X, pl. VII, 50.

Ši-ta-ri-ba, "She has increased" (cf. p. 186).
ʰšaqû, Neb. Nippur, V, 11.

Šú-uḫ-ḫu
C. T., X, pl. IV, 6.

Šu-ḫu-li-Šu-gab
s. of *Ni-bi-Ši-pak*, Susa 2, Med. 2, 7.

Šú-la-a (cf. perhaps *Šul-lu-ú-a*, Tallquist, N. B.)
f. of *Bi-e-a*, V. A. 209, IV, 9.

ᵐŠu-li-l[i]
D. E. P., VI, 43, III, 2.

Šul-ma-nu-ašaridu(MAŠ)
šar ᵐᵃᵗᵘAššur, V. A. 209, I, 1.

Šú-ma-a
1. s. of *Er-ba*, V. A. 209, III, 24.
2. s. of *ᵈMarduk-šàr-[ilâni(?)]*, C. T., X, pl. VI, 25.

Šu-ma-at(?)-ᵈŠamaš
f. of *Pi-ir-ᵈŠamaš*, D. E. P., II, 93, I, 15.

Šum-ili-a-šip-ú-uš, "The name of the god is his diviner."
O. B. I., 149, I, 8.

Šúm-ukîn(GI.NA)
f. of *Iqîšâ(BA-ša-a)*, V. A. 209, II, 19.

Šú-qa-mu-na-aḫu-iddina
s. of *Mi-li-Ḫar-be*, III R. 43, II, 13.

(Šu)-qa-mu-na-apal-iddina(-na)
s. of *Kar-zi-ab-ku*, London, 102, IV, 5.

Šu-zib-ᵈMarduk
s. of *Ardi-ᵈEa*, Susa 16, II, 8.

Ṣa-ap-ri (cf. *Za-ap-rum(ru, ri)*, in Clay, B. E., XIV, p. 55. Probably abbreviated, a derivation of *ṣapâru*, to call)

ᵈṢîr-ap-pi-li, perhaps "O Ṣir, answer."
in *Bît-ᵐᵈṢîr-ap-pi-li*, Neb. Nippur, Heading 5; III, 1.

ᵈṢîr-šum-iddina(na)
s. of *Aḫu-ba-nu-ú*, Susa 16, II, 24; III, 1.

ᵈṢîr-uṣur(ŠEŠ)
s. of *Ḫab-ban*, I R. 70, I, 13.

* Thus according to Dr. Ungnad.

† For the element *Šar-bi* cf. *ᵈSAG-mudammiq-šar-be* in this list.

T_ab-ni-e-a_ (hypocor.)
  ʰ_ḫazannu_, V. A. 209, V, 16.
Tab-nu-ta(ti)
  s. of _Be-la-ni_, London, 103, III, 11, 27, 31.
Ta-kil-a-na-ili-šu, "He is trusting in his god."
  1. ʰ_bârû_, London 103, I, 5, 7, 28, 39, 42; II, 1, 7, 10, 15; III, 43; IV, 9, 22, 32, 41; V, 22, 30, 33.
  2. _Bît-ᵐTa-kil-a-na-ili-šu_, London, 103, I, 1, 5, 36, 42; II, 7; III, 43; V, 30, 33.
Ta-qi-ša-ᵈBêlit(GAŠAN)
  s. of _ᵐRê'û-piḫâti_, III, 43, II, 7.
_Ta-qi-šu_ (abbreviated)
  s. of _Ki-in-pî-ᵈŠamaš_, Neb. Nippur, V, 12.
Tu(tam)-ma-šad(lad)-dar
  f. of _ᵈNergal-ú-šib-ši_, C. T., X, pl. III, 27.
Tu-na-mi-is-sa-aḫ(saḫ)
  1. f. of _E-ul-maš-nâṣir_, London, 102, VI, 19.
  2. in _Bît-ᵐTu-na-mi-is-sa-aḫ(saḫ)_, IV R.² 38, I, 14; I R. 70, I, 18; Susa 3, I, 45.
_Tu-un-na-a_ (cf. _Tu-na-a_, Tallquist, N. B.)
  ʰ_MUK_, V. A. 209, II, 17; IV, 44.
Ṭa-ab-a-šab-ᵈMarduk, "Good is the dwelling of Marduk" (cf. Clay, B. E., XV, 44, note 2).*
  s. of _(Ina)-E-sag-ila-zêru_, V R. 56, 22; I R. 70, I, 15, 18; I R. 66, II, 11; Stone of Amrân, II, 1.
Ṭâbu(DUG.GA)-me-lu-ú
  f. of _Mu-un-na-bit-tu_, Susa 16, I, 7; III, 10.
Ṭâbu(DUG)-mi-li-e
  f. of _Marduk-mukîn-aplu_, V R. 56, 20.
_Ṭu-bi-ia-en-na_
  ʰ_šaqû_, V R. 56, 15.

U_-bal-liṭ-su_ (abbreviated)
  s. of _Ka-šak-ti-ia-an-zi_, III R. 43, II, 9.
Uballiṭ(TI.LA)-su-ᵈGu-la
  s. of _Ardi-ᵈEa_, V R. 56, 19.
Ú-bal-liṭ-su-ᵈMarduk
  f. of _Ri-me-ni-ᵈMarduk_, IV R.² 38, II, 2.
Ul-tu-ilu (abbreviated)
  f. of _ᵈŠamaš-šum-lîšir_, Susa 3, I, 34.
ᵐ arḫuUlûla-ai
  f. of _ᵈBâniti-êreš_, V. A. 209, II, 18, 32.
Upaḫḫir(KIL)-ᵈNusku, "Nusku gave strength" (cf. _ᵈNabû-upaḫḫir (NIGIN-ir)_).
  f. of _ᵈNusku-ibni_, Neb. Nippur, II, 13; III, 10, [31].
_Up-pa...._
  D. E. P., II, 93, II, 4.
Ur-ᵈBêlit-muballiṭat (TIN)-mîtûti (BAD-ga)†
  br. of _Ta-kil-a-na-ili-šu_, London, 103, I, 6, 17, 38, 44; II, 9, 12, 19; III, 5, 14, 15, 24, 33, 38, 46; IV, 7, 11, 16, 25, 35; V, 25.
Ú-ṣal-li (abbreviated, cf. _Ninib-u-ṣal-li_)
  1. f. of _La-ba-šu_, V. A. 209, II, 20.
  2. s. of _I-sin-na-ai_, V. A. 209, III, 10.
_Uš-bu-la_
  in _Bît-ᵐUš-bu-la_, Neb. Nippur, III, 5.
_Uz-bi-ᵈ . . . ._
  D. E. P., VI, 43, II, 14.
Ú-zib-ᵈEllil
  ʰ_sukkallu_, Susa 16, III, 20.

* To this translation Prof. Hilprecht remarks: "It is doubtful to me whether the use of the ideogram in the passage quoted from B. E., XV, is sufficient to prove the writing with 'b,' _ašâbu_, 'to dwell.' In view of _Šum-ili-a-šip-ú-uš_ it is not impossible that the scribe mixed the ideograms for _ašâbu_ and _ašâpu_ (the latter also pronounced _ašâbu_ in Babylonian), so that the old translation, 'Good is the exorcism (_ašâbu_ = _ašâpu_) of Marduk,' would stand after all."

† The goddess Gula is meant, cf. her name _ᵈNIN.TIN.BAD-ga_ = _bêltum muballiṭat mîti_, see Br. 11084.

Û-zib-ia (hypocor.)
s. of *At-rat-taš*, London, 102, I, 14.
Û-zu-ub-Ši-pak
D. E. P., II, 93, I, 3.

Za(?)*-za-ku-la-te-a-dMarduk*
London, 102, VI, 23.
Zêri-ia (hypocor.)
1. s. of *Na-zi-dMarduk*, London, 102, IV, 4.
2. s. of *Nûr-dEa*, C. T., X, pl. III, 15.

Zêr-ib-ni
1. s. of *Ardi-dE-a*, Susa 14, I, 16.
2. s. of *At-rat-taš*, London, 102, I, 14.
Zêr-ukîn(GI.NA)
s. of *Kar-zi-ab-ku*, London, 102, IV, 15, 17, 26, 28, 33.
Zu-me-e-(a) (cf. *Su-me-e-a* of this list)
f. of [*Me*]*-li-Ḫa-la*, D. E. P., II, 112, 8; D. E. P., VI, 44, I, 3.

2. Names of Places.

âluA-'-a-'-zi
D. E. P., VI, 46, I, 2.
âluAk-ka-di(A.GA.DEki)
London, 103, V, 19; London, 101, II, 10; *âluA.GA.DEki*, Susa 3, I, 4; V R. 56, 50.
mâtuAkkadîki(URI)
V R. 55, 13, 44; 56, 12; IV R.² 38, I, 22; Neb. Nippur, II, 1; V. A. 2663, I, 17, 28, 38, 46; III, 14; C. T., X, pl. IV, 13, 18; V, 4; VII, 32; London, 102, IV, 27; V. A. 2663, V, 21.
mâtuAl-ni-ri-e-a
III R. 43, I, 2; III R. 45, No. 2 : 2, 3, 5.
mâtuA-mur-ri-i
V R. 55, 10.
âluAn-za-qar (cf. Hommel, *Geogr.*, p. 350)
Susa 16, I, 27.
âluAn-za-qar-meš
IV R.² 38, I, 13.
mâtuAššur
III R. 43, I, 5; II, 27; C. T., X, pl. IV, 10, [11] 12; V. A. 209, I, 1; II, 28; V, 4.

Bâbilu
(*TIN.TIR.ki*) IV R.² 38, I, 24; V R. 55, 2; 56, 18; C. T., X, pl. III, 21, 31; V. A. 208, 53; C. T., X, pl. IV, 10; V. A. 2663, II, 9, 44; III, 13, 15, 25, 37; IV, 50, 51; V. 6, 16, 18, 34; London 102, IV, 3.
(*KÀ.DINGIR.RAki*) Susa 2, I, 8; II, 29; Susa 2, Medallion 2, 4; D. E. P., II, 97, 9; Neb. Nippur, II, 20; I R. 66, I, 1; II, 17; O. B. I., 83, I, 7; C. T., IX, pl. IV, 12, 13; C. T., X, pl. III, 30; V. A. 208, 31; V. A. 2663, I, 44.
(*KÀ.DINGIR*), V. A. 2663, III, 52.
(*Bâbi-li*) V. A. 2663, I, 26.
(*DUG*) V R. 55 : 3.
(*ŠU.AN.NAki*) C. T., X, pl. IV, 16; V. A. 2663, V, 33; picture, l. 2.
Bar-sipki
V. A. 2663, III, 25; V, II; C. T., X, pl. VII, 47.
Ba-ṣi (the town Baṣ in the name of the canal *nâruḪar-ri-Ba-ṣi*)
Susa 3, I, 24.
âluBît-mA-da
III R. 43, I, 3, 15, 17, 21; II, 23, 25; III, 4, 8, 9, 10, 11, 12, 14; edge, IV, 1, 4, 6; III R. 45, No. 2, 4, 7.
Bît-a-qar-nak-kan-di
C. T., IX, pl. V, 25.
Bît-a-ša-ni-'
V. A. 2663, IV, 9.
Bît-mA-ša-ri-du
V. A. 208, 45.
Bît-mAt-na-ai
C. T., X, pl. III, 20.
Bît-mAt-rat-taš
London, 102, I, 31, 32, 33; IV, 37.

Bît-ᵐBa-zi
D. E. P., VI, 42, I, 14; C. T., IX, pl. IV, 24.
Bît-ᵐᵈBêl-šum-iškun(ŠA-un)
V. A. 209, III, 6, 21.
Bît-ᵐᵈE-a-ma-lik, ʰnangaru
Susa 3, I, 22.
Bît-ᵐᵈEllil-ki-di-ni
London, 103, IV, 29.
âluBît-ᵐḪa-'-ra-ḫu
C. T., X, pl. V, 12, 16; VI, 29.
Bît-ᵐḪab-ban(Ḫab-ba-an) (cf. Hommel, *Geographie*, pp. 267, 296)
I R. 70, I, 3, 10, 12; II, 5; V R. 56, 50.
Bît-ᵐḪa-an-bi (Delitzsch, *Kossäer*, p. 35)
III R. 41, I, 2, 3, 7, 34.
Bît-ᵐḪa-li-e . . .
C. T., X, pl. VI, 17.
Bît-ᵐḪi-ma-gu
Susa 16, I, 20.
Bît-ᵐIm-bi-ia-ti
III R. 41, I, 5.
Bît-ᵐIna-ešê-êṭir
V. A. 209, I, 34.
Bît-ᵐIr-ri-ga
Susa 3, I, 13.
Bît-ᵐIs-ba-ᵈRammân
Susa 3, I, 22.
Bît-ᵐIz-kur-ᵈNabû
Susa 16, II, 3.
Bît-ᵐKar-zi-ia-ab-ku
V R. 55, 25, 35, 45, 47; V R. 56, 4, 30.
Bît-ᵐMuq-qut-is-saḫ
Susa 2, I, 12, 18.
Bît-ᵐNa-ṣi-bi-ilu
C. T., X, pl. VI, 20.
Bît-ᵐNa-zi-ᵈMarduk
IV R.² 38, I, 10.
Bît-ᵐNûr-e-a
C. T., X, pl. VI, 24, 29.
Bît-ᵐPir'-ᵈAmurru (KUR.GAL)
Susa 3, I, 6, 25, 36; II, 40, 47; III, 17, 25, 32; IV, 45; VI, 5, 8, 12; O. B. I., 149, I, 4, 10, 13, 17; II, 5; Susa 14, I, 11; II, 4.
Bît-ᵐPir'(?)*-ᵈAmurru(MAR.TU)*, London, 101, I, 6, 7, 12.

âluBît-Sik-ka-mi-du
Susa 3, II, 23.
Bît-ᵐᵈSin-ašaridu(SAG.KAL)
Susa 2, II, 14; C. T., IX, pl. IV, 22; V. A. 213, I, 2, 3, 4.
Bît-ᵐᵈSin-ma-gir
Susa 2, I, 28; O. B. I., 83, I, 11, 12; II, 4, 6, 13.
Bît-ᵐᵈSin-še-me
Neb. Nippur, II, 20, 28; III, 1, 8, 9, 16 [30]; V, 9, 10, 11, 13, 14, 15, 17, 18, 20.
Bît-ᵐSu-ḫur-Gal-du
Neb. Nippur, Heading l. 9; III, 3.
Bît-ᵐᵈṢîr-ap-pi-li
Neb. Nippur, Heading l. 5; III, 1.
âluBît-ᵈŠamaš
V R. 56, 1.
Bît-ᵐŠEŠ-a-pa. . . .
London, 103, III, 48.
Bît-ᵐŠum-ili-a-šip-ú-uš
O. B. I., 149, I, 8.
Bît-ᵐTa-kil-a-na-ili-šu
London, 103, I, 1, 5, 36, 42; II, 7; III, 43; V, 30, 33.
Bît-ᵐTi . . . .
London, 103, III, 50.
Bît-ᵐTu-na-mis-saḫ(sa-aḫ)
Susa 3, I, 45; I R. 70, I, 8; IV R,² 38 I, 14.
Bît-ᵐUš-bu-la
Neb. Nippur, III, 5.

âlu ša ᵐDâmiq(-iq)-ᵈRammân
Susa 3, II, 24.
âluDêr (not *Dûr-iluᵏⁱ*, see references below and Delitzsch, *Lesestücke*⁴, p. 15¹)
âluDi-ri, V. A. 209, IV, 7.
âluDUR.AN.KI, V. A. 209, I, 2; II, 25, 31; III, 2, 18; IV, 25.
âlu[Di]-e-ri, O. B. I., 83, I, 2.
âluDi-e-ir maḫâz ᵈAnum, V. R 55, 14, 49.
Dil-batᵏⁱ
V. A. 208, 2, 29, 49.

$^{\hat{a}lu}$Di-in-du-bîtu (*$^{\hat{a}lu}$Dimtu-bîtu*)
  III R. 43, I, 27.

$^{\hat{a}lu}$Di-in-šarru
  C. T., IX, pl. IV, 3, 18.

$^{\hat{a}lu}$Dul-lum
  D. E. P., II, 97, 2.

$^{\hat{a}lu}$Dun-ni-edini (Hommel, *Geographie*, p. 286)
  V. A. 2663, IV, 21, 45.

Dup-li-ia-aš (not *Um-li-ia-aš*, see also Hommel, *Geographie*, p. 296)
  Susa 2, II, 9.

DUR.AN.KI (one of the names of the zikkurat of the temple Ekur at Nippur, see Commentary, p. 171f.)
  Neb. Nippur, II, 14.

$^{\hat{a}lu}$Dûr-Ku-ri-gal-zu (Hommel, *Geographie*, p. 344)
  Susa 3, I, 20.

$^{\hat{a}lu}$Dûr-^{d}Nergal
  Susa 2, II, 7.

$^{\hat{a}lu}$Dûr-^{d}Pap-sukal (Hommel, *l.c.*, p. 295)
  Susa 2, I, 37.

$^{\hat{a}lu}$Dûr-Rîm-^{d}Sin
  Neb. Nippur, V, 17, 19.

$^{\hat{a}lu}$Dûr-^{d}Šamaš-ilu-bâni(KAK)
  Susa 2, II, 12.

$^{\hat{a}lu}$Dûr-šarri (Hommel, *l.c.*, p. 296)
  Susa 2, I, 33.

$^{\hat{a}lu}$Dûr-šarru-ukîn
  C. T., IX, pl. IV, 20.

$^{\hat{a}lu}$Dûr-zi-ziki
  IV R.^{2} 38, I, 3, 19.

$^{\hat{a}lu}$Du-ú-tu
  V. A. 209, IV, 25 28.

$^{m\hat{a}tu}$Êlamtu^{ki}
  V R. 55, 41, 43; C. T., IX, pl. IV, 3, 9, 10.

E-an-na (the temple of Nanâ in Erech, cf. Code of Ḫam., II, 43–47)
  only in personal name, cf. *E-an-na-šum-iddina*.

E-kur (the temple of Ellil in Nippur)
  Neb. Nippur, II, 3, 8; IV R.^{2} 38, I, 29.

E-sag-ila (the temple of Marduk in Babylon, cf. Code of Ḫam., II, 7–12)
  D. E. P., VI, 46, IV, 4; London, 102, I, 43; V. A. 2663, II, 2; V, 9; C. T., X, pl. VII, 44.

E-šar-ra (the temple of NIN.IB in Aššur, cf. the name *Tukulti-apil-E-šar-ra* and Gula is called: *kallat E-šar-ra*)
  D. E. P., 113, 13; V R. 56, 39; I R. 70, IV, 1.

E-ul-maš (the temple of Anunît in Akkad, cf. Code of Ḫam., IV, 49–51)
  D. E. P., VI, 47, 15.

E-zi-da (the temple of Nebo in Borsippa, cf. Code of Ḫam., III, 12–15)
  IV R.^{2} 38, II, 14; D. E. P., VI, 46, IV, 3; V. A., 2663, II, 3.

$^{\hat{a}lu}$Gur-^{d}Ištar(NINNI) (Hommel, *Geog.*, 289)
  IV R.^{2} 38, I, 5, 11, 18; II, 33.

Ha-ni
  London, 101, I, 18.
  âlu ša Ḫa-ne^{ki}, D. E. P., II, 97, 6.

Ḫal-man (Hommel, *Geogr.*, 295)
  V R. 56, 22.

$^{\hat{a}lu}$Hu-da-da (not *Bag-da-da*, see Hommel, *Geogr.*, pp. 252, 273, 341, 345)
  Susa 16, I, 4; II, 1, 6, 22, 26, 28; III, 3; IV, 7; D. E. P., VI, 46, I, 4; I R. 70, I, 6.

Ḫu-da-di, Susa 16, I, 28, 30.
  piḫât mât $^{\hat{a}lu}$Ḫu-da-di(!), Susa 2, II, 4.

$^{\hat{a}lu}$Ḫar-ri-Ka-ri-e (cf. *$^{\hat{a}lu}$Ka-ri-e*)
  D. E. P., VI, 42, I, 3.

$^{\hat{a}lu}$Ḫu-uṣ-ṣi
  C. T., IX, pl. IV, 14, 22.

$^{\hat{a}lu}$Ir-ri-e-a (cf. *$^{\hat{a}lu}$Ir-ri-ia*, III R. 4, 3)
  D. E. P., 44, I, 7, 10.

mât $^{\hat{a}lu}$Ir-ri-ḫa
  D. E. P., VI, 44, I, 12.

âluI-ši-in (*Ni-ši-in*)
V R. 56 17; I R. 66; II, 7; C. T., X, pl. III, 25.
PA.ŠEki, V. A. 211, II, 2.
âluIš-nu-nak
I R. 66, II, 3.

mâtuKal-du
C. T., X, pl. V, 5, 13; VII, 33.
âluKar-dBêlit
D. E. P., VI, 42, I, 2.
mâtuKar-dDu-ni-ia-aš
C. T., IX, pl. IV, 5.
âluKar-dNabû (Delitzsch, *Paradies*, 206)
I R. 70, I, 2.
âluKa-ri-e (in the district of Upî)
Susa 2 II, 17.
Kûtû(*GÚ.DU.Aki*)
V. A. 2663, V, 13.

âluLa-ba-ṣi ša Bît-ja-[*kin?*]
C. T., X, pl. VI, 27.
âluLa-rak (only in personal name, cf. *m âluLa-rak-zêr-ib-ni*)
London, 102, I, 12.
mâtuLul-lu-bi-i
V R. 55, 9.

âluMan-du-ú
D. E. P., VI, 42, I, 9.
âlu ša Mâr-mAḫ-at-tu-ú-a
Neb. Nippur, II, 27; III, 8.
âlu šaMâr-mŠe-li-bi
Susa 3, I, 44.

âluNa-ba-ti(*tu*) (also in Neo-Babyl. Names, see Tallquist, N. B., 293)
V. A. 2663, IV, 17, 19.
mâtuNa-mar
V R. 55, 47, 48, 51, 52, 55; V R. 56, 6, 8, 10, 23, 24, 28, 29, 31, 48.
Na-ra-ni-e
D. E. P., VI, 42, I, 7, 11.

Nippur(*EN.LIL.KI*)
London, 103, I, 20, 48; III, 7, 42; Neb. Nippur, II, 3; III, 12 [32]; V. A. 2663, II, 9; III, 12.
piḫat Nippur, London, 103, III, 42.
âlu ša mNu-ur-aḫê-šu
Susa 3, I, 17.

âluPa-da-an
D. E. P., II, pl. 20, 6.
âluParak(*BAR*)-*mâri*(*TUR*)*ki**
London, 103, V, 15, 17.
âluPi-la-ri-i
Susa 2, II, 2.
âluPur-rat-taš
D. E. P., VI, 44, I, 8.

âluRi-is-ni (at the banks of the canal *Su-ri-rabû*)
Susa 2, I, 21.
âlu ša Riš-ša-gi-diki
D. E. P., II, 93, I, 2.

Sip-parki
V. A. 2663, II, 8; III, 12.
Su-bar[*-tu*] (=Mesopotamia, Winckler, *Forschungen*, I, 154f.)
D. E. P., II, 93, I, 5.
âluŠa-ḫa-neki
D. E. P., II, 97, 6.
âluŠa-ak-na-na-a
Susa 16, I, 2, 23.
âlu ša Šal-ḫi ("Rampart city")
Susa 3, I, 47.
âluŠa-lu-lu-ni (at the Royal Canal)
London, 101, I, 5.
âluŠa-an-ba-ša
V R. 56, 1.
âluŠa-sa-iki
Susa 2, I, 30.
âluŠa-sa-na-ki
O. B. I., 149, I, 6, 10, 12.
âluŠap-pi ša mSa-'....
C. T., X, pl. VI, 23.

* Cf. also Clay, B. E., XIV, 107, 3; 133, 3, 6; 148, 31. Hommel, *Geographie* p. 251; and Br. 6900, *Pa-rak-ma-ri*.

âluŠa-šar-riki
O. B. I., 149, I, 5, 6.
âluŠu-bat-šarri ("Royal residence")
Susa 16, I, 30.
mâtuŠú-me-ri
Neb. Nippur, II, 1; V. A. 2663, I, 37.
KI.EN.GIki, IV R.[2] 38, I, 22.
mâtuEME.KU, V. A. 2663, I, 27, 46; C. T., X, pl. IV, 13; VI, 32.

mat Tâmdi(A.AB.BA)
London, 101, II, 3; O. B. I., 83, I, 3, 6, 13; II, 7.
âlu ša Ta-ma-ak-ku (in the district of Akkad)
Susa 3, I, 3, 10.
âluTi-ri-qa-an (at the Ṭâban canal)
Susa 2, I, 24.
âlu TUR.ZA.GIN
Susa 2, I, 11; II, 22.

âluÛ-pi-i(e)
Susa 2, II, 19; C. T., IX, pl. IV, 19.
Uš-ti (in *ša-kin Uš-ti*)
V R. 56, 21.
Uš-tim, in *mAmel-iššakkê-ša-Uš-tim*, London, 101, I, 9.

âluZa-rat-šim-bâbâni
Susa 3, I, 23.
âlu . . . . . *dNIN.SAR*
London, 103, III, 41.

3. Names of Rivers and Canals.*

Ar-ra-ra
Susa 16, I, 34.
A-tab-dûr-dIštar (cf. Delitzsch, *Paradies*, 192)
III R. 43, I, 16.
Be-dar(?) (cf. Hommel, *Geographie*, p. 267, and B. E., XV, 102, 12)
III R. 41, I, 2, 9.
Du-ú-tu (*nâr âluDu-ú-tu*)
V. A. 209, IV, 25, 28.
Ḫa-ar-ri-Ba-ṣi, "The canal of (the city) Baṣ" (cf. Hommel, *Geographie*, p. 345).
Susa 3, I, 24.
Idiqlat (*MAŠ.TIK.ḲAR*)
IV R.[2] 38, I, 4, 7; D. E. P., VI, 42, I, 4, 17; O. B. I., 83, I, 2; Neb. Nippur, Heading, II, 28; III, 6.
Kan(Šum)-di-ri
C. T., IX, pl. IV, 23.
Ki-ba-a-ti
Susa 3, I, 50.
Ma-še-e
C. T., X, pl. III, 18.
Me-e-dan-dan (cf. Hommel, *Geographie*, pp. 273, 280, 296)
Susa 16, I, 3, 24; I R. 70, I, 3.
Mi-ga-ti (=*nâr miqâti*, see Hommel, *Geographie*, p. 296)
Susa, 2, II, 8.
Min(NIŠ)-ga-ti-rabîti(GAL-ti)
C. T., IX, pl. IV, 21.
Min(Niš)-ga-ti-rim-ma
London, 102, I, 3.
Nâr šarri
Susa 2, II, 3, 18; London, 101, I, 5, 10; Susa 3, I, 5, 54; II, 22, 29, 32; Neb. Nippur, Heading; V. A. 2663, IV, 22, 23, 31, 46; *nâr piḫâti ša šarri*, Susa 3, I, 52; III, 3; and *kišâd na-ga-ar šarri*, D. E. P., II, 112, 5. (For further references to the "royal canal," see Streck, *Deutsche Lit. Zeitung*, March 11, 1905, 618; A. J. S. L., Vol. XXII (April, 1906), p. 223; Hommel, *Geographie*, pp. 284–286; Hilpr.-Clay, B. E., IX, 73, 2; Tallquist, *Neu-Babylonisches Namenbuch*, p.299; cf. also pp.158–160 above).
Ni-ni-na
London, 103, IV, 2; also *Nin[-ni]-na* London, 103, III, 42.

* Every name is preceded by the determinative *nâru*.

Purattu (*UD.KIB.NUN^ki^*)
C. T., X, pl. VI, 17, 28; *^nâru^Pu-rat-ti*, C. T., X, pl. III, 17; V. A. 208, 11.

Ra-da-nu (cf. Hommel, *Geographie*, p. 293f.)
Susa 14, I, 6.

Ra-ki-bi
D. E. P., II, 97, 5.

Râṭi-An-za-nim
Susa 3, III, 2.

Ṣal-ma-ni (cf. Delitzsch, *Paradies*, p. 192)
I R. 66, II, 2.

Su-ri-rabû(GAL)
Susa 2, I, 22.

Su-ru(ri)
V. A. 2663, III, 49; IV, 4.

*nâr ^âlu^Ša-šar-ri^ki^*
O. B. I., 149, I, 6, 11.

Šum(kan)-di-ri
C. T., IX, pl. IV, 23.

Šum-ili . . . .
D. E. P., VI, 42, I, 4, 17.

Ṭa-ba-an (cf. Hommel, *Geographie*, p. 295f.; Delitzsch, Kossäer, p. 31, note 3)
Susa 2, I, 25, 31, 34; D. E. P., II, 97, 7.

U-la-a (cf. Hommel, *Geographie*, p. 280)
V R. 55, 28.

Zi-ir-zi-ir-ri (cf. Delitzsch, *Paradies*, p. 192)
III R. 43, I, 3, 14.

Zu-mu-un-^d^Ištar
Susa 2, II, 13.

4. Names of Deities.

^d^Ai(A.A) (consort of Shamash, cf. *Shurpu*, III, 142; worshipped chiefly at Sippar, I R. 65, II, 40, and Larsa, I R. 65, II, 42, Code of Ḫam., II, 23–31. For the older reading *Aja* see Jensen, K. B., III, 1, 20f., note *†, and Ranke, *Personal Names*, 197[2]. As *^d^GAL* she was "the queen of *Dûr-ilu*" (*šarrat Dûr-ilu*), cf. B. A., III, 238, 42).
Susa 16, V, 18; also in the personal names *^d^Ai(GAL)-bêl-šumâti*, *^d^Ai-mutakkil*.

^d^A-MAL (first mentioned by an early king of Kish, cf. Scheil, D. E. P., II, 4[1]; also on an ancient slab from Abu-Habba, cf. Hilprecht, O. B. I., pt. 1, pl. VII, Col. V, 4. Placed alongside of Nanâ on the stone of Nabû-shum-ishkun (V. A. 3031), Col. III, 1, 3. Discussed by Hommel, *Geographie*, p. 302f.).
V. A. 209, IV, 27.

^d^Amurru (called *bêl šadî*, cf. Reisner, *Hymnen*, No. 50, Rev. 17; identical with the "Ba'al of Lebanon," cf. Zimmern, K. A. T.[3], 433. The consort of Ashratu, Reisner, *Hymnen*, No. 50, Rev. 18. For the reading *^d^KUR.GAL* = *^d^Amurru*, see Clay, B. E., Vol. X, p. 8; Vol. XIV, p. VIII. For *^d^MAR.TU* = *^d^Amurru*, see Reisner, *Hymnen*, No. IV (p. 139), ll. 141 and 142).
Only in personal names, as *^d^Amurri-e-a*, *Pir'-^d^Amurru*(*^d^KUR.GAL*) and *Pir(?)-^d^Amurru* (*^d^MAR.-TU*).

^d^Anu (the chief god of the first triad in the Babylonian pantheon, worshipped chiefly in the temple *E.DIM.GAL.KALAM.MA* at Dêr, cf. *Shurpu*, II, 160; B. A., III, 262, 20; V R. 55, 14, and in the temple *E.AN.NA* at Erech., cf. Code of Ḫam., II, 43–46).

Anu(AN), IV R.[2] 38, III, 26; III R. 43, IV, 30; V. A. 209, IV, 17.

Anu(AN-nu), London, 103, V, 48; III R. 43, III, 26.

Anum(AN-num), Susa 2, IV, 2, 18; D. E. P., VI, 45, IV, 19.

dA-nu, III R. 41, II, 13; I R. 70, III, 9; O. B. I., 149, II, 18; London, 102, I, 37; Neb. Nippur, IV, 3; V. A. 2663, V, 36.

dA-num, V R. 55, 14; I R. 70, IV, 10; C. T., X, pl. VII, 38; V. A. 209, II, 8; V, 7.

dA-nu-um, London, 101, III, 9; Susa 3, VI, 16; Susa 16, V, 12.

Also in the personal name *dA-num-nâṣir.*

dA-nu-ni-tum(ti) (a title of the Ishtar of Akkad, cf. *Shurpu,* II, 169; Susa 3, I, 48; worshipped in the temple *E.UL.MAŠ,* I R. 69, II, 29, Code of Ḫam., IV, 47, 49; called *bêlit Akkadi,* V R. 56, 50).

London, 101, III, 15; Susa 16, V, 30; Susa 3, III, 48; V, 3, 24, 36; V R. 56, 50.

dA-nun-na-ki(ku) (the gods of fate in the underworld, see Zimmern, K. A. T.[3], 451–53; Morgenstern, M. V. A. G., X (1905), 161–166).

Neb. Nippur, I, 7, 11; V. A. 2663, I, 6.

dApsû (ENGUR) (a personification of the primeval ocean, cf. Zimmern, K. A. T.[3], 492; the mother of Ea, IV R. 1, II, 36; for the reading cf. C. T., XII, 26, Rev. 17f., and Thureau-Dangin, I. S. A., 263[9]).

O. B. I., 83, I, 16; II, 14, 15.

dA-ru-ru (the mother-goddess, cf. K. B., VI, 1, p. 41, l. 21, and p. 121, ll. 33, 34; identified with *dNIN.-MAḪ,* IV R. 53, III, 40, and *Bêlit ilê,* IV R. 58, III, 19; called the wife(?) of *dMU.UL.-LIL* (= *dEnlil*), cf. Craig, *Religious Texts,* I, 19, 6, and Zimmern, K. A. T.[3], 430).

Susa 2, IV, 9.

dAšur (the chief deity in the Assyrian pantheon, cf. Jastrow, "The God Ašur," *Journal of Am. Oriental Soc.,* XXIV (1903), 281–311).

Only in the personal name *dAšur-(ḪI)-aḫu-iddina.*

dAT.GI.MAḪ (a deity belonging to the court of Shamash, placed after Bunene and before Kettu and Mêsharu, perhaps, with Scheil, to be read: *Malku ṣîru* for *AT.GI* = *ma-lik,* see Br. 4170).

Susa 16, V, 20.

dBa-ú (the consort of NIN.GIR.SU, cf. Cyl. B of Gudea, Col. XI, 11, 12; or of Za-mà-mà, cf. III R. 68, 62, 63*d*; also identified with Gula, the wife of NIN.IB, cf. Zimmern, K. A. T.[3], 410).

London, 103, VI, 5; Susa 16, V, 27; D. E. P., VI, 47, [1].

dBêl(EN) (a title of Marduk, the god of Babylon).

V R. 56, 14; C. T., IX, pl. IV, 11, 12; V. A. 2663, II, 37.

dBu-ne-ne (the charioteer of Shamash, cf. V R. 65, 33*b*, forming with Ai, Kettu, Mêsharu and Daianu the court of Shamash at Sippar, V R. 65, 29*b*,ff.).

Susa 16, V, 19; D. E. P., II, 115, 4; also in the personal name *Nûr-dBunene(dḪAR).*

dBu-ri-ia-aš (the Cassite god Ubriash, identified with Ramman, cf. Cassite Vocabulary, Obv. 6).

Only in the personal name *Bur-ra-Bu-ri-ia-aš.*

dDA.MU (a Sumerian name for Bau, cf. C. T., XVII, 33 Rev. 32, 33; also identified with Gula in proper names, V R. 44, II, 19, 49; called *âšipu rabû,* cf. *Shurpu,* VII, 79).

Susa 16, V, 28.

dE-a (the chief god of Eridu, II R. 61, 46; worshipped in the temple

E.ZU.AB, together with his consort *DAM.GAL.NUN.NA*, cf. Code of Ḫam., II, 1; IV, 17, 18. She was also called *DAM.-KI.NA*, cf. *Shurpu*, III, 140).

Susa 2, IV, 6; London, 103, V, 48; London, 101, III, 11; Susa 3, VI, 18; IV R.[2] 38, III, 26; Susa 16, V, 14; Neb. Nippur, IV, 9; O. B. I., 83, I, 22; II, 17; III R. 41, II, 13; I R. 70, III, 9; III R. 43, III, 26; O. B. I., 149, II, 18; London, 102, I, 38; V. A. 2663, III, 4; V. A. 209, II, 8; V, 7; C. T., X, pl. VII, 38.

dNIN.IDI.AZAG (=*dE-a ša ni-me-ki*, II R. 58, 56*b*), V. A. 2663, III, 8.

dBE, V. A. 2663, V, 36.

dEn-lil(*Ellil*) (the chief god of Nippur, worshipped in the temple E-KUR. For the reading Ellil see above, p. 161).

Susa 2, IV, 4; Susa 3, VI, 17; VII, 44; London, 103, V, 48; London, 101, III, 10; IV R.[2] 38, III, 26; Susa 16, V, 13; Neb. Nippur, I, 1; II, 11, 13, 15; III, 11; IV, 5; III R. 41, II, 13; I R. 70, III, 9; IV, 2; III R. 43, III, 26; O. B. I., 149, II, 18; London, 102, I [37]; V. A. 209, II, 8; V, 7; C. T., X, pl. VII, 38. *dNINNÛ*, V. A. 2663, V. 36.

dEr-ia (an Elamite deity, not identical with the goddess Erûa, for *dEr-ia* was a male deity (cf. *pa-ni-šu ú-šad-gil*, C. T., IX, pl. V, 41) and his image was permanently located in the town *Ḫuṣṣi*, not in Babylon, *l.c.*, pl. IV, 15).

C. T., IX, pl. IV, 2, 11, 13, 18, 25; pl. V, 30, 40.

dErûa (*dA.EDIN.NA*) (this goddess, placed alongside of Marduk, is no doubt identical with *dA.-RÙ.'U.A* = *dE-ru-ú-a*, mentioned in the Bilinguis of Šamaš-šum-ukîn, l. 8. She was the goddess of pregnancy, also called Šêrûa, *bêlit nabnâti*, cf. Lehmann, Šamaššumukîn, II, 36ff Both are names of *Ṣarpanîtum* V R. 44, 34*c*; V R. 46*cd*, 40, 41).

V. A. 2663, V, 41.

Gal-du (doubtless a Cassite deity, see Clay, B. E., XV, pp. 4[5], 54).

Only in the personal name *Su-ḫur-Gal-du*.

dGEŠTIN.NAM (*dGEŠTIN* is identified with *d*Bêlit ṣêri, the scribe of the underworld, II R. 59, Rev. 10*c*. A temple of *dAMA.-GEŠTIN* is mentioned by Urukagina, cf. Thureau-Dangin, I. S. A., p. 92, K, Rev. II, 1, 3; also Ur-Bau built a temple (*E.ANŠU.DUN.UR*) to *dGEŠ-TIN.AN.NA*; cf. Thureau-Dangin, *l.c.*, p. 96*a*, VI, 5. She is mentioned as *dGAŠ.TIN.NAM* among the deities of Erech, cf. I R. 43, 32. We find her also alongside of *dNIN.KA.SI*, a wine goddess, cf. Reisner, *Hymnen*, IV, 64, 65, and as *dNIN.-GEŠTIN* in a list of thirteen gods, cf. K. 26, 13, Obv. II, 12 = B. A., V, 701).

Susa 16, V. 28, in a group of five goddesses.

dGirru(*BIL.GI*) (the fire god par excellence, see Zimmern, K. A. T.[3], 417f.).

Susa, 2, IV, 19.

dGU.LA (the consort of NIN.IB, III R. 43, IV, 15. That *dGU.LA* is Sumerian is shown by Reisner, *Hymnen*, IV, 49, 50,. where *AMA dGU.LA* is rendered *ummu ra-bi-tum*, hence her titles *ru-ba-a-ti ṣi-ir-ti*, cf. Nebuch., 13, II, 44, and *bi-el-ti ra-bi-ti*, cf. Nebuch., 13, II, 48, see Langdon, *Building Inscriptions*,

p. 106. On this question see Zimmern, K. A. T.[3], 410[2]. Her sacred animal was the dog, cf. p. 121[3].)

Susa 3, VII, 14; IV R.[2] 38, III, 27; D. E. P., II, 113, 13; D. E. P., VI, 43, III, 16; Susa 14, IV, 5; D. E. P., VI, 47 [11]; V R. 56, 39; Neb. Nippur, IV, 20; III R. 41, II, 29; I R. 70, IV, 5; III R. 43, IV, 15; O. B. I., 149, III, 1; London, 102, II, 20.

Ḫa-la (a Cassite goddess identified with Gula, cf. Delitzsch, *Lesestücke*[4], p. 136, 6).

In the personal name *Me-li-Ḫa-la*; and perhaps in *Šam-(Ú)-eš-Ḫa-la.*

Ḫar-be (a Cassite god identified with *d*En-lil, cf. V R. 44, IV, 1).

In the personal name *Mi-li-Ḫar-be.*

dI-gí-gí (a collective name for the gods of heaven, sometimes used for the planetary gods, hence the ideogram V + II, cf. Zimmern, K. A. T.[3], 451–453).

Neb. Nippur, I, 5; V. A. 2663, I, 5.

dIllat (for the ideogram cf. Br. 4466, perhaps to be read *dḪarrân-šadû*, as suggested by Zimmern, *Beiträge*, p. 60, for the title *âšibu šadê ellûti* is applied to this deity, cf. *Shurpu*, VIII, 22).

Only in the name *mdIllat-ai.*

dInin-ni (thus the doubtful signs of IV R.[2] 38, II, 8, are read by Peiser and others. Being placed alongside of Nabû it is at all events a name of Nanâ, the consort of Nabû, cf. *Shurpu*, II, 156).

IV R.[2] 38, II, 8.

dIš-ḫa-ra (a form of Ishtar, called *dIš-ḫa-ra tam-tim* = *dIš-tar*, cf. V R. 46, 31*b*. Some of her titles are: *bêlit dînim u bîri*, Zimmern, *Ritualtafeln*, 87, I, 6; *bêlit dadmê*, *Shurpu*, II, 171; *ummu rim-ni-tum ša'nišê*, Craig, *Religious Texts*, I, 3, 17; *šar-rat Ki-sur-ri-eki*, II R. 60, 14*ab*. Her temple in Babylon was *E.SAG.TUR.RA*, Strassm., Nebk., 247, 7; cf. Hommel, *Geographie*, 311).

Susa 2, IV, 8; D. E. P., VI, 45, IV, 8; III R. 43, IV, 28.

dIš-tar (worshipped in Babylonia chiefly at Erech under the name Nanâ, V. R. 6, 107–122, or *dIštar ša Urukki*, V R. 34, II, 33; at Akkad under the name Anunîtum, cf. *Shurpu*, II, 169, or Ishtar of Akkad, cf. Susa 3, I, 48; II, 26; at Kish in the temple *E.ME.TE.UR.SAG*, cf. Code of Ḫam., II, 59–65, and at Babylon in the temple *E.-TUR.KALAM.MA*, cf. Lehmann, *Šamaššumukîn*, pl. XXIII, 13. For her character as mother-goddess and as the goddess of love, war and hunting see Zimmern, K. A. T.[3], 420–432).

dIš-tar, Susa 2, IV, 16; V R. 55, 40; Neb. Nippur, IV, 22; III R. 41, II, 21; I R. 70, III, 22; III R. 43, IV, 12; *dNINNI*, Susa 3, I, 48; II, 26; London, 103, VI, 18; Susa 16, V, 29.

dI-šum (a fire and pest god and as such the messenger (*sukkallu*) of Nergal, IV R. 21, No. 1, Obv. 43ff. His most common titles are: *na-gir ra-bu-ú ra-bi-ṣi ṣi-i-ri ša ilâni*, C. T., XVI, 46, 179; *na-gir su-qi ša-qu-um-mi*, C. T., XVI, 15, V, 22; *na-gir mu-ši*, C. T., XVI, 49, 305. His consort was *dŠu-bu-la(l)*, IV R. 26, No. 1, 9).

Susa 16, VI, 1; also in the name *dI-šum-ba-ni.*

dKA.DI (mentioned by Entemena, cf. Thureau-Dangin, I. S.A., 62, n, I, 10; Gudea, cf. *l.c.*, 148, X, 26; Anu-mutabil, cf. *l.c.*, 250, 4, and especially by Dungi, cf. *l.c.*, 330, 7, as the goddess of Dêr (*Dûr-ilu*). On one of the boundary stones of Marduk-apal-iddina I. (Susa 16) she is placed alongside of *Tišḫu*, most likely her husband. She is closely associated with the serpent goddess *dṢîru* (Susa 2, IV, 23). In Babylon *dKA.DI* was worshipped as one of "the daughters of Esagila," cf. Reisner, *Hymnen*, p. 146, 44, and Zimmern, K. A. T.[3], 505).

Susa 2, IV, 23; Susa 16, VI, 4.

dKaš-šu-ú (the highest god among the Cassites, as Delitzsch has made probable, cf. Delitzsch, *Kossäer*, p. 51).

In the personal names, *dKaš-šu-ú-mukîn-aplu*, *dKaš-šu-ú-nâdin-aḫê* and *dKaš-šu-ú-nâdin-šumu*.

dKittu(*NIN.GI.NA*) (an attendant of Shamash at Sippar, the personification of justice, cf. Zimmern, *Ritualtafeln*, p. 104, ll. 133, 144; K. 2613, Obv. II, 15, see B. A., V, 701).

Susa 16, V, 22.

dLa-ga-ma-al (the goddess of Dilbat, V. A. 208, 2, 3. Perhaps identical with *dNIN.E.GAL*, the consort of *dIB*, "the gods of Dilbat," cf. Peiser, *Acten-Stücke*, Nos. VII, 2; IX, 2–3. In the Code of Ḫam., III, 29, *dMA.MA* takes the place of *dNIN.E.GAL*. She is also connected with *Ki-sur-ri-e^ki*, cf. II R. 60, No. 1, 15*ab*, and Hommel, *Geographie*, 397).

V. A. 208, 3, 16, 26, 33.

dLa-aṣ (the consort of Nergal, worshipped in the temple *E.ŠIT.LAM* at Kutha, Nebuch., 9, II, 36, 37, see Langdon, *Building Inscriptions*, p. 86).

Susa 16, V, 34.

dLIL (placed alongside of *dNIN.BAD*, "the mistress of the dead," Susa 16, VI, 4. *dNIN.BAD.NA* is said to be the wife of *dLUGAL.-AB.BA*, cf. III R. 68, 73*a*; but *dLUGAL.A.AB.BA* is one of the titles of Nergal, cf. II R. 59, 37, 38*e*, hence *dLIL* must be in this connection (Susa 16, VI, 4) one of the titles of Nergal and not of NIN.IB, as suggested by Scheil on the basis of II R. 57, 66*c*).

Susa 16, VI, 4.

dLUGAL.BAN.DA (the consort of *dNIN.SUN*, cf. II R. 59*e*, 24, 25, to whom Sin-gâshid built the temple *E.KAN.KAL* at Erech, IV R. 35, No. 3, 11. Also worshipped at Kullab, cf. V R. 46, 27*b*, and at Ishnunna, cf. Hommel, *Geographie*, 360, 362[3], and *Gilgamesh Epos*, VI, 192).

IV R.[2] 38, II, 9.

dLUGAL.GAZ (one of the deified weapons of NIN.IB, carried in his left hand, cf. Hrozný, *Mythen vom Gotte Ninrag*, pl. V, 20. Mentioned in the Gudea inscriptions, Statue B, V, 37–39; Cyl. A, XXII, 20; Cyl. B, VIII, 2f., etc. As stars *Šar-ur* and *Šar-gaz* appear repeatedly, cf. II R. 57, Rev. 60*a*; III R. 66, Rev. 31–32*b*, V R. 46, 32*a*, and Jensen, *Kosmologie*, 145).

Susa 2, IV, 24.

dLUGAL.GIR.RA (the companion of *ŠIT.LAM.TA.Ë*, "the twin gods," cf. Zimmern, *Ritualtafeln*, Nos. 41–42, II, 2. They represented the first and third quarters of the moon, cf. Zimmern, K. A. T.[3], 413. For their prominence in incantations see Morgenstern, M. V. A. G., X (1905), 175).

Susa 16, VI, 2.

dLUGAL.GIŠ.A.TU.GAB.LIŠ (the god of the city Baṣ, cf. V R. 34, II, 29, 30. A form of Nergal, V R. 46, 18*cd*. The name is to be read *Bêl-ṣarbi*, cf. Nebuch., 1, II, 29; 13, II, 60, and Nebuch., 9, II, 48, see Langdon, *Building Inscriptions*, pp. 64, 86, 106. His consort was dMa-mi-tum, cf. *Shurpu*, VIII, 14; Susa, 16, VI, 3. In Craig, *Religious Texts*, I, 56, 16, he is spoken of as *ra-kib nâr i-li*).

Susa 16, VI, 3.

dLUGAL.UR.UR (one of the personified weapons of NIN.IB, held in his right hand, the companion of *LUGAL.GAZ* (or *Šar-gaz*), cf. Hrozný, *Mythen*, p. 12, l. 20. For his stellar character see Jensen, *Kosmologie*, 145).

Susa 2, IV, 24.

dMa-'-me-tum (the consort of *LUGAL. GIŠ.A.TU.GAB.LIŠ* or *Bêl-ṣarbi*, the god of Baṣ, cf. K. 2866, 13. But also regarded as the consort of Nergal, cf. Böllenrücher, *Gebete an Nergal*, p. 20, No. III, 8, and *Gilgamesh Epos*, X, 6, 37).

Susa 16, VI, 3.

dMâr-bîti (*TUR.E*) (a god worshipped in Borsippa, where Nebuchadrezzar II. built him a temple, cf. I R. 55, IV, 49, which was not far from the gate of Rammân, cf. Strassm., Dar., 367, 1, 4. His title *mušabbir kakki nakiria* seems to point to a war god, cf. Weissbach in O. L. Z., VI (1903), 442. In III R. 66, Rev. 11*b*, he appears among "the gods of Esagila," Rev. 20*b*).

Occurs only in personal names, *dMâr-bîti-aḫê-iddina*, *dMâr-bîti-ša-li-ti*, etc.

dMarduk (*AMAR.UD*) (the chief god of Babylon, worshipped in the temple *E.SAG.ILA*, the consort of *Ṣarpanîtum*, cf. Langdon, *Building Inscriptions*, Nebuch., 13, I, 27–30).

Susa 2, I, 9, 15; III, 30; London, 103, VI, 3; London, 101, III, 13; Susa 3, III, 47; V, 2, 24, 35; VI, 29; IV R² 38, III, 42; D. E. P., II, 113, 4; D. E. P., II, 112, 1; Susa 14, III, 14; Susa 16, V, 23; III, R. 43, III, 31; III R. 41, II, 25; V R. 55, 11, 12; I R. 70, III, 13; O. B. I., 149, II, 21; London, 102, I [39]; V. A. 2663, I, 1; II, 1; III, 9; V, 21, 40; C. T., X, pl. IV, 8, 14.

Marut-tash (a Cassite god identified with NIN.IB, cf. Cassite Vocabulary, Obv. 8).

Only in the name *Nazi-Maruttash*.

dMêšaru(*NIN.SI*) (an attendant of Shamash at Sippar, together with Kittu and Daianu, cf. V R. 65, 29*b*. The personification of righteousness. Also associated with Rammân and Shala, cf. Craig, *Religious Texts*, I, 57, 22; 58, 24).

Susa 16, V, 22, 32 (*dMi-šar-ru*); D. E. P., VI, 46, III, 2, written *dMi-ša-ru*.

dNabû (the chief god of Borsippa, worshipped in the temple *E.ZI.DA*. His consort Nanâ (cf. Nebuch., 9, II, 18–25, see Langdon, *Building Inscriptions*, I, 84) or Tashmêtum, cf. *Shurpu*, II, 157; III, 145, Pinckert, *Hymnen*, pp. 1ff.).

dAG = *dNabû*[1], Susa 2, IV, 34; London, 101, III, 14; Susa 16, V, 24; IV R.² 38, II, 8; D. E. P., VI, 46, IV, 3; III R. 41, II, 34; III R. 43, IV, 1; I R. 70, IV, 16; London, 102, I, 44; C. T., X, pl. IV, 8, 14.

dPA = *dNabû*², V. A. 2663, II, 1; III, 8.

dNa-na-a (the goddess of Erech, worshipped in the temple *E.AN.NA*, cf. Code of Ḫam., II, 43–47, also at Borsippa as the consort of Nabû, cf. *Shurpu*, II, 156).

V R. 56, 48; Susa 16, V, 29.

dNannaru (*dŠEŠ.KI-ru*!) ("The luminary" (rt. נמר,) an epithet of the moon god Sin of Ur; cf. Zimmern, K. A. T.³, 362).

Susa 14, III, 7; V. A. 209, V, 9 (*dŠEŠ.KI-na-ra*); cf. I R. 70, III, 8.

dNergal (the god of Kutha, worshipped in the temple *E.ŠIT.LAM*, cf. Nebuch., 9, II, 36, 37, see Langdon, *Building Inscriptions*, I, 86; his consort was Laṣ (Susa 16, V, 33) or Mamêtum (see above) or Ereshkigal (Allatu), cf. II R. 59, 33f.).

dUGUR, London, 101, IV, 2; V R. 56, 48; III R. 43, IV, 21; London, 102, II, 3.

dNE.URU.GAL, Susa 16, V, 33.

dGIR = [sign] = Br. 9189; Susa I¹² (see fig. 24¹²).

dNinâ (originally the goddess of Ninâ, one of the component parts of Shirpurla, cf. brick of Eannatum, see Thureau-Dangin, I. S. A., 46, III, 1, 2. Her temple was built by Ur-Ninâ, cf. Thureau-Dangin, *l.c.*, 13, I, 6. On the boundary stones she appears as the daughter of Ea, cf. O. B. I., 83, I, 22, and as the goddess of Dêr, cf. O. B. I., 83, I, 4, 16).

O. B. I., 83, I, 4, 16, 22; II, 14, 15.

dNIN.BAD ("The mistress of the dead," a title of Allatu, the consort of Nergal, see above under *dLIL*).

Susa 16, VI, 4.

dNIN.GAL ("The great mistress," the consort of Nannar (Sin) of Ur, cf. Thureau-Dangin, I. S. A., 282*d*, II, 7; V R. 64, II, 38, 39, and *Shurpu*, III, 141. Her Semitic name was probably *Šarratu*, V R. 51, 24*b*. Her Sumerian name was later pronounced Nikkal; hence the נכל in the Nêrâb inscription, cf. Zimmern, K. A. T.³, 363).

Susa 16, V, 17.

dNIN.GIR.SU (originally the chief god of Girsu, later of Shirpurla, whose temple *E-NINNÛ* was built by Urukagina, cf. Thureau-Dangin, I. S. A., 70, IV, 8, and Gudea Cyl. A, Col. V, 18. He was a god of fertility, hence his title *bêl me-riš-ti*, *Shurpu*, IV, 80. Later identified with NIN.IB, II R. 57, 74*c*. His consort was Bau, cf. Cyl. A of Gudea XXIV, 5, 6).

London 103, VI, 5.

dNIN.E.GAL (a goddess, the consort of *dIB* (*dUraš*), worshipped in the temple *E-im-bi-dA-num* (*E.I.-NE.A.NUM*) in Dilbat, cf. Peiser, *Acten-Stücke*, VII, 2; IX, 2, 3; also Reisner, *Hymnen*, No. 47, Rev. 7, 8, add. p. 154).

London, 103, VI, 13; Susa 16, VI, 6; Susa 14, IV, 10; D. E. P., VI, 43, IV, 1; D. E. P., VI, 47, 5.

dNIN.ḪAR.SAG.GA ("The mistress of the mountain," a title of the *bêlit* of Nippur. Her temple in Nippur was *E-KI.URU*, cf. *Shurpu*, II, 145, 146; also Clay, B. E., XIV, 148, Obv. 2; in Babylon *E.MAḪ*, Nebuch., 15, IV, 14, see Langdon, *Building Inscriptions*, 126).

Susa 3, VI, 19; Susa 16, V, 15.

dNIN.IB ("The lofty son of Ellil," I R. 70, IV, 2, worshipped chiefly at Nippur, in the temple *E.ŠU.-ME.DU*, cf. Reisner, No. 18, Obv. 9; III R. 67, 54*ab*; Rm. 117, Rev. 2, 3 (see M. V. A. G. VIII (1903), p. 176), and B. E., XIV, 148, Obv. 3, and at Babylon in the temple *E.PA.ṬU.TIL.LA*, Nabop. 4, 22, see Langdon, *Building Inscriptions*, p. 58, also at Shirpurla under the name NIN.GIR.SU, cf. II R. 57, 74*c*, and at Kish under the name Zamama, cf. II R. 57, 70*c*).

Susa 3, VII, 5; London, 101, III, 16; IV R.[2] 38, III, 27; Susa 16, V, 25; D. E. P., II, 113, 3; D. E. P., VI, 46, III, 5; V R. 56, 39; Neb. Nippur, Heading 1; Col. II, 11; IV, 19, III R. 41, II, 27; I R. 70, IV, 1; III R. 43, IV, 15, 19; O. B. I., 149, III, 1; London, 102, II, 14.

dNIN.KAR.RA.AG (a title of Gula, "the mistress that spares (life)," which is evidently explained by the phrase, *e-ṭi-ra-at ga-mi-la-at na-bi-iš-ti-ia*, "who spares, who preserves my life," cf. Nebuch., 15, IV, 38, 39, see Langdon, *Building Inscriptions*, I, 126. This name exchanges with Gula and thus proves their identity, cf. Nebuch., 13, II, 41, 44, 48, see Langdon, *l.c.*, p. 106. Her chief temples were *E.SA.BE* and *E.ḪAR.SAG.EL.LA* in Babylon, cf. Nebuch., 15, IV, 40 (Langdon, *l.c.*, 126), *E.GU.LA*, *E.TIL.LA* and *E.ZI.BA.TIL.-LA* at Borsippa, cf. Nebuch., 15, IV, 54; *E.GAL.MAḪ* and perhaps also *E.RAP.RI.RI* at Isin, cf. Craig, *Religious Texts*, I, 58, 25, and Reisner, *Hymnen*, No. 47, Obv. 7, 8).

London, 101, III, 17; Susa 16, V, 26.

dNIN.MAḪ ("The great mistress," originally a title of the *bêlit* of Nippur. It exchanges with *NIN.ḪAR.SAG*, cf. Nebuch., 6, I, 6, and Nebuch., 15, IV, 14 (Langdon, *l.c.*, pp. 76, 126). Her temple in Nippur is enumerated in a list of fourteen Nippur shrines, cf. Clay, B. E., XIV, 148, Obv. 10).

I R. 70, III, 10; III R. 41, II, 13, and perhaps London, 102, II, 26, *dNIN.[MAḪ]*.

dNIN.MEN.NA ("Mistress of the tiara," a title of the *bêlit ilâni*, Sargon, Cyl. 48 (K. B., II, 47), usually applied to Ishtar, cf. Zimmern, K. A. T.[3], 360f.[3], but also to *dNIN.MAḪ* and Aruru, cf. Zimmern, *l.c.*, 429f.).

V. A. 2663, II, 52, called *bânit ilâni.*

dNIN.SAR (mentioned by Urukagina as "the sword carrier of NIN.-GIR.SU," Cone A, II, 14 (Thureau-Dangin, I. S. A., 74), and *Plaque ovale* V, 22f. (*l.c.*, 90), but also referred to as "the sword carrier (*naš paṭri*) of *E-kur*," cf. Reisner, *Hymnen*, IV, 44, and Clay, B. E., XIV, 148, Obv. 26).

Only in the name of a city, London, 103, III, 41.

dNisaba (*ŠE.ELTEG*) (a goddess of fertility, prominent in early times. Lugal-zag-gi-si calls himself the child of Nisaba, cf. Hilprecht, O. B. I., Vol. I, No. 87, I, 26, 27. She is also mentioned by Urukagina, Clay tablet, Rev. IV, 1 (Thureau-Dangin, I, S. A., 92), and Gudea, Cyl. A.V, 21–25; XVII, 15; XIX, 21).

D. E. P., VI, 43, III, 10; cf. also III R. 41, II, 33; I R. 70, IV, 12.

dNusku (*PA.KU*) ("The mighty son of E-kur" and "the sublime messenger (*sukkallu ṣîru*) of Ellil," cf. Craig, *Religious Texts*, I, 35, 7, 12. His consort was SA.DAR-NUN.NA, cf. Craig, *Religious Texts*, I, 36, Rev. 2; Susa 16, VI, 5; V R. 64, II, 18, and Jastrow, *Religion Babyloniens*, I, 488).

Susa 14, IV, 9; Susa 16, VI, 5; Susa 2, IV, 19; D. E. P., VI, 47, 5; Neb. Nippur, Heading, 2; II, 14; III, 11; IV, 25.

dPAP.NIGIN.GAR.RA (a title of NIN.IB, cf. V R. 44, 36, and *Shurpu*, VIII, 18).

London, 103, VI, 11.

dPap-sukkal (occurs on boundary stones only once after Zamama, and is no doubt identical with the god Pap-sukkal of Kish, "who dwells in E-ak-ki-il," cf. Craig, *Religious Texts*, I, 58, 10, and Hommel, *Geographie*, 251, 387).

III R. 43, IV, 25; also in the place name *Dûr-dPap-sukkal*, Susa 2, I, 37.

dRammân(IM) (the storm god, pronounced in early times Immeru, cf. Thureau-Dangin, I. S. A., 296[2], later Rammân, see p. 180f., in Assyria Adad and Addi, cf. Zimmern, K. A. T.[3], 443f. Worshipped chiefly in the temple *E.UD.GAL.GAL* at Karkar (*âluIMki*), cf. Code of Ḫam., III, 59–64, in the temple *E.NAM.ḪE* at Babylon, cf. Nebuch., 15, IV, 36, and at Ḫalmân (Aleppo), cf. K. B., I, 173, Col. II, 87. His sacred animal was the wild ox (rîmu), cf. *dRammân ša ri-mi*, III R. 67, 46*cd* (also Susa 2, IV, 17, *bu-ru ik-du ša dRammân*), and see fig. 18, p. 41).

Susa 2, IV, 17; London, 103, VI, 3, 9; London, 101, I, 3; IV, 1; Susa 16, V, 31; Susa 14, III, 9; D. E. P., II, 113, 8; D. E. P., VI, 46, III, 1; D. E. P., VI, 47, 7; V R. 55, 40; 56, 41, 48; Neb. Nippur, IV, 15; III R. 41, II, 32; I R. 70, IV, 9; III R. 43, IV, 3; London, 102, II [11].

dSA.DAR.NUN.NA (consort of Nusku, cf. Reisner, *Hymnen*, No. 48, Obv. 8, 9; II R. 59*c*, 15–17; V R. 64, II, 18, Craig, *Religious Texts*, I, 36, Rev. 2).

Susa 16, VI, 5.

dSibitti (VII-*BI*) ("Those Seven," a group of protective deities, led by Narudu, their sister, cf. Zimmern, *Ritualtafeln*, No. 54, Obv. 25. Not always the same gods, cf. III R. 66, Obv. 12–19*d*, and IV R. 21, A, Obv. I, 43–46. For their use in incantations see Zimmern, *Ritualtafeln*, Nos. 41–42, II, 13, 14; No. 45, II, 17; No. 54, Rev. 10, 22. For the reading of the ideogram see Zimmern, K. A. T.[3], 620[4]); cf. also Hehn, *Siebenzahl und Sabbat bei den Babyloniern*, pp. 19–34.

Only in the name *Ardi-dSibitti*.

dSin (the moon god, worshipped chiefly in the temple *E.GIŠ.ŠIR.GAL* at Ur; cf. Neb., 9, II, 44; see Langdon, B. I., Vol. I, 86, and *E.ḪUL.ḪUL* at Harran, cf. V R. 64, I, 46).

dEN.ZU, Susa 2, IV, 11; Susa 3, VI, 41; Susa 16; V, 16; Susa 14, III, [7]; D. E. P., II, 113, 6; D. E. P., VI, 46, III, 16.

*d*XXX, Neb. Nippur, IV, 13; V R. 56, 50; III R. 41, II, 16; I R. 70, III, 18; III R. 43, IV, 7; O. B. I., 149, III, 6; London, 102, I, [46]; V. A. 209, V, 9.

dṢar-pa-ni-tum ("The one shining (as silver)," a name of the consort of Marduk, cf. Reisner, *Hymnen*,

No. 48, 28, 29; *Shurpu*, III, 153. A personification of the rising sun or of dawn, cf. Zimmern, K. A. T.[3], 375).

Susa 16, V, 23; O. B. I., 149, II, 22; London, 102, I, 42.

dṢîru (the serpent goddess, called *râbiṣ Ešarra*, V R. 52, 19f. Closely connected with the goddess KA.DÌ, cf. Susa 2, IV, 23, and *Shurpu*, VIII, 6, with whom she is also identified, cf. II R. 59, 21*ab*, and Zimmern, K. A. T.[3], 504f. Mentioned by Esarhaddon among the gods of Dûr-ilu as a male and female deity, cf. B. A., III, 238, 42).

Susa 2, IV, 23; V R. 56, 49; I R. 70, I, 21.

dŠa-la (a goddess, the consort of Ram-mân, Craig, *Religious Texts*, I, 57, 22; 58, 24; *Shurpu*, III, 143; III R. 14, 48; III R. 66, Obv. 27f.).

Susa 16, V, 31; D. E. P., VI, 46, III, 1.

dŠamaš(UD) (the sun god, worshipped chiefly at Sippar and Larṣa, in temples of identical name, *E.BAR.RA*, cf. Neb., 9, II, 40–42, see Langdon, *Building Inscriptions*, I, 86. The name *BI.ŠE.BA*, which is used D. E. P., II, 115, 5 (cf. Br. 7299 and 7296), is his name as a planet, cf. Jensen, *Kosmologie*, 108).

Susa 2, IV, 13; Susa 3, III, 47; V, 2, 24, 35; London, 101, III, 12; London, 103, VI, 3, 9; IV R[2] 38, III, 42; Susa 14, III, 3; Susa 16, V, 17; D. E. P., II, 113, 5; 115, 5; Neb. Nippur, IV, 15; I R. 70, III, 15; III R. 41, II, 19; III R. 43, IV, 10; London, 102, II, 1.

dŠE.RU.ŠIŠ (mentioned between Bunene and Kittu, the attendants of Shamash, and belonging therefore to his court).

Susa 16, V, 21.

Ši-pak (a Cassite god identified with Marduk, cf. V R. 44, I, 27. For the pronunciation *Ši-pak* see Clay, B. E., XV, 3[4]).

Only in personal names, *e.g.*, *Ni-bi-Ši-pak*, *Ú-zu-ub-Ši-pak*, *Me-li-Ši-pak*.

dŠIT.LAM.TA.È (or perhaps *MES.-LAM.TA.È*, so Thureau-Dangin, I. S. A., 198, p, 1; 278, z, 1. One of the twin gods, representing Nergal. His companion *LUGAL.GIR.RA* (see above). Treated as his female counterpart, cf. Susa 16, VI, 2. Compare the parallel forms *dAl-mu* and *dA-la-mu šar-ri Si-bit-ti*, IV R. 21, No. 1, A, Obv. 45; V R. 46, Obv. 21, 22*b*; perhaps "young man" (עלם) and "young woman" (עלמה), see the remarks of Zimmern, K. A. T.[3], 363[7], and notice that the "Twins" are represented on the zodiac of Trichinopoly, India (fig. 43), as male and female).

Susa, 2, IV, 25; Susa 16, VI, 2.

dŠú-bu-la(l) (the goddess of Shumdula, II R. 60, 18*a*, consort of dI-šum, cf. *Shurpu*, VIII, 14. One of the lesser deities belonging to the court of Nergal, cf. IV R. 26, No. 1, 8, 9. Also referred to as the gods of the Tigris and Euphrates, cf. Craig, *Religious Texts*, I, 58, 11).

Susa 16, VI, 1.

Šu-gab (a Cassite god identified with Nergal, cf. Cassite Vocabulary, Obv. 12).

Only in personal names, *e.g.*, *Šu-ḫu-li-Šu-gab*, *Ka-šak-ti-Šu-gab*.

Šul-ma-nu (a west Semitic deity שלם or שלמן, representing perhaps a form of NIN.IB, cf. Zimmern, K. A. T.[3], 474f.).

Only in the personal name *Šul-ma-nu-a-ša-ri-du*.

dŠUL.PA.Ë (or *DUN.PA.E*, literally "the hero (*ŠUL* = *edlu*) that is brilliant" (*PA.Ë* = *šûpû*), a name of Marduk as the god of the planet Jupiter (*da-pi-nu*), cf. II R. 48, 50*ab*; II R. 51, 62*a*, and Jensen, *Kosmologie*, 125ff. Also referred to as the husband of the *bêlit ilâni*, cf. III R. 67, Obv. 14*cd*,ff.).
Susa 2, IV, 7.

dŠu-ma-li-ia (a Cassite goddess, "the lady of the shining (snowclad) mountains," V R. 56, 46. Her name is also written *Ši-i-ma-li-ia*, V R. 44, IV, 36. The consort of *Šu-qa-mu-na*, IV R.[1] 59, III, 23; Susa 16, VI, 7).
Susa 2, IV, 21; London, 103, VI, 15; Susa 16, VI, 7; London, 101, IV, 3; Susa 14, IV, 11; D. E. P., II, 113 [10]; D. E. P., VI, 43, IV, 2; D. E. P., VI, 46, III, 15; D. E. P., VI, 47, 4; V R. 56, 46.

dŠu-qa-mu-na (the Cassite god of war, identified with Nergal-Nusku, cf. Cassite Vocabulary, Obv. 13. His consort *Šu-(i)-ma-li-ia*, cf. *Shurpu*, II, 139).
Susa 2, IV, 20; London, 103, VI, 15; London, 101, IV, 3; Susa 14, IV, 10; Susa 16, VI, 7; D. E. P., II, 113, 10; D. E. P., VI, 43, IV, [2]; D. E. P., VI, 47, 4.

dTaš-me-tum (a title of Nanâ, the consort of Nabû at Borsippa, cf. *Shurpu*, II, 156, 157; III, 145; Craig, *Religious Texts*, I, 58, 13; I R. 65, II, 23, 24).
Susa 16, V, 24.

dTiš-ḫu (a form of NIN.IB, cf. III R. 67, 67*cd*, = *dNIN.IB ša ram-ku-ti*; the god of Dupliash, cf. Thureau-Dangin, I. S. A., 248, 3, 2. Placed alongside of *KA.DI*, implying most likely that he was her husband at some place, cf. Susa 16, VI, 4. For the pronunciation of his name see Ranke, *Personal Names*, pp. 169, 207).
Susa 16, VI, 4.

dUraš (*IB*) (the god of Dilbat, II R. 61, 51*b*, worshipped with his consort *dNIN.E.GAL* in the temple *E-im-bi-A-num* (*E.I.NE.A.-NUM*), cf. Peiser, *Acten-Stücke*, VIII, 1, 2, and Code of Ḫam., III, 18–22. Identified with NIN.IB, II R. 57, 31*cd*, *dIB* = *dNIN.IB ša ud-da-ni-e*, and with Nabû, II R. 60, 39*cd*, dIB = dNabû (*AG*) *ilu bal-ti*. One of the gates of Babylon was called *abullu dÚ-ra-aš*, cf. Neb., Winckler, II, 9).
London, 103, VI, 13; Susa 16, VI, 6; V. A. 208, 39.

dZa-mà-mà (the god of Kish, II R. 61, 52*b*, worshipped in the temple *E.ME.TE.UR.SAG*, cf. Code of Ḫam., II, 62. A form of NIN.IB, II R. 57, 70*c*. His consort Bau, cf. Susa 16, V, 2, or *dNIN.TU*, cf. Code of Ḫam., III, 33–35).
Susa 16, V, 27; D. E. P., VI, 47, 1; III R. 43, IV, 23; London, 102, II, 6.

5. Symbols on the Boundary Stones.

A. Arranged Chronologically.

1. **Susa I.**—Cassite dynasty (fig. 24, p. 86).

(1) A spearhead, inscribed *dMarduk* (*dAM.UD*); (2) a goddess, seated, inscribed *dG*[*u-la*]; (3) an eight-pointed star, inscription effaced, but representing Ishtar (cf. p. 88); (4) the crescent, the symbol of Sin; (5) a lamp, inscribed *dNusku*; (6) a goatfish (*su-ḫur-ma-šú*, cf. Susa, 2, IV, 5) with a shrine, inscribed *dE-a*, and a ram's head placed on the shrine; (7) an animal figure, like a crocodile, with a shrine on its back and an open vase on its head, inscription effaced; (8) a walking bird, inscribed *dBa*-[*ú*]; (9) a solar disk, inscription effaced, but representing Shamash; (10) a mace with a square top, inscribed *d*[*Šu-qa*]-*mu-na*; (11) a mace with twin lion heads, having a round knob between them, inscription effaced, but representing NIN.IB (cf. p. 87[1]); (12) a mace with a lion head, inscribed *dNergal* (*GIR*); (13) a serpent, inscribed [*a-ša*]-*ri-du*; (14) a mace with a vulture head, inscribed *dZa-mà-mà*; (15) a scorpion, inscription effaced, but representing Ishḫara (cf. p. 96).

The inscription of this stone is broken off.

2. **Susa II.**—Reign of Nazi-Maruttash (figs. 27, 28, pp. 90, 91).

(1) The crescent of Sin; (2) the sun disk of Shamash; (3) the eight-pointed star of Ishtar; (4) the goddess Gula, sitting on a shrine, with a dog at her feet; (5) the lamp of Nusku; (6) the scorpion of Ishḫara; (7–8) two shrines with tiaras, symbols of Anu and Ellil (cf. p. 89); (9) a shrine with a ram's head(?) and a goatfish(?), effaced; (10) a shrine with an Ω-like object, most likely the symbol of NIN.ḪAR.SAG (cf. pp. 95, 121[2]); (11) the spearhead of Marduk; (12) the twin lion heads, with a mace between them, the symbol of NIN.IB; (13) a mace with a vulture head, representing Zamama; (14) a mace with a lion head, representing Nergal; (15) a bird perched on a pole; (16) the lightning fork of Rammân, placed on the back of a crouching ox; (17) the serpent, the symbol of Ṣîru.

The gods mentioned in the curses are: Anu, Ellil, Ea, SHUL.PA.Ë, Ishḫara, Aruru, Sin, Shamash, Ishtar, Rammân, Girru (BIL.GI), Nusku, Shuqamuna, Shumalia, Ṣîru, KA.DI, LUGAL.UR.UR, LUGAL.GAZ, SHIT.LAM.TA.Ë.

3. **Susa IX.**—Reign of Bitiliâshu (fig. 21, p. 73).

(1) The crescent; (2) the sun disk; (3) the six-pointed star of Ishtar; (4) the sitting dog of Gula (cf. p. 121[3]); (5) a lion standing erect, holding daggers in his front paws, perhaps Nergal (Hommel).

The curses of the inscription have not been preserved.

4. **London 103.**—Reign of Meli-Shipak (symbols unpublished, described by Pinches, *Guide to the Nim-*

roud Central Saloon, London, 1886, p. 54f.).

(1) The sun disk; (2) the crescent; (3) the star of Ishtar; (4) the serpent; (5) the scorpion; (6) a curved object, perhaps the yoke of NIN.ḪAR.SAG; (7) a fox; (8) a winged dragon; (9) a scorpion-man, "with a man's head, the wings of a bird, a lion's legs and a scorpion's body and tail"; (10) a shrine with a tiara, before which is a crouching animal; (11) a shrine with a tiara, before which crouches a winged bull; (12) the lamp of Nusku, mounted on a tripod table; (13) a tortoise; (14) the figure of a god, holding in his left hand a mace against his breast and in his right hand, which is hanging down, a boomerang (*gamlu*); (15) an animal with two straight horns and two curved horns or ears and a forked tongue; (16) the lightning fork of Rammân; (17) the spearhead of Marduk.

The gods mentioned in the curses are: Anu, Ellil, Ea, Sin, Shamash, Rammân, Marduk, NIN.GIR.SU, Bau, Shamash, Rammân, PAP.NIGIN.GAR.RA = NIN.IB, IB (Urash), NIN.E.GAL, Shuqamuna, Shumalia, Ishtar.

5. **London 101.**—Reign of Meli-Shipak (symbols unpublished, but described by Pinches, *l.c.*, pp. 50–52).

(1) The scorpion-man, represented as a centaur, holding bow and arrow (cf. fig. 32, p. 98); (2) the scorpion; (3) the dog of Gula, looking toward (4) a bird perched on a pole; (5) a satyr, the upper part of his body human, the lower that of a horse, holding with both hands a long thick staff, whose head is wedge-shaped; (6) a short staff, with a conical top and tassels hanging down on each side; (7) the mace with the twin lion heads, the symbol of NIN.IB; (8) the sun disk; (9) a staff with a conical top, but without tassels; (10) the figure of a goddess, in her right hand, close to her breast, she holds a cup, and in the left an object with a thin handle; (11) a mace ending in a dragon's (lion's?) head; (12) the lightning fork of Rammân; (13) the crescent of Sin; (14) the lamp of Nusku; (15) a goddess with two wings; (16) a small staff with the head of some creature at the end, bent at the neck and looking to the right; (17) a low table, the corners of the top ornamented with lion heads, on the table a tiara, ornamented with circles; (18) the star of Ishtar; (19) the serpent of Ṣîru, coiled on top.

The gods mentioned in the curses: Anum, Ellil, Ea, Shamash, Marduk, Nabû, Anunîtum, NIN.IB, NIN.KAR.RA.AG = Gula, Rammân, Nergal, Shuqamuna, Shumalia.

6. **Susa III.**—Reign of Meli-Shipak (fig. 11, p. 28).

(1) The crescent; (2) the sun disk; (3) the eight-pointed star of Ishtar; (4–5) two shrines with tiaras, symbols of Anu and Ellil; (6) a shrine with a ram's head on it and a goatfish before it, the symbol of Ea; (7) a shrine with a nail (or a dagger?) and a reversed form of the yoke-like figure, most likely the symbol of NIN.ḪAR.SAG; (8) a winged dragon carrying the

twin lion heads, having a mace between them; (9) the mace with the vulture head, Zamama; (10) a bird looking backwards; (11) the mace with the lion head, Nergal; (12) a crouching dragon with wings; (13) the spearhead of Marduk on a shrine with a dragon before it; (14) a dragon with a shrine, on which lies a brick and a wedge, the symbol of Nabû; (15) the sitting dog, with a shrine and the bust of Gula on the shrine; (16) a crouching ox with a shrine and the lightning fork standing on the shrine, the symbol of Rammân; (17) a crouching ram with a chisel on the shrine; (18) the lamp of Nusku; (19) a plow with a double handle; (20) a walking bird; (21) a bird perched on a pole; (22) a shrine with a sea shell on it; (23) the serpent of Ṣîru; (24) the scorpion of Ishḫara.

The gods mentioned in the curses: Anum, Ellil, Ea, NIN.ḪAR.SAG.GA, Marduk, Sin, NIN.IB, Gula.

7. **London 99** (IV R.[1] 43).—Reign of Marduk-apal-iddina I. (fig. 6, p. 17).

(1) The crescent; (2) the sun disk; (3) the eight-pointed star of Ishtar; (4) the lamp of Nusku; (5) the walking bird of Bau; (6) the mace with the vulture(?) head; (7) the mace with the lion(?) head; (8) the sitting dog of Gula; (9) the scorpion of Ishḫara; (10) a shrine with the yoke(?)-like figure; (11) a bird perched on a pole; (12) the crouching ox with the lightning fork of Rammân; (13) the dragon with the spearhead of Marduk; (14) a dragon with the wedge standing erect on his back, crouching before a stage tower; (15) a horned serpent; (16) a tortoise; (17) a goatfish with a ram's head on its back, the symbol of Ea; (18) a winged dragon, walking along the body of the serpent.

The gods mentioned in the curses: Anu, Ellil, Ea, NIN.IB, Gula, Shamash, Marduk.

8. **Susa XVI.**—Reign of Marduk-apal-iddina I. (fig. 10, p. 25).

(1) The crescent; (2) the eight-pointed star of Ishtar; (3) the sun disk; (4–5) two shrines with tiaras on them, symbols of Anu and Ellil; (6) a shrine with a ram's head on it and a goatfish before it, the symbol of Ea; (7) the sitting dog of Gula; (8) the scorpion of Ishḫara; (9) the mace with the lion head, Nergal; (10) the mace with the vulture head, Zamama; (11) a shrine with four rows of bricks on it and a horned dragon before it, the symbol of Nabû; (12) the mace with the twin lion heads, having a knob between them, the symbol of NIN.IB; (13) the lamp of Nusku; (14) the crouching ox of Rammân, bearing the lightning fork on its back; (15) the spearhead of Marduk; (16) the walking bird of Bau; (17) a bird perched on a pole; (18) the serpent of Ṣîru, coiled on top.

The gods mentioned in the curses: Anum, Ellil, Ea, NIN.ḪAR.SAG, Sin and NIN.GAL, Shamash and Ai, Bunene, AT.GI.MAḪ, SHE.RU.SHISH, Kittu and Mêsharu, Marduk and Zarpanîtum, Nabû and Tashmêtum

NIN.IB and NIN.KAR.RA.AG, Zamama and Bau, DA.MU, GESHTIN.NAM, Ishtar, Nanâ and Anunîtum, Rammân and Shala, Mi-shar-ru, Nergal and Laṣ, Ishum and Shubula, LUGAL.GIR.RA and SHIT.LAM.-TA.Ë, LUGAL.GISH.A.TU.-GAB.LISH (=Bêl-ṣarbi) and Ma'mêtum, LIL and NIN.BAD, Tishḫu and KA.DI, Nusku and SA.DAR.NUN.NA, IB (Urash) and NIN.E.GAL, Shuqamuna and Shumalia.

9. Susa XIV.—Reign of Marduk-apal-iddina I. (fig. 40, p. 105).

(1) The goddess Gula, seated on a shrine, alongside the inscription *dGu-la*, and (2) her dog at her feet; (3) the walking bird of Bau; (4) the scorpion of Ishḫara; (5) apparently a priest standing before the goddess.

The gods mentioned in the curses: [Anu, Ellil, Ea], Shamash, [Sin], Rammân, Marduk, [NIN.IB], Gula, Nusku, NIN.E.GAL, Shuqamuna, Shumalia.

10. Susa IV.—Cassite dynasty (fig. 23, p. 76).

(1) The crescent; (2) the sun disk; (3) the six-pointed star of Ishtar; (4) the mace with the vulture head, Zamama; (5) the mace with the lion head, Nergal; (6) the scorpion of Ishḫara; (?) the lamp of Nusku; (8–9) two shrines with tiaras, symbols of Anu and Ellil; (10) the spearhead of Marduk; (11) the lightning fork of Rammân; (12) a centaur shooting a bow (*sagittarius*); (13) indistinct traces of a figure, perhaps the ears of the dog of Gula, but hardly an altar of incense (Hommel); (14) the goddess Gula, sitting on a shrine; (15–17) the goatfish with a shrine on its back and a ram(!) over the shrine; (18) a peculiar forked object, perhaps a plow (De Morgan); (19) a winged dragon; (20–21) a crouching dragon with a shrine on its back; (22) a bird perched on a pole; (23–24) a crouching dragon with a shrine on its back.

The curses containing the names of the gods have not been preserved.

11. Susa V.—Cassite dynasty (figs. 17, 18, pp. 40, 41).

(1) The crescent; (2) a priest of Marduk, inscribed *ṣalam ša NITAḪ dMarduk*, holding in his left hand a bowl and placing his right above (3) the spearhead of Marduk; (4) the seven-pointed star of Ishtar; (5) the god Rammân standing on a wild ox (*rîmu*, cf. fig. 94 in Jeremias, *Das alte Testament im Lichte des alten Orients*, 1st ed., p. 280), the god holding in his right hand the three-pronged lightning fork and in his left the reins; (6) the scorpion; (7) the serpent; (8) a dragon with two horns, crouching before (9) the spearhead of Marduk; (10) the walking bird of Bau.

The inscription is broken off.

12. Susa VI.—Cassite dynasty (fig. 38, p. 103; De Morgan, D. E. P., I, p. 177, fig. 383).

(1) The serpent coiled on top; (2) the crescent; (3) the solar disk; (4) the lamp of Nusku; (5) a shrine with a wedge lying on it, the symbol of Nabû; (6) the god Ea standing on a goat(!), holding against his breast a cup, from which run two streams of water.

The inscription is lost.

13. Susa VII.—Cassite dynasty (fig. 21, p. 73).

(1) The goddess Gula with the dog at her feet; (2) the serpent; (3) a dragon with a shrine and the wedge lying on the shrine, the symbol of Nabû.

The inscription is broken off.

14. Susa VIII.—Cassite dynasty (fig. 21, p. 73).

(1) The goddess Gula. The rest is broken off.

15. Susa X.—Cassite dynasty (fig. 44 (2), p. 112).

(1) The scorpion of Ishḫara; (2) the dog of Gula, with traces of the robe of Gula; (3) an animal, partly destroyed, perhaps a hare (De Morgan); (4) a lion holding a mace in his right paw, perhaps Nergal (Hommel).

The inscription has not been preserved.

16. Susa XI.—Cassite dynasty (fig. 44 (3), p. 112).

(1) A shrine with an indistinct figure, hardly the solar disk (Hommel), which never appears on boundary stones over a shrine; (2) the goddess Gula with her dog; (3) a shrine carrying the reversed yoke; (4–5) two staffs with indistinct objects on top.

The inscription is lost.

17. Susa XIII.—Cassite dynasty (fig. 29, p. 94).

(1) The crescent; (2) the eight-pointed star of Ishtar; (3) the sun disk; (4–5) two shrines, carrying tiaras, representing Anu and Ellil; (6) a shrine with an indistinct round figure, perhaps a tortoise (cf. fig. 14[13]); (7, 10) the goddess Gula with her dog; (8) the lamp of Nusku; (9) the scorpion of Ishḫara; (11) a bird perched on a pole; (12) the mace with the lion head, Nergal; (13) the mace with the vulture head, Zamama; (14) the lightning fork of Rammân; (15) the serpent of Ṣîru; (16) the spearhead of Marduk.

The inscription has been effaced.

18. Susa XV.—Cassite dynasty (fig. 2, p. 6).

(1) The solar disk; (2) the crescent; (3) the star of Ishtar; (4–5) two shrines bearing tiaras, the symbols of Anu and Ellil; (6) the goatfish carrying a shrine, the symbol of Ea; (7) a shrine with a round figure on it, which has two horns, probably a substitute for the yoke; (8) the spearhead of Marduk; (9) a dragon carrying a shrine with a pyramid-shaped figure on top, perhaps several rows of bricks, and in that case the symbol of Nabû; (10) a dragon with a shrine on its back and a square object on the shrine which shows two wedges; (11) the serpent, the symbol of Ṣîru.

The inscription has not been preserved.

19. Susa XVIII.—Cassite dynasty (fig. 4, p. 14).

(1) A crouching animal, perhaps a dog; (2) a mace with a lion(?) head; (3) a bird; (4) a mace with a vulture(?) head; (5) a crouching animal supporting a circular object; (6) a dragon with a wedge(?) on its back; (7) a dragon with the spearhead(?) on its back; (8) perhaps a plow; (9) perhaps a flying bird; (10) a shrine with a border on top, formed by two corner pieces and three knobs in the centre; (11) the walking bird of Bau; (12) the scorpion; (13) the serpent

stretched along the lower edge.

The inscription is lost.

20. Susa XIX.—Cassite dynasty (fig. 39, p. 104).

(1–2) Two shrines, carrying probably tiaras originally, which are now broken off; (3) a dragon with a shrine on its back, on which stands the spearhead of Marduk, inscribed along its side *dMarduk ilu rabû*; (4) the symbol of Rammân, broken off except the name *dRammân*.

The inscription has not been preserved.

21. Susa XX.—Cassite dynasty (figs. 16 and 30, pp. 38, 95).

(1–2) Two shrines bearing tiaras, symbols of Anu and Ellil; (3) the goatfish with a shrine on its back and a ram's head on the shrine, the symbol of Ea; (4) a shrine with the yoke reversed, the symbol of NIN.ḪAR.SAG; (5) a dragon with a shrine and the spearhead of Marduk; (6) a dragon with a shrine, on which are three rows of bricks, the symbol of Nabû; (7) a shrine with the bust of the goddess Gula; (8) a winged dragon; (9) the mace with the lion head, Nergal; (10) a bird looking backwards; (11) the mace with the vulture head, Zamama; (12) a winged dragon crouching; (13) a mace with another lion head; (14) the serpent, coiled on top, with its head lying across the last lion-headed mace; (15) the solar disk; (16) the crescent; (17) the seven-pointed star of Ishtar; (18) the lamp of Nusku; (19) the scorpion; (20) the walking bird of Bau.

This stone has no inscription.

22. London 100 (V R. 57).—Reign of Nebuchadrezzar I. (fig. 49, p. 131).

(1) The eight-pointed star of Ishtar; (2) the crescent; (3) the solar disk; (4–6) three shrines bearing tiaras, symbols of Anu, Ellil and Ea; (7) a dragon with a shrine bearing the spearhead of Marduk; (8) a dragon with a shrine bearing the wedge of Nabû; (9) a shrine with the yoke reversed, the symbol of NIN.ḪAR.SAG; (10) the mace with the vulture head, Zamama; (11) the mace with the twin lion heads, NIN.IB; (12) a low table with a horse head on it, enclosed in a shrine; (13) a bird perched on a pole; (14) the goddess Gula, seated on a shrine, accompanied by her dog; (15) the scorpion-man, having a human head and breast, below the belt the body and tail of a scorpion, holding bow and arrow in his hands; (16) the lightning fork of Rammân standing on the crouching ox; (17) a tortoise; (18) the scorpion of Ishḫara; (19) the lamp of Nusku; (20) the serpent.

The gods mentioned in the curses: "The great gods" (*i.e.*, Anu, Ellil, Ea), NIN.IB, Gula, Rammân, Shumalia, Rammân again, Nergal, Nanâ, Ṣîru, Sin and the Bêlit Akkadi.

23. Boundary Stone from Nippur.—Reign of Nebuchadrezzar I. (fig. 47, p. 120).

(1) The dragon of Marduk with the shrine and the spearhead; (2) the wedge of Nabû, standing upright; (3) a scepter, with a knob on top and an animal head in the center; (4) a shrine bearing a tiara, the symbol of Anu

(5) the mace with the lion head, Nergal; (6) a scepter with a knob on top and an animal head in the center; (7) the mace with the vulture head, Zamama; (8) a shrine with a tiara, the symbol of Ellil; (9) a scepter (like 3 and 6) with a lion(?) head in the center; (10) a shrine with the yoke reversed, the symbol of NIN.ḪAR.SAG; (11) the scorpion; (12) the crescent; (13) the five-pointed star of Ishtar; (14) the dog of Gula; (15) the solar disk; (16) the lightning fork of Rammân; (17) a pedestal with a censer(?); (18) a tortoise; (19) a bird perched on a pole; (20) the serpent, the symbol of Ṣîru.

The gods mentioned in the curses: Anu, Ellil, Ea, Sin, Shamash, Rammân, NIN.IB, Gula, Ishtar, Nusku.

24. London 105 (III R. 41).—Second Isin (PA.SHE) dynasty (fig. 14, p. 34).

(1) The dragon of Marduk with the shrine and the spearhead; (2) the mace with the twin lion heads, NIN.IB; (3) a dragon with a shrine and a wedge lying on it, the symbol of Nabû; (4) the scorpion, the symbol of Ishḫara; (5) a yoke, the symbol of NIN.ḪAR.SAG; (6) the dog of Gula; (7) the lamp of Nusku; (8) an arrow standing upright; (9) a bird perched on a pole; (10) the lightning fork of Rammân; (11–12) two shrines bearing tiaras, symbols of Anu and Ellil; (13) a shrine with a tortoise over it; (14) the crescent; (15) the solar disk; (16) the eight-pointed star of Ishtar; (17) the walking bird of Bau; (18) a mace with a globular top; (19) the serpent, the symbol of Ṣîru.

The gods mentioned in the curses: Anu, Ellil, Ea, NIN.MAḪ, Sin, Shamash, Ishtar, Marduk, NIN.IB, Gula, Rammân, Nabû.

25. Caillou de Michaux (I R. 70).—Second Isin (PA.SHE) dynasty (fig. 13, p. 33).

(1) The crescent; (2) the sun disk; (3) the star of Ishtar; (4–5) two shrines bearing tiaras, symbols of Anu and Ellil; (6) the goat-fish with a shrine, the symbol of Ea; (7) a shrine with the yoke, the symbol of NIN.ḪAR.SAG; (8) a dragon with a shrine and the spearhead of Marduk; (9) a dragon with a shrine and the wedge of Nabû lying on it; (10) the lightning fork of Rammân; (11) an arrow standing upright; (12) the serpent extending over the top; (13) the dog of Gula; (14) the lion-headed mace of Nergal; (15) the vulture-headed mace of Zamama; (16) the walking bird of Bau; (17) the lamp of Nusku; (18) a bird perched on a pole; (19) the scorpion of Ishḫara.

The gods mentioned in the curses: Anu, Ellil, Ea, NIN.MAḪ, Marduk, Shamash, Sin, Ishtar, NIN.IB, Gula, Rammân, Nabû.

26. London 106 (III R. 43).—Reign of Marduk-nâdin-aḫê (fig. 12, p. 30).

(1) The solar disk; (2) the crescent; (3) the eight-pointed star of Ishtar; (4–5) two shrines with tiaras, representing Anu and Ellil; (6) the scorpion of Ishḫara; (7) the dog of Gula; (8) the walking bird of Bau; (9) the bird perched on a pole; (10) an arrow standing upright; (11) the lamp

of Nusku; (12) a dragon with a shrine and the spearhead of Marduk; (13) a mace with a globular top; (14) the goatfish with a shrine and the ram's head on it, the symbol of Ea; (15) the lightning fork of Rammân; (16) the yoke, the symbol of NIN.ḪAR.SAG; (17) the twin lion heads, the symbol of NIN.IB; (18) the dragon with the shrine and the wedge on it, the symbol of Nabû; (19) the serpent winding around the symbols, representing Ṣîru.

The gods mentioned in the curses: Anu, Ellil, Ea, Marduk, Nabû, Rammân, Sin, Shamash, Ishtar, Gula, NIN.IB, Nergal, Zamama, Papsukkal, Ishḫara, Anu rabû.

27. Boundary Stone of 'Amrân (Berlin V. A.).—Second Isin (PA.SHE) dynasty (fig. 19, p. 45).

(1) The crescent; (2) the solar disk; (3) the star of Ishtar; (4) the scorpion of Ishḫara; (5) the serpent; (6–7) two shrines bearing tiaras, symbol of Anu and Ellil; (8) a dragon with a shrine and a wedge on it, the symbol of Nabû; (9) a shrine with a ram's head on it and traces of the goatfish before it, the symbol of Ea.

The inscription is still unpublished.

28. O. B. I., No. 149.—Reign of Marduk-aḫê-erba (symbols unpublished, described by Prof. Hilprecht, O. B. I., Vol. I, Pt. 2, p. 65f.).

(1) The tortoise on top; (2) the scorpion; (3) the crescent; (4) the solar disk; (5) the star of Ishtar; (6) the mace with the lion head, the symbol of Nergal; (7) the mace with the vulture head, the symbol of Zamama; (8) the bird perched on a pole; (9) a dragon with a shrine and the tiara on it, the symbol of Anu; (10) a shrine with a tiara, the symbol of Ellil; (11) the lightning fork of Rammân; (12) the goddess Gula, with uplifted hands; (13) the lamp of Nusku; (14) the serpent of Ṣîru.

The gods mentioned in the curses: Anu, Ellil, Ea, Marduk, Zarpanîtum, NIN.IB, Gula, Sin.

29. O. B. I., No. 80.—Second Isin (PA.SHE) dynasty, (fig. 44(1) p. 112).

(1) The dog of Gula; (2) the walking bird of Bau; (3) the lower part of what appears to be a pointed shaft (the rest is broken off).

30. O. B. I., No. 150.—Second Isin (PA.SHE) dynasty (O. B. I., Vol. I, Pt. 2, pl. XXV, No. 69).

(1) The crescent; (2) the eight-pointed star of Ishtar; (3) the solar disk (the rest is broken off).

31. Berlin V. A. 211.—(Symbols published in *Vorderasiatische Schriftdenkmäler*, Vol. I, *Beiheft*, pl. V, described by Hommel, *Aufsätze*, p. 258).

(1) A dragon with a shrine and the wedge of Nabû; (2–3) two shrines bearing tiaras, symbols of Anu and Ellil; (4) a mace with the twin lion heads, the symbol of NIN.IB; (5) a mace with a globular top; (6) a mace with the vulture head; (7) the serpent.

The curses of the inscription have not been preserved.

32. London 102.—Reign of Nabû-mukîn-aplu (symbols unpublished, described by Pinches, *Guide to the Nimroud Central Saloon*, p. 53f.).

(1) The solar disk; (2) the crescent; (3) the star of Ishtar; (4–5) two shrines bearing tiaras, symbols of Anu and Ellil; (6) a shrine with a tortoise on it; (7) a shrine with a yoke, the symbol of NIN.ḪAR.SAG; (8) a dragon with a shrine and the spearhead of Marduk; (9) a dragon with a shrine and the wedge of Nabû on it; (10) the goddess Gula, seated on a shrine, with her hands uplifted and her dog beside her; (11) the bird perched on a pole; (12) an arrow; (13) the lamp of Nusku; (14) the mace with the lion head, the symbol of Nergal; (15) the mace with the vulture head, the symbol of Zamama; (16) the lightning fork of Rammân; (17) the walking bird of Bau; (18) the scorpion of Ishḫara; (19) the serpent winding alongside of the symbols.

The gods mentioned in the curses: Anu, [Ellil], Ea, Marduk, Zarpanîtu, Nabû, Sin, Shamash, Nergal, Zamama, [Ramman], NIN.IB, Gula, Nin[-girsu?].

33. Stone of Nabû-shum-ishkun* (Berlin, V. A. 3031) (fig. 31, p. 97).

(1) The serpent winding through the center; (2) the crescent; (3) the solar disk; (4) the star of Ishtar, seven-pointed; (5) seven stars, probably the Sibitti; (6) a dragon with a shrine and the spearhead, the symbol of Marduk; (7) a dragon with a shrine and an upright wedge, the symbol of Nabû; (8) the yoke, the symbol of NIN.ḪAR.SAG; (9) the goatfish with a shrine and a ram's head on it; (10) the lion-headed mace, the symbol of Nergal; (11) the scorpion; (12) the vulture-headed mace, the symbol of Zamama; (13–14) two shrines bearing tiaras, symbols of Anu and Ellil; (15) a flying(?) bird; (16) the lamp of Nusku; (17) the lightning fork of Rammân; (18) a mace with a conical top; (19) the dog of Gula; (20–22) three fly flaps or fans; (23) the figure of a god, holding in his left the reins of a winged dragon (cf. figure of Rammân in Clay, *Light on the Old Testament from Babel*, p. 367); (24) the figure of a god (or goddess?) with uplifted hands; (25) the figure of a god with a lion(?) crouching alongside of him; (26) a dagger close to the serpent.

No gods are enumerated in the curses. We find the general statement: "The gods as many as on this inscribed stone have been caused to take a place" (*ilâni mala ina eli narî annî šuršudu nanzazu*, Edge 6, 7).

34. London 90, 922.—Reign of Nabû-apal-iddina (fig. 9, p. 23).

(1) A shrine with the spearhead of Marduk; (2) a shrine with a ram's head, the symbol of Ea; (3) a shrine with two staffs joined in the center, the symbol of Nabû (cf. p. 77[1]); (4–5) two shrines bearing tiaras, symbols of Anu and Ellil; (6) the mace with the vulture head, the symbol of Zamama; (7) the mace with the lion head, the symbol of Nergal; (8) the lightning fork of Rammân.

The inscription contains no curses.

35. Berlin, V. A. 208.—Reign of Marduk-shum-iddina (symbols pub-

* No boundary stone, but inserted for the sake of comparison.

lished in *Vorderasiatische Schriftdenkmäler*, Vol. I, *Beiheft*, pl. II, described by Hommel, *Aufsätze*, p. 256f.).

(1) A shrine with the wedge of Nabû; (2) a shrine with the spearhead of Marduk; (3) a shrine with the twin lion heads, between which is a mace, the symbol of NIN.IB; (4) a shrine, the lion(?)-headed dragon; (5) the dog of Gula; (6) a shrine with the lightning fork of Rammân; (7) the crescent; (8) the solar disk; (9) the star of Ishtar.

The inscription contains no curses.

36. Berlin, V. A. 209.—Reign of Sargon (fig. 15, p. 35).

(1) The crescent; (2) the solar disk; (3) the eight-pointed star of Ishtar; (4) the serpent coiled on top; (5) a dragon with a shrine and the spearhead of Marduk; (6) a dragon and a shrine with the stylus standing upright, the symbol of Nabû.

The gods mentioned in the curses: Anu, Ellil, Ea and Sin.

37. Berlin, V. A. 2663.—Reign of Marduk-apal-iddina II. (fig. 8, p. 20).

(1) The eight-pointed star of Ishtar; (2) the crescent; (3) the solar disk; (4) the serpent winding alongside of the inscription; (5) a dragon with a shrine and the spearhead of Marduk; (6) the goatfish with a shrine and the ram's head on it, the symbol of Ea; (7) a shrine with the yoke, the symbol of NIN.ḪAR.SAG; (8) a dragon with a shrine and a stylus standing upright on it, the symbol of Nabû; (9) the lamp of Nusku on a pedestal; (10) the lightning fork of Rammân; (11) the dog of Gula; (12) the walking bird of Bau; (13) the scorpion of Ishḫara; (14–15) two shrines bearing tiaras, symbols of Anu and Ellil; (16) a winged dragon with a shrine.

The gods mentioned in the curses: Anu, Ellil, Ea, Marduk and Erûa.

B. ARRANGED ALPHABETICALLY.

Animal figures, unclassified.*

Fig. 4[1] (crouching animal, perhaps lion or dog); fig. 4[5] (crouching animal, supporting circular object); fig. 24[7] (crouching animal, with a shrine on its back and a vase on its head); Susa 10[3] (fig. 44) (perhaps a hare); London 103[15] (animal with two straight horns, two curved horns or ears and a forked tongue).

Arrow standing erect—*Sagittarius.*

Fig. 12[10]; fig. 13[11]; fig. 14[8]; London 102[12].

Bird.

Fig. 4[3]; fig. 4[9] (perhaps a flying bird); fig. 11[10] (bird looking backwards); fig. 30[10] (bird looking backwards); fig. 31[15] (flying bird).

Bird, perched on pole—Aruru(?).†

Fig. 6[11]; fig. 10[17]; fig. 11[21]; fig. 12[9]; fig. 13[18]; fig. 14[9]; fig. 23[22]; fig. 28[15]; fig. 29[11]; fig. 49[13]; London 101[4]; London 102[11]; O. B. I., 149[8].

Bird walking—Ba[-ú].

Fig. 4[11]; fig. 6[5]; fig. 8[12]; fig. 10[16]; fig.

* The raised figures refer to the numbers given to the various symbols in the different illustrations.

† So Zimmern, see *Leipziger Semitistische Studien*, II, 2, p. 43.

11[20]; fig. 12[8]; fig. 13[16]; fig. 14[17]; fig. 18[10]; fig. 24[8]; fig. 40[8]; 44(1)[2]; London 102[17]; Susa 20[20] (fig. 16).

Censer(?)—perhaps *kinûnu*.*

Fig. 47[17] (placed on pedestal).

Centaur—*Sagittarius*.

Fig. 23[12] (centaur holding bow and arrow); London 101[1] (see fig. 32).

Chisel, standing on a shrine.†

Fig. 11[17] (before the shrine is a crouching ram).

Crescent—Sin.

Fig. 2[2]; fig. 6[1]; fig. 8[2]; fig. 10[1]; fig. 11[1]; fig. 12[2]; fig. 13[1]; fig. 14[14]; fig. 15[1]; fig. 17[1]; fig. 19[1]; fig. 21[1]; fig. 23[1]; fig. 24[4]; fig. 27[1]; fig. 29[1]; fig. 30[16]; fig. 31[2]; fig. 47[12]; fig. 49[2]; London 101[13]; London 102[2]; London 103[2]; Susa 6[2]; V. A. 208[7]; O. B. I., 149[3]; O. B. I., 150[1].

Curved object.

London 103[6] (compare perhaps yoke).

Dagger.

Fig. 31[26] (cf. fig. 11[7]).

Dog of Gula (substitute for the goddess)—perhaps *Leo*.

Fig. 6[8]; fig. 8[11]; fig. 10[7]; fig. 12[7]; fig. 13[13]; fig. 14[6]; fig. 21[4]; fig. 23[13] (uncertain); fig. 31[19]; fig. 44(1)[1]; fig. 47[14]; London 101[3]; Susa 10[2] (fig. 44(2); V. A. 208[5].

Dragon.

Fig. 2[9] (with a shrine which bears a pyramid-shaped object, perhaps some rows of bricks); fig. 18[8] (crouching before the spearhead of Marduk); fig. 23[20,21] (with a shrine on its back); fig. 23[23,24] (also with a shrine).

Dragon, winged.

Fig. 6[18] (walking along the body of a serpent); fig. 8[16] (with a shrine); fig. 11[8] (a double-headed mace standing on its back, perhaps twin lion heads); fig. 11[12] (crouching before lion-headed mace); fig. 23[19] (crouching); fig. 30[8] (crouching); London 103[8].

Fans (or fly flaps).

Fig. 31[20, 21, 22].

Fox.‡

London 103[7].

Goatfish (with ram's head) Ea—*Capricorn*.

Fig. 2[6] (with a shrine on the goatfish); fig. 6[17] (with a ram's head over the goatfish); fig. 8[6] (goatfish crouching before a shrine with a ram's head); fig. 11[6] (*idem*); fig. 12[14] (*idem*); fig. 13[6] (goatfish and shrine); fig. 19[9] (goatfish with shrine and ram's head); fig. 23[15, 16, 17] (*idem*); fig. 24[6] (*idem*, shrine inscribed *d*E-a); fig. 28[9] (ram's head and goatfish effaced); fig. 30[3] (goatfish with shrine and ram's head); fig. 31[9] (*idem*); fig. 9[2] (shrine and ram's head without goatfish).

Gods.

Fig. 5[1]; fig. 31[23] (holding reins of dragon); fig. 31[24] (hands uplifted); fig. 31[25] (with a lion(?) crouching at his side); Susa 6[6] (see fig. 38), the god Ea standing on a goat, holding a cup against his breast, from which flow two streams); London 103[14] (holding a mace against his breast with

* For the star *kinûnu*, which appears near the Capricorn, see Hommel, *Aufsätze*, p. 241.

† This symbol can hardly be a substitute for the shrine with the stylus or the wedge, because the latter appears on the same stone at another place (cf. fig. 11[14, 17]).

‡ For the "fox star" (*kakkab šêlibi* (*LUL.A*), see II R. 49, 8*d*; III R. 53, 66, and Hommel, *Aufsätze*, p. 423.

16

the left hand and in the right hand a *gamlu*).

Goddess.

London 101[10] (holding a cup in the right and an object with a thin handle in the left hand); London 101[15] (winged).

Goddess Gula—perhaps *Virgo*.

Fig. 11[15] (the bust of the goddess on a shrine borne by a dog); fig. 23[14] (seated on a shrine and accompanied by her dog, partly effaced); fig. 24[2] (seated on a shrine, inscribed *dG[u-la]*); fig. 27[4] (seated on a shrine, with the dog at her feet); fig. 29[7, 10] (*idem*); fig. 30[7] (the bust of the goddess on a shrine); fig. 40[1,] (the goddess with the dog and the accompanying inscription *dGu-la*); fig. 49[14] (on a shrine, with her dog beside her); Susa 7[1] (see fig. 21); Susa 8[1] (fig. 21 only partly preserved); Susa 11[2] (fig. 44, with dog, partly effaced); O. B. I., 149[12]; London 102[10].

Horse head.*

Fig. 49[12] (standing on a table, enclosed in a shrine).

Indistinct figures.

Fig. 4[9]; fig. 23[13]; fig. 44(1)[3]; Susa 11[1] (fig. 44); Susa 11[4, 5] (fig. 44).

Lamp of Nusku.

Fig. 6[4]; fig. 8[9] (on pedestal); fig. 10[13]; fig. 11[18]; fig. 12[11]; fig. 13[17]; fig. 14[7]; fig. 23[7]; fig. 24[5]; fig. 27[5]; fig. 29[8]; fig. 31[16]; fig. 49[19] (on a pedestal); London 101[14]; London 102[13]; London 103[12] (mounted on a tripod); Susa 6[4]; Susa 20[18] (see fig. 16); O. B. I., 149[13].

Lightning fork of Rammân.

Fig. 6[12] (standing on a crouching ox); fig. 8[10]; fig. 9[8]; fig. 10[14] (on a crouching ox); fig. 11[16] (standing on a shrine borne by crouching ox); fig. 12[15]; fig. 13[10]; fig. 14[10]; fig. 23[11]; fig. 29[14]; fig. 18[5] (held by the god Rammân who is standing on the wild ox); fig. 28[16] (standing on the crouching ox); fig. 31[17]; fig. 39[4] (symbol broken off, only the name *dRammân* (*dIM*) preserved); fig. 47[16]; fig. 49[16] (on crouching ox); London 101[12]; London 102[16]; London 103[16]; O. B. I., 149[11]; V. A. 208[6].

Lion, standing erect.†

Fig. 21[5] (Susa 9) (holding daggers in front paws); fig. 44 (Susa 10[4]) (holding a mace in right paw).

Mace, with conical top.

London 101[6] (tassels hanging down on each side, probably a substitute for the spearhead of Marduk which is missing).

Mace, with globular top.

Fig. 12[13]; fig. 14[18]; fig. 31[18]; London 101[9]; V. A. 211[5].

Mace, with lion head—Nergal (cf. p. 87[1]).

Fig. 4[2] (doubtful); fig. 6[7]; fig. 9[7]; fig. 10[9]; fig. 11[11]; fig. 13[14]; fig. 23[5]; fig. 24[12] (inscribed *d*Nergal (GIR)); fig. 28[14]; fig. 29[12]; fig. 30[9]; fig. 31[10]; fig. 47[5]; London 101[11]; London 102[14]; O. B. I., 149[6]; V. A. 208[4] (shrine with the head of a dragon, perhaps = lion).

Mace, with square top—Shuqamuna.

Fig. 24[10] (inscribed *d*[Shu-qa]-muna).

Mace, with twin lion heads—NIN.IB (cf. pp. 87[1], 88)—*Gemini*(?).

Fig. 10[12] (projecting knob between the two heads); fig. 11[8] (mace standing on a winged dragon,

* For the "horse star" see V R. 46, 20*ab*, and Hommel, *Aufsätze*, p. 262.

† Perhaps a representation of Nergal (so Hommel, *Aufsätze*, p. 445). In that case it is a variant of the mace with the lion head.

also a knob between the two heads); fig. 12^{17}; fig. 14^{2}; fig. 24^{11} (with a knob between the two heads); fig. 28^{12} (the same); fig. $30^{12, 13}$ (winged dragon before the mace with the lion head = twin lion heads*) (cf. fig. 11^{8}); fig. 49^{11}; V. A. 211^{4}; London 101^{7}; V. A. 208^{3} (placed on a shrine, a knob between the two heads).

Mace, with vulture head—Za-mà-mà.
Fig. 4^{4} (doubtful); fig. 6^{6}; fig. 9^{6}; fig. 10^{10}; fig. 11^{9}; fig. 13^{15}; fig. 23^{4}; fig. 24^{14} (inscribed ᵈZa-mà-mà); fig. 28^{13}; fig. 29^{13}; fig. 30^{11}; fig. 31^{12}; fig. 47^{7}; fig. 49^{10}; O. B. I., 149^{7}; London 102^{15}; V. A. 211^{6}.

Plow.
Fig. 4^{8}; fig. 11^{19}; fig. 23^{18} (doubtful).

Priest.
Fig. 17^{2} (standing before the spear-head of Marduk in the act of anointing it, inscribed *ṣalmu ša zikari* (*NITAḪ*) ᵈ*Marduk*); fig. 40^{5} (standing before the goddess Gula).

Satyr.
London 101^{5} (the upper part of the body is human, the lower that of a horse with a short tail; he holds a long thick staff in both hands).

Scepter.
Fig. $47^{3, 6, 9}$ (three scepters with knobs on top and animal heads in the center).

Scorpion—Ishḫara.
Fig. 4^{12}; fig. 6^{9}; fig. 8^{13}; fig. 10^{8}; fig. 11^{24}; fig. 12^{6}; fig. 13^{19}; fig. 14^{4}; fig. 18^{6}; fig. 19^{4}; fig. 23^{6}; fig. 24^{15}; fig. 27^{6}; fig. 31^{11}; fig. 40^{4}; fig. 47^{11}; fig. 49^{18}; Susa 10^{1} (cf. fig. 44(2)); Susa 20^{19} (cf. fig. 16); London

* This identification is established by a comparison of Susa No. 3 (fig. 11) with Susa No. 20 (fig. 30). The arrangement of the symbols on these two stones is almost identical. The first four symbols of fig. 30 (Anu, Ellil, Ea and Ninḫarsag) correspond to the first section of fig. 11, the next three symbols of fig. 30 (Marduk, Nabû, Gula) correspond to the third section of fig. 11, repeating even the curious bust of Gula on a shrine (fig. 11^{15} and 30^{7}) which is found only here. The next six symbols of fig. 30 (winged dragon, Nergal, bird looking backwards, Zamama, winged lion, followed by the mace with the lion head) correspond exactly to section 2 of fig. 11, where we find instead of the last two symbols the winged lion with the twin-headed mace standing on its back. This shows that the winged lion, followed by the lion-headed mace, exchanges with the winged lion having the twin lion heads on its back. The last three symbols of Susa No. 20 are separated from the rest and are found on fig. 16, first view. They are the lamp, the scorpion and the walking bird, which correspond to Nos. 18, 20, 24 on Susa No. 3 (fig. 11). This remarkable similarity of Susa No. 3 (a stone of Meli-Shipak) and Susa No. 20 (an uninscribed boundary stone) cannot be accidental. The latter (Susa No. 20) belongs undoubtedly to the reign of the same king and was made perhaps by the same sculptor. It may also explain why this stone (Susa No. 20) is not inscribed. Perhaps before the inscription could be engraved the invasion of Sutruk-naḫunte took place, by which most likely all the boundary stones found by the French at Susa were carried away, for it should be noted that the inscription which this Elamite king put on another monument (see fig. No. 5) states distinctly: "the land of Qarin. . . . I took and the stele of Me-li-[Shi-pak] I found," see Scheil, D. E. P., IV, p. 146, B. 6, 7.

101^{2}; London 102^{18}; London 103^{5}; O. B. I., 149^{2}.

Scorpion-man—*Sagittarius.*

Fig. 49^{15} (having a human head and breast, a body and tail of a scorpion, holding in his hands a bow and arrow); London 103^{9} (having a man's head, wings, a scorpion's body and tail, and a lion's legs).

Serpent—Ṣîru.

Fig. 4^{13}; fig. 6^{15} (horned serpent); fig. 8^{4}; fig. 10^{18} (serpent coiled on top); fig. 11^{23}; fig. 12^{19} (winding along lower edge of symbols); fig. 13^{12} (winding across top); fig. 14^{19}; fig. 15^{4}; fig. 18^{7}; fig. 19^{5}; fig. 24^{13} (inscribed [*a-ša-*]*ri-du*); fig. 28^{17}; fig. 29^{15}; fig. 30^{14} (coiled on top); fig. 31^{1}; fig. 47^{20}; fig. 49^{20}; Susa 6^{1} (coiled on top); Susa 7^{2} (cf. fig. 21); London 101^{19} (coiled on top); London 102^{19}; London 103^{4}; O. B. I., 149^{14}; V. A. 211^{7}.

Shrine, with sea shell.

Fig. 11^{22}.

Shrine, with two staffs—Nabû.

Fig. 9^{3} (two staffs, joined in the center, standing on a shrine, cf. fig. 26^{10}).

Shrines with tiaras—Anu, Ellil (Ea).

Fig. 2^{4,5}; fig. 8^{14,15}; fig. 9^{4,5}; fig. 10^{4,5}; fig. 11^{4,5}; fig. 12^{4,5}; fig. 13^{4,5}; fig. 14^{11,12}; fig. 19^{6,7}; fig. 23^{8,9}; fig. 28^{7,8}; fig. 29^{4,5}; fig. 30^{1,2}; fig. 31^{13,14}; fig. 39^{1,2} (tiaras broken off); fig. 47^{4,8}; fig. 49^{4,5,6} (Anu, Ellil, Ea); London 103^{10} (a crouching animal alongside of the shrine); London 103^{11} (a winged bull alongside of shrine); London 102^{4,5}; V. A. 211^{2,3}; O. B. I., 149^{9} (shrine with dragon); O. B. I., 149^{10} (shrine without dragon).

Shrines with indistinct objects.

Fig. 29^{6}; Susa 11^{1} (cf. fig. 44, 3)

Shrines with various figures.

Fig. 2^{7} (a shrine with a round figure having two horns, perhaps a substitute for the yoke); fig. 2^{10} (a dragon with a shrine, having a square object (brick?) on it, marked with two wedges); fig. 4^{10} (a shrine with a border on top, formed by two corner pieces and three knobs in the center).

Solar disk—Shamash.

Fig. 2^{1}; fig. 6^{2}; fig. 8^{3}; fig. 10^{3}; fig. 11^{2}; fig. 12^{1}; fig. 13^{2}; fig. 14^{15}; fig. 15^{2}; fig. 19^{2}; fig. 21^{2} (Susa 9); fig. 23^{2}; fig. 24^{9}; fig. 27^{2}; fig. 29^{3}; fig. 30^{15}; fig. 31^{3}; fig. 47^{15}; fig. 49^{3}; Susa 6^{3}; London 101^{8}; London 102^{1}; London 103^{1}; O. B. I., 149^{4}; O. B. I., 150^{3}; V. A. 208^{8}.

Spearhead of Marduk—perhaps *taurus.*

Fig. 2^{8}; fig. 4^{7} (crouching dragon with a spearhead(?) on its back); fig. 6^{13} (spearhead standing on a dragon); fig. 8^{5}; fig. 9^{1} (standing on a shrine); fig. 10^{15}; fig. 11^{13}; fig. 12^{12} (standing on a shrine flanked by a dragon); fig. 13^{8} (*idem*); fig. 14^{1} (*idem*); fig. 15^{5} (*idem*); fig. 17^{3} (priest standing before spearhead); fig. 23^{10}; fig. 24^{1} (inscribed *d*Marduk) (AM. UD); fig. 28^{11}; fig. 29^{16}; fig. 30^{5} (standing on a shrine with a dragon); fig. 31^{6} (*idem*); fig. 39^{3} (on a shrine with a dragon, inscribed *dMarduk ilu rabû*); fig. 47^{1} (standing on a shrine with a dragon); fig. 49^{7} (*idem*); London 103^{17}; London 102^{8}; V. A. 208^{2}.

Staff.

Susa 11^{4} (cf. fig. 44, a staff with an indistinct object on top, partly broken off); Susa 11^{5} (a staff, whose top is broken off); London 101^{16} (a staff with the head of some animal on top).

Star of Ishtar—Venus.

Fig. 2[3]; fig. 6[3] (eight-pointed); fig. 8[1] (*idem*); fig. 10[2] (*idem*); fig. 11[3]; fig. 12[3] (*idem*); fig. 13[3]; fig. 14[16] (*idem*); fig. 15[3] (*idem*); fig. 18[4] (*idem*); fig. 19[3]; fig. 21[3] (Susa 9) (six-pointed); fig. 23[3] (*idem*); fig. 24[3] (eight-pointed); fig. 27[3] (*idem*); fig. 29[2] (*idem*); fig. 30[17] (seven-pointed); fig. 31[4] (*idem*); fig. 47[13] (five-pointed); fig. 49[1] (eight-pointed); London 101[18]; London 102[3]; London 103[3]; O. B. I., 149[5]; O. B. I., 150[2]; V. A. 208[9].

Stars—Sibitti.

Fig. 31[5] (seven stars, probably representing the seven planets).

Stylus (substitute for wedge)—Nabû.

Fig. 8[8] (on a shrine with a dragon); fig. 15[6] (*idem*).

Table.

London 101[17] (the corners ornamented with lion heads, a tiara on the table, perhaps a substitute for the shrine with the tiara).

Tortoise.

Fig. 6[16]; fig. 14[13] (placed over shrine); fig. 29[6] (doubtful, but cf. fig. 14[13]); fig. 47[18]; fig. 49[17]; O. B. I., 149[1]; London 102[6].

Wedge (and bricks)—Nabû—perhaps *aries*.

Fig. 2[9] (a dragon bearing a shrine with a pyramid-shaped object, perhaps bricks); fig. 4[6] (a crouching dragon with a wedge(?) on its back); fig. 6[14] (wedge on the back of a dragon, crouching before a stage tower); fig. 10[11] (a horned dragon before a shrine with four rows of bricks); fig. 11[14] (a dragon carrying a shrine with a brick and a wedge); fig. 12[18] (a wedge on a shrine with a dragon); fig. 13[9] (*idem*); fig. 14[3] (*idem*); fig. 19[8] (*idem*); fig. 30[6] (a dragon before a shrine on which are three rows of bricks); fig. 31[7] (wedge on a shrine with a dragon); fig. 47[2] (wedge alone, standing upright); fig. 49[8] (dragon with shrine and wedge); V. A. 208[1]; V. A. 211[1]; London 102[9]; Susa 6[5] (shrine with wedge lying on it); Susa 7[3] (cf. fig. 21, wedge on shrine with dragon).

Yoke (perhaps plaits of hair*)—Ninḫarsag (cf. fig. 48).

Fig. 6[10] (standing on a shrine); fig. 8[7] (*idem*); fig. 11[7] (shrine with nail (dagger?) and reversed yoke on top); fig. 12[16] (yoke alone); fig. 13[7] (on shrine); fig. 14[5] (yoke alone); fig. 28[10] (on shrine); fig. 30[4] (on shrine, yoke reversed); fig. 31[8] (yoke alone); fig. 47[10] (shrine with yoke reversed); fig. 49[9] (*idem*); Susa 11[3] (cf. fig. 44, shrine with reversed yoke, partly broken off); London 102[7] (yoke on shrine).

* Prof. W. Max Müller kindly informs me that the part of the Egyptian picture which corresponds to the Babylonian really represents the plaits of hair (*ḥnskt*) of the goddess *Ḥat-ḥor*, which, according to him, play an important part in Egyptian mythology.

GLOSSARY.

abu, father.

cstr., (*Anu*) *a-bi ilâ*[*ni*], London, 101, III, 9; *šarru abi*(*AD*) *ilâni*, Neb. Nippur, IV, 3; (*Sin*) *a-bi ilâni rabûti*, D. E. P., II, 113, 6; *zi-kir a-bi a-li-di-šu*, V. A., 2663, II, 42; *ša a-bi a-bi-šú*, whose grandfather, IV R.[2] 38, I, 33; *a-bí bâbi*, gatekeeper, Susa, 3, I, 19; *bît abi*(*AD*) *la-bi-ri*, C. T., X, pl. V, 12; c. suff., *abu*(*AD*)-*ú-a*, London, 102, I, 20; IV, 13; *bît abi-ia*, London, 102, IV, 21; C. T., X, pl. III, 4, 6, 7; *a-bu-ka*, London, 103, IV, 31; (Bunene) *ma-lik a-bi-šu*, D. E. P., II, 115, 6; *i-na muḫ-ḫi abi-i-nu*, V. A., 209, IV, 20; *bît abi-ni*, V.A., 209, IV,22; pl., *bît abê*(*AD.MEŠ*)-*e-a*, C. T., X, pl. V, 2.

abûbu, storm flood.

(Ištar) *ša ru-ub-ša a-bu-bu*, Neb. Nippur, IV, 22.

אבב$_1$, **abâbu,** be clean.

I, 1 pret., *ai i-bi-ib*, III R. 41, II, 17.

אבך$_2$, **abâku,** turn away (Hebr. הפך).

I, 1 pret., *i-bu-uk-šú-nu-ti*, he turned them off, London, 103, I, 33.

I, 2 *i-na kišitta*(-*ta*)*ša im-qut-ma i-ta*[*bak-ma*] *i-na pân . . . . šarri . . . . di-na lu-ša*(-*ad*)-*bu-ba*, because of the property which he claimed he brought (his wife) and before . . the King . . they (dual) instituted a lawsuit. London, 102, VI, 5.

ablu, boundary.

dNin-ib be-el ab-li šú-ú-mi u ku-dur-ri, Susa 3, VII, 6; *na-ṣir ku-dur-ri-ti mu-kin-nu ab-li-e*, V R. 55, 5 (cf. *iš-ta-at-tu-um ib-li-e ú-ki-in-nu-um ki-su-ur-ri-im*, Nabop. (Hilpr.), II, 30; O. B. I., Vol. I, Pt. 1, p. 42[1], compares Hebr. חַבְלֵי; see also Lau, J. A. O. S., Vol. 27 (1906), p. 301f.).

abullu, city gate.

abulli(*KÁ.GAL*)-*âli-šú*, Susa, 16, VI, 16.

אבן$_1$, **abnu,** stone.

abnu(*TAQ*) *la ta-a-ra ù la ra-ga-mi . . . . iṣ-ba-at*, London, 103, III, 30; *abnu šú-a-tu i-na aš-ri-šú ú-nak-ka-ru*, London, 101, III, 2; *i-na abni ú-ab-bit-su*, London, 101, III, 4; *na-ra-a ša abni eš-ša*, Susa, 2, Med., II, 9; *ina abni i-naq-qa-ru*, V R. 56, 35; *ina abni* (NA) *ub-ba-tu*, III R. 41, II, 11; I R. 70, III, 3; III R. 43, I, 34; London, 102, V, 2, *ina ab-ni ub-ba-ṣu*, Susa, 16, V, 2; *ina ab-ni ú-pa-sa-su*, V. A., 2663, V, 30; *ina abni* (*an*)-*na-a šùm-šu-nu* [*zak-ru*], London, 102, V, 6.

ubânu, finger.

ubâni(*ŠU-SI*)-*šú a-na limutti i-tar-ra-ṣu*, Neb. Nippur, III, 24.

אבץ, **abâṣu,** break (cf. **napâṣu**).

II, 1 pres., *i-na ab-ni ub-ba-ṣu*, Susa, 16, V, 2.

abqallu, wise man, leader.

(Marduk) *abqal*(*NUN.ME*) *ilâni*, London, 101, III, 13; *abqal šamê u irṣiti*, Susa, 14, III, 14; *abqal kiš-šat šamê*(-*e*) *u irsitim*(-*tim*), V. A., 2663, I, 8.

אבר$_3$, **abâru,** enclose, bind.

II, 1 inf., cstr., *ub-bur meš-ri-e-ti*,

lameness of limbs, V. A. 2663, V, 38; Susa, 14, III, 5.

ibru, friend.
i-bir bêli-šu, Neb. Nippur, II, 17.

אבר$_4$, **ebêru,** pass over.
III, 1 part., *mê ša mu-še-bi-ri,* the waters of the connecting canal, Susa, 3, III, 1.

abšênu, vegetation.
abšênu(AB.SIM) la šú-zu-za-at-ma, Neb. Nippur, II, 30.

אבת$_1$, **abâtu,** destroy (Hebr. אבד).
I, 1 prec., *išid-su li-bit,* London, 101, III, 15; *li-bu-tu ku-dur-ra-šú,* V R. 56, 40.
I, 2 pres., *i-ta-ba-at uḫ-tal-lik,* Susa, 3, V, 56.
II, 1 pret., *i-ga-ru 'u-a-bit-ma 'u-ḫe-pi,* Susa, 2, Med., II, 6; pres., *i-na abni ub-ba-tu,* III R. 41, II, 11; I R. 70, III, 3; III R. 43, I, 34; London, 102, V, 2; *ši-pir ni-kil-ti ub-ba-tu,* C. T., X, pl. VII, 36; *i-na abni ú-ab-bit-su,* London, 101, III, 4.
IV, 1 pret., *in-na-bi-tu-ma,* he fled, D. E. P., II, pl. 20, 3; *in-na-bi-tu-nim-ma,* they fled, C. T., IX, pl. IV, 6; part., *mu-un-na-bi-it-tum,* a fugitive, D. E. P., II, pl. 20, 1.

abtu, fallen, dilapidated.
bîtâti(E.MEŠ) abtûti(GUL.MEŠ) (cf. Br. 8954), V. A. 209, III, 17.

agû, crown.
(Sin) *bêl agê(MIR) na-me-ru-ti,* Neb. Nippur, IV, 13.

אגג, **aggu,** anger.
i-na ag-gi libbi-šú-nu, London, 103, VI, 1.

aggiš, angrily, in anger.
ag-giš li-ru-ru-šú, V R. 56, 38; [*ag-giš li-ḫal*]-*liq-šú,* London, 101, III, 9.

igigallu, open-minded, wise.
(Marduk) *igi(ŠI)-gal(IG) ilâni,* V. A., 2663, I, 3.

agalatillû, dropsy.
a-ga-lâ(NU)-til-la ša ri-ki-is-su la ip-paṭ-ṭa-ru, Susa, 3, VI, 44; III R. 41, II, 25; *a-ga-lâ-til-la(-a) ri-ki-is-su la pa-ṭe-ra,* I R. 70, III, 13; III R. 43, III, 31; London, 102, I, 41; *a-gal-la-til-la-a li-šam-ri-ṣu-šú-ma,* Susa, 16, VI, 20; *a-ga-lâ-til-la-a lišiššu(-šu)-šu-ma,* V. A., 2663, V, 43; [*ina zumri-šu li-ša*]-*aš-ši-šu-ma,* D. E. P., VI, 43, III, 12; D. E. P., II, 113, 18.

igisû, gift.
ina igisê(ŠI.DI) ḫab-ṣu-ú-ti, Neb. Nippur, II, 9.

אגר, **igirru,** plan.
lu mu-lam-me-nu i-gir-ri-šu šú-nu-ma, Neb. Nippur, IV, 17; *i-gir-ra-*[*šu*] *l*[*i-la*]*m-man,* O. B. I., 149, II, 23.

אגר$_3$, **igaru,** wall.
i-na i-ga-ri ip-te-ḫi, Susa, 3, V, 54; *i-na i-ga-ri i-p*[*i-ḫu*], D. E. P., II, 113, 17.

ugâru, communal land.
ugâr âli, Susa, 2, I, 21, 24, 30, 33; II, 2, 7, 12, 17; London, 101, I, 5; London, 103, III, 41; Susa, 3, I, 4; IV R.[2] 38, I, 3, [19]; Susa, 16, I, 2; D. E. P., VI, 42, I, [2]; D. E. P., VI, 46, I, 2; Neb. Nippur, II, 27; III, 8; C. T., IX, pl. IV, 20, 22; O. B. I., 83, I, [2]; I R. 70, I, 2; III R. 43, I, 2; O. B. I., 149, I, 5; London, 102, I, 2; V. A. 2663, IV, 19, 21, 45; *ú-ga-ri-šú,* D. E. P., II, 113, 9; *ugâr-šú,* D. E. P., VI, 46, III, 3; *ugâr qân appari,* C. T., IX, pl. IV, 19; *ugâru ša-nam-ma,* Susa, 3, III, 10; *ugâr-šú li-ir-ḫi-iṣ-ma,* III R. 41, II, 32, I R. 70, IV, 11.

אד$_3$, **edû,** a single one.
ma-am-ma e-di-i, Susa, 3, II, 46; *e-du amelu la i-zib-ma,* V. A., 2663, III 26.

אדה$_4$, **adi**, unto, including.
a-di IV alâni, Susa, 2, I, 13; *a-di ti-tur(!)-ri*, Susa, 14, I, 3; *a-di ûm(-um) bal-ṭu*, Susa, 3, VI, 52; VII, 23; V R. 56, 59; London, 102, II, 22; *a-di ûm(-um) bal-du*, Susa, 16, VI, 18; *a-di šamê ù irṣiti ba-šú-ú*, V R. 56, 60; *a-di ûm(-um) ṣa-a-ti*, I R. 70, IV, 25; *a-di* ^d^*Nabû-ku-dur-ri-uṣur*, O. B. I., 83, I, 7; *a-di XII* ^ta-a-an^*i-ta-nap-pal*, V. A. 208, 47; V. A., 209, II, 5; London, 102, IV, 40; *a-di eqli-šu*, C. T., X, pl. V, 16; *a-di ištên(-en) ṣubâtu KUR.RA*, V. A., 209, IV, 33.

אדל, **edlu**, man.
ed-li qar-di, V R. 55, 21; *ed-lu bêl* ^iṣu^*narkabti*, the charioteer, V R. 55, 34; *ed-lu dan-nu*, V. A., 2663, II, 33.

אדם$_1$, **admânu**, dwelling.
bêl ad-ma-ni, D. E. P., VI, 45, IV, 5.
dadmu, dwelling.
kal da-ad-me, Neb. Nippur, I, 15; *ma-ḫa-az da-[a]d-me*, Neb. Nippur, II, 2; *da-ad-mi*, D. E. P., VI, 45, IV, 9; ^d^*Iš-ḫara bêlit le-ti da-ad-ma*, III R. 43, IV, 28; *gi-mir kal da-ád-me*, V. A., 2663, I, 23; *nišê da-ád-me saplḫâ-ti(BIR.ME)*, V. A., 2663, II, 28.

I. **אדר**, **adâru**, fear.
I, 1 pret., *la i-dur-ma taḫâzi*, V R. 55, 38; pres., *ul id-dar dan-na-at eqli*, V R. 55, 24; part., *la a-di-ru taḫâzi*, V R. 55, 8.

II. **אדר**, **adâru**, be dark.
IV, 1 perm., *na-'-du-ru pân* ^d^*Šam-ši(-ši)*, the face of the sun was obscured, V R. 55, 31.

drânu, weeds.
ki-mu ur-ki-ti id-ra-nu, III R. 41, II, 33; *ki-mu-ú mê id-ra-na*, London, 102, II, 13; *eqlâti-šú id-ra-[nu] li-ša-as-ḫi-ma*, Susa, 14, III, 10.

אדש$_3$, **edêšu**, be new.
II, 1 inf., *a-na ud-du-uš eš-rit*, to renew the sanctuaries, Neb. Nippur, II, 2; *a-na ud-du-šu [eš]-rit*, V. A., 2663, II, 22; part., *mu-ud-diš ka-liš ašrâti(AŠ.ME)*, V. A. 2663, II, 6.
eššu, new.
na-ra-a ša abni eš-ša, Susa, 2, Med., II, 9; *dul-la eš-ša*, Susa, 3, III, 28; *i-na eš-ši il-la-a*, shall raise up anew, Susa, 3, III, 39; *i-na muḫ-ḫi nâri eš-šit*, V. A., 209, I, 11.

או$_1$, **ú**, and, *passim*.
lu-ú—ù, either—or, Susa, 2, III, 8; *ù lu-ú*, or, London, 103, V, 46; London, 102, I, 31, etc.

אוץ, **iṣu**, few.
a-di ûmi(-mi) i-ṣu-ti šá bal-ṭa, IV R.[2] 38, III, 40.

אור$_1$, **urru**, light.
ur-ra u mu-šá, III R. 41, II, 23; V R. 56, 44.

אזב$_4$, **ezêbu**, to leave, spare.
I, 1 pret., *i-zi-ib*, Susa, 3, III, 54; *i-zi-bu*, Susa, 3, IV, 10; *e-zi-bu*, Susa, 3, IV, 42; V, 7, 26; *e-du amelu la i-zib-ma*, V. A. 2663, III, 27; *ai i-zi-bu da-ad-da-šú*, Susa, 16, VI, 27; *la i-zi-bu ar-[ki-i]*, C. T., X, pl. V, 7; *i-zi-bu-ú-ni*, Susa, 3, IV, 25; prec., *u ar-ki-i lu-zi-bu*, C. T., X, pl. V, 9.

azugallatu, great (lady) physician.
(^d^*Gula*)*a-zu-gal-la-tu rabîtum*, Susa, 14, IV, 5; *a-zu-gal-la-tu be-el-tu rabîtu(-tu)*, III R. 41, II, 29.

אזז$_4$, **uzzu**, wrath, anger.
na-aš-par-ta-ša šá uz-zi, III R. 41, II, 22.
uzzatu, anger.
i-na uz-za-at libbi(-bi), V R. 56, 51.
izzu, terrible.
^d^*Girru(BIL.GI) iz-zu*, Susa, 2, IV, 18; (^d^*Sin*) *be-lum iz-zu*, Susa, 3,

VI, 41; f., *qaštu iz-zi-ti*, V R. 55, 8; pl., *i-na bu-ni-šú-nu iz-zu-ú-ti*, Susa, 3, VI, 24.

izziš, in anger, angrily.

iz-zi-iš lik-kil-mu-šú, IV R.[2] 38, III, 32; Susa, 16, VI, 11; D. E. P., VI, 47, 2; O. B. I., 149, II, 19; V R. 56, 38; III R. 41, II, 14; I R. 70, III, 11.

אזן₁, **uznu**, ear.

sa-ka-ak uz-ni, Susa, 3, VII, 37; Susa, 14, III, 4; *ú-zu-un-šú i-šak-ka-nu*, directs his mind to, III R. 41, I, 35; *i-šak-ka-nu uznâ(PI[2])-šu*, V. A., 2663, V, 23; *uznâ-šu i-šak-ka-nu*, V. A., 2663, V, 35; *i-šak-ka-nu ú-zu-uš-šú*, V. A. 211, III, 7; *ba-ša-a uznâ-šu*, V. A., 2663, II, 25; *rap-ša uznâ*, V. A., 2663, II, 48; *ú-zu-un ni-kil-tu*, clever understanding, V. A., 2663, III, 3; *sa-kak uznâ(PI[2])*, V. A., 2663, V, 38; *uzun(PI)-šu ib-ši-ma*, V. A., 2663, III, 14.

אח₁, **aḫu**, brother.

aḫi, London, 103, I, 7, 39; c. suff., *aḫu-ú-a*, London, 103, IV, 23; *a-ḫi-i-a*, London, 103, IV, 33; pl., *aḫê*, London, 103, I, 22; V, 28; London, 102, IV, 36; I R. 70, II, 2; III R. 43, III 2; London, 102, I, 30; V. A., 208, 43; V. A., 209, I, 32; pl. c. suff., *ilâni aḫê-šú*, III R. 43, IV, 26; *i-na âli aḫê-šu*, London, 102, I, 11, 22; *i-na nazâzi(-zi) ša aḫê-šu*, London, 102, I, 25.

aḫâtu, sister.

a-na aḫât(NIN)-ia a-nam-din, London, 102, I, 24; *a-na aḫâti(NIN)-šu*, London, 102, I, 36.

aḫḫûtu, brotherhood.

a-na aḫ-ḫu-ti, London, 103, I, 28; *a-na aḫ-ḫu-ú-ti . . . . ul qu-ru-ub*, London, 103, IV, 24; *a-na aḫ-ḫu-ú-ti la qir-bu*, London, 103, IV, 42.

aḫameš, each other, both.

it-ti a-ḫa-meš, London, 103, IV, 18, 37; *a-na a-ḫa-meš ul i-rag-gu-mu*, they will not sue each other, London, 102, IV, 35; V. A. 209, I, 30; II, 40; III, 16, 28; V. 2.

aḫu, side.

ai ir-šú-u ni-da a-ḫi, Susa, 2, III, 29.

aḫânu, another.

iš-tar-ra-qu a-ḫa-nu, C. T., X, pl. V, 5; *a-na a-ḫa[-nu] i-šar-ra-[qu]*, C. T., X, pl. VI, 33.

aḫû, hostile, strange.

amelu a-ḫa-am, a strange man, Susa, 3, V, 47; *ú-ma-'-a-ru a-ḫa-a sak-ku*, V. A., 2663, V, 25; *na-ka-[ra(?)] lu a-ḫa*, IV R.[2] 38, III, 10; *na-ka-ra a-ḫa-a*, I R. 70, II, 22; pl., *par-ga-niš bašê(-e) a-ḫu-ú-ti*, V. A., 2663, III, 18.

אחז₁, **aḫâzu**, take.

III, 1 *ina lim-ni-ti ú-šá-ḫa-zu*, Neb. Nippur, III, 23; *ú-ma-'-a-ru ú-ša-aḫ-ḫa-zu*, London, 103, V, 36; *ša-na-am-ma ú-ša-aḫ-ḫa-zu*, commissions another one, Susa, 16, IV, 25; *šá-nam-ma ú-ša-aḫ-ḫa-zu-ma*, III R. 41, II, 8; *ma-am-man ú-ša-ḫa-zu*, V. A., 2663, V, 25; *pu-uz-ru ú-ša-ḫa-zu*, puts it in a secret place, V. A., 2663, V, 31.

III, 2, *pu-uz-ra uš-ta-ḫi-iz*, Susa, 3, V, 44.

UḪ.ME.ZU.AB, a class of priests (cf. p. 170f.).

Neb. Nippur, II, 14; III, 11.

אחר₁, **aḫrû**, future.

pl. fem., *a-na ni-ši aḫ-ra-a-ti*, London, 101, II, 13; *a-na aḫ-rat nišê a-pa-ti*, Neb. Nippur, III, 18.

aḫrâtaš, adv., in future.

ṣi-i-ti aḫ-[ra]-taš, a late descendant, C. T., X, pl. IV, 14.

aḫartiš, forever.

a-ḫar-ti-iš i-ri-mu, London, 101, I,

15; *a-ḫar-ti-iš i-rim-šú*, IV R.[2] 38, II, 29.

אטה$_4$, **eṭû,** be dark.

II, 1 *bu-ni-šú liṭ-ṭe-šú-ma*, may he darken his face, Neb. Nippur, IV, 14.

eṭemmu, shade, departed spirit.

[*eṭemmu-šu*] *a-na eṭemmi*, Susa, 16, VI, 22.

אטר$_4$, **aṭru,** support (cf. Hilprecht, *Assyriaca*, p. 5, f.[3]).

a-na aṭ-rı ḫa-ma-aṭ ša ša-kin, V R. 56, 10.

אי$_1$, **ai,** not.

Neb. Nippur, IV, 14, 18, 23; Susa, 2, III, 28; Susa, 3, VII, 4, 13; IV R.[2] 38, III, 44; Susa, 16, VI, 19, 21, 22, 27; Susa, 14, III, 13; IV, 17; D. E. P., VI, 43, III, 14; III R. 41, II, 17; London, 102, II, 19, etc.

ê, not.

e te-ti-iq, O. B. I., 83, II, 22; *e tu-saḫ-ḫi*, O. B. I., 83, II, 23.

aiumma, any one.

u lu ai-um-ma, London, 101, II, 15; *lu ai-am*[*-ma*], IV R.[2] 38, III, 13; *ai-um-ma*, Susa, 16, IV, 11; *šakkanakku ai-um-*[*ma*], O. B. I., 83, II, 12; *ai-um-ma ki-pu*, III R. 41, I, 33; Susa 3, II, 39; *ù lu-ú ai-um-ma*, I R. 70, II, 6; O. B. I., 149, II, 4; *ilu ai-um-ma*, Neb. Nippur, I, 10; *ai-um-ma ša . . i-kap-pu-du limutta*, V. A., 211, III, 1.

ê, o, indeed.

e be-li rubû na-a-du, O. B. I., 83, I, 20.

איב$_1$, **aibu,** enemy.

a-na ai-bi li-tur-šu, London, 102, II, 31.

אין$_1$, **ia'nu,** there was not.

ia-'-nu mê saḫ-ḫi, there was no water of cisterns, V R. 55, 19.

אין$_4$, **înu,** eye.

qup-pu-ú i-na i-ni-šu, V R. 56, 54; *dSin în(-in) šamê(e) ù irṣi-tim(-tim)*, O. B. I., 149, III, 6; [*dSin în*] *šamê(-e) ù irṣitim(-tim)*, London, 102, I, 46; *tur-ti înâ(ŠI[2]) sa-kak uznâ(ŠI[2])*, V. A., 2663, V, 38.

איר$_1$, **âru,** go forth.

II, 2, *ú-ta-'-ir-šú-ma šàr ilâni*, sent him forth the king of the gods (perhaps = *um-ta-'-ir*), V R. 55, 12.

urtu, command.

ur-ta ú-ma-'-ir-šú-nu-ti-ma, O. B. I., 83, II, 8; *na-dan ur-ti-šú*, Neb. Nippur, I, 5; *kiš-šat nišê ú-kan-ni-šu a-na ur-ti-šu*, V. A., 2663, I, 40; *iš-te-'-u-ma* [*ur*(?)]*-ti bêl ilâni*, V. A., 2663, II, 20.

Airu, the month Iyyar.

III R. 43, I, 27; V. A., 209, II, 25.

iku, ditch of irrigation.

i-ku la šap-ku, Neb. Nippur, II, 29; *i-ka mi-iṣ-ra ù ku-dur-ra*, Susa, 3, II, 12; *i-ka mi-iṣ-ra it-ti-ku*, Susa, 16, IV, 18.

ú-ki-e.

ú-ki-e bi-lam-ma, London, 102, IV, 21 (or does the original read *ú-di*(!)*-e*, vessels?).

אכד, **ekdu,** powerful.

bu-ru ek-du, Susa, 2, IV, 17; *ik*(?)*-di-e a-ma-ti*, London, 103, IV, 46.

אכי$_1$, **akî,** instead of.

a-ki ½ MA.NA kaspi, V. A., 209, IV, 5; *a-ki kaspi-ka bîtâti-ia . . . . pa-ni-ka lid-gu-la*, V. A., 209, IV, 7.

אכל$_1$, **akâlu,** consume.

III, 1 *išâti(NE) ú-ša-ka-lu*, O. B. I., 150, II, 4.

ikîlu, have usufruct (cf. p. 176).

I, 1 inf., *a-na i-ki-li ri-'-ti*, Neb. Nippur, III, 21.

aklu, secretary, agent (cf. p. 176).

ak-lu, Neb. Nippur, III, 19; III R. 41, I, 31; III R. 43, III, 14; *aklu(PA)*, D. E. P., II, 97, 11;

Susa, 16, III, 27; IV R.[2] 38; III, 1; O. B. I., 83, II, 12.

êkallu, palace.

amel bâb êkalli(E.GAL), Neb. Nippur, V, 10; *amelu ša bâb êkalli*, V R. 56, 16; *ʰnâgir êkalli*, V. A., 2663, V, 7; *ʰṭup-šar êkalli*, V. A., 2663, V, 15; *amelu ša pân(ŠI) êkalli*, C. T., X, pl. VII, 43.

אכל₃, **eklîtu,** darkness.

bît ik-li-ti, IV R.[2] 38, III, 7.

אכם₄, **ekêmu,** take.

I, 1 pret., *i-na da-na-ni i-ki-im-ma*, London, 103, IV, 15; prec., *li-kim-šú-ma*, Neb. Nippur, IV, 11; Susa, 3, VII, 11; Susa, 14, IV, 2; [*naq mê li*]*-kim-šu*, D. E. P., IV, pl. 16, I, 6; pres., *eqlu šú-a-tu ik-ki-mu*, Neb. Nippur, III, 28.

êkurru, temple.

pl., *gi-mir e-kur-re*, V. A., 2663, II, 6.

ul, not.

London, 103, V, 38; Neb. Nippur, III, 29, 32, 33, IV, 1, 2; O. B. I., 149, II, 7; V. A., 209, I, 28, 29, 30; II, 3; III, 15, 16, 27, 28; V, 1, 2, 3, etc.

אל₁, **ilu,** god, *passim*.

iltu, goddess.

cstr., *ilat ba-ri-ri-ta*, III R. 41, II, 22.

ilûtu, deity.

pa-liḫ ilu-ti-šu, V. A., 2663, I, 28; *la um-daš-ša-lu ilu-su* (=*ilûti-šu*), Neb. Nippur, I, 17.

אלה₄, **elû,** rise up.

I, 1 pres., *i-na eš-ši il-la-a*, Susa, 3, III, 39; *ša il-lam-ma*, London, 103, V, 32; London, 101, II, 16; Susa, 16, IV, 12; III R. 43, III, 4; I R. 70, II, 7; London, 102, IV, 38; O. B. I., 149, II, 5; Susa, 14, II, 6; III R. 41, I, 33; *ša illamma(DUL.DU-ma)*; V. A., 209, I, 35; V. A., 208, 45; inf., *a-na âli la e-li-e*, C. T., IX, pl. V. 35; *a-na e-li ù pa-ki-ri*, D. E. P., II, pl. 20, 9.

II, 1 inf., *ul-lu-ú rubû(NUN)-us-su*, to elevate his lordship, V. A., 2663, I, 30.

III, 1 prec., *apil-šú na-qa mê-šú li-še-li*, may he snatch away his son, his libator, III R. 43, IV, 20; *li-še-lu-ú na-an-nab-šú*, III R. 43, III, 30; *li-še-la-šum-ma*, D. E. P., IV, pl. 16, II, 3.

eli, over, above.

eli šarri a-lik maḫ-ri, Neb. Nippur, II, 7; *eli ili šarri*, before god, London, 101, IV, 12; *a-na eli*, on, London, 102, IV, 22; *eli ša pa-ni*, more than before, V. A., 2663, III, 29; *i-na eli*, against, Susa, 2, III, 11; London, 101, II, 16, etc.; *i-na eli na-ri-e an-ni-i*, upon that stone, Susa, 2, III, 17; Susa, 2, Med., II, 5, etc.

eliš, above.

eliš(AN.TA) ù šapliš(KI), IV R.[2] 38, I, 31.

elû, upper.

in the phrases *šiddu elû*, and *pûtu elû*, *passim*; pl. fem., *bêl e-la-ti*, lord of that which is above, V. A., 2663, I, 10.

ullû, distant.

ultu ul-la, from of old, Neb. Nippur, II, 18.

elênû, upper.

pa-na-at ⁱṣᵘkirî e-li-ni-i, before the upper orchard, V. A., 2663, IV, 34.

têlîtu, crop, revenue.

ur-bu ù te-li-tu ma-la ba-šu-ú, V. A., 208, 4.

âlu, city, town.

su-ú-uq âli-šu, Susa, 3, VI, 39; *abulli âli-šu*, Susa, 16, VI, 16; *ka-mat âli-šu*, Susa, 16, VI, 17; O. B. I., 149, III, 8; V. A., 209,

V, 12; *ri-bi-it âli-šu*, III R. 41, II, 24; *a-na âli la e-li-e*, C. T., IX, pl. V, 35; *a-na âli(ER.KI)-šu a-na la e-ri-bi*, III R. 45, No. 2, 6, 7; *âlu ša ᵈEr-ia*, C. T., IX, pl. V, 25, and *passim*.

אלך$_2$, **alâku**, go, march.

I, 1 pret., *il-lik*, London, 103, I, 3; *a-na ḫur-ša-an la il-lik*, London, 103, V, 4; *illiku(DU-ku)*, Susa, 16, II, 28; *a-na* ^{mâtu}*Êlamti*^{ki} *il-li-ku-ma*, C. T., IX, pl. IV, 10; pres., *il-lak šarru na-as-qu*, then advances the valiant king, V R. 55, 22; imper., *a-lik-ma VII a-mi-lu-ta a-na* ^{m}*Bu-[ru-ša i-din(?)]*, London, 102, VI, 10; part., *eli šarri a-lik maḫ-ri*, Neb. Nippur, II, 7; *šarru a-[lik] pa-ni-ia*, Susa, 3, IV, 2; *a-lik da-i-li šú-a-tim*, IV R.^{2} 38, II, 30; ^{h}*âlik(DU)pâni*, London, 102, IV, 23; *a-lik ki-ši-ir-ri ilâni aḫê-šú*, III R. 43, IV, 26; *a-lik ar-ki*, the younger, Susa, 16, I, 18.

I, 2, *ša ina tu-kul-ti ilâni rabûti it-tal-la-ku-ma*, who marches about, V. A. 2663, II, 27.

III, 1 perm., *a-na me-riš-ti la šú-lu-ku-ú-ma*, Neb. Nippur, II, 31; prec., *li-ša-li-ku-šu a-na mim-ma la ba-še-e*, may they cause him to come to naught, London, 103, VI, 25.

alkakâtu, ways.

al-ka-ka-tu-šu nak-la, Neb. Nippur, I, 19.

allaku, messenger.

gir-gi-lu al-la-ku ša ᵈEn-lil, Susa, 2, IV, 3.

ilku, tax, service (cf. p. 177).

a-na il-ki la ú-še-ri-bu, Susa, 3, IV, 6, 22, 33, 58, V, 31; *a-na i-lik* ^{mâtu}*Na-mar i-ru-bu*, V R. 55, 48; *i-na i-lik* ^{mâtu}*Na-mar gab-bi-šu*, V R. 55, 51; 56, 6, 31; *ut-te-ru-ma il-ka il-tak-nu*, V R. 56, 32; *il-ki ṭup-ši-ki*, forced labor, C. T., IX, pl. V, 38; *il-ka ma-la ba-šú-ú*, I R. 66, II, 1.

אלך, **alâku,** throw down (syn. *maqâtu*).

I, 2, *ag-giš li-tal-lik-šu-ma*, Neb. Nippur, IV, 3 (cf. p. 179).

I. אלל$_1$, **allu,** basket.

zakûtum(?) i-na al(-lu) du-up-ši-ki, freedom from the baskets of forced labor, III R. 45, No. 2, 2.

alîlu, powerful.

ᵈMarduk a-li-lu, Susa, 2, III, 30.

II. אלל$_1$, **ulâlu,** imbecile.

sa-ma-a ú-la-la, Susa, 14, II, 15; *ú-la-la ù la še-ma-a*, III R. 43, I, 31.

III. אלל, **ellu,** shining.

pl., *šadê el-lu-ti*, V R. 56, 46; *šamê ellûti(AZAG.*^{pl}*)*, III R. 41, II, 16; *ᵈSin a-šab(!) šamê(-e) el-lu-ti*, III R. 43, IV, 7.

IV. אלל, **alâlu,** rejoicing, hilarity.

a-la-la ṭa-a-ba, London, 103, VI, 6.

alpu, ox.

ṣibit alpê u ṣi-e-ni, V R. 55, 55; *alpi-šu imêri-šu la ra-ka-si*, C. T., IX, pl. V, 36; *I alpu libbi alpi*, III R. 41, I, 20; London, 102, III, 26; IV, 24; *imêru ù al-pi*, III R. 45, No. 2, 8; *a-la-ad a-me-lu-ti alpê ù ṣênê*, London, 102, II, 27.

ul-lap(b) (cf. אלף, II, 1 pres., join?)

iš-ka-ra-a-ti ul-lap(b), V R. 55, 24.

אלץ$_4$, **elêṣu,** rejoice.

III, 1, *ú-ša-li-iṣ kab-ta-as-su-nu*, V. A., 2663, III, 30.

אלת, **tâlittu,** despair.

ᵈIš-tar . . . . ta-li-tum liš-pur-šú-ma, III R. 41, II, 21.

ultu, from, after.

ul-tu a-na-ku ṣi-iḫ-ri-ku, London, 103, IV, 27; *ul-tu . . . i-mu-tu*, London, 103, IV, 11; V, 7; *ul-tu bîti*, London, 103, IV, 43; *ul-tu âli-šu*, Susa, 3, II, 41; *ul-tu paṭ-ru i-na kišâdi-šu,* V R. 56, 54; *ul-tu Bâbili,* C. T., IX, pl. IV, 13; [*ul*]*tu GUL.KI.ŠAR,* O. B. I., 83, I, 6; *ultu ul-la,* Neb. Nippur, II, 18; *ultu*(*TA*) *ûmi*(*-mi*) *pa-na,* Neb. Nippur, II, 29.

iltânu, north.
ideogram *IM.SI.DI, passim.*

ema, while, with.
e-ma ^d^*Šamaš u* ^d^*Marduk i-ša-as-su-ú,* IV R.[2] 38, III, 42; *e-ma purîmê ṣêri li-ir-pu-ud,* Susa, 14, IV, 3.

אמד$_4$, **emêdu,** stand.
I, 2, *i-te-mid kúr-šu,* fate overtook him, V R. 55, 41, cf. *kuršu.*
II, 1, *še-ir-ta-šú ra-bi-i-ta lim-is-su-ma,* Susa, 3, VI, 34; his heavy punishment may he inflict upon him; *še-ri-*[*it-su li-*]*mi-is-su,* London, 101, III, 10.
IV, 1, *in-nin-du-ma šarrâni,* the kings stood up, *i.e.,* gathered, V R. 55, 29.

אמה$_1$, **amû,** speak.
I, 1 pret., *i-mu šar*[*ru*], D. E. P., II, 93, II, 14.
III, 2, *šarru ilu uš-tim*(?)*-mi-e-šú,* the king caused him to swear by god, C. T., X, pl. V, 14.

amâtu, word.
la še-ma ša a-ma-ti, D. E. P., VI, 45, V, 21; cstr., *a-mat ki-bi-ti-šú-nu,* Susa, 3, VI, 21; *ina a-ma-at* ^d^*En-lil,* Susa, 3, VII, 43; *ina amât*(*KA*) *šarri,* because of the prayer of the king, Neb. Nippur, II, 12; *a-mat nišê li-gi-sa-šú,* Neb. Nippur, IV, 8; *mim-ma a-ma-at limutti*(*-ti*), anything evil, Susa, 16, V, 9; pl., *a-ma-ta iš-tu-ru-ma,* Susa, 3, IV, 24; *a-ma-a-ti šá i-na* ^abni^*narî an-ni-i aš-tu-ru-ma,* Susa, 3, IV, 40, 59; *ik-*(?)*-di-e a-ma-ti,* London, 103, IV, 46.

atmu, word.
at-mu-šú na-as-qu-ma, his word was weighty, Neb. Nippur, II, 19; *li-ma-'-i-da at-mi-šú,* may she multiply his words, cries(?), III R. 41, II, 23.

^h^**U.MUK,** title of an official.
V. A., 209, II, 17.

amelu, man.
amelu šú-ú, Susa, 3, IV, 52; V, 20; VI, 1; *amelu šú-a-tum,* Susa, 3, VI, 15; IV R.[2] 38, II, 24; Susa, 16, IV, 21; III R. 43, I, 35; V. A., 2663, V, 36; III R. 41, II, 13; I R. 70, III, 8; *amelu šá-a-šú,* V R. 56, 37; *e-du amelu,* a single one, V. A., 2663, III, 26; *amelu ša bit-ḫal-li,* master of the (riding) horse, V R. 55, 58; *amelu ša pân êkalli,* C. T., X, pl. VII, 43; *amel bâb êkalli,* Neb. Nippur, V, 10; *amelu ša bâb êkalli,* V R. 56, 16; pl., *a-mi-lu-ú-tum,* Susa, 3, VI, 13; *amelûti ša ṭe-mi-šú,* Susa, 3, II, 37; *a-la-ad a-me-lu-ti,* London, 102, II, 27; *VII a-mi-lu-ta,* London, 102, VI, 10, 12; *a-na libbi*(*-bi*) *a*[*-mi-lu-ti*] *im-ru-uq*(?), London, 102, VI, 13.

ameltu (SAL), woman.
mâr mâri ameltu(*SAL*) *ša Bît-*^m^*Ta-kil-a-na-ili-šú,* London, 103 I, 42.

ummu, mother.
um-mi a-ša-ra, London, 101, II, 9; *um ma-šú la zu-uk-ku-ra-*[*at*], London, 103, I, 31.

umma, thus, as follows.
ki-a-am iq-bi um-ma-a, London, 102, IV, 20; *i-qa*[*b*]*-bu-*[*ú*] *um-ma-a,* London, 102, I, 32; [*iq-bi*] *um-ma-a,* London, 102, I, 20; *be-el šu u*[*š-'-*]*id-ma um-ma,* C. T., X, pl. III, Obv. 3; *i-qab-bu-ú um-ma,* V. A., 208, 46; *i-qab-bu-ú um-ma-a,* London, 102 IV 38; *ki-a-am iq-bi um-ma,*

V.A., 209, I, 5; IV, 6, 19; London, 102, VI, 10; C. T., X, pl. V, 11; *um-ma qaq-qa-ru i-ba-aš-ši*, V. A., 209, I, 7; *ú-paq-qa-ru um-ma*, V. A., 209, II, 2; *um-ma*, V. A., 209, IV, 20; C. T., X, pl. V, 1.

umâmu, animal.
ú-ma-am ṣi-ri, Susa, 3, VII, 1; *ú-ma-am ṣêri*, D. E. P., VI, 47, 16.

ummânu, army.
ummân(ZAB) nakru(PAP), the army of the enemy, V. A., 2663, III, 16.

ammatu, cubit.
ina ammatu(Ú) rabîtu(GAL-tu(m), *passim*; *i-na am-ma-ti ra-bi-i-ti*, D. E. P., II, pl. 20, 5.

אמק$_4$, **emûqu**, strength.
ša a-na e-piš taḫâzi kit-pu-da e-mu-qa-šu, whose resources are devoted to battle, V R. 55, 7; *i-na e-muq ^{d}Bêl(EN)*, V. A., 2663, II, 37; *šarru ša a-na e-muq ^{d}Nabû u ^{d}Marduk [it-ka-lu]*, C. T., X, pl. IV, 14.

nîmequ, wisdom.
ni-me-ki ša ^{d}Nabû, IV R.[2] 38, II, 7; *ni-me-ki ^{d}Nabû ù ^{d}Marduk*, C. T., X, pl. IV, 8; *ina ni-me-ki ip-še-ti-šu*, V. A., 2663, III, 2.

אמר$_1$, **amâru**, see.
I, 1 pret., *i-mu-ur-šú-[ma] i-ri-im-[šú]*, D. E. P., II, 93, I, 7; *šarru bêli-šu i-mu-ru-šu-ma*, V R. 55, 46; inf., *a-šar la a-ma-ri*, a place where it cannot be seen, IV R.[2] 38, III, 6; Susa, 16, IV, 35; D. E. P., VI, 45, V, 18; D. E. P., VI, 46, III, 10; III R. 41, II, 12; O. B. I., 150, II, 4; I R. 70, III, 7; Neb. Nippur, V, 4; *eqlu la a-ma-ri*, O. B. I., 149, II, 13; *a-šar la a-ma-ru išakkanû(ŠA. MEŠ)*, V. A., 2663, V, 31; *ina eqli la a-ma-ri i-tam-mi-ru*, V R. 56, 36; *a-šar la a-(ma!)-ri pu-uz-ri [i-tam-me-ru]*, C. T., X, pl. VII, 37.

amâru, construct.
I, 1 inf., *ḫarrâna ù ti-tur-ra . . . . la a-ma-ri*, Susa, 3, III, 27; *ti-tur-ra la e-pi-ši ḫarrâna la a-ma-ri*, V R. 56, 2.

imêru, ass.
imêri-šú ù ameli-šú la na-še-e, Susa, 3, II, 51; *bît rê'û-tum imêrê*, grazing place of the asses, Susa, 16, I, 27; *I imêru amurrû*, III R. 41, I, 17, 18; *I imêru KIL.DA*, III R. 41, I, 19; *imêru ù al-pi*, III R. 45, No. 2, 8; *I imêru rabû(-ú)*, London, 102, IV, 24.

imêru, a measure of capacity = חֹמֶר.
pu-lu-uk(g) u imêr burâši, V R. 55, 56, 57; *IV imêrê*, London, 102, III, 11; *I imêru*, London, 102, III, 14, 16, 17.

amurrû (IM.MAR.TU), west, *passim*.

immeru, lamb.
immerê(LU.ARAD.Ú.ZUN)-šu la ṣa-ba-ti, C. T., IX, pl. V, 37; *immeru(LU.ARAD) šîru taḫ-ši-e šîru šûni(UR)*, V. A., 208, 5.

anu, condition.
an ka-bit-ta, a serious condition, Susa, 16, VI, 14.

ana, prep., to, for, *passim*.
a-na eli, concerning; *a-na muḫ-ḫi*, to, occur frequently.

ina, prep., in, at, with.
i-na eli, against, over; *i-na libbi*, of; *i-na muḫ-ḫi*, against, occur often.

inu, time.
i-nu-šu, at that time, V. A., 2663, I, 43; C. T., X, pl. V, 10; *i-nu*, when, V. A., 2663, I, 1; *e-nu-ma*, when, D. E. P., II, 113, 14; D E. P., VI, 45, V, 8; V R. 55, 1.

enûtu, lordship.
e-nu-us-su ú-ša-ti-ru, V. A., 2663, I, 41.

אנב$_1$, nannabu, offspring, descendant.
šùm-šu zêr-šu pi-ri-'-šú na-an-nab-šú, III R. 41, II, 38; *li-še-lu-ú na-an-nab-šú,* III R. 43, III, 30; *na-an-nab-šu i(-na) pî nîšê li-ḫal-liq,* London, 102, II, 17.

unûtu, vessel, property.
pl., *ša-tam bît ú-na-ti,* keeper of the treasury, V R. 56, 20; London, 102, IV, 9; *ša(g)-tam bît ú-na-a-ti,* I R. 66, II, 16.

אנה$_4$, enû, to annul.
I, 1 pres., *ša . . . . aš-tu-ru-ma e-zi-bu la in-ni,* Susa, 3, IV, 43; *mi-iṣ-ra in-nu-ú ku-dur-ra ú-na-ka-ru,* O. B. I., 150, II, 1; *ša in-nu-ú ki-bi-su,* D. E. P., II, 115, 6; *ú-šad-ba-bu innû(BAL-ú) ú-paq-qa-ru,* V. A., 209, II, 1; *ša da-ba-bi an-na-a innû(BAL-ú) ú-paq-qa-ru,* V. A., 209, II, 7; V. A., 2663, V, 6; inf., *a-na-ku la e-nu-ú ù la uš-pi-lu . . . . la e-pu-šú-ma,* Susa, 3, IV, 11; *mi-lik[-šu-nu] la i-nu-ú,* O. B. I., 80, 3; prec., *pi-lik-šu li-ni,* may he alter his plot, III R. 41, II, 28.
I, 2, *sú-ú la i-te-ni ù la im-taš,* he does not annull and does not disregard, Susa, 3, V, 8; inf., *i-ta-ni-e i-šá-lu-ma,* annulment he asked for, O. B. I., 83, II, 9.
IV, 1, *šá ki-bit pi-i-šú la in-ni-en-nu-ú,* the command of whose mouth cannot be annulled, Susa, 3, VII, 46; *la in-nin-nu-ú ki-bit-su,* V. A., 2663, I, 16.

אנח$_1$, tâniḫu, sighing.
ta-ni-ḫi, D. E. P., VI, 45, V, 7.

anâku, I.
London, 103, IV, 27; Susa, 3, IV, 11; London, 102, I, 21.

annû, this.
Frequently in the phrase *narî an-ni-i,* London, 101, IV, 5; Susa, 3, IV, 41, 60; V, 23, etc.; or *narâ an-na-a,* O. B. I., 149, II, 8; Neb. Nippur, IV, 28; *eqlu an-nu-ú,* London, 103, V, 37; *eqla an-na-a,* D. E. P., II, 97, 15; *eqli an-ni-i,* III R. 43, III, 22; *ku-dur-ri an-ni-i,* London, 103, VI, 22; London, 101, I, 2.
fem., *a-su-mi-it-tu an-ni-i-tu,* London, 103, VI, 26; pl. m., *ilâni rabûti an-nu-tu,* V R. 56, 51; *[nap]-ḫar an-nu-tu ^{h}mu-kin-nu$^{pl.}$,* V. A., 209, V, 20; pl fem., *ar-ra-a-tum an-na-a-tum,* Susa, III, VII, 42; *ar-ra-a-ti a-na-ti,* London, 101, III, 5; *qaq-qa-ra-tim an-na-tim,* Susa, 2, III, 10; *eqlâti an-na-a-tú,* C. T., X, pl. VI, 29; emphatic, *an-nu-um-ma lu-ú rê'û,* V. A. 2663, I, 32.

אנן$_3$, anânu, be gracious.
II, 2 inf., *ina ut-ni-ni-šú,* because of his prayer, Neb. Nippur, II, 16.

annu, grace.
an-na-šú ki-i-nu, Susa, 3, VII, 47.

unninu, supplication.
un-ni-ni-šú ai im-ḫu-ur-šú, V R. 56, 56.

inanna, now.
i-na-an-na, O. B. I., 83, II, 3; *e-nin-na,* C. T., X, pl. V, 8.

אנף$_1$, appu, face.
ap-pa i-lab-bi-nu, Neb. Nippur, I, 6; *ina li-bi-en ap-pi,* Neb. Nippur, II, 10; *ap-pa . . . li-il-bi-in,* D. E. P., VI, 46, III, 19; *ap-pa-šú lil-bi-im-ma,* V R. 56, 55.

אנש$_1$, aššatu, wife.
^{fd}SAG-mudammiq-šar-be mârti-šu aššati(DAM)-šu ša ^{md}Šamaš-nâdin-šumu, London, 102, I, 17; *a-na aḫâti-šu aššâti-šu ša . . . ,* London, 102, I, 36.

aššûtu, marriage.
a-na aš-šu-tú i-[il-qi], London, 102, VI, 4.

אנש$_1$, tênišêti, mankind.
muš-te-ši-ru te-ni-še-e-ti, V. A., 2663, I, 13.

us(s)u, confines, limits.
ú-sa mi-iṣ-ra ù ku-dur-ra, I R. 70, II, 13; *ú-sa mi-iṣ-ra ù ku-dur-ra-šú,* III R. 43, III, 20; IV, 1; *us-su mi-ṣir-šú u ku-dur-ra-šu,* I R. 70, IV, 3.

אסה$_1$, **asû,** physician.
^{h}*asû(A.ZU),* III R. 43, II, 28.

asaku, darkness (=*asakku,* cf. Jensen, K. B., VI, 433).
a-na bît a-sa-ki a-šar(!) *la a-ma-ri,* D. E. P., VI, 45, V, 17.

אסק$_4$,
II, 1 pret., *us-siq is-ki-e-tú,* possessions he granted, V. A., 2663, III, 35.
isqu, portion, income, property.
a-na is-ki-šú li-šá-kin-nu, Susa, 3, V, 19; *ša is-ki ma-ḫir,* London, 102, III, 11, 14, 15; *is-qu bît* ^{d}*La-ga-ma-al,* income of the temple of L., V. A., 208, 3; pl., *us-siq is-ki-e-tú,* V. A., 2663, III, 35; pl., *ana tabâli esqêti(GIŠ.-RU.BA.MEŠ) ša-ši-na,* V. A., 211, III, 5.

usqaru, the crescent (cf. *asqaru,* Del., H. W., 717*b*).
us-qa-ru bu-gi-na ma-qur-ru ša ^{d}*Sin,* Susa, 2, IV, 10.

אסר, **esiru,** street(?).
e-sir mu-ta-qa-tu, V. A., 209, IV, 30.

mêsiru, bond.
mêsir(ḪU) maqlûti (= Br. 10,873) *li-ik-mi-*[*šu*], D. E. P., II, 113, 19.

אפל, **apâlu,** pay, restore.
I, 1 perm., *maḫ-ru ap-lu za-ku-ú,* London, 102, IV, 34; *ma-ḫir a-pil, za-ku,* V. A., 209, I, 27; II, 39; III, 14, 26.
I, 3, *a-di XII* $^{ta\text{-}a\text{-}an}$*i-ta-nap-pal,* restore, V. A., 208, 48; London, 102, IV, 40; V. A., 209, II, 5.

aplu, son.
ap-la-am na-aq mê li-ki-im-šú-ma, Susa, 3, VII, 9; *apil-šu na-qa mê-šú li-še-li,* III R. 43, IV, 20; *aplu ù* [*na-a*]*q mê ai ú-šar-ši-šu,* London, 102, II, 18.

apsû, abyss, ocean.
^{d}*E-a šar apsî,* Neb. Nippur, IV, 9.

אפר$_4$, **epiru,** dust.
i-na e-pi-ri ú-ša-at-ma-ru, London, 103, V, 46; *i-na e-pi-ri i-tam-me-ru,* Neb. Nippur, IV, 29; III R. 43, I, 33; *i-na epirê(IŠ.-ZUN) i-tam-mi-ru,* I R. 70, III, 2; V. A., 2663, V, 29; *i-na epiri(IŠ) i-te*[*-mi-ru*], O. B. I., 150, II, 3.

אפר, **atpirtu,** covering(?), adjoining(?).
at-pi-ir-tu pa-an gi . . . . London, 103, IV, 4.

אפר, **epêru,** support.
la e-pi-e-ri su-ú-uq âli-šú li-is-sa-aḫ-ḫar, without being fed may he wander through the streets of his city, Susa, 3, VI, 38.

uprû, perhaps = *epartu,* cover.
I ^{ṣubâtu}*up-ru-ú,* III R. 41, I, 25.

apparu, thicket.
qan(GI) appari(SUK), reed thicket, C. T., IX, pl. IV, 19.

אפש, **epêšu,** do, make.
I, 1 pret., *e-pu-šú-ma* (1st pers.), Susa, 3, IV, 18; pres., *ip-pu-šú taḫâzi,* they offer battle, V R. 55, 29; *ip-pu-šú* (relative sentence), Susa, 3, III, 35; *bîtu ip-pu-šú li-bi-el šá-nu-um-ma,* V R. 56, 53; *ina* ^{mâtu}*Akkadî*^{ki} *ip-pu-šu be-lu-tú,* V. A., 2663, V, 22; inf., *i-piš pî-šú,* decree, Neb. Nippur, I, 9; *ti-tur-ra la e-pi-ši,* V. R. 56, 2; *la e-pi-ši du-ul-li,* Susa, 3, II, 28; *dul-la šú-a-tu la e-pi-ši,* Susa, 3, III, 41; *a-na e-piš taḫâzi,* V R. 55, 7; *II bitâti abtûti ša na-qa-ru ú e-pi-*[*šu*], two dilapidated houses which are to be torn down and to be (re)built, V. A., 209, III, 17; *bîtu šú-a-tu ša na-qa-ru u e-pi-šu,* V. A., 209, IV, 23; part.,

e-piš ku-um-mu ki-iṣ-ṣi u si-ma-ku, V. A., 2663, II, 11.

I, 2, *ki-i pi-i rabûti ma-li-ki-šú . . . . la i-te-pu-uš-ma*, Susa, 3, V, 12.

ipšu, built.

bîtu ip-šu, a built-up plot, V. A., 208, 12.

epištu, deed.

pl., *i-na ni-me-ki ip-še-ti-šu*, with the wisdom of his deeds, V. A., 2663, III, 3.

אפשׁ₃, meditate (cf. Hebr. חפשׂ and Hilprecht, B. E., XX, 1, p. xii[7]).

itpêšu, prudent.

ma-al-ku it-pi-šu, V. A., 2663, II, 47; [*šar*] *ilâni it-pi-šu rim-nu-ú*, C. T., X, pl. IV, 15.

אץ₄, **'iṣu,** wood.

Used frequently as determinative; *lu-ú iṣê lu-ú šammê*, Susa, 3, II, 48.

אקל₃, **eqlu,** field.

Used frequently in the phrases *eqlu šú-a-tum*, IV R.² 38, III, 3, 15; Susa, 16, I, 11; II, 10, etc.; *eqla an-na-a*, III R. 43, III, 18; III R. 43; edge IV, 2, 5; *eqlu ša-a-šu*, London, 102, II, 33; *bêl eqli*, Susa, 2, III, 31; IV R.² 38, III, 15; *ba-ab eqli-ia*, Susa, 16, II, 18; *eqil mu-li-gi*, I R. 70, I, 4; *eqlu ki-i mu-lu-gi*, I R. 70, II, 17; *eqil piḫâti*, IV R.² 38, I, 17; *eqil še-pir-ti*, C. T., IX, pl. IV, 15; *eqlu la a-ma-ri i-te-mi-ru*, O. B. I., 149, II, 13; *itti eqli lib-bu-ú eqli*, V. A., 209, II, 34; III, 19; IV, 10; pl., *eqlâtim(-tim)*, Susa, 2, III, 11; *eqlâti ši-na-ti*, III R. 41, II, 2; *eqlâti an-na-ti*, III R. 41, I, 35; C. T., X, pl. VI, 29; *eqlâti(A.ŠÀ.ME) ša-ši-na*, C. T., X, pl. V, 6.

aqqullu, pickaxe.

ta-dan[*-nun?*] *aq-qu-ul-lu*, V R. 55, 17.

אקץ, **aqṣu,** evil, painful.

si-im-ma aq-ṣa la-az-za, Susa, 14, IV, 6.

ארב₅, **erêbu,** enter.

I, 1 pret., *a-na i-lik* ^{mâtu}*Na-mar i-ru-bu*, under the tax of Namar had come, V R. 55, 48; *qâtâ-šu ṭi-ṭa li-ru-ba*, may his hands get into the mire, V R. 56, 58; inf., *a-na âli la e-ri-bi*, V R. 55, 52; *a-na âli-šu a-na la e-ri-bi*, III R. 45, No. 2, 7, 10; *a-na âlâni la e-ri-e-bi*, V R. 55, 58; *bît* ^{âlu}*Ša-an-ba-ša la e*[*-ri-bi*], V R. 56, 1.

I, 2, *a-na nakri bêli-šú i-te-ru-ub*, against the enemy of his lord he advanced, V R. 55, 39.

III, 1, *a-na il-ki l*[*a*] *ú-še-ri-bu*, Susa, 3, IV, 7, 23; *a-na il-ki la ú-šer-rib*, Susa, 3, IV, 33; *a-na* ^{âlu}*Ḫu-uṣ-ṣi ú-še-ri-ib*, C. T., IX, pl. IV, 14; *a-na bît ik-li-ti ú-še-ir-ri-bu*, IV R.² 38, III, 8; *a-šar la a-ma-ri ú-še-ri-bu*, D. E. P., VI, 45, V, 19; inf., *a-na libbi(-bi) âlâni la šú-ru-bi*, V R. 55, 54.

III, 2, *a-na il-ki uš-te-ri-ib*, Susa, 3, V, 31; *a-na il-ki la uš-te-rib*, Susa, 3, IV, 58.

irbu, income.

ir-ba u ki-ša-a-ti, V. A., 2663, II, 17.

urbu, income.

ur-bu ù te-li-tu ma-la ba-šu-ú, V. A., 208, 4.

ardu, servant.

arad-su . . . . i-ri-im, Neb. Nippur, III, 12; Susa, 3, I, 40; II, 5; D. E. P., II, 112, 9; IV R.² 38, II, 4; Susa, 16, I, 8; D. E. P. VI, 42, I, 21; D. E. P., VI, 44, I, 4; III R. 43, I, 6; edge IV, 5; O. B. I., 149, I, 22; C. T., X, pl. III, 22; *ardi-šu*, I R. 66, II, 3; III R. 43, I, 12; *ardu pa-liḫ-šu*, V. A., 2663, III, 37; pl., *ar-di-en u ki-na-a-ti*, I R. 70, II, 4.

ארה, urû, horse.
ʰrab ú-ri-e, master of horse, V R. 55, 53; *ú-ra-a ù ᶠurâte* (*ˢᵃˡsisûᵖˡ*), stallions and mares, V R. 55, 53, 59; *ᶠurâte,* III R. 43, edge IV, 2.

ארח₁, II, 1 pret., *ur-ri-iḫ-ma,* he hastened, V R. 55, 28.

ארך₁, arâku, be long.
I, 1 prec., *li-rik ri-nin-šú-ma,* London, 101, IV, 13.

irnittu, victory.
ik-šú-du ir-nit-tuš, V. A., 2663, II, 28.

ארץ₁, irṣitu, earth, land.
šamê ù irṣiti(-ti), London, 101, III, 12; Susa, 3, III, 50; Neb. Nippur, I, 1, 20; *ša-kan irṣiti,* Neb. Nippur, I, 21; *i-na irṣiti i-qab-bi-ru,* IV R.² 38, III, 20; *irṣitim šú-a-tum,* IV R.² 38, III, 28; *ina irṣiti,* Susa, 16, VI, 21; *ina su-up-pu irṣitim(-tim)* *ⁱṣᵘgi-šimmari šadî,* V. A., 209, II, 30; *irṣitim(-tim),* V. A., 209, III, 18.

ארר₁, arâru, curse.
I, 1 pret., *ar-ra-ta i-ru-ur-ma,* London, 102, I, 26; prec., *li-ru-ru-šú,* Susa, 2, III, 24; Neb. Nippur, V, 7; London, 101, IV, 6; III R. 43, III, 25; IV, 35; edge II, 2; IV R.² 38, III, 34; Susa, 16, VI, 13; Susa, 14, III, 2; III R. 41, II, 15; I R. 70, IV, 24; O. B. I., 149, II, 17; V R. 56, 38; London, 102, I, 39; C. T., X, pl. VII, 40; V. A., 209, II, 10; V, 9; *li-ru-ru-uš,* Susa, 3, VI, 28; pres., *i-ra-ru-šu,* D. E. P., II, pl. 20, 11.
I, 2, *li-te-ir-ru-šú,* Susa, 16, VI, 12.
arratu, curse.
ar-rat limutti(-ti), Susa, 2, III, 23; Neb. Nippur, V, 7; *ar-rat la nap-šú-ri,* London, 101, IV, 6; III R. 43, III, 25; IV, 34; edge II, 2; *arrat(AŠ) la nap-šu-ru,* V. A., 2663, V, 37; *ar-rat la na-ap-šú-ri li-mut-ta,* Susa, 14, III, 1; Susa, 3, VI, 26; I R. 70, IV, 23; O. B. I., 149, II, 16; *ar-ra-at la nap-šú-ri-im ma-ru-uš(us)-ta,* Susa, 16, VI, 12; III R. 41, II, 15; London, 102, I, 38; V. A., 209; II, 9; V, 8; *ar-rat la pa-ša-ri,* IV R.² III, 33; *ar-ra-ta i-ru-ur-ma,* London, 102, I, 26; *i-na ar-rat lim-ri-ru,* Susa, 14, IV, 17; pl., *aššu(MU) ar-ra-a-ti a-na-ti,* London, 101, III, 5; *ar-ra-a-ti ši-na-a-ti,* Susa, 3, V, 45; Susa, 16, IV, 22; *ar-ra-a-tum an-na-a-tum,* Susa, 3, VII, 41; *ar-ra-a-ti šá ina ᵃᵇⁿⁱnarî an-ni-i aš-tu-ru-ma,* Susa, 3, V, 22; *aš-šú ar-ra-ti,* III R. 41, II, 8; *aš-šu ar-ra-ti limutti(-ti),* I R. 70, II, 19; *aš-šu ar-r[a-ti] i-pal-la-ḫu-ma,* London, 102, V, 3.

ארר₃, arâru, burn.
I, 1 part., *a-ri-rum ka-ru-bu,* Neb. Nippur, IV, 25.
arratu, drought.
ûm(-um) su-gi-e ù ar-ra-ti, III R. 41, II, 34.
arurtu, drought.
ûmê a-ru-ur-ti šanâti ḫu-šá-aḫ-ḫi, London, 101, IV, 9.

irrû, bitterness.
i-na(!) ir-ri-i im-[lu]-ú, D. E. P., VI, 45, V, 16.

ארש, erêšu, decide(?), plant(?).
tib(?)-da-a a-na la e-ri-ši, III R. 45, No. 2, 10.

ארש₅, erêšu, plant.
III, 1 part., *mu-še-ri-šú lu-ú gù-gal-lu,* a planter, Susa, 3, VI, 10; III R. 41, I, 32.
irrišu, farmer, cultivator.
ir-ri-ši ša âli-šú, Susa, 3, II, 34.
mêrištu, cultivation (cf. p. 174).
a-na me-riš-ti la šú-lu-ku-ú-ma, Neb. Nippur, II, 30.

אש₁, išâtu, fire.
ina išâti(NE) i-qal-lu-ú, Neb. Nippur, V, 1; C. T., X, pl., VII,

37; London, 102, V, 3; *i-na išâti i-qa-al-lu-ú*, III R. 41, II, 11; *i-na i-ša-ti i-qal-lu-ú*, O. B. I., 149, II, 12; III R. 43, I, 34; *išâti ú-šaq-lu*, V R. 56, 36; *i-ša-ta ú-ša-aq-qa[-lu]*, London, 103, V, 44; *i-na išâti i-šar-ra-pu*, I R. 70, III, 4; *išâti ú-ša-ka-lu*, O. B. I., 150, II, 4; *i-na išâti iqallû(GIBIL-ú* = Br. 10,867); V. A., 2663, V, 29; *a-na išâti inadû(-ú)*, London, 101, III, 3; *lu i-na [mê] lu a-na išâti i-na-ad-du-[ú]*, D. E. P., II, 113, 16; *a-na išâti i-na-[ad-du-ú]*, D. E. P., VII, 45, V, 12; *a-na me-e u išâti it-ta-di*, Susa, 3, V, 51; *a-na mê ù išâti i-nam-du-ú*, Susa, 16, IV, 31; *a-na mê a-na išâti ú-šad-da(!)-ú*, IV R.[2] 38, III, 18; *ki-i i-ša-ti*, V R. 55, 17; *in-na-pi-iḫ i-ša-tu*, V R. 55, 30.

išdu, foundation.
išid-su lissuḫu(ZI-ḫu), London, 103, VI, 4; Neb. Nippur, V, 7; *[išid-su] li-iz-zi-ḫu*, Susa, 16, VI, 25; *išid-su li-bit*, London, 101, III, 15; *išid-su li-is-su-ḫu*, I R. 70, III, 12; *e-ši-is-su li-is-su-ḫu*, III R. 43, III, 27; *mu-kin iš-di ma-a-ti*, Neb. Nippur, II, 24; *mu-kin išdi mâti*, V. A., 2663, II, 44; C. T., X, pl. IV, 13.

אשה, **ešîtu**, disturbance, revolution.
ina e-ši-tú u saḫ-maš-ti ša ^{mâtu}Ak-kadî^{ki}, C. T., X, pl. V, 3.

אשך$_3$, **ušaku**, misfortune (cf. Hebr. חֹשֶׁךְ and Jensen on *asakku*, K. B., VI, 433f).
ai ú-ṣi ina ú-ša-ki, Neb. Nippur, IV, 24 (cf. p. 183).

iškaru, a span of horses.
pl., *iš-ka-ra-a-ti ul-lap*, V R. 55, 24.

ušumgallu, sovereign.
ušumgal(GAL.UŠU) ^{d}Igigê, V. A., 2663, I. 5.

ašamšatu, hurricane.
a-šam-ša-tu iṣ-ṣa-nun-da, a hurricane sweeps along, V R. 55, 32.

ašnân, grain.
li-za-am-mi ^{d}Aš-na-an ai ú-še-ṣi ur-ki-ti, Susa, 14, III, 12.

UŠ.SA.DU, adjoining (cf. p. 160).
London, 103, III, 48, 50; London, 101, I, 7, 9, 12; IV R.[2] 38, I, 9, 13, 17; Susa, 16, I, 20, 22, 26, 29; II, 2; III R. 41, I, 3, 5, 7, 9; I R. 70, I, 5, 7, 10, 12; III R. 43, I, 15, 17, 19, 21; O. B. I., 149, I, 7; C. T., X, pl. VI, 18, 21, 22, 23, 25, 26, 27, 28; V. A., 208, 9, 10, 11, 14; C. T., X, pl. III, 12, 14; London, 102, I, 4, 6, 7, 9; V. A., 2663, III, 44, 47, 54; IV, 26, 28, 35, 38. *UŠ.SA.DU*, neighbor, Susa, 16, IV, 5; Susa, 14, II, 5; *UŠ.SA.DU-šu*, its adjoining (field), V. A., 209, I, 8, 18.

išparu, weaver.
^{m}Bêl(EN)-am-ma apil ^{h}išpari(UŠ-BAR), V. A., 2663, IV, 29.

išpartu, female weaver.
London, 102, IV, 23.

אשר$_1$, **ašru**, place.
i-na aš-ri-im ša-ni-im-ma, Susa, 3, V, 41; *a-šar la a-ma-ri*, IV R.[2] 38, III, 6; Neb. Nippur, V, 4; III R. 41, II, 12; London, 101, III, 7; Susa, 3, V, 43; I R. 70, III, 7; O. B. I., 150, II, 4; London, 102, V, 5; Susa, 16, IV, 35; D. E. P., 45, V, 18; *a-šar la a-ma-ru*, V. A., 2663, V, 31; *a-šar la a-(ma!)-ri pu-uz-ri*, C. T., X, pl. VII, 37; *a-šar qa-tuš u ta-ḫa-zi*, London, 103, VI, 18; *ú-tir-ru aš-ru-uš-šin*, he returned them to their abodes, V. A., 2663, II, 30.

aširtum, sanctuary.
a-ši-ir-tum rabîtum(GAL), Susa, 2, IV, 6; pl., *muš-te-'-ú aš-ra-ti-šu*, Neb. Nippur, I, 24; pl. cstr., *aš-rat ^{d}Nabû(PA) u ^{d}Marduk*,

V. A., 2663, III, 8; *ša aš-rat ilâni . . . .*, C. T., X, pl. IV, 8; *mu-ud-diš ka-liš ašrâti (AŠ.ME)*, V. A., 2663, II, 7.

ešrêti, sanctuaries.
eš-ri-tu-šú-nu ud-da-a, IV R.[2] 38, III, 31; cstr., *ina eš-rit ma-ḫa-zi*, V. A., 2663, II, 45; *a-na ud-du-uš eš-rit ma-ḫa-az da-ad-me*, Neb. Nippur, II, 2.

išrubû, leprosy(?).
iš-ru-ba-a ki-ma ṣu-ba-ti pa-ga-ar-šú li-la-bi-iš-ma, Susa, 3, VI, 48; *iš-ru-ba-a mûti(BAD-ti) an ka-bit-ta zu-mur-šu lil-la-ib[-biš]-ma*, Susa, 16, VI, 14; *iš-ru-ba-a la te-ba-a*, III R. 41, II, 16; *iš-ru-ba-a ki-i lu-ba-ri li-la-ab-bi-su-ma*, I R. 70, III, 19; *išrubâ(SU.-ḪUR.ŠÚ.ŠAB-a) ki-ma lu-ba-ri li-li-bi-ša zu-mu-ur-šú*, III R. 43, IV, 8; *iš-ru-ba-a i-na zu-um-ri-šu li-šab-šú-ma*, O. B. I., 149, III, 6; *iš-ru-ba [ki-ma lu-ba-ri li-lab-bi-iš]-šu*, London, 102, I, 46; *iš-ru-pa-a li-lab-bi-is-su-ma*, V. A., 209, V, 10.

ašaridu, first.
mâru ašaridu(SAG.KAL) ša [Aš-šur-aḫu-iddina], C. T., X, pl. IV, 9.

aššu, concerning.
aš-šú X gur, London, 103, II, 13; *aš-šu ar-ra-a-ti ši-na-a-ti*; Susa, 3, V, 45; Susa, 16, IV, 22; *aššu (MU) ar-ra-a-ti a-na-ti*, London, 101, III, 5; *aš-šu âlâni Bit mKar-zi-ab-ku*, V R. 55, 47; *aš-šú ar-ra-ti*, III R. 41, II, 8; I R. 70, II, 19, London, 102, II, 3; *aš-šu paq-ri la ra-še-e*, London, 102, II, 34; *aš-šu la ra-ga-mu*, C. T., X, pl. V, 9; *aš-šu ru-gu-um-[mi]*, C. T., X, pl. V, 10.

iššakku, prince, representative.
lu-ú ḫa-za-an-nu lu-ú iššakku(PA.-TE.SI), Susa, 16, IV, 3; *iššakku qar-du*, V R. 55, 3; *iššak šarri*, III R. 41, II, 3; *iššak hša-kin*, III R. 41, II, 4; *iššak bît ṭe-mi-šu*, III R. 41, II, 4; *lu-ú hšakin(-in) ṭe-mi lu-ú iššakku(PA.TE.SI)*, O. B. I., 149, II, 4.

ištu, from, since.
ištu(TA) il-lik, London, 103, I, 3; *iš-tu âluDi-e-ir ma-ḫa-az dA-num*, V R. 55, 14; *ištu(TA) i-na li-ti . . . . a-na Akkadî i-tu-ra*, V R. 55, 44; *ištu(TA) i-na i-lik mâtuNa-mar*, V R. 56, 6.

ištên, one.
ûma(-ma) iš-tin, London, 101, IV, 7; *ki-i išten ûmi(-mi) la balâṭ-su liq-bu-ú*, O. B. I., 149, III, 10.

ištêniš, in the same manner.
ṣiḫra u rabâ(-a) ki-i ištêniš(I-iš) ú-ša-aṣ-bit-ma, V. A., 2663, III, 28.

ištaru, goddess.
pl., *dNinâ bêlit eš-[t]a-ra-tu*, O. B. I., 83, II, 15.

אתה$_1$, **atû,** see.
II, 1, *mim-ma ut-tu-ú a-na ḫur-ri pi-šu la i-kaš-šad*, whatsoever he seeks for his throat may he not secure it, I R. 70, IV, 19; *gi-mir kal da-ád-me ki-niš ut-tu-ú-ma*, he paid careful attention, V. A., 2663, I, 24.

itû, overseer(?).
laputtû lu-ú i-tu-ú, I R. 70, II, 6.

itû, boundary.
30 (gur) *i-te-e Bît-mMa-zi nâr šarri*, C. T., IX, pl. V, 24; *e te-ti-iq i-ta-[a]*, O. B. I., 83, II, 22.

אתל, **etellu,** lord.
amelu šú-ú lu-ú etellu(BE) lu-ú rabû ma-lik šarri, Susa, 3, VI, 1; *e-til šamê(-e) u irṣiti*, Neb. Nippur, I, 1; (Nebuchadrezzar I.) *e-til šarrâni*, V R. 55, 2; fem., (Gula) *e-til-li-it ka-la be-li-e-ti*, Susa, 3, VI, 16.

אתק$_4$, **etêqu,** remove.

I, 1 pret., *a-na-ku la e-mi-e-šú*(מאש) *ú la e-ti-qu,* Susa, 3, IV, 27; *e te-ti-iq i-ta-*[*a*], O. B. I., 83, 22; pres., *i-ka mi-iṣ-ra it-ti-qu,* Susa, 16, IV, 18.

IV, 1, pres., *an-na-šú ki-i-nu la in-ni-ti-qu,* whose grace is constant and cannot be surpassed, Susa, 3, VII, 49.

mêtequ, inroad(s).

a-na me-te-iq mê šaknu(-nu), to the inroads of the waters exposed, Neb. Nippur, II, 31.

mêtiqtu, road.

a-di ti-tur(!)*-ri mi-ti-iq-ti šarri,* Susa, 14, I, 4.

itti, prep., with, alongside of.

it-ti a-ḫa-meš i-šal-šú-nu-ti, London, 103, IV, 18; *it-ti a-ḫa-meš,* London, 103, IV, 37; *it-ti,* London, 103, II, 19; V, 12; *ša-na-a ša it-ti-šu,* the companion who is with him, V R. 55, 34; *lu-ú ra-ki-is it-ti-šu,* V R. 56, 44; *it-ti-šu a-na* ^{mâtu}*Êlamti*^{ki} *il-li-ku-ma,* C. T., IX, pl. IV, 9; *it-ti* ^{d}*Bêl(EN) a-na Bâbili iš-ša-a,* C. T., IX, pl. IV, 12; *it-ti* ^{d}*E-a,* O. B. I., 83, II, 17; *it*(!)*-ti mu-lu-gi,* London, 102, I, 15; *it-ti-šu,* London, 102, III, 17; *it-ti* ^{mâtu}*Akkadî*^{ki} . . . . *ir-ša-a sa-li-me,* V. A., 2663, I, 17; *itti(DA),* alongside of, C. T., X, pl. III, 18; V. A., 208, 9, 10, 11, 13, 16, 17, 19; V. A., 2663, IV, 7, 11, 14, 25; V. A., 209, II, 32, 33, 35, 35; III, 3, 4, 6, 7; IV, 9, 10, 11, 12, 25, 26, 28, 30; O. B. I., 150, I, 2, 3, 4, 5.

באל$_4$, **bêlu,** possess.

I, 1 prec., *bîtu ip-pu-šu li-bi-el ša-nu-um-ma,* V R. 56, 53.

bêlu, lord, *passim.*

pl., *be-lu-ú irṣitim šú-a-tum,* IV R^2 38, 28.

bêltu, mistress.

(Gula) *be-el-tu rabîtu(-tu),* III R. 41, II, 29; *bêltu rabîtu,* I R. 70, IV, 5; III R. 43, IV, 15; Neb. Nippur, IV, 20; D. E. P., VI, 47, 11; London, 102, II, 20; (Zarpanîtum) [*bêltu*] *rabî-tum(-tum),* O. B. I., 149, II, 22; *bêlit E-sag-ila,* London, 102, I, 42; (Ištar) *bêlit šamê(-e) ù irṣiti(-ti),* III R. 43, IV, 12; I R. 70, III, 22; (Ištar) *bêlit mâtâti,* Neb. Nippur, IV, 22; Susa, 2, IV, 16; (Gula) *bêltu šur-bu-tum,* Susa, 3, VII, 15; (Išḫara) *bêlit le-ti da-ad-ma,* III R. 43, IV, 28; (Šumalia) *be-lit šadê el-lu-ti,* V R. 56, 46; (Ištar) *be-el-tu ru-ba ilâni,* III R. 41, II, 21; *ša belti* ^{d}*Ninâ,* O. B. I., 83, I, 22; [*a-na*] ^{d}*Ninâ be-el-ti-šú,* O. B. I., 83, I, 4; *bêlat(NIN-at) ilâni,* D. E. P., II, 113, 1; pl., *e-til-li-it ka-la be-li-e-ti,* Susa, 3, VII, 17.

bêlûtu, lordship, rule.

ša . . ina ^{mâtu}*Akkadî*^{ki} *ip-pu-šu be-lu-tú,* V. A., 2663, V, 22; *be-lut-su la iš-ša-na-nu,* Neb. Nippur, I, 17.

ba'ûlâti, kingdoms.

ka-bit mâtâti mut-tar-ru-ú ba-'-ú-la-ti, Neb. Nippur, I, 12.

bêlu, weapon.

pl., ^{d}*Nergal bêl be-li-e ù qa-ša-ti,* III R. 43, IV, 21.

באר$_1$, **ba'âru,** catch.

I, 1 part., ^{h}*bâ'iru(ŠÚ.ḪA),* C. T., X, pl. III, 13.

באר$_1$, **bûru,** well.

a-na bûri(PU) i-na-as-su-ku, III R. 41, II, 11; *a-na bûri(PU) i-(na)-as-su-ku,*London, 102,V, 2.

באת, **bâtu,** pass night.

I, 2, *ki-ma kalbi li-ib-ta'-i-ta i-na ri-bi-it âli-šú,* III R. 41, II, 24.

bâbu, gate.

du-ul-li bâb nâr šarri, Susa, 3, II,

29; *ba-ab eqli-ia*, Susa, 16, II, 18; *bâb eqli*, Susa, 16, II, 31; *amelu ša bâb êkalli*, V R. 56, 16; *amel bâb êkalli*, Neb. Nippur, V, 10; *ba-ab-šú li-par-ri-ki*, III R. 43, IV, 27; pl., *ba-ba-at ḫar-ri* ^{âlu}*Šá-sa-na*^{ki}, O. B. I., 149, I, 9.

Bâbilû, the Babylonian.
^{h}*Bâbilû(TIN.TIR*^{ki} *ME)*, V. A., 2663, III, 45, 48; *Bâbilû (TIN.-TIR-ú)*, V R. 56, 3.

bubûtu, hunger.
bu-bu-ta še-ir-ta-šu ra-bi-i-ta lim-is-su-ma, Susa, 3, VI, 33; *murṣu bu-[bu]-ti*, D. E. P., VI, 47, 20; *bu-bu-ta ù ḫu-ša-aḫ-ḫa liš-kun-šú-um-ma*, V R. 56 43.

bugina, basket.
us-qa-ru bu-gi-na maqur-ru ša ^{d}*Sin*, Susa, 2, IV, 10.

בול, **bûlu,** cattle.
bu-ul šarri u ša-kin, Susa, 3, III, 15.

בור, **bûru,** ox.
bu-ru ek-du ša ^{d}*Rammân*, Susa, 2, IV, 17.

בחל, **buḫalu,** stallion.
XXX sisê XXV bu-ḫa-lu V ^{f}*urâte* (^{f}*sisû*), III R. 43, edge IV, 2.

בטל, **baṭâlu,** cease.
I, 1 inf., *la ba-ṭa-la at-riš a-na du-um-mu-ki*, IV R.[3] 38, II, 25.

בין, **bânu,** give.
I, 1 imper., *UŠ.SA.DU-šu ina pa-ni-ka bi-nam-ma*, V. A., 209, I, 9; *ṭuppa-šu ku-nu-uk-ma bi-in-ni*, V. A., 209, I, 14; *V šiqlu kaspi bi-na-an-na-ši-ma*, give us, V. A., 209, IV, 21.

בית, **bîtu,** house, *passim*.

בלה, **balû,** perish; II, 1, destroy.
II, 1 prec., *nap-ša-tuš li-bal-li*, Neb. Nippur, IV, 4.

belû, ragged garment (Hebr. בְּלוֹאִים).
II ṣubâtu elîtu be-lu-ú, III R. 41, I, 23.

billudû, command.
par(?)-su-šú šit-ru-ḫu billudû(PA +AN)-šú ṣîru, Neb. Nippur, I, 18.

בלט, **balâṭu,** live.
I, 1 perm., *a-di ûm(-um) bal-ṭu*, Susa, 3, VI, 52; VII, 23; V R. 56, 59; London, 102, II, 23; *ûm [b]al-ṭu*, O. B. I., 149, III, 4; *a-di ûm(-um) bal-du*, Susa, 16, VI, 18 *a-di ûmi(-mi) i-ṣu-ti ša bal-ṭa*, IV R.[2] 38, III, 41.

balâṭu, life.
ûma(-ma) iš-tin la balâṭ(TI)-su liq-bu-ú, London 101, IV, 7; *ki-i ištên ûmi(-mi) la balâṭ(TI)-su liq-bu-ú*, O. B. I., 149, III, 10; *[bal-a]ṭ ûmi(-mi) ma-'-du-ti*, Susa, 3, V, 17; *la ba-la-az-zu [liq-b]u-ú*, Susa, 16, VI, 23; *ši-mat balâṭi(TI.LA) li-ši-ma-šú*, O. B. I., 83, II, 18; *balâṭ(TI.LA) ûmê da-ru-ú-ti*, Neb. Nippur, II, 6; *ûmê-šu la ba-laṭ-su iq-[bu-ú]*, London, 102, V, 7.

בלת, **baltu,** riches.
nu-uḫ-ši ù ḫe-gal a-di bal-tu, Susa, 3, V, 19.

בנה, **banû,** do, make, create.
I, 1 pres., *i-ban-nu-ú ni-kil-tú*, (who) practices mischief, V. A., 2663, V, 24; part., cstr., ^{d}*E-a ba-an ka-la*, O. B. I., 83, II, 17; *mu-um-mu ba-an ka-la*, the prototype, the creator of all, V. A., 2663, III, 5; (Nusku) *[ilu] ban-nu-ú-a*, Neb. Nippur, IV, 26 (Lugal-banda) *ilu ba-ni-šú*, IV R.[2] 38, II, 10; part. fem., ^{d}*NIN.-MEN.NA ba-nit ilâni*, V. A., 2663, II, 52; *bêlat (NIN-at) ilâni ba-na-at nap-[ḫa-ri]*, D. E. P., II, 113, 1.

bûnu, face, features.
pl., *ina bu-ni-šu nam-ru-ti*, Neb. Nippur, I, 22; *bu-ni-šu nam-ru-ti(tu)*, C. T., X, pl. III, 9; pl. V, 15; V. A., 2663, III, 40; *i-na bu ni-šú-nu iz-zu-ú-ti*, Susa, 3,

VI, 23; *bu-ni-šú liṭ-ṭe-šú-ma,* Neb. Nippur, IV, 14.

nabnîtu, birth.
ú-šar-ri-ḫu nab-nit-su, V. A., 2663, II, 54.

בקן, **baqânu,** cut off (cf. p. 177).
I, 1 inf., *ba-qa-an šam-mi,* Neb. Nippur, III, 26; *šammê eqli-šú la ba-qa-ni,* Susa, 3, III, 14.

ברא, **nibrêtu,** hunger.
su-gà-a u ni-ib-ri-ta liš-ku-na-aš-šum-ma, I R. 70, IV, 17.

ברה, **barû,** see.
I 1 pret., *ib-ri-e-ma kul-la-tan nišê i-ḫi-iṭ,* he looked around and everywhere he examined men, V. A., 2663, I, 20.

bârû, seer.
ʰbârû(ḪAL), London, 103, I, 1, 39; II, 10, 15; IV, 8, 22, 32; V, 22; V R. 56, 26; Neb. Nippur, V, 14; O. B. I., 149, I, 16; V. A., 209, V, 18 (so acc. to Dr. Ungnad).

bîrit, prep., between.
bi-rit ⁿᵃʳᵘIdiqlat u ⁿᵃʳᵘŠum-ili, D. E. P., VI, 42, I, 4, 17; *i-na bi-ri-šú-nu,* V R. 55, 30.

ברה, **birû,** luxuriant growth, pasture.
ši-ir bi-ra-a li-kab-bi-sa še-pa-šu, III R. 43, IV, 6.

birîtu, luxuriant pasture.
ši-ir-a bi-ri-ta li-kab-bi-sa šêpâ-šú, I R. 70, IV, 14.

ברח, **barruḫu,** luxuriant.
zur-šu bar-ru-ḫu, V. A., 2663, II, 16.

ברם, **barâmu,** seal.
I, 1 inf., *i-na ša-a-me ša-ṭa-ri ù ba-ra-me,* London, 102, IV, 41; perm., *ṭup-pi bar-mu,* the tablet has been sealed, V. A., 2663, V, 50.

ברר, **barîritu**, rise of the stars.
(Ištar) *ilat ba-ri-ri-ta,* III R. 41, II, 22 (cf., however, Delitzsch, H. W., 188*a*).

burrurtum, shining (Zimmern).
ⁱṣᵘqar-ru-ur-tum bur-ru-ur-tum ša ᵈIš-tar, Susa, 2, IV, 15.

burâšu, cypress.
imêr burâši(ŠIM.LI) la na-da-ni, V R. 55 56.

בשה, **bašû,** be.
I, 1 pret., [*ilâni mala*] *ib-ši-mu li-ru-ru-šú-ma,* C. T., X, pl. VII, 40; *uzun(PI)-šu ib-ši-ma,* V. A., 2663, III, 14; *šumu lâ(NU) ibši(IG),* London, 103, I, 3; *šumu lâ ibšê-(IG-e),* relat., London, 103, II, 9; IV, 33, *šumu lâ ibšû(IG-ú),* relat., London, 103, IV, 23; pres., *la i-ba-aš-šú-ú ilu ša-nin-šú,* Neb. Nippur, I, 4; *um-ma qaq-qa-ru i-ba-aš-ši,* V. A., 209, I, 8; inf., *ma-la ba-šú-ú,* as much as there is, V R. 55, 47; 56, 8, 29; I R. 66, II, 1; C. T., IX, pl. V, 38; V. A., 2663, III, 32; V, 24; V. A., 208, 4; C. T., X, pl. V, 16; London, 103, V, 32, 40; *a-na mim-ma la ba-še-e li-šá-li-ku-šú,* may they cause him to come to naught, London, 103, VI, 24; *a-di šamê ù irṣiti ba-šú-ú,* V R. 56, 60; *a-na paq-ri la bašê(IG),* V. A., 2663, IV, 53; *par-ga-niš bašê(-e) a-ḫu-ú-ti,* V. A., 2663, III, 18; *a-na ud-du-šu* [*eš*]-*rit . . . ba-ša-a uznâ(PI²)-šu,* V. A., 2663, II, 25.
III, 1, *i-na zumri(SU)-šú li-šab-ši-ma,* III R. 41, II, 30; [*i-n*]*a zu-um-ri-šú li-šab-šú-ma,* O. B. I., 149, III, 4, 7; *ina zu-um-ri-šu li-šab-ši-ma,* London, 102, II, 22; *ki-mu-ú mê id-ra-na li-šab-ši,* London, 102, II, 14; *ú-šab-ši,* London, 102, II, 10.

bušû, property.
i-na eli buši (ŠA.ŠU) ú-ṭib-ú-ma, London, 102, VI, 13.

bitḫallu, riding horse.
amelu ša bit-ḫal-li, master of the (riding) horse, V R. 55, 58; *urâte(ⁱṣisê) bit-ḫal-la,* mares as riding horses, V R. 55, 59.

בתק, **batâqu,** cut off.
II, 1 perm., *bu-ut-tu-qu maš-qu-ú,* the drinking places were cut off, V R. 55, 19.
butuqtu, inundation (Talm. בדקא).
šá a-na bu-tuq-ti šaknu(-nu), Neb. Nippur, II, 26.

gabbu, entire, total.
i-na i-lik ^{mâtu}*Na-mar gab-bi-šú,* V R. 55, 51.

gabarû, gabrû, copy.
na-ra-a šá abni eš-šá ga-ba-ri-e la-bi-ri-šu iš-ṭur-ma, Susa, 2, Med., II, 10; *ki ga-ba-[ri-i] li'i(GIŠ.LI),* D. E. P., II, 93, II, 8, 11; *a-su-mi-it-tu an-ni-i-tu ga-ba-ri-e šá-lal-ti,* London, 103, VI, 27; *gabri(GAB.RI) kunuk šarri,* I R. 66, II, 19.

gugallu, regent, chief.
gù-gal-lu ša piḫât Bît-^{m}*Pir-*^{d}*Amurru,* Susa, 3, VI, 11; (Rammân) *gù-gal ilâni,* D. E. P., II, 113, 8; (Rammân) *gù-gal šamê(-e) ù irṣitim(-tim),* III R. 41, II, 32; I R. 70, IV, 9; III R. 43, IV, 3; V R. 56, 41; Susa, 14, III, 9; *lu mu-še-ri-šú lu gù-gal-lu,* III R. 41, I, 33.

גמל, **gimillu,** preservation.
a-na tur-ri gi-mil-li, to avenge, V R. 55, 13.

גמר, **gamâru,** complete.
I, 1 pret., *pa-gu-mi a-na Bi-ti-li-ia-a-šú ig-mu-ur-ma,* D. E. P., II, pl. 20, 5; part., *ga-mir šú-luḫ-ḫi,* the most perfect commander, V. A., 2663, I, 7.
gamrûtu, completion, fulness.
šîmi-šu gam-ru-tu, its full price, V. A., 209, II, 37; III, 13, 26; *V šiqlu kaspi šîm gam-ru-tu,* V. A., 209, IV, 34.
gimru, totality.
(Marduk) *šàr gi-im-ri,* V. A., 2663, I, 4; (Ellil) *bêl gim-ri* Neb. Nippur, I, 2; *šàr(?) gim(?)-ri,* London, 101, III, 10; *gi-mir la-ni-šú,* III R. 41, II, 17; *gi-mir kal da-ád-me,* V. A., 2663, I, 23; *gi-mir e-kur-re,* V. A., 2663, II, 5.

GAN, a surface measure.
$\frac{1}{18}$ *GAN 30 qa I ammatu rabîtu,* Susa, 2, I, 26, 35; II, 5, 10, 15; Neb. Nippur, pl. 1; III, 7; London, 103, III, 40; London, 101, I, 4; Susa, 3, I, 2; Susa, 16, I, 1; D. E. P., VI, 42, I, 1; D. E. P., VI, 46, I, 1; C. T., IX, pl. V, 26; O. B. I., 83, I, 1; III R. 41, I, 1; I R. 70, I, 1; III R. 43, I [1], 11; O. B. I., 149, I, 1; C. T., X, pl. III, 11, 19; V. A., 2663, IV, 3, 18, 20, 32, 42, 47, etc.

GÚ.EN.NA, title of an official.
London, 103, I, 20, 48; III, 7, 26, 35, 37.

girgilu, a symbol of Ellil.
gir-gi-lu al-la-ku ša ^{d}*En-lil,* Susa, 2, IV, 3.

girru, road.
pl., *tu . . . ša gir-ri-e-ti,* V R. 55, 18.

gurru, measure of area, Hebr. כר.
gur $^{she'}$*uzêru, passim.*

GIŠ.BAR, rent.
London, 103, III, 19, 20; III R. 41, I, 21, 22; London, 102, IV, 25.

gišḫabbu, rascal.
nu-a giš-ḫab-ba, III R. 41, II, 9.

gišimmaru, date palm.
eqlu ^{iṣu}*gišimmaru zaq-qu,* a field planted with date palms, V. A., 208, 35; ^{iṣu}*kirû(SAR) gišimmaru,* V. A., 2663, IV, 21; C. T., X, pl. VI, 24; ^{iṣu}*gišimmaru šadî,* V. A., 209, II, 30; III, 1; ^{iṣu}*kirû* ^{iṣu}*gišimmarê 40 gišimmaru ina bilti(GU.UN) ina lib-bi-šu,* the date palm grove in which are forty date palms with fruit, V. A., 209, IV, 24.

נשר, **gašru**, strong.
ᵈNusku bêl ga-aš-rum, Neb. Nippur, IV, 25; *i-na e-muq ᵈBêl(EN) gaš-rat*, V. A., 2663, II, 38; pl., *ᵈŠamaš u ᵈRammân ilâni ga-aš-ru-tu*, Neb. Nippur, IV, 15.

gašrûtu, strength, power.
ša ina dun-ni u [gaš]-ru-tú la [i-]šú-u tam-šil-šu, V. A., 2663, II, 32.

gutaku, title of an official.
gu-ta-ku ša Bît-ᵐA-da, III R. 43, III, 12.

Dûzu, month of Tammuz.
V R. 55, 16; V. A., 2663, V, 16.

דא₂ם, **da'ummatu**, darkness.
ûmi-šú nam-ru a-na da-um-ma-ti li-tur(?)-šú, III R. 41, II, 20.

דבב, **dabâbu**, raise a claim.

I, 1 pret., *id-bu-bu*, London, 103, I, 16; *i-na mu-uḫ [eqli šú-a-tu] id-bu-um-ma*, London, 103, I, 43; *id-bu-um-ma*, Susa, 16, II, 17; pres., *i-na eli eqlatim(-tim) ši-na-a-tim i-dib-bu-bu-ma*, Susa, 2, III, 13; *i-na mu-uḫ Bît-ᵐTa-kil-a-na-ili-šú i-da-ab-bu-bu i-rag-gu-mu*, London, 103, V, 34; *i-na eli eqlu šú-a-tum i-da-ab-bu-bu*, London, 101, II, 17; Susa, 16, IV, 14; Susa, 14, II, 8; III R. 43, III, 5; *šà eqlu šú-a-tum i-dab-ba-[bu]*, IV R.² 38, III, 4; *muḫ-ḫi eqlê šú-a-tu i-da-bu-bu*, C. T., IX, pl. V, 32; *i-na muḫ-ḫi eqlu šú-a-tu i-da-bu-bu*, O. B. I., 149, II, 6; *i-na muḫ-ḫi [bîtâ]ti šú-a-tu i-dib-bu-bu*, V. A., 209, I, 36; inf., *bêl da-ba-bi*, impostor, Susa, 2, IV, 31; *ṭuppu la ta-a-ru ù la da-ba-bu ik-nu-uk-ma*, V. A., 209, IV, 14, 37; *ša da-ba-bi an-na-a*, V. A., 209, II, 6; V, 6; part., *lu-ú bêl da-ba-bi da-bi-bi*, Susa, 2, IV, 32.

III, 1 pret., *di-na lu-ša-(ad)-bu-ba*, London, 102, VI, 8; pres., *ú-ša-aḫ-ḫa-zu ú-šad-ba-bu ú-šat-ba-lu eqlu an-nu-ú*, London, 103, V, 36; *ša rubû ú-šad-ba[bu] eqla an-na-a*, D. E. P., II, 97, 14; *i-na eli eqlu šú-a-tum i-da-ab-bu-bu ú-šad-ba-bu*, London, 101, II, 17; Susa, 14, II, 9; *i-dab-ba-bu ú-šad-ba[-bu]*, IV R.² 38, III, 5; O. B. I., 149, II, 7; III R. 43, III, 6; *ú-[šad-ba-bu(?)]-ma eqlu šú-a-tu ik-ki-mu*, Neb. Nippur, III, 27; *i-dib-bu-bu ú-šad-ba-bu*, V. A., 209, II, 1; part., *mu-še-id-bi-bi*, plotters, seducers, Susa, 3, IV, 17; *mu-šad-bi-bi*, Susa, 3, IV, 38; V, 12.

dibbu, lawsuit.
di-ib-bi tap-qir-ta ù ru-gu-um-ma-a, Susa, 3, II, 15.

דגל, **dagâlu**, see.

I, 1 prec., *pa-ni-ka lid-gu-la*, V. A., 209, IV, 8.

III, 1, *pa-ni-šu ú-šad-gil*, to him he entrusted, C. T., IX, pl. V, 41; *pa-ni ᵐKi-di-ni mâri-šu kut-tin-nu ú-šad-gil*, V. A., 208, 6, 21; *pa-ni ṣâbê ki-din-nu . . . ú-šad-gil*, V. A., 2663, III, 26; *ú-šad-gil pa-n[i-šu]*, C. T., X, pl. V, 6; *pa-ni-ka nu-šad-gi-[il]-ma*, V. A., 209, IV, 22.

daddu, child.
a[i] i-zi-bu da-ad-da-šú, Susa, 16, VI, 27.

dûru, wall.
dûru ša ᵃˡᵘBît-ᵈŠamaš, V R. 56, 1.

דור, **dârû**, everlasting.
zêru da-ru-ú ša [šarrûti], of ancient royal seed, C. T., X, pl. IV, 13; *zêru šarru-u-ti da-ru-ú*, V. A., 2663, II, 41; pl., *balâṭ ûmê da-ru-ú-ti*, Neb. Nippur, II, 6; *ana ûmê(-me) da-ru-ú-ti*, Neb. Nippur, III, 17; pl. fem., *a-na ku-dur da-ra-a-ti*, for an everlasting boundary stone, Susa, 3, III, 53; *mu-ki-in ku-dur-ri da-ra-ti*, III R. 41, heading 3, II, 40;

a-na da-ra-a-ti, forever, Susa, 3, V, 39.

dâriš, forever.

^{d}Rammân limuttu(?) *pa-at-ti-nu da*(?)*-riš*, London, 101, I, 3.

דחד, **daḫâdu**, be abundant.

II, 1 part., *mu-daḫ-ḫi-id ši-gar-šu-nu*, who fills with plenty their gates, V. A., 2663, II, 4.

duḫdu, plenty.

šanâte duḫ-di, Susa, 3, V, 18.

dailu (= *daialu*), title of official.

a-lik da-i-li šú-a-tim, IV R^{2}. 38, II, 30.

דין, **dânu**, judge.

I, 1 pret., *di-in kit-ti u me-ša-ri ai i-di-nu-šu*, Neb. Nippur, IV, 18; *ša di-in mi-ša-ri i-din-nu*, V R. 55, 6; prec., *lu-ú-di-in kul dîni*(*DI*)*-šu*, may he decree the denial(?) of his right, I R. 70, III, 16; *lu-ú-di*(*-in*) *kul dîni*(*DI*)*-šú-ma*, III R. 43, IV, 11.

dînu, right, lawsuit.

di-in mi-ša-ri, V R. 55, 6; *di-in kit-ti u me-ša-ri*, Neb. Nippur, IV, 17; (Šamaš and Rammân) *bêlê di-ni*, London, 103, VI, 9; *di-in-šú la uš-te-eš-še-ru*, London, 103, VI, 10; *di-in-šu ù purus-si*(*EŠ.BAR*)*-šu ai ip-ru-us*, London, 102, II, 2; *di-na lu-ša-*(*ad*)*-bu-ba*, they brought suit, London, 102, VI, 8; *di-ni il*(?)[*-li-ku*], V. A., 209, IV, 2; *ka-nik di-nim*, London, 103, VI, 28; pl. cstr., *di-na-at*, D. E. P., 43, IV, 10.

dainu (= *daianu*), judge.

(*Šamaš*) *daianu rabû*, Susa, 2, IV, 13; Susa, 14, III, 3; *daianu*(*DI.-KUD*) *rabû šamê*(*e*) *u irṣi-tim*(*-tim*), I R. 70, III, 15; *^{d}Šamaš daianu kaš-kaš nišê*, III R. 43, IV, 10; *^{d}Šamaš daian šamê u irṣiti*, London, 101, III, 12; III R. 41, II, 19; London, 102, II, 1; (Šamas and Rammân) *daianê* (*DI.KUD.MEŠ*) *ṣîrûti* (*MAḪ.MEŠ*), Neb. Nippur, IV, 16; *lu-ú daianu lu-ú bêl paḫâti*, III R. 45, No. 2, 3; *lu laputtu lu dai*[*anu*], D. E. P., II, 97, 11.

דכה, **dakû**, overthrow.

I, 2, *šú-ú id-di-ki-ma i-na aš-ri-im ša-ni-im-ma ki-i limutti*(*-ti*) *il-ta-ka-an*, Susa, 3, V, 40.

דכה, **dikû**, levy, be ready.

I, 1 pret., [*ina*] *bu-ni-šú nam-ru-tu id-ki-ma*, with shining face he was ready (willing), C. T., X, pl. V, 15; inf., *la di-ki-im-ma*, not to levy, Susa, 3, II, 27.

dikû, levymaster.

lu-ú di-ku-ú lu na-gi-ru, D. E. P., II, 97, 12.

dikûtu, levy, conscription.

i-na il-ki di-ku-ti, Neb. Nippur, III, 25; *it-ti di-ku-tu ṣa-bit âlâni*, Susa, 3, II, 25.

דל, **daltu**, door.

dal-[*ti*] *ù ašar*(*KI*) *mi-il-ti nâri-šú i-si-ik-ki-ru-ma*, the sluice, the place of filling his canal, Susa, 16, V, 6.

דלל, **dullu**, work.

du-ul-li pit-ki mi-iḫ-ri nam-ba-'-i, Susa, 3, II, 18; *du-ul-li bâb nâr šarri*, Susa, 3, II, 29; *du-ul-la eš-ša*, Susa, 3, III, 28, 36; *du-ul-la šú-a-tu*, Susa, 3, III, 40.

dâmu, blood.

dâma(*BE*) *u šarqa*(*BE.UD*) *kîma mê li-ir-muk*, Neb. Nippur, IV 21; London, 102, II, 23; *da-ma u šar-ka*, I R. 70, IV, 7; O. B. I., 149, III, 4; *šar-ka u da-ma*, Susa, 3, VII, 24; *šarqa*(*BE.UD*) *ù dâma*(*BE*), III R. 41, II, 31; *ša-ar-ka u da-ma*, III R. 43, IV, 17; *da-a u šar-ka*, D. E. P., IV, pl. 16, II, 4.

דמק, **damâqu**, be merciful.

II, 1 inf., *at-riš a-na du-um-mu-ki*, for an exceedingly great favor,

IV R.² 38, II, 26; part., *mu-dam-me-iq zi-kir a-bi a-li-di-šu*, who keeps unstained the name of the father, his begetter, V. A., 2663, II, 41.

damqu, gracious.

ina nûr pânû(ŠI.MEŠ)-šu damqûti(ŠI.BIR.MEŠ), Neb. Nippur, I, 22.

damqiš, graciously.

[damqiš] lip-pal-su-šú-ma, Susa, 3, V, 16.

damiqtu, favor.

i-na [ṭûb lib]-bi u da[miqti iš]-pur, Susa, 16, I, 10.

דנן, **danânu,** force.

ina da-na-ni, by force, London, 103, IV, 14.

dannu, powerful, mighty.

šarru dan-nu, V R. 55, 28; C. T., X, pl. IV, 10, 12; *ed-lu dan-nu*, V. A., 2663, II, 33; *i-na ta-ḫa-zi da-an-ni*, III R. 43, IV, 29; *dan-na* ^{mâtu}*Lul-lu-bi-i*, V R. 55, 9; *[ta]-ḫa-zi dan-ni*, D. E. P., VI, 45, IV, 14.

dannatu, difficulty.

ul id-dar dan-na-at eqli, V R. 55, 24.

dunnu, strength.

ina dun-ni u [gaš]-ru-tú, V. A., 2663, II, 31.

dannu, document (cf. *dannitu*).

a-na šarri dan(-an)-ni iq-bi-ma, III R. 43, I, 10; *dan(-an) [-ni] ka-ni-ki*, the document was sealed, III R. 43, I, 23.

דרך, **diriktu,** diminution (cf. *dirku*, small).

i-na di-ri-ik-ti mê, at the low water level, Susa, 3, II, 54.

דשא, **dišû,** widely extended.

nišê(UN) di-ša-a-ti, people far and near, III R. 41, II, 39.

$יאד_4$, **âdu,** inform.

III, 1 pret., *šarru uš-id-ma it-ti a-ḫa-meš i-šal-šú-nu-ti-ma*, London, 103, IV, 18; *šarru . . . uš-id-ma*, Susa, 16, II, 21; *šarru bêli-šu . . . uš-id-ma*, V R. 55, 49; *šarru be-el-šu u[š-'-]id-ma um[-ma]*, C. T., X, pl. III, 3.

ובל, **abâlu,** carry, bring.

I, 1 prec., *li-ib-bi-el*, D. E. P., VI, 47, 8; imper., *ú-ki-e bi-lam-ma*, London, 102, IV, 21.

II, 1 pres., *ši-ki-iz-zu ub-ba-lu*, (who) diverts its irrigation, Susa, 16, V, 8.

III, 2 pres., *pân bêl eqli uš-ta-ba-lu*, in the presence of the owner of the field causes it to be taken, London, 101, III, 8.

biltu, (1) tribute, (2) fruit.

(1) tribute, *bilat(GUN)-su kabittim(DUGUD-tim)*, V. A., 2663, II, 14; (2) fruit, *XL* ^{iṣu}*gišimmaru ina bilti(GU.UN)*, V. A., 209, IV, 24.

ודה, **adû,** fix, appoint.

II, 1 part., *mu-ad-du-ú ša-kan irṣiti*, Neb. Nippur, I, 21.

adû, law.

a-na la a-di-šu-nu, contrary to their law, V R. 55, 48.

ולד, **alâdu,** beget.

I, 1 inf., *a-la-ad a-me-lu-ti alpê u ṣênê*, the birth of men, oxen and sheep, London, 102, II, 27; part., *a-bi a-li-di-šu*, V. A., 2663, II, 42.

ilittu, child, offspring.

i-lit-ti ^{m}*Er-ba-*^{d}*Marduk*, V. A., 2663, II, 43.

וסם, **asumittu,** a sculptured and engraved stele.

a-su-mi-it-tu an-ni-i-tu, London, 103, VI, 26.

simtu, decoration.

pl., *simâti*, *ina eš-rit ma-ḫa-zi ilâni rabûti iš-tak-ka-nu si-ma-tu*, works of art, V. A., 2663, II, 47.

ופא, šûpû, brilliant.
(Sin) *šá i-na ilâni rabûti šú-pu-u,* Susa, 3, VI, 43; *^{ilu}Ṣîru ilu šú-pu-ú mâr bîti ša ^{âlu}Di-e-ir,* V. R., 56, 49.

ופה, aptu, dwelling.
pl., *nisê a-pa-ti,* Neb. Nippur, III, 18; *a-pa-a-ti i-na nap-ḫar ṣal-mat qaqqadi,* V. A., 2663, I, 21.

יצא, aṣû, go forth.
I, 1 pret., *ai ú-ṣi ina ú-ša-ki,* Neb. Nippur, IV, 23; pres., *ana ṣi-i-ti la uṣ-ṣi,* C. T., X, pl. III, 8; inf., *mê la a-zi-im-ma,* Susa, 3, III, 7.
II, 2, *i-na qât ^{md}Marduk-zâkir-šumu ù zêri-šu ú-tu-ṣu-ú,* IV R.[2] 38, III, 22.
III, 1, *ai ú-še-ṣi ur-ki-ti,* Susa, 14, III, 13; *lu-ú a-na našû(ZI.GA) ú-še-iṣ-ṣu-ú,* I R. 70, II, 11; *i-na zu-um-ri-šú li-še-ṣi,* Susa, 14, IV, 9; inf., *ul-tu âli-šu la šú-zi-im-ma,* Susa, 3, II, 42.

ṣîtu, that which goes forth.
ṣi-it pi-šu, command, Susa, 3, VI, 30; *ša ṣi-it pi-i-šu la uš-te-pi-il,* V. A., 2663, I, 14; *iq-bi ina ṣi-it pi-i-šu,* V. A., 2663, I, 31; *ṣi-it Bâbili,* offspring of B., V R. 55, 2; *ṣi-i-ti aḫ-[ra]-taš,* late off-spring, C. T., X, pl. IV, 14; *a-na ṣi-i-ti lu uṣ-ṣi,* may he not let go out (of my hands), C. T., X, pl. III, 8.

ṣâtu, eternity.
*a-di ûm(-um) ṣa-a-ti,*I R.70, IV, 25; *a-na ûmê ṣa-a-ti,* Neb. Nippur, III, 12; I R. 66, II, 4; *a-na ûm(-um) ṣa-a-ti,* London, 103, V, 26; Susa, 16, III, 25; I R. 70, I, 17; London, 102, I, 29; C. T., IX, pl. IV, 16; *a-na ûmê(-me) ṣa-a-tu,* V. A., 2663, IV, 55; C. T., X, pl. VI, 30; *a-na ûmê ṣa-ti,* III R. 43, edge IV, 6; *a-na ûm(-mu) ṣa-ti,* V. R. 56, 9; *a-na ṣa-a-at ûmi(-mi),* Susa, 3, VII, 39; *a-na ṣa-a-ti,* Susa, 3, III, 55; *a-na ṣa-ti,* III R. 43, I, 13.

ירד, arâdu, go down.
I, 2, *it-ta-rad a-na ^{h}nakri,* V R. 55, 38.

ירה, arû, lead.
I, 2 part., *mut-tar-ru-ú ba-'-ú-la-ti,* ruler of kingdoms, Neb. Nippur, I, 12.
II, 1 part., *mu-ir-ru,* captain, Susa, 16, IV, 4; Susa 14, II, 3.
III, 2, *muš-ta-ru-ú Sip-par^{ki},* who rules S., V. A., 2663, II, 8.

ירח, arḫu, month.
ar-ḫi ša ši-ṭa-ru-da, months that hasten, IV R.[2] 38, II, 21.

ירך, arki, afterwards.
ar-ki. . . . iq-bi-ma, III R. 43, edge IV, 3; *ar-ki,* London, 103, I, 34; II, 5; *ša ar-ki-šú,* his successor, Susa, 16, II, 26.

arkû, a later one.
bêl bîti ša Bît-^{m}A-da ar-ku-ú, III R. 43, III, 8; edge IV, 1; *man-nu arkû(EGIR-ú),* V. A., 2663, V, 18; C. T., X, pl. VII, 32; D. E. P., II, 97, 10; *ṭuppu bîti ar-ku-ú ù maḫ-ru-ú,* V. A., 209, I, 24; *u ar-ki-i lu-zi-bu,* C. T., X, pl. V, 9; *la i-zi-bu ar-[ki-i],* C. T., X, pl. V, 7; pl., *arkûti, ki-pu-tu ša Bît-^{m}A-da ar-ku-tu,* III R. 43, III, 15; III R. 45, No. 2, 4; pl. fem., *arkâtu,* future, *a-na arkât ûmê,* Susa, 2, III, 2; London, 101, II, 12; D. E. P., VI, 45, V, 8; London, 102, IV, 36; *a-na ar-kat ûmi(-mi),* London, 103, V, 27; V R. 56, 26; O. B. I., 83, II, 11; III R. 41, I, 31; *i-na ar-kat ûmê,* Susa, 3, III, 29; *i-na arkât(EGIR) ûmê,* D. E. P., II, 112, 10; V. A., 209, I, 31; I R. 70, II, 1; London, 102, I, 29; *i-na (ar)-kat ûma(-ma),* V. A., 208, 43; *i-na ar-ka-ti*

ûmi(-mi), III R. 43, III, 1; *likkisû arkât(EGIR)-su*, V. A., 2663, V, 47.

arkânu, adv., later.

ar-ka-nu šattu V ^{md}*Nabû-mukîn-aplu*, London, 102, I, 18.

arkâniš.

i-na ar-ka-niš, in later times, C. T., IX, pl. V, 31.

ירק, **urqîtu,** green herbs.

ai ú-še-ṣi ur-ki-ti, Susa, 14, III, 13; *ki-mu ur-ki-ti id-ra-nu*, III R. 41, II, 33.

ושב, **ašâbu,** dwell.

I, 1 part., *lu-ú qa-at-ti-ni lu-ú a-sib âli*, Susa, 3, II, 36; *a-šib âli-šú*, his citizen, V R. 56, 45; *a-šib šamê(-e) ellûti*, I R. 70, III, 18; *Sin a-šab (šib?) šamê(-e) el-lu-ti*, III R. 43, IV, 7; *ṣâbê a-šib âlâni šú-a-tum*, V R. 56, 9; ^{d}*A-nu-ni-tum a-ši-bat* [*šamê*], London, 101, III, 15; *a-ši-bat šamê(-e)*, D. E. P., VI, 45, IV, 12; (*Šumalia*) *a-ši-bat ri-še-e-ti*, V R. 56, 47; perm., *ma-la ina âlâni . . . . aš-bu*, V R. 56, 4.

III, 1 inf., *šu-šu*[*-ub ma*]*-ḫa-zi*, the preservation of cities, V. A., 2663, II, 23.

šubtu, seat.

šub-tum ù šú-ku-zu ša ^{d}*A-num*, Susa, 2, IV, 1; *ú-na-ka-ru ina šub-ti-šu*, V. A., 2663, V, 28; pl., *šú-ba-tum-šú-nu ud-da-a*, Susa, 2, III, 21; *šú-ba-at-šu-nu ud-da-a*, Susa, 3, VII, 30; *šú-ba-tu-šu-nu ud*(!)*-da-a*, D. E. P., IV, pl. 16, II, 7.

ושר, **ašriš,** submissively.

aš-riš šú-ḫar-ru-ru, Neb. Nippur, I, 8.

ותר, **atâru,** exceed.

III, 1, *ú-ša-tir šùm-šu*, he magnified his name, Neb. Nippur, II, 7; *e-nu-us-su ú-ša-ti-ru*, V. A., 2663, I, 41; *eli ša pa-ni ú-ša-tir-ma*, he enlarged more than it was before, V. A., 2663, III, 30.

atru, earnest money.

ki-i pi-i atri(DIR) lud-dak-ka, as earnest money I will give thee, V. A., 209, I, 15, 21; *ki-i pi-i at-ru*, V. A., 209, IV, 33; *šiqlu ḫurâṣi atru(DIR)*, Susa, 14, I, 14.

atriš, exceedingly.

at-riš a-na du-um-mu-ki, IV R.[2] 38, II, 26.

atarta, powerfully.

i-ṭe-ru-ub a-tar-ta, V R. 55, 39.

atartu, that which has been added, property.

a-tar-ti eqli Bît-^{m}*Ir-ri-ga*, Susa, 3, I, 12; *a-tar-ta eqli âlu ša . . . .*, Susa, 3, I, 16.

זוז, **zâzu,** divide.

I, 1 pret., *ṭup-pi zitti ša . . . a-na mâri-šu i-zu-zu*, the tablet of the share which N. assigned to his son, V. A., 208, 3.

zu'uztu, allotment.

še-pi-it zu-'-uz-tu ša ^{m}*Er-ba-*^{d}*Marduk*, V. A., 2663, III, 51.

zûtu, blindness.

zu-ut pa-ni sa-ka-ak uz-ni, Susa, 14, III, 4.

זיר, **zâru,** hate.

I, 1, imp., *limutta(-ta) zi-ir-ma kit-ta ra-*[*am*], O. B. I., 83, II, 24.

I, 2 pres., *ki-it-ta ir-tam-ma qu-ul-lul-ta iz-zi-ir*, Susa, 3, IV, 54; *ki-it-te iz-zi-ir-ma*, V, 20.

זכה, **zakû,** be free.

I, 1 pret., ^{md} *Marduk-kudur-uṣur iz-kam-ma*, London, 103, V, 18; ^{m}*Zêr-ukîn iz-kam-ma*, London, 102, IV, 17; perm., *ša ina šarri pa-na za-ku-ma*, which under a former king had been freed, V R. 55, 48; *maḫ-ru ap-lu za-ku-ú*, London, 102, IV, 34; *ma-ḫir a-pil za-ku*, it has been received, it has been paid, he is freed, V A., 209, I, 27; II, 39; III, 14, 26; V, 1.

II, 1 pret., *a-na ûm(-um) ṣa-ti ú-zak-ki*, forever he freed, V R. 56, 31; *ú-zak-ku-ú*, I R. 66, I, 5; *ú-za-ki-šú-nu-ti-ma*, he freed them, C. T., IX, pl. V, 39; inf., *zu-uk-ki ša ^{âlu}Bît-Sik-ka-mi-du*, the safety of . . . ., Susa, 3, II, 22; perm., *ra-ša-a ul zak-ki*, the creditor has not been satisfied, London, 102, IV, 39.

zakûtu, freedom.

za-ku-ut âli-šu . . . . iš-ku-nu-ma, Susa, 3, III, 43; *za-ku-tu iš-ku-nu*, Susa, 3, IV, 5, 21; *za-ku-tú aš-ku-nu*, Susa, 3, IV, 32, 57; V, 31; *za-ku-us-su iš-kun*, Susa, 3, II, 7; *i-na za-ku-ut âlâni šú-a-tum*, V R. 56, 11; *za-ku-tu-šu-nu*, V R. 55, 50; *za-ku-tu ša . . . . ú-zak-ku-ú*, I R. 66, I, 1; perhaps also III R. 45, No. 2, 1.

I. זכר, **zakâru,** name, mention.

I, 1 perm., *šùm-šu-nu za-ak-ru*, Susa, 2, III, 19; Susa, 3, VII, 29; I R. 70, IV, 23; London, 103, VI, 22; London, 102, V, 6; London, 101, IV, [5]; V R. 56, 37; O. B. I., 149, II, 15; III, 10; III R. 41, II, 36; V. A., 2663, V, 46; *šú-un-šú-nu za-ak-ru*, III R. 43, III, 24; IV, 33; III R. 43, edge II, 1; *šumâti-šú-nu za-ak-ru*, Susa, 16, VI, 10; D. E. P., VI, 43, IV, 9; *i-[na narî] za-ak-ru*, D. E. P., II, 113, 21.

II, 1 *um-ma-šú la zu-uk-ku-ra-[at]*, London, 103, I, 31.

zikru, name, naming.

zi-kir ^dApsû i-pal-la-ḫu, O. B. I., 83, II, 14; *a-na zi-kir šumi-šu*, at the mention of his name, V. A., 2663, II, 34; *mu-dam-me-iq zi-kir a-bi*, V. A., 2663, II, 42.

II. זכר, **zikru,** hero.

zi-ik-ru qar-du, V R. 55, 7.

זמה, **zamû,** bar, keep back.

II, 1 prec., *bît-su li-za-mi-ma*, from his house may he bar him, Susa, 3, VI, 53; *li-za-am-mi ^dAš-na-an*, may he keep back the grain, Susa, 14, III, 12.

זמר, **zumru,** body.

i-na zu-um-ri-šú liš-ku-un-ma, Susa, 3, VII, 21; *i-na zu-um-ri-šu liš-kum-ma*, I R. 70, IV, 6; D. E. P., VI, 47, 13; *i-na zu-'u-ri-šú li-iš-kum-ma*, III R. 43, IV, 16; *i-na zumri(SU)-šu liškun (ŠA)-ma*, Neb. Nippur, IV, 21; *i-na zumri(SU)-šú li-šab-ši-ma*, III R. 41, II, 30; *[i-n]a zu-um-ri-šú li-šab-šú-ma*, O. B. I., 149, III, 3, 7; *ina zu-um-ri-šu li-šab-ši-ma*, London, 102, II, 21; *liq-ta-a zumur(SU)-šu*, V. A., 2663, V, 44; *zu-mur-šú lil-la(!)-ib-[biš]-ma*, Susa, 16, VI, 15; *li-bi-bi-ša zu-mu-ur-šú*, III R. 43, IV, 9; *i-na zu-um-ri-šú li-še-ṣi*, Susa, 14, IV, 8.

I. זנן, **zanânu,** preserve.

II, 1 prec., *li-za-nin-ma ḫa-zi-ni-šú*, O. B. I., 80, 1.

II. זנן, **zunnu,** rain.

(Rammân) *bêl naq-bi ù zu-un-ni*, V R. 56, 41.

זקף, **zaqpu,** cultivated.

a-di ^{iṣu}kirî zaq-pi, V. A., 208, 8; *eqlu ^{iṣu}gišimmaru zaq-pu*, V. A., 208, 35; *^{iṣu}kirû ^{iṣu}gišimmaru zaq-pu u pi-i [šul-pi]*, C. T., X, pl. VI, 24.

זקר, **tizqaru,** sublime.

šarru ti-iz-qa-ru, D. E. P., II, 115, 5.

זרא$_4$, **zarû,** beget, create.

I, 1 part., *za-ri-i-šu*, V. A., 2663, I, 10.

zêru, (1) seedfield.

^{she'u}zêru, passim.

(2) seed, offspring.
Susa, 2, III, 26; Susa, 3, IV, 3, 19, 30, 55; V, 28; London, 101, III, 17; IV, 8; IV R.[2] 38, III, 22, 37; *zi-i-ri-šu*, Susa, 14, IV, 14; D. E. P., IV, pl. 16, II, 9; V R. 56, 40, 60; III R. 41, II, 38; I R. 70, IV, 25; O. B. I., 149, II, 20; V. A., 2663, II, 40; V, 46; C. T., X, pl. IV, 13; Neb. Nippur, V, 7.

זרב, **zarâbu,** be pressed (cf. p. 170).
II, 1 inf., *ina zu-ru-ub ZI-ŠAG-GAL-li,* because of the utterance of supplication, Neb. Nippur, II, 12.

זרש, **zuršu,** abundance, plenty.
zur-šu ba-ru-ḫu, V. A., 2663, II, 16.

ZI.ŠAG.GAL=li, supplication (cf. p. 170).
ik-ri-bi u ZI.ŠAG.GAL-li, O. B. I., 83, I, 17; *ina zu-ru-ub ZI.SAG.-GAL-li,* Neb. Nippur, II, 12.

zittu, share.
ṭup-pi zitti(ḪA.LA), V. A., 208, 1; *a-na zittu* (*ḪA.*[*LA*]) *ú-tir-am-ma,* to the (original) possession (owners) he returned them, V. A., 2663, III, 23; *zi-it-ti ma-na*[*-ma*], no share, C. T., X, pl. V, 13.

חבץ, **ḫabâṣu,** be abundant.
I, 1 inf., *na-ḫa-ša ḫa-ba-ṣa li-kim-šú-ma,* abundance and overflowing may he take from him, Neb. Nippur, IV, 11.

ḫabṣu, rich (cf. p. 169).
ina igisê(ŠI.DI) ḫab-ṣu-ú-ti, Neb. Nippur, II, 9.

Ḫabirai, the Habirean.
Ku-dur-ra mâr ^{m}Ḫi(?)-ri-šú-ru Ḫa-bir-ai, O. B. I., 149, I, 22.

ḫegallu, affluence.
šanâti duḫ-di nu-uḫ-ši u ḫé-gál, years of plenty, abundance and affluence, Susa, 3, V, 18; *šar ḫé-gál-lim,* D. E. P., VI, 43, III, 7; D. E. P., II, 116, 6.

חדה, **ḫadû,** to rejoice.
II, 1 inf., *libbi be-li-šú . . . ḫu-ud-di-i,* to gladden the heart of his lord, IV R.[2] 38, II, 19; *i-na ḫu-ud libbi(-bi)-šu,* V. A., 209, I, 23; *i-na li-ti u ḫu-ud libbi(-bi),* V R. 55, 44.

ḫadiš, joyfully.
ḫa-diš ip-pa-lis-ma, C. T., X, pl. III, 10; *ḫa-diš ip-pal-su-šu-ma,* V. A., 2663, I, 29; *ḫa-diš ip-pa-lis-su-ma,* V. A., 2663, III, 41.

חוז, **maḫâzu,** city.
^{âlu}Di-e-ir ma-ḫa-az ^{d}A-num, V R. 55, 14; *ma-ḫa-az da-*[*a*]*d-me,* Neb. Nippur, II, 2; pl., *i-na ma-ḫa-ze rabûti,* V. A., 2663, II, 13; *šu-šu-*[*ub ma*]*-ḫa-ze,* V. A., 2663, II, 23; *ina eš-rit ma-ḫa-ze,* V. A., 2663, II, 45.

חזן, **ḫazannu,** magistrate.
^{h}ḫa-za-an-nu Ḫa-ni, London, 101, I, 18; *^{h}ḫa-za-an Bît-^{m}Pir-^{d}Amur-ru,* Susa, 14, I, 10; Susa, 3, I, 35; *ḫa-za-an piḫâti ša Bît-^{m}Pir-^{d}Amurru,* Susa, 3, VI, 7; *^{h}ḫa-za-an Bît-^{m}A-da,* III R. 43, II, 25; *lu-ú ḫa-za-an-ni ša Bît-^{m}A-da,* III R. 43, III, 10; III R. 45, No. 2, 4; *lu-ú ḫa-za-an-na ša ^{mâtu}Al-ni-ri-e-a,* III R. 45, No. 2, 5; *^{h}ḫa-za-an ^{âlu}Nippur^{ki},* Neb. Nippur, III, 12, 32; *ḫa-za-an ^{âlu}Dûr-Rîm-^{d}Sin,* Neb. Nippur, V, 19; *ḫa-za-an-nu,* Susa, 14, II, 2; III R. 41, I, 32; IV R.[2] 38, III, 2; Neb. Nippur, III, 20; O. B. I., 149, I, 19; II, 3; V. A., *^{h}ḫa-za-an-nu(na),* 208, 41; V. A., 2663, V, 6, 20; C. T., X, pl. VII, 33; V. A., 209, V, 16; pl., *^{h}ḫa-za-an-na-ti,* Susa, 2, I, 17; *ḫa-za-an-na-tim,* Susa, 2, III, 7.

חטט, **ḫaṭṭu,** scepter.
^{işu}ḫaṭṭu i-šar-ti, V. A., 2663, I, 34.

חיט, **ḫâṭu,** inspect, examine.
I, 1 pret., *kul-la-tan nišê i-ḫi-iṭ,* V.

A., 2663, I, 21; *L šiqlu kašpi ša i-ḫi-iṭ-ma id-da-aš-šu-nu*, V. A., 209, IV, 32; *V šiqlu kaspi šîm gam-ru-tu ša . . . i-ḫi-iṭ-ma . . id-din*, V. A., 209, IV, 35.

חיר, **ḫîrtu,** consort.
ᵈGu-la bêltu rabîtu(-tu) ḫi-rat ᵈNIN.IB, III R. 43, IV, 15; *ḫi-rat Šamaš-šûtu(UD.GAL.LU)*, I R. 70, IV, 5.

חלף, **naḫlaptu,** mantle.
IX ṣubâtu naḫlaptu(TIK.UD.DU), III R. 41, I, 24.

חלק, **ḫalâqu,** destroy.
I, 1 prec., *zêra-šu li-iḫ-liq*, V R. 56, 60.
II, 1 pres., *ku-dur-ri eqlu šú-a-tu . . . ú-na-ak-ka-ru ú-ḫal-liq-qu*, London, 103, V, 43; prec., *šùm-šú li-ḫal-li-qu*, Susa, 2, III, 25; Susa, 16, VI, 24; London, 103, VI, 23; D. E. P., VI, 47, 14; *li-ḫal-liq šùm-su*, London, 101, III, 12; *li-ḫal-li-qu zêra-šú*, V R. 56, 40; *[aggiš li-ḫal]-liq-šú*, London, 101, III, 9; *zêra-šu liḫal-liqû(ḪA.A.ME*, for which text has *A.ḪA.ME*), Neb. Nippur, V, 7; *li-ḫal-li-qu piri'-šu*, I R. 70, III, 12; *li-ḫal-li-qu pi-ri-iḫ-šú*, III R. 43, III, 28; *ᵈNisaba(ŠE.ELTEK) li-ḫal-li-qa*, I R. 70, IV, 12; *mârê zêri-šu li[-ḫal]-li-[qu]*, O. B. I., 149, II, 20; *ina pî nišê di-ša-a-ti li-ḫal-li-qu*, III R. 41, II, 39; *i-(na) pî nišê li-ḫal-liq*, London, 102, II, 18; *ina pî nišê liḫalliqû(ḪA.A.ME)*, V. A., 2663, V, 47.
II, 2 (*abnu narû*) *i-ta-bat uḫ-tal-liq*, Susa, 3, V, 56.

I. חמט, **ḫamâṭu,** hasten.
I, 1 inf., *a-na aṭ-ri ḫa-ma-aṭ*, V R. 56, 10, for the support (cf. Hilprecht, *Assyriaca*, p. 5f, note 3).
III, 1 inf., *šú-uḫ-mu-ṭu ma-ḫar bêl bêlê iš-te-'-u-ma*, V. A., 2663, II, 18.

ḫanṭiš, quickly.
ḫa-an-ṭi-iš lik-ki-sa na-ap-šat-[su], V R. 56, 57.

II. חמט, **ḫamâṭu,** be hot.
I, 1 pres., *i-ḫa-am-ma-ṭu ki nab-li*, V R. 55, 18.

חנב, **ḫanâbu,** grow up in abundance.
I, 1 prec., *pu-qut-tu li-iḫ-nu-bi*, III R. 41, II, 33.

חסס, **ḫasâsu,** think, remember.
I, 2, *a-na limutti(-ti) li-iḫ-ta-as-su-šú-ma*, V R. 56, 52.

ḫasisu, understanding.
ḫa-si-sa pal-ka, V., 2663, III, 6.

חפה, **ḫapû,** break, destroy.
I, 1 pret., *lu i-iḫ-pu-ú*, D. E. P., II, 113, 15; *lu iḫ-p[i-i]*, D. E. P., VI, 45, V, 11; *iḫ-pi mâtu Êlamtu*, C. T., IX, pl. IV, 10; inf., *ana ḫa-pi-e abnu narû šú-a-tu*, V. A., 2663, V, 22; *i-na ḫi-pi-e bîti-šú*, V R. 56, 58.
II, 1 *i-na eli na-ri-e šú-a-tum i-ga-ru 'u-a-bit-ma 'u-ḫe-pi*, Susa, 2; Med., II, 6.

חצב, **ḫaṣbu,** terra cotta (cf. p. 21[3]).
na-ra-a ša ḫa-aṣ-bi, Susa, 2; Med., I, 3.

ḫiṣbu, wealth.
ḫi-ṣib tam-tim rapaštim (DAGAL-tim), V. A., 2663, II, 15.

חצן, **ḫazinnu,** axe.
li-za-nin-ma ḫa-zi-ni-šú, O. B. I., 80, 1.

חצץ, **ḫiṣṣatu,** enclosure, dyke.
ku-šá-ar-ti ù ḫi-iṣ-ṣa-ti šá nâr šarri, Susa, 3, II, 21.

חרה, **ḫirû,** dig.
I, 1 inf., *ḫi-ru-ut nâr šarri la ḫi-ri-e*, Susa, 3, II, 33; *amel ḫi-ri-e nâra*, a canal-digger, Neb. Nippur, III, 25.

ḫirû, canal.
a-na eli ḫi-ru âlu Man-du-u, D. E. P., VI, 42, I, 9.

ḫirûtu, digging, excavation.
ḫi-ru-ut nâr šarri la ḫi-ri-e, Susa, 3, II, 32.

ḫirîtu, canal.
lu a-na na-ri i-na[-ad-du-ú] lu a-na ḫi-ri-ti i-na[-as-su-ku], D. E. P., VI, 45, V, 15.

ḫarrânu, road.
harrâna(KAS) ù ti-tur-ra . . . la a-ma-ri, Susa, 3, III, 22; *iṣ-ṣa-bat ḫa-ra-a-na,* V R. 55, 16; *ḫarrâna(KAS) la a-ma-ri,* V R. 56, 2; *ḫar-ra-an-na pa-ri-ik-ta li-še-iṣ-bi-su,* III R. 43, IV, 30.

ḫurâṣu, gold.
šîm MA.NA ša ḫurâṣi, London, 103, III, 21; *šiqlu ḫurâṣi,* Susa, 14, I, 12, 14; *šuššu(KU) ḫurâṣi(AZAG.GI),* London, 102, IV, 25.

חרר, **ḫarru,** canal.
ba-ba-at ḫar-ri ^{âlu}*Šá-sa-na*^{ki}, O. B. I., 149, I, 10; *ḫa-ar-ri* ^{âlu}*Šá-sa-na*^{ki}, O. B. I., 149, I, 5; *[ḫar]-ri ša* ^{m}*Amel . . . .,* C. T., X, pl. VI, 22; *ḫar-ri ša* ^{m}*Nâdin . . . .,* C. T., X, pl. VI, 26; cf. also *Ḫa-ar-ri-Ba-ṣi,* Susa, 3, I, 24.

ḫurru, hole.
ḫur-ri pi-šu, his throat, I R. 70, IV, 19.

ḫuršânu, compromise(?).
ṭuppâni(?) a-na ḫur-ša-an il-tu-ra-aš-šú-nu-tim-ma, London, 103, IV, 38; *ṭuppâni(?) a-na ḫur-ša-an a-na* ^{âlu}*Parak-mâri*^{ki} *il-tu-ra-aš-šú-um-ma,* London, 103, V, 14; *a-na ḫur-šá-an la il-lik,* London, 103, V, 4; *i-na ḫur-ša-an i-na* ^{âlu}*Parak-mâri* ^{m}*Marduk-kudur-uṣur iz-kam-ma,* London, 103, V, 17; *a-na ḫur-ša-an iš-pur-ma* ^{m}*Zêr-ukîn iz-kam-ma,* London, 102, IV, 16 (cf. K. B., IV, 168, II, 6–7, *di-in-šu-nu u-par-su-ma ḫur-ša-an ina muḫ-ḫi-šu-nu ip-ru-su*).

חשח, **ḫušaḫḫu,** famine, want.
šanâte ḫu-ša-aḫ-ḫi, London, 101, IV, 10; *bu-bu-ta u ḫu-ša-aḫ-ḫa,* V R. 56, 43; *[mârê]-šu a-na ḫu-šaḫ-ḫi [li-ir-te-id-di(?)],* London, 102, I, 45.

חתח, **ḫatû,** defeat.
I, 1 pret., *ša* ^{mâtu}*Aššur(AŠ) iḫtû(?)* III R. 43, I, 5; II, 27.

טא$_4$ם, **ṭêmu,** report, command.
ṭe-im-šú . . . ú-tir-ma, he brought his report, London, 103, III, 1; V, 10, 19; *ṭe-im-šú-nu ú-tir-ru-ma,* London, 103, III, 38; *ṭe-e-ma iš-kun-šú-ma,* he gave him command, London, 103, III, 8; *amelûti ša ṭe-mi-šú,* men of its council, Susa, 3, II, 38; ^{h}*ša-kin ṭe-mi mât* ^{âlu}*Ir-ri-ḫa,* D. E. P., VI, 44, I, 12; ^{h}*ša-kin ṭe-me,* commander, Neb. Nippur, III, 15; V, 17; *šakin(GAR-in) ṭe-mi,* Susa, 16, III, 30; ^{h}*šakin(GAR-in) ṭe-mi,* O. B. I., 149, II, 3; *šakin(GAR) ṭe-mi mâti,* V R. 56, 13; *šakin(GAR) ṭe-mi ša Bît-*^{m}*A-da,* III. R. 43, III, 43, 11.

טוב, **ṭâbu,** be good.
II 1 pret., *i-na eli buší ú-ṭib-u-ma,* regarding the property they made good, London, 102, VI, 13; inf., *i-na li-mu-ut-ti ù la ṭûb(DUG-ub) šêri,* in misery and discomfort of body, IV R.[2] 38, III, 39; *i-na [ṭûb lib]-bi ù da[miqti iš]-pur,* Susa, 16, I, 9.

ṭâbu, good.
a-la-la ṭa-a-ba a-na ši-im-ti-šú la i-man-nu-ú, London, 103, VI, 6.

ṭâbtu, prosperity.
a-na limutti(-ti) ù lâ ṭâbti(DUG-ti) li-ir-te-id-du-šú, III R. 41, II, 37.

טחה, **ṭiḫû,** approach.
I, 1 pret., *a-na ni-ši-šú ai iṭ-ḫi,* Susa, 16, VI, 19; *ma-ḫar šarri bêli-šú iṭ-ḫi-ma,* O. B. I., 83, I, 19.

טיט, **ṭîṭu,** mire.

qâtâ-šu ṭi-ṭa li-ru-ba, V R. 56, 58; *ni-is-ḫi ša ṭi-i-ṭi,* extract of the clay (tablet), C. T., IX, pl. V, 42.

ṭuppu, tablet.

i-na ka-na-ak li-ú u ṭup-pi eqli, Susa, 16, III, 11, 15; *i-na ka-nak ṭup-pi šú-a-tu,* I R. 66, II, 5; *i-na ka-nak* ^{abnu}*ṭuppi(DUB) šú-a-tu,* C. T., X, pl. III, 23; V. A., 208, 48; *i-na ka-nak ṭuppi(IM.DUB) šú-a-tu,* V. A., 209, II, 11; V, 13; *ina ka-nak ṭuppi(IM) šumâtu(MU.MEŠ),* V. A., 2663, IV, 56; C. T., X, pl. VII, 41; *ṭuppâni a-na ḫur-ša-an il-tu-ra-aš-šú-nu-tim-ma,* London, 103, IV, 38; V, 14; *ṭup-pi zitti(ḪA.LA),* V. A., 208, 1; ^{h}*ṭup-šar ša-ṭir* ^{abnu}*ṭuppu(DUB),* V A., 208, 52; *ṭup-pi eqli,* V. A., 208, 32; *ṭup-pi bar-mu,* V. A., 2663, V, 50; *ṭuppa(IM.DUB)-šu ku-nu-uk-ma bi-in-ni,* V. A., 209, I, 14; *ṭuppu(IM.DUB) bîti ar-ku-ú u maḫ-ru-ú,* V. A., 209, I, 24; *ṭuppu(IM.DUB) la ta-a-ru u la da-ba-bu ik-nu-uk-ma,* V. A., 209, IV, 13, 36. (For the reading *ṭuppu* cf. Hebr. טפסר; Sab. טף (Hommel, *Aufsätze,* p. 141); see also Zimmern, K. A. T.[3], p. 400[5], and Hilprecht, B. E., XX, Pt. 1, p. 17[5]).

ṭupšikku, forced labor.

il-ki ṭup-ši-ki, C. T., IX, pl. V, 38; *al-(lu) du-up-ši-ki,* III R. 45, No. 2, 2 (cf. *tu-up-ši-kam* and *tu-up-ši-ka-a-ti,* O. B. I., Vol. I, No. 84, cols. II, 58; III, 5, 22).

ṭupšarru, scribe (Hebr. טפסר).

ṭup-šar ša mâti, London, 101, I, 19; *ṭup-šar šarri,* Susa, 16, II, 9; *ṭup-šar,* Susa, 16, III, 5; Neb. Nippur, V, 18; O. B. I., 149, I, 16, 17; (Nabû) *ṭup-šar E-sag-ila,* D. E. P., VI, 46, IV, 4; *ṭup-šar ša-ṭi-ir* ^{abnu}*narî an-ni-i,* V R. 56, 25; ^{h}*ṭup-šar ša-ṭir* ^{abnu}*ṭup-pu(DUB),* V. A., 208, 28, 52; V. A., 209, II, 22; ^{h}*ṭup-šar êkalli,* V. A., 2663, V, 15.

טרד, **ṭarâdu,** drive away.

I, 2, *ûmi(-mi) šá na-ka-da ar-ḫi šá ši-ṭa-ru-da,* days that pass quickly(?), months that hurry on(?), IV R.[2] 38, II, 21.

IV, 1 prec., *abulli âli-šu ka-meš liṭ-ṭa-rid,* may he be driven away, Susa, 16, VI, 16; *ina pâni-šu lim-niš iṭ-ṭa-ra-du,* V. A., 2663, II, 36.

יד, **idu,** side.

a-na i-di li-mut-ti iz-za-az-zu-ma, III R. 41, II, 1; *a-na i-di ram-ni-šu-nu ú-tir-ru-ma,* they turned them (the fields) to their own use, C. T., X, pl. V, 5; *a-na i-di ram-ni-šu ú-tar-ru,* C. T., X, pl. VI, 34.

ידא$_4$, **idû,** to know.

II, 1 perm., *šú-ba-tum-šú-nu ud-da-a,* whose seats are made visible, *šú-ba-at-šu-nu ud-da-a,* Susa, 3, VII, 30; *eš-ri-tu-šú-nu ud-da-a,* IV R.[2] 38, III, 31; *šu-ba-tu-šu-nu ud(!)-da-a,* D. E. P., IV, pl. 16, II, 7; *ni-ši-ir-ti gi-iṣ-ṣa-a-tu ud-da[a],* C. T., X, pl. VII, 34.

III, 1, *ú-še-id-di-šú-nu-ti,* inform, London, 103, I, 35; *ú-še-id-di,* London, 103, II, 6; *aḫê-šu i-šal-ma ú-šá-ad-di-ma,* London, 103, V, 3 (cf. וא$_4$ר).

mûdû, intelligent.

lâ mu-da-a, a witless man, London, 103, V, 42; Susa, 3, V, 50; Susa, 16, IV, 27; Susa, 14, II, 16; I R. 70, II, 23; V. A., 2663, V, 26; *mu-du-u kal šip-ri,* who understands everything, V. A., 2663, II, 49.

יום, **ûmu,** day, *passim.*

ûmišamma, daily.

ûmi(-mi)-šam-ma, I R. 70, III, 23.

ימן, **imittu**, right hand.
šà *^{iṣu}ma-ša-ra-šú bît*(?) *i-mit-ti šarri*, V R. 55, 26, 36.

יצר, **eṣêru**, form, sculpture.
II, 1 perm., *ú-ṣu-ra-tu-šu-nu uṣ-ṣu-ra*, Susa, 3, VII, 34; D. E. P., II, 113, 21; D. E. P., IV, pl. 16, II, 8.
uṣurtu, picture, bas relief.
pl., *ú-ṣu-ra-tu-šu-nu uṣ-su-ra*, Susa, 3, VII, 33; D. E. P., II, 113, 21; *uṣurâti*(*GIŠ.ḪAR*)-*šú-nu uṣ-ṣu-ra*, D. E. P., IV, pl. 16, II, 8.

ia=a=ši, me.
šu-ú ia-a-ši la u-qal-la-la, Susa, 3, IV, 28.

ישה, **išû**, have.
I, 1 pret., *šâninu la*(*NU*) *išû*(*TUK*), relat., V R. 55, 23; *i-na i-lik ^{mâtu}Na-mar išî*(*AN.TUK-i*) *gab-bi-šú*, V R. 56, 6; *lil-li ai îši*, Neb. Nippur, IV, 14; *na-da-na ul i-ši-ma*, London, 102, IV, 19; *ru-gu-um-ma-a lâ i-šú-u*, pl., London, 102, IV, 34; *ša . . . la* [*i*]-*šú-u tam-šil-šu*, V.A., 2663, II, 32; *ru-gam-ma-a ul i-ši*, V. A., 209, I, 28; II, 39; III, 15, 27; V, 1.

ישר, **ašâru**, to be right.
III, 2, *di-in-šú la uš-te-eš-še-ru*, may they not let his cause succeed, London, 103, VI, 10; part., *muš-te-ši-ru te-ni-še-e-ti*, the ruler of mankind, V. A., 2663, I, 12.
išaru, righteous.
f., *^{iṣu}ḫaṭṭu*(*PA*) *i-šar-ti*, V. A., 2663, I, 34.
mêšaru, righteousness.
di-in me-ša-ri, V R. 55, 6; *di-in kit-ti u me-ša-ri*, Neb. Nippur, IV, 18; *šàr me-ša-ri*, Neb. Nippur, IV, 18; *šanâti mi-ša-ri*, O. B. I., 83, II, 19.

כבב, **kabâbu**, burn.
I, 1 pres., *i-kab-ba-bu ki-i i-ša-ti*, V R. 55, 17

כבס, **kabâsu**, tread, walk.
I, 1 pret., *ri-bi-it âli-šú ai ik-bu-us*, Susa, 3, VII, 4; part., (Šumalia) *ka-bi-sa-at kup-pa-a-ti*, V R. 56, 47.
II, 1 prec., *mi-ṣir-šú li-ka-bis*, III R. 41, II, 28; *li-kab-bi-sa šêpâ-šú* I R. 70, IV, 15; *ši-ir bi-ra-a li-kab-bi-sa* (dual) *še-pa-šú*, III R. 43, IV, 6.

כבת, **kabtu**, heavy, mighty.
ka-bit mâtâti, Neb. Nippur, I, 12; f., *iš-ru-ba-a mûti*(*BAD-ti*) *an ka-bit-ta*, a serious condition, Susa, 16, VI, 14; *bilat*(*GUN*)-*su kabittim*(*DUGUD-tim*), V. A., 2663, II, 15; *še-rit-su kabit-tu*(*DUGUD-tu*), V. A., 2663 V, 42.
kabittu, mind.
nu-gu ka-bit-ti nu-mur lib-bi, Neb. Nippur, IV, 10; *ú-ša-li-iṣ kab-ta-as-su-nu*, V. A., 2663, III, 31.

*^{h}*KAD, title of an official.
London, 101, I, 22.

kidûdê, temples, shrines.
a-na ud-du-šu [*eš-*]*rit . . .u šul-lum ki-du-di-e*, V. A., 2663, II, 24.

כדן, **kidin(n)u**, protection.
ṣâbê ki-di-nu, clients, V. A., 2663, III, 11, 24, 32.

כדר, **kudurru**, boundary stone.
^{d}Nabû-nâṣir-kudur-eqlâti, Susa, 2, IV, 34; *bêl ku-dur-ri*, London, 103, VI, 11; D. E. P., II, 113, 3; *bêl mi-iṣ-ri ù ku-dur-ri*, O. B. I., 149, III, 2; III R. 41, II, 27; D. E. P., IV, pl. 16, I, 7; Neb. Nippur, IV, 19; *ku-dur-ri eqlu šú-a-tu*, London, 103, V, 39; *kudurra-šu lissuh*(*ZI-uḫ*), Neb. Nippur, IV, 19; *ku-dur-ra-*[*šu*] *li-is-su-ḫu*, IV R.[2] 38, III, 35; *ku-dur-ra-šú li-is-su-uḫ*, III R. 41, II, 27; *ku-dur-ri an-ni-i*, London, 103, VI, 21; I R. 70,

II, 8; *ú-sa mi-iṣ-ra ù ku-dur-ra*, III R. 43, III, 20; IV, 2; I R. 70, II, 13; *us-su mi-ṣir-šú u ku-dur-ra-šu*, I R. 70, IV, 4; *ku-dur-ra ú-na-ka-ru*, O. B. I., 150, II, 1; *kudurri(ŠA.DU)-ši-na nu-uk-ku-ru-ma*, V. A., 2663, III, 21; *ku-dur-ra ú-na-ak-ka-ru*, Susa, 16, IV, 19; *ku-dur-ra-ša ul ut-ta[k-k]ar*, O. B. I., 83, II, 2; *ku-dur-ra-ša ut-tak-kir*, O. B. I., 83, II, 5; *li-bu-tu ku-dur-ra-šú*, V R. 56, 40; *ku-dur-ra-šu li-na-qir*, London, 103, VI, 12; *be-el ab-li šu-ú-mi ù ku-dur-ri*, Susa, 3, VII, 8; *šùm ku-dur-[ri]*, London, 101, I, 1; *[d]NIN.IB u [d]Nusku mu-kin ku-dur-ri šumišu(MU.-NE)*, Neb. Nippur, heading 2; *a-na ku-dur da-ra-a-ti*, Susa, 3, III, 53; pl., *bêl ku-dur-ri-e-ti*, III R. 43, IV, 19; *na-ṣir ku-dur-ri-ti*, V R. 55, 5.

כול, **kâlu,** hold, sustain.

II, 1 part., *mu-kil mâtâti*, Neb. Nippur, I, 20.

כום, **kûm,** prep., instead of.

ku-um 887 *kaspê*, London, 102, IV, 29.

kêmu, place, instead of.

ki-mu eqlu la i-nam-di-na-aš-šum-ma (kîmû = ina kêmi), Susa, 3, IV, 48; *eqlu ki-mu la uš-ta-an-na-aš-šum-ma*, Susa, 3, V, 13; *ki-mu ur-qi-ti id-ra-nu*, III R. 41, II, 33; *[ki]-mu-ú ŠE.BAR la ši-ri-iš*, London, 102, II, 11; *ki-mu-ú mê id-ra-na*, London, 102, II, 12.

kummu, sanctuary.

e-piš ku-um-mu ki-iṣ-ṣi u si-ma-ku, V. A., 2663, II, 11.

כון, **kânu,** establish, fix.

II, 1 pret., *iš-ṭur-ma ú-kin*, Susa, 2; Med., II, 11; *a-na da-ra-a-ti ú-ki-in-nu*, relat., Susa, 3, V, 39; *a-na [m]Mu-un-na-bit-ti ú-kin-nu*, Susa, 16, II, 12; *ú-kin kudurru*, V. A., 2663, III, 29; part., *mu-kin iš-di ma-a-ti*, Neb. Nippur, II, 24; V. A., 2663, II, 44; C. T., X, pl. IV, 13; *mu-ki-in ku-dur-ri da-ra-ti*, III R. 41, heading 2, II, 40; *mu-kin-nu ab-li-e*, V R. 55, 5; *[d]NIN.IB u [d]Nusku mu-kin ku-dur-ri*, Neb. Nippur, heading 2.

kênu, faithful.

rê'û kênu(GI.NA), V. A., 2663, II, 25; *rê'û ki-nu*, Neb. Nippur, I, 21; *rê'î ki-ni*, Neb. Nippur, II, 15; *an-na-šú ki-i-nu*, Susa, 3, VII, 48; pl., *šàr ki-na-a-ti*, king of justice, V R. 55, 6.

kîniš, faithfully.

ki-niš ip-pa-lis-ma, Neb. Nippur, I, 24; *ki-niš ippalis(ŠI.BAR)-su-ma*, Neb. Nippur, II, 16; *ki-niš lip-pal-sa-šú-ma*, O. B. I., 83, II, 16; *ki-niš ut-tu-ú-ma*, V. A., 2663, I, 24; *šum-šu ki-niš im-bu-u*, V. A., 2663, II, 55; *ki-niš iš[-'-al-]šu*, C. T., X, pl. V, 11.

kittu, righteousness.

ki-it-ta ir-tam-ma, Susa, 3, IV, 53; *ki-it-te iz-zi-ir-ma*, Susa, 3, V, 20; *kit-ta ra-[am]*, O. B. I., 83, II, 23.

mukinnu, witness.

an-nu-tu mu-kin-nu[pl], V. A., 209, V, 20.

kizû, bodyguard, servant.

na-an-za-az maḫ-ḫar šarri ki-zu-ú, Neb. Nippur, II, 18.

כי, **kî,** as.

ki[-i] a-na]-ku, Susa 3, IV, 1; *ki-i pi-i*, according to the word, Susa, 3, IV, 13, 34, 44; V, 10; III R. 43, I, 10, 22; London, 102, III, 10; *ki-i pi-i atri(DIR)*, as earnest money, V. A., 209, I, 15; *ki-i pi-i at-ru*, V. A., 209, IV, 33; *ki-i mê*, I R. 70, IV, 8;

aš-ri-im ki-i limutti(-ti), Susa, 3, V, 42; *ki-i purîmi*, London, 102, I, 47; *ki-i I MA(-NA)*, for, V. A., 208, 38; *ki-i šiqlu kaspi*, London, 102, IV, 23, 24, 25; V. A., 209, I, 6; II, 36; *bîta ki-i(!) bîti*, house for house, V. A., 209, I, 10, 20; *ki-i išteniš(I-iš)*, alike, V. A., 2663, III, 28.

kîâm, thus.
ki-a-am iq-bu-ú, D. E. P., II, 93, II, 17; V. A., 209, IV, 18; *ki-am iq-bi*, London, 103, IV, 21; *ki-a-am iq-bi um-ma*, London, 102, IV, 20; VI, 9; C. T., X, pl. V, 11; V. A., 209, I, 5; IV, 6; *ki-a-am iq-bi-šú*, O. B. I., 83, I, 19; *ki-a-am iš-kun*, Susa, 3, II, 8.

kîma, as.
ki-ma me-e, Susa, 3, VII, 25; D. E. P., IV, pl. 16, II, 4; III R. 43, IV, 18; London, 102, II, 23; Neb. Nippur, IV, 21; Susa, 2, III, 34; III R. 41, II, 31; *ki-ma ši-ṭi-ir šamê(-e)*, IV R.[2] 38, II, 27; *ki-ma ṣu-ba-ti*, Susa, 3, VI, 49; *ki-ma ú-ma-am ṣi-ri*, Susa, 3, VII, 1; *ki-ma* *imêrupurîmi*, III R. 41, II, 18; V. A., 209, V, 11; *ki-ma lu-ba-ri*, III R. 43, IV, 8; *ki-ma ili*, V. A., 2663, III, 41; *ṣu-pur kîma (GIM)* *abnukunuk-ki(DUB)-šu*, V. A., 208, 55; V. A., 209, II, 27.

kakku, weapon.
iṣukakku(KU)-šú-nu kul-lu-mu, Susa, 2, III, 20; *iṣukakkê-šú-nu ku-ul-lu-mu*, Susa, 3, VII, 31; *ina iṣukakki*, V R. 55, 9; *ú-šat-ba-a iṣukakkê-šú*, V R. 55, 13; *ka-ak-ke-šú li-še-bir*, III R. 43, IV, 22.

כלב, **kalbu**, dog.
ki-ma kalbi(UR.KU), III R. 41, II, 24.

I. כלה, **kalû**, drive forward(?).
II, 2, *iṣuma-šá-ra-šú uk-til-la*, V R. 55, 27, 37.

II. כלה, **kalû**, end, cease.
I, 1 prec., *ina limutti(-ti) li-ik-la*, London, 101, IV, 14.

kala, all.
e-til-li-it ka-la be-li-e-ti, Susa, 3, VII, 17; *ka-la si-ḫi-ip ša-ma-me*, Neb. Nippur, I, 14; *dE-a ba-an ka-la*, O. B. I., 83, II, 17; *mu-um-mu ba-an ka-la*, V A., 2663, III, 5; *ilâni ka-li-šú-nu*, O. B. I., 149, III, 9; cstr., *gi-mir kal da-ád-me*, V A., 2663, I, 23; *kal da-ad-me*, Neb. Nippur, I, 15; *mu-du-u kal šip-ri*, V. A., 2663, II, 49; *šàr kal šarrâni*, C. T., X, pl. IV, 10.

kališ, altogether.
mu-ud-diš ka-liš ašrâte(AŠ pl.), V. A., 2663, II, 7.

kullu, denial(?), end(?).
lu-ú-di-in kul dîni(DI)-šu, I R. 70, III, 16; *lu-ú-di(-in) kul dîni(DI)-šú-ma*, III R. 43, IV, 11.

kallû, name of an official (cf. p. 177).
kal-li-e šarri, V R. 55, 51; *kal-li-e nâri u ta-ba-li*, Neb. Nippur, III, 26; *kal-li nâri kal-li ta-ba-li*, C. T., IX, pl. V, 33; *kal-li-e nâri kal-li-e ta-ba-li*, I R. 66, I, 6, 7; *ka-al-li-e nâri ka-al-li-e ta-ba-li*, III R. 45, No. 2, 2.

kallatu, bride.
dGu-la kal-lat E-šar-ra, D. E. P., II, 113, 13; V R. 56, 39; *kal-lat(E.GE.A)* *mTâb-a-šab-dMar-duk*, I R. 70, I, 15; *kal-lat-i-šu ša mBu-ru-ša*, London, 102, I, 28; *kal-lat-šu*, London, 102, I, 35.

כלל, **kilallân**, roundabout.
šarrâni ki-lal-la-an ip-pu-šú taḫâzi, V R. 55, 29.

kullatân, everywhere.
kul-la-tan nišê i-ḫi-iṭ, V. A., 2663, I, 20.

כלם, **kalâmu,** see.
II, 1 prec., *nam-ra-ṣa li-kal-lim-šu-ma,* Neb. Nippur, IV, 23; perm., *[iṣu]kakkê-šú-nu ku-ul-lu-mu,* Susa, 3, VII, 32; *kul-lu-mu,* Susa, 2, III, 20; *ú-[kal-lim],* D. E. P., II, 93, II, 10.

כלמא, IV, 1, look upon.
i-na ag-gi lib-bi-šú-nu li-ik-kil-mu-šú, London, 103, VI, 2; *i-na bu-ni-šú-nu iz-zu-ú-ti li-ik-ki-el-mu-šu-ma,* Susa, 3, VI, 25; *iz-zi-iš lik-kil-mu-šú,* IV R.[2] 38, III, 32; D. E. P., VI, 47, 2; V R. 56, 38; III R. 41, II, 14; I R. 70, III, 11; O. B. I., 149, II, 19.

I. כמה, **kamû,** enclose.
II, 1 perm., *ku-um-ma* 696 *šanâte,* 696 years had passed, O. B. I., 83, I, 8 (but see Winckler, *Forschungen,* I, 130[3], 267[2]; Jensen, Z. A., VIII, 221[3]).

kamâtu, enclosure, wall.
i-na ka-mat âli-šu, Susa, 16, VI, 17; III R. 41, II, 18; I R. 70, III, 20; O. B. I., 149, III, 8; V. A., 209, V, 12.

kameš, bound, captive.
abulli âli-šú ka-meš liṭ-ṭa-rid, Susa, 16, VI, 16.

II. כמה, **kimtu,** family.
i-na aḫê mârê kimti (IM.RI.A), I R. 70, II, 2; III R. 43, III, 3; London, 102, I, 30; IV, 37; V. A., 208, 43 (*IM.RI*); V. A., 209, I, 32.

כמל, **kammalu,** anger.
ina na-ṭa-al ka-am-ma-li, Susa, 3, VI, 36.

kimiltu, anger.
ša ki-mil-tuš (=*ina kimilti-šu*) *is-bu-su,* V. A., 2663, I, 18.

כנה, **kinîtu,** female servant.
pl., *ar-di-en u ki-na-a-ti,* I R. 70, II, 4.

כנש, **kanâšu,** subject.
II, 1 pret., *ú-kan-ni-šu a-na ur-ti-šu,* V. A., 2663, I, 39.

Kisilîmu, Kislev, ninth month.
V. A., 208, 53.

כסף, **kaspu,** silver.
London, 103, III, 22; III R. 41, I, 15, 16, 17, 18, 19, 20, 21, 22, 23, 24, 25, 26, 27; London, 102, III, 25, 26; IV, 23, 24, 25, 27; V. A., 208, 46; C. T., X, pl. V, 2; V. A., 209, I, 6, 15, 21; II, 3, 4; IV, 5, 19, 20, 32, 33.

כסר, **kisurru,** boundary.
ki-sur-ri-ši-na im-ma-šu-ma, V. A., 2663, III, 19.

כפד, **kapâdu,** plan, devise.
I, 1 pres., *mim-ma a-ma-at limutti(-ti) i-ka-ap-pa-du,* Susa, 16, V, 10; *ša lib-bu-uš-šu i-kap-pu-du limutta,* V. A. 211, III, 3.
I, 2, *ša a-na epêš taḫâzi kit-pu-da e-mu-qa-šu,* whose forces are devoted to battle, V R. 55, 7.

kuppu, spring.
pl., *ka-bi-sa-at kup-pa-a-ti,* V R. 56, 47.

kiṣṣu, dwelling, temple.
e-piš ku-um-mu ki-iṣ-ṣi u si-ma-ku, V. A., 2663, II, 12; pl., *adi eqli ki-iṣ-ṣa-a-ti ša i-na libbi Na-ra-ni-e,* D. E. P., VI, 42, I, 6.

kirû, garden.
[iṣu]kirû(SAR) [âlu]Ša-ak-na-na-a, Susa, 16, I, 23; *[iṣu]kirê u šaggu-lâni,* V R. 55, 60; *[iṣu]kirê(SAR. MEŠ) eqli Bît-[m]At-na-ai,* C. T., X, pl. III, 20; *a-di [iṣu]kirî zaq-pi,* V. A., 208, 8; *[iṣu]kirû gišimmaru,* V. A., 2663, IV, 21; *[iṣu]kirû,* V. A., 2663, IV, 29, 33, 36, 43; C. T., X, pl. VI, 24; V. A., 209, IV, 24.

כרב, **ikribu,** prayer.
i-na ik-ri-bi ù ZI.ŠAG.GAL-li, O B. I., 83, I, 17.

karûbu, powerful.
(Nusku) *a-ri-rum ka-ru-bu,* Neb. Nippur, IV, 25.

כרה, **karû**, undertake.
I, 1 pres., *i-kir-ru-ma ip-pu-šú ù lu-ú du-ul-la . . . i-na eš-ši il-la-a*, Susa, 3, III, 34.

KUR.RA, a kind of garment.
a-di ištên ṣ*ubâtu*[*ṣubâtu*] *KUR.RA*, V. A., 209, IV, 33.

I. כרש, **kar(a)šu**, body, mind.
li-ṣa-an ka-ra-as-su(= *karaši-šu*), III R. 41, II, 26; *ka-raš ši-tul-ti*, of thoughtful mind, V. A., 2663, II, 50.

II. כרש, **kuršu**(= **karâšu**), ruin.
i-te-mid kúr-šu, fate overtook him, V R. 55, 41 (cf. Sennach., prism, II, 37; *Aššurb. Annals*, II, 81; *Synchronistic History*, II, 30; III [8], 26; and Winckler, *Forschungen*, I, 105, 241; Delitzsch, *Lesestücke*[4], p. 170*b*).

KAŠ.BU(KAŠ.GID), double mile.
ši-iḫ-ṭa iš-ta-ka-an a-na XXX KAŠ.BU, V R. 55, 15; *i-ni-is-su-u* 3660 *KAŠ.BU*, V. A., 2663, II, 37.

kišâdu, (1) bank of river.
Susa, 2, I, 22, 25, 31, 34; II, 3, 8, 13, 18; London, 103, III, 42; IV, 2; London, 101, I, 5; Susa, 3, I, 5, 24, 50, 54; IV R.[2] 38, I, 4; Susa, 16, I, 3, 24; C. T., IX, pl. IV, 21, 23; III R. 41, I, 2, 9; I R. 70, I, 3; London, 102, I, 2; C. T., X, pl. III, 17; V. A., 2663, IV, 16, 22, 23, 31, 46, etc.
(2) neck, *paṭ-ru i-na kišâdi(TIK)-šu*, V R. 56, 54.

כשד, **kašâdu**, reach, overtake.
I, 1 pret., *ik-šú-du ir-nit-tuš*, he gained his victories, V. A., 2663, II, 27; prec., *li-ik-šú-da-šú*, Susa, 3, VII, 51; pres., *mim-ma ut-tu-ú . . . la i-kaš-šad*, I R. 70, IV, 20; part., *ka-šid* mâtu*A-mur-ri-i*, V R. 55, 10; perm., *lâ kul-du* (= *kušdu*), had not been taken, London, 103, I, 29; *ku-ša-ad ša-ai-ma-a-ni*, London, 103, III, 17.
I, 2, *ik-ta-šad a-na kišâd* nâru*Ú-la-a*, V R. 55, 28.

kišittu, property.
i-na kišitta(KUR-ta) ša im-qut-ma, because of the property which he claimed, London, 102, VI, 5.

כשה, **kištu**, grove.
kištu(TIR) ša m*Mar-duk*, V. A., 2663, IV, 26.

kaškaš(š)u, most powerful.
d*Šamaš daianu kaš-kaš nišê*, III R. 43, IV, 10; d*Za-mà-mà kaš-kaš ilâni*, London, 102, II, 6.

כשר, **kiširru**, perhaps support.
a-lik ki-ši-ir-ri ilâni aḫê-šú, III R. 43, IV, 26.

ku-ši-ri.
D. E. P., II, 113, 23.

kušartu, preservation.
ku-ša-ar-ti ù ḫi-iṣ-ṣa-ti ša nâr šarri, Susa, 3, II, 20.

Kaššû, the Cassite.
šá-li-lu Kaš-ši-i, V R. 55, 10.

כשש, **kiššatu**, universe, world.
(Nazi-Maruttash) *šàr kiššati(KIŠ)*, Susa, 2, I, 2; (*ŠAR.RA*), Susa, 2, II, 27; (Marduk-apal-iddina I.), Susa, 2; Med., II, 3; IV R.[2] 38, I, 21; D. E. P., VI, 42, I, 24; (Rammân-šum-uṣur), D. E. P., II, 97, 8; (Meli-Shipak), London, 101, I, 13; (Nebukudurri-uṣur), Neb. Nippur, II, 23; (Nabû-mukîn-aplu), London, 102, IV, 2, 12; C. T., X, pl. IV, 10, 11, 12; *rê'u ki-iš-šat*, D. E. P., VI, 46, IV, 5; *abkal kiš-šat šamê(-e) u irṣitim(-tim)*, V. A., 2663, I, 8; *purussû(EŠ.BAR) kiš-šat nišê*, V. A., 2663, I, 38.

ki-ta-a-ti.
d*Rammân bêl ki-ta-a-ti*, D. E. P., VI, 47, 7.

כתם, **katâmu**, cover.
I, 1 perm., *ša-qum-mat-su mâtâti ka-at-ma*, Neb. Nippur, I, 16.

kuttinnu, younger (cf. Hebr. קָטוֹן).

mKi-di-ni mâri-šu kut-tin-nu, V. A., 208, 3, 21; *mâri-šu kut-tin-nu*, placed between *mâri-šu rabî(-i)* and *mâri-šu šal-ša-ai*, London, 102, IV, 32.

lâ, not, *passim*.

li'û, tablet (cf. p. 10).
li(𒁹)*-ú ù ṭuppi eqli*, Susa, 16, III, 11; *i-na ka-na-ak li*(𒁹)*-ú ù ṭup-pi eqli*, Susa, 16, III, 15; *i-na ka-nak li*(𒁹)*-ú šú-a-tu*, Neb. Nippur, V, 8; *^{iṣu}li'û(LI)*, D. E. P., II, 93, II, 9, 12.

לאה, lîtu, power, victory.
it-ta-ši-iz i-na li-ti, he stood in triumph, V R. 55, 42; *i-na li-ti u ḫu-ud libbi(-bi)*, V R. 55, 44; *lit-ti par-si-e i-ta-ni-e i-ša-lu-ma*, he asked for the annulment of the decrees in force, O. B. I., 83, II, 9; *i-na le-ti*, III R. 43, I, 5; *^{d}Iš-ḫa-ra bêlit le-ti da-ad-ma*, III R. 43, IV, 28; *tal-bi-iš ina le-ti*, V. A., 2663, II, 40.

לבב, libbu, heart.
nu-mur libbi, Neb. Nippur, IV, 10; *i-na ḫu-ud libbi-šu*, V. A., 209, I, 23; *ma-la lib-bu-uš(= ina libbišu) im-ṣu-u*, V. A., 2663, II, 38; *i-na ag-gi libbi-šú-nu*, London, 103, VI, 2; *libbi be-li-šú*, IV R.[2] 38, II, 17; used as prep., *a-na libbi(-bi) eqlu ša-a-šu*, against, London, 102, II, 33; *i-na libbi*, of, from, Susa, 3, I, 7; V. A., 208, 5; V R. 55, 59; I R. 70, II, 16; C. T., X, pl. VII, 35, *a-na libbi(-bi) âlâni*, into, V R. 55, 54; *ina lib-bi-šu*, within it, V. A., 209, IV, 24; *ša lib-bu-uš-šu i-kap-pu-du*, V. A. 211, III, 2.

libbu, young(?).
I alpu libbu alpi, III R. 41, I, 20; *I alpu libbu alpi ša rit-ti*, London, 102, III, 26; IV, 24.

libbû, demarcation(?).
itti lib-bu-ú eqli, V. A., 2663, IV, 25; *pa-na-at ^{iṣu}kirî e-li-ni-i lib-bu-ú eqli*, V. A., 2663, IV, 34; *UŠ.SA.DU lib-bu-ú eqli*, V. A., 2663, IV, 37; *itti(DA) eqli libbû(bu) eqli*, V. A., 209, II, 34; *itti eqli (lib!)-bu-ú eqli*, V. A., 209, III, 19; *itti eqli lib-bu-ú eqli*, V. A., 209, IV, 10; *UŠ.SA.-DU libbu-ú eqli*, London, 102, I, 5, 8, 9.

לבן, labânu, libênu, throw down, prostrate.
I, 1 prec., *ap-pa li-il-bi-in*, D. E. P., VI, 46, III, 20; *ap-pa-šú lil-bi-im-ma*, V R. 56, 55; pres., *ap-pa i-lab-bi-nu*, Neb. Nippur, I, 6; inf., *ina li-bi-en ap-pi*, Neb. Nippur, II, 10.

lubnu, calamity.
lu-ub-nu ma-ku-ú u li-mi-nu, V R. 56, 44; *lu-ub-na ni-el-me-na a-mat nišê li-gi-sa-šú*, Neb. Nippur, IV, 7.

לבר, labâru, become old.
I, 1 inf., *a-na la-bar ûmi(-mi)*, to distant days, Susa, 16, III, 26; *ûmê la-ba-ri*, old age, O. B. I., 83, II, 19.

labiru, old.
ga-ba-ri-e la-bi-rišu, a copy of its original, Susa, 2; Med., II, 10; *ul-tu la-bi-ri*, from of old, Susa, 3, III, 37; *bît abi(AD) la-bi-ri ma-ḫi-ra-a[-ti]*, C. T., X, pl. V, 12; *ki i-na la-bi-ri*, as was of old, V R. 55, 50; pl., *parsê(BAR.-SUD) la-bi-ru-ti*, Susa, 16, II, 27; fem., *eqlâti mârê Bâbili^{ki} la-bi-rat*, V. A., 2663, III, 15; *eqlâti bît abê-e-a labirâti(Ù.RA.-ME)*, C. T., X, pl. V, 2.

lubâru, garment.
iš-ru-ba-a ki-i lu-ba-ri, I R. 70, III, 19; *išrubâ(-a) ki-ma lu-ba-ri*, III R. 43, IV, 8; *iš-ru-ba[-a ki-*

ma lu-ba-ri li-lab-biš-]šu, London, 102, I, 46.

לבש, **labâšu,** clothe.

II, 1 prec., *iš-ru-ba-a . . pa-ga-ar-šú li-la-bi-iš-ma*, Susa, 3, VI, 51; *zu-mur-šú lil-la-ib-[biš]-ma*, Susa, 16, VI, 15; *la-ni-šú li-lab-biš-ma*, III R. 41, II, 17; *ki-i lu-ba-ri li-la-ab-bi-su-ma*, I R. 70, III, 19; *li-li-bi-ša zu-mu-ur-šú*, III R. 43, IV, 9; *iš-ru-ba[-a ki-ma lu-ba-ri li-lab-biš]-šu*, London, 102, I, 47; *iš-ru-pa-a li-lab-bi-is-su-ma*, V. A., 209, V, 11.

talbišu, garment.

tal-bi-iš ina le-ti, clothed in strength, V. A., 2663, II, 39.

לו, **lû,** (1) adv., truly.

Neb. Nippur, IV, 16, 26; Susa, 2, IV, 31, etc.

(2) conj., either, or.

lu-ú . . . ù, Susa, 2, III, 4; *lu-ú . . . lu-ú*, London, 102, V, 1, 2, 3; London, 101, II, 13–15; III, 3, 6, etc.

לזז, **lazzu,** destructive, evil (cf. p. 181).

si-im-ma la-az-za, Susa, 14, IV, 6; D. E. P., IV, pl. 16, II, 3; D. E. P., VI, 47, 12; Neb. Nippur, IV, 20; III R. 41, II, 30; London, 102, II, 21; *si-im-ma la-az*, Susa, 3, VII, 19; III R. 43, IV, 16.

ליף, **lîpu,** descendant.

li-pu ri-bu-ú, fourth descendant, IV R.[2] 38, II, 1.

lîlu, laughter(?), merriment(?).

lil-li ai îši(TUK), Neb. Nippur, IV, 14.

למן, **lamânu, limênu,** be evil.

I, 1 inf., *lu-ub-nu ma-ku-ú u li-mi-nu*, distress, frailty and evil, V R. 56, 44.

II, 1 prec., *šîmti-šu li-lam-min*, make his fate evil, London, 101, III, 11; *i-gir-ra[šu] l[i-l]am-min*, O. B. I., 149, II, 23; part., *daianê ṣîrûti lu mu-lam-me-nu i-gir-ri-šu*, Neb. Nippur, IV, 16.

limnu, evil.

fem., *ina lim-ni-ti ú-ša-ḫa-zu ubâni-šu*, Neb. Nippur, III, 23.

limniš, miserably, with evil intent.

ina pâni-šu lim-niš iṭ-ṭar-ra-du, V. A., 2663, II, 35; *nu-'-a . . . lim-niš ù-ma-'-a-ru*, V. A., 2663, V, 27.

limuttu, the evil.

ar-rat limutti(ḪUL-ti) li-ru-ru-šu, Susa, 2, III, 23; Neb. Nippur, V, 6; *ar-rat la nap-šú-ri limutta(-ta)*, I R. 70, IV, 24; Susa, 14, III, 2; *li-e-mu-ut-ta*, Susa, 3, VI, 27; *li-mut-ta*, O. B. I., 149, II, 16; *ar-ra-ti limutti(ḪUL-ti)*, I R. 70, II, 19; *ina limutti(ḪUL) li-ir-di-šu*, London, 101, III, 13; *a-na limutti(-ti) li-ir-te-id-di-šu*, I R. 70, III, 24; III R. 43, IV, 14; London, 103, VI, 14; *i-na li-mu-ut-ti . . . ša bal-ṭa liq-ti-ma*, IV R.[2] 38, III, 38; *ul-te-is-ḫi-ir limutte(-te)*, V R. 55, 41; *a-na limutti(-ti) li-iḫ-ta-as-su-šú-ma*, V R. 56, 52; *limutta(-ta) zi-ir-ma*, O. B. I., 83, II, 24; *i-di li-mut-ti*, III R. 41, II, 1; *a-na limutti(-ti) u la ṭâbti(DUG-ti) li-ir-te-id-du-šú*, III R. 41, II, 37; *ki-i limut-ti(-ti) il-ta-ka-an*, Susa, 3, V, 42; *ubâni-šu a-na limutti(-ti) i-tar-ra-ṣu*, Neb. Nippur, III, 24; (Nusku) *lu rabiṣu limutti-šu šú-ma*, Neb. Nippur, IV, 26; *^{d}Rammân limuttu pa-at-ti-nu da(?)-riš*, London, 101, I, 3; *i-kap-pu-du limutta(ḪUL.MEŠ)*, V. A. 211, III, 4.

lamassu, tutelary deity.

ilu šarri ù ^{d}lamassu(KAL) šarri, Susa, 16, VI, 8.

lânu, body.

gi-mir la-ni-šú, III R. 41, II, 17.

לפת, **liptu,** work, construction (cf. p. 198).

pl., *^{d}Marduk bêl lip-te-ti*, O. B. I., 149, II, 21.

lipittu, enclosure (cf. p. 184).
i-na lipitti(LIBIT) it-te-'i, Susa, 3, V, 53; *ina ^{iṣu}lipitti(LIBIT) i-pi-ḫu-ú*, Neb. Nippur, V, 2.

la(u)puttû, chief (cf. p. 171).
lu-pu-ut-tu-ú, III R. 43, III, 13; *NU.TUR*, London, 101, II, 14; IV R.[2] 38, III, 1; Susa, 16, III, 28; D. E. P., II, 97, 11; O. B. I., 83, II, 12; *NU.TUR.DA*, III R. 41, I, 32; I R. 70, II, 5.

לקא$_3$, **laqû,** seize, take.
I, 1 prec., *ni-is-sa-tu li-ilqi(ŠÚ.TI)-šú*, Neb. Nippur, IV, 12; *a-na aš-šu-ti i[-il-qi]*, London, 102, VI, 4; pres., *ša ultu libbi nâr piḫâti ša šarri i-liq-qa-a*, Susa, 3, I, 52.
I, 2, *eqlu bît abi-[ia al-ti]-ki*, C. T., X, pl. III, 4.

לקת, **laqâtu,** snatch away.
I, 1 prec., *i-na zêri-šú lil-qut*, London, 101, III, 17; *zêri-šu lil-qu-tum*, IV R.[2] 38, III, 37; *[zêri-šu] li-il-ku-tum*, Susa, 16, VI, 26.

ma, part. of emphasis, *passim*.
mi, *na-din-mi*, London, 101, III, 1; London, 103, V, 38; *šarri-mi*, O. B. I., 149, II, 7; *šú-mi*, Susa, 16, II, 32; *ma-ḫi-ir-mi*, Neb. Nippur, IV, 2.
mu, *[ma]-la ib-ši-mu*, C. T., X, pl. VII, 40; *iš-me-e-mu*, V. A., 209, I, 17; *i-tur-ru-mu*, V. A., 209, II, 39; III, 27; *ik-nu-ku-ú-mu*, V. A., 209, IV, 37.

mê, water.
a-na mê i-nam-du-u, I R. 70, III, 1; III R, 43, I, 33; Susa, 16, IV, 31; O. B. I., 149, II, 11; V. A., 2663, V, 28; IV R.[2] 38, III, 18; London, 103, V, 45; London, 101, III, 3; Neb. Nippur, V, 1; C. T., X, pl. VII, 36; *ki-i mê li-ir-muk*, I R. 70, IV, 8; Neb. Nippur, IV, 21; Susa, 3, VII, 25; III R. 41, II, 31; O. B. I., 149, III, 5; D. E. P., IV, pl. 16, II, 4; *ki-ma mê lit-bu-uk*, Susa, 2, III, 34; *mê saḫ-ḫi*, V R. 55, 19; *apil-šu na-qa mê-šú*, III R. 43, IV, 20; *aplu u [na-a]q mê*, London, 102, II, 19; *na-aq mê*, Susa, 3, VII, 10; D. E. P., VI, 45, IV, 10; *ki-mu-ú mê id-ra-na*, London, 102, II, 13; *mê ša mu-še-bi-ri*, Susa, 3, III, 1; *mê nâr ši-qi-ti-šú*, Susa, 3, III, 4; *mê la a-zi-im-ma*, Susa, 3, III, 7.

מאד$_1$, **ma'âdu,** be much.
II, 1 prec., *li-ma-'-i-da at-mi-šú*, may he multiply his words; III R. 41, II, 23.
ma'du, much.
ûmi(-mi) ma-'-du-ti, many days, Susa, 3, V, 17.

מאר$_2$, **ma'âru,** send.
II, 1 pret., *me-gir-šú ú-ma-ir-ma*, Neb. Nippur, II, 21; *ú-ma-'-ir-šú-nu-ti*, O. B. I., 83, II, 8; pres., *ú-ma-'-a-ru ša-nam-ma*, Neb. Nippur, III, 22; *ú-ma-'-a-ru*, London, 103, V, 35; Susa, 16, IV, 28; V R. 56, 35; Neb. Nippur, III, 22; III R. 41, II, 9; I R. 70, II, 23; V. A., 2663, V, 25, 27; *ú-ma-a-ru-ú-ma*, III R. 43, I, 32; part., *mu-ma-'-ir šamê(-e) ú irṣiti*, Neb. Nippur, I, 20.
II, 2 pret., *la mu-da-a um-ta-'-ir-ma*, Susa, 3, V, 50.

mâru, son, *passim*.
mârtu, daughter.
mârti(TUR.SAL)-šu aššati(DAM)-šu ša, London, 102, I, 17; *a-na mârti-šu id-di-nu*, London, 102, I, 21.
mêru, child.
^{d}Girru iz-zu me-ru ša ^{d}Nusku, Susa, 2, IV, 19; *^{d}Ṣîru me-ru ša ^{d}KA.DI*, Susa, 2, IV, 23.

מאש, **mêšu,** disregard.
I, 1 pret., *a-ma-ta iš-tu-ru-ma . . . a-na-ku la e-mi-e-šú,* Susa, 3, IV, 26.
I, 2, *šú-ú la i-te-ni ù la im-taš,* Susa, 3, V, 9.

מגר, **magâru,** be gracious.
I, 1 pret., *^dAššur-aḫ-iddina šàr bêli-šu im-gur-šu-ma,* C. T., X, pl. V, 6.
migru, favorite.
rubû me-gir-šú, Neb. Nippur, I, 23; II, 21; *me-gir ^dEn-lil,* Neb. Nippur, II, 15.
mitgurtu, agreement.
i-na mi-it-gur-ti-šú, London, 103, III, 16.

מדד, **madâdu,** measure.
I, 1 pret., *GÙ.EN.NA in-du-ud-ma,* London, 103, III, 26.

מות, **mâtu,** die.
I, 1 pret., *i-mu-ut-ma,* London, 103, V, 6; *i-mu-tu,* London, 103, IV, 12; V, 8.
mûtu, death.
iš-ru-ba-a mûti(BAD-ti) an ka-bit-ta, Susa, 16, VI, 14.

meḫû, storm.
i-sa-ar me-ḫu-ú, a storm rages, V R. 55, 32; *i-na me-ḫi-e ta-ḫa-zi-šú-nu,* V R. 55, 33.

muḫḫu, prep.
i-na muḫ-ḫi, against, III R. 43, III, 23; IV, 32; edge II, 1; O. B. I., 149, II, 6; V. A., 209, I, 35; IV, 20; *i-na muḫ-ḫi nâri eš-šit,* at, V. A., 209, I, 10; *i-na muḫ-ḫi-šú-nu,* in their behalf, C. T., IX, pl. IV, 8; *a-na muḫ-ḫi,* to, C. T., IX, pl. IV, 4; D. E. P., II, pl. 20, 2.

מח, **maḫâṣu,** smite, break.
I, 1 prec., *pa-ni-šú lim-ḫaṣ-ma,* III R. 41, II, 19.
I, 2 part. pl., *mun-daḫ-ṣu-ti,* warriors, V R. 55, 46.
II, 1 perm., *ku-dur-ri-ši-na nu-uk-ku-ru-ma la mu-uḫ-ḫu-ṣa,* their boundary stones were changed, but not broken, V. A., 2663, III, 22.

מחר, **maḫâru,** receive.
I, 1 pret., *im-ḫur,* London, 103, III, 36; V. A., 209, II, 4; London, 102, IV, 26; *im-ḫu-ru,* relat., London, 102, IV, 40; V. A., 208, 47; III R. 41, I, 12; *ai im-ḫu-ur-šú,* V R. 56, 56; *im-ḫur[-šu],* D. E. P., II, 93, II, 7; *am-ḫu-ru,* C. T., X, pl. V, 3; *an-ḫu-ru,* V. A., 209, I, 13; part., *ša is-ki ma-ḫir,* London, 102, III, 11, 14, 15; perm., *kaspu ul ma-ḫir,* V. A., 208, 46; V. A., 209, II, 3; *ma-ḫi-ir-mi,* Neb. Nippur, IV, 2; *kaspu maḫ-ru,* V. A., 208, 38; *maḫ-ru aplu za-ku-u,* London, 102, IV, 34; *ma-ḫir a-pil za-ku,* V. A., 209, I, 27; II, 39; III, 14, 26; IV, 39, V, 1.
I, 2, *ina qâtâ . . . im-taḫ-ḫu-ru,* V. A., 208, 34; *ki-i LV šiqlu kaspi [am-]da-ḫar,* V. A., 209, I, 7; perm., *a-na šîmi V she'uzêru mi-taḫ-ḫu-ru,* he received, III R. 41, I, 30.

maḫru, before.
maḫ-ri En-lil, Neb. Nippur, II, 9; *ina maḫ-ri šakkanakki,* Neb. Nippur, II, 19; *eli šarri a-lik maḫ-ri,* Neb. Nippur, II, 7; *ma-ḫar bêl bêlê,* V. A., 2663, II, 18; *ma-ḫar ili-šú,* Susa, 2; Med., I, 5; *ma-ḫar ^dŠamaš,* Susa, 3, III, 47; V. 2, 24, 35; *ma-ḫar šarri,* O. B. I., 83, I, 18; *na-an-zaz maḫ-ḫar šarri,* Neb. Nippur, II, 18; *a-na ma-aḫ-ri ilâni,* III R. 43, IV, 13; *a-na ma-ḫar ili u šarri,* I R. 70, III, 23; *a-na ma-ḫar šarri,* C. T., X, pl. V, 10.

maḫrû, former.
ša-kin ^aluHu-da-da ma-ḫa-ra-a, Susa, 16, II, 23; *ṭuppu bîti ar-ku-ú ù maḫ-ru-ú,* V. A., 209, I, 25.

miḫru, bulwark.
mi-iḫ-ri nam-ba-'-i, Susa, 3, II, 19.

miḫirtu, front.
eqlâti ša miḫirti(ŠI-ti) $^{\hat{a}lu}$*Bâbili,* opposite, Susa, 2, I, 7.

maḫîru, price.
ŠE.BAR maḫîrê(KI.LAM.MEŠ) *mâtuAkkadî,* London, 102, IV, 27; *ameli-šu ma-ḫi-ri kaspi,* C.T., X, pl. VI, 24; *ki-i LVI šiqlu kaspi maḫîri(KI.LAM) im-bi-e-ma i-šam,* V. A., 209, II, 37; 5 *šiqlu šibirtu(AZAG.PAD.DU) maḫîri im-bi-e-ma i-šam,* V. A., 209, III, 25; 4 *šiqlu kaspi maḫîru im-bi-e-ma i-šam,* V. A., 209, III, 12; *eqlâti bît abê-e-a labirâti(Ù.RA.ME) u maḫîrâti (KI.LAM.ME) kaspi,* C. T., X, pl. V, 2; *bît abi(AD) la-bi-ri u m[a-ḫ]i-ra-a[-ti],* C. T., X, pl. V, 12.

maḫarûtu.
V urâte i-na libbi(-bi) II ma-ḫa-ru-tu, IV R. 43, edge IV, 3.

^{h}**MUK,** title of an official.
London, 102, I, 17, 28, 35, 37; II, 32; IV, 29, 30; VI, 3, 7; V. A., 209, II, 33.

מכה, **makû,** frailty.
lu-ub-nu ma-ku-ú u li-mi-nu, V R. 56, 44; *ma-ki-i qât-su lim-gu-ug,* V R. 56, 45.

makkaltu, perhaps enclosure or hedge.
[ma]-ak-kal-ti ^{iṣu}*kirê la na-ka-si,* V R. 55, 60 (cf. *ma-kal-li-e,* dam, Neb., 760; B. A., IV, 21; Winckler, *Forschungen,* I, 453; Peiser, *Verträge,* 231; *makallû,* suburb).

מכס, **mâkisu,** tax-gatherer.
a-na ^{h}*ma-ki-si la na-da-ni,* V R. 55, 57; *ma-ki-su a-na âli-šú a-na la e-ri-bi,* III R. 45, No. 2, 9.

I. מכר, **mikêru,** irrigate.
I, 1 inf., *la mi-ki-e-ri,* Susa, 3, III, 11.

II. מכר, **makkûru,** possession.
i-iš-ta-lal makkûra(ŠÀ.GA), V R. 55, 43.

mala, as many as, as much as.
Susa, 2, III, 16; London, 103, V, 32, 40; Susa, 3, VI, 14; VII, 27; IV R.² 38, III, 29; Susa, 16, VI, 9; Susa, 14, IV, 15; D. E. P., II, 113, 2, 20; D. E. P., IV, pl. 16, II, 5; V R. 55, 47; 56, 4, 8; Neb. Nippur, V, 5; C. T., IX, pl. V, 38; III R. 41, II, 36; I R. IV, 22; III R. 43, III, 23, 24; IV, 33; O. B. I., 149, II, 14; III, 9; V. A., 208, 4; London, 102, V, 6; V. A., 2663, II, 38; III, 32; V, 24, 45; C. T., X, pl. VII, 40.

מלא$_1$, **malû,** be full.
I, 1, *lu i-na(!) ir-ri-i im-[lu]-ú,* D. E. P., VI, 45, V, 16.
II, 1 prec., *nârâte-šú li-mil-la-a sa-ki-ki,* V R. 56, 42; *nârâte sa-ki-ki li-mi-li,* III R. 43, IV, 4; *ta-mi-ra-ti-šú li-mi-la-a pu-qut-ta,* III R. 43, IV, 5; *li-ma-li-šú,* Susa, 14, III, 8.

miltu, filling.
dal-[ti] ašar mi-il-ti nâri-šú, Susa, 16, V, 6.

tamlîtu, terrace.
pûtu šaplû šâr III UŠ.SA.DU ta[m]-li-ta$^{pl.}$, V. A., 2663, IV, 1.

מלג, **muli(u)gu,** dowry.
eqil mu-li-gi, I R. 70, I, 4; *eqlu ki-i mu-lu-gi,* I R. 70, II, 17; *it-ti mu-lu-gi ù nu-dun-ni-e,* London, 102, I, 15.

מלל, **melultu,** pleasure, happiness.
me-lul[-ta?] ni-me-ki ša ^{d}*Nabû,* IV R.² 38, II, 7.

מלך, **malâku,** counsel.
I, 1 part., *ma-li-ku ram-ni-šu,* V. A., 2663, II, 51; *ma-li-ki-ia,* Susa, 3, IV, 14; *ma-li-ki-šú,* Susa, 3, IV, 35; V, 10; *ma-lik šarri,* Susa, 3, VI, 2; *ma-lik a-bi-šu,*

D. E. P., II, 115, 6; (Marduk) *ma-lik ilâni*, V. A., 2663, I, 9.

I, 2 part., *mun-tal-ku*, the wise, V. A., 2663, I, 45.

malku, prince.
ma-al-ku it-pi-šu, V. A., 2663, II, 47; *ina pu-ḫur šu-ut ma-al-ku* (= *malkû*), V. A., 2663, I, 42.

milku, counsel.
mi-lik *mâtuŠú-me-ri u Akkadî*ki, V. A., 2663, I, 37; *mi-lik*[*-šu-nu*], O. B. I., 80, 2.

melammu, splendor.
ilu ša melammi (*ME.LAM*)*-šú saḫ-*(?)*-pu-ú*, Neb. Nippur, I, 13.

mu-um.
mu-um u su-ḫur-ma-šú . . . ša *dE-a*, Susa, 2, IV, 5.

mummu, prototype.
mu-um-mu ba-an ka-la, V. A., 2663, III, 5 (cf. B. A., V, 280).

מנה, **manû,** count.

I, 1 prec., *a-na* *iṣukakki na-ki-ri li-im-nu-uš*, may she surrender him to the weapon of the enemy, London, 103, VI, 20; pres., *a-na ši-im-ti-šú la i-man-nu-ú*, London, 103, VI, 8; *lu-ú a-na pi-ḫat i-man-nu-ú*, C. T., X, pl. VII, 34.

minûtu, number.
mi-nu-ut šanâti, D. E. P., VI, 46, IV, 7.

manû, mine.
šîm MA.NA ḫurâṣi, London, 103, III, 21; *a-ki* ½ *MA.NA kaspi* ⅔ *MA.NA V šiqli pa-ri-ṣi*, V. A., 209, IV, 5; *I MA.NA XIII šiqlu kaspuka*, V. A., 209, IV, 1, 19; *II MA.NA V šiqlu kaspi*, V. A., 209, IV, 34.

mu-ne.
sisê mu-ne(*MU.NE*), III R. 43, edge IV, 1.

mamma, anyone.
ma-am-ma e-di-e, Susa, 3, II, 46; *ilu ma-am-ma*, Susa, 3, VI, 31; *ma-am-ma ša-nu-um-ma*, any other one, V R. 56, 27; III R. 41, II, 5; London, 102, I, 31.

mammâna, anyone.
lu ai-am-[*ma*] *lu ma-am-ma-na*, IV R.² 38, III, 14.

manâma, anyone.
ma-na-ma arkû(*-ú*), C. T., X, pl. VII, 32; *zi-it-ti ma-na*[*-ma*], C. T., X, pl. V, 13.

mamman, anyone.
ni-kil-tu ma-am-man ú-ša-ḫa-zu, V. A., 2663, V, 24.

mammanâma, anyone whatsoever.
lu ai-mu-ma mâr ma-am-ma-na-ma, London, 101, II, 15; *na-ka-ra mâr ma-am-ma-na-ma*, Susa, 3, V, 48.

mimma, any whatsoever.
lu-ú mim-ma maš-ši-ta, any harvest, Susa, 3, II, 50; *mim-mu id-di-nu-šú*, whatever he gave him, Susa, 3, III, 45; *mim-ma šá i-na* *abnunâri-šu iš-tu-ru-ma*, Susa, 3, IV, 8; *u mim-ma a-ma-at limutti*(*-ti*), Susa, 16, V, 9; *a-na mim-ma la ba-še-e li-šá-li-ku-šú*, London, 103, VI, 24; *ina mim-ma šumi-šu ma-la ba-šu-u*, V. A., 2663, V, 23.

mannu, whoever.
man-nu arkû(*-ú*), V. A., 2663, V, 18.

mu-ni-ri.
hsukkallu mu-ni-ri, London, 101, I, 14.

masabbu, censer (Zimmern).
ma-sab ru-ba-ti, Susa, 2, IV, 26.

מסך, **masâku,** set aside, annul (cf. p. 163).

III, 1, *ša i-piš pî-šu la ú-šam-sa-ku ilu ai-um-ma*, Neb. Nippur, I, 9.

ma-su-uš-še-e.
30 *ugâr Dûr-šarru-ukîn ma-su-uš-še-e*, C. T., IX, pl. IV, 20.

מצא₁, **maṣû,** find, gain.

I, 1 pret., *ma-la lib-bu-uš im-ṣu-u*, he gained all that was in his heart, V. A., 2663, II, 39.

מצר, **miṣru,** boundary.
bêl mi-iṣ-ri, Neb. Nippur, IV, 19; *bêl mi-iṣ-ri ù ku-dur-ri,* O. B. I., 149, III, 1; III R. 41, II, 27; *i-ka mi-iṣ-ra ù ku-dur-ra,* Susa, 3, II, 12; *i-ka mi-iṣ-ra it-ti-qu,* Susa, 16, IV, 18; *mi-ṣir-ša us-saḫ-ḫi,* O. B. I., 83, II, 5; *e tu-saḫ-ḫi mi-iṣ-ra,* O. B. I., 83, II, 23; *mi-ṣir-ša ul us-saḫ-ḫa,* O. B. I., 83, II, 1; *mi-ṣir-šú li-ka-bis,* III R. 41, II, 28; *ú-sa mi-iṣ-ra ù ku-dur-ra,* I R. 70, II, 13; III R. 43, III, 20; IV, 1; *us-su mi-ṣir-šú ku-dur-ra-šu,* I R. 70, IV, 3; *mi-iṣ-ra in-nu-ú,* O. B. I., 150, II, 1.

מקק, **magâgu,** fasten.
I, 1 prec., *ma-ki-i qât-su lim-gu-ug,* may frailty fasten its grip, V R. 56, 45.

maqurru, ship (Zimmern).
ma-qur-ru ša ^dSin, Susa, 2, IV, 11.

I. מקת, **maqâtu,** fall down.
I, 1 perm., *ša ul-tu la-bi-ri i-na qa-ti ma-aq-tu-ma,* which from of old had completely fallen down, Susa, 3, III, 38.
III, 1 pret., *šá dan-na ^mâtu Lul-lu-bi-i ú-šam-ki-tu,* overthrew, V R. 55, 9.
miqtu, fall.
mi-iq-ta la ta-ba-a, a fall without rising, Susa, 14, IV, 7.

II. מקת, **maqâtu,** claim(?).
I, 1 pret., *i-na kišitta(-ta) ša im-qut-ma,* London, 102, VI, 5.

^h **MIR.GAL,** title of an official.
London, 101, II, 11.

I. מרץ, **marâṣu,** be sick.
III, 1, *a-ga-lâ-til-la-a li-šam-ri-ṣu-šú-ma,* may they afflict him with leprosy, Susa, 16, VI, 20; *qaqqadsu(SAG.NI) li-šam-ri-ṣu-šu,* Susa, 14, IV, 12; *li-šam-ri-is-su,* D. E. P., VI, 43, IV, 11; *[ilâni] šarrûti u mâti-šu li-šam-ri-ṣu-šu(?),* D. E. P., VI, 47, 6.
marṣu, sick.
qaqqadu(SAG) [mar]-zi-ma a-ga-lâ-[til-la-a] mêsir maqlûti li-ik-mi-[šu], D. E. P., II, 113, 18.
murṣu, sickness.
mu-ur-ṣa, D. E. P., VI, 45, V, 5; *murṣu bu[-bu]-ti,* D. E. P., VI, 47, 20.

II. מרץ, **namraṣu,** difficulty.
nam-ra-ṣa li-kal-lim-šu-ma, Neb. Nippur, IV, 23.

מרק, **marâqu,** pay in full (Aram. מְרַק, finish).
I, 1 pret., *a-na libbi(-bi) a[-mi-lu-ti] im-ru-uq,* London, 102, VI, 14 (cf. B. E., IX, Nos. 48 : 19; 82 : 20, **II, 1,** *ú-mar-raq-qa-am-ma,* and **IV, 1,** *im-me-ri-ik-ku-u,* B. E., IX, 64 : 9).

מרר, **marâru,** be bitter.
I, 1 prec., *i-na ar-rat lim-ri-ru,* Susa, 14, IV, 17.

מרש, **maruštu, marustu,** evil.
ma-ru-uš-ta li-iš-du-ud, V R. 56, 59; *ši-mat ma-ru-uš-ti li-šim-šú-ma,* Neb. Nippur, IV, 6; *ar(-rat) la nap-šú-ri ma-ru-uš-ta li-rú-ru-šú,* III R. 41, II, 15; London, 102, I, 39; *ar-rat la nap-šur marušta(ŠA.GIG) li-ru-ru-šu,* V. A., 209, II, 10; V, 8; *ar-ra-at la nap-šú-ri-im ma-ru-us-ta li-ru-ru-šú,* Susa, 16, VI, 13; *liš-du-ud ma-ru-uš-ti,* V. A., 2663, V, 40.

MAŠ.DA.MEŠ.
I R. 66, I, 4.

I. משה, **mašû,** forget.
IV, 1, *ki-sur-ri-ši-na im-ma-šu-ma,* V. A., 2663, III, 19.

II. משה, **mûšu,** night.
ur-ra ù mu-ša, V R. 56, 44; III R. 41, II, 23.

משח, **mašâḫu,** measure.
I, 1 pret., *eqlu šú-a-tum im-šú-ḫu-ma,*

London, 101, I, 21; Susa, 16, II, 10; III, 8; D. E. P., VI, 44, I, 15; *iš-pur-ma im-šú-ḫu-ma*, Susa, 3, I, 38; C. T., IX, pl. V, 28; *eqlu im-šú-uḫ-ma*, Susa, 14, I, 17; *im-šú-uḫ-ma a-na ṣa-ti i-ri-en-šú*, III R. 43, I, 13; inf., *i-na ma-ša-ḫi eqli*, Susa, 14, I, 8; perm., *eqlu [šu-a-tum ul ma-ši-iḫ]*, Neb. Nippur, III, 33.

mašiḫânu, surveyor.

ma-ši-ḫa-an eqli, III R. 41, I, 14.

משל, **mašâlu,** be equal.

II, 2, *la um-daš-ša-lu ilu-su*, whose divinity cannot be equaled, Neb. Nippur, I, 17.

tamšîlu, equal.

la [i]-šú-u tam-šil-šu, V. A., 2663, II, 33; (*kunukku*) *ša la tam-šil* (the royal seal), which has no like, V. A., 2663, V, 49; *^{abnu}ku-nukku šarru-ú-ti-šu ša la tam-ši-li*, C. T., X, pl. V, 8; VI, 30.

maššitu, harvest(?).

lu-ú tibnu(IN.NU) lu-ú ŠE.BAR ù lu-ú mim-ma maš-ši-ta, Susa, 3, II, 50.

mâtu, land, *passim*.

מתי, **matîma,** whenever.

Susa, 2, III, 1; London, 103, V, 27; London, 101, II, 12; Susa, 3, III, 55; Susa, 16, III, 24; D. E. P., II, 112, 10; V R. 56, 26; Neb. Nippur, III, 17; O. B. I., 83, II, 11; III R. 41, I, 31; V. A., 208, 43; London, 102, IV, 36; V. A., 209, I, 31; *matîma(UD.-ME.DA)*, D. E. P., II, 97, 10; *im-ma-ti-ma*, I R. 70, II, 1; III R. 43, III, 1; *ma-te-ma*, O. B. I., 149, II, 1.

$נא_1ד$, **nâdu,** lofty, sublime.

rubû na-a-du, V R. 55, 1; O. B. I., 83, I, 20; *rubû [na]-'i-du*, V. A., 2663, II, 31.

$נא_2ר$, **nâru,** river.

a-na nâri i-na-du-ú(i-nam-du-ú), O. B. I., 150, II, 2; London, 102, V, 1; III R. 41, II, 10; *^{h}ḫi-ri-e nâra*, Neb. Nippur, III, 25; *nâr piḫâti ša šarri*, Susa, 3, I, 52; III, 3; for the *nâr šarri* cf. p. 219; for *kišâd nâri* cf. *kišâdu*; *nâri-šú i-si-ik-ki-ru-ma*, Susa, 16, V, 7; *nâri-šú a-na la sa-ka-ri*, III R. 45, No. 2, 8; *[nârât]e-šú li-is-kir-ma*, O. B. I., 149, II, 21; *nârâte sa-ki-ki li-mi-li*, III R. 43, IV, 3; V R. 56, 42; *ka-al-li-e nâri ka-al-li-e ta-ba-li*, III R. 45, No. 2, 2; cf. C. T., IX, pl. V, 33; Neb. Nippur, III, 26; I R. 66, I, 6, 7; *i-na muḫ-ḫi nâri eš-šit*, V. A., 209, I, 11; *itti nâri ^{âlu}Du-ú-tu*, V. A., 209, IV, 25.

I. $נב_1א$, **nabû,** call.

I, 1 pret., *šùm-šu ke-niš im-bu-u*, V. A., 2663, III, 1; *V šiqlu šibirtu maḫîri im-bi-e-ma i-šam*, for five sheqels as purchase price he offered to buy, V. A., 209, III, 25, cf. V. A., 209, II, 37; III, 12; pres., *i-nam-bu-šú-ma a-na ri-'-ut ma-ti i-na-aš-šú-šú*, Susa, 3, III, 58; *^{d}Marduk šùm-šu i-nam-bu-u*, V. A., 2663, V, 21; part., *na-bu-ú rê'û ki-nu*, relat., Neb. Nippur, I, 21; perm., *lu-ú a-mi-lu-ú-tum ma-la šú-ma na-bi-a-at*, Susa, 3, VI, 14.

II. $נב_4א$, **namba'u,** inundation.

mi-iḫ-ri nam-ba-'-i ku-ša-ar-ti u ḫi-iṣ-sa-ti šá nâr šarri, Susa, 3, II, 19.

נבט, **nabâṭu,** light up.

II, 1, *ûmi(-mi)-is nu-ub-bu-ṭi*, lit up like day, IV R.^{2} 38, II, 16.

נבל, **nablu,** flame.

ḫa-am-ma-ṭu ki nab-li, V R. 55, 18.

$נג_2א$, **nigû,** be light.

II, 1, *nu-gu ka-bit-ti*, cheerfulness of heart, Neb. Nippur, IV, 10.

nâgiru, commander.
lu-ú di-ku-ú lu na-gi-ru, D. E. P., II, 97, 12; *ʰnâgiru(LIGIR) a-na âli la e-ri-bi,* V R. 55, 52; *ša-kin* *mâtuNa-mar ʰnâgiru,* V R. 56, 10, 24; *ʰnâgir(LIGIR) êkalli (E.GAL),* V. A., 2663, V, 7.

nangaru, carpenter.
Susa, 3, I, 22; V. A., 208, 9.

נגש, **nagâšu,** oppress, overwhelm.
I, 1 prec., *a-mat nišê li-gi-sa-šú,* Neb. Nippur, IV, 8 (cf. p. 180).

נדה, **nadû,** throw, overthrow.
I, 1 pres., *a-na mê ù išâti i-nam-du-ú,* Susa, 16, IV, 32; *a-na me-e lu a-na išâti inamdû(RU-ú),* London, 101, III, 3; *a-na mê inamdû(RU-u),* Neb. Nippur, V, 1; V. A., 2663, V, 28; *a-na mê i-nam-du-ú,* I R. 70, III, 1; O. B. I., 149, II, 11; C. T., X, pl. VII [36]; *a-na nâri i-nam-du-ú,* London, 102, V, 1; III R. 41, II, 10; *a-na nâri i-na-du-ú,* O. B. I., 150, II, 2; D. E. P., VI, 45, V, 14; *a-na mê i-na-du-ú,* III R. 43, I, 33; *lu a-na išâti i-na-du-[ú],* D. E. P., II, 113, 16; D. E. P., VI, 45, V, 12; *ša-ar-qi eqlu šú-a-tum i-nam-du-ma,* who overthrows the grant of this field, Neb. Nippur, III, 21.
I, 2, *a-na me-e u išâti it-ta-di,* Susa, 3, V, 51.
III, 1, *a-na me-e ú-ša-ad-du-ú,* London, 103, V, 45; *a-na mê a-na išâti(NE) ú-šad-du-ú,* IV R.² 38, III, 19.

nidû, throwing down.
zêr-šú a-na šú-li-i ai ir-šú-ú ni-da a-ḫi, throwing down of side, *i.e.*, rest may he not have, Susa, 2, III, 29.

נדן, **nadânu,** give.
I, 1 pret., *id-din,* London, 103, III, 5, 14, 28; IV, 10; V, 26; London, 102, I, 18, 29, 35, 37; IV, 25; V. A., 209, I, 22, 26; IV, 15; *id-di-in-ma,* Susa, 2, I, 10; Susa, 16, III, 14; *iddin(SE)-ma,* Susa, 2, I, 15; I R. 70, I, 18; *id-di-nu,* C. T., IX, pl. V, 30; V. A., 209, IV, 38; *i-din-nu,* D. E. P., II, pl. 20, 8; *id-di-in-nu-ma,* London, 103, II, 11; *eqlu ad-di-nu* (relat.), Susa, 3, IV, 50; c. suff., *id-di-nu-šu,* Susa, 3, III, 45; *id-di-nu-niš-šum-ma,* C. T., X, pl. V, 7; *ad-di-na-aš-šu,* Susa, 3, V, 14, 33; pret., *iddan;* c. suff., *id-da-aš-ši,* V. A., 209, I, 19; *id-da-aš-šu-nu,* V. A., 209, IV, 32; prec., *lid-di-nam-ma,* C. T., X, pl. V, 9; *bîtu ki-i bîti . . . lud-dak-ka,* V. A., 209, I, 11, 16; pres., *a-na aḫât-ia a-nam-din,* London, 102, I, 24; pres., c. suff., *i-nam-di-na-aš-šum-ma,* Susa, 3, IV, 49; imper., *a-na mBu-[ru-ša] i-din,* London, 102, VI, 11; inf., *na-da-an kaspi,* Susa, 14, I, 14; *na-dan ur-ti-šú,* Neb. Nippur, I, 5; *la na-da-ni,* V R. 55, 56, 57; *eqlu ul na-dan i-qa-bu-ú,* III R. 43, III, 6; *na-da-na ul i-ši-ma,* London, 102, IV, 19; *na-da-na,* London, 102, VI, 11; *a-na na-dan eqlâti,* V. A., 2663, III, 10; perm., *ul na-din-mi i-qab-bu-ú,* London, 103, V, 38; London, 101, III, 1; I R. 70, II, 17; *ul na-di-in ul ma-ḫi-ir-mi i-qab-bu-ú,* Neb. Nippur, IV, 1; *bîtâti šú-a-tu ul nadinû(SE.MEŠ)-ma kaspu ul ma-ḫir,* V. A., 209, II, 3; *kaspu ul nadin(SE-in),* London, 102, IV, 39; *eqlu ul na-din,* V. A., 208, 46; *ša a-na šîmi eqli nad-nu(?),* London, 102, IV, 23; *ša a-na mBe-la-ni na-ad-nu,* London, 103, III, 4; *a-na šîmi na-ad-nu-ma,* London, 103, III, 45; *ša a-na bêl mâtâti*

nadnu(*SE-nu*), Neb. Nippur, III, 5.

2, *arad-su . . . i-ta-ad-di-nu*, III, R. 43, edge IV, 6; *it-ta-din*, London, 102, IV, 14; *šarru it-ta-din*, C. T., X, pl. III, 6.

nadinânu, seller.

na-di-na-an eqli, Susa, 16, II, 23; *na-din-an*, London, 102, III, 3.

nidintu, nidittu, gift.

ul ni-di-it-ti šarrâni, Susa, 16, IV, 20; *ul ni-di-it-ti šarri*, Susa, 14, II, 12; III R. 41, II, 7; O. B. I., 149, II, 7; *eqlu ul ni-di-it šarri*, III R. 43, edge IV, 2; *ša ni-din-ti šú-a-tu ú-ša-an-nu-ú*, C.T., X, pl. VII, 33; *ul ni-din-ti šarri-im-ma i-gab-bu-*[*ú*], C. T., X, pl. VII, 35.

nudunnû, dowry.

it(!)-*ti mu-lu-gi ù nu-dun-ni-e*, London, 102, I, 16.

נזז, **nazâzu,** stand.

I, 1 pres., *iz-za-az-zu*, are present, Susa, 16, III, 23; I R. 66, II, 16; III R. 41, II, 1; D. E. P., VI, 43, II, 19; C. T., X, pl. III, 30; London, 102, IV, 10; I R. 70, II, 9; *iz-za-zu*, Neb. Nippur, V, 25; *iz-za-zi*, V. A., 2663, V, 15; *izzazû*(*DU.MEŠ-zu*), V R. 56, 24; London, 101, II, 11; prec., *ina pa-rik-ti li-iz-zis-su*, with violence proceed against him, I R. 70, III, 17; inf., *i-na nazâzi* (*GUB.BA*), III R. 43, I, 29; II, 1, 5, 7, 11, 13, 15, 17, 19, 21, 24, 26, 28, 29; *i-na nazâzi*(*GUB-zi*) *ša aḫê-šu*, London, 102, I, 25.

III, 1 pret., *ma-ḫar ili-šú uš-zi-iz*, before his god he set up, Susa, 2; Med., I, 5; perm., *šú-zu-uz-zu ina maḫ-ri šakkanak Bâbili*, (whose word) had standing before the potentate of B., Neb. Nippur, II, 19; *abšênu*(*AB.SIM*) *la šú-zu-za-at-ma*, vegetation had not grown up, Neb. Nippur, II, 30.

IV, 1 perm., *na-zu-uz-zu ša-aḫ-tiš*, Neb. Nippur, I, 8.

ušuzzu, stand.

IV, 2, *ni-is-qu ša rabûti sisê it-ta-ši-iz-zu*, the excellence of the horses stood still, *i.e.*, disappeared, V R. 55, 20; *it-ta-ši-iz i-na li-ti*, he stood in might, *i.e.*, he triumphed, V R. 55, 42.

manzazu, nanzazu (p. 172), highest dignitary.

ma-an-za-az pân(*ŠI*) *šarri*, D.E. P., II, 97, 13; *na-an-za-az maḫ-ḫar šarri*, Neb. Nippur, II, 18 (cf. Nabû-shum-ishkun, edge 7, *ilâni ma-la ina eli narî an-ni-i šur-šu-du na-an-za-zu*; IV R.[2] 31*, No. 1(c), Col. III, 11, *ti-ru u na-an-za-z*[*u*]).

^{h}**Na-ḫas-si-pa-ni.**

Susa, 16, I, 32.

נחש, **naḫâšu,** be full.

I, 1, *na-ḫa-ša ḫa-ba-ṣa li-kim-šú-ma*, Neb. Nippur, IV, 10.

nuḫšu, abundance.

šanâte duḫ-di nu-uḫ-ši ù ḫegalli (*ḪÉ.GÁL*), Susa, 3, V, 18.

נטל, **naṭâlu,** see.

I, 1 inf., *i-na na-ṭa-al ka-am-ma-li*, Susa, 3, VI, 35; *ši-ma-at la na-ṭa-li*, a fate of not seeing, *i.e.*, blindness, Susa, 3, VII, 36; part., *la na-ṭil ša pâni-ša*, a short-sighted man, V. A., 2663, V, 26 (cf. Sippar tablet of Nabû-apal-iddina, I, 12, *la na-ṭil ma-na-ma*, not seeing anything).

nuḫatimmu, baker.

^{h}*nuḫatimmu*(*MU*), V.A., 209, II, 16.

ניא, **nî'u,** enclose.

I, 2, *i-na lipitti it-te-'i*, Susa, 3, V, 53.

nu'u, weakling, feeble.

nu-'-a giš-ḫab-ba, III R. 41, II, 9; *nu-'-a la pa-liḫ ilâni*, V. A., 2663, V, 27; *sak-la sak-ka nu-'-a*, V. A., 211, III, 9.

נכד, **nakâdu,** pass quickly(?).
ûmi(-mi) ša na-ka-da arḫi ša ši-ṭa-ru-da, IV R.² 38, II, 20.

נכל, **nakâlu,** be skilful, wonderful.
I, 1 perm., *al-ka-ka-tu-šu nak-la,* Neb. Nippur, I, 19.

naklu, skilful.
par-su-u nak-lu, V. A., 2663, II, 48.

nikiltu, cleverness, mischief.
ú-zu-un ni-kil-tú, a mind of cleverness, V. A., 2663, III, 4; *i-ban-nu-ú ni-kil-tú,* he practices mischief, V. A., 2663, V, 24; *ši-pir ni-kil-ti,* by a mischievous deed, C. T., X, pl. VII, 36.

נכם, **nakintu,** treasure (cf. p. 170).
ina na-kin-ti maḫ-ri ^d^*En-lil,* Neb. Nippur, II, 9.

נכס, **nakâsu,** cut off.
I, 1 prec., *lik-ki-sa na-ap-šat-[su],* V R. 56, 57; inf., ^iṣu^*kirê u* ^iṣu^*šag-gulâni la na-ka-si,* V R. 55, 60.
II, 1 prec., *lunakkisû (TAR.ME) arkat(EGIR)-su,* V. A., 2663, V, 47.

נכר, **nakâru,** change.
II, 1 pres., *i-na aš-ri-šú ú-nak-ka-ru-ma,* London, 101, III, 3; *ú-na-ak-ka-ru ú-ḫal-liq-qu,* London, 103, V, 43; *ku-dur-ra ú-na-ak-ka-ru,* Susa, 16, IV, 19; *ku-dur-ra ú-na-ka-ru,* O. B. I., 150, II, 2; *ú-na-ka-ru ina šub-ti-šu,* V. A., 2663, V, 28; perm., *kudurri-ši-na nu-uk-ku-ru-ma,* V. A., 2663, III, 22.
II, 2 pres., *a-mat ki-bi-ti-šú-nu la ut-ta-ak-ka-ru,* Susa, 3, VI, 22; *ku-dur-ra-ša ul ut-ta[k-k]ar,* O. B.I., 83, II, 2; pret., *ku-dur-ra-ša ut-tak-kir,* O. B. I., 83, II, 5.

nakaru, enemy.
na-ka-ra a-ḫa-a la mu-da-a ú-ma-'-a-ru-ma, I R. 70, II, 22; *a-ḫa-am na-ka-ra . . . um-ta-'-ir-ma,* Susa, 3, V, 48; *lu na-ka(-ra) lu a-ḫa,* IV R.² 38, III, 10.

nakiru, enemy.
^iṣu^*kakku na-ki-ri,* London, 103, VI, 19; ^iṣu^*kakku na-ki-ri-šú ú-šib-bir-ma,* Neb. Nippur, II, 4.

nakru, hostile, enemy.
a-na nakri(KÚR) bêli-šu i-te-ru-ub, V R. 55, 39; *it-ta-rad a-na* ^h^*nakri,* V R. 55, 38; *ṣir-rit nakri-šú,* Neb. Nippur, II, 5; ^h^*nakri-šu ina pâni-šu lim-niš iṭ-ṭar-ra-du,* V. A., 2663, II, 35; *ummân(ZAB) nakri,* V. A., 2663, III, 16; pl., *i-na nakru-ú-ti ù mun-daḫ-ṣu-ti,* V R. 55, 46, 48.

נמר, **namâru,** shine.
I, 1 pres., *bît i-mit-ti šarri bêli-šu la im-mir-šú-ma,* V R. 55, 27, 37.
II, 1 part., *mu-nam-mir gi-mir e-kur-re,* who makes brilliant all temples, V. A., 2663, II, 5.

namru, shining.
ûmi-šu nam-ru, III R. 41, II, 20; pl., *i-na bu-ni-šú nam-ru-ti,* Neb. Nippur, I, 22; C. T., X, pl. III, 9; V. A., 2663, III, 41; C. T., X, pl. V, 15.

namerûtu, splendor.
^d^*Sin bêl agê na-me-ru-ti,* Neb. Nippur, IV, 13.

numru, gladness.
nu-mur libbi, Neb. Nippur, IV, 10.

namrir(r)u, glory.
ni-ip-ḫu nam-ri-ru, flaming disk, Susa, 2, IV, 12; *ilu ša melammi-šú . . nam-ri-ir-ri ṣa-'-nu,* Neb. Nippur, I, 13.

nannaru, lamp.
^d^*Sin na-an-nar šamê ellûti,* III R. 41, II, 16; ^d^*Sin na-an-na-ru a-šib šamê(-e) ellûti,* I R. 70, III, 18; ^d^*Sin nannara(*^d^*ŠEŠ.KI-na-ra) šamê(-e) u irṣitim(-tim),* V. A., 209, V, 9.

נסא₄, **nisû,** depart, move away.
I, 1 pres., *i-ni-is-su-u* 3660 *kaš-bu i-na e-muq* ^d^*Bêl(EN),* V. A., 2663, II, 36.

Nisaba, grain.
ki-mu *^{d}Nisaba(ŠE.ELTEG)* *pu-qut-tu li-iḫ-nu-bi*, III R. 41, II, 33; *^{d}Nisaba li-ḫal-li-qa pu-qut-tu li-iš-mu-uḫ*, I R. 70, IV, 12.

נסח, **nasâḫu,** tear out.
I, 1 prec., *ku-dur-ra-[šu] li-is-su-ḫu*, IV R.[2] 38, III, 36; *ku-dur-ra-šú li-is-su-uḫ*, I R. 70, IV, 4; III R. 41, II, 27; *li-is-suḫ*, London, 102, II, 16; *kudurra-šu lis-suḫ(ZI-uḫ)*, Neb. Nippur, IV, 19; *išid-su li-is-su-ḫu*, I R. 70, III, 12; *e-ši-is-su li-is-su-ḫu*, III R. 43, III, 27; *išid-su lissuḫû(ZI-ḫu)*, Neb. Nippur, V, 7; *[išid-su] li-iz-zi-ḫu*, Susa, 16, VI, 25; *pi-ri-iḫ-šu li-is-su-uḫ-ḫu*, III R. 43, III, 29; *pir'-šu li-is-su-ḫu*, D. E. P., IV, pl. 16, II, 10; *li-su-uḫ-šu-ma*, D. E. P., II, 115, 7; *li-su-ḫu-šú-ma*, D. E. P., II, 113, 22; inf., *na-saḫ ku-dur-ri an-ni-i*, I R. 70, II, 8.

nisḫu, extract.
a-na pi-i ni-is-ḫi ša ṭi-i-ṭi, C. T., IX, pl. V, 42.

נסך, **nasâku,** appoint, put.
I, 1 pres., *a-na nâri i-na-su-ku* (relat.), V R. 56, 36; *a-na bûri i-na-as-su-ku*, III R. 41, II, 11; London, 102, V, 2; part., *na-sik šarrâni*, V R. 55, 11.

nisakku, priest.
nisak(NU.AB) ili bêl bîti, London, 103, I, 47; *nisak(NU.AB) ^{d}En-lil*, Neb. Nippur, II, 13; *ina amât šarri nisakki*, Neb. Nippur, II, 12; *^{m}Kaš-šú-ú ṭup-šar nisak (NISAG.GA) Bît-^{md}Sin-še-me*, Neb. Nippur, V, 18.

Nîsannu, first Babylonian month.
C. T., X, pl. III, 30.

נסס, **nissatu,** lamentation.
ni-is-sa-tu li-ilqi(ŠU.TI)-šú Neb. Nippur, IV, 12.

נסק, **nasâqu,** respect.
I, 1 perm., *at-mu-šú na-as-qu-ma*, Neb. Nippur, II, 19.

nasqu, noble.
rubû na-a-du na-as-qu, V R. 55, 2; *šarru na-as-qu*, V R. 55, 22.

nisqu, excellence.
ni-is-qu ša rabûti sisê, V R. 55, 20.

^{h}**NI.SUR,** title of an official.
V. A., 209, III, 20.

נפח, **napâḫu,** kindle.
IV, 1, *in-na-pi-iḫ i-ša-tu*, V R. 55, 30.

nipḫu, flaming rise (of sun).
ni-ip-ḫu nam-ri-ru, flaming sun disk, Susa, 2, IV, 12.

^{h}**nappaḫu,** smith.
V. A., 209, III, 6, 21.

נפץ, **napâṣu,** crush, destroy.
I, 1 prec., *lip-pu-ṣu zêr-šu*, I R. 70, IV, 25.

Nippurû, the Nippurian.
ṣâbê Nippurû(EN.LIL-ú), V R. 56, 3.

נפש, **napištu,** soul, life.
na-piš-ta-šú ki-ma mê lit-bu-uk, Susa, 2, III, 33; *lik-ki-sa na-ap-šat-[su]*, V R. 56, 57; *nap-ša-tuš li-bal-li*, Neb. Nippur, IV, 4; *na-p[i-iš-ta-šu] aplê zêri-šú li-[ḫal]-li[-qu]*, O. B. I., 149, II, 19.

נצר, **naṣâru,** guard, protect.
I, 1 part., *^{d}Nabû nâṣir(ŠEŠ) ku-dur eqlâti*, Susa, 2, IV, 34; *ilu na-ṣir-ri-šú*, Susa, 14, IV, 13; *na-ṣir ku-dur-ri-ti*, V R. 55, 5.

נקב, **naqbu,** fountain.
šar naqbê, D. E. P., VI, 43, IV, 4; (Rammân) *bêl naq-bi u zu-un-ni*, V R. 56, 41.

נקה, **naqû,** pour out water.
I, 1 part., *na-aq me-e*, libator, Susa, 3, VII, 10; D. E. P., VI, 45, IV, 10; *aplu ù n[a-a]q mê*, London, 102, II, 19; *apil-šu na-qa mê li-še-li*, III R. 43, IV, 20.

niqû, libation.
ina niqê(SIGIŠ) šum-du-li, Neb. Nippur, II, 8.

נקר, **naqâru**, destroy.

I, 1 prec., *ku-dur-ra-šu li-na-qir*, London, 103, VI, 12; pres., *ú-ša-aq-qa-ru i-na-aq-qa-ru*, IV R.[2] 38, III, 17; *ina abni i-na-aq-qa-ru*, V R. 56, 35; inf., *II bîtâti abtûti(GUL.MEŠ) ša na-qa-ra u e-pi-[šu]*, V. A., 209, III, 17; *bîtu šú-a-tu ša na-qa-ru ù e-pi-šu*, V. A., 209, IV, 23.

I, 2, *it-ta-qar i-ta-bat uḫ-tal-liq*, Susa, 3, V, 55.

III, 1 pres., *ú-ša-aq-qa-ru*, London, 103, V, 42; IV R.[2] 38, III, 16.

narû, inscribed stone.

na-ri-i, Susa, 2, III, 17; *na-ri-e*, Susa, 2, IV, 33; Susa, 2; Med., II, 5; III R. 43, IV, 32; *na-ra-a*, Susa, 2; Med., I, 3; Med., II, 9; III R. 43, III, 32; D. E. P., VI, 45, V, 9; *abnuNA.RÚ.A*, London, 101, IV, 5; Susa, 3, III, 51; IV, 9; VII, 28; IV R.[2] 38, III, 9, 30; Susa, 14, IV, 16; Susa, 16, IV, 29; VI, 9; D. E. P., VI, 43, IV, 8; D. E. P., II, 113, 20; D. E. P., VI, 45, V, 9; D. E. P., VI, 47, 19; V R. 56, 25, 35; III R. 41, II, 36, 40; I R. 70, II, 24, IV, 22; III R. 43, III, 23; O. B. I., 149, II, 8, 14; London, 102, V, 1; V. A., 2663, V, 45; V. A., 209, V, 5; Neb. Nippur, heading 1; IV, 28; V, 5; *abnuRÚ.A*, Susa, 3, IV, 9, 41, 60; V, 22, 34, 46; C. T., X, pl. VII, 36.

nurzu.

nu-ur-zu kisâd nâr šarri, V. A., 2663, IV, 31.

nišu, spirit.

ni-iš ilâni rabûti is-qur, I R. 70, I 21.

nišu, people.

pl., *nišê, a-na ni-ši aḫ-ra-a-ti* London, 101, II, 13; *dE-a pa-ti-ik ni-ši*, London, 101, III, 11; *a-na ni-ši-šú ai iṭ-ḫi*, Susa, 16, VI, 19; *mu-šam-mi-ḫu ni-ši-šú*, V R. 55, 4; *nišê(UN.MEŠ) a-pa-ti*, Neb. Nippur, III, 18; *a-mat nišê li-gi-sa-šú*, Neb. Nippur, IV, 8; *nišê di-ša-a-ti*, III R. 41, II, 39; *(Šamaš) kaš-kaš nišê*, III R. 43, IV, 10; *i(na) pî nišê li-ḫal-liq*, London, 102, II, 17; V. A., 2663, V, 47; *nišê (UN.ME) i-ḫi-iṭ*, V. A., 2663, I, 21; *ši-bir-ru mu-šal-lim nišê (UN.ME)*, V. A., 2663, I, 36; *kiš-šat nišê*, V. A., 2663, I, 39; *nišê da-ad-me ṣapḫâti(BIR.ME)*, V. A., 2663, II, 28.

נשא, **našû,** take up.

I, 1 pret., *ri-eš eqli šú-a-tum iš-šú-ma*, Susa, 16, III, 6; *reš(SAG) eqli iš-šú-ma*, O. B. I., 149, I, 20; *reš(SAG) eqlu šú-a-tu [iš]-ši-ma*, London, 103, II, 46; *rêš(SAG) eqlâti ša Bît-mSin-ma-gir . . . iš-ši-ma*, O. B. I., 83, I, 13; *dEr-ia it-ti dBêl(EN) a-na Bâbi-liki iš-ša-a* (Dual), C. T., IX, pl. IV, 12; *mârê-šú ša mBe-la-ni iš-šá-am-ma* (Dual), they brought, London, 103, III, 13; pres., *i-na-aš-šú-šu a-na ri-'-ut mâti*, they raised him, Susa, 3, III, 60; inf., *imêri-šú ù ameli-šu la na-še-e*, Susa, 3, II, 53; *a-na la na-še-e ša mâtuAl-ni-ri-e-a*, III R. 45, No. 2, 3; *a-na našê (ZI.GA) ú-še-iṣ-ṣu-ú*, I R. 70, II, 11; part., *na-aš išuqašti iz-zi-ti*, V R. 55, 8; *ilâni na-šú-šú*, the gods urging him on, V R. 55, 22; *la na-še-šú-nu*, I R. 66, I, 8.

III, 1, *ú-ša-aš-šú-ma*, London, 101, III, 7; Susa, 16, IV, 30; Neb. Nippur, V, 3; London, 102, V, 5; III R. 41, II, 10; O. B. I., 149, II, 10; *ú-ša-aš-šú-ú*, III R. 43, I, 32; Neb. Nippur, III, 27; I R. 70, II, 24; prec., *ri-ki-is-su la* *pa-ṭi-ra li-šiš-ši-šú*, I R. 70, III, 14; *a-ga-lâ-til-la-a lišiššu(GA.-TU-šu)-šu-ma*, V. A., 2663, V, 43; *ša ri-ki-is-su la ip-paṭ-ṭa-ru li-še-eš-ši-šu*, Susa, 3, VI, 47; *ri-ik-su la pa-ṭe-ra [li-šiš-ši-šú]*, III R. 43, III, 32; London, 102, I [41]; *li-ša-aš-ši-šu*, D. E. P., IV, pl. 16, I, 2.

III, 2, *uš-taš-ši-ma a-na me-e u išâti it-ta-di*, Susa, 3, V, 5, 13.

III, 3, *eqlu ki-mu uš-ta-an-na-aš-šum-ma*, Susa, 3, V, 13.

IV, 3, *eqlu ki-mu it-ta-na-aš-šum-ma*, Susa, 3, V, 32.

nišûtu, nisûtu, relatives, family.
aḫê mârê nišûti(IM.RI.A) u sa-la-ti, London, 103, V, 29; *i-na kimti(IM.RI.A) nišûti(IM.RI.-A) ù salâti(IM.RI.A)*, III R. 43, III, 3; London, 102, I, 30; IV, 37; V. A., 209, I, 33; *kimti (IM.RI.A) ni-šu-ti u sa-la-ti*, I R. 70, II, 3; *ni-su-ta ù sa-la-ti*, V. A., 208, 44.

nišru, diminution.
cstr., *[ni-š]i-er* $^{she'uzêru}$ *ig-zu-uz-ma*, O. B. I., 83, I, 14.

נשר, niširtu, diminution.
ni-šir-ta qi-za-ta i-šak-ka-nu, Susa, 2, III, 14; *ni-ši-ir-ta u qi-iṣ-ṣa-ta la ša-ka-ni*, Susa, 3, II, 9; *ni-(ši)-šir-tu il-ta-kan*, Susa, 3, V. 29; *ni-šir-ta qi-iṣ-ṣa-tu*, Susa, 16, IV, 16; *qi-iṣ-ṣa-ta ni-šir-ta i-šak-ka-nu*, III R. 41, II, 6; *ni-šir-ta qi-iṣ-ṣa-ta i-na lib-bi i-šak-ka-nu*, I R. 70, II, 15; *ni-ši-ir-ta qi-iṣ-ṣa-ta*, III R. 43, III, 21; *ni-ši-ir-ti gi-iṣ-ṣa-a-tu ud-da[a]*, C. T., X, pl. VII, 34.

nušurrû, diminution.
nu-šur-ra-a la ša-ka-ni, Susa, 3, III, 5.

nuširtu, loss(?).
nu-šir-ti, London, 102, III, 20; *[nu]-šir-ti-šu-nu ultu šatti* V^{kan} *adi šatti* 24^{kan}, London, 102, III, 12.

^{h}*SA*, probably a worker in leather.
D. E. P., II, pl. 20, 8 (cf. *âlu (ša)* ^{h}*SA.MEŠ*, B. E., IX, 70, 7; 97, 4, 6; etc.).

סבס, sabâsu, turn away, be angry.
I, 1 pret., *ša ki-mil-tuš is-bu-su*, V. A., 2663, I, 18 (cf. Nabû-apal-iddina, Sippar tablet, III, 14, *is-bu-su kišâd-su*).

סגה, sugû, want.
ûm(-um) su-gi-e u ar-ra-ti, III R. 41, II, 34; *su-ga-a u ni-ib-ri-ta liš-ku-na-aš-šum-ma*, I R. 70, IV, 17.

סדר, sadâru, set in order.
I, 1 inf., *ina sa-dar satuk E-kur*, Neb. Nippur, II, 3, 8.

סון, sûnu, thigh.
šîr taḫ-ši-e šîr sûni(UR), V. A., 208, 5.

סוק, sûqu, street.
su-u-uq âli-šú, Susa, 3, VI, 39; *itti sûqi(SILA) kad-ni*, V. A., 208, 13; *itti sûqi(SILA) u bîti*, V. A., 208, 16, 17.

סחה, saḫû, destroy.
II, 1 pret., *e tu-saḫ-ḫi mi-iṣ-[ra]*, O. B. I., 83, II, 23; inf., *ku-dur-ra la su-uḫ-ḫi-i*, Susa, 3, II, 14.

II, 2, *mi-ṣir-ša ul us-saḫ-ḫ[a]*, O. B. I., 83, II, 1; *mi-ṣir-ša us-saḫ-ḫi*, O. B. I., 83, II, 5.

III, 1, *eqlâti-šú id-ra-[nu] li-ša-as-ḫi-ma*, Susa, 14, III, 11.

saḫḫu, cistern (Hebr. שׁוּחָה) (Haupt).
ia-'-nu mê saḫ-ḫi, V R. 55, 19.

saḫmaštu, revolt.
i-na e-ši-tú u saḫ-maš-ti ša ^{mâtu}*Akkadî*^{ki}, C. T., X, pl. V, 3.

סחף, siḫpu, extent (cf. p. 165).
ka-la si-ḫi-ip ša-ma-me, Neb. Nippur, I, 14.

סחר, saḫâru, turn.
I, 2, *su-ú-uq âli-šú li-is-sa-aḫ-ḫar*, Susa, 3, VI, 40.

III, 2, *ul-te-is-ḫi-ir limutte(-te) lu ana šàr mâtuÊlamti,* he caused disaster to enclose the king of Elam, V R. 55, 41.

suḫurmašu, goatfish (Zimmern).
mu-um u su-ḫur-ma-šú a-ši-ir-tum rabîtum ša dE-a, Susa, 2, IV, 5.

סיר, rage.
I, 1 pres., *i-sa-ar me-ḫu-ú,* V R. 55, 32.

סכך, sakâku, stop up.
I, 1 inf., *sa-ka-ak uz-ni,* stopping up of ears, *i.e.*, deafness, Susa, 3, VII, 37; Susa, 14, III, 4; *sa-ka-ak,* D. E. P., VI, 43, III, 4; *sa-ka-ak [uz-ni],* D. E. P., II, 116, 3; *sa-kak uznâ(PI²),* V. A. 2663, V, 38.

sakku, deaf.
hsa-ak-la sa-ak-ka, London, 103, V, 41; Susa, 14, II, 14; Neb. Nippur, V, 3; Susa, 16, IV, 26; O. B. I., 149, II, 9; *sak-la lu sak-[ka],* IV R.² 38, III, 11; *sak-la sak-ka,* III R. 41, II, 9; I R. 70, II, 21; III R. 43, I, 31; V R. 56, 34; V. A. 211, III, 9; *sa-ak-ka sak-la,* D. E. P., VI, 45, V, 20; *sak-ka sak-la,* Susa, 3, V, 49; *sak-ku sak-lu,* V. A., 2663, V, 25.

sukkuku, a deaf man.
lu sak-lam lu suk-ku-ka, London, 101, III, 6.

sakîkê, šakîkê, mud.
nârâte-šu li-mil-la-a sa-ki-ke, V R. 56, 42; *nârâte sa-ki-ke li-mi-li,* III R. 43, IV, 4; *lu-ú šá-ki-i-ik-ki dal[-ti] ù ašar(KI) mi-il-ti nâri-šú i-si-ik-ki-ru-ma,* Susa, 16, V, 5.

סכל, saklu, fool.
hsa-ak-la sa-ak-ka, London, 103, V, 41; Susa, 16, IV, 26; Susa, 14, II, 14; O. B. I., 149, II, 9; Nippur, V, 2; *sak-la lu sak[-ka],* IV R.² 38, III, 11; *sak-lam lu suk-ku-ka,* London, 101, III, 6; *sak-la sa-ma,* Susa, 3, V, 49; *lu-ú sak-la lu-ú sak-ka,* V R. 56, 34; *sak-la sak-ka sa-ma-a,* I R. 70, II, 21; III R. 43, I, 31; *sa-ak-ka sak-la,* D. E. P., VI, 45, V, 20; *sak-la la še-ma-a,* London, 102, V, 4; *sak-la sak-ka,* III R. 41, II, 9; V. A. 211, III, 9; *sak-ku sak-lu,* V. A., 2663, V, 26.

suk(k)allu, minister.
dPap-sukal su-kal-li ilâni rabûti, III R. 43, IV, 25; *hsukallu (LUḪ),* IV R.² 38, I [11]; II, 35; Susa, 16, III, 18; V R. 56, 14; I R. 70, I, 17, 19, I R. 66, II, 12; III R. 43, I, 9; edge IV, 4, 5; London, 102, IV, 5; VI, 19; C. T., X, pl. III, 27; pl. VII, 42; *hsukallu mu-ni-ri,* London, 101, I, 14; *dNabû sukallu ṣi-ru,* III R. 41, II, 34; III R. 43, IV, 1; *suk-kal-lu ṣi-i-ru,* I R. 70, IV, 16.

si-kil-la.
mar-ka-su rabû(-ú) ša bît si-kil-la (Zimmern suggests that it may stand for E-sag-ila), Susa, 2, IV, 28.

סכף, sakâpu, throw down.
I, 1 pret., *is-kip-šu-ma,* D. E. P., VI, 45, IV, 6.

סכר, sakâru, sikêru, stop up, dam.
I, 1 prec., *[nârât]e-šú li-is-kir-ma,* O. B. I., 149, II, 22; pres., *ašar mi-il-ti nâri-šú i-si-ik-ki-ru-ma,* Susa, 16, V, 7; inf., *nâri-šú a-na la sa-ka-ri,* III R. 45, No. 2, 8; *lu-u ša si-ki-e-ri lu-ú ša pi-te(!)-e,* Susa, 3, II, 30.

סלם, salîmu, favor.
ša . . . ir-ša-a sa-li-me, who granted favor, V. A., 2663, I, 19 (cf. Napû-apal-iddina, Sippar tablet, III, 17, *sa-li-ma ir-ši-ma*).

salatu, household.
nišûti u sa-la-ti, London, 103, V, 29; *ni-šu-ti u sa-la-ti,* I R. 70, II, 3; *ni-su-ta ù sa-la-ti,* V. A., 208, 44; *kimti(IM.RI.A) nišûti*

(*IM.RI.A*) *u salati*(*IM.RI.A*), III R. 43, III, 4; London, 102, I, 30; IV, 37; V. A., 209, I, 33.

סמה, **samû,** blind.
sak-lam lu suk-ku-ka lu sa-ma-a, London, 101, III, 6; *sak-la sak-ka sa-ma,* Susa, 3, V, 49; *sak-ka sa-ma-a,* Susa, 16, IV, 27; V R. 56, 34; I R. 70, II, 21; III R. 43, I, 31; *sa-ak-ka sa-ma-a,* Susa, 14, II, 15; O. B. I., 149, II, 9.

simaku, shrine.
e-piš ku-um-mu ki-iṣ-ṣi u si-ma-ku, V. A., 2663, II, 12.

simmu, sickness (cf. p. 181).
si-im-ma la-az-za, Neb. Nippur, IV, 20; III R. 41, II, 30; I R. 70, IV, 6; *si-im-ma la*[*-az-za*], O. B. I., 149, III, 3; *si-im-ma aq-ṣa la-az-za,* Susa, 14, IV, 6; *si-im-ma la-az,* Susa, 3, VII, 19; III R. 43, IV, 16.

סנק, **sanâqu,** press.
I, 1 pret., *rit-ti-šu ai is-ni-iq,* Susa, 16, VI, 22; prec., *a-di ûm*(*-um*) *bal-du lit*(!)*-niq* (= *lisniq*?) *ma-a-ta,* Susa, 16, VI, 18.

sisû, horse.
ni-is-qu ša rabûti sisê (*imêrKUR.-RA.MEŠ*), V R. 55, 20; *salsisê,* see *urâte,* V R. 55, 53, 59; *rak-kab sisê,* riding saddles(?), III R. 41, I, 16; *sisê mu-ne*(*MU.-NE*), III R. 43, edge IV, 1; *xxx sisê,* III R. 43, edge, IV, 2; *rê'û sisê,* London, 102, III, 11, 13, 15, 23.

ספח, **sapḫu,** scattered.
mu-pa-aḫ-ḫi-ru sapḫâti(*BIR.ME*), *i.e., nišê,* V. A., 2663, I, 33; *nišê da-ad-me sapḫâti,* V. A., 2663, II, 29.

suppu.
ina su-up-pu irṣitim(*-tim*) *iṣugi-šimmaru šadî,* V. A., 209, II, 30.

סקר, **saqâru,** swear (perhaps = זכר).
I, 1 pret., *ni-iš ilâni rabûti . . . . is-qur,* I R. 70, I, 22.

surtu, wickedness (Aram. סְיוְרָא).
i-na su-ur-ti ma-la ba-šú-ú, London, 103, V, 40.

סתק, **satukku,** temple dues, tithes.
satuk(*ŠÀ.DUG*) *E-kur,* Neb. Nippur, II, 3, 8.

פאל,
III, II, 1 pret., *a-na-ku la e-nu-ú ù la uš-pi-lu,* I have not annulled, have not revoked, Susa, 3, IV, 12; *ša ṣi-it pi-šú ilu ma-am-ma la uš-pi-el-lum,* Susa, 3, VI, 32; *uš-pi-lum,* O. B. I., 150, II, 1.
III, II, 2 pret., *ša ṣi-it pi-i-šu la uš-te-pil-lu,* V. A., 2663, I, 15.

pagumu, object made of leather.
pa-gu-mi a-na Bi-ti-li-ia-a-šú ig-mu-ur-ma, D. E. P., II, pl. 20, 4 (cf. *mâshkupa-gu-mu,* Amarna Letters, Berl. 26, I, 48).

פגר, **pagru,** body.
iš-ru-ba-a . . . pa-ga-ar-šú li-la-bi-iš-ma, Susa, 3, VI, 50.

pûtu, front.
pûtu(*SAG*) *elû* and *pûtu šaplû, passim.* For orientation of fields cf. pp. 39–41.

פזר, **puzru,** concealment.
pu-uz-ra uš-ta-ḫi-iz, Susa, 3, V, 43; *pu-uz-ru ú-ša-ḫa-zu,* V. A., 2663, V, 30; *a-šar la a-*(*ma-*)*ri pu-uz-ri* [*i-tam-me-ru*], C. T., X, pl. VII, 37.

I. פחה, **piḫû,** enclose.
I, 1 pres., *ina iṣulipitti*(*LIBIT*) *i-pi-ḫu-ú,* (relat.), Neb. Nippur, V, 2; *i-na i-ga-ri i-p*[*i-ḫu-ú*], D. E. P., II, 113, 17.
I, 2 *i-na i-ga-ri ip-te-ḫi,* Susa, 3, V, 54.

II. פחה, **paḫâtu,** provincial district.
bêl paḫâti(*EN.NAM*), governor, Susa, 16, III, 23; IV, 1; Neb. Nippur, V, 15; V R. 56, 19; I R. 66, II

14; III R. 43, II, 4; III, 9; O. B, I., 149, II, 2; London, 102, IV. 8; VI, 21; IV R.[2] 38, I, 28; V. A., 2663, V, 3; *bêlê paḫâti(EN.-NAM.MEŠ)*, Susa, 2, III, 6.

piḫâtu, district, province.

pi-ḫat šarri, V. A., 2663, IV, 14, 49; *ana pi-ḫat i-man-nu-ú*, C. T., X, pl. VII, 34; *piḫâtu(NAM)*, Susa, 2, I, 28, 37; II, 9, 14, 19; London, 103, III, 42; London, 101, I, 6; Susa, 3, I, 52; III, 3, 16, 24, 31; IV, 16, 37, 51; V, 11, 14, 33; VI, 4, 7, 12; D. E. P., II, 112, 7; IV R.[2] 38, I, 5; Susa, 16, I, 4; IV, 6; Neb. Nippur, II, 28; III, 1, 8; O. B. I., 83, I, 15; O. B. I., 83, II, edge; III R. 41, II, 2; III R. 43, II, 23.

פחר, paḫâru, gather, collect.

II, 1 pret., *nišê da-ad-me sapḫâti ú-paḫ-ḫi-ru*, V. A., 2663, II, 29; part., *mu-pa-aḫ-ḫi-ru sapḫâti*, V. A., 2663, I, 33.

puḫru, assembly.

ina pu-ḫur šu-ut ma-al-ku, V. A., 2663, I, 42.

napḫaru, totality, all.

nap-ḫar qin-ni-e u kal da-ád-me, Neb. Nippur, I, 15; *ba-na-at nap-[ḫa-ri]*, D. E. P., II, 113, 1; *ina nap-ḫar ṣal-mat qaqqadi*, V. A., 2663, I, 22; *napḫar(PAP)*, Susa, 2, I, 26, 35; Neb. Nippur, III, 7; C. T., IX, pl. V, 26; III R. 41, I, 27; C. T., X, pl. III, 19; V. A., 102, IV, 27; V. A., 2663, IV, 2, 17, 42; V. A., 209, IV, 34; C. T., X, pl. VI, 29; *napḫar napḫar*, V. A., 2663, IV, 46.

פטר, paṭâru, break, free.

I, 1 pret., *eqlu šú-a-tu ip-tu-ur*, London, 103, III, 29; *mUr-dBêlit-muballiṭat-mîtûti ip-tu-ur*, London, 103, III, 46; inf., *ri-ki-is-su la pa-ṭi-ra*, an unbreakable bond, I R. 70, III, 14; *ri-ik-su la pa-ṭe-ra*, III R. 43, III, 32; *ša rik-su la pa[ṭe-ra]*, London, 102, I, 41.

IV, 1, *ša ri-ki-is-su la ip-pat-ṭa-ru* Susa, 3, VI, 46; III R. 41, II, 26

paṭru, dagger.

ul-tu paṭ-ru ina kišâdi-šu, V R. 56, 54.

פי, pû, mouth.

ṣi-it pi-šú, command, Susa, 3, VI, 30; *ṣi-it pi-i-šu*, V. A., 2663, I, 14, 31; *qi-bit pi-i-šú*, Susa, 3, VII, 45; *i-piš pî-šu*, Neb. Nippur, I, 9 *ki-i pi-i*, according to the word of, Susa, 3, IV, 13, 34, 44, V, 10; London, 102, IV, 27; III R. 43, I, 10; *a-na pi-i ni-is-ḫi*, according to the extract, C. T., IX, pl. V, 42; *i-na pi-i nišê li-ḫal-li-qu*, from the mouth of men, III R. 41, II, 39; London, 102, II, 17; V. A., 2663, V, 47; *ṣi-bit pi-i*, the holding of the mouth, *i.e.*, dumbness, Susa, 3, VII, 38; *ša pi-i nâruṢal-ma-ni*, the mouth of the river Ṣ., I R. 66, II, 2.

pi-i.

in the phrase *pi-i šú-ul-pi*, V. A., 208, 36, uncultivated or pasture land; the opposite is *eqlu zaq-pu*, cf. V. A., 208, 7, 8, 35, 36; *iṣukirû iṣugišimmarê zaq-pu u pi-i [šul-pi]*, C. T., X, pl. VI, 24.

פלה, palû, reign.

i-na palê(BAL-e) dMarduk-apal-iddina, Susa, 2; Med., II, 1; *ina ûmê(-me) palê-š[u]*, C. T., X, pl. IV, 15.

פלח, palâḫu, fear.

I, 1 pres., *aš-šu ar-r[a-ti] i-pal-la-ḫu-ma*, London, 102, V, 4; *aššu (MU) ar-ra-ti a-na-ti i-pal-la-ḫu-ma*, London, 101, III, 5; *zi-kir dENGUR dNinâ i-pal-la-ḫ[u]*, O. B. I., 83, II, 14; part., *pa-li-ḫu ilâni-šú*, O. B. I., 83,

I, 21; *pa-liḫ ilu-ti-šu*, V. A., 2663, I, 28; *pa-liḫ* ^d^*Nabû u* ^d^*Marduk*, V. A., 2663, II, 1; *ardu pa-liḫ-šu*, V. A., 2663, III, 37; *la pa-liḫ ilâni*, V. A., 2663, V, 27.

I, 2, *šú-ú la ip-ta-la-aḫ-ma*, Susa, 3, V, 27; *ša i-na* ^abnu^*narî ša-aṭ-ra ip-ta-laḫ-ma*, Susa, 3, V, 47; *šarru u ilâni-šu la ip-tal-ḫu-ma* (relat.), V R. 56, 32.

palḫiš, reverently.
ú-taq-qu-ú pal-ḫiš, Neb. Nippur, I, 6; *ana* ^d^*En-lil u* ^d^*NIN.IB pal-ḫi-iš ú-taq-qu-ú*, Neb. Nippur, II, 11.

פלך, **palâku,** fix limits.
I, 1 pret., *pil-ki ip-lu-uk-ma*, O. B. I., 83, I, 5; part., *pa-lik eqlu šú-a-tu*, Neb. Nippur, III, 13.

pilku, plot.
ki-i pil-ki ip-lu-uk-ma, O. B. I., 83, I, 5; *a-na pil-[ki]-šú ú-tir-ru*, O. B. I., 83, II, 10; *pi-lik-šú li-ni*, III R. 41, II, 28.

pulukku, boundary.
pu-lu-uk-ku la šit-ku-nu, V. A., 2663, III, 20; *pu-luk-ka-šu-un iš-ni-ma*, C. T., X, pl. V, 4.

pu-lu-uk(g), perhaps a measure.
pu-lu-uk(g) u imêru burâši, V R. 55, 56.

פלכה, **palkû,** wide, comprehensive.
ḫa-si-sa pal-ka, of wide intelligence, V. A., 2663, III, 7.

פלס, **palâsu,** look.
IV, 1 pret., *ki-niš ip-pa-lis-ma*, Neb. Nippur, I, 24; *ki-niš ippalis-(ŠI.BAR)-su-ma*, Neb. Nippur, II, 16; *arad-su ip-pa-li-is-ma*, III R. 43, I, 7; *ḫa-diš ip-pa-lis-ma*, C. T., X, pl. III, 11; *ḫa-diš ip-pal-su-šu-ma*, V. A., 2663, I, 29; *ḫa-diš ip-pa-lis-su-ma*, V. A., 2663, III, 42; prec., *lip-pal-su-šú-ma*, Susa, 3, V, 16; *ki-niš lip-pal-sa-šú-ma*, O. B. I., 83, II, 16; pres., *ul ip-pal-la-sa ša-na-a-ša it-ti-šu*, V R. 55, 34.

pânu.
(1) face, *zu-ut pa-ni*, blindness, Susa, 14, III, 4; *la na-ṭil ša pâni-(ŠI)-ša*, V. A., 2663, V, 26; *pa-ni-šú lim-ḫaṣ-ma*, III R. 41, II 19; *pân* ^d^*Šamši(-ši)*, V R. 55, 31; (2) presence, *pân*, before, in presence of, Susa, 16, 1, 25; London, 101, III, 8; London, 102, VI, 6; V. A., 208, 22, 49, 50, 51; *i-na pa-an*, before, in presence of, London, 103, III, 23, 24; VI, 16; *i-na pa-ni*, from his presence, C. T., IX, pl. IV, 3; V. A., 2663, II, 35; *ina pa-ni-ka*, at thy disposal, V. A., 209, I, 9; *pa-an iltânu (šûtu, amurrû, šadû)*, towards north, etc., London, 103, III, 47, 49; IV, 1, 3, 4; London, 101, I, 7, 8, 10, 11; Susa, 14, I, 2, 7; D. E. P., II, 112, 2, 6; with the verb *dagâlu*, cf. *pâni-šu ú-šad-gil*, he entrusted to him, C. T., IX, pl. V, 41; C. T., X, pl. V, 6; V. A., 209, IV, 8, 22; V. A., 2663, III, 24; V. A., 208, 6, 21; (3) former time, *ultu ûmi(-mi) pa-na*, from former days, Neb. Nippur, II, 29; *šarru pa-na*, a former king, V R. 55, 48; cf. *šarru a[-lik] pa-ni-ia*, my predecessor, Susa, 3, IV, 2; *eli ša pa-ni*, more than formerly, V. A., 2663, III, 29; also in the titles: *man-za-az pân šarri*, D. E. P., II, 97, 13; and *amelu ša pân(ŠI) êkalli*, C. T., X, pl. VII, 43.

pânâtu, in front of, before.
tap-tu-u pa-na-at ^išu^*kirû*, V. A., 2663, IV, 33; *a-di tap-te-e ša pa-na-at* ^išu^*kirû*, V. A., 2663, IV, 44.

pânû, title of an official.
^h^*pa-nu-ú* ^h^*šanû*(?) ^h^*ṣu-ḫi-li*, C. T., IX, pl. V, 34.

פסס, **pasâsu,** destroy.
II, 1 pres., *ú-pa-sa-su*, O. B. I., 150, II, 3; *ina abni ú-pa-sa-su*, V. A., 2663, V, 30.
II, 2, *up-te-is-si-is-ma it-ta-qar*, Susa, 3, V, 55.

פקד, **paqâdu,** govern, establish.
I, 1 pret., *ši-bir-ru . . . ip-qid qa-tuš-šu*, a scepter he handed over to his hand, V. A., 2663, I, 36; inf., *pi-iq-da . . . la pa-qa-di*, a government not to establish, III R. 45, No. 2, 7; part., *dNabû pa-qid kiš[šat] ni-ši*, who governs all men, London, 101, III, 14; *dNabû pa-[qid šamê u irṣiti(?)]*, London, 102, I, 44.
piqdu, government.
pi-iq-da ša Bît-mA-da a-na âli-šú la pa-qa-da, III R. 45, No. 2, 7.

puquttu, thorn.
ki-mu dNisaba pu-qut-tu li-iḫ-nu-bi, III R. 41, II, 33; *dNisaba li-ḫal-li-qa pu-qut-tu li-iš-mu-uḫ*, I R. 70, IV 13; *ta-mi-ra-ti-šú li-mi-la-a pu-qut-ta*, III R. 43, IV, 5.

פקר, **paqâru,** raise a claim.
I, 1 pret., *šarru ip-qir-ma a-na qâti . . . id-din*, the king reclaimed (the field) and gave it to . . ., London, 103, III, 4; pres., *i-paq-qi-ru ú-šap-qa-ru*, reclaims, III R. 41, I, 36; inf., *ku-nu-uk šarri ša la pa-qa-ru*, C. T., X, pl. V, 7; *ša la tam-ši-li ù la pa-qa-ra*, C. T., X, pl. V, 9; VI, 30; *ša la tam-šil u la pa-qa-ri*, V. A., 2663, V, 49; *a-na e-li u pa-ki-ri*, for the purpose of opposing and reclaiming, D. E. P., II, pl. 20, 9.
II, 1 pres., *ú-šad-ba-bu innû(BAL-ú) ú-paq-qa-ru*, V. A., 209, II, 1, 7.
III, 1 pres., *i-paq-qi-ru ú-šap-qa-ru*, III R. 41, I, 36.
paqru, reclamation.
a-na paq-ri la ra-še-e, I R. 70, I, 20; *aš-šu paq-ri la ra-še-e*, London, 102, II, 34; *a-na paq-ri la bašê(IG)*, V. A., 2663, IV, 52; *[pa]-ak(?)-ri išukirî id-bu-um-ma* Susa, 16, II, 17.
tapqirtu, claim.
tap-qir-ta ù ru-gu-um-ma-a, Susa, 3, II, 15.

פרא₃, **pir'u,** offspring.
she'uzêru ù pi-ir-a, Susa, 3, VII, 12; *pi-ri ai ir-šu*, Susa, 14, IV, 17; *zêr-šu u pir'(!)-šu li-is-su-ḫu*, D. E. P., IV, pl. 16, II, 9; *pi-ir-'-šú*, D. E. P., II, 113, 2; *pi-ir-šu*, D. E. P., VI, 45, IV, 16; *zêr-šu pi-ri-'-šú na-an-nab-šú*, III R 41, II, 38; *zêr-šu pir'-šu u na-an-nab-šu*, London, 102, II, 16; V. A., 2663, V, 46; *li-ḫal-li-qu pir'i-šu*, I R. 70, III, 12.

pargâniš, undisturbed(?).
par-ga-niš bašê(e) a-ḫu-ú-ti, V. A., 2663, III, 18.

purîdu, leg.
ša ed-li qar-di pu-ri-da-šú it-tu-ra, the legs of the valiant man turned, *i.e.*, failed, V R. 55, 21 (cf. Jensen, K. B., VI, 1, 428, 508).

פרח, **pirḫu,** offspring.
pi-ri-iḫ-šú li-is-su-uḫ-ḫu, III R. 43, III, 29.

פרך, **parâku,** lock, bolt.
II, 1 prec., *ba-ab-šú li-par-ri-ki*, III R. 43, IV, 27.
parku, barred.
ḫar-ra-an-na pa-ri-ik-ta (fem.) *li-še-iṣ-bi-su*, may he cause him to take a road that is barred, III R. 43, IV, 31.
pariktu, violence.
ina pa-rik-ti li-iz-zis-su, with violence proceed against him, I R. 70, III, 16; *i-na pa-ar(-ik)-ti li-iz-zi-su*, III R. 43, IV, 11.

פרכה, cease.

IV, 1, *la na-par-ka-a*, without fail, IV R.² 38, II, 23.

purîmu, wild ass.

e-ma *imêrupurîmê ṣêri li-ir-pu-ud*, Susa, 14, IV, 3; *ki-ma imêrupu-rîmi(EDIN.NA)*, III R. 41, II, 18; V. A., 209, V, 11; *ki-i purîmi(-mi)*, I R. 70, III, 20; London, 102, I, 47.

פרס, parâsu, decide.

I, 1 pret., *di-in-šu u purussî-šu ai ip-ru-us*, London, 102, II, 3; prec., *ina bîti(-ti)-šu [li]-ip-ru-us*, D. E. P., II, 115, 3; part., *pa-ri-is purussê*, Susa, 14, III, 7.

parsu, decision.

par(?)-su-šu šit-ru-ḫu, Neb. Nippur, I, 18; pl., *lit-ti pár-si-e i-ta-ni-e i-šá-lu-ma*, O. B. I., 83, II, 9.

parsû, decider, judge.

šarru parsê (BAR.SUD.MEŠ)i-šal-ma, the king asked the judges, V R. 55, 50; *parsê(BAR.SUD) la-bi-ru-ti illikû šarru . . i-šal-šú-nu-ti-ma*, Susa, 16, II, 27; *par-su-u nak-lu*, skilful arbitrator, V. A., 2663, II, 48.

purussû, judgment, decision.

pa-ri-is purussê(EŠ.BAR.MEŠ), Susa, 14, III, 7; *di-in-šu ù purussî(EŠ.BAR)-šu ai ip-ru-us*, London, 102, II, 2; *purussû (EŠ.BAR) kiš-šat nisê*, V. A., 2663, I, 38; *bêlê purussî*, C. T., X, pl. VII, 39.

פרץ, parâṣu, decide.

I, 1 perm., *a-ki ½ ma-na kaspi ⅔ ma-na V šiqlu pa-ri-ṣi*, V. A., 209, IV, 5.

parṣu, command.

a-na paraṣ(GARZA) šarri, Susa, 3, II, 43; *paraṣ ša-kin*, Susa, 3, II, 44; *paraṣ ma-am-ma*, Susa, 3, II, 45.

פשט, pašâṭu, efface.

I, 1 pres., *šú-mi šá-aṭ-ra i-pa-aš-ši-ṭu* (relat.), Susa, 16, V, 4; *šùm šaṭ-ru i-pa-aš-ši-ṭu*, V. A., 2663, V, 32.

I, 2, *šu-mi šaṭ-ra ip-ta-ši-iṭ*, Susa, 3, V, 57.

II, 1, *ú-pa-aš-ša-ṭu-ma ša-nam-ma i-šaṭ-ṭa-ru* (relat.), I R. 70, III, 5.

II, 2, *šú-um ili ù šarri ša šaṭ-ru up-taš-ši-ṭu-ma*, V R. 56, 33.

פשר, pašâru, loosen.

I, 1 inf., *ar-rat la pa-ša-ri*, IV R.² 38, III, 33.

IV, 1, *ar-rat la nap-šú(šu)-ri*, London, 101, IV, 6; Susa, 3, VI, 26; Susa, 16, VI, 12; I R. 70, IV, 23; III R. 43, III, 25; IV, 34; III R. 43, edge II, 2; O. B. I., 149, II, 16; London, 102, I, 39; *arrat(AŠ) la nap-šu-ru*, V. A., 2663, V. 37; *ar-rat la nap-šur marušta li-ru-ru-šu*, V. A., 209, II, 9; V, 8.

פתח, pitû, open.

I, 1 inf., *lu-ú šá si-ki-e-ri lu-ú šá pi-te(!)-e ḫi-ru-ut nâr šarri la hi-ri-e*, Susa, 3, II, 31.

פתן, patânu, keep off.

II, 1 imp., *dRammân limuttu(?) pa-at-ti-nu da(?)-riš*, London, 101, I, 3.

patinnu, some kind of dress.

I ṣubâtupa-tin-nu, III R. 41, I, 26.

פתק, patâqu, make, create.

I, 1 part., (Ea) *pa-ti-iq ni-ši*, London, 101, III, 11; (Šamaš) *pa-ti-iq šamê(e) u [irṣitim](-tim)*, D. E. P., II, 113, 5.

pitqu, building.

du-ul-li pit-ki, Susa, 3, II, 18.

צ₁אן, ṣênu, sheep.

ṣibit alpê u ṣi-e-ni, V R. 55, 55; *ina(?) ṣi-bit ṣi-en-ni(=ṣêni) ma-ki-su a-na âli-šú la e-re-bi*, III R. 45, No. 2, 9; *a-la-ad a-me-lu-ti alpê u ṣênê ('U.LU.ZUN.-MEŠ)*, London, 102, II, 28.

צאן, ṣânu, fill.

I, 1 prec., *li-ṣa-an ka-ra-as-su*, III R.

41, II, 26; perm., *nam-ri-ir-ri ṣa-'-nu*, Neb. Nippur, I, 13.

צא$_2$ר, **ṣêru,** field.

û-ma-am ṣi-ri, Susa, 2, VII, 1; *û-ma-am ṣêri(EDIN)*, D. E. P., VI, 47, 11; *ṣi-ra li-ir-pu-ud*, Susa, 2, VII, 2; *pa-an ṣêri (EDIN)*, Susa, 16, I, 25; *purîmê ṣêri*, Susa, 14, IV, 4; *i-na âli ù ṣêri*, V R. 56, 5.

ṣîru, lofty.

billudû(GARZA)-šú ṣi-ru, Neb. Nippur, I, 18; ^{d}*Nabû sukallu ṣi-ru*, III R. 41, II, 34; I R. 70, IV, 16; III R. 43, IV, 1; (Ninib) *mâr* ^{d}*En-lil ṣi-i-ru*; pl., (Šamaš and Rammân) *daianê ṣîrûti (MAḪ.MEŠ)*, Neb. Nippur, IV, 16.

צבא, **ṣâbu,** soldier.

ṣâb(ZAB) šarri, V R. 56, 3; pl., *ṣâbê (ZAB.MEŠ)* ^{âlu}*Nippurû(-ú)*, V R. 56, 3; *ṣâbê a-šib âlâni šu-a-tum*, V R. 56, 9; *ṣâbê(ZAB.ME) ki-din-nu*, V. A., 2663, III, 11; *pa-ni ṣâbê ki-din-nu . . . ú-šad-gil*, V. A., 2663, III, 24, 31.

צנב, **ṣûmbu,** wagon.

^{išu}*ṣumbi (MAR.GID.DA)-šú* ^{išu}*ṣi-mitti(LAL)-šú*, Susa, 3, II, 51.

צבה, **ṣabû,** desire, want.

I, 1 pret., *a-na ma-ta iṣ-bi-i*, IV R.^{2} 38, II, 28.

צבת, **ṣabâtu,** seize.

I, 1 pret., *iṣ-ba-at*, he took, London, 103, III, 33; *qât* ^{d}*Bêl(EN) iṣ-ba-ta* (Dual), C. T., IX, pl. IV, 11; pres., *i-na ta-ḫa-zi qât-su la i-ṣa-bat*, III R. 43, IV, 24; inf., *ina il-ki di-ku-ti ṣa-bat amelu ḫi-ri-e nâra*, Neb. Nippur, III, 25; *i-na âli ù ṣêri ṣa-bat amelu*, V R. 56, 5; *la ṣa-ba-ti*, V R. 55, 55, 59; C. T., IX, pl. V, 37; perm., *ṣa-bit âlâni ša mât* ^{d}*Ištar A.GA.DE*^{ki}, Susa, 3, II, 26; *ṣa-ab-tu*, London, 103, IV, 30.

I, 2, *iṣ-ṣa-bat ḫa-ra-a-na*, he undertook the march, V R. 55, 16; *iṣ-ṣa-bat* ^{mâtu}*Êlamtu*, V R. 55, 43.

III, 1 prec., *ḫar-ra-an-na pa-ri-ik-ta li-še-iṣ-bi-su* (= *lišeṣbit-su*), III R. 43, IV, 31; *ki-i išteniš (I-iš) ú-ša-aṣ-bit-ma*, V. A., 2663, III, 28.

ṣibtu, holding, increase.

(1) *ṣi-bit pi-i*, holding of the mouth (= dumbness), Susa, 3, VII, 38; (2) revenue, increase, *ṣibit(BIR) alpê ù ṣi-e-ni*, V R. 55, 55; *ina ṣibit ṣi-en-ni(ṣêni)* III R. 45, No. 2, 9.

ṣubâtu, garment.

ki-ma ṣu-ba-ti pa-ga-ar-šú li-la-bi-iš-ma, Susa, 3, VI, 49; *ṣubâtu elîtu(MUḪ) be-lu-ú*, III R. 41, I, 23; *I ṣubâtu ša qab-lu*, III R. 41, I, 24; ^{ṣubâtu}*naḫlaptu(TIK.-UD.DU)*, III R. 41, I, 24; ^{ṣubâtu}*up(b)-ru-ú*, III R. 41, I, 25; ^{ṣubâtu}*pa-tin-nu*, III R. 41, I, 26; *a-di ištên ṣubâtu KUR.RA*, V. A., 209, IV, 33.

ṣabitânu, captor.

a-na ṣa-bi-ta-ni-šú ap-pa-šú lil-bi-im-ma, V R. 56, 55.

צוד, **ṣâdu,** chase.

I, 3, *a-šam-ša-tu iṣ-ṣa-nun-da*, V R. 55, 32.

ṣuḫilu, title of an official.

^{h}*ṣu-ḫi-li*, C. T., IX, pl. V, 34.

צחר, **ṣeḫêru,** be little.

I, 1, *ul-tu a-na-ku ṣi-iḫ-ri-ku*, since I was little, London, 103, IV, 27.

ṣiḫru, little.

ištu ṣi-ḫir ra-bi, great or small, V R. 56, 29, *ṣiḫra(TUR) u rabâ(-a)*, V. A., 2663, III, 27.

צלה, **ṣiltu,** war.

i-na ṣi-il[-tu] ša Su-bar[-tu], D. E. P., II, 93, I, 3.

צלל, **ṣillu,** protection.

ša ina ^{išu}*ṣilli(MI) bêli-ia am-ḫu-ru*, C. T., X, pl. V, 3.

ṣulûlu, protection.
eli ṣâbê ki-din-nu . . . iš-ta-kan ṣu-lu-li, V. A., 2663, III, 33.

I. צלם, **ṣalmu,** picture.
ṣa-lam ^{m}*Ardi-*^{d}*Sibitti*, London, 102, III, 1, 4; *ṣa-lam* ^{d}*Nabû-mukîn-aplu* London, 102, IV, 1; *ṣa-lam* ^{d}*Marduk-apal-iddina*, V. A., 2663, at picture, l. 1.

II. צלם, **ṣalmu,** black.
ṣal-mat (sc. *nišê*) *qaqqadi*(*SAG.-DU*), Neb. Nippur, I, 11; *ina nap-ḫar ṣal-mat qaqqadi*, V. A., 2663, I, 22; *ṣal-mat qaqqadi*, V. A., 2663, II, 55.

צמד, **ṣimittu,** team.
^{iṣu}*ṣumbi*(*MAR.GID.DA*)*-šú* ^{iṣu}*ṣi-mitti*(*LAL*)*-šú*, Susa, 3, II, 51.

ṣuppâti, orchards.
ṣu-up-pa-a-ti ša ^{h}*Na-ḫas-si-pa-ni*, Susa, 16, I, 31.

צפר, **ṣupru,** finger-nail.
ṣu-pu-ri-šú, D. E. P., II, 113, 7; *ṣu-pur* ^{m}*Iddinâ*, V. A., 208, 54; *ṣu-pur* ^{m}*Ina-ešê-êṭir*(*-ir*), V. A., 209, II, 26.

צרר, **ṣarru,** opponent, enemy.
(Gula) *za-ar-ri-ša si-im-ma la-az . . i-na zu-um-ri-šú liš-ku-un-ma*, Susa, 3, VII, 18; *za-ar-ri-ša si-im-ma la-az-za li-še-la-šum-ma*, D. E. P., IV, pl. 16, II, 1.

ṣirru, opponent.
ṣir-ri-šu, D. E. P., 43, IV, 5.

ṣirritu, scepter.
ṣir-rit ^{h}*nakri-šú qa-tu-uš-šú it-muḫ*, Neb. Nippur, II, 5.

ṣurru, heart, mind.
ṣur-ru šad-lu, of broad mind, V. A., 2663, II, 49.

קבא, **qabû,** speak.

I, 1 pret., *ki-a-am iq-bi* (*um-ma-a*), London, 102, IV, 20; VI, 9; C. T., X, pl. V, 11; V. A., 209, I, 5; IV, 6; London, 103, IV, 21; *ki-a-am iq-bi-šú*, O. B. I., 83, I, 19; *a-na šarri i-iq-bi-ma*, III R. 43, edge IV, 4; *iq-bi-ma*, III R. 43, I, 10; Susa, 16, II, 18; *la ba-laṭ-su iq-*[*bu-ú*], London, 102, V, 7; *iq-bi ina ṣi-it pi-i-šu*, V. A., 2663, I, 31; *ki-a-am iq-bu-ú*, D. E. P., II, 93, II, 18; V. A., 209, IV, 19; *iq-bu-ú-ma*, Susa, 16, II, 33; prec., *la balâṭ-su liq-bu-ú*, O. B. I., 149, III, 11; London, 101, IV, 7; *la ba-la-az-zu* [*liq-b*]*u-ú*, Susa, 16, VI, 24; pres., *ul na-din-mi i-qab-bu-ú*, London, 103, V, 38; London, 101, III, 1; *ul ni-di-it-ti šarrâni i-qa-ab-bu-ú*, Susa, 16, IV, 21; Susa, 14, II, 13; *i-qa-bu-ú*, III R. 43, III, 6, 7, 16, 17; edge IV, 3; O. B. I., 149, II, 8; *i-qab-bu-ú*, III R. 41, II, 7; I R. 70, II, 18; London, 102, I, 32; IV, 38; Neb. Nippur, IV, 2; III [32]; V. A., 209, II, 4; V. A., 208, 45, 47; C. T., X, pl. VII, 35; inf., *ina qa-bi-e šàr me-ša-ri*, Neb. Nippur, II, 22.

II, 1 prec., *lu-ú-qa-bu-ú*, London, 101, IV, 4.

qibîtu, command.
šá a-mat qi-bi-ti-šú-nu, Susa, 3, VI, 21; *šá qi-bit pi-i-šú*, Susa, 3, VII, 45; *ša in-nu-ú qi-bi-su*, D. E. P., II, 115, 7; *i-na qibît*(*KA*) ^{d}*Ištar*, V R. 55, 40; *la in-nin-nu-u qi-bit-su*, V. A., 2663, I, 16.

קבל, **qablu,** midst, battle.
(1) midst, *i-na qabal*(*MURU*) ^{arḫu}*Dûzu*, V R. 55, 16. (2) battle, ^{d}*Šú-qa-mu-na ù* ^{d}*Šú-ma-li-ia ilâni qabli ta-mu*, Susa, 2, IV, 22; *ṣubâtu ša qab-lu*, III R. 41, I, 24; ^{d}*Nergal bêl qab-li ù ta-ḫa-zi*, London, 102, II, 4.

qabaltu, midst.
ina qa-bal-ti âli, V. A., 208, 12.

קבר, **qabâru,** bury.

I, 1 pres., *i-na irṣi*[illegible] [illegible]*-qab-bi-ru*, IV R.[2] 38, III, 20.

IV, 1 pret., [*šalamta*]-*šú ai iq-qi-bir*, D. E. P., VI, 43, III, 14; *ša-lam-ta-šú i-na irṣiti ai iq-qi-bir*, Susa, 16, VI, 21.

qibîru, grave.
qi-bi-ra ai [*ú-šar-ši-šu*], London, 102, II, 25.

קיף, **qîpu,** official.
qi-pu ai-um-ma, Susa, 3, II, 39; *ai-um-ma qi-pu*, III R. 41, I, 33; ^h^*qi-i-pi ša E-sag-ila*, C. T., X, pl. VII, 44; ^h^*qi-i-pu lu-ú* ^h^*šak-nu*, V. A., 2663, V, 19; pl., *qi-pu-ú-tim ša qaq-qa-ra-tim*, Susa, 2, III, 8; *qi-pu-tu ša Bît-*^m^*A-da ar-ku-tu*, III R. 43, III, 14; *qi-pu-tu lu-ú ḫa-za-an-nu Bît-*^m^*A-da ar-ku-tu*, III R. 45, No. 2, 4, 5; *qi-pu-ut* ^mâtu^*Na-mar*, V R. 56, 29 (cf. "The Ḳêpu," A. J. S. L., XXII (1905), pp. 81–88).

קיש, **qâšu,** present.
I, 1 pret., *ša* ^d^*E-a* . . *i-qi-šu-šu*, V. A., 2663, III, 6; *qi-ša-a-tu i-qis-su-nu-ti-ma*, V. A., 2663, III, 34.

qîštu, present.
pl., *ir-ba u qi-ša-a-ti*, V. A., 2663, II, 17; *qi-ša-a-tú i-qis-su-nu-ti-ma*, V. A., 2663, III, 34.

קלה, **qalû,** burn.
I, 1 pres., *i-na išâti*(*i-ša-ti*) *i-qal-lu-ú*, Neb. Nippur, V. 1; O. B. I., 149, II, 12; London, 102, V, 3; C. T., X, pl. VII, 37; *i-na išâti*(*NE*) *iqallû*(*ŠU*+*AŠ-ú*), V. A., 2663, V, 29; *i-na i-ša-ti i-qa-lu-ú*, III R. 43, I, 34.
III, 1 *išâti ú-šaq-lu*, V R. 56, 36; *i-ša-ta ú-ša-aq-qa-*[*lu*], London, 103, V, 44.

קלל, **qalâlu,** despise.
II, 1 pres., *šú-ú ia-a-ši la ú-qal-la-la*, Susa, 3, IV, 29.

qullultu, wrongdoing.
qu-ul-lu-ul-ta iz-zi-ir, Susa, 3, IV, 54; V, 21.

קמה, **qamû,** burn.
II, 1 prec., *li-qa-am-me šur-ši-šú*, Neb. Nippur, IV, 27.

I. קנה, **qanû,** perhaps acquire.
II, 1 prec., *li-ga-an-ni-ma*, D. E. P., VI, 43, III, 8.

II. קנה, **qanû,** reed.
qan(*GI*) *appari*(*SUK*), reed thicket, C. T., IX, pl. IV, 19.

קנן, **qinnu,** habitation, family.
(1) habitation, *nap-ḫar qin-ni-e u kal da-ad-me*, Neb. Nippur, I, 15; (2) family, *qin-ni* ^m^*Aḫu-ni-e-a*, Susa, 16, IV, 9; *qin-ni*, D. E. P., 46, IV, 11.

קנק, **kanâku,** seal.
I, 1 pret., *ik-nu-uk-ma*, London, 103, III, 36; IV, 6, 34, V, 23; Susa, 16, II, 13; III, 12; C. T., IX, pl. IV, 16; V. A., 209, I, 25; IV, 14; C. T., X, pl. VI, 30; V. A., 2663, IV, 54; *ik-nu-uk*, D. E. P., VI, 42, I, 24; *i-ik-nu-uk-ma*, III R. 43, edge IV, 5; *ik-nu-kam-ma*, London, 102, I, 15, 26, 34; *ik-nu-ku-ma*, London, 102, I, 21; *ik-nu-ku-ú-ma*, V. A., 209, IV, 37; pres., *a-kan-nak-ma*, London, 102, I, 24; imper., *ṭuppa-šu ku-nu-uk-ma bi-in-ni*, V. A., 209, I, 14; inf., *i-na ka-nak ṭuppi šú-a-tu*, I R. 66, II, 5; V. A., 209, II, 11; V, 13; C. T. X, pl. VII, 41; V. A., 2663, IV, 56; C. T., X, pl. III, 23; *i-na ka-nak li*( )-*ú ù ṭup-pi eqli*, Susa, 16, III 14; *i-na ka-nak* ^abnu^*ṭup-pi šu-ma-tu*(?) (so Dr. Ungnad), V. A., 208, 48; *i-na ka-nak kan-gi šu-a-tu*, London, 102, VI, 14; *i-na ka-nak li*( )-*ú šú-a-tu*, Neb. Nippur, V, 8; perm., *kunuk-ku ul ka-nik-ma i-qa-bu-ú*, III R. 43, III, 7; *kunukku ul ka-ni-ki i-qa-bu-ú*, III R. 43, III, 17; *dan*(*an*)[-*ni*] *ka-ni-ki*, III R. 43,

I, 23; *ul ka-nik-ma*, D. E. P., VI, 42, I, 22.

kân(i)ku, document.

ka-nik di-ni, Susa, 16, III, 11; *i-na ka-nak kan-gi šu-a-tu*, London, 102, VI, 14; *ka-nik di-nim*, London, 103, VI, 28.

kunukku, seal.

ku-nu-uk šîmi eqli, London, 103, III, 9; *abnukunuk(DUB) di-ni šú-a-tum*, Susa, 16, III, 16; *ku-nu-uk šarri*, C. T., X, pl. III, 32, V, 7; *abnukunuk šarru-ú-ti-šu*, C. T., X, pl. V, 8; VI, 30; *i-na abnukunuk(DUB) šarri ša šip-ri-e-ti*, V. A., 2663, V, 48; I R. 66, II, 19; *kunukku ul ka-nik-ma i-qa-bu-ú*, III R. 43, III, 7; *kunukku ul ka-ni-ki i-qa-bu-ú*, III R. 43, III, 17; *kîma abnukunukki-šu*, V., 208, 55; V. A., 209, II, 27; *abnukunukku ši-ṭir šumi-šu ik-nu-uk-ma*, V. A., 2663, IV, 53.

quppû, poniard, knife.

ul-tu paṭ-ru i-na kišâdi-šu ù qup-pu-ú i-na i-ni-šu, V R. 56, 54.

קצץ, **qaṣâṣu,** cut off.

I, 1 pret., *[ni-š]i-er she'uzêru ig-zu-uz-ma*, O. B. I., 83, I, 14.

qiṣṣatu, curtailment.

ni-šir-ta qi-ṣa-ta i-šak-ka-nu, Susa, 2, III, 14; *ni-ši-ir-ta ù qi-iṣ-ṣa-ta la ša-ka-ni*, Susa, 3, II, 10; *ni-šir-ta qi-iṣ-ṣa-tu*, Susa, 16, IV, 16; *ni-šir-ta qi-iṣ-ṣa-ta i-na libbi(-bi) i-šak-ka-nu*, I R. 70, II, 15; III R. 43, III, 21; *ni-ši-ir-ta gi-iṣ-ṣa-a-tu ud-da-[a]*, C. T., X, pl. VII, 34; *qi-iṣ-ṣa-ta ù ni-(ši)-šir-tu*, Susa, 3, V, 29; *qi-iṣ-ṣa-ta ni-šir-ta i-šak-ka-nu*, III R. 41, II, 6.

qaqqadu, head.

qaqqad(SAG)-su li-šam-ri-ṣu-šu, Susa, 14, IV, 12; *qaqqadu(SAG) [mar(?)]-zi-ma . . . li-ik-mi-[šu]*; D. E. P., II, 113, 18; *ṣal-mat qaqqadi*, the blackheaded, Neb. Nippur, I, 11; V. A., 2663, I, 22; II, 55.

קקר, **qaqqaru,** piece of land.

i-na qaq-qa-ri it-te-mi-ir, Susa, 3, V, 52; *i-na qaq-qa-ri i-ta-im-me-ru*, Susa, 16, IV, 33; *qaq-qar mâtuNa-mar*, V R. 55, 47; 56, 8; *qaq(?)-qar-šu*, I R. 66, I, 11; *qaq-qa-ru šu-ú*, V. A., 209, I, 5; *um-ma qaq-qa-ru i-ba-aš-ši*, V. A., 209, I, 7; *qaq-qar ša i-na qâtâ(ŠÚ²) mIddina-dNabû an-ḫu-ru*, V. A., 209, I, 12; pl., *qi-pu-ú-tim šá qaq-qa-ra-tim*, Susa, 2, III, 9.

I. קרב, **qarâbu,** approach.

I, 1 perm., *a-na aḫ-ḫu-ti . . . la qir-bu*, London, 103, I, 29; IV, 42.

II, 1, pres., *ú-qar-ra-bu-ma ú-ša-aš-šú-ma*, O. B. I., 149, II, 10; perm., *a-na aḫ-ḫu-ú-ti . . . ul qu-ru-ub*, London, 103, IV, 26; *qu-ru-ub ibšê(-e)*, London, 103, III, 20.

qirbu, midst.

a-na ki-rib Bâ[bili i-tur-ma], C. T., X, pl. IV, 16; *ša ki-rib Dêriki*, V. A., 209, II, 31; III, 2, 18; IV, 25.

II. קרב, **qirubû,** arable land (Aram. כרובא, cf. p. 173).

eqlu qi-ru-ba-a šá a-na bu-tuq-ti šaknu(-nu), Neb. Nippur, II, 25.

qarbâti, plowed fields.

qar-ba-ti kudurri(ŠA.DU)-ši-na nu-uk-ku-ru-ma, V. A., 2663, III, 21.

קרד, **qardu,** strong, powerful.

ti-iz-qa-ru qar-du, D. E. P., II, 115, 5; *iššakku qar-du*, V R. 55, 3; *zi-ik-ru qar-du*, V R. 55, 7; *ed-li qar-di*, V R. 55, 21; *dRam-mân . . . mâr dA-num qar-du* I R. 70, IV, 10.

qarrurtum, torch(?) (Zimmern).
ișuqar-ru-ur-tum bur-ru-ur-tum ša dIštar, Susa, 2, IV, 14.

qaštu, bow.
na-aš ișuqaštu(BAN) iz-zi-ti, V R. 55, 8; pl., *dNergal bêl be-li-e ù qa-ša-ti,* III R. 43, IV, 21.

qâtu, hand.
qa-ti . . . ú-tir-ru, compensate, Susa, 2, I, 18; *ana qâti . . . id-din,* London, 103, III, 5; *i-na qât mMarduk-zâkir-šumu,* IV R.[2] 38, III, 21; *qât dBêl(EN) iș-ba-ta,* C. T., IX, pl. IV, 11; *i-na qât,* from the hand of, III R. 41, I, 10; V. A., 208, 33, 37; London, 102, IV, 28, 30; *ina qâtâ(ŠU[2]),* V. A., 209, I, 6, 12; c. suff., *qa-tu-uš-šu* (= *ina qâti-šu*) *it-muḫ,* Neb. Nippur, II, 5; *qât-su la i-șa-bat,* III R. 43, IV, 24; *a-šar qa-tuš,* London, 103, VI, 18; *qa-az-zu tur-rat,* compensation has been given, Susa, 3, I, 26; *ti-ri-iș qa-ti-šu,* V. A., 2663, I, 27; III, 38; *ši-bir-ru ip-qid qa-tuš-šu,* V. A., 2663, I, 36; *qâtâ-šu ṭi-ṭa li-ru-ba* (Dual), V R. 56, 58.

קתה, **qatû,** complete, end.
I, 1 prec., *ûmi(-mi) i-șu-ti šá bal-ṭa liq-ti-ma,* IV R.[2] 38, III, 41; *liq-ta-a zumur(SU)-šu,* may his body perish, V. A., 2663, V, 44.
qati, adv., completely.
i-na qa-ti ma-aq-tu-ma, Susa, 3, III, 38.

קתן, **qattinu,** a class of farmers.
ir-ri-ši ša âli-šú lu-ú qa-at-ti-ni lu-ú a-šib âli, Susa, 3, II, 35 (cf. B. E., XV, 37: 1).

$ר_{8}$אב, **rêbitu,** street.
ri-bi-it âli-šú, Susa, 3, VII, 3; *li-ib-ta-'-i-ta i-na ri-bi-it âli-šú,* III R. 41, II, 24.

$ר_{4}$אה, **rê'u,** feed, pasture.
I, 1 inf., *šammê la ri-'-e,* Susa, 3, III, 21.

rê'û, shepherd.
(Nabû) *rê'û(SIB) kiš-šat šamê(-e) u irșitim,* D. E. P., VI, 46, IV, 5; *na-bu-ú rê'û(SIB) ki-nu:* Neb. Nippur, I, 21, [*a*]*-na šarri rê'î ki-ni,* Neb. Nippur, I, 15I; *lu-ú rê'û(SIB) lu-ú šakkanakku,* Neb. Nippur, III, 19; *rê'û(SIB) mu-pa-aḫ-ḫi-ru sapḫâti,* V. A., 2663, I, 32; *rê'û kênu(GI.NA),* V. A., 2663, II, 25; *rê'û sisê,* London, 102, III, 11, 13, 15, 23.

rê'ûtu, rule.
a-na rê'û-ut mâtuŠú-me-ri u Ak-kadíki, Neb. Nippur, II, 1; *ri-'-ut ma-ti,* Susa, 3, III, 59; *a-na rê'û-ut șal-mat qaqqadi,* V. A., 2663, II, 54; *ina la rê'û-tu,* in the rulerless time, V. A., 2663, III, 17.

rî'tu, rittu, pasture.
a-na i-ki-li ri-'-ti, Neb. Nippur, III, 21; *al-pu libbu alpi ša rit-ti,* London, 102, III, 26; IV, 24 (cf. Clay, B. E., XIV, 123: *I alpu ri-it-ti*).

$ר_{3}$אם, **râmu,** (1) love, (2) present, give.
I, 1 (1) love, imper., *kit-ta ra-*[*-am*], O. B. I., 83, II, 24.
(2) present, **I, 1** pret., *i-ru-um,* Susa, 2, II, 24; *arad-su i-ri-mu,* Susa, 2, II, 33; D. E. P., II, 97, 10; D. E. P., VI, 44, I, 4; O. B. I., 149, I, 22; C. T., X, pl. III, 22; *i-ri-mu,* V. A., 2663, V, 35; *arad-su i-ri-im,* Susa, 3, I, 40; Susa, 16, I, 8; V. A., 2663, IV, 52; *arad-zu i-ri-e-mu,* D. E. P., II, 112, 9; *arad-su i-ri-im-ma,* D. E. P., VI, 42, I, 21; *ana ûmê(-me) șa-a-ti i-ri-im,* Neb. Nippur, III, 13; *a-na ûmê șa-ti i-ri-in-šú,* III R. 43, edge IV, 6; *a-ḫar-ti-iš i-ri-mu,* London, 101–I, 15; *a-ḫar-ti-iš i-rim-šú,* IV R[2]., 38, II, 29; *i-ri-im-*[*šú-ma*], D. E. P., II, 93, I, 8; *i-ri-en-šú,* III R.

43, I, 13; *i-ri-mu-šú*, D. E. P., II, pl. 20, 6; *ša . . . i-ri-mu*, Susa, 3, II, 5; prec., *šarru li-ri-man-ni-ma*, C. T., X, pl. III, 7.

I, 2, *ki-it-ta ir-tam-ma*, (who) loves righteousness, Susa, 3, IV, 53; *qu-ul-lu-ul-ta ir-tam*, Susa, 3, V, 21.

rîmûtu, grant, gift.

II she'uzêru ri-mut ^{md}*Sin-bêl-ilâni*, O. B. I., 149, I, 2; *a-na ta-bal eqli ri-mut* ^{d}*Marduk-apal-iddina . . uznâ-šu i-šak-ka-nu*, V. A., 2663, V, 33.

rîmnû, merciful.

[*šar*] *ilâni it-pi-šu rim-nu-ú*, C. T., X, pl. IV, 15.

narâmu, beloved.

na-ra-am ^{d}*Marduk*, V R. 55, 11; *na-ram-šu*, C. T., X, pl. IV, 17.

ראק₃, **rûqu,** distant.

pl., *a-na ûmê ru-qu-ú-ti*, Susa, 3, III, 56.

ראש₁, **rêšu,** (1) head, (2) boundary stone.

(1) head, *amêlu ša rêši*(*SAG*) *ša mâtâti*, III R. 43, II, 2.

(2) boundary stone (cf. p. 197), *reš*(*SAG*) *eqli šú-a-tu iš-ši-ma*, London, 103, II, 21; *ri-eš eqli šú-a-tum iš-šú-ma*, Susa, 16, III, 6; *rêš*(*SAG*) *eqlâti ša mâti tâmdi iš-ši-ma*, O. B. I., 83, I, 12; *rêš*(*SAG*) *eqli iš-šú-ma*, O. B. I., 149, I, 20.

rêštu, top.

pl., (^{d}*Šumalia*) *a-ši-bat ri-še-e-ti*, V R. 56, 47.

rêštû, first.

i-na šatti rêštî, Susa, 16, II, 13; *šak-ku-šu riš-tu-ú*, Neb. Nippur, I, 19; ^{d}*Nabû* [*mâru*] *reš-tu-ú ša E-sag-ila*, London, 102, I, 44.

רבה, **rabû,** great, prince.

daianu rabû, Susa, 2, IV, 13; Susa, 14, III, 3; *rabû ma-lik šarri*, Susa, 3, VI, 2; (^{d}*Šamaš*) *ràb šamê*(*-e*) *u irṣiti*(*-ti*), III R. 43, IV, 10; *Anu rabû bêlu rabû*, III R. 43, IV, 30; *mar-ka-su rabû*(*-ú*), Susa, 2, IV, 27; *mâri-šu rabî*(*-i*), London, 102, IV, 31; *ištu ṣi-ḫir ra-bi*, V R. 56, 29; ^{h}*ràb ú-ri-e*, master of the horse, V R. 55, 53; fem., *rabîtum*, *a-ši-ir-tum rabîtum ša* ^{d}*E-a*, Susa, 2, IV, 6; *a-zu-gal-la-tu rabîtum*. Susa, 14, IV, 6; *še-ir-ta-šú ra-bi-i-ta*, Susa, 3, VI, 34; *i-na am-ma-ti ra-bi-i-ti*, D. E. P., II, pl. 20, 6, and *passim*; *bêltu rabîtu*, Neb. Nippur, IV, 20; *be-el-tu rabîtu*(*-tu*), III R. 41, II, 29; ^{d}*Nina mârat* ^{d}*E-a rabî-ti*(*-ti*), O. B. I., 83, I, 22; pl., *ilâni rabûti*, Susa, 2, III, 16; IV, 30; Susa, 14, III, 3; London, 103, VI, 1, etc.

rubû, prince.

(Ellil) *rubû*(*NUN*) *bêl gim-ri*, Neb. Nippur, I, 2; *rubû me-gir-šu*, Neb. Nippur, I, 23; II, 21; *rubû me-gir* ^{d}*En-lil*, Neb. Nippur, II, 15; *rubû mun-tal-ku*, V. A., 2663, I, 45; pl., *i-na pa-an šarri ù rubûti*(*NUN.MEŠ*), London, 103, VI, 47; *eli šarri* [*bêli*?] *ù rubî*, London, 101, IV, 12; *rubû*, D. E. P., II, 97, 14; *rubû na-a-du*, V R. 55, 1; V. A., 2663, II, 31; O. B. I., 83, I, 20; ^{d}*Iš-tar be-el-tu ru-ba ilâni*, III R. 41, II, 21; fem., *ma-sab ru-ba-ti*, Susa, 2, IV, 26.

rubûtu, lordship.

ul-lu-ú rubû(*NUN*)*-us-su iq-bi*, V. A., 2663, I, 30.

šurbû, sublime, glorious.

f., ^{d}*Gu-la bêltu*(*-tu*) *šur-bu-tum*, Susa, 3, VII, 15.

רבץ, **rabâṣu,** crouch.

I, 1 pret., *i-na ka-mat âli-šú ai ir-bi-iṣ*, O. B. I., 149, III, 8.

III, 1 prec., *li-šar-bi-ṣu-šú-ma*, Susa, 16, VI, 17.

rabiṣu, demon.
lu rabiṣu(MAŠKIM) limutti-šu šú-ma, Neb. Nippur, IV, 26.

tarbaṣu, court.
bîtu šûtu tar-ba-ṣu, V. A., 209, II, 29.

רגם, **ragâmu**, raise a claim.
I, 1 pres., *i-da-ab-bu-bu i-rag-gu-mu*, London, 103, V, 34; *i-rag-gu-mu ú-šar-ga-mu*, Susa, 14, II, 10; *a-na a-ḫa-meš ul i-rag-gu-mu*, London, 102, IV, 35; V. A., 209, I, 30; II, 40; III, 16, 28; V, 3; inf., *aš-šu la ra-ga-mu*, C. T., X, pl. V, 9; *la ta-a-ra u la ra-ga-mi*, London, 103, III, 30.
III, 1 pres., *ú-šar-ga-mu*, London, 103, V, 35; Susa, 14, II, 11.

rugummû, reclamation.
tap-qir-ta ù ru-gu-um-ma-a, Susa, 3, II, 16; *ru-gu-um-ma-a lâ i-šú-ú*, London, 102, IV, 34; *ru-gam-ma-a ul i-ši*, V. A., 209, I, 28; II, 39; III, 14, 27; V, 1; *aš-šu ru-gu-um-[mi-i] an-ni-i ki-niš iš-['-al-]šu*, C. T., X, pl. V, 10.

I. רדה, **ridû**, march.
I, 1 pres., *il-lak šarru . . . i-rid-di ᵈNabû-kudurri-uṣur*, V R. 55, 23.

II. רדה, **ridû**, drive, lead.
I, 1 prec., *i-na limutti(-ti) li-ir-di-šú*, London, 101, III, 13.
I, 2 prec., *a-na limutti(-ti) ù la ṭâbti(-ti) li-ir-te-id-du-šú*, III R. 41, II, 37; *a-na li-mut-ti li-ir-te-di-šú*, III R. 43, IV, 14; *i-na limutti(-ti) lirtedûšu(UŠ-UŠ-šú)*, London, 103, VI, 14; *a-na limutti(-ti) li-ir-te-id-di-šu*, I R. 70, III, 24.
III, 1 inf., *a-na ta-mi-ir-ti-šú la šú-ru-di-im-ma*, Susa, 3, III, 20.

rîdû, leader, captain (cf. p. 176).
lu ri-du-ú lu ḫa-za-an-nu, Neb. Nippur, III, 20.

ridûtu, government.
Bît-ᵐTu-na-mi-is-sa-aḫ ša ri-du-ti, IV R.² 38, I, 15.

רוב.
II, 1 inf., *ša ru-ub-ša a-bu-bu*, whose destruction (or perhaps anger, ראב) is a stormflood, Neb. Nippur, IV. 22 (cf. p. 182).

ריץ, **rêṣu**, helper.
ri-ṣu-šu-ma, D. E. P., VI, 47, 21.

רחץ, **raḫâṣu**, flood.
I, 1 prec., *ᵈRammân . . . ugâr-šú li-ir-ḫi-iṣ-ma*, III R. 41, II, 32; I R. 70, IV, 11.

ריח, **rîḫu**, remaining.
206 she'uzêru ri-ḫu, Susa, 2, II, 25; *ul ri-ḫu . . .*, Neb. Nippur, III, 29; *ù ri-ḫi eqli bît abi-ia*, C. T., X, pl. III, 6.

רכב, **rakkabu**, saddle(?).
rak-kab sisê, III R. 41, I, 16; *rak-kab imêru amurrû*, III R. 41, I, 18.

narkabtu, chariot.
bêl ⁱˢᵘnarkabti, charioteer, V R. 55, 34; *ⁱˢᵘnarkabtu la ra-ka-si*, C. T., IX, pl. V, 37; III R. 41, I, 15.

רכס, **rakâsu**, hitch up, attach.
I, 1 inf., *imêri-šu la ra-ka-si, ⁱˢᵘnar-kabtu la ra-ka-si*, C. T., IX, pl. V, 36, 37; *[imêrê]-šu-nu a-na la ra-ka-si-im-ma*, I R. 66, I, 9; part., *li-mi-nu . . . lu-ú ra-ki-is it-ti-šu*, V R. 56, 44.

riksu, bond, hold.
ša ri-ki-is-su la ip-paṭ-ṭa-ru, Susa, 3, VI, 45; III R. 41, II, 25; *ri-ki-is-su la pa-ṭi-ra*, I R. 70, III, 14; *ri-ik-su la pa-ṭe-ra*, III R. 43, III, 32; *ša rik-su la pa-[ṭe-ra]*, London, 102, I, 41.

markasu, band.
mar-ka-su rabû(-ú), Susa, 2, IV, 27.

רמך, **ramâku**, pour out.
I, 1 prec., *ki-ma mê li-ir-mu-uk*, Susa, 3, VII, 25; *kîma mê li-ir-muk*,

D. E. P., IV, pl. 16, II, 4; *ki-[ma] mê li-ir-muk*, O. B. I., 149, III, 5; London, 102, II, 24; *ki-i-ma mê li-ir(-mu)-muk*, III R. 43, IV, 18; *ki-i mê li-ir-muk*, I R. 70, IV, 8.

I, 2 prec., *ki-ma mê li-ir-tam-muk*, III R. 41, II, 31.

ramânu, ramnu, self.

a-na ra-ma-ni-šu i-šak-ka-nu, I R. 70, II, 12; III R. 43, III, 19; *ma-li-ku ram-ni-šu*, V. A., 2663, II, 51; *a-na i-di ram-ni-šu-nu ú-tir-ru-ma*, C. T., X, pl. V, 5; *a-na i-di ram-ni-šu ú-tar-ru*, C. T., X, pl. VII, 34.

רנן, **rinînu,** whining.

li-rik ri-nin-šú-ma, London, 101, IV, 13.

רפד, **rapâdu,** lie down.

I, 1 prec., *ki-ma ú-ma-am ṣi-ri ṣi-ra li-ir-pu-ud*, Susa, 3, VII, 2; *e-ma purîmê ṣêri li-ir-pu-ud*, Susa, 14, IV, 4.

I, 2 prec., *i-na ka-mat âli-šú li-ir-tap-pu-ud*, III R. 41, II, 18; I R. 70, III, 21; *li-ir-ta-pu-ud*, D. E. P., VI, 43, III, 15; *i-na ka-mat âli-šu liš-tap-pu-ud*, V. A., 209, V, 12.

רפש, **rapšu,** wide.

rap-ša uznâ(PI²), broad minded, V. A., 2663, II, 48; fem., *ḫi-ṣib tam-tim rapaštim(DAGAL-tim)*, V. A., 2663, II, 16.

riqqu, [cuneiform sign], gardener.

ᵏriqqu ša ili rabî, V. A., 209, IV, 17. (For the ideogr. cf. Clay, B. E., XIV, List of Signs, No. 129.)

רשב, **rašubbu,** powerful.

ra-šub-bi ᵈA-nun-na-ku, Neb. Nippur, I, 11.

רשה, **rašû,** take possession, have.

I, 1 pret., *ai ir-šú-ú ni-da a-ḫi*, may he not have a resting place, Susa, 2, III, 27; *pi-ri ai ir-šu*, Susa, 14, IV, 17; *ir-ša-a sa-li-me* (relat.), granted favor, V. A., 2663, I, 19; inf., *a-na paq-ri la ra-še-e*, not to make reclamation, I R. 70, I, 20; *ru-gu-um-ma-a la ra-še-e*, Susa, 3, II, 17; *aš-šu paq-ri la ra-še-e*, London, 102, II, 34.

III, 1 pret., *ˢʰᵉ'uzêra u pi-ir-a ai ú-šar-ši-šú*, may he not let him have, Susa, 3, VII, 13; *na-aq mê [ai ú]-šar-šu*, D. E. P., VI, 45, IV, 11; *ai ú[-šar]-šu-[ú]*, D. E. P., VI, 46, III, 4, 7; *šumu ai u-šar-šu-šu*, D. E. P., VI, 47, 3; *[na-a]q mê ai ú-šar-ši-šu*, London, 102, II, 19.

râšû, creditor.

ᵐZêr-ukîn mâr ᵐKar-zi-ab-ku ra-šú-ú, London, 102, IV, 33; *ra-ša-a ul zak-ki*, the creditor has not been satisfied, London, 102, IV, 39.

rittu, hand.

[eṭemmi-šu] a-na eṭemmi rit-ti-šú ai is-ni-iq, Susa, 16, VI, 22.

ša, (1) who, (2) of, *passim*.

šâšu, that, he.

i-na šatti ša-a-ši, London, 103, V, 5; *ša i-na eqli ša-šu ša-ak[-nu]*, D. E. P., VI, 45, V, 10; *ša-a-šu šumi-šu ù zêri-šú*, he himself, London, 101, IV, 8; *amelu ša-a-šú*, V R. 56, 37; *a-na libbi(-bi) eqlu ša-a-šu*, London, 102, II, 33; pl. fem., *eqlâti ša-ši-na*, C. T., X, pl. V, 6; *esqêti ša-ši-na*, V. A. 211, III, 5.

šu'atu, that, *passim*.

Usually *šú-a-tu*, Neb. Nippur, III, 13, 20, 27, etc.; *i-na šú-'-a-ti*, whereupon, London, 103, IV, 30; *ᵃᵇⁿᵘṭuppi šu-ma-tu*(?) (so Dr. Ungnad), V. A., 208, 48; *ina ka-nak ṭuppi(IM) šumâti(MU.-MEŠ)*, V. A., 2663, IV, 56.

א$_4$ש, šattu, eternity.
a-na šat-ti, forever, Neb. Nippur, I, 22.

še'u, seed.
Only found as a determinative for *she'uzêru*, seedfield, Susa, 2, I, 14; Neb. Nippur, II, 25, III, 7, etc., and in *she'uBAR*, London, 103, III, 18, 19, etc.

שאה$_4$, šê'u, to see.
I, 2 pret., *aš-rat* *^{d}Nabû u ^{d}Marduk iš-te-e-ma*, he looked after (cared for) the sanctuaries, V. A., 2663, III, 10; *iš-te-'-u-ma [ur-(?)]-ti bêl ilani*, he paid attention to the law of the lord of the gods, V. A., 2663, II, 19; part., *muš-te-'-ú aš-ra-ti-šu*, Neb. Nippur, I, 24.

שאל$_1$, ša'âlu, ask.
I, 1 pret., *it-ti a-ḫa-meš i-šal-šú-nu-ti-ma*, London, 103, IV, 19; *i-šal-šú-nu-ti-ma*, London, 103, I, 25; *aḫê-šú i-šal-ma*, London, 103, V, 2; *parsê(BAR.SUD) la-bi-ru-ti . . . i-šal-šú-nu-ti-ma*, Susa, 16, II, 30; *šarru parsê i-šal-ma*, V R. 55, 50; *i-ta-ni-e i-šá-lu-ma*, O. B. I., 83, II, 9.

šitultu, decision.
a-na ši-tul-ti-šú ^{d}A-nun-na-ku aš-riš šú-ḫar-ru-ru, Neb. Nippur, I, 7; *ka-raš ši-tul-ti*, of thoughtful mind, V. A., 2663, II, 50.

שאר$_4$, šâru, cardinal point.
šâru(IM) I, V. A., 2663, III, 44; IV, 15, 23, 35; *šâru(IM)*II, V.A., 2663, III, 47; IV, 14, 25, 36; *šâru(IM)* III, V. A., 2663, III, 54; IV, 11, 30, 41; *šâru(IM)* IV, V. A., 2663, III, 50, IV, 6, 28, 38.

שאר$_1$, šîru, (1) flesh, (2) body.
(1) *šîr(UZU) taḫ-ši-e šîr sûni*, the meat of a ram, the meat of the thigh, V. A., 208, 5; (2) *lâ-ṭûb(-ub) šîri*, ill health of body, IV R.^{2} 38, III, 39; *ina ši-ḫat šîri*, with the bloating of the body, V. A. 2663, V, 44.

שאר, šêrtu, punishment.
bu-bu-ta še-ir-ta-šú ra-bi-i-ta, Susa, 3, VI, 33; *še-rit-su kabittu (DUGUD-tu) a-ga-lâ-til-la-a lišiš(GA.TU)-šu-šu-ma*, V. A., 2663, V, 42.

שאת$_3$, šêtu, leave, escape.
I, 1 pres., *ar-ra-a-tum an-na-a-tum . . . la i-še-it-ta-šú li-ik-šú-da-šú*, may these curses not miss him, but overtake him, Susa, 3, VII, 50.

Šabâṭu, the month Shebâṭ.
I R. 66, I, 2; II, 17; V. A., 208, 30.

ŠÀ.BAL.BAL, grandson, descendant.
Neb. Nippur, III, 14; Susa, 2, I, 3; IV R.^{2} 38, I, 25; II, 3; C. T., X, pl. IV, 12 (cf. p. 174f.).

שבר, šabâru, break.
II, 1 pret., *^{iṣu}kakku na-ki-ri-šú ú-šib-bir-ma*, Neb. Nippur, II, 4; prec., *ka-ak-ke-šú li-še-bir*, III R. 43, IV, 22.

šibirtu, purchase price (Hebr. שבר, buy).
V šiqlu šibirtu(AZAG.PAD.DU) maḫîri(KI.LAM) im-bi-e-ma, V. A., 209, III, 25.

šibirru, staff.
ši-bir-ru mu-šal-lim nišê, V. A., 2663, I, 35.

ŠE.BAR, barley.
(The meaning of this word is definitely determined by the rendering שערן pl., which found in the Aramaic endorsements of the Murashû tablets, according to Prof. Clay), London, 103, III, 18, 19; Susa, 3, II, 49; London, 102, IV, 27.

šaggullu, palm grove(?).
pl., *^{iṣu}kirê u ^{iṣu}šaggulâni(SAG.-KAL*, cf. Br. 8046), parks and palm groves(?), V R., 55, 60.

שגר, šigaru, lock, gate.
mu-daḫ-ḫi-id ši-gar-šu-nu, who fills

with plenty their gates, V. A., 2663, II, 4.

שדד, **šadâdu,** draw, drag.

I, 1 prec., *ma-ru-uš-ta li-iš-du-ud,* may he drag along misery, V R. 56, 59; *liš-du-ud ma-ru-uš-ti,* V. A., 2663, V, 40; *šá-di-id eqli,* probably "the one who drew the line," *i.e.,* measured the field, London, 101, I, 17.

šiddu, side of a field, *passim.*

šiddu(UŠ) elû and *šiddu(UŠ) šaplû.*

שדה, **šadû,** (1) mountain.

dŠú-ma-li-ia be-lit šadê(KUR-MEŠ) el-lu-ti, mistress of the shining (*i.e.,* snowclad) mountains, V R. 56, 46.

(2) east, *passim.*

šadû(IM.KUR.RA).

שדל, **šadlu,** wide.

ṣur-ru šad-lu, of broad intelligence, V. A., 2663, II, 50.

šumdulu, magnificent.

niqê šum-du-li, Neb. Nippur, II, 8.

šû, he.

šú-ma, he is, Neb. Nippur, IV, 26; *šú-mi* (emph. *mi*), Susa, 16, II, 32; *šú-ú,* he, Susa, 3, IV, 28; V, 8; used as adj., *amelu šú-ú,* Susa, 3, IV, 52; V, 20; VI, 1; *qaq-qa-ru šú-ú,* V. A., 209, I, 5; pl., *eqlâti ši-na-ti,* these fields, III R. 41, II, 2; *ar-ra-a-ti ši-na-a-ti,* Susa, 3, V, 45; Susa, 16, IV, 23.

šûmu, boundary, limit.

be-el ab-li šú-ú-mi ù ku-dur-ri, Susa, 3, VII, 7.

שוף, **šêpu,** foot.

Dual. *li-kab-bi-sa še-pa-šú,* III R. 43, IV, 6; *li-kab-bi-sa šêpâ (NER² pl) šú,* I R. 70, IV, 15.

šêpîtu, foot end.

še-pi-it zu-'-uz-tu, V. A., 2663, III, 51.

שור, **mašâru,** wheel.

ša išuma-ša-ra-šú, whose charioteer, V R. 55, 26; *ša išuma-ša(ma)-ra-šú,* V R. 55, 36; *išuma-ša-ra-šu uk-til-la,* V R. 55, 27, 37.

šûtu, south, *passim.*

šûtu(IM.ER.LU).

šût, genetive particle, of.

ina pu-ḫur šu-ut ma-al-ku, V. A., 2663, I, 42; *mârê Sippar . . . u šu-ut ma-ḫa-zi ša mâtuAkkadîki,* V. A., 2663, III, 13.

ši-ḫi.

itti(DA) ši-ḫi ša dIB (Peiser proposes the reading *papaḫi(-ḫi),* which cannot be substantiated thus far), V. A., 208, 39.

שחט, **šiḫṭu,** march.

ši-iḫ-ṭa iš-ta-ka-an, a march he made, V R. 55, 15; *šiḫ(?)-ṭa ina muḫ-ḫi-šú-nu i-pu-uš-ma,* an expedition(?) he made in their behalf, C. T., IX, pl. IV, 7.

שחת(ט), **šaḫât(ṭ)u,** fear, reverence.

I, 1 pret., *bêl ilâni [i]š-ḫu-ṭu* (cf. the adj. *ša-aḫ-ṭu,* Delitzsch, H. W., 651*a*), V. A. 2663, II, 21.

šaḫtiš, submissively.

na-zu-uz-zu ša-aḫ-tiš, Neb. Nippur, I, 8.

שחרר, **šuḫarruru,** tremble.

I, 1 perm., *aš-riš šú-ḫar-ru-ru,* Neb. Nippur, I, 8.

שטר, **šaṭâru,** write.

I, 1 pret., *iš-ṭur-ma,* Susa, 2; Med., I, 4; II, 11; *iš-ṭur-ma,* Susa, 3, III, 51; *iš-tu-ru-ma,* Susa, 3, IV, 10, 24; *aš-tu-ru-ma,* Susa, 3, IV, 42; V, 1; V, 23, 34; *il-tu-ra-aš-šú-nu-ti-ma,* London, 103, IV, 39; *il-tu-ru-ú-ma,* D. E. P., II, pl. 20, 7; *il-tu-ra-aš-šu-um-ma,* London, 103, V, 16; pres., *ša-nam-ma i-šaṭ-ṭa-ru,* I R. 70, III, 6; inf., *i-na ša-a-me ša-ṭa-ri ù ba-ra-me,* London, 102, IV, 41; part., *hṭup-šar ša-ṭir abnuṭuppu,* V. A., 208, 28, 52; V. A., 209,

II, 22; *ša-ṭi-ir* ^{abnu}*narî an-ni-i*, V R. 56, 25; perm., *šú-mi šaṭ-ra*, Susa, 3, V, 57; Susa, 16, V, 3; *šùm ša-aṭ-ra*, Susa, 14, IV, 16; *ša šaṭ-ru*, V R. 56, 33; *šá i-na* ^{abnu}*narî ša-aṭ-ra*, Susa, 3, V, 46; pl. fem., *šùm šaṭ-ru i-pà-aš-ši-ṭu*, V. A., 2663, V, 32.

I, 2, *ša-nam il-ta-aṭ-ru*, V R. 56, 33.

II, 1 pres., *lu a-na ili lu a-na rubî*(?) *ú-ša-ṭa-ra-ma*, IV R.² 38, III, 25.

šiṭru, writing.

ki-ma ši-ṭi-ir šamê(-e), IV R.² 38, II, 27; ^{abnu}*kunuk ši-ṭir šumi-šu ik-nu-uk-ma*, V. A., 2663, IV, 53.

שיח, šîḫtu, bloating(?).

ina ši-ḫat šîri liq-ta-a zumur(-SU)-šu, V. A., 2663, V, 44.

I. שים, šâmu, fix, determine (cf. Hebr. שִׂים).

I, 1 prec., *a-na ši-ma-ti-šú li-šim-šú*, III R. 41, II, 35; *a-na ši-ma-ti-šú li-ši-mu*, London, 101, IV, 11; *li-ši-mu-šú*, Susa, 3, VII, 40; *ši-mat balâṭi li-ši-ma-šú* (Dual), O. B. I., 83, II, 18; *ši-mat ma-ru-uš-ti li-šim-šú-ma*, Neb. Nippur, IV, 7.

II, 1 part., *mu-šim ši-mat ilâni*, who determines the fate of the gods, Neb. Nippur, IV, 5; *bêlê mu-šim-mu šim-ti*, V. A., 2663, V, 41.

šîmtu, fate.

bêlê mu-šim-mu šim-ti, V. A., 2663, V, 42; *a-na ši-im-ti-šu*, London, 103, VI, 7; *šîmti(NAM.TAR)-šu li-lam-min*, London, 101, III, 11; *a-na ši-im-[ti]*, D. E. P., VI, 46, IV, 10; pl., *šîmâte*, *a-na ši-ma-ti-šú li-ši-mu*, London, 101, IV, 11; III R. 41, II, 35; *ša ši-ma-ti*, D. E. P., IV, pl. 16, I, 3; *ši-mat balâṭi(TI.LA) li-ši-ma-šu* (Dual), O. B. I., 83, II, 18; *ši-ma-at la na-ṭa-li*, Susa, 3, VII, 35; *ši-mat ilâni*, Neb. Nippur, IV, 6; *ši-mat ma-ru-uš-ti*, Neb. Nippur, IV, 6.

tasîmtu, wisdom.

(Ea) *bêl ta-šim-ti*, Neb. Nippur, IV, 9.

II. **שים, šâmu,** pay (cf. Talm. שׂוּם).

I, 1 pret., *i-šam šîmi-šu gam-ru-tu*, he paid its full price, V. A., 209, II, 37; III, 13, 26; *ša . . . i-ša-a-mu*, C. T., X, pl. III, 16; inf., *i-na ša-a-me ša-ṭa-a-ri u ba-ra-me*, during the paying of the price, writing and sealing, London, 102, IV, 41.

šîmu, price.

ku-nu-uk šîm eqli, London, 103, III, 9; *šîm MA.NA ša ḫurâṣi*, London, 103, III, 21; *a-na šîmi na-ad-nu-ma*, London, 103, III, 45; *ša a-na šîmi eqli nad-nu*, London, 102, IV, 22; *a-na šîmi im-ḫu-ru*, III R. 41, I, 12, 30; *šîmu gam-ru-tu*, full price, V. A., 209, IV, 34; *šîmi-šu gam-ru-tu ma-ḫir a-pil za-ku*, V. A., 209, II, 37; III, 13, 26.

šai(a)mânu, taxer, valuer.

ku-ša-ad ša-ai-ma-a-ni, London, 103, III, 17.

šakkû, law.

šak-ku-šú riš-tu-u, Neb. Nippur, I, 19.

שכן, šakânu.

I, 1 pret., *za-ku-us-su ki-a-am iš-kun*, its freedom he thus established, Susa, 3, II, 8; *za-ku-tu iš-ku-nu*, Susa, 3, IV, 5, 21; *za-ku-tu aš-ku-nu*, Susa, 3, IV, 32, 57; *za-ku-ut âli-šú . . . iš-ku-un-ma*, Susa, 3, III, 46; *šarru ṭe-e-ma iš-kun-šú-ma*, the king gave him a command, London, 103, III, 8; *iš-kun-ma*, London, 102, IV, 18; prec., *si-im-ma la-az . . i-na zu-um-ri-šu liš-ku-un-ma*, Susa, 3, VII, 22; *i-na zu-'-ri-šú li-iš-kum-ma*, may she put into his body, III R. 43, IV, 17; *i-na* *zu-um-ri-šu liš-kum-ma,* I R. 70, IV, 7; *ina zumri-šu liškun-(ŠA)-ma,* Neb. Nippur, IV, 21; *su-ga-a u ni-ib-ri-ta liš-ku-na-aš-šum-ma,* may he bring want and famine upon him, I R. 70, IV, 18; *ḫu-ša-aḫ-ḫa liš-kun-šu-um-ma,* V R. 56, 43; pres., *ni-šir-ta ki-za-ta i-šak-ka-nu,* who shall cause dismemberment and diminution, Susa, 2, III, 15; cf. I R. 70, II, 16; III R. 43, III, 22; C. T., X, pl. VII, 35; Susa, 16, IV, 17; III R. 41, II, 6; *a-šar la a-ma-ri i-ša-ka-nu,* places it in an invisible place, Neb. Nippur, V, 4; I R. 70, III, 8; Susa, 16, V, 1; *a-šar la a-ma-ru iškkanu(ŠA.MEŠ),* V. A., 2663, V, 31; *i-šak-ka-nu ú-zu-un-šu,* who puts his mind to, III R. 41, I, 36; V. A., 2663, V, 23, 35; *i-šak-ka-nu ú-zu-uš-šú,* V. A. 211, III, 6; *a-na ra-ma-ni-šu i-šak-ka-nu,* puts it to his own use, I R. 70, II, 12; III R. 43, III, 19; inf., *ni-ši-ir-ta ù qi-iṣ-ṣa-ta la ša-ka-ni,* Susa, 3, II, 11; *nu-šur-ra-a la ša-ka-ni,* Susa, 3, III, 5; *ṣa-bat amelu la ša-ka-na,* V R. 56, 5; perm., *a-na bît šá ᵐBe-la-ni ša-ak-nu,* it had been placed, London, 103, III, 10; *bîtu ša a-na UŠ.SA.DU-šu šak-nu,* V. A., 209, I, 18; *na-ra-a ša i-na eqli ša-šu ša-ak[-nu],* D. E. P., VI, 45, V, 10; *šá a-na bu-tuq-ti šaknu(ŠA-nu),* which had been exposed to flooding, Neb. Nippur, II, 26; *a-na me-te-iq mê šaknu(-nu),* Neb. Nippur, II, 31.

I, 2, *ši-iḫ-ṭa iš-ta-ka-an,* an advance he made, V R. 55, 15; *iš-ta-kan ṣu-lu-li,* he established protection, V. A., 2663, III, 33; *iš-tak-ka-nu si-ma-tu,* he puts works of art (in the temples), V. A., 2663, II, 46; *ni-(ši)-šir-tú i-na libbi(-bi) il-ta-ka-an,* he inflicts diminution upon it, Susa, 3, V, 30; *i-na aš-ri-im šá-ni-im-ma . . . il-ta-ka-an,* puts it in another place, Susa, 3, V, 42; *il-ka il-tak-nu,* imposes taxes, V R. 56, 32; perm., *pu-lu-uk-ku la šit-ku-nu,* the boundary had not been established, V. A., 2663, III, 20.

II, 1 pres., *a-šar la a-ma-ri ša-nam-ma ú-ša-ka-nu,* O. B. I., 150, II, 5; prec., *a-na is-ki-šú li-ša-kin-nu,* as his portion may they appoint, Susa, 3, V, 19.

III, 1 pres., *ú-ša-aš-šú-ma a-šar la a-ma-ri ušaškanu(ŠA-nu),* London, 101, III, 7; prec., *i-na pa-an šarri ù rabûti li-ša-aš(!)-ki-nu-šú,* before king and princes may they cause him to stand, London, 103, VI, 17.

IV, 1 pret., *bêl bîti . . . ša iš-ša-ki-nu-ma,* (who) has been appointed, III R. 43, edge IV, 1; III R. 45, No. 2, 6; cf. III R. 43, III, 15; London, 102, I, 32; V R. 56, 28; pres., *iš-ša-ka-nu-ma,* (who) will be appointed, III R. 41, I, 34; Susa, 3, III, 18, 26, 33; IV, 46; VI, 6; Susa, 16, IV, 8.

šaknu, governor.

ʰ*šak-nu,* V. A., 2663, V, 20; often followed by name of city or country, ʰ*ša-kin . . .,* Susa, 16, II, 6, 22, 25; III, 3; Susa, 14, II, 4; D. E. P., VI, 43, II, 18; D. E. P., VI, 44, I, 7; IV R.[2] 38, II, 33; V R. 55, 52, 55; V R. 56, 10, 18; Neb. Nippur, II, 20; III, 9; O. B. I., 83, I, 11; II, 4, 6, 7; O. B. I., 149, I, 4, 17; C. T., X, pl. III, 25; V. A., 209, I, 2; I R. 66, II, 7; this title occurs also in the list of officials, *lu-ú ša-kin lu-ú bêl paḫâti,* O. B. I., 149,

II, 2; cf. C. T., X, pl. V, 4, 13; VII, 32; Susa, 3, VI, 4; cstr., either *ša-kin,* Susa, 3, II, 44; III, 15, 24, 30; IV, 44; VI, 4; C. T., X, pl. VII, 42, 49; or *ša-kan,* C. T., X, pl. V, 4, 13; VII, 32; Neb. Nippur, I, 21; in titles of officials, as *ša-kin mâti,* Susa, 2, III, 5; ^{h}*ša-kin ṭe-mi,* commander, D. E. P., VI, 44, I, 12; ^{h}*ša-kin ṭe-me,* Neb. Nippur, III, 15; V, 16; *šakin(GAR-in) ṭe-mi,* Susa, 16, III, 30; O. B. I., 149, I, 18; II, 3; III R. 43, III, 11; Susa, 3, VI, 9; I R. 66, II, 13; *šakin(GAR) ṭe-mi mâti,* V R. 56, 13; *šakin(GAR) ṭe-mi ša mâtâti,* III R. 43, II, 6; ^{h}*ša-kin bu-ši,* Neb. Nippur, V, 13; (*šaknu* is represented by סגן in the Aramaic endorsements of the Murashû tablets, according to Prof. Clay).

šak(i)nûtu, government.

ša a-na ša-kin-ú-ti ša ^{mâtu}*Na-mar iš-šak-ki-nu,* V R. 56, 28; *eqil bît ša-ak-nu-ti,* III R. 43, I, 15.

šakkanak(k)u, potentate.

šakkanak(NER.ARAD) Bâbili, Neb. Nippur, II, 20; C. T., X, pl. IV, 10 [12]; *šakkanak* ^{âlu}*DUG* (=*Bâbili*), V R. 55, 3; *šakkanak* ^{mâtu}*Šumêri u Akkadî*^{ki}, V. A., 2663, I, 27; *šakkanak A.GA.-DE*^{ki}, London, 101, II, 10, *lu-ú šakkanakku,* Susa, 14, II, 1; Neb. Nippur, III, 19; *lu-ú šakkanakku ša i-na piḫât* ^{âlu}*Ḫu-da-da iš-šak-ka-nu,* Susa, 16, IV, 6; *šakkanakkê ša piḫâti,* Susa, 3, IV, 15, 36, V, 11; *šakkanak-ni-šú,* O. B. I., 83, I, 20; *šakkanakku ai-mu[-ma],* O. B. I., 83, II, 12.

שלא$_3$.

II, 1 inf., *a-na šú-li-i ai ir-šu-u ni-da a-ḫi,* for reposing(?) he shall not have a resting place, Susa, 2, III, 27.

šuluḫḫu, command, commander.

ga-mir šú-luḫ-ḫi, the most perfect commander, V. A., 2663, I, 7.

שלל, **šalâlu,** spoil.

I, 1 part., *ša-li-lu Kaš-ši-i,* V R. 55, 10.

I, 2 pret., *i-iš-ta-lal makkûra(ŠA.-GA)-šá,* he carried off as spoil its possessions, V R. 55, 43.

שלם, **šalâmu,** be whole.

II, 1 part., *ši-bir-ru mu-šal-lim nišê,* a scepter which prospers people, V. A., 2663, I, 35; *mu-šal-lim par-ṣi-šu-nu,* he carries out their laws, V. A., 2663, II, 10; inf., *šul-lum ki-du-di-e,* the care of shrines, V. A., 2663, II, 24.

šalamtu, corpse.

ša-lam-ta-šú i-na irṣiti ai iq-qi-bir, Susa, 16, VI, 21; [*ša-lam-ta*]-*šú ai iq-qi-bir,* D. E. P., VI, 43, III, 14.

šulpu.

in *pi-i šu-ul-pi,* uncultivated or pasture land, V. A., 208, 7, 36; C. T., X, pl. VI [24]. Its opposite is *eqlu zaq-pu, q.v.*

שלש, **šalšai,** third in order.

mâri-šu šal-ša-ai, following *mâri-šu rabî(-i)* and *mâri-šu kut-tin-nu,* London, 102, IV, 32.

šalaltu, three.

ga-ba-ri-e ša-lal-ti, London, 103, VI, 27.

שם, **šumu,** name, *passim.*

The most common phrases are: *šùm* ^{abnu}*narî an-ni-i,* Neb. Nippur, heading 1; *šumi(-mi) na-ri-e,* Susa, 2, IV, 33; *šùm ku-dur[-ri] an-ni-i,* London, 101, I, 1; cf. III R. 41, I, 3; *šùm-šú-nu za-ak-ru,* D. E. P., VI, 43, IV, 9; Susa, 3, VII, 29; Susa, 16, VI, 10; London, 103, VI, 22; III

R. 41, II, 36; I R. 70, IV, 23; O. B. I., 149, II, 15; III, 9; London, 102, V, 6; V. A., 2663, V, 46; also *šú-un-šú-nu za-ak-ru*, III R. 43, III, 24; IV, 33; *šú-mu-un-šú-nu za-ak-ru*, III R. 43, edge II, 1; *šu-um ili u šarri*, V R. 56, 33; *li-ḫal-liq šumi-šu*, London, 101, III, 12; cf. Susa, 16, VI, 24; III R. 41, II, 38; London, 102, II, 16; *šú-mi šaṭ-ra*, Susa, 3, V, 57; Susa, 16, V, 3; Susa, 14, IV, 16; *šumu la ibšû(-ú)*, relat., London, 103, IV, 23; cf. London, 103, I, 3; II, 9; *šumi-šu(MU.NI)*, London, 101, IV, 8; *šumi-šu(MU.-NE)*, Neb. Nippur, heading, 2.

א₄שמ, šemû, hear.

I, 1 pret., *iš-me-e-mu*, V. A., 209, I, 17; *iš-me-e-šú-nu-ti-ma*, V. A., 209, IV, 31; *iš-mi-ma*, Susa, 14, I, 15; *ai iš(!)-mu-šú*, IV R.[2] 38, III, 44; pres., *la i-še-mi-šú*, III R. 43, IV, 29.

III, 1 pret., *ú-še-eš-mi-ma*, he announced, London, 103, III, 35.

šêmû, intelligent.

la še-ma-a la na-ṭil ša pâni-ša, an imprudent man, V. A., 2663, V, 26; *sak-la la še-ma-a*, London, 102, V, 4; III R. 43, I, 31; *la še-ma ša a-ma-ti*, D. E. P., VI, 45, V, 21; *lâ šêmâ(ŠI.NU.TUK)*, IV R.[2] 38, III, 12; V R. 56, 34; Neb. Nippur, V, 3; III R. 41, II, 9; O. B. I., 149, II, 9; *lâ šêmâ(ŠI.NU.GAL.LA)*, I R. 70, II, 22.

שמה, šamû, heaven, *passim*.

šamâmu, heaven.

ka-la si-ḫi-ip ša-ma-me, Neb. Nippur, I, 14.

שמח, šamâḫu, be prosperous, luxuriant.

I, 1 prec., *ᵈNisaba li-ḫal-li-qa pu-qut-tu li-iš-mu-uḫ*, may thorns grow luxuriantly, I R. 70, IV, 13.

II, 1 part., *mu-šam-mi-ḫu ni-ši-šú*, who makes prosperous his people, V R. 55, 4.

šammu, plant, herb.

lu-ú iṣê lu-ú šammê(ŠAM.MEŠ), Susa, 3, II, 48; *šammê eqli-šú*, Susa, 3, III, 13; *šammê la ri-'-e*, Susa, 3, III, 21; *ba-qa-an šam-mi*, Neb. Nippur, III, 26.

šumma, if.

Susa, 3, IV, 52; V, 20.

שמן, šamnu, oil.

40 (*qa*) *šamni(NI)*, III R. 41, I, 22.

שמש, ᵈŠamšu, sun.

pân ᵈŠamši(-ši), V R. 55, 31; *ᵈŠamaš mâti-šú*, V R. 55, 4.

שן, šattu, year.

i-na šatti(MU.AN.NA) ša-a-ši, London, 103, V, 5; *ina šatti rêštî*, Susa, 16, II, 13; *šanâte ḫu-ša-aḫ-ḫi*, London, 101, IV, 10; *šanâte duḫ-di*, Susa, 3, V, 18; *šattu*, I R. 66, I, 2; II, 17; III R. 43, I, 28; Neb. Nippur, V, 26; London, 102, I, 9, 18; II, 35, 36, 37; VI, 1, 24; III, 9, 10, 12, 13, 14, 22; V. A., 209, I, 1; II, 28; V, 4; C. T., X, pl. III, 31; V. A., 208, 30, 53.

šattišam, yearly.

ša-at-ti-šam, IV R.[2] 38, II, 22; *šat-ti-šam-ma*, V. A., 2663, II, 14.

šangû, priest.

šangû(E.MAŠ) ᵈEr-ia, C. T., IX, pl. IV, 2, 18; V, 30; *šangû ᵈENGUR u ᵈNinâ*, O. B. I., 83, I, 16; *šangû ᵈMarduk*, V. A., 208, 52; *ʰE.MAŠ ᵈA-e*, V. A., 209, IV, 27; *ʰšangû(ŠID) ᵈRammân*, V. A., 2663, IV, 40.

שנה, šanû, change.

I, 1 pret., *pu-lu-uk-ka-šu-un iš-ni-ma*, C. T., X, pl. V, 4.

II, 1 pres., *ša ni-din-ti šú-a-tu ú-ša-an-nu-ú*, C. T., X, pl. VII, 33; *ku-dur-ra ú-ša-an-nu-ú*, I R. 70,

II, 14; III R. 43, III, 21; prec., *ku-dur-ra-šú li-še-in-ni*, III R. 43, IV, 2; inf., *ši-qit-ta la šú-un-nim-ma*, Susa, 3, III, 9; part., *mu-ša-na an-ni-i*, O. B. I., 83, II, 21.

šanû, the second.

ʰšanû (cf. Br. 4821), Susa, 16, III, 18; C. T., IX, pl. V, 34; and perhaps also I R. 66, I, 4.

šanû, the other one.

ša-na-a ša it-ti-šu, the companion that was with him, V R. 55, 34.

šanamma, any other one.

ša-nam-ma, Susa, 3, III, 10; Susa, 16, IV, 24; III R. 41, II, 8; O. B. I., 150, II, 5; Neb. Nippur, III, 22; *ša-nam*, V R., 56, 33; *ša-nam-ma i-šaṭ-ṭa-ru*, (who) writes anything else, I R. 70, III, 6.

šanimma, any other.

ša-ni-im-ma, Susa, 3, V, 41.

šanumma, another, any other.

ša-nu-um-ma, V R. 56, 53; *ma-am-ma ša-nu-um-ma*, V R. 56, 27; III R. 41, II, 5; London, 102, I, 31.

שנן, **šanânu,** be equal.

I, 1 part., *la i-ba-aš-šú-ú ilu ša-nin-šú*, Neb. Nippur, I, 4; *šâni-nu(GAR.RI) lâ išû(NU.TUK)*, V R. 55, 23; inf., *šarru la ša-na-an*, the king without equal, IV R.² 38, I, 26; [*šarru la*] *ša-na-an*, C. T., X, pl. IV, 11.

IV, 1, *be-lut-su la iš-ša-na-nu*, whose rule will not be equaled, Neb. Nippur, I, 17.

שסה, **šasû,** call.

I, 1 pret., *a-na ma-ḫar šarri il-su-ma*, C. T., X, pl. V, 10; pres., *e-ma i-ša-as-su-ú*, when he calls, IV R.² 38, III, 43.

שפך, **šapâku,** throw up.

I, 1 perm., *i-ku la šap-ku*, a ditch had not been thrown up, Neb Nippur, II, 29.

שפל, **šaplû,** lower.

in the phrases *šiddu šaplû(KI.TA)* and *pûtu šaplû, passim*; pl. fem., *bêl e-la-ti u šap-la-a-ti*, lord of all that is above and below, V. A., 2663, I, 11.

šapliš, below.

eliš(AN.TA) ù šapliš(KI.TA), IV R.² 38, I, 31; D. E. P., VI, 43, III, 9; D. E. P., II, 93, I, 14.

שפר, **šapâru,** send.

I, 1 pret., *iš-pur-ma*, Susa, 3, I, 37; Susa, 16, III, 6; C. T., IX, pl. V, 27; London, 102, IV, 16; [*iš*]*-pur*, Susa, 16, I, 10; *iš-pur-šú-ma*, London, 103, II, 20; *iš-pur-šú-nu-ti-ma*, Susa, 16, II, 9; *iš-pu-ru-ma* (relat.), O. B. I., 149, I, 20; prec., *liš-pur-šú-ma*, III R. 41, II, 22.

šipru, work.

mu-du-u kal šip-ri, V. A., 2663, II, 49; *ši-pir ni-kil-ti*, a mischievous deed, C.T., X, pl. VII, 36.

šâpiru, scribe (cf. p. 176).

aklu lu šá-pi-ru, D. E. P., II, 97, 11; *lu-ú ʰlaputtû lu-ú šá-pi-ru*, Susa, 16, III, 29; *lu ak-lu lu ša-pi-ru*, Neb. Nippur, III, 19; *ʰša-kan ʰša-pi-ru*, C. T., X, pl. V, 4, 13; VII, 32.

šepirtu, disposition, gift.

eqlu še-pir-ti ᵈNabû-kudurri-uṣur, C. T., IX, pl. IV, 15; *še-pir-ti*, C. T., X, pl. VI, 31; pl., *kunuk šarri ša šip-ri-e-ti*, the administrative(?) seal of the king, C. T., X, pl. III, 32; V. A., 2663, V, 48; I R. 66, II, 20.

našpartu, message.

na-aš-par-ta-ša ša uz-zi, III R. 41, II, 22.

שקה, **šaqû,** lofty.

bêl ša-qu-ú, Neb. Nippur, IV, 5; *ʰšaqû(SAG)*, Neb. Nippur, V,

11; D. E. P., VI, 43, II, 8, 13; V R. 56, 15; I R. 66, II, 8; London, 101, II, 5, 6, 13; London, 102, VI, 16; ^{h}*šaq bîti*, Susa, 16, III, 19; ^{h}*šaq šarri*, London, 101, I, 20; Susa, 3, I, 14, 32; VI, 3; D. E. P., VI, 42, I, 20; III R. 41, I, 11, 29; ^{h}*šaq-šup-par*, Neb. Nippur, V, 9; I R. 66, II, 10; III R. 43, I, 30; II, 6; III R. 43, edge IV, 4; London, 102, IV, 48; VI, 17; *ša-ku mâti*, London, 102, IV, 6; ^{h}*ša-ku mâti*, C. T., X, pl. III, 28; ^{h}*ša-ku Dil-bat*, V. A., 208, 2, 49; ^{h}*ša-ku Bâbili*, V. A., 2663, III, 36; IV, 51; V, 34; ^{h}*ša-ku Bar-sip^{ki}*, V. A., 2663, V, 11; C. T., X, pl. VII, 47; ^{h}*ša-ku Kûtî*, V. A., 2663, V, 13.

שקה, **šaqû,** irrigate.
la mi-ki-e-ri u la ša[-qi-e] šammê eqli-šú, Susa, 3, III, 12.

šiqîtu, irrigation.
mê nâr ši-qi-ti-šú, Susa, 3, III, 4; *ši-qi-iz-zu ub-ba-lu*, Susa, 16, V, 8; *ši-qit-ta*, Susa 3, III, 9.

mašqû, drinking place.
bu-ut-tu-qu maš-qu-ú, the drinking place was cut off, V R. 55, 19.

mašqîtu, place of irrigation.
ina nâri maš-qi-ti-šú, Susa, 3, III, 6.

שקל, **šiqlu,** shekel.
Susa, 14, I, 12; London, 102, III, 25; IV, 23, 25, 26; V. A., 209, I, 6, 15, 21; IV, 5, 19, 20, 32, 33.

שקם, **šaqummatu,** majesty (cf. p. 166).
ša-qum-mat-su mâtâti ka-at-ma, Neb. Nippur, I, 16.

שקץ, **šukuzu,** cap(?) (Zimmern).
šub-tum ù šú-ku-zu ša ^{d}A-num, Susa, 2, IV, 1.

שקש, **šaqâšu,** destroy.
I, 1 prec., *i-na taḫâzi-šu liš-gi-is-su*, London, 102, II, 5.

šaqaštu, destruction.
^{d}Nergal i-na šá-ga-aš-ti pir'i-šú . . . ., London, 101, IV, 2.

šiqiltu, bloodshed.
ina ši-qil-ti it-ba-lu-ma, with bloodshed they had taken away, V. A., 2663, III, 16.

שרא, **šer'û,** vegetation.
ši-ir bi-ra-a li-kab-bi-sa še-pa-šú, III R. 43, IV, 6; *ši-ir-a bi-ri-ta*, I R. 70, IV, 14.

širiš, fruitful.
[ki]-mu-ú ŠE.BAR la ši-ri-iš, instead of grain unfruitfulness, London, 102, II, 12.

mešrêti, limbs.
ub-bur meš-ri-e-ti, paralysis of limbs, V. A., 2663, V, 39; Susa, 14, III, 5.

שרב, **šuribtu,** terror.
pl., *xvii šú-ri-pat ša ilâni rabûti*, Susa, 2, IV, 29.

שרח, **šarâḫu,** be exceedingly large.
I, 2 perm., *par(?)-su-šu šit-ru-ḫu*, whose law is powerful, Neb. Nippur, I, 18.
II, 1 pret., *ba-nit ilâni ú-šar-ri-ḫu nab-nit-su*, (Bêlit) the creator of the gods made glorious his birth, V. A., 2663, II, 53.

שרף, **šarâpu,** burn.
I, 1 pres., *i-na išâti(NE) i-šar-ra-pu*, I R. 70, III, 4.

שרק, **šarâqu,** present, give.
I, 1 pret., *iš-ru-ku*, Susa, 3, IV, 3, 19; *iš[-ru-uq]*, D. E. P., II, 93, II, 2; *iš-ruq-šum-ma*, Neb. Nippur, II, 6; *iš-ru-uq-šú-nu-ti*, C. T., IX, pl. V, 40; *aš-ru-ku*, Susa, 3, IV, 30, 55; V, 28; prec., *li-iš-ru-uq*, D. E. P., VI, 43, III, 6; *liš-ri-iq*, D. E. P., VI, 47, 9; *liš-ruq-šú*, Susa, 14, III, 6; D. E. P., II, 116, 5; D. E. P., VI, 46, IV, 2; *liš-ru-ku-šum-ma*, V. A., 2663, V, 39; *a-na ši-riq-ti liš-ru-qa-šú* (Dual), O. B. I., 83, II, 20;

pres., *i-šar-ra-qu*, III R. 41, II, 5; C. T., X, pl. VII, 33; *a-na ili i-šar-ra-ku*, III R. 43, III, 18; perm., *ul ša-ri-iq*, Neb. Nippur, IV, 1.

I, 2, *iš-tar-ra-ku a-ḫa-nu*, C. T., X, pl. V, 5.

III, 1 pres., *a-na ili ú-ša-aš-ra-ku*, I R. 70, II, 10.

šarqu, gift.

ša-ar-qi eqlu šú-a-tu i-nam-du-ma, Neb. Nippur, III, 20.

šeriqtu, gift.

ši-ri-iq-ti liš-ruk-šu, D. E. P., II, 116, 4; *a-na še-ri-iq-ti liš-ru-[uq]-šu*, D. E. P., VI, 46, IV, 1; *a-na ši-riq-ti liš-ru-qa-šú*, O. B. I., 83, II, 20; *[ši]-riq-ti liš-ruq-šu*, Susa, 14, III, 6.

šarqu, bright red blood (cf. p. 182).

ša-ar-ka u da-ma, III R. 43, IV, 17; *šar-ka u da-ma*, Susa, 3, VII, 24; *šarqa(BE.UD) ù da-ma*, III R. 41, II, 31; *da-ma ù šar-ka*, I R. 70, IV, 7; O. B. I., 149, III, 4; *da-a u šar-ka*, D. E. P., IV, pl. 16, II, 4; *dâma(BE) u šarqa(BE. UD)*, Neb. Nippur, IV, 21.

שרר, **šarru,** king, *passim*.

šarru(LUGAL.E), I R. 66, I, 3; II, 18; III R. 43, I, 4, 10, 23, 28; II, 27; IV, 13; III R. 43, edge IV, 2; O. B. I., 149, I 14; *šàr apsî*, Neb Nippur, IV, 9; *šàr E-zi-da*, D. E. P., VI, 46, IV, 3; *šàr ilâni*, D. E. P., II, 93, II, 16; V R. 55, 12; Neb. Nippur, I, 3; *šàr Bâbili*, Susa, 2, II, 29; D. E. P., II, 97, 9; O. B. I., 83, I, 7; London, 102, IV, 3; V. A., 2663, I, 26; *šàr gim-ri*, V. A., 2663, I, 4; *šàr ḫe-gal-lim*, D. E. P., II, 116, 6; D. E. P., VI, 43, III, 7; *šàr ki-na-a-ti*, V R. 55, 6; *šàr kiššati*, Susa, 2, I, 2; II, 27; Med., II, 3; D. E. P., II, 97, 8; IV R.^{2} 38, I, 21; D. E. P., VI, 42, I, 24; C. T., IX, pl. IV, 15; Neb. Nippur, II, 23; V R. 56, 7; London, 102, IV, 2, 12; *šàr me-ša-ri*, Neb. Nippur, II, 22; *šàr mât tâmdi*, O. B. I., 83, I, 3, 6; *šàr naqbê*, D. E. P., VI, 43, IV, 4; *šàr šamê*, Susa, 2, IV, 2; *šàr šamê u irṣiti*, V R. 56, 39; III R. 41, II, 25; V. A., 2663, III, 1; *šàr Šumêri u Akkadî*, IV R.^{2} 38, I, 22; *šàr ta-ḫa-zi*, III R. 43, IV, 23.

šarrûtu, kingdom.

šarru-u-tu a-na zi-i-ri-šú li-tir-ru-šú, Susa, 14, IV, 14; *[ilâni] šarrûti u mâti-šu*, D. E. P., VI, 47, 6; ^{abnu}*kunuk(DUB) šarru-ú-ti-šu*, C. T., X, pl. V, 8; *zêr šarru-ú-ti da-ru-ú*, V. A., 2663, II, 40; *šar-ru-ti*, IV R.^{2} 38, II, 5.

šarûru, glory.

šá-ru-ru-šú ka-la si-ḫi-ip ša-ma-me . . . lit-bu-uš-ma, Neb. Nippur, I, 14.

שרש, **šuršu,** root.

li-qa-am-me šur-ši-šú, Neb. Nippur, IV, 27.

šuššu, a soss, sixty.

šuššu(I ŠÚ) $^{she'u}$*zêru*, Susa, 2, II, 1; *šuššu(KU) ḫurâṣi*, London, 102, IV, 25.

šatammu, a title of an official, perhaps overseer.

ša-tam bît ú-na-ti, keeper of the treasure house, V R. 56, 20; London, 102, IV, 9; *ša(g)-tam bît ú-na-a-ti*, I R. 66, II, 16; ^{h}*šá-tam E-sag-ila*, V. A., 2663, V, 9; ^{h}*ša-tam*, V. A., 2663, V, 20; C. T., X, pl. VII, 48; *ša(?)-tam Bît-di-bi-na*, London, 101, II, 4.

ti'ûtu, equipment(?).

I ^{iṣu}*narkabtu a-di ti-'-ú-ti-ša*, III R. 41, I, 15.

תא$_2$ם, **tâmtu, tâmdu,** sea.

ú-la-la tâmdi(A.AB.BA) ù la mu-da-a, Susa, 14, II, 16; *ina libbi tâmdi,* D. E. P., VI, 42, I, 5; *šàr mât tâmdi,* O. B. I., 83, I, 3, 6; *ša mât tâmdi,* O. B. I., 83, I, 13; *ḫi-ṣib tam-tim rapaš-tim(-tim),* V. A., 2663, II, 15.

*h*TU **bîti,** a title of a class of priests.
mA-qar-dNabû TU bîti, C. T., X, pl. III, 2; *TU dLa-ga-ma-al,* V. A., 208, 26; *hTU bît dLa-ga-ma-al,* V. A., 208, 33; *hTU [bit]* . . . C. T., X, pl. VII, 46 (cf. "The Assyrian-Babylonian *ameluTU bîti,*" in A.J.S.L., XXII (1905), October, pp. 46–62).

תבא, **tebû, tabû,** come out, rise.
I, 1 part., *si-im-ma la te-e-ba-a,* Susa, 3, VII, 20; *iš-ru-ba-a la te-ba-a,* III R. 41, II, 16; *mi-iq-ta la ta-ba-a,* a fall without rising, Susa, 14, IV, 7.
III, 1 pret., *ú-šat-ba-a išukakkê-šú,* he caused him to draw his weapons, V R. 55, 13.
tîbu, approach.
pûtu šaplû ti-ib âluŠá-sa-naki, O. B. I., 149, I, 12.

tibdû.
tib-da-a a-na la e-ri-ši, III R. 45, No. 2, 10.

תבך, **tabâku,** pour out.
I, 1 prec., *ki-ma mê lit-bu-uk,* Susa, 2, III, 35.
tabku, poured out, perhaps stored.
GIŠ.BAR tab-ki, London, 103, III, 20 (cf. Clay, B.E., XV, 10:7; XV, 29:5; 115:1, 4; *tab-ku,* B.E., XIV, 37:2; 125:1; XV, 80:11; *tu-bu-uk-ku-ú,* B. E., XIV, 144:4).

תבל, **tabâlu,** take away.
I, 1 pret., *at-ba-lu* (relat.), Susa, 3, IV, 4, 20; *ina ši-qil-ti it-ba-lu-ma,* V. A., 2663, III, 17; pres., *eqlu . . la i-tab-ba-lu ú-šat-ba-lu* (relat.), Susa, 16, IV, 15; III R. 41, I, 37; inf., *la ta-bal eqli-šú,* Susa, 3 II, 6; III, 42; *a-na ta-bal eqli-šu,* I R. 70, II, 7; *a-na ta-bal eqlâti an-na-ti,* III R. 41, I, 35; *a-na ta-bal eqli . . . . uznâ-šu i-šak-ka-nu,* V. A., 2663, V, 32; *ana tabâli(TÚM,* cf. Br. 9062) *esqêti ša-ši-na,* V. A., 211, III, 4.
I, 2 pres., *eqlu a-na zêri-ia aš-ru-ku la it-ta-bal,* Susa, 3, IV, 56; V, 28.
III, 1 pres., *i-tab-ba-lu ú-šat-ba-lu,* Susa, 16, IV, 15; III R. 41, I, 37; *ú-šat-ba-lu eqlu an-nu-ú,* London, 103, V, 37.

tabalu, land (Hebr. תֵּבֵל) (cf. p. 178).
kal-li-e nâri u ta-ba-li, Neb. Nippur, III, 26; C. T., IX, pl. V, 33; I R. 66, I, 7; III R. 45, No. 2, 2.

תבן, **tibnu,** straw.
lu-ú tibnu(IN.NU) lu-ú ŠE.BAR, Susa, 3, II, 49.

תור, **târu,** return.
I, 1 pret., *a-na Akkadî i-tu-ra,* V R. 55, 44; *i-tur-ma . . i-na nazâ-zi(GUB-zi) ša aḫê-šu eqlu ik-nu-kam-ma,* London, 102, I, 24; *i-tur-ma,* London, 102, II, 32; pres., *ul i-tur-ru-ú-mu,* V. A., 209; II, 39; III, 15, 27; V, 2; *ul i-tur-ru-ú-ma,* V. A., 209, I, 29; *ul i-tur-ru-ma,* they shall not reopen the case, London, 102, IV, 35; *ana piḫâti(NAM) i-t[u-ur-ru],* secularize, Neb. Nippur, III, 28; prec., *ana da-um-ma-ti li-tur(?)-šu,* III R. 41, II, 20; *a-na ai-bi li-tur-šu,* London, 102, II, 31; inf., *la ta-a-ra u la ra-ga-mi,* London, 103, III, 30; *[la] ta-a-ri,* D. E. P., IV, pl. 16, I, 4; *ṭuppu la ta-a-ru u la da-ba-bu(bi) ik-nu-uk-ma,* V. A., 209, IV, 13, 36.
I, 2, *ša ed-li qar-di pu-ri-da-šu it-tu-ra,* the legs of the strong man turned, *i.e.,* failed, V R. 55, 21.
II, 1 pret., *a-na piḫâti u-te-ir,* to the crown he returned, O. B. I., 83, I, 15; *ṭe-im-šú ú-tir-ma,* his

report he brought, London, 103, III, 2; V, 11, 21; *ṭe-im-šu-nu ú-tir-ru-ma*, London, 103, III, 39; *ú-tir-ru aš-ru-uš-šin*, V. A., 2663, II, 30; *a-na zitti(ḪA.LA) ú-tir-am-ma*, V. A., 2663, III, 23; *a-na i-di ram-ni-šu-nu ú-tir-ru-ma*, they turned them to their own use, C. T., X, pl. V, 5; *eqlâti ša-ši-na ú-tir-am-ma*, those fields he returned, C. T., X, pl. V, 6; *qâti . . . ú-tir-ru*, they compensated, Susa, 2, I, 19; prec., *li-tir-ru-šú*, Susa, 14, IV, 15; pres., *eqlu a-di-nu a-na piḫâti la ú-tar*, Susa, 3, IV, 51; *ana piḫâti-ši-na u-tar-ru*, III R. 41, II, 2; [*ú*]-*ta*-[*ra*], O. B. I., 83, II, edge; *a-na i-di ram-ni-šu ú-tar-ru*, C. T., X, pl. VII, 34; inf., *eli bît abi-ia a-na tur-r*[*i*], to make restitution to the house of my father, C. T., X, pl. III, 5; *a-na tur-ri gi-mil-li*, to avenge, V R. 55, 13.

II, 2, *ut-te-ru-ma il-ka il-tak-nu*, again lays taxes, V R. 56, 32; *a-na piḫâti ut-te-ir*, Susa, 3, V, 14; *a-na piḫâti ut-tir*, Susa, 3, V, 33.

taḫâzu, battle.

a-šar qa-tuš ù ta-ḫa-zi, London, 103, VI, 19; *a-na e-piš taḫâzi*, V R. 55, 7; *la a-di-ru taḫâzu*, V R. 55, 8, 38; *ip-pu-šu taḫâzu*, V R. 55, 29; *bêlê taḫâzi*, V R. 55, 40; *i-na mi-ḫi-e ta-ḫa-zi-šú-nu*, V R. 55, 33; (Zamama) *šàr ta-ḫa-zi*, III R. 43, IV, 23; *i-na ta-ḫa-zi*, III R. 43, IV, 24, 29; (Nergal) *bêl qabli ù ta-ḫa-zi*, London, 102, II, 4; *i-na taḫâzi-šu liš-gi-is-su*, London, 102, II, 5.

taḫšû, ram (Hebr. תַּחַשׁ).

šîr(UZU) taḫ-ši-e šîr sûni(UR), mutton, V. A., 208, 5.

תכל, **tukultu,** help.

ša ina tu-kul-ti ilâni rabûti it-tal-la-ku-ma, V. A., 2663, II, 26.

תלם, **talâmu,** present.

III, 1 pret., *ḫa-si-sa pal-ka ú-šat-li-mu-šu*, the wide understanding which he imparted to him, V. A., 2663, III, 7.

talîmu, twin brother.

(*Šamaš-šum-ukîn*) *aḫu ta-li-mu ša* ^{d}*Aššur-bân-apal*, C. T., X, pl. IV, 11.

תמה, **tamû,** speak, call.

I, 1 pret., *it-ma*, spoke, London, 103, I, 45; perm., *ilâni qabli ta-mu*, Susa, 2, IV, 22 (according to Zimmern = *tu'amû*, twins).

תמח, **tamâḫu,** take.

ṣir-rit ^{h}*nakri-šú qa-tu-uš-šu it-muḫ*, Neb. Nippur, II, 5.

תמר, **tamâru,** hide.

I, 1 pres., *ina eqli la a-ma-ri i-tam-mi-ru*, V R. 56, 36; O. B. I., 149, II, 13; *i-na e-pi-ri i-tam-me-ru*, Neb. Nippur, IV, 30; III R. 43, I, 33; *i-na epiri(IŠ) i-te*[*-mi-ru*], O. B. I., 150, II, 3; *i-na epirê (IŠ.ZUN) i-tam-mi-ru*, I R. 70, III, 2; V. A., 2663, V, 29; *i-na qaq-qa-ri i-ta*(!)*-im-me-ru*, Susa, 16, IV, 34; *i-na irṣiti i-tam-mi-ru*, III R. 41, II, 12; (*ina*) *a-šar la a-ma-ri i-*[*tam-mi-ru*], London, 102, V, 5.

I, 2, *i-na qaq-qa-ri it-te-mi-ir*, Susa, 3, V, 52.

III, 1 pres., *i-na e-pi-ri ú-ša-at-ma-ru*, London, 103, V, 47.

tamirtu, environs of a city.

ta-mir-ti âli . . ., D. E. P., II, 97, 2, 3, 6; *ta-mi-ir-ti âli*, Susa, 3, I, 9; *a-na ta-mi-ir-ti-šú*, Susa, 3, III, 19, 44; pl., *ta-mi-ra-ti-šú li-mi-la-a pu-qut-ta*, III R. 43, IV, 4.

taptû, cultivated field(?) (perhaps from פתח, to open, cultivate).
tap-tu-ú pa-na-at $^{i\c{s}u}$*kirû*, V. A., 2663, IV, 33; *a-di tap-te-e ša pa-na-at* $^{i\c{s}u}$*kirû*, V. A., 2663, IV, 44.

תקה, **taqû**, pay homage (cf. p. 162).
II, 1, *ú-taq-qu-ú pal-ḫiš*, Neb. Nippur, I, 6; *pal-ḫi-iš ú-taq-qu-ú*, Neb. Nippur, II, 11.

turpu'tu, tumult.
i-na tur-pu-'-ti-šu-nu, V R. 55, 31.

תרץ, **tarâṣu**, stretch out.
I, 1 pres., *ubâni-šú a-na limutti(-ti) i-tar-ra-ṣu*, Neb. Nippur, III, 24.
tarṣu, direction.
a-na tar-ṣi ^{âlu}*Na-ba-ti*, towards, V. A., 2663, IV, 17.

tirṣu, stretching (of the hand).
i-na ti-ri-iṣ qa-ti, Susa, 3, VI, 37; *ti-ri-iṣ qa-ti-šu*, guided by his hand, V. A., 2663, I, 26; III, 38.

turtu, blindness.
tur-ti înâ(ŠI²) sa-kak uznâ(PI²) ub-bur meš-ri-e-ti liš-ru-ku-šum-ma, V. A., 2663, V, 38 (cf. the parallel expression: *zu-ut pa-ni sa-ka-ak uz-ni*, Susa, 14, III, 4).

Tašrîtu, the month Tishri.
London, 102, IV, 11.

titurru, bridge.
ḫarrâna ù ti-tur-ra . . . la a-ma-ri, Susa, 3, III, 22; *a-di ti-tur(!)-ri mi-ti-iq-ti šarri*, Susa, 14, I, 3; *ti-tur-ra la e-pi-ši*, V R. 56, 2.

ADDITIONS AND CORRECTIONS.

p. xxii, No. XXIX. "Perhaps Nippur."—There seems to be some difference of opinion as to the place where this stone was discovered. While the author of the official catalogue of the Royal Museums (*Verzeichnis der Vorderasiatischen Altertümer und Gipsabgüsse*, Berlin, 1889, p. 66, No. 213) assigns this boundary stone thus: "*Aus Nippur (heute Niffer) in Südbabylonien,*" and while nothing is known of any authorized change in this designation, yet according to information received from one of the officials of the Museums more recently (June, 1905), the statement in the Catalogue rests solely upon what the dealer, who sold the stone to the Berlin authorities in 1885, said. Moreover, according to the records of the Museums, the stone was not excavated by the dealer, but purchased by him. In view of this, and in the absence of any internal evidence, it seems that an attitude of reserve is advisable.

p. 5, l. 2, and p. 10, ll. 15f. For *duppu* read *ṭuppu*; see Glossary, s. v.

p. 11, l. 2. The "sealing" of the boundary stones is evidently a stereotyped phrase, derived from the period when clay tablets were still in use. Only in one case we may possibly have an instance of an autograph signature. The name of King Meli-Shipak is scratched under the inscription on Susa, No. 2.

p. 27, l. 2 from below. Instead of "sojourners," see Glossary under *qattinu*.

p. 58, l. 2 from below. For *lilamman* read *lilammin*. "Br. 9946, *MIN* has the same phonetic value also in Assyrian, which is required grammatically in the above passage. Cf. also Delitzsch, A. G.², p. 40" (Prof. Hilprecht). The same correction also on p. 66, l. 16; p. 192, II, 23; p. 199, ll. 10, 11.

p. 69, ll. 3, 4. Instead of *ekimmu* read *eṭemmu*. For *e-di-im-mi, e-te-im-mi-im* and *e-GIM-mu* = *eṭemmu*, see Ungnad, V. S., Vol. I, p. VIII*b*, and Zimmern in Pinckert, *Hymnen und Gebete an Nebo*, p. 14. The writing of *du-up-pu* and *tu-up-pu* (Muss-Arnolt, Dict., p. 263*a*) = *ṭuppu* is a perfect parallel.

p. 78, note 10. For "fig. 12^{14}, p. 29," read "fig. 12^{14}, p. 30."

p. 92, l. 20. For "London 106" read "London 105," also p. 137, last line.

p. 92, l. 22. For "London 105" read "London 106."

p. 97, fig. 31. Alongside of the figures found on the Babylonian boundary stones may be placed the figures on an unbaked cylinder which was recently found by Mr. MacAlister at Gezer, in débris belonging to the El Amarna period, and published by him in the October number of the "Quarterly Statement of the Palestine Exploration Fund," p. 262. It shows two bands of figures in relief, made by the rolling of a seal cylinder over the clay. The complete design appears twice in each band. It represents certain constellations, some of which certainly belong to the zodiac, but (as on the Babylonian boundary stones) they are not arranged in regular order. Beginning at the left hand corner of the lower band we find, after a partial picture of the sun, what looks like a tree, but is probably intended for an ear of grain and thus represents *spica*, the most prominent star in the *virgo*. Below it is the *scorpion;* alongside of it an upturned vessel, most likely the *amphora*, a name for the *aquarius*. Then follows a ladder with an upturned vase on top. The next figure is a horned animal, perhaps the *aries*. Immediately above it is a small animal which cannot be identified. Alongside is a bird with a little triangle. It reminds us of the walking bird on the Babylonian boundary stones. Over the three last figures is a curiously ribbed animal, perhaps intended for *leo* or *taurus*. This is followed by an animal which looks like an antelope. It is perhaps meant for the *capricorn*. Beneath it is a figure, resembling an inverted T, which may stand for the *libra*. Above the antelope is an indistinct, clumsy figure, which the artist intended perhaps for the *cancer*. Between antelope and lion is another T-shaped figure. Next comes a serpent, perhaps the *hydra*. Near its tail is a star, most likely *Venus*. Alongside of it is the crescent and the sun, beneath which are

FIG. 52.—The zodiac tablet from Gezer.

the clear figures of a fish and a scorpion. In all there are eighteen figures, of which the little triangle under the bird and the upper T-shaped figure are perhaps only inserted to fill out space. Of the remaining figures we can clearly recognize the sun, moon, Venus star, fish, scorpion, amphora and ear of grain, while the ram, capricorn, lion, balance and cancer are less clearly represented. Finally the ladder with inverted vase, the small animal between ram and lion and the bird with the triangle under it are still unclear. But they may stand in some relation to the *sagittarius*, *taurus* and *gemini*, which are not otherwise represented.

p. 105, last line. Franz X. Kugler in his excellent work, *Sternkunde und Sterndienst in Babel*, I. *Buch*, Münster, 1907, shows, pp. 261–263, that in the late (Arsacide) period the star of Gula corresponded to our waterman. This can hardly be applied to the picture of the goddess Gula on the boundary

21

stones, which is always associated with the dog. Now the "great dog," called *UR.GU.LA* (evidently also a play on the name of the goddess), is identical with *leo*, the zodiacal sign of the month *Abu;* hence the goddess Gula on the boundary stones is either an explanatory addition to the symbol of the "lion" or stands for the next zodiacal sign, the "virgin." In the lists given by Kugler on p. 229 the zodiacal sign for the month *Ulûlu* is either called *AB.SIM*(*šer'u*) or *ŠU.PA*(*namru*), which is identical with *spica* or *a virginis* (Kugler, p. 251). Thus far, however, the picture of an ear of grain has not appeared on the boundary stones. It is, therefore, *possible* that the picture of Gula represents the "virgin." That the Babylonians associated a goddess with the month *Ulûlu* is evident from the list of months with their patron deities, where we read: *arḫuUlûlu Iš-tar be-lit.* . .

p. 106, l. 13. For NIN.IB read Nergal.

p. 106, l. 14. For Nergal read NIN.IB. The investigations of Kugler (*Sternkunde und Sterndienst in Babel*, pp. 215–225) have shown that the names of the Babylonian planets and the gods associated with them were *not* exchanged, as has been argued by Hommel and Winckler.

p. 202, Col. II, 1. Instead of *A-šab-šu*, Prof. Hilprecht prefers the reading *A-šap-šu* in view of *Bît-Šum-ili-a-šip-ù-uš.*

p. 209, Col. II, 17. Instead of *Nabû*-[*êriš*](*-iš*), Prof. Hilprecht suggests *Nabû*-[*ga*]*-mil* as the preceding name. The form *Nabû*-[*êriš*](*-iš*) had been chosen in view of *Ilu-êriš*(*PIN-iš*), *Rammân-êriš*(*PIN-iš*), *Sin-êriš*(*PIN-iš*), *Šamaš-êriš*(*PIN-iš*), etc., found in Clay, B. E., Vols. XIV, XV.

p. 213, Col. II. Instead of *dṢîr-ap-pi-li*, Prof. Hilprecht suggests the reading *dṢîr-ap-pi-LI*(*SUB*) as a possibility. *LI* is ideogram for *ellu*, therefore probably also for *alâlu*, "to be shining"; hence "O Ṣir, make my face shining," *i.e.*, "joyful."

p. 217, Col. I, 1. For *âluDi-in-du-bîtu* = *âluDintu-bîtu* = *âluDimtu-bîtu* Prof. Hilprecht remarks: "For *dintu* = *dimtu* cf. (1) *âluDi-in-tu ša mSu-la-ai*, Sennach., IV, 56; (2) Hommel, *Geographie*, p. 350[6]; (3) *nakamtu*, *nakantu*, *nakandu*, cf. the list on p. 215: *Bît-a-qar-nak-kan-di*."

p. 248, l. 6 from below. For **drânu** read **idranu.**

p. 264, Col. II, 19. For *GÚ.EN.NA* see also Clay, B. E., XIV, 39 : 1; 136 : 1.

p. 277, Col. II, after l. 5 insert:

kalû, magician, priest.

hka-lu, C. T., X, pl. III, 26; *ka-lu*, V R. 56, 12.

p. 277, Col. II, after *kallatu* insert:

*imêru***KIL.DA,** III R. 41, I, 19.

p. 295, Col. II, l. 22. For *mâshkupa-gu-mu* read *mashkupa-gu-mu.*

p. 299, Col. II, after *pašâru* insert:

pîtu(bîtu ?), in the phrase *p*(*b*)*ît i-mit-ti šarri*, V R. 55, 26, 36, perhaps with Muss-Arnolt, Dict., p. 853*a*, to be rendered: "In front of the right hand of the king."

p. 309, Col. I, l. 13. In support of the identity of *šadû*, mountain, and *šadû*, east, which I owe to Prof. Hilprecht, he remarks: "(1) Cf. Hebr. יָם, (*a*) sea, (*b*) west. (2) In 1900, while at Nippur, I convinced myself by repeated observation that on clear days the eastern mountains beyond the Tigris are easily visible in Babylonia at the latitude and longitude of Nippur."

p. 312, Col. 1, l. 3 from below. Prof. Hilprecht explains *a-na šú-li-i* differently. "In view of the fact that *elû* in the contract literature is also used of the 'emporschiessen, aufgehen, wachsen,' of plants (*ina qaqqari*) and of fruit on trees (*ina gišimmarê*), I propose to translate *šûlû*, standing here in connection with *zêru*, as Inf. III, 1 of *elû*: "May they destroy his name and may (= so that) his seed not have (find) a resting place where one lets it grow up."

ADDITIONAL CORRECTIONS.

---

p. 169, l. 4. For *panûšû* read *pânûšu*.

p. 182, l. 6. For " consumptoin " read consumption.

p. 184, l. 11. For *ú-ša-aš-ša-ma* read *ú-ša-aš-šu-ma*.

p. 281, Col. I, l. 11 from below. For **Ilu** read **lillu**.

p. 283, Col. I, l. 7 from below. For כמח read כמחץ.

p. 308, Col. II, l. 12 from below. " is " has dropped out.

www.ingramcontent.com/pod-product-compliance
Lightning Source LLC
LaVergne TN
LVHW020527100826
845148LV00010B/1375

* 9 7 8 1 6 0 8 9 9 0 9 9 3 *